THE
TIMES
COOK
BOOK

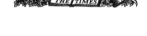

By the same author

A COOK'S CALENDAR
THE PLEASURES OF COOKERY
TEN DINNER PARTIES FOR TWO
SAINSBURY'S BOOK OF FOOD
ORIENTAL FLAVOURS
THE REAL MEAT COOKBOOK

THE TIMES COOK BOOK

Frances Bissell

Chatto & Windus
LONDON

First published in 1993 by
Chatto & Windus Limited
Random House, 20 Vauxhall Bridge Road, London SW1V 2SA

This Paperback Edition First Published 1995

1 3 5 7 9 10 8 6 4 2

© Frances Bissell 1993

Frances Bissell has asserted her right under
the Copyright, Designs and Patents Act, 1988
to be identified as the author of this work

The Times is the registered proprietor of the trade mark shown
on the previous page and is reproduced by permission of
Times Newspapers Limited

Illustrations © Diana Leadbetter
Designed by Terry Jeavons

Random House Australia (Pty) Limited
20 Alfred Street, Milsons Point, Sydney,
New South Wales 2061, Australia

Random House New Zealand Limited
18 Poland Road, Glenfield
Auckland 10, New Zealand

Random House South Africa (Pty) Limited
PO Box 337, Bergviei, South Africa

Random House UK Limited Reg. No. 954009

A CIP catalogue record for this book
is available from the British Library

ISBN 0 7011 6366 6

Typeset in Simoncini Garamond by
SX Composing Limited, Rayleigh, Essex
Printed in Great Britain by
Butler & Tanner Ltd, Frome, Somerset

For Tom, with love

CONTENTS

Introduction

On one of my bookshelves, I have a small, somewhat stained, spiral-bound book with turquoise-blue card covers. When published in 1960, 'as a result of continued and encouraging requests from readers', the first edition of *The Times Cookery Book* cost ten shillings and sixpence. It was already well thumbed and annotated when I found it in a second-hand bookshop, a familiar friend, for I had had the paperback edition of the same book since my final year at university. It saw me into the first couple of years of setting up home with Tom, my husband. I remember using the cheese cake recipe to great acclaim. Then, when Tom and I moved into a small cold-water flat in north London's Crouch End, I used some of the bread recipes, making a note in the margin that there were '44 level teaspoons of dried yeast in a 4 oz tin'. The *faisan normand* recipe was a great success too.

The material for the first *The Times Cookery Book* was drawn from *The Times* 'Women's Page', which had started five years earlier on 26 September 1955, the same year as Elizabeth David's first book, *Mediterranean Food*, appeared in the Penguin edition. Although the author is anonymous, I feel sure that the book was written by one person, perhaps Muriel Forbes who was in charge of the page, as the recipes and style are of a piece. There is a detailed knowledge of, and love for, the Italian way with food, that reads in an entirely contemporary way, except that there are no pasta recipes and only a few for risotto. An occasional hint of personal involvement crept past the copy editor, indicating that the author had indeed been in someone's kitchen, watching the dishes being made. In the recipe for *torta pasquale casalinga* we are told to put it 'into a fairly hot oven (*un forno gaio* was the phrase at Frascati)'. When I re-read this, I imagine the author going to Frascati by train from Rome, as we did one Easter Sunday, to sample the new wine, signalled by a bunch of twigs over the doorway of the tavernas, before going off for lunch at one of the restaurants famous for their *abacchio*.

Portugal was also a favourite source of recipes for the author of the original *The Times Cookery Book*. In 1971 after a first visit to Portugal, where I discovered an entirely new kind of cooking, I recognized in the book the *pasteis de Belem* and *bacalhau de creme* recipes. I cooked those first recipes, and then went on to recreate other dishes we had enjoyed in Portugal.

Food became a focal point in our travels; I began to cook without recipes, and Tom started to build up a wine cellar. My cooking developed, as did my tastebuds, and my palate memory, or my ability to recall exact tastes and textures in food that I have eaten. An appreciation of wine, and the recognition that it is inextricably linked to the enjoyment of good food, has also given focus to my cooking and writing.

Over the last twenty-five years, our travels have taken me into kitchens from China to Colombia and from Paris to Pittsburgh. In the early years our travelling was mainly in America, in France, where I was an *assistante* in Albi, in Germany, where I studied at the University of Freiburg, and in other parts of Europe for holidays. Later, when I worked for The British Council, I travelled, as Regional Officer for Southern Europe, to Portugal, Spain, Italy, Malta and Yugoslavia. By the mid 1980s, I was writing about food, as well as cooking it, and then I was invited as guest cook to hotels abroad, sometimes to participate in British food festivals, or simply to present my own cooking.

I seized every opportunity, and still do, to visit markets, farms, factories and restaurants. I learned about pasta in Liguria, visiting the small museum devoted to spaghetti, and the factory where the grain, shipped in from Canada and Argentina, was milled into strong flour, and then made into various pasta shapes. The arcana of tea tasting was explained to me in Lipton's headquarters in Colombo, Sri Lanka. And I saw fresh spices being harvested in Kandy. In Bogotá I learned about chocolate, about potatoes and pre-Colombian cooking. The dark bodegas of Jerez in southern Spain yielded not only suave and ancient sherries but the secrets of sherry vinegar. In Shanghai I discovered, by watching women in the market, how to fold the intricate *jao zi* dumplings, how to fillet small eels, and how to peel bamboo shoots. In Hong Kong I learned Cantonese home-cooking from my sister-in-law. And in the kitchens of the Mandarin Oriental Hotel, where I was twice invited as guest cook, I found out how to adapt my domestic recipes to the setting of a grand hotel. At The Dusit Thani Hotel in Bangkok, when I was not preparing beef and pigeon cobbler and 'Frances' little oyster pies' for the Tiara Restaurant, I was in the Benjarong Restaurant kitchens learning how to make Thai green and red curries. In a village near Modena I learned to make authentic 'tortellini in brodo'. In Pittsburgh my mother-in-law, Edith Bissell, taught me to make nut rolls and stuffed cabbage leaves. I discovered different types of corn dishes, including fermented drinks, in Quito, Ecuador. In Manila I was fascinated by the cross-cultural aspects of the food, Spanish blended with Chinese, underpinned by local traditions. It was in Camden, Maine, that I learned how to deal with fresh lobsters and in Birmingham, Alabama how to make cornbread and Brunswick stew. On the small island of Gozo, over the years, I have learned about each season's produce in the southern Mediterranean and how to preserve the abundant harvest of figs and tomatoes for the winter.

And, of course, I spend much time exploring closer to home. Some happy summers have been spent looking after a farmhouse in Oxfordshire, while our friends were away. There I have had first-hand experience of an abundant vegetable garden and gluts of soft fruit, which inspired me to create some of my recipes for jams and jellies. When I was researching my book on meat, *The Real Meat Cookbook*, I visited many farms. I went to see herds of goats in Somerset and a fine herd of cross-bred wild boar in Hampshire. In Ireland, where I taught a summer course at Ballymaloe Cookery School, I watched that night's dinner being landed in the small harbour at Ballycotton, and I went further west to County Cork to visit a small dairy farm and meet cheesemakers who make cheeses in the traditional way.

Many of the recipes in this book are inspired by dishes I have learned to cook in other people's kitchens. I have learned, and continue to learn, so much from so many generous cooks, chefs and food writers that they are too numerous to mention, but I thank them all and here acknowledge the debt I owe them.

My travels are not the only influences on my cooking. Seasonality in food is very important to me and always has been. The food I ate at home as a child was fresh and unprocessed. We ate whatever was available and in season. It still matters to me now that the English asparagus season begins May 1st, and the pheasant season on October 15th. This is reflected in my weekly *Times* cook column, as I describe seasonal food and seasonal themes, since this is what inspires my cooking. August is the time to make the most of the last of the season's wild salmon. I will buy a whole fish and have my fishmonger fillet it. The head and bones will make good stock, and the two tail pieces can be made into gravad lax. The rest of the fillets can be trimmed into 6 or 8 neat serving pieces, and the offcuts go into a salmon and cucumber broth. I enjoy the wild salmon while I can, as I know there will be no more until the next spring. A visit to my local greengrocer in early winter is like a geography lesson. Kumquats from Israel, quinces from Cyprus, pomegranates and cherimoyas from Spain and persimmons from Italy. Some of the fruit is with us for such a short season that it is good to have the chance to eat it fresh before it disappears from the shelves. But sometimes there is a glut, and I like to preserve some fruits for Christmas, persimmon and cranberry jam, kumquats in *eau de vie*, for example. January then sees the appearance of forced rhubarb, a truly native delicacy that comes from Yorkshire and Humberside. I welcome its fresh, tart qualities in my kitchen after months of imported fruit.

Recognizing the realities of today's shopping and eating habits, with a global market to draw upon, I realize that some people will want to eat asparagus in November, for instance (and very good it usually is too), and others will not mind eating game out of season. Thus, *The Times Cookbook* has a traditional list of chapters, with soups, salads, fish dishes, puddings, exactly where you would expect to find them. Pasta, grains, and pulses play a large part in our style of eating today, and in my style of cooking, and there is a good deal of space devoted to them, as there is to vegetables. And there are plenty of puddings, cakes, pies and other sweet things. Many recipes are suitable for vegetarians, and these are highlighted in the index, together with those recipes that will be suitable for them with only a little adaptation.

This book has undergone much pruning, and I thank Rowena Skelton-Wallace and Carmen Callil at Chatto and Windus, and my editor Vicky Hayward and copy editor, Cecile Landau. It is not just for the pruning that I thank them, but for their kindness, patience, intelligent and constructive criticism and assistance in controlling an unwieldy mass of material. In draft, the book came to 1,800 pages; much had to be left out. Many recipes have been written down in short form as variations to a main recipe. What this shows is that my recipes can be adapted, played around with, and altered to produce new recipes. Perhaps a recipe title will inspire you, as I am often inspired, to create an entirely new dish from a particular combination of ingredients.

A chapter about the perfect kitchen and the essential *batterie de cuisine* would be out of place, since I have never had a 'perfect kitchen'. My kitchen is small, along the lines of a galley. It has a few full-size units but also a couple of silly half-width cupboards, scarcely wide enough to take even a good-size casserole. I have solved the storage problem partially by having a shelf put along each of two walls. Underneath the shelves and across the kitchen, three sturdy poles are suspended, on which I have hung butcher's hooks. These, in turn, support the heavy casseroles, fish kettle, stock pot, sieves and colanders, wok, whisks and ladles – the contents, in fact, of three cupboards. It is a very practical storage system, and it looks good too. In order to conserve valuable worktop space, all jars of pulses and pasta have been banished to a dark cupboard, which is where they should be. No more decorative pots of pickled kumquats and sun-dried tomatoes to clutter up precious space.

The size of the kitchen has made me think very carefully about the 'essential' gadgets and so-called labour-saving devices. The food processor is used regularly. For small jobs, such as chopping herbs and nuts, it works very efficiently. However, it is such a palaver washing it afterwards when the end result is only a tablespoon or two of chopped parsley, it is often quicker to use a sharp knife or pestle and mortar.

Pots and pans, of various materials, have been acquired over the years, often while travelling. A neat brush for scrubbing clean the insides of a gutted fish and a sturdy wire mesh trivet are very useful kitchen souvenirs from a visit to Norway. I have a fearsomely sharp pair of steel knives roughly set in plain, wooden handles bought from a shop next to the market in Santiago de Compostela, the larger one of which is perfect for slicing Iberian ham. My pasta bowl comes from Stephen Pearce, a potter with a studio in Shanagarry, near Cork in southern Ireland. I first used his pots at Ballymaloe Cookery School, and I loved the contrast between the unglazed red earthenware and the cool, greyish-white interior glaze. Recently, I bought a solid copper Georgian preserving pan. Until now I have always made jams, jellies and marmalades in my wok.

A mechanical pasta maker, a small ice cream maker and an electric hand-blender are useful gadgets, although on a desert island, I dare say, I would get by without them. I like my ridged, rectangular cast-iron grill which is large enough to cook a whole meal. The electric cooking pot and the raclette set, handsome though they are, in matt black cast-iron, are not used enough to warrant work-top space and have been banished until I have my 'perfect kitchen'.

A word about ingredients. Fresh food should be fresh, and stored dry goods should not be ancient. Apart from that, I buy food that has undergone as little processing as possible. I prefer to do the processing in my own kitchen, where I can control how much salt, sugar or fat is added to a dish. When I can, I buy organic fruit and vegetables, unpasteurised dairy produce, and free-range or organic meat and poultry, or food that has come from a similar source, where the producers, growers and farmers use conservation-based, extensive methods, rather than intensive, factory-like methods. Whenever a recipe requires eggs, I will have used free-range eggs. And the ingredients I use are not, on the whole, expensive ones. I have mentioned caviar perhaps once in my column over the years, oysters on two occasions, and only now, as I write this have I just written in a recent *Times* cook column about lobsters. I am sometimes chided for using esoteric ingredients, such as wild venison or wild boar. It is usually the case, however, that today's uncommon ingredients become part of tomorrow's shopping basket. Wild venison, for instance, is now available in one of our largest supermarket chains.

Over the years, letters from readers of *The Times* have provided me with endless encouragement and inspiration, as well as good advice. Three times my column has given rise to correspondence on *The Times* 'Letters Page' about subjects as diverse as samphire, the origins of crème brûlée and wild boar. There is a long tradition of letters to the Editor of *The Times* about such matters. For example, at the end of 1935, a French visitor complained that he could not get Stilton cheese in England because, as he was told, it was out of season. The ensuing correspondence to *The Times* ranged from issues of seasonality to differences of opinion as to where the credit for the invention of Stilton should be given which, in turn, prompted Sir John Squire, in 1937, to write a book about English cheeses.

My correspondents write to me with suggestions for articles, requests for recipes, appeals for simplicity, pleas for incredibly complex recipes for special occasions, and asking for last week's recipe because the dog ate *The Times*, or the baby had other ideas about what to do with *The Times* 'Weekend' section. A research scholar at my old university wrote to ask for my help in cooking a Passover lamb the way it would have been cooked in Biblical times. Countless readers write to me about marmalade. One wrote to me with a squirrel recipe. Another, my most distant correspondent from

St Helena in the south Atlantic, sent me a small batch of tiny, green chillies, which she claimed were the hottest in the world.

A gentleman from Liverpool wrote asking if I would write a column of recipes 'for men who like to cook'. I was rather taken aback at this one. Do men who like to cook, cook differently from women who like to cook? I think the distinction is between those who are habitués of the kitchen and those who are not. Habitués, men and women alike, are prepared to take on all kitchen and cooking tasks, the glamorous and the tedious. Those who only cook occasionally are perhaps impatient, want immediate effect and immediate satisfaction. My recipes are for both kinds of cooks.

There are readers who would wish me to write only about fish or vegetarian food, and leave out our traditional puddings, baked goods and roasts, and concentrate on what is currently viewed to be healthy and correct. In doing this, they are asking me to ignore two thousand years of culinary tradition. I firmly believe, and this is reflected in my recipes, that a varied diet is a healthy diet.

I am grateful to all those who have written to me at *The Times* for their support, encouragement and suggestions. I owe similar gratitude to all at *The Times*, past and present, who have helped and supported me, particularly to Sally, Les, Colette, Alison, Louise, to all the copytakers, to Robin Young who, in July 1987, launched me in a feature article as the new *Times* cook, to Brian MacArthur, to Nicholas Wapshott, to Phil Lawlor, to Lisa Brown, to Melanie Aspey, the archivist, to Andrew Harvey who took me into colour, and, not least, to Mark Law who was my first editor and told me my brief as the new *Times* cook was to give the readers a square meal. I thank my current editor, Jane Owen and her deputy, Clare Brennan, and two previous editors of the *Weekend Times*, Sue Peart and Rebecca Nicolson. I am grateful to the editor of *The Times*, Peter Stothard, for his continued support and encouragement, and to the two previous editors, Simon Jenkins and Charles Wilson, who were also strong supporters of the *The Times* cook column. I would especially like to thank Diana Leadbetter for enhancing my column every week with her beautiful illustrations.

It makes me proud to know that I am one in a long line of *The Times* cooks. My immediate predecessors, Shona Crawford-Poole and Katie Stewart were not easy to follow, and I thank them for their support. I am lucky enough to meet them from time to time. I wish I could meet the earlier *Times* cooks as well. In 1910 the then proprietor, Lord Northcliffe, thought that a women's supplement might be a source of extra advertising revenue, and thirteen issues appeared between October and December. The earliest food articles were 'An Old English Recipe for Pheasant' by a Mr Schlosser of Kew, and, under the rubric, 'Some Vegetarian Recipes', one for cheese pie by Miss Dunham. In a later issue, Miss Dunham gave some more vegetarian recipes, curry cakes and tomato pie. Even then *The Times* cookery writers were concerned both with seasonality and presenting something for everyone. Harold Child, drama critic of *The Times* and assistant editor of its literary supplement, wrote about salad plants, and Lady Edward Cecil wrote about shooting lunches and tea in a country house. It was not until 1920 that the women's supplement reappeared in *The Times*, lasting less than a year when it was amalgamated with the magazine *Eve*. It was during this time that Lady Jekyll wrote about food. Between November 1937 and July 1940, Jane Carlton, a former social editor of *The Times*, was reappointed to take charge of the women's page. She proposed a *Times Cookery Book* in response to reader demand, but the idea did not get very far. It was not until 1955 that cookery became a regular feature of the women's page, under Muriel Forbes. The first food column was entitled, 'A change in the cook's routine: variations on a plain menu'. The recipes were for baked onions, trout and almonds and green apple purée. Even then, the brief was to give the reader a square meal.

As I leaf through the original *The Times Cookery Book* of thirty years ago and see that a previous owner has scribbled in the margin against the Friar's omelet (sic) recipe, 'delicious with v. dull c. apples', the nicest thing I can imagine happening to this *The Times Cookbook* is for someone to find it thirty or more years from now, battered and worn, with pencil notes in the margin.

Frances Bissell
Hampstead, June 1993

Soups

Received wisdom has it that in order to make soup, you need to start with stock. But according to the domestic science teacher in the first and only cookery lesson I had at school, this is not so.

We were to make soup. We chopped up some onions, carrots, celery and turnip, and put these in a saucepan with a pint or so of water, some salt and white pepper. I remember the white pepper vividly. It was, of course, the only pepper we knew at the time. And then we boiled and boiled. I took the result home in a thermos flask, knowing that praise would not be heaped on my head for this little creation. Soup was popular at home, but this was not considered soup. Thereafter, I transferred to needlework lessons, and learned to make soup under my mother's supervision.

The soup we used to make was simple and very tasty, a homely English version of minestrone. Flavour came not from stock but from bacon rinds, which we fried until the fat ran. This was used for browning the onions and vegetables. Beans or other pulses were added, together with whatever greens were available, such as the leaves torn from cauliflower ribs or some cabbage leaves. Gravy, left over from the Sunday joint or roast chicken, would go into the pot, together with some broken spaghetti. The Bean, Pasta and Vegetable Soup recipe which you will find on page 19, is not very different, although it is stock-based.

But in one respect my domestic science teacher was right. Not all soup recipes use a pre-prepared stock. In many cases, such as the Fresh Tomato Soup with Quenelles recipe on page 15, the ingredients themselves have enough flavour to provide what is needed. In other soups, extra depth of flavour comes from the judicious addition of a few spices, providing a counterpoint to the starchy sweetness of root vegetables, for example. Herbs will enhance the flavour of delicate vegetable soups, which can be overwhelmed if a meat stock is used.

If you want to make a stock-based soup, but have no pre-prepared stock or time to make it, there are now some good instant substitutes which are free of artificial flavour enhancers, gluten and lactose, as well as artificial colouring and preservatives.

Fish stocks take little time to make, not much more than about 30–40 minutes after coming to simmering point. Follow the method given for the stock in the Fish Soup recipe on page 22. This stock can be reduced, cooled and then frozen, so that you always have a supply in your freezer, ready for use any time.

Chicken or other meat stocks are made in a similar fashion to fish stock, but need to simmer for much longer, usually several hours. A dark stock is made by browning the bones first in a hot oven. Leftover bones from roast beef are good for this. Refrigerate the stock after cooling, so that any fat solidifies on the surface and can easily be scraped off. Freeze if appropriate.

The Vegetable Broth recipe which follows can be used to make a base for all the vegetable soups in this chapter, and indeed for some of the vegetable, rice and grain recipes in other chapters if you are cooking for vegetarians. It also makes an excellent lunchtime snack.

Vegetable Broth

Makes 3 pt / 1.70 l

1 tsp olive oil
1 onion, peeled and finely chopped
1 carrot, peeled and thinly sliced
2 celery stalks, trimmed and sliced
1 leek, trimmed and sliced
8 oz / 230 g tomatoes, peeled and
  chopped
6 parsley stalks

6 watercress stalks
1 oz / 30 g lentils
1 oz / 30 g dried beans
1 oz / 30 g chick peas
4 pt / 2.30 l water
salt
freshly ground black pepper

Heat the olive oil in a large saucepan. Add the onion and fry gently until it begins to brown and caramelize. This will give the broth a good colour. Add the rest of the vegetables, the parsley and watercress. Rinse the lentils, beans and chick peas, and add to the saucepan together with 3 pt / 1.70 l water and salt and pepper to taste. Bring to the boil, and simmer for 2–3 hours, partially covered. Strain into a bowl. Return the debris to the pan with 1 pt / 570 ml water. Bring to the boil and cook for 15 minutes, then strain into the rest of the broth, pressing down well on the debris in the sieve. Cool and chill until required.

VEGETABLE AND BEAN SOUPS

Asparagus Soup

Serves 4

This is a good recipe for using up the tougher ends of the stalks or a bundle of mixed asparagus of different sizes. It can be served hot or chilled.

1 lb / 455 g asparagus	salt
2 shallots	freshly ground black pepper
½ tbsp olive oil, if serving the soup chilled *or* ½ oz / 15 g butter, if serving it hot	2 ripe tomatoes, peeled, deseeded and chopped
1½ pt / 850 ml vegetable stock	1 tbsp balsamic or sherry vinegar
1 tsp marjoram leaves	1 tbsp single cream
	chives, to garnish

Wash the asparagus thoroughly, chop off the ends, and peel off any coarse outer skin with a potato peeler. Cut off and reserve the four best-looking tips for garnishing, and cut the rest into 1 in / 2.5 cm chunks. Peel and chop the shallots, and sweat in the oil or butter in a large saucepan. Add the asparagus, the vegetable stock and the marjoram. Bring to the boil, lower the heat, and simmer gently until the asparagus is tender. Allow the soup to cool slightly, and then blend it in a food blender or processor. Sieve it, and either return to the pan if serving it hot, or cool and then chill it. Season to taste.

Make a purée of the raw tomatoes, sieve them, and stir in the vinegar. Quickly steam or boil the reserved asparagus tips. Pour the soup into bowls, hot or chilled, as desired. Carefully spoon a swirl of the tomato vinaigrette and a swirl of cream into each bowl, and garnish with the chives, chopped or left long, and with the asparagus tips.

Variations ∾ For a thicker soup, add a potato or two, peeled and diced, as the asparagus is cooking.

For a more unusual variation, the soup can be thickened by stirring in 2–3 tablespoons ground almonds, after sieving. Heat the ground almonds gently in a frying pan before adding, to release the flavour. Toasted almond flakes can be scattered on the soup to garnish before serving.

Aubergine, Corn and Tomato Soup

Serves 6–8

This soup is based on one served at Colettes, an unexpected haven for simple home-cooking on Wilshire Boulevard in Beverly Hills.

1 medium onion
1 aubergine, about 12 oz / 340 g
6 firm ripe tomatoes, peeled,
   deseeded and chopped
2½ pt / 1.45 l chicken or vegetable
   stock

2–3 corn cobs
salt
freshly ground black pepper
1–2 tbsp finely chopped parsley

Peel and finely chop the onion. Slice and then dice the aubergine into about ½ in / 1 cm cubes. 'Fry' the onion and aubergine in a large non-stick pan until soft and wilted and beginning to brown a little. Add the tomatoes and stock, and continue cooking until the flavour has begun to develop. Husk the corn cobs, and cut the kernels from the cobs by standing each one vertically on a chopping board and slicing down with a sharp knife, cutting off as much of the flesh as possible. Add the corn kernels to the soup, together with salt and pepper to taste. Bring to the boil, and simmer for a few minutes, until the corn is just tender. Stir in the chopped parsley and serve.

The flavour of the soup can be heightened with a dash of lemon juice, balsamic vinegar or fino sherry. Extra body can be added to the soup by putting a handful or so of rice in the pot when you have first brought the stock to the boil.

Black Bean Soup

Serves 4–6

One of our very favourite winter soups.

8 oz / 230 g black kidney beans
1 medium onion
1 tbsp sunflower or olive oil
1 tbsp ground cumin
1 tbsp paprika
¼ tsp cayenne pepper or chilli
   powder
3 cloves *or* ¼ tsp ground cloves

1 tbsp tomato purée
1 pt / 570 ml stock or water
salt
4–6 tbsp good dry or medium sherry
   (optional)
4–6 thin slices of lemon
1 tbsp finely chopped parsley
4–6 tbsp soured cream *(optional)*

Soak the beans in cold water overnight. Next day, drain and rinse them, place them in a saucepan and cover with at least 2 in / 5 cm water. Boil for 15 minutes. Drain and return them to the pan with fresh water. Bring slowly to the boil, cover and barely simmer for 2–2½ hours, until the beans are tender.

Meanwhile, peel and finely chop the onion, and fry it in the oil in a heavy saucepan until beginning to brown. Add the cumin, paprika, cayenne pepper or chilli and cloves, and cook for 2–3 minutes. Stir in the tomato purée, and cook until the mixture thickens and darkens as the water evaporates. Pour on half the stock or water, bring to the boil, cover and simmer for 30 minutes or until the onions are soft.

Allow the cooked beans to cool slightly in their liquid before making a purée of them in a food processor or blender. It is best to do this in two batches, unless you have a large-capacity machine. Add the bean purée to the onion and spice mixture, together with the rest of the stock or water. Stir until thoroughly mixed, bring to the boil, and add salt to taste. If the consistency is too thick for you, gradually add a little more water or stock and appropriate seasoning, until the taste and consistency are as you want them.

There are several ways of serving this soup – with or without sherry, a thin slice of hard-boiled egg, or a thin slice of lemon, in any combination. I like to serve the soup very hot, pouring it when practically boiling into earthenware soup bowls containing a splash of sherry (or, even better, rum) so that the heat of the soup evaporates most of the alcohol, leaving the spirity flavour behind. I then add to each bowl a very thin slice of lemon, a sprinkling of finely chopped parsley and perhaps a tablespoonful of soured cream.

Spiced Carrot and Parsnip Soup

Serves 4–6

The idea of making the two main ingredients into two separate soups, and then pouring them into the soup bowl so that they swirl together in a pattern, keeping their colours distinct, comes from Alice Waters' restaurant in Berkeley, Chez Panisse, where her chef, Paul Bertolli, is, in her words, 'very strong on soups'. It looks and tastes very good, and is only a little more trouble to make than combining all the ingredients together, which of course, you can do for a more homely dish. Either way, inexpensive and humble ingredients are transformed into a delicious soup.

½ oz / 15 g unsalted butter
1 medium onion, peeled and sliced

1 celery stalk, trimmed and thinly sliced

Carrot soup
8 oz / 230 g carrots, peeled and
  thinly sliced
¼ tsp ground cardamom
¾ pt / 430 ml vegetable or meat
  stock
¼ pt / 140 ml full-cream milk or
  single cream
salt
freshly ground black pepper

Parsnip soup
8 oz / 230 g parsnips, peeled and thinly
  sliced
¼ tsp freshly grated nutmeg
¾ pt / 430 ml vegetable or meat stock
¼ pt / 140 ml full-cream milk or single
  cream
salt
freshly ground black pepper

Use two saucepans. Melt half the butter in each. Divide the onion and celery between the two pans and gently sweat them in the butter. Add the carrots and cardamom to one pan and the parsnips and nutmeg to the other. Cook for 2–3 minutes, and then pour on the stock, ¾ pt / 430 ml into each pan. Cover and let it simmer gently for 15–20 minutes or until the vegetables are tender. Allow to cool slightly.

Blend the parsnip mixture with ¼ pt / 140 ml milk or cream in a blender or food processor, sieve it, and pour it back into a clean saucepan. Rinse the blender goblet or food processor bowl, and blend the carrot mixture in the same way. Reheat the two soups, season to taste, pour some of each into heated soup bowls, and swirl together gently to form a pattern. For a denser, chewier texture, serve the soup without sieving it.

Lettuce and Mint Soup

Serves 6

2 oz / 60 g butter
4 oz / 110 g onions, peeled and
   diced
5 oz / 140 g potatoes, peeled and
   diced
½ tsp salt

freshly ground white pepper
6 oz / 170 g lettuce leaves, chopped
2 pt / 1.15 l vegetable or light chicken
   stock
2 tsp finely chopped mint
1 tbsp whipping cream *(optional)*

Melt the butter in a heavy saucepan. When it foams, add the onions and potatoes, and turn them until well coated. Sprinkle with salt and pepper. Cover, and sweat on a gentle heat for 10 minutes. Add the chopped lettuce leaves and stock. Boil until just tender, but do not overcook or the lettuce will lose its colour and flavour. Make a purée in a blender or food processor (after cooling slightly first), then sieve and add the mint, the cream, if using it, and more salt and pepper, if necessary. Bring back to the boil and serve immediately.

Mushroom Soup

Serves 4

2 oz / 60 g smoked streaky bacon
1 small onion, peeled and finely
   chopped
1 lb / 455 g mushrooms, wiped and
   thinly sliced
1½ pt / 850 ml vegetable or chicken
   stock

1 bay leaf
salt
freshly ground black pepper
cream *(optional)*

Remove the rind from the bacon, cut it into small strips, and fry it in a large saucepan until the fat runs. Add the onion, and fry it until golden brown, then add the mushrooms, stir, and cook over a high heat for a minute or two. Pour in the stock, and add the bay leaf, salt and pepper. Bring to the boil, and simmer for 20 minutes. You can either serve the soup as it is or thicken it, by making a purée of most of the mushrooms, with or without cream, stirring this into the soup remaining in the pan, and reheating it. Serve very hot.

Nettle and Barley Soup

1½ pt / 850 ml vegetable stock
2 oz / 60 g pearl barley
sprig of sage and 1 bay leaf

2 oz / 60 g fresh young nettle tops
salt
freshly ground black pepper

Bring the stock to the boil in a large saucepan, and throw in the barley and herbs. Lower the heat and simmer until the barley is tender. Remove the herbs. Roughly chop the nettles, and add to the pan. Bring to the boil, season to taste, and serve immediately.

Onion and Cheese Soup under a Soufflé

1 lb / 455 g onions, peeled and
   chopped
½ pt / 280 ml chicken or vegetable
   stock
2 pt / 1.15 l milk
3 oz / 85 g butter
3 oz / 85 g plain flour

12 oz / 340 g farmhouse Lancashire
   cheese, grated
salt
freshly ground black pepper
freshly grated nutmeg
3 eggs, separated

Using a non-stick pan, sweat the onion until transparent and just beginning to caramelize, but do not burn. Add the stock, and cook until the onion is soft.

Meanwhile, pre-heat the oven to 200 °C / 400 °F / Mark 6, bring the milk to the boil and, in another saucepan melt the butter. Stir the flour into the butter, and cook for 5 minutes. Slowly add ¼ pt / 140 ml boiled milk, whisking it to prevent any lumps forming. Stir in the cheese until melted. Set aside 3 tablespoons of this roux mixture, and add the remaining milk to the roux remaining in the pan, stirring continuously. Add the onion and stock and mix well. Bring to the boil, and add salt, pepper and nutmeg to taste.

Divide the mixture between six ovenproof soup bowls placed on a baking sheet. Beat the egg yolks into the roux that you have set aside, whisk the whites to firm peaks, and gently fold the two together. Spoon this soufflé mixture on top of the soup bowls, and bake in the preheated oven for 10–12 minutes. Serve at once.

Pea and Herb Soup

Serves 6

½ oz / 15 g butter *or* 1 tbsp
  sunflower oil
2 shallots *or* 1 small onion, peeled
  and chopped
1 celery stalk, trimmed and
  chopped
8 oz / 230 g pea pods, chopped
  (optional)
1 small lettuce, chopped
1 small cucumber, chopped

3–4 oz / 85–110 g potatoes, peeled and
  diced
2 pt / 1.15 l vegetable or chicken stock
handful of any of the following: parsley,
  chervil, purslane, rocket, basil,
  watercress, chopped
6 oz / 170 g fresh peas
salt
freshly ground black pepper
cream *(optional)*

Heat the butter or oil in a large saucepan, and gently fry the shallots or onion without browning. Add the celery, pea pods (if using), lettuce, cucumber, potatoes and stock. Bring to the boil, and simmer until the celery and potatoes are tender. Add half the herbs, and cook for a few minutes more. Make a purée of the soup in a blender or food processor, and sieve into a clean saucepan. Add the fresh peas and the remaining herbs, and cook until the peas are tender. Season to taste just before serving, and stir in cream if desired.

Potato, Onion and Herb Soup

Serves 4–6

2 mild onions, peeled and thinly
  sliced
2 tbsp extra virgin olive oil
1 lb / 455 g potatoes, peeled and
  sliced
1 celery stalk, trimmed and sliced
sprigs of herbs, such as parsley,
  chervil, basil, tarragon and
  coriander

3–4 spring onions, trimmed and
  chopped
2 pt / 1.15 l vegetable or chicken stock
pinch of freshly grated nutmeg
salt
freshly ground black pepper

In a large saucepan, sweat the onions in the oil until soft and translucent, then add the potatoes and celery. Strip the leaves from the herbs, and put to one side. Tie the stalks together, and put them in the pan, together with the spring onions and stock. Bring to the boil, and simmer until the celery and potatoes are tender.

Finely chop the leaves of the herbs. Use them in combinations that will not cancel out the flavours – coriander and parsley, basil and parsley, chervil, tarragon and parsley – and use enough to give 2–3 tablespoons when chopped. Stir half the herbs into the soup. Make a purée in a blender or food processor, sieve, and return to the pan. Bring back to the boil, stir in the rest of the herbs, and season with nutmeg, salt and pepper. Serve immediately.

Variations ∾ A particularly good version of this soup can be made using fresh lovage instead of a mixture of herbs. Hardly available commercially, it is something you have to grow yourself or beg from a friend. Its yeasty, celery-like flavour marries well with potato. You can substitute celery tops if you wish.

Also, in the summer when there is a glut of it, try making the soup using basil as the sole herb, and serve chilled.

Pumpkin and Almond Soup

Serves 4–6

*This is from Italian friends, based on a Renaissance recipe, with
delicate, subtle flavours and almonds to thicken it.*

2 lb / 900 g piece of butternut
   squash or pumpkin
2 shallots
1 tbsp grapeseed or almond oil
4 oz / 110 g blanched almonds
juice and grated zest of 1 orange

1½ pt / 850 ml chicken, turkey or
   vegetable stock
salt
freshly ground black pepper
freshly grated nutmeg
2–3 oz /60–85 g Parmesan cheese,
   freshly grated

Remove the seeds and filaments from the squash or pumpkin and bake in the
oven at 180°C / 350°F / Mark 4 in a roasting tin until tender. Meanwhile, peel and
chop the shallots, and sweat in the oil in a large saucepan until transparent. Chop
the almonds finely and stir into the shallots. Add the baked pumpkin flesh together
with the orange juice and zest and ½ pt / 280 ml stock. Cook for 5 minutes or until
the shallots are tender, and then make a purée in a blender or food processor.
Return to the saucepan with the rest of the stock and reheat. Season to taste with
salt, pepper and nutmeg (for me, nutmeg and pumpkin go together like rhubarb
and ginger or apple and cinnamon, and I tend to use a lot of it). Just before serving
this thick soup in small heated soup bowls or plates, stir in the Parmesan so that it
will have melted into the soup by the time you eat it.

Pumpkin and Cheese Soup

3 rashers smoked streaky bacon, derinded and cut into matchsticks
1 large Spanish (or other mild) onion, peeled and thinly sliced
3 lb / 1.35 kg piece of pumpkin
1½ pt / 850 ml milk
2 bay leaves
3 cloves
14 oz / 395 g can borlotti beans
1½ pt / 850 ml vegetable or chicken stock or water

3 oz / 85 g Lancashire or White Stilton cheese, crumbled
3 oz / 85 g Gruyère, Jarlsberg or Gouda cheese, diced
salt
freshly ground black pepper
freshly grated nutmeg
1 tbsp finely chopped parsley
2 oz / 60 g Parmesan cheese, freshly grated

Put the bacon in a heavy flameproof casserole or saucepan, and cook gently until the fat runs. Add the onion, and cook it with the bacon until soft and translucent, but do not let it brown. Discard any seeds and stringy filaments from the pumpkin, and cut the rind away. Cut the flesh into 1 in / 2.5 cm chunks, and add to the pan. Pour on the milk, and add the bay leaves and cloves. Cover, and simmer gently until the pumpkin and onion are tender. The pumpkin will start to collapse, but this does not matter since that is what gives body to the soup.

Drain the beans, and add them to the soup, together with the stock or water. Stir in the first two cheeses, and season to taste with salt, pepper and nutmeg. Scatter the parsley and Parmesan on top, and serve immediately.

Cream of Spinach Soup

Serves 4

This simple soup recipe can be adapted to many vegetables – broccoli, lettuce, chard, watercress, sorrel and cauliflower (add a pinch of curry powder), for example. Add potato during cooking for a thicker soup.

1 small onion or shallot, peeled and finely chopped
½ oz / 15 g butter, if serving hot *or* ½ tbsp olive oil, if serving cold
1½ lb / 680 g spinach, washed and drained

1¼ pt / 710 ml vegetable or chicken stock
¼ pt / 140 ml whipping cream
salt
freshly ground black pepper
freshly grated nutmeg

In a large saucepan, sweat the onion or shallot in the butter or oil until soft and translucent. Stir in the spinach. As it wilts, it will gradually lose its volume. Pour on half the stock, and cook for approximately 4–5 minutes or until the spinach is just tender.

Allow to cool slightly, and place in a blender or food processor. Pour on half the remaining stock, and blend until smooth. It can be sieved or not, as you wish (this may depend on whether the spinach was very stalky or not). Stir in the cream and the rest of the stock. Season to taste with salt, pepper and nutmeg, then bring to the boil and serve, or chill until required.

Fresh Tomato Soup with Quenelles

Serves 4

Use the tastiest, ripest, sweetest tomatoes you can find.

1½ lb / 680 g ripe tomatoes
1 oz / 30 g chilled butter, cut into
    cubes
1 tbsp, or more if you like, finely
    shredded basil

salt
freshly ground black pepper

Peel and deseed the tomatoes in a sieve over a basin to catch the juices. Cut the tomatoes into very thin, short slivers, and place in a heavy saucepan with the sieved juice. Heat gently until the tomatoes begin to 'sweat' and give off their liquid. Stir in the cubes of butter, one at a time, so that each blends with the tomato before adding the next. Stir in the basil, season to taste, and serve immediately. It should still have a very fresh, uncooked flavour.

At Leith's, where I first tasted it, this soup is served with basil-flavoured cream cheese quenelles (see below). These are quite tricky, and the mixture should be made the day before. If you do not have time, mix some finely chopped basil into seasoned cream cheese, and place a spoonful in each bowl of soup as you serve it.

Quenelles

Serves 4

1 oz / 30 g butter
2 egg yolks
1½ oz / 40 g soft white
    breadcrumbs

3½ oz / 100 g cream cheese
1 tbsp finely chopped basil

Beat the butter and egg yolks together until smooth. Add the rest of the ingredients, and allow the mixture to rest overnight. Form into small dumplings or sausages, and slide them gently into a large pan of water, held just at the boil. When they float to the surface, they are cooked, and should be removed with a slotted spoon and served immediately with the hot soup.

Tomato and Jerusalem Artichoke Soup

Serves 4

1 small onion, peeled and thinly
  sliced
1 tbsp olive oil
1 lb / 455 ripe tomatoes, roughly
  chopped
8 oz / 230 g Jerusalem artichokes,
  scrubbed, trimmed and sliced

1½ pt / 850 ml vegetable or chicken
  stock
salt
freshly ground white pepper

Sweat the onion until translucent in the olive oil. Add the tomatoes (with any juice), the artichokes and half the stock, and simmer gently until the artichokes and onion are soft. Allow to cool slightly, then make a purée in a blender or food processor, and sieve into a clean saucepan. Stir in the remaining stock, bring to the boil, and simmer for 8–10 minutes. Season to taste, and serve hot. Cream and herbs can be stirred in if desired.

Variations ～ To make a fragrant tomato and garlic soup, sweat 20–30 peeled cloves of garlic (this is not a mistake – garlic loses its powerful smell when cooked with tomato, becoming sweet and mild in flavour) with the onion in the olive oil, making sure the garlic does not brown. Add a tablespoon of freshly grated ginger root with the chopped tomatoes and half the stock, and simmer until the garlic and onion are soft. Continue as above. Shredded basil leaves can be added just before serving, or this soup can be served chilled, garnished with chopped chives and watercress.

I also make a rich, velvety, red tomato and beetroot soup, substituting cooked beetroot (*not* pickled) for the artichokes. Cook this soup with a generous tablespoon of chopped dill, and add a swirl of soured cream to each serving.

Charred Plum Tomato and Plum Soup

This is one of my favourite vegetable and fruit soup combinations, and is best made at the end of the summer when tomatoes are at their sweetest and plums just coming into season.

Serves 4–6

8 ripe plum tomatoes,
  about 1½ lb / 680 g
2 tbsp olive oil
1 small onion, peeled and finely
  chopped
1 celery stalk, trimmed and finely
  chopped
1½ pt / 850 ml vegetable stock

3–4 pieces sun-dried tomato
8 oz / 230 g ripe plums, stoned and
  chopped
basil
salt
freshly ground black pepper
4–6 tbsp soured cream or thick yoghurt

Halve four of the plum tomatoes lengthways, and roughly chop the rest. Using a frying pan and a saucepan, put a tablespoon of olive oil in each. In the saucepan, cook the chopped tomatoes and vegetables with the pieces of sun-dried tomato until soft, but without really browning them. Fry the halved tomatoes in the frying pan until the skin has turned dark brown and then transfer them to the saucepan. Pour a little of the stock into the frying pan, and scrape up all the cooking residues, which will give you quite a dark golden-brown liquid. Pour it into the saucepan. This and the charred tomato skins give the soup an unusual depth of flavour.

Poach the plums in some of the remaining vegetable stock until just tender. When cool, put them in a blender or food processor with the soft vegetables and tomatoes, the remaining stock and some basil leaves. Blend until smooth and sieve. The soup can be served chilled or hot. Season to taste just before serving, and serve with some more fresh basil leaves, shredded just before use, and a swirl of soured cream or thick yoghurt.

Vegetable Gumbo

This is more of a meal than a soup. There are enough vegetables to stand a spoon up in it, and the okra thickens the broth to a silky-rich texture. You can vary the other vegetables according to what is available, and a knuckle of bacon or half a chicken can be added, if you are not making the soup for vegetarians.

1 large onion, peeled and chopped
4 ripe tomatoes, peeled, deseeded and chopped
3 celery stalks, trimmed and thinly sliced
2 tbsp olive oil
4 oz / 110 g okra, trimmed and sliced
1 red or green pepper, deseeded and sliced
3 pt / 1.70 l vegetable or chicken stock

8 oz / 230 g bobby beans, trimmed
8 oz / 230 g courgettes, thickly sliced
kernels of 2–3 corn cobs *or* 6 oz / 170 g baby corn
8 oz / 230 g chick peas or black-eyed beans, soaked and cooked, plus their cooking liquid
sprigs of coriander, thyme, parsley and bay leaves
salt
freshly ground black pepper
finely chopped parsley or coriander

Fry the onion, tomatoes and celery in the oil until the onion and celery are translucent and the tomatoes collapsed. Add the sliced okra and pepper, together with the stock. Bring to the boil, and simmer for 20–30 minutes. Add the rest of the vegetables, the chick peas or black-eyed beans and their cooking liquid, and the herbs (tied together). Continue cooking until the vegetables are done to your liking. Remove the bundle of herbs, season the soup, and stir in the chopped parsley or coriander before serving. You might like to add a dash of hot pepper sauce.

Bean, Pasta and Vegetable Soup

Serves 8

*This is a particularly delicious and satisfying soup, which closely
resembles Italian minestrone. It is a good way of using up cooked
beans from another dish, but is also well worth making from scratch.
If you use canned beans, they should be added only 5 minutes before
the end of cooking.*

¼ pt / 140 ml extra virgin olive oil
2 onions, peeled and finely chopped
1 celery stalk, trimmed and finely
  sliced
2 carrots, peeled and finely sliced
3 garlic cloves, peeled and finely
  chopped
1 tbsp tomato purée
14 oz / 395 g can tomatoes
3 pt / 1.70 l turkey, duck, ham or
  vegetable stock
¼ pt / 140 ml dry red or white wine
  (optional)
2 leeks, trimmed and finely sliced

12 oz / 340 g Savoy cabbage, finely
  shredded
2 courgettes, trimmed and thinly sliced
4 oz / 110 g green beans, broken into
  ½ in / 1 cm pieces
6 oz / 170 g broken spaghetti or pasta
  shapes
8 oz / 230 g dried beans or chick peas,
  soaked, cooked and drained
finely chopped herbs, such as basil,
  chives or parsley
salt
freshly ground black pepper

Heat 3–4 tablespoons of the olive oil in a large saucepan or flameproof
casserole, and gently fry the onions, celery, carrots and garlic until soft. This will
take 20–30 minutes, and is what gives the soup its underlying depth of flavour. Stir
in the tomato purée, and cook until most of the liquid from it has evaporated. Add
the tomatoes, and let that liquid boil off too. Add the stock and wine, if using, and
bring to the boil. Simmer for 10–15 minutes.

Add the leeks, cabbage, courgettes and green beans to the simmering stock,
together with the pasta, and cook until vegetables and pasta are just done. Stir in
the beans or chick peas and chopped herbs. Bring back to the boil, season to taste,
and ladle into hot soup bowls. Pour the remaining olive oil into the soup in each
bowl, and serve immediately. Instead of olive oil, you may prefer to stir in a
spoonful of pesto.

Leftovers are extremely good reboiled the next day and served over a thick
toasted slice of wholemeal bread and a little olive oil. This is almost identical to the
Tuscan *ribollita*.

Spring Vegetable Soup

Serves 4–6

1 small carrot
2 celery stalks
1 leek
1 small turnip
3 oz / 85 g mixture of asparagus
   tips, green beans and mangetout
bunch of watercress
2 tbsp dried cannellini or haricot
   beans, well rinsed

parsley stalks
2 ripe tomatoes, roughly chopped
mushroom peelings
1 bay leaf
1 sprig of thyme
3 pt / 1.70 l water
salt
freshly ground black pepper
pinch of ground mace

First prepare the garnish by washing and peeling or trimming the carrot, celery, leek and turnip. Reserve the outer peelings. Finely shred about a tablespoon of the white part of the leek, and finely dice enough celery, carrot and turnip to give you another 2 tablespoons of vegetables. Cover and put to one side with the asparagus tips, green beans and mangetout. Reserve a few of the watercress sprigs. Put the rest of the ingredients, including the dried beans and the reserved vegetable peelings, in a saucepan with the water, bring to the boil, and cook for 1 hour. Put the prepared garnish in a clean saucepan with the reserved watercress. Strain the broth on top of it, and bring to the boil. Season to taste, and serve when the vegetables are just tender.

Variations ⁓ When forced rhubarb is available in early spring, it makes a welcome addition to this clear vegetable broth. Cut the rhubarb into 1 in / 2.5 cm pieces, then cut each piece into four thin batons. Add these to the garnish mixture of asparagus tips, green beans, mangetout and chopped vegetables.

For a summer version, use chopped spring onions, shredded lettuce and spinach or sorrel, watercress, young peas and a handful of herbs as garnishing.

FISH AND SHELLFISH SOUPS

Fresh Scallop and Jerusalem Artichoke Soup

Serves 4

I have tasted versions of this now classic soup in many restaurants and dining rooms. Margaret Costa, author of the classic Four Seasons Cookery Book, *was one of the first to write down the recipe, and may well have been its creator.*

1 lb / 455 g Jerusalem artichokes	1 pt / 570 ml water
½ tsp vinegar	4 scallops
½ oz / 15 g butter	sea salt
1 medium onion, peeled and chopped	freshly ground white pepper
	chopped dill or parsley
½ pt / 280 ml milk	

Scrub the Jerusalem artichokes, cut off the knobbly bits, and then peel them. Slice the artichokes, and drop them into a bowl of water to which you've added the vinegar. Melt the butter in a saucepan, and cook the onion until it is soft. Drain the artichokes, add them to the pan with the milk and water. Simmer gently until the artichokes are soft. Pass through a fine sieve into a clean saucepan, rubbing the vegetables through. This gives the soup a better texture than if you make a purée of it in a food processor or blender.

Wash the scallops, remove the thick pads of muscle and dice them, including the coral. Add them to the soup, and poach them gently for 2–3 minutes. Season the soup to taste, add some herbs, and serve immediately. The soup can be rich or plain depending on whether you use full-cream, skimmed or semi-skimmed milk.

Fish Soup

*Excellent fish soup can be made wherever fresh fish is available. I cook
my fish soup in three stages. First the base is made which provides the
underlying flavours of herbs, garlic and tomatoes, then the stock is
made, and finally the two are cooked together and the fish added at
the third stage for the last few minutes. The stock is best made with
the bones from monkfish, sole, plaice, brill, turbot, ling, catfish, coley
and other white fish. Salmon bones and head can also be used, as can
lobster and crab shells if available. Prawn shells should, I feel, be used
with discretion, for they have a sweet, powerful flavour. Fish bones
can be frozen until you have enough to make stock.*

Base
4 tbsp extra virgin olive oil
1 onion, peeled and chopped
2 leeks, trimmed and sliced
1 small fennel bulb, trimmed and
    diced *(optional)*

Stock
3–4 lb / 1.35–1.80 kg fish bones and
    trimmings
7 oz / 200 g can plum tomatoes, or
    equivalent of ripe fresh tomatoes,
    peeled and chopped
sprig of thyme
1 bay leaf
1–2 tbsp extra virgin olive oil
4 pt / 2.30 l water

½ celery stalk
1 bay leaf
1 thin slice of fresh root ginger, peeled
    (optional)

Flavouring
pinch of saffron threads
Pernod

Fish
2–3 lb / 900 g–1.35 kg fish (prepared
    weight – without skin and bone)

For the base, heat the oil in a large heavy saucepan or flameproof casserole, and
sweat the vegetables and herbs until the fennel, if using, and onion are soft.

For the stock, chop the bones into manageable pieces, and fry them gently in
the olive oil for a few minutes. Add the water, celery, bay leaf and ginger, if using.
Bring to the boil, skim any foam from the surface, and simmer for about 30–40
minutes. There is no merit in cooking fish bones any longer, as all the flavour will
have been extracted from them. Sieve into a bowl or jug through a very fine mesh
sieve, through a coffee filter paper or a scalded muslin cloth placed over a sieve.

To flavour the soup, use a good pinch of saffron steeped in a little of the hot fish stock or, especially nice if you have used fennel in the base, a good slug of Pernod. Both or either can be used. Stir into the vegetable base, and pour in the strained stock. Bring to the boil, and season to taste. Simmer the broth gently while you prepare the fish.

Use any firm white fish, such as cod, ling, coley and monkfish. One small red mullet, scaled and filleted or chopped into three or four pieces, will add extra flavour. Crustacea can be left whole. Mussels should be scrubbed, and barnacles knocked off the shells. Cut the fish into 2–3 in / 5–7.5 cm pieces.

The final preparation and cooking is simple, and takes less than 10 minutes. Thus the base, the stock, the flavourings and the accompaniments (see below) can be prepared well in advance. Put the prepared fish pieces into the simmering broth. It will immediately stop simmering. Bring back to simmering point, and hold there for 3–4 minutes. This is sufficient to cook the fish, which will continue to cook in the hot liquid even when the pan is removed from the heat. Serve the soup from the pan in which it was cooked, or quickly transfer it to a heated soup tureen, and from there to heated soup bowls. Garnish with parsley if desired, and hand the other accompaniments separately for people to stir in as they wish.

This fish soup is a large rustic dish, ideal as a main course. If you want a more elegant version for a first course, place a few thin slices of raw fish in the bottom of a heated soup plate, and pour the strained boiling broth over it, which will be hot enough to cook the fish. In this case, 1½ lb / 680 g fish will be ample.

Accompaniments ∾ Chopped parsley can be used for garnish, but is not essential. A thick, garlicky rouille, made like mayonnaise with the addition of cayenne pepper, is a good accompaniment, but so is a herb and garlic mayonnaise. Croûtons or breadsticks also go well with the soup.

Monsieur Furlan's
'Minestrone de Coquillages'
(Shellfish Minestrone)

Serves 6

Le Chandelier in Montpellier serves some of the best food I have ever eaten, and this recipe is based on one of those simple, exquisite dishes that causes you to wonder, 'Why didn't I think of that?'

2 tbsp extra virgin olive oil
4 oz / 110 g streaky bacon, derinded and cut into matchsticks
1 onion, peeled and thinly sliced
2 carrots, peeled and thinly sliced
1 leek, trimmed and sliced
2 pt / 1.15 l fish, vegetable or light chicken stock
8 oz / 230 g spring or Savoy cabbage, shredded

4 oz / 110 g green beans, topped and tailed and cut into ½ in / 1 cm pieces
4 oz / 110 g raw queen scallops, shelled
4 oz / 110 g fresh cockles or venus clams, steamed and shelled
8 oz / 230 g fresh mussels, steamed and shelled
handful of basil, chopped
salt
freshly ground black pepper

In a large saucepan, fry the bacon in the olive oil with the onion, carrots and leek, until the bacon has lost its rawness and the vegetables are golden brown. Pour on half the stock, bring to the boil, and simmer for 20 minutes. Add the cabbage and the beans, and cook for about another 10 minutes or until the vegetables are just tender. Add the shellfish and basil. Season to taste and serve very hot. Chef Furlan serves the soup with a crisp golden puff pastry lid. Slices of good bread fried in olive oil would also be nice.

Shellfish and Saffron Broth

Serves 4–6

pinch of saffron threads
3 lb / 1.35 kg fresh mussels
1 lb / 455 g prawns in their shells
1 small onion, peeled and halved
2 cloves
1 leek
handful of parsley stalks

2–3 dill stalks
1 tsp peppercorns
1 pt / 570 ml dry white wine
¼ pt / 140 ml water
1 carrot
freshly ground black pepper
dill fronds, to garnish

Soak the saffron in 2–3 tablespoons boiling water. Scrub the mussels, tug off
the beards, knock off any barnacles with the back of a knife, and rinse thoroughly.
Discard any which do not close. Put them in a bowl, and put to one side. Shell the
prawns, and put them to one side, reserving the shells. Put the prawn shells in a
saucepan with the onion halves studded with the cloves. Trim and thoroughly wash
the leek, cut it in half and slice the top half into rings. Add these to the saucepan,
together with the parsley stalks, dill, peppercorns, wine and water. Bring to the boil
and simmer gently for 20 minutes.

Meanwhile, peel the carrot (the carrot peeling can go into the simmering
broth), and cut into fine strips. Slice the bottom half of the leek lengthways, and
shred it in a similar fashion. Put these vegetables in a sieve, and pour boiling water
over to soften them. Rinse under cold running water, and put to one side.

Put the mussels in a heavy, lidded saucepan, and pour the hot broth over them.
Cover, bring to the boil, and simmer for 2–3 minutes or just until all the mussels
open. Discard any which fail to open. Carefully drain the broth into a clean
saucepan, through a sieve lined with muslin wrung out in hot water. When the
mussels are cool enough to handle, remove them from their shells. Divide the
prawns and mussels between heated soup plates, and scatter over them the carrot
and leek shreds. Pour the saffron liquid into the broth, bring to the boil, and add
pepper to taste. Pour into soup plates, garnish with dill fronds, and serve at once.

Light Salmon Soup

Serves 4

1½ pt / 850 ml salmon stock
3½ fl oz / 100 ml white wine
3½ fl oz / 100 ml crème fraîche
salt
2 small carrots, peeled and cut into
  matchsticks

3 oz / 85 g small broccoli florets
⅔ cucumber, cut into matchsticks
8–10 oz / 230–280 g piece of salmon,
  skinned and filleted
chopped dill

Bring the salmon stock and wine to the boil in a large saucepan. Beat in the crème fraîche, and add salt to taste. Blanch the vegetables separately in a small amount of water. Thinly slice the salmon, and divide between four warm soup bowls. Pour the boiling broth over the salmon in each bowl, so that it will be cooked by it. Place some of the blanched vegetables in each bowl, add the dill, and serve immediately.

Salmon and White Bean Soups with Basil and Garlic Oil

Serves 4–6

*One of the best soups I have made came about through a coincidence
of leftovers. I had cooked jumbo lima beans and made them into a
smooth, white purée as a change from hummus. I served it with a
pungent basil and garlic-flavoured olive oil spooned on top. For the
main course, I poached a piece of grilse, young wild salmon. With the
leftover fish and purée, I planned to make a smooth, creamy, pale pink
soup. Then I remembered how Alice Waters serves soup at Chez
Panisse in Berkeley, California. Taking complementary flavours,
textures and colours, the two soups are kept separate as they are
poured into the bowls. It is a most attractive presentation, and the
basil and garlic oil finished it off well. The simplified version, blending
all together, is also good, and the first time I made the soup, I served it
chilled, which would be perfect for a summer evening.*

8 oz / 230 g cooked salmon
1 pt / 570 ml salmon stock
12 oz / 340 g cooked white beans,
    such as haricots, cannellini or
    navy beans
salt
freshly ground white pepper

1 pt / 570 ml bean cooking liquor
pinch of ground mace
2 garlic cloves
pinch of coarse sea salt
few basil leaves
3 tbsp extra virgin olive oil

In a food processor or blender, blend together the salmon, salmon stock and
2 oz / 60 g beans. Put in a saucepan, heat and season to taste. Then blend the
remaining beans and bean cooking liquor, and heat in a separate saucepan. Season
with salt, pepper and mace. Peel and roughly chop the garlic cloves, and crush to a
paste with the sea salt in a mortar. Tear up the basil leaves, crush these into the
garlic paste, and then blend in the olive oil.

Bring the soups to the boil, and carefully pour into a heated soup tureen or
individual soup bowls. Pour each soup into opposite sides of the tureen or bowl, so
that they do not blend completely. Dribble a little basil and garlic oil in the centre
and serve immediately. If serving the soup cold, simply blend the ingredients as
described, without heating or boiling, and serve in a chilled tureen or soup bowls.

Smoked Haddock and Potato Soup

This is based on the Scottish Cullen Skink.

Serves 4–6

1 lb / 455 g piece of undyed
    smoked haddock
1 pt / 570 ml milk
parsley stalks
6 peppercorns
1 onion, peeled and finely chopped

1½ pt / 850 ml water
6 oz / 170 g mashed potatoes
¼ pt / 140 ml single cream
2 tbsp finely chopped parsley
freshly ground black pepper

Skin the fish and put it in a saucepan or frying pan, cutting it in two if necessary. Cover with the milk, and bring gently to the boil. Remove from the heat. When the fish is cool enough to handle, remove the flesh, cut into small pieces, and put it to one side. Reserve the milk, and put the fish bones, parsley stalks, peppercorns and half the onion in a saucepan with the water. Simmer for 30–40 minutes.

Meanwhile, simmer the remaining onions in the reserved milk in a large saucepan. Strain the fish stock into the saucepan. Mix the potatoes, cream and parsley, and stir this into the soup. Add pepper to taste, bring to the boil, stir in the pieces of fish and serve immediately.

Variation ⏤ For a creamy smoked haddock and garlic soup, use all the onion to make the stock, omit the mashed potato, and simmer 15–20 garlic cloves and a peeled and diced potato in the milk until soft. Blend the stock with the milk, cooked potato and garlic, and pieces of fish, in a blender or food processor until smooth. Reheat, stir in the chopped parsley and cream, season with pepper to taste, and serve immediately.

Golden Fish Chowder

2 tbsp extra virgin olive oil *or* 1 oz /
  30 g butter
1 onion, peeled and chopped
1 lb / 455 g potatoes, peeled and
  diced
2 pt / 1.15 l fish stock
pinch of saffron threads

handful of coriander, stalks separated
  and leaves chopped
1 bay leaf
1 lb / 455 g undyed smoked haddock
  fillet
8 oz / 230 g cod fillet
freshly ground black pepper

Heat the oil or butter in a large saucepan or flameproof casserole, and gently cook the onion and potatoes, without browning, until the onion is transparent. Pour on the fish stock, add the saffron, coriander stalks and bay leaf, and simmer until the potatoes are soft. Remove the herbs. (At this stage, you can, if you want a thicker soup, mash some of the potatoes.)

Skin the fish fillets, and cut into 2–3 in / 5–7.5 cm squares. Put into the soup, and let it barely simmer for 2–3 minutes, until the fish is just cooked through. Season to taste with pepper, and chopped coriander leaves. Serve at once.

MEAT SOUPS

Avgolemono Soup

Serves 6

*This rice-based soup from Greece has a distinct lemon flavour. I often
serve rice with pot-roast chicken and make this soup from the chicken
and leftover rice.*

2–2½ pt / 1.15–1.45 l chicken stock	2–3 tbsp lemon juice
3 tbsp long grain rice	salt
2 egg yolks	freshly ground black pepper

Put the stock in a saucepan and bring to the boil. Scatter in the rice, lower the
heat, and simmer until the rice is tender. Beat the egg yolks and lemon juice
together in a small bowl, then beat in a ladleful of simmering broth. Remove the
soup from the heat, and stir in the egg and lemon mixture. Let it heat through
without simmering, otherwise the eggs will curdle. Season to taste, and serve.

Turkey and Barley Soup

Turkey stock is often plentiful after Christmas. Here is a very good recipe for using it up. Chicken, duck and goose stock can be used in the same way.

3–4 tbsp pearl barley
3 pt / 1.70 l turkey stock
1 small onion or shallot, peeled and finely chopped
1 celery stalk, trimmed and finely sliced
½ small fennel bulb, trimmed and finely chopped

1 bay leaf
2 tbsp finely chopped parsley
salt
freshly ground black pepper
2 tbsp dry sherry *(optional)*

Simmer the barley in the stock until almost tender. Add the vegetables and bay leaf, and continue to simmer until the vegetables are cooked to your liking. Stir in the parsley, and season to taste. Add the sherry, if using, a few minutes before the vegetables are cooked to allow the alcohol to evaporate.

If you do not have, or like, barley, dice some raw potato and cook it with the vegetables. Shreds of turkey can also be added to the soup, in the last few minutes of cooking.

Bacon and Lentil Soup

Serves 4–6

1–1½ lb / 455–680 g knuckle of
  bacon
1 leek, trimmed and thinly sliced
1 carrot, peeled and thinly sliced
2 onions, peeled and thinly sliced
1 celery stalk, trimmed and thinly
  sliced

1 bay leaf
½ tbsp peppercorns
8 oz / 230 g blonde lentils
1 tbsp olive oil
salt

Soak the knuckle of bacon in water for 20 minutes. Put all the prepared vegetables except for one onion, in a large saucepan. Put the bacon knuckle on top, and cover with plenty of water. Add the bay leaf and peppercorns, and bring slowly to the boil. Simmer for 2 hours, until you have plenty of good stock and the meat is tender.

While the stock is simmering, soak the lentils for 30 minutes, then drain them. Fry the remaining onion in the olive oil until golden, then add the lentils. Cover with water, and simmer very gently until the lentils are tender, adding a little more water as necessary.

Remove the bacon, and strain the stock. Allow the stock to cool slightly, and then put 1 pt / 570 ml in a blender with three-quarters of the lentils. Blend until smooth, and pour into a saucepan together with another 1 pt / 570 ml stock and the remaining lentils. Shred a little of the cooked bacon into the saucepan. Bring the soup to the boil, add salt if necessary, and pour into heated soup bowls.

Variation ∾ For a creamy bacon and potato soup, substitute 1 lb / 455 g potatoes for the lentils. When the stock is almost ready, peel and dice them, and cook them gently in the olive oil with the remaining onion for 8–10 minutes. Pour on 2 pt / 1.15 l stock, and simmer for 30–45 minutes. Allow to cool slightly, then purée in a blender or food processor. Add ¼ pt / 140 ml single cream, reheat, season to taste, and serve hot, garnished with chopped parsley. I particularly like this soup with thick slices of hot buttered toast.

See also Linsenspeck on page 219.

Split Pea and Sausage Soup

Very inexpensive to make, this is a real winter warmer, to serve when the budget is stretched. Rye bread and beer are perfect accompaniments.

6 oz / 170 g streaky bacon in a
 piece, smoked or unsmoked to
 taste
1 onion, peeled and chopped
1 carrot, peeled and chopped
1 leek, trimmed and sliced
1 celery stalk, trimmed and sliced

1 lb / 455 g dried split peas, soaked for
 1–2 hours
4 pt / 2.30 l ham stock
freshly ground black pepper
1 frankfurter or other boiling sausage
 per person

Remove the rind from the bacon and dice the meat. Fry the bacon gently in a large, heavy flameproof casserole until the fat runs. Add the vegetables, and fry them until lightly browned. Add the split peas, stock and a little pepper. Simmer for about 45 minutes, until the peas and vegetables are soft. Purée in a blender or food processor, or rub through a sieve, and return to the casserole. Poach the sausages in water until heated through, and then place in heated soup bowls. Ladle the soup over the sausages in the bowls. Serve with fried bread triangles, wholemeal rolls, or your favourite bread.

Lamb and Spring Vegetable Broth

Serves 4–6

If you can get lambs' tongues and a pair of sweetbreads, blanch and poach them, and then peel and dice, and add to the soup for the last few minutes. Otherwise, make the soup with vegetables and lamb.
The recipe is based on the one we were served at Kokejane in Belgium, cooked by Solange de Brouwer. The stock is best made the day before, so that it can be de-greased by chilling and removing the layer of fat.

2 lb / 900 g middle or scrag end of
  lamb, chopped
1 leek
2 celery stalks
1 carrot
1 small turnip
1 bay leaf

sprig of thyme or lemon thyme
6 peppercorns
piece of lemon zest
4–5 pt / 2.30–2.85 l water
salt
freshly ground black pepper

Remove as much fat as possible from the meat, and brown the pieces in a large heavy saucepan. Clean and trim or peel the vegetables, and add some of the peelings to the pan, together with the bay leaf, thyme, peppercorns and lemon zest. Pour on the water. Bring to the boil, skim the surface, and simmer on the lowest heat, partially covered, for 3–4 hours.

Meanwhile, finely dice the vegetables. Strain the stock, cool, and then chill it, and remove the layer of fat which will have congealed on the surface. Put the stock back in a saucepan with the diced vegetables, and cook until the vegetables are just tender, adding the tongue and sweetbreads, if using, or a little diced cooked lamb. Season to taste.

Game Soup

*This is a soup to make late in the game season, say in January when
the price of pheasant comes down.*

1 hen pheasant	sprig of thyme
1–2 wood pigeons	4 pt / 2.30 l water
3 fl oz / 85 ml port	5 oz / 140 g fat belly pork, derinded
pinch of ground mace	1 oz / 30 g unsalted butter
freshly ground black pepper	1 tbsp plain wholemeal flour
1 onion	6 oz / 170 g soft breadcrumbs
8 oz / 230 g carrots	1 egg
1 medium celeriac root, about	butter or oil for frying
12 oz / 340 g	salt
2–3 parsley stalks	freshly ground black pepper

Remove the breasts from the birds, and marinate them in the port and spices
while you make the stock. Chop the carcasses, and brown them well in a frying pan
before transferring to the stockpot. Halve the onion without peeling it, and brown
one half, cut side down, in the frying pan until well caramelized. Put with the
carcasses, one of the carrots, sliced, and a piece of peeled celeriac, no more than
2–3 oz / 60–85 g. Add the parsley stalks and thyme and cover with the water. Bring
to the boil, skim any foam from the surface, and simmer for 3–4 hours, until you
have a rich brown stock. Strain it, and put to one side. The recipe can be prepared
to this stage the day before required. It will not spoil the meat to marinate it for
even up to 48 hours (refrigerated).

Dice half the marinated meat, and mince the rest. Also mince the belly pork.
Fry the diced meat in the 1 oz / 30 g butter in a large, clean saucepan. Peel the
remaining onion, carrot and celeriac, dice them finely and fry with the meat.
Sprinkle on the flour, and stir in so that it absorbs the fat and any cooking juices.
Moisten with about ¼ pt / 140 ml stock, and stir until there are no lumps of flour.
Add up to 3 pt / 1.70 l stock in all, and simmer until the meat and vegetables are
tender. Mix the minced game and pork with the breadcrumbs and egg to bind. Roll
this forcemeat mixture into marble-sized balls, and fry until a deep golden brown.
Add to the simmering soup, and cook for a further 20 minutes or so. Season to
taste, and serve.

Pheasant Consommé

*This clear soup is dark amber-coloured, from the onion skin and the
browning of the bones used to make the stock. Its deep flavour is
obtained by cooking fresh pheasant and vegetables in the stock before
clarifying it. Consommé is time-consuming to prepare, but well worth
it for special occasions. It can be made in advance, and stored for up to
2 days in the refrigerator. It can also be frozen.*

2 hen pheasants	6 peppercorns
2 onions	3 cloves
2 carrots	twist of orange zest
1 leek	4 pt / 2.30 l water
2–3 ripe tomatoes	1 egg white
8–10 parsley stalks	salt
2 bay leaves	freshly ground black pepper

Remove the meat from the birds, keeping the breasts for another dish, and
finely mince or shred the meat from the thighs and drumsticks, and put it on one
side. Chop up the carcasses, and brown in a hot oven or large heavy saucepan.
Take one onion, quarter it but do not peel, and add to the carcasses in the pan.
Take one carrot, the leek and the tomatoes, and wash and trim as appropriate.
Then slice them, and add to the pan, together with 6–8 parsley stalks, one bay leaf,
the peppercorns, the cloves and the orange zest. Cover with the water, and bring
slowly to the boil. Skim off the grey foam that rises to the surface, partially cover
with a lid, and cook on the lowest possible heat for 3–4 hours. Do not let the stock
boil, as this makes it cloudy. Skim off the foam from time to time. Carefully strain
through a fine sieve lined with scalded muslin into a bowl, and then cover, cool and
refrigerate. The recipe can be prepared to this stage the day before, but remember
also to refrigerate the meat until needed.

When ready to prepare the consommé, remove the layer of fat that will have
congealed on the surface of the chilled stock, and put the stock in a large saucepan.
Peel or trim and very finely chop the remaining vegetables, and add to the pan with
the the minced pheasant, remaining bay leaf and parsley stalks and the egg white.
Heat gently, whisking continuously, until the egg white has formed a foamy mass
on the surface. Lower the heat, and simmer very gently for 1½–2 hours. Do not let

the contents of the pan boil or the foam will break up and cloud the stock once more. Place a scalded jelly bag or a sieve lined with scalded muslin over a clean bowl, and carefully pour the contents of the pan through it. The foamy cooked egg white will be left in the muslin. Carefully pour the consommé through it once more into another clean bowl or saucepan, leaving any remaining impurities trapped in the foam. Reheat, season to taste, and serve with toast or croûtons.

Variations ∞ Chicken and beef consommés can be made the same way.

CHILLED SOUPS

Carrot and Peach Soup

Serves 4

This soup has a wonderfully soothing quality, both in its delicate colour and its velvety texture. The peach flavour is barely there, but just enough to intrigue.

2 shallots, peeled and finely sliced
8 oz / 230 g carrots, peeled and
  thinly sliced
1¼ pt / 710 ml vegetable stock
1 large or 2 small ripe peaches

good pinch of ground cardamom
salt
freshly ground white pepper
2–3 tbsp yoghurt or single cream
  (optional)

Put the shallots and carrots in a saucepan with a quarter of the stock. Cook until soft. Cool slightly. Stone the peach(es), roughly chop the fruit and place in a food processor or blender with the carrot and shallot mixture. Add a little more stock and the cardamom. Process until smooth. Sieve and mix with the rest of the stock. Cool rapidly, and chill until ready to serve. Season to taste just before serving. If you want to enrich it, also stir in the yoghurt or cream just before serving.

Variation ∞ Substitute mango for the peach, and before cooking the vegetables in the stock, fry them in sunflower oil with the cardamom and a teaspoon of ground cumin until the shallots are golden brown.

Summer Vichyssoise

Serves 4–6

1 medium potato, peeled and
  chopped
1 onion, peeled and chopped
1 tbsp sunflower oil
1½ lb / 680 g green vegetables, such
  as fennel, celery, courgettes, peas,
  asparagus, broad beans

2 pt / 1.15 l vegetable or light chicken
  stock
handful of fresh herbs, such as parsley,
  chives, chervil and sorrel
salt
freshly ground black pepper
3–4 tbsp yoghurt or single cream
  (*optional*)

Fry the potato and onion gently in the oil for a few minutes without browning.
Wash, trim and roughly chop the green vegetables as appropriate. Any tough ones,
such as fennel or celery, should be put on to cook at this stage. Add about ¼ pt /
140 ml stock, and cook until the vegetables are soft. Add the rest of the greens and
half the herbs, and cook until the greens are done. Allow to cool slightly, make a
purée in a blender or food processor, sieve, and stir in the rest of the stock. Finely
chop the remaining herbs, and stir these in. Chill until ready to serve. Just before
serving, season to taste, and, if using, stir in the yoghurt or single cream.

Chilled Courgette and Potato Soup

Serves 4

1 medium onion, peeled and finely
  chopped
2 tbsp sunflower oil
12 oz / 340 g courgettes, trimmed
  and diced
1 medium potato, peeled and diced

1½ pt / 850 ml vegetable stock
handful of fresh basil
salt
freshly ground white pepper
¼ pt / 140 ml single cream

Sweat the onion in the oil in a large saucepan until soft. Add the courgettes and
potato to the saucepan, pour on half the stock, bring to the boil, and simmer until
the vegetables are tender. Put most of the basil, leaves and stalks, in a blender or
food processor, keeping a little for garnish. Pour on the vegetables, and process
until smooth. Sieve if necessary, season lightly, stir in the remaining stock and the
cream, and chill until required. Check seasoning, garnish with basil and serve.

Cucumber Soup

1 cucumber
1 small onion
½ pt / 280 ml chicken or vegetable
   stock
1 bay leaf
1 tbsp roughly chopped parsley

½ pt / 280 ml full-cream milk
7 fl oz / 200 ml single or double cream,
   depending on how rich a soup you
   want
salt
freshly ground white pepper

Peel the cucumber, cut it in half lengthways, and remove the seeds. Roughly chop. Peel and thinly slice the onion, and cook gently in a large saucepan with a little of the chicken or vegetable stock until soft. Add the cucumber pieces, the rest of the stock, the bay leaf and parsley, and cook for 10–12 minutes. Put in a blender or food processor, and blend until smooth. Allow the mixture to cool, stir in the milk and cream, and then chill until required. Season to taste just before serving.

Variations ∾ Tomato soup can be made in the same way, substituting 1 lb / 455 g ripe tomatoes, peeled and roughly chopped, for the cucumber.

A creamy avocado soup can be made by replacing the cucumber with the flesh of 2 large ripe avocados, but use single cream or milk instead of double cream, or the soup will be too rich. Make at the last minute, so that the avocado does not have time to discolour.

To prepare a delicious and unusual cucumber, prawn and buttermilk soup, simply put the peeled, deseeded and roughly chopped cucumber in a blender or food processor with 1 pt / 570 ml buttermilk, ½ pt / 280 ml semi-skimmed milk, ½ pt / 280 ml peeled prawns and a little fresh dill, basil or coriander leaf, and blend until smooth. Chill, season to taste, stir in a handful of whole peeled prawns and serve. For an oriental version of this, use coconut milk, coriander, mint or basil and a little grated fresh ginger and lime zest.

THE TIMES COOK IN SINGAPORE
AND MALAYSIA

ONE OF THE most interesting styles of cooking to be found in Singapore and Malaysia's exquisite food is that of the Nonyas. These are women of the Straits' Chinese families, descended from the original Chinese settlers who went to the Malay Peninsula and married into the local Muslim population. Their cooking is a heady blend of the subtle and varied textures and cooking methods of the Chinese from Hokkien mixed with the powerful and aromatic spices of Malacca and the Spice Islands. Indeed, Malacca is the home of the Nonya Baba or Peranakan culture, and is where the first Chinese settlers arrived in the sixteenth century. Now you can find this marvellous food throughout Malaysia and Singapore.

Those who enjoy curries will enjoy the spicy heat of the chillies. But other flavourings are also used, particularly coconut milk, which gives a mellowness to the finished dish. It is quite simple to make at home using desiccated coconut, and keeps well in the refrigerator for 2–3 days (see page 41).

Fresh turmeric, galangal (a member of the ginger family), tamarind, lemon grass, lime leaves and kaffir limes or makrut are also used, and can now be found in many Indian and Chinese shops and city markets in the West as can canned coconut milk and coconut cream.

Some of Singapore's best-known dishes are essentially street-food. Eating in Singapore at one of the hawker stalls or *kopi tiams* is a hugely social occasion, and people are most knowledgeable about where to get the best *hokkien mee* (see recipe on page 194) or the most succulent satay. People will travel from all over the island to go to one particular stall. For this reason, standards are very high and competition fierce.

The Nonya Chicken Curry recipe given on page 43 is based on one cooked at The Regent Hotel in Kuala Lumpur by Mr Kasim, the Malaysian sous chef. They serve it on the Palm Terrace, next to the clear blue, free-form swimming pool, surrounded by palm trees. The curry, however, tastes only slightly less wonderful away from this tropical paradise. My Beef Rendang recipe (see page 44) is based on one we ate at Aziza's in Singapore, but I also checked the ingredients for the dish, originally from Sumatra, with Sri Owen's *Indonesian and Thai Cookery*. Chutneys, flat breads, hard-boiled eggs, spring onions and cucumber sticks can be served as accompaniments to these main dishes.

After all this flavour and spiciness, sliced pineapple, mango and papaya set on a bed of crushed ice would be a perfect way to finish. If you prefer something richer, serve chilled tapioca pudding, made with coconut milk and served with a topping of brown sugar syrup, for a typical Malaysian *gula melaka*. The banana, date and coconut tart fillings given on pages 546-547 were also inspired by my visits to Malaysia.

Coconut Milk

1 lb / 455 g desiccated coconut
1½ pt / 850 ml water

Put the coconut and water in a saucepan, bring to the boil, and simmer for 5 minutes. Allow to cool until you can hold your finger in it without burning. Pour through a fine sieve into a bowl, pressing out as much liquid as possible from the coconut trapped in the sieve. Cool and refrigerate until required, but no longer than 2–3 days. 'Cream' will form on the top, which should be stirred back into the liquid before using.

Laksa
(Coconut Soup with Chicken and Rice Noodles)

Serves 6–8

Sambal Sauce
4 shallots *or* 1 medium onion, peeled and finely chopped
8 garlic cloves, peeled and crushed
6 tbsp groundnut (peanut) oil
4 dried chillies, soaked
5 oz / 140 g ripe tomatoes, roughly chopped
1 tsp sugar
1 tsp ground coriander
1 tsp ground cumin

Soup
4 oz / 110 g thin rice noodles *or* vermicelli
8 oz / 230 g chicken breast meat
1 pt / 570 ml chicken stock

1 pt / 570 ml coconut milk (see page 41)
½ oz / 15 g tamarind paste *or* 2 tbsp lemon juice
½ oz / 15 g fresh root ginger, peeled and grated
4 kaffir lime leaves *or* a piece of lemon grass, if available
3 tbsp shrimp paste
½ lb / 230 g prawns, peeled
3 oz / 85 g bean sprouts
3 oz / 85 g cucumber, cut into matchsticks

Accompaniments
chilli slices
fried onion rings
coriander leaves

To make the sambal sauce, gently fry the shallots or onion and garlic in the groundnut oil until soft. Add the rest of the ingredients, bring to the boil, cook for a few minutes, then rub through a sieve. Put in a bowl, and cover until required. (It will keep for a few days in the refrigerator.)

To make the soup, blanch the noodles in boiling water for 3–4 minutes, drain and refresh under cold water, and put to one side. Poach the chicken meat for 8 minutes, and then shred it. Put the stock and coconut milk in a saucepan, add the tamarind paste or lemon juice, ginger, lime leaves or lemon grass and shrimp paste. Simmer for 5 minutes, then add the prawns, chicken, bean sprouts, cucumber and noodles. Bring to the boil and serve immediately.

Hand the sambal sauce and the other accompaniments separately for people to stir into their soup as they wish.

Nonya Chicken Curry

Serves 4–6

3½ lb / 1.35 kg free-range chicken
4 tbsp groundnut (peanut) oil
3 onions, peeled and chopped
½ tsp salt
red chillies, deseeded, to taste
1 in / 2.5 cm fresh turmeric root,
   peeled and chopped
10 blanched almonds

2 lime leaves *(optional) or* 1 bay leaf
4 lemon grass stalks
4–6 tbsp good quality curry powder or
   paste
1½ pt / 850 ml coconut milk (see
   page 41)
juice of 1 lime

Joint the chicken quite small, using poultry shears to cut thighs into two and breasts into several pieces. In a heavy frying pan, heat the oil, and fry one of the chopped onions with the salt until lightly browned. Grind together the red chillies, turmeric root, almonds, lime leaves or bay leaf, lemon grass and curry powder or paste, and add this paste to the pan. Fry for 5–8 minutes until fragrant, adding a little coconut milk if the mixture shows signs of catching. Add the chicken pieces, and turn them well in the spice mixture. Fry for 5–10 minutes, and then pour in the remaining coconut milk. Bring to the boil, partially cover, and simmer for 30–35 minutes or until the chicken is tender and cooked through. Just before serving, stir in the lime juice. Add more salt if necessary, and serve with rice or one of the Indian flat breads.

Beef Rendang

Serves 6–8

2 lb / 900 g flank or shin of beef in a piece

4–5 garlic cloves, peeled and roughly chopped

2 medium onions, peeled and roughly chopped

2–3 (or more to taste) red chillies, deseeded and chopped

1 in / 2.5 cm fresh root ginger, peeled and chopped

1½ pt / 850 ml coconut milk (see page 41)

2 tsp freshly grated turmeric root *or* 1 tsp ground turmeric

1 tsp freshly grated galangal root *or* ½ tsp dried galangal

1 bay leaf

1–2 lemon grass stalks, shredded

salt

Cut the beef into 2 in / 5 cm chunks, removing any excess fat and gristle. Grind the garlic, onions, chillies and ginger together into a paste. Stir the meat into this paste and put it all in a heavy saucepan, deep frying pan or wok. Cover with coconut milk, and stir in the turmeric and galangal. Add the bay leaf and the lemon grass, bring to the boil, and simmer, uncovered, for 1½ to 2 hours. You can start to season the meat with salt towards the end of this cooking time, but use a light hand since the stew has to cook until almost dry.

If you have cooked it so far in a saucepan, transfer the stew to a frying pan or wok, and continue cooking. By now you will have quite a dark, fragrant stew with the oil beginning to separate out from the coconut milk in which the meat has cooked. Cook for a further 20–30 minutes, stirring fairly frequently to stop the stew from catching, until the oil and liquid have almost all been reabsorbed into the meat. Serve with plain boiled rice or rice cooked in coconut milk. This dry stew is, as you might imagine, even better when reheated the next day.

Short Eats

I hope my Sri Lankan friends will forgive me for borrowing their term for this chapter, and that my Nigerian friends will forgive me for not borrowing theirs, 'small chop', which was a close second choice. 'Short eats' is far more expressive of the food I have written about than canapés, hors d'oeuvre or starters. Within this chapter you will find dishes suitable for the first course of a meal, and for serving with drinks before dinner alongside food suitable for snacks, or for a break when you do not have the time or the energy to prepare a meal. 'Grazing food' is another similar notion, except that I do not like the term much; it sounds faddish, and fads pass.

You will find here recipe ideas which can be prepared using little more than the contents of your store-cupboard. I have included food suitable for picnics of all kinds from the rough hike in the country to the most elegant of Glyndebourne picnics, and the 'en cas' that you might need to take with you while travelling.

Some recipes in the chapter use up leftovers. In other recipes, I deliberately create leftovers so that I can use them in entirely new and appetizing ways. Some of the food is designed to be eaten hot, some cold. Quite a number of the recipes can be prepared in advance and stored in the refrigerator, making them invaluable aids to the cook faced with unexpected guests, or when an impromptu supper party is suggested.

A common theme to many of the dishes is that they consist of a bland staple and something savoury. The fillings are also, in many cases, interchangeable. I would not recommend quail eggs in filo pastry 'overcoats', unless you have great manual dexterity. It can be done, and would not be unlike a miniature Tunisian *brik à l'oeuf*. But the snail and garlic butter filling from the Snail Puffs (see page 48) can be baked in the Savoury Batter Pudding batter (see page 52), the stuffed vine leaf filling (see page 65) in wonton wrappers, the mussels (see page 54) in potato 'treasure chests' (see page 62) and the oriental wonton filling (see page 53) in puff pastry, or, indeed, in the Savoury Batter Pudding batter. The permutations are numerous. For example the recipe on page 52 can also be increased and baked in a larger container to allow you to cut it into serving portions. The larger Savoury Batter Pudding is particularly good with mussels and lightly cooked sliced leeks.

There are many more versions of the staple-plus-savoury theme: blini (see page 57) with soured cream and caviar; pizzas, large or small, with a traditional or unusual topping (I like cream cheese and smoked salmon on mine. This goes on *after* the pizza has baked – see Glamorous Pizzas on page 450); and small filled bread cases. Make the latter by stamping out rounds of sliced buttered bread, pressing them into buttered bun tins, and baking them until crisp. A spoonful of scrambled egg mixed with chopped ham, smoked salmon, herbs or cheese, for example, makes a good filling. (See also Stir-fried Vegetable and Toasted Sesame Tartlets on page 61.)

If preparing food for a drinks party or buffet, I suggest that 'spoon food' should re-place the usual fork or finger food. For food that is too wet, hot, slippery, crumbly or otherwise difficult to eat in the hand, such as Hot Stuffed Vine Leaves (see page 65), Deep-fried Oyster and Potato Bundles (see page 69), Chicken Liver Mousse (see page 77) and steamed Wontons (see page 53), put mouthfuls into Chinese soup spoons and arrange these on a platter or tray. The food is eaten from the spoon. No plates or forks are needed, and it is easy to manage with the spoon in one hand and a glass in the other.

Spoon food, finger food, fork food, buffet food, appetizers, snacks, sandwiches – they are all here, and they are all 'short eats'.

HOT PASTRIES

IF YOU are planning to serve any of these at a drinks party, over a period of about 2–3 hours, you need to allow for approximately 8–12 mouthfuls per guest. Depending on how many people you are inviting, you can work out if you need to start the preparation the day before or a few hours before.

Snail Puffs

Makes 12

8 oz / 230 g puff pastry, thawed if
  frozen
12 medium shelled snails
3–4 garlic cloves, peeled and
  crushed

3 oz / 85 g salted butter, softened
freshly ground black pepper
salt *(optional)*
finely chopped parsley
beaten egg yolk and water, to glaze

Roll out the pastry, and cut it into twelve 3 in / 7.5 cm squares. Place a snail in the centre of each. Mash the crushed garlic into the butter and add a portion to each snail. Season with pepper, a little salt, if you wish, and add finely chopped parsley. Dampen the edges of the pastry, fold the corners to the centre, and pinch to seal along the four edges, completely enclosing the snail and butter. (You can prepare to this point well in advance, in the morning or even the night before. Refrigerating the pastries does in fact help them to remain sealed tight during baking.)

When ready to bake, brush the pastries with the beaten egg yolk and water, and bake in a preheated oven at 200 °C / 400 °F / Mark 6 for 12 minutes.

Little Oyster Pies

Makes 6

6 oysters
freshly ground black pepper
6 lettuce leaves, blanched
4 oz / 110 g flaky pastry
3 oz / 85 g butter, softened
3 anchovy fillets, chopped

good pinch of ground mace
2 tbsp soft white breadcrumbs
juice and grated zest of ½ lemon
beaten egg yolk and water, to glaze
  (optional)

Remove the oysters from their shells, keeping the juice. Season lightly with pepper, and wrap in the lettuce leaves. Roll out the pastry and use to line six tartlet tins, reserving a third of the pastry to make 'lids' for the pies. Mix the remaining ingredients together with a little lemon juice and the strained oyster juice. Place some of the mixture in the lined tart tins, put the wrapped oysters on top and add the remaining butter mixture. Top the tarts with pastry lids. Brush with egg yolk and water if you wish and bake in a preheated oven at 200°C / 400°F / Mark 6 for 10 minutes. Serve hot or warm.

Variation ∾ Spinach or blanched streaky bacon can replace the lettuce leaves.

Minced Meat Pastries

Small savoury pastries can be served with soup to turn them into a substantial lunch or supper dish. I like to experiment with sweet and savoury mixtures, something like the traditional mince pies when meat was added to the fruit mixture. I have used cooked minced game; they would also work very well with cooked minced lamb (either raw lamb, minced and then cooked, or cooked lamb that has been finely chopped or minced).

8 oz / 230 g puff pastry
4 oz / 110 g cooked minced meat
2 tbsp olive oil
2 tbsp grated apple
1 tbsp finely chopped onion
1 tbsp dark muscovado or other
   unrefined sugar

¼ tsp ground cardamom
¼ tsp ground cinnamon
freshly grated nutmeg
salt
freshly ground black pepper
milk, to glaze

Roll out the pastry and use it to line 12 tartlet tins, also cutting out 12 pastry lids. Mix together the rest of the ingredients, season to taste with nutmeg, salt and pepper, and divide the mixture between the pastry cases. Cover with pastry lids and brush with milk to glaze. Bake in a preheated oven at 180°C / 350°F / Mark 4 for 15–18 minutes.

Spicy Sausage Roll

Makes 12–16 slices

*Buy the best sausages you can find, with plenty of meat, and you will
find this makes an excellent accompaniment to a tasting of red wines,
as an alternative to cheese.*

1 lb / 455 g sausages	1 tsp ground allspice
2 tbsp port, red vermouth or sherry	freshly ground black pepper
2 shallots *or* 1 small onion, peeled and finely chopped	12 oz / 340 g puff pastry
1 tbsp finely chopped parsley or watercress	2–3 tbsp Dijon mustard
	milk or beaten egg, to glaze *(optional)*

Slit open the sausages and squeeze the meat into a bowl. Mix in the port,
shallots or onion, parsley or watercress and spice, and blend thoroughly. You may
like to add some black pepper, but it is unlikely that you will need to add salt. Roll
the pastry out to a rectangle measuring about 8 × 12 in / 20.5 × 30.5 cm, and
spread with the mustard. Spoon the sausage meat in a line along the length of the
pastry and brush the long edges with water. Carefully roll up, press the pastry edge
to seal, and place the roll on a greased and floured baking sheet, with the join
underneath. Slash with a knife point in two or three places on top to let steam
escape, brush with milk or egg, if wished, and bake for 20–25 minutes in a
preheated oven at 190 °C / 375 °F / Mark 5. Cut into slices to serve.

Variation ∾ A salmon roll can be made by mixing flaked cooked salmon with
cooked rice, chopped hard-boiled eggs, herbs (such as dill or chervil) and some
chopped onion fried in butter, with a little white wine and seasoning. Construct
and bake in exactly the same way.

Cheese and Asparagus Pastries

Makes 8

*Buying asparagus loose during the short season, one is often left with
an assortment of different sizes. Here is one way of using them up.*

8 oz / 230 g trimmed fresh
  asparagus (the tender green parts
  and tips only)
1 lb / 455 g puff pastry
8 oz / 230 g cheese, grated
4 ripe tomatoes, peeled, deseeded
  and chopped

salt
freshly ground black pepper
juice of ½ lemon
8 basil leaves
2 oz / 60 g butter
milk or beaten egg, to glaze

Bring a saucepan of salted water to the boil and throw in the asparagus. Boil
vigorously for 5 minutes, or until just beginning to become tender. Drain and
refresh under cold running water. Roll out the puff pastry, and cut out eight circles.
Divide the asparagus between the eight circles, arranging it on one half only.
Divide the cheese into eight and heap it up on top of the asparagus. Top this with
the chopped tomatoes. Season to taste with salt, pepper and a little lemon juice.

Tear the basil leaves into shreds, and arrange on top of the tomato, together
with a small knob of butter. Moisten around the edges of the pastry circles with
water, fold them over and seal the parcels. Place on a greased baking sheet and
brush with milk or egg. Pierce the top of each pastry with a fork to let the steam
escape, and bake for 15 minutes in a preheated oven at 190 °C / 375 °F / Mark 5.

Savoury Batter Puddings

Makes 12

1 heaped tbsp plain flour
1 egg
¼ pt / 140 ml milk or milk and
  water mixed
2 ripe tomatoes

2 oz / 60 g black olives
1 garlic clove, peeled and crushed
  (optional)
6 anchovy fillets, chopped

Beat the flour, egg and liquid together to make a smooth batter. Let it stand
while you prepare the rest of the ingredients. Peel, deseed and dice the tomatoes.

Remove the stones from the olives,and chop them. Mix the tomatoes and olives with the rest of the ingredients. Lightly oil a bun tin, or use a non-stick tin. Put a teaspoonful of the mixture in each tin, pour on the batter, and bake in a preheated oven at 200 °C / 400 °F / Mark 6 for 30–35 minutes. They should be quite dark golden brown and puffed up when cooked, though will sink somewhat when removed from the oven. Serve warm.

This can also be baked in one large container, and cut into individual serving portions. You will need to bake it for 45–50 minutes.

Wontons

Makes 24

*Buy Wonton wrappers in Oriental markets to make
these savoury parcels.*

4 spring onions *or* 1 small leek,
   trimmed and finely sliced
3 oz / 85 g bean sprouts, blanched
   and roughly chopped
2 garlic cloves, peeled and crushed
1 tsp freshly grated ginger
1 tbsp groundnut (peanut) oil
2 tbsp soy sauce
2 tsp clear honey
1 tbsp rice vinegar

3 oz / 85 g cooked chicken meat,
   chopped or shredded
2 oz / 60 g peeled prawns, roughly
   chopped
2 oz / 60 g shiitake or button
   mushrooms, finely chopped
salt
freshly ground black pepper
24 wonton wrappers

Mix the vegetables with the garlic and ginger, and then add the oil, soy sauce, honey and vinegar. Mix in the chicken meat, prawns and mushrooms. Season to taste. Spoon a little of the mixture into the centre of one wonton wrapper, floury side up, dampen the edges, and pinch it together to seal it. Fill the rest in the same way. The wontons can then be deep-fried, steamed or simmered in soup.

Mussels in Overcoats

Makes 12

3 sheets filo pastry	salt
12 spinach leaves	freshly ground white pepper
12 mussels, lightly steamed and	juice of ½ lemon
shelled	1 oz / 30 g unsalted butter, melted

Cut each sheet of pastry into four strips, and pile them, one on top of the other, on a damp tea-towel. Wrap the towel around the pastry to prevent it from drying out. Remove the central rib from the spinach leaves, and blanch them by draping them over a colander and pouring boiling water over them. Refresh under cold running water, and dry them carefully. Wrap each mussel carefully in a spinach leaf, lightly seasoning with salt and pepper and a drop of lemon juice.

Preheat the oven to 200 °C / 400 °F / Mark 6. Unwrap the pastry, and brush the top strip with some of the melted butter. Place a wrapped mussel at the bottom right-hand corner of the strip, the edge nearest you. Fold the pastry over the mussel so that the bottom edge now meets the left hand side, to form a triangular shape. Now fold that triangle over so that the parcel is sealed, and continue folding over until the strip completely encloses the mussel in a triangular parcel. Place on a baking sheet. Make the other parcels in the same way and bake in the oven for 8–10 minutes.

Variation ∾ Raw oysters or queen scallops can be substituted for the mussels, and the 'overcoat' can be made with blanched lettuce leaves instead of spinach.

Spanakopitta

Serves 6–8

The next dish, based on a Greek recipe, is very good hot, cold or warm. It is also as at home in a picnic basket as on the dining-table. I like to use a mixture of cheeses – feta for sharpness, ricotta or cottage cheese for mellowness and a hard cheese, which melts and holds the filling together.

2¼ lb / 1 kg spinach
6 oz / 170 g butter
salt
freshly ground black pepper
freshly grated nutmeg

3 oz / 85 g ricotta or cottage cheese
2 oz / 60 g feta cheese, crumbled
2 oz / 60 g Parmesan, Pecorino,
    Cheddar or Gruyère cheese, grated
10 sheets filo pastry

Wash and pick over the spinach, and remove any tough central stalks. Shake dry, and put in a large saucepan with a third of the butter. Cover and cook until the spinach has wilted and collapsed. Drain and cool the spinach, and season with salt, pepper and nutmeg. Stir in the cheeses.

Thickly butter a square or round cake tin, about 1–1½ in / 2.5–4 cm deep and 8 in / 20.5 cm across. Melt the remaining butter and brush each sheet of filo pastry with it before peeling the sheet off the pile. Line the tin with five sheets of buttered filo, butter side down, and spoon in the spinach mixture. Cut the remaining five sheets of pastry to fit the top of the pie. Lay two sheets on top, and then bring the overlapping lining sheets over the top layer of pastry. To finish the pie, lay the last three sheets of pastry on top. Bake in a preheated oven at 180°C / 350°F / Mark 4 for about 45 minutes, increasing the heat for the last 10 minutes or so to brown the top. Remove from the oven and allow to cool slightly. Remove from the tin by inverting a plate over the pie, turning it out, and then putting another plate over the base of the pie and turning it the right way up.

Roquefort Profiteroles

Makes 18

¼ pt / 140 ml milk and water mixed
2 oz / 60 g butter
3 oz / 85 g plain flour, sifted
pinch of salt

2 large eggs
2 oz / 60 g Roquefort cheese, finely
diced

Put the liquid and butter in a saucepan, heat gently until the butter has melted, and then bring to a strong boil. Remove from the heat, and tip in the flour and salt. Beat vigorously until the mixture becomes a stiff paste and leaves the sides of the pan. Cool for 5–10 minutes, and then beat in the eggs, one at a time, stirring in vigorously until the dough becomes smooth and glossy. Stir in the cheese. Drop teaspoonfuls of the mixture on to a greased baking sheet, and bake for 10–12 minutes in the top half of a preheated oven at 200 °C / 400 °F / Mark 6. Switch off the heat, open the oven door slightly, and leave the profiteroles in the oven for another 3–5 minutes. Remove and serve while hot.

Gougère

Serves 6–8

Using the standard choux pastry recipe, (see page 471), you can make a versatile cheese dish to be served as a cheese course with salad, as a starter or to serve warm in slices with drinks. Gruyère is the cheese used in the authentic version, but you could substitute other hard cheeses. Individual gougères made with Gruyère are traditionally served in the cellars of Burgundy and Chablis when wine-tasting.

3 oz / 85 g Gruyère cheese, finely diced
12 oz / 340 g choux pastry

Mix the diced cheese with the pastry and spoon it into a ring on a greased baking sheet. To make it rise even more by creating a steam oven, invert a deep roasting tin or cake tin over the pastry. Bake the pastry in a preheated oven at 220 °C / 425 °F / Mark 7 for 15 minutes, then turn the heat down to 180°C / 350°F / Mark 4 for another 12–15 minutes. Remove and serve hot or warm.

Variation ⁓ Mix diced mature goat's cheese with the pastry before baking and, when cool, split the gougère horizontally and sandwich it back together with a filling of fresh goat's cheese mixed with yoghurt or cream and fresh herbs.

Blini

Makes 12–16

1 egg
½ pt / 280 ml warm milk
1 tsp sugar
1 heaped tsp dried yeast

6 oz / 170 g plain flour and 2 oz / 60 g buckwheat flour *or* 8 oz / 230 g plain flour
1 tsp salt
oil for frying

Beat the egg and milk together, and stir in the sugar and yeast. Sift the flours and salt into a warm bowl, and whisk in the liquid. Cover the bowl and leave it to stand in a warm place for about 45 minutes, until the mixture has doubled in size.

Heat a heavy-based frying pan or griddle, and wipe it over with a few pieces of kitchen paper dipped in oil. Pour on a ladleful of batter and cook until the surface looks dry, with holes in it. Turn the blin over and cook quickly on the other side. It should not take more than 1–2 minutes for each blin. If you have a very large pan, or can manage two pans, you can cook several blini at a time. Keep them warm on a heatproof plate set over a pan of hot water. Serve each with a spoonful of soured cream and caviar.

TOASTS

IF YOU do not have time to make fancy snacks or finger food to accompany drinks, tri-angles of hot toast spread with spiced anchovy butter are a good standby. About 4 oz / 110 g softened butter blended with a 2 oz / 60 g can of anchovy fillets, a crushed garlic clove, a tablespoon of spicy chutney and a pinch of cayenne pepper will make enough spiced butter to spread on approximately 15–20 average-sized triangles of toast. The butter can be prepared in advance, and kept in the refrigerator until needed.

The other suggestions in this section will take a little more time to prepare, but are well worth it.

Toast Rothschild

Serves 2

I base this recipe on a dish I ate at Le Grand Véfour in Paris. This was my first visit to a Michelin three-star restaurant, as it was then. The food was memorable, but this dish particularly so.

2 slices of bread, 2 in / 5 cm thick	1 bay leaf
2½ oz / 70 g unsalted butter	sprig of thyme and parsley
2 tbsp olive or grapeseed oil	¼ pt / 140 ml dry white wine
8 oz / 230 g unpeeled prawns	¼ pt / 140 ml water
1 shallot, peeled and finely chopped	1 tbsp cognac
1 carrot, peeled and finely chopped	1 tbsp double cream
1 celery stalk, trimmed and finely chopped	salt
	freshly ground black pepper
2 ripe tomatoes, roughly chopped	1 tbsp Gruyère cheese, grated

Trim the crusts from the bread to make neat squares. Remove some of the crumb from each slice, leaving a hollow in the centre. Melt 1 oz / 30 g of the butter, mix it with the oil and brush over the bread squares. Place on a baking sheet. Peel the prawns, reserving the shells, and put the flesh to one side. Sweat the prawn shells with the shallot, carrot and celery in half the remaining butter. When the vegetables are soft, add the tomatoes and herbs. Pour on the wine and water, and let it all bubble gently for 20 minutes or so. Strain it into another saucepan, and boil to reduce by half. Meanwhile, bake the prepared bread squares in the oven preheated to 200°C / 400°F / Mark 6 for 8–10 minutes or until crisp and golden, and keep them warm on a plate. Add the cognac to the sauce, and flame it before stirring in the cream. Whisk in pieces of the remaining butter, and season to taste. Stir in the prawns, let them heat through, and then spoon the sauce into the toasted bread squares. Sprinkle with the grated Gruyère, and brown under a hot grill. Serve immediately.

Raisin Tapenade Cigarillos

Makes 24

*This is a recipe I came across in California, when I went to the
Central Valley during the harvesting of grapes for the raisin industry.*

12 thin slices fresh white bread
4 oz / 110 g cream cheese, softened
melted butter or olive oil for
　brushing

Raisin Tapenade
4 oz / 110 g black olives, pitted and
　finely chopped

2 oz / 60 g seedless raisins, finely
　chopped
1 tbsp paprika mixed with ½ tsp
　cayenne pepper
2 tbsp extra virgin olive oil
1 garlic clove, peeled and crushed
1 tbsp capers
2 anchovy fillets

To make the tapenade, pound the olives and raisins to a paste with the rest of the ingredients, or blend all together in a food processor or blender.

Trim the crusts from the bread, and then slightly flatten the slices with a rolling pin. Cut each slice into two rectangles. Spread each with cream cheese and then with the tapenade. Roll up tightly lengthways. Brush the rolls with butter or oil, dip one end into the paprika mix, and place on a baking sheet, seam-side down. Bake the cigarillos in preheated oven at 200 °C / 400 °F / Mark 6 for 5–8 minutes, until crisp and brown.

Asparagus and Prawns on Toast

Serves 2–4

*My friend Margaret Andrews introduced me to this tasty piece of
decadence. It is very good indeed.*

4 slices bread   1 tbsp mustard
8 oz / 230 g can asparagus spears or   3 oz / 85 g prawns, peeled
  cooked asparagus   1 egg white
1 oz / 30 g butter, softened   3 tbsp mayonnaise

Toast the bread on one side. Drain the asparagus spears. Mix the butter and
mustard, and spread on the untoasted side of the bread slices. Arrange the
asparagus on the same side and prawns on top. Whisk the egg white, and fold it
into the mayonnaise. Spread on top of the prawns and asparagus. Heat the grill,
but put the grill pan on a lower shelf to that normally used for making toast. Grill
the toasts until the topping is just turning golden brown. Serve immediately.

Stir-fried Vegetables and Toasted Sesame Tartlets

24 thin slices bread
2–3 tbsp groundnut (peanut) oil, plus extra for frying
1 tbsp toasted sesame oil
2 tbsp sesame seeds
1 in / 2.5 cm piece of fresh root ginger, peeled and sliced
2–3 star anise
2 in / 5 cm cinnamon stick

1 lb / 455 g prepared vegetables, selected from thin slices of carrot, mushrooms, baby corn cobs, broccoli florets, mangetout and spring onions
1 tbsp soy sauce
1 tbsp amontillado sherry or rice wine
1 tbsp sherry vinegar or rice vinegar
pinch of freshly ground black pepper or crushed Szechuan peppercorns

Cut the bread slices into 24 rounds with a pastry cutter. Brush 24 bun tins with some of the groundnut oil, and mix the rest with half the sesame oil. Use this to brush the bread, and press each piece into a bun tin. Sprinkle a few sesame seeds into each. Lightly toast the rest of the sesame seeds in a small frying pan and set aside. Bake the tartlets in a preheated oven at 200 °C / 400 °F / Mark 6 for 10–15 minutes, until crisp and golden.

Meanwhile, put 2–3 tablespoons groundnut oil in a frying pan or wok, and gently fry the ginger, star anise and cinnamon for 5 minutes. Remove from the oil, and then add the vegetables to the pan, starting with those that take longest to cook, and finishing with the mushrooms and spring onions. Stir continuously as the vegetables are frying, and when all have been added, splash in the soy sauce, sherry or wine, vinegar and pepper, together with 1–2 tablespoons of cold water. Cover with the lid and steam for a few minutes, shaking occasionally. When the vegetables are just cooked, but still crisp and vivid, stir in the remaining sesame oil, and spoon them into the hot tartlet cases. Sprinkle with toasted sesame seeds before serving.

OTHER HOT SNACKS

Treasure Chests

Makes 6

6 large potatoes
2 oz / 60 g butter, melted, *or*
    4 tbsp extra virgin olive oil
1 oz / 30 g ground almonds

1 oz / 30 g fresh breadcrumbs
good pinch of salt
freshly ground black pepper

Peel the potatoes and shape them into deep rectangular blocks. Cut a smaller rectangle out of the centre of each, leaving a good ¼ in / 0.5 cm wall. Brush the potato boxes inside and out with butter or oil. Mix the almonds, breadcrumbs and seasoning, and coat the boxes with it, also sprinkling the mixture inside. Put on a baking sheet, and bake in a preheated oven at 180°C / 350°F / Mark 4 until the potato is cooked crisp and golden. Remove and allow to cool slightly before filling (see below). If you want to make lids for the boxes, cut thin rectangles of potato, and prepare in the same way, balancing them on top when you have added the filling.

Suggested fillings

Soured cream, Greek yoghurt or crème fraîche topped with caviar or salmon roe

Soured cream, Greek yoghurt or crème fraîche mixed with grated horseradish and strips of smoked salmon

Soured cream, Greek yoghurt or crème fraîche mixed with diced cucumber and smoked haddock

Scrambled eggs and truffles

Scrambled eggs and caviar

I have also served, as an accompaniment to salmon, baked potato boxes filled with creamy mashed potatoes and topped with salmon roe.

Variations ⮞ Select very large potatoes and clean but do not peel them. Bake at 200 °C / 400 °F / Mark 6, until soft, about 1–1½ hours then take a thin slice off one broad surface of each to form a level base, and scoop out most of the potato from the top, leaving a sturdy layer next to the skin. Fill each hollowed-out potato with hot soup, and serve. Once the soup has been eaten, the remaining potato skin is delicious. Use the potato you have scooped out for another dish.

Use small new potatoes. Wash and scrub them, and then remove a thin slice from the bottom of each to allow it to stand flat, and, with a melon baller, scoop out a hollow in the top large enough to hold a quail's egg. Boil until just cooked in salted water. Drain, arrange on an oiled baking sheet, brush with melted butter, and sprinkle lightly with salt and pepper. Crack a quail's egg into each potato, and bake for 8–10 minutes at 180°C / 350°F / Mark 4. Serve immediately.

See also Baked Potatoes with Oysters on page 314.

Llapingachos
(*Potato and Cheese Cakes*)

Makes 16–20

These come from Ecuador. We ate them frequently in La Choza, a lovely restaurant in Quito. Serve these small ones as hot appetizers to accompany drinks.

2 lb / 900 g floury potatoes
salt
freshly ground black pepper
2 oz / 60 g butter

1 onion, peeled and finely chopped
2 tbsp olive oil
4 oz / 110 g hard cheese, such as
      Jarlsberg, Gruyère or Cheddar, grated

Peel, boil and mash the potatoes with salt, pepper and half the butter. Fry the onion in half the olive oil until soft and golden. Allow to cool slightly, and then mix with the cheese. Form the potato into small patties, and bury some of the cheese and onion mixture in the centre. Heat the remaining butter and olive oil in a frying pan, and fry the potato cakes on both sides until golden brown.

Variation ❧ A meal-size version uses the same ingredients to make 6 cakes, which are fried as described and served with a fried egg on top of each. Sliced avocados and a peanut sauce are the other accompaniments.

Snail and Mushroom Stew

*A hunt through your store-cupboard may well provide the ingredients
for this quick dish.*

8 oz / 230 g can shelled snails
¼ pt / 140 ml good dry white wine
1 small onion, peeled and chopped
1 celery stalk, trimmed and
　chopped
1 tbsp olive oil
½ oz / 15 g butter
1 level tsp cornflour or potato flour
¾ pt / 430 ml single cream or full-
　cream milk

1 jar (about 14 oz / 395 g) wild
　mushrooms
2 oz / 60 g tender greens, shredded
juice and grated zest of ½ lemon
salt
freshly ground black pepper
freshly grated nutmeg

Drain and thoroughly rinse the snails. Put them in a bowl and cover them with the white wine. Fry the onion and celery in the olive oil and butter until soft. Drain the snails, reserving the wine. Mix the cornflour or potato flour with a little of the white wine, and pour the rest over the onion and celery. Bring to the boil, and simmer for 2–3 minutes. Stir in the blended cornflour or potato flour until the mixture thickens. Add the cream, the mushrooms and the snails. Bring gently to simmering point, then stir in the greens. Once the mixture simmers again, add a little lemon juice and grated lemon zest, salt, pepper and nutmeg to taste.

Serve the stew on toast or in shallow bowls with bread fried in olive oil or butter, or with steamed new potatoes. The greens you use can, of course, be varied depending on the time of year. Try lettuce, spinach, rocket, watercress, sorrel, or even nettles and dandelions, provided you pick them far away from our lead-polluted roadsides.

Hot Stuffed Vine Leaves

Makes 24

A cucumber, mint and yoghurt salad (see page 98) makes a good
accompaniment to these. They are also very good cold.

24 vine leaves
8 oz / 230 g cooked lamb, finely
  chopped or minced
8 oz / 230 g cooked rice
2 oz / 60 g chopped tomatoes
1 tbsp finely chopped onion
1 tbsp pinenuts

1 tbsp finely chopped mint, sage or
  coriander
crushed garlic *(optional)*
sea salt
freshly ground black pepper
olive oil

Bring a large pan of water to the boil, and drop in the vine leaves. Bring back
to the boil, drain, rinse, and pat the leaves dry. Mix the lamb with the rest of the
ingredients, except the olive oil. Spoon a little on to a leaf, fold over the sides, and
roll into a cork shape. Place in an oiled ovenproof dish. Fill the rest of the leaves in
the same way. Sprinkle with olive oil, and bake in a preheated oven at 180°C /
350°F / Mark 4 for 20–30 minutes.

The filling can be varied to use up other leftovers. I like to make a vegetarian
filling, mixing cooked chick peas and couscous or lentils and quinoa, chopped
mint, grated lemon zest, raisins and pinenuts.

Grilled Polenta Slices with Mushrooms

This recipe is based on one from Antonio Carluccio's excellent book,
An Invitation to Italian Cooking. *If fresh ceps are hard to find,*
ordinary field mushrooms combined with a few dried ceps still give a
wonderful flavour to this dish. It is best to start your preparation the
day before, to allow sufficient time for the polenta to set.

Polenta Slices
3 pt / 1.70 l water
salt
13 oz / 370 g packet polenta *or*
    10 oz / 280 g yellow polenta flour

1 oz / 30 g butter
2 oz / 60 g Parmesan cheese, freshly
    grated
2 tbsp olive oil

Put the water in a large saucepan, add salt and bring to the boil. Very carefully add the polenta, stirring constantly to prevent lumps forming. Continue to stir until you see the golden mass start to come away from the sides of the pan (5 minutes for polenta; 30 minutes for ordinary polenta flour). Stir in the butter and the Parmesan cheese, and, while it is still hot, pour into an oiled mould with straight sides, such as a loaf tin. Leave to cool and set, ideally overnight.

Next day, turn out the polenta, and cut it into slices about ¾ in / 2 cm thick. Brush each slice with olive oil, and put under a hot grill until well browned on both sides. Serve with a small spoonful of the mushroom sauce (see below) on top of each slice.

Mushroom sauce
12 oz / 340 g fresh ceps *or* 12 oz /
    340 g field mushrooms plus
    1 oz / 30 g dried ceps
1 small onion, peeled and finely
    chopped
3 tbsp olive oil

1 oz / 30 g butter
7 oz / 200 g can peeled plum tomatoes,
    puréed
salt
freshly ground black pepper
6 basil leaves, chopped *(optional)*

Clean and slice the mushrooms, and, if using dried ceps, soak them in lukewarm water for 10 minutes. Fry the onion in the olive oil and butter until translucent, then add the mushrooms, and cook over a high heat for 10 minutes.

Add the tomatoes, lower the heat slightly, and continue cooking for another 20 minutes, so that most of the water from the tomatoes evaporates. Season to taste with salt and pepper, and, if using, stir in the basil.

Variations ∽ Grilled polenta slices make a good 'bed' for all manner of savouries. Try them with creamed salt cod or smoked haddock, aubergine purée, olive paste, or any of the toppings, spreads, pâtés, sauces and fillings found in this chapter and throughout the book.

See also Creamy Cep Polenta on page 215.

Roasted Garlic, Gorgonzola and Toasted Pinenuts

Per person

I have tasted various versions of this dish in California and I am fairly sure that Alice Waters, of Chez Panisse in Berkeley, is the originator.

1 large head of garlic
1 tbsp extra virgin olive oil
2–3 oz / 60–85g slice of Gorgonzola
  cheese

1 tbsp pinenuts
greenery, to garnish

Peel off any loose skin, but leave the garlic bulb whole. With a sharp knife, slice off a shallow cap from the top of the bulb. Put the garlic in a baking tin and sprinkle the cut surface with the olive oil, letting the rest dribble into the tin. Replace the cap, and bake in the centre of a preheated oven at 190 °C / 375 °F / Mark 5 for 20 minutes. Lower the heat to 150°C / 300°F / Mark 2, and continue cooking until the garlic is creamy and tender, which may take 1 hour altogether. Meanwhile, put the cheese on a heatproof plate and toast the pinenuts in a dry frying pan.

Just before you are ready to serve the garlic, melt the cheese in the oven or under the grill. Put the garlic on the plate, cap removed, and scatter the pinenuts on the cheese. Garnish the plate with greenery.

Given the length of time taken to cook the garlic in the oven, this is a good dish to serve as a starter, if you're also cooking a casserole in the oven.

Winni's St Helenian Fish Cakes

Makes 15–20

This recipe came to me from Mrs Winni Scipio in St Helena, who sent me a pungent package of extremely *hot chillies, some of which I still had, several years later, bottled in oil. Mrs Scipio uses fresh tuna, but fresh mackerel, rainbow trout or salmon would be suitable alternatives.*

1½ lb / 680 g potatoes, peeled
2 oz / 60 g back bacon, finely chopped
1 large onion, peeled and finely chopped
3 small fresh chillies, deseeded and finely chopped

2 tbsp finely chopped parsley
1 tsp chopped thyme
fat or oil for frying
2 lb / 900 g skinned fish fillets
1 egg, beaten
salt
freshly ground black pepper

Boil and mash the potatoes. They should be smooth, but do not add any milk. Fry the bacon, onion, chillies and herbs in a little fat or oil without browning them, then transfer to a bowl. Mince the raw fish, add it to the bowl and mix everything well together. Add the beaten egg, and season to taste. Let the mixture rest for 10 minutes. Make into cakes 1½ in / 4 cm deep and 2 in / 5 cm across. Pour slightly less than 1 in / 2.5 cm oil into a frying pan and, when hot, fry the fish cakes for 3 minutes on each side. They should, according to Mrs Scipio, be quite a dark brown colour when cooked.

Variations ∾ Delicious tuna fish cakes can also be made using poached fish. Omit the bacon, herbs and egg, leave the chillies and onion raw, and mix these with the cooked, flaked fish and 2 lb / 900 g mashed potatoes. Shape into cakes, and fry as above. These fish cakes can be dipped in flour and then beaten egg and breadcrumbs before frying.

Make the mixture from 1 lb / 455 g cooked smoked haddock, 1½ lb / 680 g mashed potato, 8 oz / 230 g cooked leeks and 2 tbsp finely chopped parsley. Then fry this as one large cake, in an omelette or frying pan, for about 10 minutes on each side. Cut into wedges to serve. The other fish cake mixtures can also be cooked in this way.

Deep-fried Oysters and Potato Bundles

Makes 12

*If you like your oysters hot, here is a very elegant, albeit rather
intricate, recipe based on a Japanese dish.*

2–3 medium potatoes
1 sheet dried nori seaweed
12 oysters

groundnut (peanut), grapeseed or
    sunflower oil for deep frying

Peel the potatoes and cut them into very small chips, about 1½–2 in / 4–5 cm
long and no more than ¼ in / 0.5 cm thick. Soften the seaweed by placing it
between a folded damp tea-towel. Shuck and drain the oysters, carefully wiping
them free of any shell or grit. Heat the oil to 190 °C / 375 °F, and fry the potatoes,
as if cooking chips, for 1 minute without letting them colour. Remove, drain and
allow to cool by spreading them out on kitchen paper.

Cut the seaweed sheet into 12 ribbons, about ¼ in / 0.5 cm wide. Now for the
fiddly bit: lay a ribbon of seaweed on a work surface, and lay six or eight chips
across it. Place the oyster on top and three more chips lengthways on top of the
oyster. Draw the two ends of the ribbon carefully over the oyster and chips and tie
to secure the bundle. Repeat with the remaining ingredients to make 12 bundles.
Reheat the oil and fry the bundles for no more than 20–30 seconds. Remove, drain
and serve.

Grilled Scallop and Bacon Skewers

Makes 6 large or 12 small skewers

12 rashers smoked streaky bacon,
    derinded
12 scallops, cleaned
1 oz / 30 g butter, melted
2 tbsp soft white breadcrumbs

12 button or cup mushrooms, trimmed
    and wiped
12 cherry tomatoes
sprigs of fresh watercress or parsley, to
    garnish

Cut each bacon rasher in half, and blanch in boiling water for about 2 minutes.
Drain and dry on kitchen paper. Separate each scallop from its roe, and remove the
black thread from around the scallop and the pad of white muscle. Roll the scallops
and roes in melted butter, and then in the breadcrumbs, pressing them well in. Roll
up the bacon rashers. Thread the bacon rolls, scallops, mushrooms and tomatoes
alternately on to oiled skewers. Brush the mushrooms with a little melted butter,
and nick the tomato skins with the point of a knife to prevent them from bursting.
Place under a preheated moderately hot grill, and grill for 5–6 minutes. Garnish
and serve hot with triangles of toast or fried bread.

Spiced Chicken Parcels

Makes 12

This is excellent picnic food.

1 tbsp coarsely ground black
    pepper
1 tsp ground Szechuan peppercorns
    (*optional*)
2 tsp grated fresh root ginger
2 tsp clear honey
2 tsp toasted sesame oil

2 tbsp soy sauce
2 tbsp rice wine or dry amontillado
    sherry
1 tbsp rice vinegar or sherry vinegar
12 free-range chicken wings, thighs or
    drumsticks

Mix all the ingredients, except the chicken, together to make a marinade. Place
the chicken in a large bowl and pour the marinade over. Stir well to make sure
each piece is coated. Cover, refrigerate, and leave for 2–3 hours, or overnight if this
is convenient.

Take 12 roasting bags or squares of foil or baking parchment, cut to the right size, place a chicken piece on each, and wrap the chicken up carefully, so that the juices will not leak out. Place the parcels on a baking sheet, and bake in a preheated oven at 200 °C / 400 °F / Mark 6 for 30–40 minutes. Remove from the oven, allow to cool, and do not open the parcels until you are ready to eat them. If you chill them in an ice-pack before serving, a delicious, dark, clear jelly will have formed around the chicken.

Spiced Quail and Quail Eggs

Serves 8

24 quail eggs
8 quail
2 oz / 60 g butter, melted
1 tbsp plain flour
1 tsp ground coriander
1 tsp ground cumin
½ pt / 280 ml chicken or quail
  stock

½ tsp each of crushed cardamom seeds,
  ground cinnamon, ground cloves,
  Madras curry powder, coarsely
  ground black pepper, sea salt and
  mustard powder
oil for frying
lemon juice *(optional)*

Boil the quail eggs, and shell when cool enough to handle. Put to one side. Cut the quail into four pieces (two breasts, two legs) each and use the back and trimmings to make stock. Brush the pieces with melted butter. Put the flour and dry seasonings in a polythene bag, add the quail pieces and shake to coat them in the spice mixture. In a heavy frying pan, fry the quail pieces in a little oil until just done, which will take about 8–10 minutes with such small pieces. Remove from the pan, and put to one side. Pour the stock into the pan, and boil, scraping up the cooking residues. Adjust the seasoning, and add a drop of lemon juice, if wished. Pile the quail eggs in the middle of a dish with the pieces of quail around them. Strain the sauce, pour over meat and eggs, and serve.

DIPS, MOUSSES, PÂTÉS AND POTTED FOODS

Vegetables with Dips and Dressings

Vegetables
A mixed selection from:
miniature carrots
blanched baby leeks
baby corn
boiled new potatoes
blanched green beans
blanched mangetout or sugar snap
   peas

blanched or raw cauliflower and
   broccoli florets
celery
chicory
cherry tomatoes
radishes
cooked or raw baby artichokes, thinly
   sliced
fennel bulb, cut into wedges

Serve one or more of the following dips or dressings:

Bagna Cauda

Serves 4–6

2 oz / 60 g butter
4–5 garlic cloves (or to taste),
   peeled and thinly sliced

2 oz / 60 g can anchovy fillets, drained
6 fl oz / 170 ml extra virgin olive oil

Melt the butter in a small heavy saucepan, and cook the garlic until soft but not at all browned. Add the anchovy fillets, each cut into two or three pieces. Stir and crush with a wooden spoon, then gradually stir in the olive oil, heating gently. When the mixture is thoroughly blended, set the pan over a small spirit or candle burner, and take it to the table to serve hot with the vegetables.

Pinzimonio

Serves 4–6

8 fl oz / 230 ml extra virgin olive oil
sea salt
freshly ground black pepper

Mix thoroughly, adding salt and pepper to taste, and serve in a small bowl to accompany the vegetables.

Herb, Walnut and Lemon Dressing

Serves 4–6

1 tbsp finely chopped chives
1 tbsp finely chopped parsley
1 tsp thyme leaves
2 garlic cloves, peeled and chopped
2 oz / 60 g chopped walnuts

½ tsp sea salt
freshly ground black pepper
2 fl oz / 60 ml walnut oil
¼ pt / 140 ml sunflower or grapeseed oil
juice of ½ lemon

Mix the herbs together in a bowl. Crush the garlic and walnuts with the salt and mix into the herbs. Add pepper to taste, then slowly add the oils and finally the lemon juice.

Radishes with Three Butters

Serves 8, as a starter

*I imagine eating this lovely summery snack in a shaded garden or
taking it on a picnic.*

3–4 bunches of radishes, trimmed
8 oz / 230 g salted butter, at room
  temperature
1 ripe tomato, peeled, deseeded and
  chopped

few sprigs of watercress, blanched and
  finely chopped
2 oz / 60 g mushrooms, fried and
  chopped
freshly ground black pepper

Pile the radishes into a serving bowl. Divide the butter into three, and into each
portion, mix one of the next three ingredients. Season with pepper, and pack each
butter into a small ramekin. Serve with crusty bread and a bowl of coarse salt.

Instead of using butter, you can serve yoghurt dips flavoured with the
ingredients above, adding appropriate herbs; for example, basil with the tomato,
and chives with the mushrooms. Ripe avocados and cucumber can also be used to
make flavoured butters or yoghurts.

Hummus

Serves 4–6, as a starter

*The sesame oil used in this recipe is not the toasted light brown
sesame oil of Chinese cooking, but clear virgin sesame oil. The sesame
paste is available at good delicatessens and Cypriot shops.*

1 lb / 455 g cooked or canned chick
  peas, drained
2 garlic cloves, peeled and crushed
juice of ½ lemon
2½ fl oz / 70 ml extra virgin olive
  oil

1 tbsp sesame oil or sesame paste
  (tahina)
salt
freshly ground black pepper
coriander leaves, to garnish

Put the chick peas in a blender or food processor with the rest of the
ingredients. Process until smooth, then spoon into a bowl and trickle a little more
olive oil on top. Garnish with coriander, and serve with olives, hot pitta bread,
sesame bread sticks and raw vegetables.

Brandade of Smoked Trout

Serves 4, as a starter

*With the same smooth texture and pale cream colour, this does
indeed resemble the classic 'brandade', made from salt cod, olive oil
and hot milk.*

2 smoked trout	salt
2 tbsp crème fraîche or soured cream	freshly ground black pepper
1 tbsp lemon juice	freshly grated nutmeg
3½ fl oz / 100 ml extra virgin olive oil	

Skin the trout and carefully remove the fillets. Pick out any remaining bones (I keep a pair of tweezers in my kitchen drawer for just this sort of job), and put the flesh in a food processor or blender with the cream and half the lemon juice. Process until smooth, then, with the motor still running, pour the olive oil in a thin stream on to the creamed trout. It should amalgamate and form a thick, shiny cream. Alternatively, you can do the whole thing by hand, first mashing the fish with a fork, mixing in the cream and lemon juice, and then beating in the oil until you have a rich glossy mass. Season to taste with salt, pepper and nutmeg, and add more lemon juice if you think it is needed. Serve with hot toast.

Variations ∾ You can prepare smoked salmon and smoked mackerel in the same way.

See also potted smoked trout, under *Variations* for Potted Crab on page 78.

Snails with Chilled Garlic Mousse

Serves 8, as a starter

I devised this recipe as part of an elegant summer garden meal.

48 cherry tomatoes or 24 larger
  ones
48 small or medium shelled snails
6 garlic cloves, peeled and crushed
6 spring onions (bulbs only), finely
  chopped

bunch of chervil, finely chopped
1 tbsp tarragon mustard
sea salt
freshly ground black pepper
½ pt / 280 ml whipping cream, whipped

If you can bear to skin the larger tomatoes, do so. Cut them in half and scoop out the seeds. Cherry tomatoes just need a cap cut off and the seeds scooped out. (Do not waste the seeds and pulp. Rub it through a sieve, and use the liquid as a base for a marvellous vinaigrette to mix with a nut oil or extra virgin olive oil.) Rinse and drain the snails, and put one into each tomato cup. Mix the garlic, onions, chervil, mustard and seasoning, and fold into the whipped cream. Pipe or spoon over the snails, and refrigerate until required.

Chicken Liver Mousse

Serves 12–15, as a starter

*This chicken liver mousse requires long, slow cooking. I would
prepare it a day or two in advance when the oven might be on for
other slow-cooking dishes. Since it keeps, you can make a large
quantity and serve the rest at another meal.*

2 lb / 900 g chicken livers
½ pt / 280 ml milk
3 eggs
¼ pt / 140 ml double cream or
   crème fraîche

salt
freshly ground black pepper
pinch of ground mace or nutmeg
oil for frying

Trim and clean the livers carefully, removing any green bits and sinews. Soak
them in the milk for about 2 hours to lighten them. Lightly oil a 2 lb / 900 g loaf
tin. Preheat the oven to 110°C / 225 °F / Mark ¼.

Drain and dry the livers on kitchen paper. Put the livers, eggs and cream in a
blender or food processor, and blend until smooth. Rub the mixture through a
sieve and season it with salt, pepper and mace or nutmeg. Fry a teaspoonful of the
mixture in a little oil, and taste to check that the seasoning is sufficient. Pour it into
the loaf tin, bang the tin sharply on the worktop to settle the mixture, and then
pack it down. Place the tin on a baking sheet and bake in the oven for 2 hours.
When cooked, remove the mousse from the oven and allow to go cold. The mousse
should have a soft texture and, therefore, need not be weighted down as it cools.
To serve, scoop out and shape the portions with two dessertspoons.

Potted Crab

Serves 6–8, as a starter

2 freshly cooked crabs	good pinch of ground mace
6 oz / 170 g unsalted butter	fine sea salt
juice of 1 lemon	freshly ground white pepper

Crack the crabs open and remove the feathery gills and stomach sacs. Pick out all the meat, keeping the white meat separate from the creamy brown flesh. Divide the butter into three 2 oz / 60 g portions. Pound the white crab meat with one portion of the butter, the brown meat with another, seasoning both portions to taste with lemon juice, mace, salt and pepper. Spoon the mixtures in alternate layers in a glass or pottery container. Melt the remaining portion of butter over a gentle heat. Let it cool a little, and spoon it over the crab to seal the surface. Cover and refrigerate until required.

Variations ⁓ Lobster, crayfish, sardines, shrimps, oysters and smoked trout, mackerel and salmon are also good potted.

For potted lobster or crayfish, season the pounded fish and butter mixture in the same way as the crab.

For potted sardines, season with a little grated apple, a few finely chopped shallots and a sprinkling of finely chopped dill.

For devilled potted shrimps, season with salt, cayenne pepper and lemon juice.

For potted oysters, use shucked and drained raw oysters, thoroughly dried on a tea-towel, and pound them into the butter together with two anchovy fillets to every six oysters. Season with mace or nutmeg and lemon juice. Potted oysters should be treated in the same way as raw oysters, and eaten within a few hours of preparation; they should not be kept overnight, even in a refrigerator.

For potted smoked trout, mackerel and salmon, pound the fish and butter together with a few anchovy fillets (one or two anchovy fillets to every average-sized trout), and season with nutmeg or mace, pepper and lemon juice. Potted smoked fish is very good served with a cucumber and horseradish relish. Make this by mixing the finely chopped flesh of a medium-sized cucumber with four finely chopped spring onions, three finely chopped sprigs of mint and a tablespoon of grated horseradish. Stir this into ¼ pt / 140 ml thick Greek yoghurt, and season to taste with freshly ground black pepper.

Potted Cheese

Serves 4–6, as a starter

12 oz / 340 g farmhouse cheese,
   grated or crumbled
4 oz / 110 g unsalted butter,
   softened

2–3 tbsp port or oloroso sherry
good pinch of ground mace
clarified butter

Make sure that the cheese is at room temperature, and mix it with the butter. Add the port or sherry and mace, and mix thoroughly once more. Pack into individual ramekins, and run a spoonful or two of clarified butter over the top to seal it. Refrigerate until required, but allow to come to room temperature before serving with fingers of hot toast. Alternatively, spoon into celery stalks or chicory leaves.

Variation ~ Chopped walnuts can be added for further refinement. Potted gorgonzola is excellent. Blend it with an equal quantity of ricotta, and half the quantity of butter. Season with nutmeg and add grappa instead of port or sherry. If using Roquefort, flavour it with Armagnac.

Rillettes de Porc

Serves 12–15, as a starter

*Belly pork is the cut traditionally used for this dish, with as much fat
as lean. It is becoming increasingly difficult to find, however, with
modern breeds of slimline pigs. The whole point of* rillettes *is the
texture and flavour supplied by the fat. No one says you have to eat
the whole potful in one go!* Rillettes *keep well in the refrigerator for a
week or so, and make a good sandwich filling. A scoop of* rillettes *with
lettuce salad, a pickle or two, bread and a glass of wine makes for a
good lunch, or they can be spread on fingers of hot toast as appetizers
to serve with drinks. Goose, duck, rabbit or mixed meats, such as duck
and pork or rabbit and pork, can also be used.*

2¼–2½ lb / 1–1.10 kg fat belly pork
¼ pt / 140 ml water
½ tsp salt
freshly ground black pepper
1 bay leaf

1 sprig of thyme
1 sage leaf *(optional)*
a pinch each of ground nutmeg or mace,
  cloves and cinnamon

Cut the meat into 1 in / 2.5 cm chunks, and put it in an earthenware casserole
or other ovenproof dish. Add the rest of the ingredients, cover and cook in the
bottom of a preheated oven at 110°C / 225°F / Mark ¼ for at least four hours. This
can be done overnight, if you are sure of your oven. The meat will be cooked,
swimming in fat with the water evaporated.

Pour the contents of the casserole into a large sieve set over a bowl. Remove
any bones and the herbs, and transfer the meat to a board. Shred the meat with
two forks and pack it into straight-sided pots or jam jars. Pour on the fat so that it
seeps into the meat and covers the surface. Cool, cover and refrigerate.

It is worth making double quantities of this recipe to give as presents, and for
buffet lunches.

SANDWICHES

RACE MEETINGS, cricket matches, a day's fishing or simply a hike in the country, all require sustenance of a kind that satisfies an appetite sharpened by the open air and is easy to transport without getting in the way of the main event. We have the gambling habits of an eighteenth-century English aristocrat to thank for the solution. In order not to have his play at the card table interrupted, John Montagu, Earl of Sandwich, called for cold meat between two slices of bread, thus devising the meal-between-covers which now bears his name. Since then, the sandwich has earned a permanent place in our gastronomic life, for better or worse. With some honourable exceptions, especially amongst city sandwich bars, the public sandwich is a rather dull fellow. I know we've gone beyond the listless, curling, white bread filled with a slice of processed ham or cheese, but there is so much more that can be done with the sandwich. The 'BLT' and the Chicken Tikka are on the right lines, but be adventurous. Rather than consider what is suitable to put between slices of bread, consider everything suitable until proved otherwise. Also, experiment by using different types of bread with the same filling (see bread recipes in the chapter on baking).

One of my favourite sandwiches (Summer Sybarite would be a good name for it) is something of a labour of love, since it requires the cracking and picking over of a freshly boiled crab. I mix the soft meat to a paste with a little softened butter or mayonnaise, and spread it on both slices of bread. A layer of white crabmeat goes on top of one slice, followed by cooked asparagus, cut to fit, or steamed slices of courgette, then lightly cooked spinach or shredded lettuce and watercress and finally the second slice of bread. This is not a dainty sandwich. It takes two hands to hold it together. Yes, you can skewer it like a club sandwich, and eat it with a knife and fork, but that defeats the purpose, and a sandwich never tastes as good as when eaten in the hand.

What follows are not recipes but ideas for unusual sandwiches, which, with some fresh fruit and a piece of cheese, make a substantial meal. Add some bitter chocolate and a bottle of champagne, and you have a feast indeed.

The Viking

Layer thick slices of gravad lax with slices of dill cucumber and a spread of softened butter or polyunsaturated margarine mixed with chopped dill and sweet mustard sauce. Use rye bread.

The Gondolier

Split a ciabatta bun or loaf, line it with shredded lettuce, and pile on a seafood salad of squid, prawns and monkfish, mixed with a well-flavoured lemon, herb and garlic mayonnaise. Clamp the top of the bun back on.

The Hill Club Sandwich

Make a spiced spread by mixing finely chopped mango chutney and mango pickle with softened butter or polyunsaturated margarine. Use sourdough bread, and build up layers of minced or sliced curried lamb, devilled egg salad, curried chicken or potted curried ham and plenty of watercress.

Asparagus and Egg Sandwiches

Boil sufficient free-range eggs and shell them into a bowl. Mash them with softened unsalted butter, fromage frais, mayonnaise or polyunsaturated margarine. Cut enough slices of fresh wholemeal bread, not too thin and not too thick, and spread them with a smear of whatever you have used with the eggs. Spread the egg mixture on the bread, and arrange rows of fairly well-cooked, well-drained and dried asparagus on top. Season with salt and pepper if you have not seasoned the egg mixture and top with another slice of bread.

The Country Cousin

This is what to do with leftovers from a roast stuffed loin of pork. Make a fruit butter by mixing chopped pickled plums or apple sauce with softened butter or polyunsaturated margarine. Spread it on thick slices of cottage loaf. Line the sandwich with mixed salad leaves, and lay sliced pickled onion and gherkins between slices of meat and the bread.

The Pittsburgh Fish Sandwich

This is not my own invention, but an institution, from the Oyster House, itself a Pittsburgh institution. Fillets of cod, for which you could substitute haddock, coley or indeed almost any white fish, are dipped in egg and then cornmeal, fried and put inside a soft bun from which the fish overhangs generously. The whole is sprinkled liberally with a hot pepper sauce. Eat hot.

The Tsar

Fill rye bread with layers of hard-boiled egg or egg mayonnaise, sliced raw onion, sliced gherkin, sliced marinated mushrooms and a pickled herring.

The Sultan

Spread pitta or olive bread with hummus, and pile up with slices of roast lamb, cucumber, yoghurt and garlic salad and chopped dried apricots or apricot chutney.

South of the Border

Fill tortillas or bread made with cornmeal and chopped chillies with slices of marinated beef, a purée of refried beans, sliced avocado and a fruity chilli salsa.

The Lancastrian

For this, I like to use a wholemeal bap, spread with butter mixed with finely chopped pickle. Slice the first of the English apples, brush with lemon juice to stop them browning, and layer with slices of mature Lancashire cheese.

The Penang

Peanut butter mixed with polyunsaturated margarine, finely grated ginger and chopped pineapple makes the ideal spread for an oriental-flavoured sandwich filled with chicken marinated in pineapple juice, sesame oil and soy sauce. Crunch is added with blanched bean sprouts and mangetout.

Lunch-in-a-bun

Some breads are more suitable for individual servings, such as pitta, whereas a ciabatta loaf will do for 2–4 people. These are not small, neat sandwiches, but two-handers with deep fillings. The fillings depend on what you have available, but here are some combinations that work well (all with leftovers from Sunday in mind):

Sliced roast chicken, sliced courgettes, watercress and caper mayonnaise to spread on the bread.

Pink roast lamb, ratatouille, lettuce and pitted black olives chopped into mayonnaise or butter for spreading on the bread.

Roast beef slices, potato and carrot salad bound in mustard mayonnaise and horseradish butter for spreading.

Roast pork, sliced apple, watercress, butter flavoured with chutney or rosemary.

Salmon, spinach mixed with mayonnaise and lemon, and dill-flavoured butter.

Mushroom sandwiches

Lightly fry 8 oz / 230 g sliced field mushrooms with two finely chopped shallots in a little olive oil until soft. Raise the heat and allow any liquid from the mushrooms to evaporate, then season to taste, allow to cool, and mash together with 3 oz / 85 g butter. Sandwich this thickly, garnished with some flat-leaved parsley, between thick slices of crusty white bread. It is also good in pitta bread. Try adding pitted black olives, chopped spring onions and finely sliced tomato.

THE TIMES COOK IN SPAIN

THE SPANISH way with short eats is well known. *Tapas* long since left the dark cool bars of the Barrio Gotico in Barcelona and the dazzling, sun-dappled alleyways of Seville to colonize the restaurant and café culture of the waiting world. But Spain is still where you will find the widest variety of tapas reflecting the regions and their local produce. In Cadiz, small shark or *cazón* are sliced, dipped in sherry vinegar, floured and deep-fried. In Galicia, you will find the sweet hot peppers, the small green *pimentos del Padron* of which I will always have a vivid memory in the Bar Escuela in Bayona.

The bars in Spain are not, of course, called tapas bars, but a *tapa* or *pincho* is what you are served, often free, when you order a drink. Larger portions are *raciónes*.

In southern Andalusia, around Jerez and the Atlantic coast, both fish and egg dishes are specialities. Softly scrambled eggs made with a variety of flavourings – wild asparagus, shrimps, ham, beans or mushrooms – are called *huevos revueltos*. *Ajo caliente* or *sopa di ajo* is an earthenware bowl of hot soup of bread, water and garlic with an egg lightly cooked in it. In Bar Juanito in Jerez, with a lovely outdoor patio in La Pescadería, we ate a very fine tortilla with herbs and *canutilla* or calf spinal cord, a typical gypsy dish. At Bar Bigote, on the waterfront in Sanlucar, Fernando and Paco served the freshest fish and shellfish, caught in the waters off Cadiz, including sole-like fish called *acedias*, little bigger than a child's hand. In other bars we ate different sorts of eggs and *huevos de pescado* or fish roe. These were the smaller roes of hake, not the large cod roes we are familiar with. In Andalusia they are simply floured, seasoned and deep-fried or grilled, and are excellent.

The best dish of all was Manolo's *ensaladilla* at Bar las Bridas in Jerez. We turned our noses up at it to begin with. Who wants egg mayonnaise when you can have *calamares*, *salmonetes* (baby red mullet), monkfish liver and *revuelto de camarones*? Then we noticed, over a two-hour period, how everyone who came into the bar ordered a *ración de ensaladilla* before anything else. We weakened, much to Manolo's amusement. It was sublime, a suave, smooth, rich mouthful of Russian salad with prawns, potatoes and carrots in a creamy mayonnaise. Our friends were amused when we told them the story. 'But it is the best, everyone goes there for the *ensaladilla*.'

Madrid is, to my mind, one of the few cities in the world which has outdoor living and eating and drinking down to a fine art. When the light dims and bats take the place of swifts and house martins, the doors open and Madrileños pour into the streets and squares to sit and talk, but more often to walk from bar to bar sipping *fino* or quenching their thirst with beer. In the Calles del Prado, de León and de las Huertas, counters are laden with earthenware bowls of tempting food: bean stews, *calamares*, snails in spicy sauce, pigs' ears, black pudding, anchovy fillets in vinaigrette, all of which are spooned on to small oval plates as *tapas* or on to slightly larger plates as *raciónes*. *Chorizos* and *jamón serrano*, the spicy sausages and cured ham, hang from the ceiling, but there will be a ham already lying in a rack behind the counter ready to be carved for one of the best *tapas*, and one to which visitors to Spain quickly become addicted. Unlike Parma ham, it is not sliced on a machine, paper thin, but with a sharp knife into small uneven slices. Sweet, succulent and tender, it has a unique flavour which comes from the lengthy curing process and the excellent natural diet on which the Iberian pig feeds itself.

The following recipes, as well as many of the short eats, can be served Spanish-style, outdoors if possible, as a selection of small tasty dishes on which to nibble rather than a full-scale elaborate meal that will keep you too long in the kitchen. For a summer meal with a Spanish flavour, gazpacho is almost *de rigueur*. I have included a novel reinterpretation from Patrick Buret, executive chef at The Ritz in Madrid, much in demand in the Jardin Ritz, the lovely outdoor restaurant in the Ritz garden at the foot of the elegant terrace. Here you sit in a cool green oasis, surrounded like a peninsula on three sides by the roaring ocean of Madrid's traffic.

With all these dishes, I would recommend a cool *fino*, such as Valdespino's Inocente or Osborne's Quinta, bearing in mind the Jerezano saying, 'One before 11, and eleven after 1'. In the south the first *copita* of the day is often not a *fino*, which some find too acid, but a dry amontillado or oloroso. It is a nice convention.

Gazpacho de Melon
(Chilled Melon Soup)

Serves 4–6

This fresh green soup is really very refreshing, and looks good too.

4 tbsp extra virgin olive oil

2–3 leeks (white parts only), trimmed and sliced

8 oz / 230 g potatoes, peeled and diced

½ pt / 280 ml vegetable or chicken stock

1 green pepper

1 cucumber

1 ripe honeydew or Galia melon

2 tbsp sherry vinegar

2 pt / 1.15 l water

salt

freshly ground black pepper

Garnish

sliced or diced strawberries

diced kiwi fruit

flaked or slivered almonds, lightly toasted

small cubes of dried bread, toasted or fried

Put half the olive oil in a saucepan, add the leeks and potatoes and fry gently until the leeks are wilted. Add the stock, and cook until the vegetables are tender. Meanwhile, cut the pepper into quarters, remove the seeds, and blanch it in boiling water for 1–2 minutes. Roughly chop the pepper and cucumber, and put into a blender with the rest of the olive oil. Add the cooked vegetables and stock and blend until smooth. Transfer to a bowl or jug, sieving if you wish. Cut the melon in half, remove the seeds and cut the flesh into cubes, taking care to retain as much juice as possible. Put the melon and juice in with the sherry vinegar and half the water. Blend until smooth, then stir it into the vegetable mixture. Add enough extra water to give the soup the consistency you prefer. Season and chill the soup until required but for no longer than 2–3 hours, as it loses its freshness. Just before serving, adjust the seasoning. Serve the garnishes in separate bowls.

Empanada
(Savoury Fish Pie)

Serves 6–8

Dough

2 tbsp dried yeast
pinch of sugar
Up to ½ pint / 280 ml warm water
12 oz / 340 g strong plain white
 flour
4 oz / 110 g fine cornmeal, polenta
 or plain flour

1 tsp salt
4 tbsp olive oil
2 eggs
extra flour for kneading
beaten egg or milk, to glaze

Filling

1 large onion, peeled and chopped
2–3 tbsp olive oil
12 oz / 340 g firm ripe tomatoes,
 peeled, deseeded and chopped
1 green or red pepper, peeled,
 deseeded and chopped
2½ fl oz / 70 ml dry white wine

pinch of powdered saffron
salt
freshly ground black pepper
8 oz / 230 g freshly cooked mussels *or* 4
 fresh sardines *or* 8 oz / 230 g tuna fish
 or 1–2 cans sardines in olive oil *or*
 7 oz / 200 g can tuna fish in brine

To make the dough, sprinkle the yeast and sugar on the warm water, and let it stand for 10–15 minutes. Put the flours, salt, oil and eggs in a food processor with the yeast liquid, and process until combined to a dough. Turn out and knead until smooth on a lightly floured surface, then put the dough in a greased bowl, inside a large polythene bag, or cover with a clean, damp tea-towel. Put in a warm place to rise for an hour or so. While the dough is rising, prepare the filling.

Cook the onion in some of the olive oil until soft and transparent, and add the tomatoes and pepper, the white wine, saffron and a little seasoning. Cook gently for 30–40 minutes until you have a well-flavoured stew. Allow it to cool. If using fresh sardines or tuna fish, fry in another pan in a little more olive oil. Fillet the sardines or flake the tuna fish. Canned sardines or tuna will simply need draining.

When the dough has risen sufficiently, put it on a floured work surface and knock it back. Cut it in two, and roll out one piece to a 10–12 in / 25.5–30.5 cm circle. Place it on a greased, floured baking sheet. Spoon half the tomato and pepper stew on to the dough and spread it to within ½ in / 1 cm or so of the edge.

Arrange the fish on top, and cover with the remaining stew. Wet the edges of the dough. Roll out another circle of the same size, and lay it on top, pressing it down to seal it. Make one or two slits in the top for steam to escape. Brush with egg or milk and bake in a preheated oven at 180°C / 350°F / Mark 4 for 30 minutes or until risen and golden brown. Serve cut into wedges. It tastes best when served warm or just cold.

Variation ∾ If you are lucky enough to be able to get salt cod, then instead of a tomato and pepper stew, onions only can be cooked until soft and then moistened with the wine and saffron. The flaked, cooked salt cod can then be arranged on top with raisins or sultanas.

Mussel Salad

Serves 6

5–6 lb / 2.30–2.70 kg mussels in the shell
2 tbsp extra virgin olive oil
1 mild onion, peeled and thinly sliced
4 firm ripe tomatoes (fresh plum tomatoes, if available) peeled, deseeded and diced

2 tbsp flat-leaved parsley
lemon juice or cider vinegar, to taste
salt
freshly ground black pepper

Scrub the mussels and knock off any barnacles. Rinse thoroughly in a colander held under running water to get rid of any grit and sand, and discard any mussels that remain open when tapped. Put the mussels in a large saucepan, cover with a tight-fitting lid or foil, and set the pan over a high heat for 3–4 minutes, during which time the mussels will cook in their own steam and open. Remove from the heat and, to stop the mussels at the bottom from cooking in the residual heat, carefully tip the mussels into the colander set over a bowl to catch the juices. Discard any which have failed to open. When they are cool enough to handle, shell the mussels, and put them into a large bowl. Mix in the olive oil, then add the onion, tomatoes and parsley. Season with lemon juice, salt and pepper to taste.

Tuna Fish Salad

Serves 6–8

Any cooked fish can be used in the same way. If fresh fish is not available, canned fish is a good standby. Look for fish canned in brine rather than in vegetable oil.

1 lb / 455 g cooked tuna
12 oz / 340 g ripe tomatoes, peeled, deseeded and finely chopped
1 cucumber, peeled, deseeded and chopped
1 green pepper, deseeded and chopped

6 spring onions, trimmed and finely sliced, *or* 1 mild onion, peeled and finely sliced
extra virgin olive oil
sherry vinegar
salt
freshly ground black pepper
1 tsp chopped flat-leaved parsley

Flake the tuna into a bowl and carefully mix in the vegetables. Pour on olive oil and vinegar to taste, season, and stir in the parsley before serving.

Patatas Alioli

(Potatoes with Garlic and Olive Oil)

Serves 6–8

4 garlic cloves, peeled
¼–½ tsp salt, to taste
¼ pt / 140 ml olive oil

lemon juice, to taste
1 lb / 455 g new potatoes, boiled and diced

Have all your ingredients at room temperature. Pound the garlic in a mortar until it becomes a fine paste. Adding a pinch of salt at the beginning will help give the garlic a 'grip' in the mortar. Add the oil slowly but constantly, stirring all the time until the sauce thickens. Mix the lemon juice with a few drops of water and add to the sauce with more salt if necessary. Mix with the potatoes and serve. If the sauce separates rather than emulsifies, it still tastes very good.

Salads

As long ago as the seventeenth century, Giacomo Castelvetro wrote *A Brief Account of the Fruit, Herbs and Vegetables in Italy*. He was born in Modena, but left as a young man for travels in Europe, and finally settled in England. It was to his wealthy English patrons (or to those whom he hoped might become his patrons) that he addressed his description of seasonal produce with the advice on how to prepare it. He felt that the English needed a good deal of advice, particularly on salads. After castigating the Germans 'and other uncouth nations', he went on to say that the English were even worse and served up badly washed, soggy salad leaves, swamped in vinegar which prevented them taking up oil, 'so to make a good salad the proper way, you should put the oil in first of all, stir it into the salad, then add the vinegar and stir again'.

I think Castelvetro is right to assume that oil, vinegar and a little seasoning make the correct dressing for a salad. Stocks, nut oils, herbs, fruit juice, garlic and spices are all optional additions but do not, I think, improve on the simple vinaigrette. However, the few ingredients needed for a good vinaigrette are worth choosing with care. Look for the best oils and vinegars, that is those that you like best.

It was after a visit to Liguria that the consumption of olive oil in our household began to increase dramatically. At a Mediterranean Food Fair, I had the chance to taste the greeny-gold oil (more gold than green in Liguria) from a number of producers. Each tasted better than the last, and I was addicted. By a happy coincidence, the olive oil from this fish and rice area of Italy is considered the finest for fish cookery, but perhaps only by the Ligurians. I am sure the Greeks, the Portuguese, the French and the Spanish consider their oil best. I have catholic tastes when it comes to olive oil. That is not to say I do not discriminate, but I am not one of those who maintain that the only olive oil is the finest from Tuscany. For a long time, our favourite was Portuguese extra virgin olive oil, bought from Lisbon. Not much is produced, and that is mainly for home consumption. At one time, the little that found its way abroad usually went to Brazil, but it is now more widely exported. I have also had lovely Tunisian olive oil, labelled Carthage, and from Crete, where they have been making olive oil for 2,000 years, I like the Kydonia oil. Extra virgin olive oils from Catalonia and Andalusia in Spain are well worth looking out for, as of course, are the oils from the south of France in the Vaucluse.

And what vinegar to use with this exquisite oil? Choose a traditionally made wine vinegar from France, or perhaps an equally traditional balsamic vinegar from Modena, or consider sherry vinegar.

The cool, fragrant bodegas of Jerez and Sanlucár have other treasures amongst their elegant *finos* and delicate *manzanillas*. Tucked away so that they will not pass on their yeasts and characteristics to those fine wines are to be found small barrels full of sherry vinegar. Made, cared for and aged in *soleras* in the same way as sherry is made, this rich, dark, mellow, fragrant nectar smells not unlike an old dry *oloroso*, and, indeed, a sip of it will reveal the same depth and complexity. I do wish the sherry producers would not be so shy about it; no one in their right mind could possibly think of it as failed sherry. It is a fine ingredient in its own right, and it goes so well with the good extra virgin olive oils we can now buy quite readily. Of course, not much is produced, and being connoisseurs of fine food and wine, the sherry producers probably prefer to keep most of it for themselves. I have tasted some, sadly not available commercially, which was drawn from a small barrel 60 or 70 years old.

Only a little sherry vinegar is needed to give an exquisite nutty flavour to whatever you use it in. It is a particularly good match for tomatoes or a green salad when mixed with a fruity extra virgin olive oil. In fact, good sherry vinegar is so good that I often eat sliced tomatoes sprinkled only with that, and no olive oil.

VEGETABLE, BEAN AND FRUIT SALADS

Aubergine Salad

Serves 4

1 aubergine, about 1 lb / 455 g
garlic cloves, to taste
3 heaped tbsp finely chopped
  parsley
pinch of fresh or dried thyme or
  oregano

extra virgin olive oil
salt
freshly ground black pepper

Slice the aubergine in half lengthways. Preheat the grill until very hot, and put the aubergine under it, skin-side up. Grill for 15 minutes, until the skin is wrinkled and charred, but not burnt. This is, of course, difficult to see, but your sense of touch and smell will tell you when it is charred. Remove from the grill, and when cool enough to handle, scoop out the softened flesh with a pointed teaspoon. Put this in a sieve over a bowl so that some of the liquid drains away. The flesh tends to come away in long strands, so snip these up with kitchen scissors. Transfer the aubergine to a bowl. Peel and crush the garlic cloves, and stir into the aubergine. Add the herbs, olive oil and season to taste. Serve as it is, with hot toast or warm pitta bread, or on a plate of salad leaves garnished with olives and tomatoes.

Carrot and Cumin Salad

Serves 4

12 oz / 340 g carrots
2 tsp cumin seeds
4 tbsp extra virgin olive oil

1 tbsp sherry vinegar
freshly ground black pepper
salt

Peel or scrape the carrots, and slice them, not too thinly or they will break up. Drop them into boiling water, and boil until just tender. Drain and, while they are still hot, mix them with the rest of the ingredients, adding pepper and salt to taste. This is best served cold, but not straight from the refrigerator.

Variations ∽ Omit the cumin, and stir a mixture of chopped fresh herbs and crushed garlic into the warm carrots, then mix in finely chopped spring onion and the rest of the ingredients.

For a refreshing carrot and peach salad, leave the carrots raw, grate them, and mix with sliced or diced fresh peaches and some finely shredded spring onions. Dress this with olive oil and lemon juice or walnut oil and sherry vinegar.

Fennel and Pomegranate Salad

Serves 6

*Pomegranates are at their best in the middle of winter, and are perfect
for dressing this crisp, light salad which I often serve at Christmas.*

about 1¼ lb / 570 g fennel bulb(s),
  trimmed
juice of ½ lemon
1 large pomegranate

3 tbsp extra virgin olive oil
sea salt
freshly ground black pepper

Slice the fennel thinly and turn the pieces in lemon juice to keep them white.
Cut the pomegranate in half. Extract the seeds whole from one half, and put to one
side. Squeeze the other half on a lemon squeezer, and mix the juice with the olive
oil and seasoning. Stir into the fennel, add the pomegranate seeds and serve
immediately. Any green feathery fennel top can be used for garnish.

Lentil Salad

Serves 4–6

8 oz / 230 g green or Puy lentils
4–5 tbsp hazelnut oil or extra virgin
  olive oil
1–2 tbsp balsamic vinegar
salt

freshly ground black pepper
1–2 shallots, peeled and finely chopped
1–2 garlic cloves, peeled and crushed
  (optional)

Put the lentils in a saucepan, cover with water and cook until just tender. Drain
if necessary. While still hot, stir in the oil and vinegar, and season lightly. Stir in the
shallots and garlic, if using.

Mushroom Salad

Serves 4–6

4 tbsp extra virgin olive oil
1 lb / 455 g button or cup
  mushrooms, wiped and sliced
2 tbsp good red or white wine

thinly pared rind of ½ lemon, lime or
  orange
½ tsp coriander seeds
1 small onion, peeled and thinly sliced

Heat half the olive oil in a frying pan and quickly stir-fry the mushrooms for no more than 1 minute. Remove from the heat, and transfer to a flat serving dish. Blend the rest of the oil with the wine, and pour it over the hot mushrooms. Stir in the lemon peel and the coriander seeds. Add the onion and allow to cool before serving. The hot mushrooms absorb the flavour of the wine and olive oil and give off their own juices to form a delicious dressing.

Orange, Onion and Olive Salad

Serves 4–6

This salad would make an excellent starter to a meal of Mediterranean or Moroccan flavours, including such dishes as couscous (see pages 160 and 214) and bstila (see page 344).

2–3 navel oranges
2 mild onions, peeled and thinly
  sliced
2–3 tbsp extra virgin olive oil

1 tbsp orange juice
salt
freshly ground black pepper
black olives

Peel the oranges, carefully removing all the white pith, and slice them thinly. Arrange alternating slices of orange and onion on a large serving platter. Sprinkle over the olive oil and orange juice, season to taste, and scatter on a handful of black olives.

Cucumber and Mint Salad

Serves 4

2 cucumbers
1 tbsp sea salt
2 heaped tbsp thick plain yoghurt
½ tsp chilli paste, or to taste

2–3 garlic cloves, peeled and crushed
1 tbsp chopped fresh mint
mint leaves, to garnish

Peel the cucumbers, cut them in half lengthways, and scoop out and discard the seeds. Thinly slice the cucumber and place in a sieve set over a bowl. Sprinkle with salt, turning the slices with a spoon to make sure that all the cucumber is well salted. Leave it to disgorge its juices for 4–5 hours, or even overnight. A great deal of liquid will be given off. Rinse the cucumber thoroughly, and dry it well in a clean tea-towel. Mix the cucumber into the yoghurt with the chilli paste, garlic and chopped mint and leave it to stand for 30–40 minutes before serving in order for the flavours to blend. Garnish with mint leaves.

Variations ∾ Omit the chilli paste and mint, use 4 garlic cloves and 8 tablespoons yoghurt, and stir in a handful of finely chopped, mixed, fresh herbs.

Mix the prepared cucumber slices with 2 tablespoons finely chopped chives, 1 tablespoon finely chopped fresh dill and a light dressing of extra virgin olive oil, lemon juice and a little sugar and freshly ground black pepper to taste.

Dice, rather than slice, the cucumber, disgorge as above, and then mix with an equal quantity of diced melon (watermelon would give a nice colour contrast). Sprinkle with a little sugar and freshly ground white pepper, and stir in 4 tablespoons thick plain yoghurt and 1 tablespoon white wine vinegar.

Salad Elona is a classic mixture of sliced cucumber (prepared as above) and sliced strawberries, arranged in alternating concentric circles, seasoned with freshly ground white pepper, and sprinkled with balsamic vinegar and a little extra virgin olive oil.

Pear and Herb Salad with Raspberry Dressing

Serves 6

Based on a Castelvetro recipe, this comes from our friends the
Lancellotis. Chervil, tarragon, salad burnet, chives, flat leaf parsley,
and basil are the herbs I like to use.

6 ripe conference pears	1 tbsp extra virgin olive oil
juice of ½ lemon	salt
6 tbsp raspberries, thawed if frozen	freshly ground black pepper
herbs	salad leaves
1 tbsp balsamic vinegar	

Peel, core and slice the pears, and sprinkle them with lemon juice. Rub the
raspberries through a sieve, and mix the purée with the pears. Strip the leaves of
the herbs from their stems, shred or leave whole as appropriate, and mix with the
pears. Stir in the balsamic vinegar, olive oil and seasoning. Line a large bowl with
salad leaves, heap the pear salad in the middle, and garnish with more fresh herbs
and edible flowers if you wish.

Grilled or Roasted Pepper Salad

Serves 6

1½ lb / 680 g red, green or yellow
  peppers
2–3 garlic cloves, peeled
½ tsp salt

freshly ground black pepper
extra virgin olive oil
sherry vinegar
2 oz / 60 g pinenuts, toasted (*optional*)

Quarter the peppers and remove the seeds, pith and stalks. Char the peppers by grilling or roasting, and then peel off the blackened skin. Put to one side. Crush the garlic in a bowl with the salt. Add the pepper and then the olive oil and vinegar to make a dressing to your taste. Stir in the peppers, and let them stand at room temperature for at least 30 minutes to absorb the flavours of the dressing. Scatter with pinenuts before serving, if liked. If you prepare this salad well in advance and refrigerate it, remember to bring it to room temperature before serving.

Variations ∽ Instead of the olive oil and vinegar dressing, just sprinkle the peppers with a little lime or lemon juice and salt and pepper to taste. You may add a few thin slices of mild onion and a sprinkling of crushed garlic instead of the pinenuts, if you wish.

Potato and Wild Mushroom Salad

Serves 4

8 oz / 230 g waxy potatoes
4 oz / 110 g chanterelle, shiitake or
  oyster mushrooms

3–4 tbsp extra virgin olive oil
2 shallots, peeled and finely chopped
2 tbsp sherry vinegar

Peel, boil and drain the potatoes. Cut them into approximately ½ in / 1 cm cubes, and place in a serving bowl. Clean the mushrooms, and fry them lightly in the olive oil for about 5 minutes. Add to the potatoes in the bowl. Sprinkle on the chopped shallots and the sherry vinegar, mix well, and serve.

A 'Grand Sallet'

John Nott, John Evelyn and Gervase Markham, all great gardeners and herbalists in their time, encouraged their fellow Englishmen to eat greens with the creation of 'Grand sallets' for spring and summer. And very showy creations they were. Even under the plain-living Commonwealth, we know that Joan Cromwell had her own recipe for a rather elaborate salad. 'Landscapes' were a favourite form for this dish, the ingredients arranged in 'steps' and 'terraces', leading to a gilded 'castle' in the centre carved from a turnip and gilded with egg yolk or gold leaf, surrounded by 'trees' and 'flowers'.

However, we should bear in mind the advice of Yuan Mei, the cultured eighteenth-century gourmet of the Manchu Ching dynasty. He was not impressed by mere display which, he said, had little to do with gastronomy. 'Do not,' he admonished, 'fuss with the natural state of the food just to show that you are a clever cook.' It is possible, nevertheless, to create an imaginative, appetizing and, above all, edible, centrepiece of salad stuffs, herbs and flowers as a change from the usual bowl of green salad. Make either a 'landscape' form with different levels – 'trees', 'terraces' and 'steps', or a tighter 'flower bouquet' form. For a flat arrangement, consider using slices of tightly furled fennel to represent buds, radicchio as rose petals, chicory as waterlily petals. Feathery fennel and carrot tops can provide dense background; young crinkly spinach leaves a foreground. A bowl of *bagna cauda* (see page 72), half hidden in the centre, can be a murky pond. If I was making a 'bouquet', I would look out for baby artichokes still attached to their stems. These I would peel down to the edible core, and then boil or steam them whole before using as the centrepiece of the arrangement. Use a large white loaf rather as you might use florists' foam to give the 'bouquet' some height. Slice off the crust, and allow the loaf to dry out slightly, which will give a firm base into which you can poke tufts of celery, bunches of green beans, long curving leaves of Treviso radicchio, young dandelion leaves and flowers.

Salade Niçoise

Ask six cooks for their salade niçoise recipe, and they will give you six different versions. Consult six or even ten cookery books on the subject, and you will read as many recipes. Some authorities, such as *Larousse Gastronomique* maintain that, with the possible exception of hard-boiled eggs, nothing cooked should go into the salad, particularly potatoes. Waverley Root, author of *Food in France*, argued in correspondence in *Le Monde* that lettuce had no place in the salad. Henri Pellaprat, on the other hand, whose *Cuisine Familiale et Practique* is still widely used, suggests green beans and potatoes, both, of course, cooked, as well as lettuce. Escoffier's version has tuna fish in oil, tomatoes, anchovy fillets, chopped herbs and vinaigrette. *Le Repertoire de la Cuisine* gives the ingredients as French beans, tomato quarters, potatoes, fillets of anchovies and capers; olives garnish the salad and vinaigrette dresses it.

Richard Olney has the best advice, suggesting that we forget about following 'any of the endless and precisely defined classical recipes for composed salads [Niçoise, Waldorf, Andalouse, etc.]', and realize instead 'how much more valuable and exciting is the imaginative and playful, self-renewing invention of a giant composed salad, never once repeated, its composition dictated by the materials at hand'. Here is the thinking behind my version of salade niçoise. It takes very little detective work to arrive at some ingredients, at least, of a dish that surely started life as a simple, robust, seasonal, local salad. The dressing will be made of fruity olive oil, since the hinterland of Nice is still rich in olive groves. Little black olives will also garnish the salad. Garlic and anchovies complete the trinity, which provides the underlying flavours. Capers and sun-ripened field tomatoes are abundant in Provence, and will also go into the salad. One thing that everyone agrees on is that the tomatoes should not be sliced but cut into wedges.

Now, whether the rest of your vegetables are raw or cooked or a mixture of both, depends on whether you have a garden full of vegetables that you can pick when tender enough to need no cooking, or access to a market as good as the one in Nice, where vegetables are fresh, young and tender. For most of us who rely on greengrocers or supermarkets for our vegetables, a quick boiling or steaming may well improve the flavour and texture of green beans, broad beans or quartered baby artichoke hearts. I would certainly add lettuce to the salad, halved or quartered Little Gems for preference. Freshly cooked new potatoes, halved and just cool, are so very good in salads, especially with lettuce, tomato, garlic and anchovies, that I would have to include them. Hard-boiled eggs, I can leave out. If I were serving the salad as a main course, canned tuna fish would be a nice addition, but I would drain off the oil it was canned in, as this would almost certainly not be anywhere near as good as the olive oil I would use. Green peppers often figure in salade niçoise, but not in mine, as I do not much like them. Here it is, in summary:

Essential	*Extras*
tomatoes	hard-boiled free-range eggs
olives and olive oil	tuna fish (canned)
capers	
anchovies	*Vinaigrette* (to be added at the table)
	fruity olive oil
Suggested	garlic
lettuce	wine vinegar
green beans	seasoning
broad beans	
artichoke hearts	
new potatoes	

Note: Although anchovies are an essential part of a classic salade niçoise, and I have suggested adding tuna fish, I have included the recipe here because it is largely a vegetable salad. Vegetarians may omit the anchovies, as well as the tuna, if they wish.

Salade Huguette

Serves 4

8 oz / 230 g asparagus
8 oz / 230 g French beans
4 artichoke bottoms
salt
freshly ground black pepper

2 Little Gem lettuces, washed
2 hard-boiled eggs, finely chopped
chopped chervil, chives or parsley
mayonnaise or vinaigrette, to serve

Trim the tough ends off the asparagus, and use the tender parts and the tips only. Break each stem into two or three pieces. Top and tail the beans. Ideally the three vegetables should be cooked separately, just for a few minutes until barely tender for the beans and asparagus, and longer for the artichoke bottoms, which should be quite tender but not breaking up. Drain the vegetables and season lightly. Slice the artichoke bottoms. Separate the outer leaves from the lettuces, and use them to line a salad bowl. Pile the vegetables in the middle, and place the two lettuce hearts on either side. Scatter with chopped hard-boiled egg and herbs, and serve the dressing separately.

Salad of Peas and Beans

Serves 8

some of the following, about 2 lb /
900 g prepared weight in all:

Fresh
French beans, topped and tailed
runner beans, topped, tailed and
    sliced
broad beans, shelled
garden peas, podded
mangetout, topped and tailed
sugar snap peas, topped and tailed

Dried
green lentils, cooked and drained
chick peas, soaked, cooked and drained
flageolets, soaked, cooked and drained
soissons, haricot or cannellini beans,
    soaked, cooked and drained

2 garlic cloves, peeled and crushed
sea salt
freshly ground black pepper
juice of ½ lemon
2½ fl oz / 70 ml walnut oil

Cook the fresh vegetables as briefly as possible and drain them. In a large salad bowl, mix the garlic, seasoning, lemon juice and oil. Stir in the freshly cooked green vegetables and the pulses.

Coleslaw

8 oz / 230 g red cabbage
8 oz / 230 g white winter cabbage
2 carrots
2 celery stalks
2 shallots or 1 medium onion
1 Cox's apple
2 tsp lemon juice
1–2 tbsp finely chopped
  parsley

Salad Cream
1 tsp caster sugar
1 tsp mild olive oil
1 tsp salt
scant tsp mustard powder
1 hard-boiled egg yolk
1 tbsp wine vinegar
7 fl oz / 200 ml single cream
2–3 tbsp milk

Cut the central stems out, and finely shred the cabbages. Peel and grate or shred the carrots. Trim and thinly slice the celery. Peel and finely chop the shallots or onion. Peel, core and chop the apple, and mix with the lemon juice. Mix all the ingredients together with the parsley, and then stir in some mayonnaise, a yoghurt or soured cream dressing or some authentic salad cream.

To make authentic salad cream mix the first four ingredients to a smooth paste. Sieve the egg yolk into the mixture, and blend well. Stir in the vinegar. Set the bowl over a pan of simmering water, and gradually add the cream and milk, stirring with a wooden spoon until the mixture lightly coats the back of the spoon. Cool and refrigerate until required.

White Root Salad

*A cool, crisp, pale contrast, this salad is a perfect dish to follow a spicy
meat stew, such as chilli.*

8 oz / 230 g mooli (white radish)
8 oz / 230 g celeriac
8 oz / 230 g young parsnips
8 oz / 230 g fennel
lemon juice
2 tbsp Dijon mustard

6 tbsp cream or plain yoghurt
1 garlic clove, peeled and crushed
½ tsp ground cumin
coarse sea salt

Peel the vegetables, then slice them and cut them into fine shreds. As you deal
with each piece, drop it into a bowl of salted water with lemon juice added to stop
it becoming discoloured. Mix the mustard, cream or yoghurt, garlic and cumin.
Drain the vegetables thoroughly and mix with the dressing. Sprinkle coarse sea salt
on top and serve immediately. It is best to make this salad just before required so
that the vegetables will not be in the water too long, thus losing much of their
flavour, texture and nutrients.

Chick Pea and Vegetable Salad

4 small courgettes
4 oz / 110 g green beans, topped
   and tailed
4 oz / 110 g broccoli florets
8 spring onions, trimmed and
   chopped
2–3 garlic cloves, peeled and
   crushed

4 tbsp extra virgin olive oil
2 tsp balsamic or sherry vinegar
2 tsp finely chopped parsley
8 oz / 230 g cooked chick peas
salt
freshly ground black pepper

Bring a saucepan of water to the boil. Trim the ends off the courgettes, and
break the beans into pieces, if necessary. Drop them and the broccoli into the
boiling water, bring back to the boil, and simmer for 3 minutes. Drain and mix
while still hot with the onions, garlic, oil, vinegar and parsley. Allow to stand for
30–45 minutes, then mix with the chick peas, and season to taste before serving.

FISH AND MEAT SALADS

MANY EXCELLENT fish and meat salads can be made quickly from leftovers or the contents of your store-cupboard, by simply combining flakes or small strips of cooked meat or fish with a base such as pasta, beans or potatoes. Smoked or cooked salmon, haddock, chicken or ham are good with pasta shells or spirals; add chopped onion and seasoning, and moisten with yoghurt or soured cream to finish. Smoked fish and meat are also good with diced, cooked potato; add blanched, shredded white cabbage or Chinese leaves, chopped onions, a few capers or chopped gherkin, and stir in a dressing of olive oil and lemon juice, seasoned with salt, pepper and mustard.

One of the best standbys for an impromptu meal is bean and tuna fish salad. Simply open a can of cannellini or haricot beans and a can of tuna fish. Drain both, and flake the fish. Put the beans in a large serving bowl, top with thin slices of onion, add a dash of Worcestershire sauce, stir in an olive oil, vinegar and garlic dressing, arrange the tuna on top, and serve. The recipes I have given below will take a little more time to prepare, but are well worth it. Also see the recipes given for marinated and cured fish on pages 302–306.

Skate and Samphire Salad with Hazelnut and Tomato Vinaigrette

Samphire is in season in June, July and sometimes part of August. If you only have a little, make it go further by combining it with other ingredients, as in this salad.

1½ lb / 680 g skate
12 oz / 340 g fresh samphire
small salad leaves
3 ripe tomatoes, peeled and roughly
   chopped
1 garlic clove, peeled and crushed
   (optional)

salt
freshly ground black pepper
2½ fl oz / 70 ml hazelnut oil
1 oz / 30 g flaked hazelnuts, lightly
   toasted

Poach the skate in lightly salted water until just cooked. Carefully remove from the pan, and put to one side until cool enough to handle. Pick over the samphire, discard any bruised branches, and cut off any discoloured ends. Wash thoroughly under cold running water to remove any mud. Blanch the samphire briefly in boiling water, or leave it raw, as you prefer. Arrange the salad leaves on individual plates and the samphire on top of them. Skin the skate, and carefully remove the strands of flesh from the cartilage. Arrange the fish on top of the salad. To make the dressing, rub the tomatoes through a sieve into a bowl. Add the garlic, if using, then season lightly and beat in the oil. Pour the dressing over the salad, and scatter the hazelnuts on top.

Variation ∾ Omit the samphire, and simply arrange the skate on top of the salad leaves. Top with a mint and honey dressing, made by grinding 2 garlic cloves to a paste with a little salt, and then gradually stirring in a pinch of cumin, a handful of chopped fresh mint, 2 tablespoons clear honey, 4 tablespoons cider vinegar, 6 tablespoons grapeseed or mild olive oil and a little pepper to taste.

Smoked Salmon and Lentil Salad with Hazelnut Vinaigrette

Serves 6–8

8 oz / 230 g green lentils
2–3 shallots, peeled and chopped
2 tbsp sunflower oil
1–2 tbsp hazelnut oil
2 tsp sherry vinegar or balsamic
  vinegar

salt
freshly ground black pepper
crushed garlic, to taste *(optional)*
3 oz / 85 g smoked salmon, finely
  chopped

Cover the lentils with one and a half times their volume of water and cook until tender. If the lentils are very old and dry, you may need to add more water during cooking. Drain the lentils and mix with the shallots. Stir in the oils, vinegar, seasoning and garlic while the lentils are still hot, and they will absorb the flavours of the dressing. Allow to cool before stirring in the smoked salmon.

Squid Salad

Serves 4

6 squid body cavities, prepared as
  on page 320
juice of ½ lemon
salt
freshly ground black pepper
4 tbsp extra virgin olive oil
3 garlic cloves, peeled and crushed

4 spring onions, trimmed and sliced
2 firm ripe tomatoes, peeled, deseeded
  and chopped
12 black or green olives, pitted and
  halved
shredded basil or coriander leaves

Slice the squid into ¼ in / 0.5 cm rings, and toss them in a little lemon juice, salt and pepper. Heat half the olive oil in a frying pan, add half the squid rings and stir-fry for about 5 minutes, lowering the heat after about 2 minutes. Transfer the squid to a bowl, keeping the cooking juices in the pan. Reheat it and cook the second batch of squid in the same way. When done, put in the bowl with the first batch. Mix the garlic, spring onions, tomatoes and olives with the squid, together with the rest of the olive oil and a little more lemon juice, to taste. Allow to stand for 30 minutes or so and then stir in the herbs before serving. This salad can be stretched by adding cooked pasta shapes and a little more olive oil and seasoning.

Aïoli
(Cod and Vegetables with Garlic Sauce)

Serves 6–8

*Traditionally, salt cod was used for this Southern French dish,
requiring up to 48 hours soaking and then very gentle simmering for
10–15 minutes. A very large, thick piece of fresh cod would also be
very good. The version of aïoli given here requires no eggs. It should
be thick and glossy, with a marvellous flavour.*

Vegetables
a mixed selection from new
  potatoes, small artichokes, green
  beans, garden peas or mangetout,
  cauliflower, broccoli florets,
  spring onions, radishes, olives,
  tomatoes and lettuce hearts

Cod
2 lb / 900 g cod fillet
salt

freshly ground black pepper
1 tbsp extra virgin olive oil

Aïoli
1 ripe tomato
1 tsp sea salt
10 garlic cloves
freshly ground black pepper
½ pt / 280 ml olive oil

Prepare the vegetables as appropriate. The potatoes and artichokes should be boiled or steamed until tender, and allowed to cool. The beans, peas or mangetout, cauliflower and broccoli should be steamed or boiled for just a few minutes to retain their crispness and colour. The rest of the vegetables are used raw. Arrange the vegetables either on one large serving platter or on individual plates, leaving enough room for the fish and the aïoli.

Season the fish lightly all over. Oil a large piece of foil or greaseproof paper, and wrap the fish in it carefully. Put the parcel on a baking sheet and cook in a preheated oven at 190 °C / 375 °F / Mark 5 for 15–20 minutes. Let the fish cool in the parcel to retain all the juices. Unwrap and arrange the fish, in fairly large pieces, on the plate with the vegetables.

To make the aïoli, peel, deseed and chop the tomato, and place in a sieve. Sprinkle with half the salt and leave to drain for 30 minutes. Meanwhile, prepare the garlic by peeling and roughly chopping, then placing in a mortar with the remaining salt and pounding to a paste. This takes time and patience. Add the drained tomato, and work into the garlic so that the two are well blended. Add about ½ teaspoon black pepper. Then, working in a smooth clockwise motion, blend in the oil, drop by drop to begin with, and then in a thick stream as the mixture begins to emulsify and thicken. If the mixture separates, it will still taste good, even if it doesn't look quite so impressive served as a dip with the fish and vegetables.

Celeriac and Mushroom Salad with Mussels

Serves 4

If you cannot get celeriac, finely sliced celery heart makes a good substitute.

24 large mussels
8 oz / 230 g button mushrooms, wiped
juice of 1 lemon
8 oz / 230 g celeriac
4 oz / 110 g mixed lettuce leaves and watercress

2 garlic cloves
3 tbsp thick Greek yoghurt or mayonnaise
2 tbsp Dijon, tarragon or mild mustard
salt
freshly ground black pepper
fresh herbs (as available)

Scrub and rinse the mussels very thoroughly under cold running water, knocking off any barnacles with the back of a knife blade. Tug off the 'beards'. Discard any mussels that remain open when tapped. Put the mussels in a saucepan, cover tightly and place over a high heat. Steam for 2–3 minutes, until the mussels open. Discard any that remain closed. Remove from the heat, strain off the cooking liquor and reserve. When cool enough to handle, remove the mussels from their shells and place in a bowl of cool water to stop them drying out.

Slice or quarter the mushrooms and sprinkle some of the lemon juice over them. Peel the celeriac and cut into matchsticks, or shred in a food processor. Drop straight into water with lemon juice added to stop the celeriac discolouring while you quickly prepare the rest of the salad.

Arrange the mixed salad leaves on four plates. Peel and crush the garlic and stir it into the yoghurt or mayonnaise. Beat in the mustard and season with salt and pepper. Drain the celeriac and stir it into the dressing. Add the mushrooms. You can, if you like, add a little of the mussel liquor for flavouring. Spoon the celeriac and mushroom salad over the salad leaves. Drain the mussels, arrange these on top, and garnish with such fresh herbs as you have available.

Duck, Olive and Garlic Salad

Serves 4–6

Poached duck breasts make an easy main course, hot or cold. New potatoes and fresh garden peas are classic accompaniments to a hot duck dish. Here I serve the meat in a salad with whole garlic cloves and an olive dressing for plenty of flavour.

4 duck breasts
½ pt / 280 ml good dry white wine
2–3 cloves
black peppercorns
2–3 allspice berries
1 bay leaf
1 celery top

1 head of garlic, cloves separated and peeled
24 black olives
1 tbsp capers
¼ pt / 140 ml homemade seasoned mayonnaise
salad leaves, to serve

Skin the duck breasts and put them in a deep frying pan with the wine, enough water to cover and the spices, bay leaf, and celery top. Simmer very gently until the duck is just done, preferably still slightly pink. Remove from the pan. While the duck is cooking, ladle a little of the cooking broth into a saucepan, add the garlic cloves and simmer until tender. Stone and pound half the olives with half the capers. Mix into the mayonnaise, together with the garlic cloves.

Slice the duck breasts, and serve on salad leaves with the mayonnaise and the rest of the olives and capers. This is excellent with a rice, pasta or new potato salad, just dressed with olive oil and herbs and a splash of sherry vinegar or lemon juice.

WARM SALADS

I'M ALL FOR warm salads at any time of the year. They are especially good in winter to serve as a starter in place of a soup or a rich pâté, but are, if anything, even better as a light main course, served with some appropriate salad leaves. A consommé to start with, either of fish or meat, or a clear Chinese-style vegetable soup, and a bowl of tropical fruit salad to finish makes for a light yet sustaining and very attractive meal.

Wilted Dandelion Salad

Serves 4

*In France and Belgium, dandelion is cultivated as a salad vegetable.
It is a favourite bistro salad, and is often served with a poached
egg on top.*

3–4 good handfuls of young
  dandelion leaves
4 rashers smoked streaky bacon

freshly ground black pepper
2 tbsp wine vinegar or sherry vinegar

Wash the leaves in several changes of warm water, and dry them in a salad
spinner or clean tea-towel. Place in a salad bowl. Fry the bacon until crisp, and
crumble over the salad. Pour the hot fat over the leaves, too, and mix well,
seasoning with pepper. Deglaze the frying pan with the vinegar, and stir into the
salad. Serve immediately before the bacon fat has time to congeal.

Variation ∽ This is also very good if you add young tender spinach leaves.

Warm Leek and Courgette Salad

Serves 4

8 oz / 230 g baby leeks
8 oz / 230 g baby courgettes
6 tbsp walnut oil
1 tbsp wine vinegar or cider vinegar

1 garlic clove, crushed
sea salt
freshly ground black pepper
about 4 oz / 110 g salad leaves

Wash and trim the leeks and courgettes and drop them into a large saucepan of
boiling salted water. Bring back to the boil and hold there for 3 minutes.
Meanwhile, make a dressing with the oil, vinegar, garlic, salt and pepper. Drain the
vegetables, put them in a bowl and while they are still hot, pour over the dressing
and mix well. Arrange the salad leaves on individual plates and place the leeks and
courgettes on top. Serve at once.

Variation ∽ Prepare a warm baby carrot and baby sweetcorn salad in the
same way, but cook the carrots first for 5 minutes or so, before adding the
sweetcorn and cooking the two together for a further 2–3 minutes.

Warm Green Bean, Garlic and Potato Salad

Serves 4–6

1 lb / 455 g new potatoes, scrubbed
2–3 heads of garlic, cloves
  separated and peeled
8 oz / 230 g slim green beans,
  topped and tailed
4 tbsp extra virgin olive oil

sea salt
freshly ground black pepper
sherry vinegar, balsamic vinegar or wine
  vinegar
basil leaves

Drop the new potatoes into a large saucepan of boiling, lightly salted water. Add the garlic after 5 minutes. Add the beans after another minute or so. Bring everything back to the boil and simmer until the vegetables are just tender. Drain and toss in the olive oil. Season with salt and pepper, and add a little vinegar. Tear the basil leaves, and stir these into the salad. Serve warm or tepid, either in a large bowl or heaped on individual plates.

Grilled Aubergine, Onion and Pepper Salad with Warm Garlic and Pinenut Cream

Serves 4

1–2 aubergines
¼ pt / 140 ml extra virgin olive oil
1 large mild onion
1 lb / 455 g green, red and yellow
  peppers
salad leaves *(optional)*
coarse sea salt

freshly ground black pepper
1–2 tbsp sherry vinegar
herbs, to garnish
3 oz / 85 g peeled garlic cloves
7 fl oz / 200 ml milk
1 oz / 30 g toasted pinenuts

Slice the aubergines lengthways, and brush liberally with olive oil. Peel the onion and slice into four even slices. Brush with oil. Quarter and deseed the peppers and brush with oil. Under a hot grill or in a heavy cast-iron frying pan, cook the vegetables until nicely charred and tender, turning them frequently to stop them burning. Peel the skin from the peppers. Arrange the vegetables on individual plates or on a serving platter, with salad leaves if you wish. Sprinkle with half the remaining olive oil, salt, pepper and the sherry vinegar, and garnish with herbs. Meanwhile, simmer the garlic cloves in the milk. When soft, blend them to a purée with the toasted pinenuts, a tablespoon of milk and the remaining olive oil. Spoon into a bowl and serve with the vegetables.

Warm Mackerel and Cucumber Salad

Serves 4

Initial preparation should be done an hour or so before final cooking.

1 cucumber	6 tbsp extra virgin olive oil
salt	4 oz / 110 g salad leaves, washed and
1 lb / 455 g mackerel fillets	dried
2 tsp Dijon mustard	freshly ground black pepper
2½ fl oz / 70 ml apple juice	
1 small onion, peeled and thinly	
sliced	

Cut the cucumber in half lengthways and scoop out the seeds. Slice the cucumber very thinly on a mandolin or use the slicing disc of a food processor. Place the slices in a colander or sieve, sprinkle with a little salt, and leave to drain for 1 hour. Meanwhile prepare the fish. Remove any bones with tweezers, and cut the fillets into neat oblique slices about 1 in / 2.5 cm wide. Mix the mustard and apple juice, and pour into a shallow dish. Lay the onion in the dish, and place the pieces of fish on top, skin-side up. Press well down so that the fish is in contact with the onions and the marinade. Leave for 1 hour.

Rinse and dry the cucumber very thoroughly, squeezing it in a clean tea-towel if necessary. Fry it in 1 tablespoon of the olive oil for about 2 minutes, until it wilts and the colour brightens. Put it to one side. Remove the mackerel from the marinade, and pat it dry on kitchen paper. Fry in a little more olive oil for 1–2 minutes on each side. Arrange the salad leaves on four plates. Spoon the cucumber into the centre and arrange the pieces of smoked mackerel around it. Add the rest of the oil and 2 tablespoons of the marinade to the frying pan, add a pinch of salt and pepper, bring to the boil and pour it over the salad. Fresh dill, coriander or chervil can be used to garnish and flavour.

Warm Skate, Cod's Roe and Bacon Salad

Serves 4–6

2 oz / 60 g smoked streaky bacon,
  derinded and cut into matchsticks
12 oz / 340 g cooked cod's roe
1 skate wing, about 10 oz / 280 g
green salad leaves, washed and
  dried

3 tbsp olive oil
1 tbsp balsamic vinegar or cider vinegar
1 tbsp capers *(optional)*
salt (if required)
freshly ground black pepper

Fry the bacon until the fat runs, then remove with a slotted spoon, leaving the bacon fat in the frying pan. Slice the cod's roe and fry it in the bacon fat. Meanwhile, poach or steam the skate until just cooked. The timing will depend on the thickness of the fish. When cooked, put it to one side until just cool enough to handle, then remove the fish in shreds from the cartilage. Divide the salad leaves and arrange on individual plates. Arrange the slices of cod's roe on top and then the warm skate. Put the olive oil in the pan with the remaining bacon fat and the pieces of bacon. When the pan is sizzling, add the vinegar and capers, if using, and season lightly. Pour the hot dressing over the salad, and serve immediately.

Steamed Smoked Haddock,
Leek and Potato Salad

Serves 4

2 shallots, peeled and finely
  chopped
2 tbsp sherry vinegar
4 tbsp hazelnut oil
2 tbsp sunflower oil
coarse sea salt
freshly ground black pepper

1 lb / 455 g small waxy potatoes, such as
  Belle de Fontenay, Asperges or Pink
  Fir Apple
12–16 baby leeks, trimmed and halved
salad leaves *(optional)*
1½ lb / 680 g undyed smoked haddock
  fillet

Mix the shallots, vinegar, oils and a little seasoning, and put to one side while you prepare the rest of the dish. Steam the potatoes and leeks until just tender. Arrange salad leaves, if using, on individual plates with the vegetables, halving or slicing the potatoes, if preferred. Skin the haddock fillet and cut it into four even pieces. Steam the fish and, when done, carefully transfer a piece to the centre of each salad plate. Spoon the dressing over the fish and vegetables and serve immediately.

A further embellishment to this salad recipe, which I developed from a light main course served by the chef at the Café Royal, Herbert Berger, is to spoon a little caviar into hollows made in the potato halves.

Asparagus and Mangetout Salad with Shellfish and Warm Sesame Dressing

Serves 4–6

12 oz / 340 g asparagus (not too thick)
6 oz / 170 g mangetout
2–3 garlic cloves
1 tbsp toasted sesame oil
2 tbsp olive oil
salad leaves, to serve

12 oz / 340 g prawns, peeled, *or* 8 scallops, halved
1 tbsp fruit vinegar, such as blackcurrant, raspberry or blackberry, *or* you could use cider vinegar, lime or lemon juice or rice vinegar instead

Snap off the tips and the tenderest parts of the asparagus stems, about 4–5 in / 10–12.5 cm. Top and tail the mangetout, and pull off the stringy edges if necessary. Bring a pan of lightly salted water to the boil and drop the asparagus in it. Boil for 5 minutes, then add the mangetout and boil for a further 3 minutes. Meanwhile, peel and crush the garlic. Heat the oils in a frying pan and, when hot, add the garlic. Remove it immediately from the heat.

Drain the vegetables, reserving the cooking water. Rinse the vegetables under cold running water and arrange on individual plates on a bed of salad leaves. (Use dinner plates, not side plates, or everything will look too crowded.) Heat the oil again and add the prawns or scallops. Stir-fry for 3–4 minutes, until just cooked through. Add the flavoured vinegar to the pan, shake, remove from the heat and divide the shellfish between the plates, arranging them on the salad leaves. Pour the warm dressing over the salad and serve immediately.

Use the rest of the asparagus stalks for soup, or peel if necessary, cut up small and use in a risotto. The cooking liquid is a good base for soup or risotto.

Chicken Liver and Roquefort Salad

Serves 4

8 oz / 230 g chicken livers
4 oz / 110 g Roquefort cheese
extra virgin olive oil or walnut oil
lemon juice

salt
freshly ground black pepper
lettuce, radicchio, endive, watercress
  and chicory, prepared as appropriate

Clean and trim the livers, carefully removing any greenish parts and the sinews. (Soaking them in milk for a few hours in advance will improve their colour and flavour.) Slice the large pieces of liver in two, and dry all the livers on kitchen paper. Cut the cheese into cubes.

Make a dressing to your taste with the oil, lemon juice, salt and pepper. Toss the salad vegetables in the dressing and add the cheese. Arrange on individual plates. Heat a few drops of the oil (just enough to prevent sticking) in a frying pan and fry all the chicken livers for 2–3 minutes, shaking the pan a few times, not stirring as this tends to break them up. When the livers are coloured on the outside but still slightly pink in the middle when you stick a knife point in, remove them from the pan and arrange them on top of the salad. Pour over any pan juices, and serve while still warm.

Warm Pigeon and Lentil Salad

Use small blue-green Puy lentils if you can get them. The stock can be made and the lentils cooked the day before required.

4 wood pigeons	4 tbsp extra virgin olive oil
¼ pt / 140 ml good red wine	2 tbsp freshly squeezed orange juice
1 onion, peeled and sliced	2 garlic cloves, peeled and crushed
1 carrot, peeled and sliced	salt
1 celery stalk, trimmed and finely sliced	freshly ground black pepper
	green salad leaves
few parsley stalks	herbs – torn sage leaves, to garnish
6 oz / 170 g green lentils	*(optional)*

Remove the breasts from the wood pigeons, put them in a bowl, pour over the red wine and leave to marinate while you prepare some pigeon stock. Chop the rest of the pigeon carcasses into pieces and fry in a little oil in a heavy frying pan until well browned all over. Put the pieces in a saucepan. Fry the onion, carrot and celery until beginning to brown, and add to the pigeon pieces in the saucepan with the parsley stalks. Cover with cold water, bring slowly to the boil, skim the surface and simmer, uncovered, for about 1 hour.

Meanwhile, rinse the lentils, removing any stones, drain and tip into a clean saucepan. Once the stock has a good flavour, strain it over the lentils, bring to the boil, cover and simmer for about half an hour or until the lentils are tender. Drain the lentils, reserving the stock. Mix the lentils while still warm with the olive oil, orange juice, garlic and seasoning.

Remove the pigeon breasts from the marinade and dry them thoroughly. Heat a non-stick or well-seasoned frying pan, and fry the pigeon breasts for 3 minutes on one side, 2 minutes on the other. Remove from the pan and leave to rest for 5 minutes or so. Arrange the salad leaves on individual dinner plates and heap the lentils in the centre. Slice the pigeon breasts and arrange around the lentils.

Variations ∾ Serve the lentils and pigeon hot, without salad leaves but with a hot potato, garlic purée and a couple of spoonfuls of reduced pigeon stock.

Lentils and pork also make a good combination. Cook the lentils in water or any stock you may have, and, while still warm, stir in 4 tablespoons olive oil. While the lentils are cooking, dice 6 oz / 170 g belly pork, fry until well browned, then pour off the fat and mix in a little dark muscovado sugar, Dijon mustard and red wine vinegar. Leave to stand for 30 minutes, season, and mix with the warm lentils.

Warm Leek and Black Pudding Salad

Serves 4

*My father invented this recipe which has become a favourite addition
to his and my repertoire.*

1½ lb / 680 g thin leeks *or* 12 oz /
    340 g ready-trimmed baby leeks
8 oz / 230 g black pudding
4 tbsp extra virgin olive oil
1 tbsp wine vinegar

1 garlic clove, peeled and crushed
2 sage leaves, finely chopped
freshly ground black pepper
sea salt

Wash and trim the leeks, and split them down the middle if necessary. Steam or
boil them until just tender, and place in a shallow dish. Slice and fry the black
pudding, and lay it over the leeks. Put the rest of the ingredients in the frying pan,
and heat to sizzling point. Pour over the salad and serve immediately.

Variation ∾ A warm leek salad with a nut oil dressing is also very good with
chunks or slices of salami or ham instead of black pudding.

THE TIMES COOK IN HONG KONG

IN THE COURSE of my many visits to Hong Kong, I have been lucky enough to spend a good deal of time in other people's kitchens, some the professional kitchens of the European and Chinese chefs and some domestic kitchens, like that of my sister-in-law, Bettina.

I love shopping with Bettina in Wanchai's street markets. We buy Chinese wind-dried sausages, called *ap cheung*, from the shop that sells all manner of dried foods, and barbecued pork and spare ribs from the pork butcher. The sausage and barbecue will be added to fried rice to form part of the evening meal. The spare ribs will be cooked in a homely stew with 'hairy cucumbers'. For fish, it is difficult to choose between the pearly, mottled squid and the groupers swimming in a tank. We choose a grouper, which, simply steamed with ginger, garlic and spring onions for flavouring, will be the highlight of the meal, in true Cantonese fashion. We will have vegetables, too, perhaps stir-fried broccoli or a Chinese leaves and mangetout dish that I learned with Chan Fat Chee, chef at the Fung Lum in Shatin. He has allowed me into his kitchen on several occasions, and is an excellent teacher despite the fact that we speak not a word of each other's language. I was fascinated to watch how he used his fist as a piping bag, taking a handful of shrimp paste and squirting it neatly into mushroom caps, first adding that all-important dab of cornflour to hold mushroom and filling together.

After our food shopping, we might buy some auspicious flowers, slender wands of peach blossom, or a small orange tree for the balcony. Perhaps we'll buy some red and gold New Year decorations and the traditional *lai see*, or red packets, in which to tuck a crisp new banknote or two for the children. The pungent smell of dried fish mingles with that of barbecued meat; the smell of fresh oranges is tempered by a compound spiciness coming from the herbal medicine shop.

Hong Kong is a melting pot of culinary ideas and practices, with a huge enthusiasm for food, tireless energy and a vivid imagination. Its style of cooking used to be called 'East meets West cuisine', a fusion of oriental and western ingredients and cooking techniques drawn from Chinese and European kitchens. Thus, one might be offered roast lamb marinated in oriental spices and served not with roast potatoes, mint sauce and two veg, but with steamed *bok choy*, stir-fried vegetables and a dipping sauce of ginger, chillies and soy sauce.

More wonderful dishes are to be found in the restaurants of the fine hotels, where European chefs have a wealth of ingredients to draw on, which, when coupled with newly-learned Chinese cookery techniques, produces exceptional results. Thus, you might find a soy-flavoured mousseline served with shellfish, a roast pigeon caramelized with lavender honey and Chinese spices, braised skate with pink basil and lemon grass butter, or scallops marinated in lemon juice, fresh mint and sesame oil.

The 'East meets West' tag has tended to disappear in favour of 'Pacific rim cooking', a style favoured by European chefs in the Far East, by Asian and Australian chefs in Australia and by American chefs in California.

But borrowing from other cuisines has its pitfalls. We might have seen just one too many wontons filled with goat's cheese and sun-dried tomatoes. Culinary marriages are not always happy ones. I shall never forget the time I ordered, in France, a delectable *crème au citron avec sa sauce au thé.* I was expecting a pool of clear, amber, tea-flavoured sauce, surrounding the just-set delicate lemon cream. Instead, the lemon cream looked and tasted as if someone had just poured a cup of cold tea over it. So it is a good idea not only to familiarize yourself with unusual ingredients, but to learn how they are used authentically before launching into experiments. Much of my travelling in the Far East has had this as its objective, and, as a result, I feel more confident about using the wide range of oriental ingredients now available in the West.

Of all the dishes I cook which marry oriental and western ingredients and techniques, I find that salads are amongst the most appetizing and successful. This applies to both warm and cold salads, as well as to raw and cooked ones. The piquancy and fragrance of lemon grass, kaffir limes and garlic chives add an extra dimension to cold dishes; the rich nuttiness of toasted sesame oil and the salty tang of soy sauce enhance a simple meat salad quite surprisingly.

With the salad recipes given here, I could not resist including a recipe for *da bin lo* (see page 126). This is a favourite Hong Kong dish for casual entertaining, both at home and in restaurants. Shopping and cooking take some time, but all the cooking is done at the table. Put a large pot of boiling stock on a burner, arrange the platter of food around it, and let everyone help themselves.

I have also included an unusual sweet recipe to demonstrate that the experimentation is not all in one direction.

Oriental Fish Salad

Serves 4

Skate, salmon, cod, plaice or sole can be used for this recipe.

6 oz / 170 g salad leaves
1 leek *or* 3 spring onions
3 oz / 85 g bean sprouts, blanched
2 garlic cloves, peeled
1 tbsp soy sauce
2 tbsp sunflower or groundnut
 (peanut) oil

2 tsp toasted sesame oil
2 tsp rice vinegar, sherry vinegar or
 wine vinegar
8 oz / 230 g skinned fish fillet
sunflower and sesame oil for frying
1 tbsp toasted sesame seeds

Arrange the salad leaves on individual serving plates. Trim, shred, wash and dry the leek, or trim and shred the spring onions, and mix with the beansprouts in a bowl. Crush the garlic, and mix with the soy sauce, oils and vinegar. Pour over the vegetables, and let them stand while you prepare the fish. Slice the fish as thinly as possible. Heat a non-stick frying pan, brush it with a little sunflower and sesame oil, and fry the fish for just a few seconds on each side; it should barely cook through. Arrange the bean sprout mixture on the salad leaves and the fish on top. Spoon over any remaining dressing, and sprinkle with the toasted sesame seeds.

Lamb Salad with Oriental Dressing

Serves 4

2–3 neck fillets of lamb, about
   12 oz / 340 g–1 lb / 455 g in all
1 tbsp soy sauce
½ tsp five–spice powder
2 tbsp sunflower or groundnut
   (peanut) oil
4 oz / 110 g shiitake or oyster
   mushrooms
4 oz / 110 g bean sprouts
1 firm mango
4 large Chinese leaves
coriander leaves or fresh chillies, to
   garnish

Dressing
1 tsp clear honey
2 tsp rice vinegar or sherry vinegar
2 tsp soy sauce
4 tbsp sunflower or groundnut (peanut)
   oil
2 tsp sesame oil
1 small fresh chilli, deseeded and
   chopped *(optional)*

Trim any excess fat from the meat. Rub it all over with soy sauce and five-spice powder. Cover and leave it for at least 30 minutes or for as long as overnight if convenient. Heat half the oil in a frying pan, and fry the meat until well browned on the outside, leaving it as pink as you like inside. Remove and put to one side. Put the rest of the oil in the pan, and fry the mushrooms, slicing them first if you prefer. Blanch the bean sprouts in boiling water for 2 minutes, rinse under running cold water, and drain. Peel and slice or dice the mango. Place the large Chinese leaves on a serving platter, and arrange the bean sprouts and mushrooms on them. Slice the meat on the oblique, and lay in overlapping slices on the salad. Top with the mango. Mix the ingredients for the dressing in the order given, adding any meat juices to it, and spoon it over the lamb. Garnish with coriander leaves, or fresh chillies if you have used them in the dressing.

Chicken and Melon Salad with Warm Sesame Dressing

Serves 6

Melon partners cold cooked meats very well. Arrange a bed of salad leaves on the plates first, if you wish.

three 5 oz / 140 g skinless, boneless
chicken breasts
1 small honeydew melon, sliced,
deseeded and peeled
2 tbsp sesame seeds

3 tbsp sunflower oil
1 tbsp rice vinegar
2 tsp shredded fresh root ginger
2 garlic cloves, peeled and crushed
2 tsp toasted sesame oil

Poach or steam the chicken for 8 minutes. When cool enough to handle, slice, and arrange the slices on plates, alternating with slices of melon, or put a fan of chicken slices on one side of each plate and a fan of melon slices on the other. In a small, heavy frying pan, toast the sesame seeds until golden brown. Scatter them over the chicken and melon. In the same pan, mix all the remaining ingredients, except the sesame oil and bring to the boil. Remove from the heat, stir in the sesame oil, and spoon over the salad. Serve immediately.

Da Bin Lo
(Oriental Dip-Dip)

Serves 8–10

Meats

8 oz / 230 g fillet steak (this can be taken from the less expensive tail end)

8 oz / 230 g pork tenderloin

8 oz / 230 g lamb fillet

8 oz / 230 g skinless chicken breast *or* 12 chicken wings

Fish

1 lb / 455 g raw, peeled prawns or skinless white fish fillet

2–3 tsp cornflour

2 spring onions, trimmed and finely chopped *or* 4 garlic chives, finely chopped

1 tsp finely grated orange zest or dried peel (if making fish balls)

1 egg white, lightly beaten

uncooked prawns in their shells

fresh scallops or queen scallops

Vegetables

a selection from the following: mangetout, fine green beans, Chinese leaves and/or *bok choy*, oyster mushrooms, shiitake mushrooms, baby corn cobs, bunches of watercress

Noodles

1 lb / 455 g thin rice or wheat noodles

Flavoured vinegars

12 tbsp rice vinegar

6 tbsp water

3 tbsp sugar

1–2 chillies, finely sliced

2 tbsp finely grated fresh root ginger

2–3 garlic cloves, peeled and crushed

salt

Coconut sauce

1 small onion, peeled and thinly sliced

2–3 in / 5–7.5 cm thick end of lemon grass stalk, thinly sliced

1 tsp crushed coriander seeds

1 tsp groundnut (peanut) oil

3 oz / 85 g creamed coconut

3 fl oz / 85 ml vegetable or chicken stock

Stock

4 pt / 2.30 l chicken or vegetable stock

1–2 tbsp chopped coriander leaves

3 in / 7.5 cm thin end of lemon grass stalk, thinly sliced

2–3 spring onions, trimmed and finely sliced

First prepare the meats. Firm up the meat fillets and chicken breast by putting them in the freezer or ice-making compartment of the refrigerator, well wrapped, for 1 hour. With a very sharp knife, slice into paper-thin slices (or as close to that as you can get), and arrange each meat in a neat pattern on a separate plate. If using chicken wings, cut off and discard the wing tips, and divide the remaining parts in two at the joint. Cover each plate of meat with cling film, stack one on top of the other, and refrigerate until required.

To make prawn or fish balls, put the prawns or fish in a food processor with 2 teaspoons cornflour, and process until smooth. Mix in the spring onions or chives and, for fish balls, the orange zest or peel. Stir in the egg white and remaining cornflour, if necessary, to bind the mixture, which should be firm enough to handle. Wet your hands, and roll the mixture into walnut-sized balls. Put on a plate with the whole prawns and scallops, cover lightly with cling film and refrigerate until required.

Prepare the vegetables and cut into bite-sized pieces, as appropriate. Arrange in bowls or on plates, and keep covered until required. Cook the noodles according to the directions on the packet. Refresh under cold running water, drain and put to one side until required.

For the flavouring vinegars, mix the vinegar, water and sugar, and divide between three bowls. Add the chillies to one bowl, the ginger to another, and the garlic and a little salt to the third.

To make the coconut sauce, fry the onion, lemon grass and coriander in the oil until the mixture is fragrant. Stir in the creamed coconut and, when it has melted, add enough stock to give the sauce a good consistency for dipping. Transfer to a bowl.

To make the stock, put the stock, coriander, lemon grass and spring onions in a large flameproof casserole, fondue pot or hotpot and bring to the boil. When ready to serve, transfer to a table candle or spirit burner and keep at simmering point. Pieces of meat, prawn or fish balls, whole prawns, scallops or vegetables are picked up with fondue forks, chopsticks or those small mesh baskets on long handles which so resemble fishing nets, and held in the simmering stock until cooked, when they are transferred to the individual bowl or plate, being dipped into the coconut sauce or one of the vinegars en route, and then eaten. You can also thread two or three different ingredients on a long wooden skewer as they do in Malaysia, and dip it into the stock to cook. The stock, of course, gets better and better as the dipping progresses. When all the morsels have been cooked, put the noodles in a colander, and pour boiling water over them to warm them up. Swirl them in the pot of stock, and serve as a clear noodle soup.

Rose and Almond 'Bean Curd'

Serves 4–6

*An almond-flavoured jelly, called 'bean curd' because it has a similar
texture, is sometimes served at the end of a Chinese meal. In
Shanghai, I came across a stunning combination of oriental and
western flavours when Chef Lo at the Shanghai Hilton served such a
sweet in a syrup of* crème de menthe. *This led me to experiments of
my own, and to a rose and almond 'bean curd'.*

4½ leaves gelatine *or* 4½ tsp
  powdered gelatine
1 pt / 570 ml milk *or* ½ pt / 280 ml
  milk and ½ pt / 280 ml single
  cream

caster sugar, to taste
few drops of pure almond essence
3 tbsp triple distilled rose water

Soften the gelatine in ¼ pt / 140 ml milk. Bring another ¼ pt / 140 ml to the
boil, and pour it over the softened gelatine, stirring until dissolved. Sweeten the
warm milk to taste, and add the rest of the milk or the cream, the almond essence
and the rose water. Wet a shallow dish or cake tin, pour in the liquid and
refrigerate until set. Cut the jelly or 'bean curd' into shapes, place in individual
glass bowls and serve, perhaps with a little more single cream or preserved
kumquats, peeled fresh lychees or other appropriate fruit.

Vegetables

I have an image of my friend Joe wearing a Breton beret and pushing an old black bicycle along the Pantiles in Tunbridge Wells. He invited us for a late lunch one autumn weekend and we found him in the garden plaiting shallots into small bundles. The recent acquisition of an allotment was responsible for this; and for the treasure trove of Pink Fir Apple potatoes and bundles of Swiss chard he gave us to take home, as well as sorrel, shallots and coriander seeds. Autumn is a marvellous time of year to be a vegetarian. We do not have to rely on tasteless imports from Dutch greenhouses or green beans that have travelled thousands of miles after harvest. Tomatoes, courgettes, beans, peppers, corn, plums, greens, freshly dug potatoes, and more, are here in rich full-flavoured profusion. For a few short weeks, I like to enjoy this harvest; I put meat and fish dishes to one side and instead make vegetables and fruit the focal point of our meals. They go into soups, pies, omelettes, casseroles, crumbles and sauces. They add colour, flavour and texture to pasta, grain and pulse dishes, and they combine in intriguing sweet and savoury dishes.

With the Swiss chard, a too-often neglected vegetable, I was able to use both leaf and stem. The leaves, by then quite coarse, I blanched and used to line my Aubergine and Pepper Terrine (see page 162). Alternatively, I could have made them into a pie or tart like those favoured in Nice. In these the chard is mixed with sugar, eggs, spices, pinenuts and raisins and baked in an olive oil pastry. Niçois ravioli is also quite likely to contain chard rather than spinach, and it makes a good filling when mixed with ricotta (prepare and fill ravioli dough as in the Pumpkin Ravioli recipe on page 175). Keep some of the raisins and pinenuts in it, too. Chard stems can be steamed and eaten like asparagus with melted butter or an orange hollandaise sauce. There is also a very pleasant and easy dish from the Dauphiné in France in which the stems are chopped, simmered in salted water until tender, drained, fried in butter and sprinkled with grated Gruyère. Beaten eggs are stirred into the pan, and the dish is served when the eggs set to a soft scramble.

Many of the recipes in this chapter are suitable for vegetarians. The Aubergine and Pepper Terrine is based on one I was served as part of the best vegetarian meal I have ever eaten, cooked by Chef Mark Henry at the Milton Inn in Maryland, near Baltimore. I had been planning a meal around the local delicacy of soft shell crabs, but the 'two course vegetable and grain dinner' sounded so good that I chose it instead. After the terrine came a 'gâteau of spaghetti squash, brown rice with black beans, grilled onion and fried tomato salad, mixed spring vegetables and sautéed wild mushrooms'. It tasted as good as it looked, an exciting colourful plate, with each vegetable retaining its smell, flavour and shape, each cooked by a different method to achieve different textures. It was a meal which demonstrated the compatibility of vegetables with each other, and not just as accompaniments to main dishes.

Compatible is a good word to describe the potato which is so thoroughly adaptable that it is suited to the homeliest dishes as well as to the grandest. Caviar and *foie gras* are favourites in the restaurant world for putting with potatoes; the first served with a baked potato, the second thinly sliced and layered with thinly sliced potatoes and baked into a rich 'gâteau'. I have included rather simpler, more homely recipes here.

Although it is possible to track down exotic and unusual potatoes in the shops (and it is, of course, possible to grow your own), the likelihood is that you will have little to choose from in most shops. This is hardly surprising when you consider that only five varieties go to make up about 50 per cent of commercially grown potatoes not destined for the crisp packet. These are Maris Piper, a maincrop potato, usually described as a good all-rounder suitable for baking, boiling, mashing and roasting; Estima, a second early, which means it is harvested in July and August but has good keeping qualities, even into the spring; Wilja, also a second early and, like Estima, suitable for most cooking methods, but particularly good for chips; Pentland Squire, a maincrop potato with a floury texture that makes it suitable for baking; and Cara, a relatively new variety of maincrop potato, which resembles the King Edward in size and colouring (white skin, pink around the eyes), and is good for baking but suitable for all cooking methods. Asperges (also known as La Ratte and Cornichon), Belle de Fontenay, Bintje, Charlotte, Desirée, Elvira, Epicure, Maris Peer, Pink Fir Apple and Roseval are varieties to look for if you want to serve more unusual potatoes. These varieties have plenty of flavour, a firm waxy texture and good colour, and are excellent in salads. It is increasingly possible to find these 'designer' potatoes in supermarkets. Unless you are buying potatoes for immediate use, store them in a brown paper bag in a cool, dry, dark place, and definitely not in the polythene bag in which they are usually sold. Exposure to light will cause the potato to turn green, which is an indication that the toxin solanin is forming under the skin; green potatoes should not be eaten.

So often are we tempted by the exotic and the expensive that we tend to ignore the familiar and inexpensive. Mangetout and baby corn catch our eye, and we forget about the knobbly celeriac, tasty leeks and the great variety of cabbages. The root vegetables particularly are much more versatile than we might imagine. Beetroots are not only a tasty vegetable, but I have capitalized on their sweetness by using them in a cake, modelled on the traditional carrot cake (see page 460).

Parsnips are the main ingredient in a lovely spring tart I came across in Dorothy Hartley's *Food in England*. Described as 'Parsnip pie for February', it calls for boiled and sieved parsnips sweetened with honey, spiced with ginger and allspice, and mixed with lemon rind and juice and egg, before being poured into a pastry case. A pastry lattice is arranged on top, and the pie baked. A light meringue is piped around the edge, the pie returned to the oven to set it, and then the pie is served cold, garnished with primroses. It would look very attractive indeed. But only use garden or pot primroses as the wild flowers are protected, and it is illegal to pick them.

Jerusalem artichokes are often made into a soup with scallops (see page 21). I have also used their nutty, earthy sweetness in a seafood pie which would make an unusual main course (see page 292).

As well as our own native roots or 'neps', which are often neglected, sweet potatoes are more and more available in city greengrocers and supermarkets. These dusky pink, elongated tubers lend themselves to all manner of sweet and savoury dishes. They can be made into spiced pie fillings, like the pumpkin (see page 561), and are also served with glazed meats. Chicken baked with sweet potatoes (see variation in Chicken with Garlic Potatoes on page 333) is an American favourite.

TWO VEGETABLE STARTERS

HERE ARE two of my favourite vegetable starters. Several of the other dishes featured in this chapter would also be suitable to serve as a first course at a dinner party, as would some of the dishes in the Short Eats chapter.

Vegetable Fondue

Serves 4

1 small can anchovy fillets, drained
3 plump garlic cloves, peeled
10 pitted black or green olives
2 pieces dried tomato *(optional)*
¾ pt / 430 ml olive oil
sprig of thyme, rosemary or
    marjoram

1 lb / 455 g mixed, prepared vegetables,
    chosen from cherry tomatoes, broccoli
    and cauliflower florets, courgettes,
    mushrooms, baby sweetcorn and
    mangetout.

Chop the anchovies finely with the garlic, olives and dried tomato, if using. Mix with the olive oil in a small heavy saucepan. Add the herbs and heat gently. Transfer the oil to a flameproof casserole, fondue pot or hotpot, set over a table candle or spirit burner. Thread the vegetables on to wooden skewers or satay sticks, and let each person cook their own in the oil when it comes to boiling point. Alternatively you could pile the vegetables on a platter, and let each person prepare their own sticks of vegetables.

Vegetable and Tofu Creams with Tomato and Basil Vinaigrette

Serves 6–8

1 onion, peeled and finely chopped
1 tbsp sunflower oil
1 small fennel bulb, trimmed and finely chopped
4 oz / 110 g celeriac *or* 1 celery stalk, trimmed and finely chopped
2 carrots, peeled and finely chopped
2 courgettes, trimmed and finely chopped

1 small aubergine, trimmed and finely chopped
1 small turnip, trimmed and finely chopped
1–2 tbsp chopped parsley
3 eggs
4 oz / 110 g silken tofu
3 fl oz / 85 ml single cream
salt
freshly ground black pepper

Sweat the onion in the oil until soft, then add the rest of the vegetables. Moisten with 2–3 tablespoons water (or dry white wine if you have a bottle opened), cover with a lid, and cook until the vegetables are soft. Add the parsley and put the vegetables in a blender with the eggs, tofu and cream. Blend until smooth, then rub through a sieve and season to taste. Oil or butter six or eight dariole moulds or ramekins, and spoon in the vegetable cream. Steam over a low heat, or cook in a bain-marie in a preheated oven at 170°C / 325°F / Mark 3 until set, when a knife point inserted in the middle will come out clean. Allow the creams to cool a little before turning them out on to plates. Serve with Tomato and Basil Vinaigrette.

Tomato and basil vinaigrette
2–3 ripe tomatoes
4 tbsp extra virgin olive oil
2 tbsp sherry vinegar

sprigs of basil
salt
freshly ground black pepper

Roughly chop the tomatoes, and put in a blender or food processor with the olive oil, vinegar and a few basil leaves. Process and sieve. Season to taste and spoon around the vegetable creams. Garnish with basil leaves, shredded or whole.

LIGHT AND SIDE DISHES

MOST OF the recipes given here are for side dishes, although some would make a good starter, or even a light main course.

Artichoke and Asparagus Casserole in Butter and Cider Sauce

Serves 8

This is best served on its own, and makes an excellent starter.

12 small or 4 medium globe
   artichokes
2 lb / 900 g green asparagus
3 oz / 85 g unsalted butter
2 oz / 60 g shallots, peeled and
   finely chopped
2 fl oz / 60 ml good dry white wine
¼ pt / 140 ml dry cider

¼ pt / 140 ml vegetable stock or water
6 oz / 170 g diced tomato flesh
8 basil leaves, torn into shreds
3 tbsp crème fraîche (*optional*)
salt
freshly ground black pepper
chervil or parsley

If using medium artichokes, remove all the leaves and the chokes. Put the artichoke bottoms in a bowl of acidulated water. Small artichokes need only the outer leaves and the leaf tips removing. Quarter small artichokes, or slice artichoke bottoms into four or five pieces or cut into wedges. Blanch in boiling water for 5 minutes, then drain. Remove and discard any woody stems from the asparagus, and break into 1½ in / 4cm pieces. Blanch the asparagus pieces in boiling water for 4–5 minutes, then drain and refresh under cold running water. Reserve the tips for garnish. Melt 1 oz / 30 g butter in a flameproof casserole, and add the shallots, artichoke pieces, white wine and cider. Bring to the boil and cook briskly for a few minutes. Add the stock or water and continue cooking until the artichokes are tender but still firm. Remove the artichokes and boil the cooking liquor until reduced by half. Put the artichokes back in the casserole with the asparagus pieces and bring back to the boil. Add the tomato and basil, stir in the crème fraîche, if using, and season to taste. Warm the asparagus tips by pouring boiling water over them. Divide the vegetables between eight individual dishes, and garnish with asparagus tips and chervil or parsley.

Variations ‿ Courgettes could be used if artichokes are not available, although you would need to adjust the cooking time.

Cook some small new potatoes in the casserole, and serve with some lightly boiled or poached eggs, even quail eggs, to make a marvellous main course for a vegetarian dinner.

Carciofi all Romana
(Roman-style Artichokes)

Serves 4

1 lemon	salt
4 globe artichokes	freshly ground black pepper
few stems of mint	3 tbsp extra virgin olive oil
few stems of parsley	4 tbsp white wine

Grate the zest from the lemon, and cut the lemon in half. If the artichokes have long stalks, break these off near the base, and rub the broken surfaces with the cut lemon to keep them from browning. Peel the stalks down to the tender centre, and drop in a bowl of water to which you have added some lemon juice. Break off the coarse outer leaves of the artichokes, and then snip off the coarse tips of the remaining leaves until you have removed all the tough fibrous part. Each cut surface should be rubbed with the lemon to prevent it darkening. The choke is dealt with later. (There is no need to cut off the leaf tips unless you have artichokes with sharp spiny points to the leaves.)

Strip the mint and parsley leaves from the stems. Chop the leaves and put the stems, together with some of the lemon zest, in a large saucepan of water. Season lightly and bring to the boil, then add the artichokes and cook for 15–20 minutes. Drain, and when cool enough to handle, open out the centre and remove the hairy choke without removing the tender base, which is the best part of the artichoke. Put the artichokes back in the pan with the olive oil and white wine, chopped herbs and zest, keeping a little of the green herbs and yellow zest back to sprinkle on the artichokes before serving. Cover and cook over a low heat until the artichokes are tender. Serve in shallow soup plates, scattered with the remaining herbs and zest. Eat with a knife and fork or your fingers.

The peeled stalks can be cooked with the artichokes and then used in soup or as a salad ingredient.

Baked Jerusalem Artichokes

Serves 4

*The following recipe is excellent with roast beef or a pot-roast chicken,
and makes an interesting change from potatoes.*

2 lb / 900 g Jerusalem artichokes   1 oz / 30 g butter
½ pt / 280 ml thin béchamel sauce   salt
    or cream   freshly ground black pepper

This may seem a large quantity for four people, but because of all the knobbly
bits, there is often quite a lot of waste with Jerusalem artichokes. I find that if you
scrub them well, cutting off any bruised knobs, it is not necessary to peel them.
Since making this discovery, I serve Jerusalem artichokes often in the autumn and
winter. I love this nutty flavour. Cut the vegetables into ¼ in / 0.5 cm slices and
drop into a large pan of boiling water. Simmer for 2–3 minutes. Drain and layer
them in a buttered baking dish with the béchamel sauce and seasoning, finishing
with a layer of sauce on top. Bake for 25–30 minutes at 200°C / 400°F / Mark 6.

Asparagus and Almonds in Filo

Serves 4–6

To suggest at the beginning of the English asparagus season, which opens in early May, that you might cook and eat this silky, green delicacy, long awaited through winter and spring, any other way than quickly boiled or steamed until just tender, and then served warm, dressed in nothing more than a little good oil or butter and lemon juice, would be seen by some as sacrilege. But once the asparagus season is in full swing, the shops are full of it, and it is so easy to get carried away, buy too much, and then find it a few days later looking somewhat fridge-worn. This is a good recipe for such times.

5 oz / 140 g butter
1 onion, peeled and finely chopped
1 lb / 455 g asparagus, trimmed and
   blanched
4 oz / 110 g flaked almonds, toasted

6 tbsp single cream
4 oz / 110 g Cheddar cheese, grated
salt
freshly ground black pepper
5 sheets filo pastry

Make the filling first. Melt 1 oz / 30 g of the butter and fry the onion until softened. Cut the asparagus into 1 in / 2.5 cm pieces, and fry briefly with the onion without letting it colour. Remove the pan from the heat, and stir in the almonds, cream and cheese. Season to taste, and cool. Meanwhile, melt the remaining butter and preheat the oven to 200°C / 400°F / Mark 6. Lay one sheet of filo pastry on a work surface. Cover the remaining sheets with a clean, damp cloth. Brush the first sheet with melted butter and cover with a second. Brush with melted butter again, and repeat with the remaining three sheets. Spread the asparagus filling over the pastry, leaving a 1 in / 2.5 cm border around the edge. Fold in the two shorter sides and then roll up. Carefully brush with the remaining butter, and bake in the oven for 20 minutes. Turn the oven down to 180°C / 350°F / Mark 4, and cook for a further 10 minutes, until crisp and golden brown.

Variation ∽ Halve the amount of asparagus, and substitute 8 oz / 230 g diced, cooked chicken breast for the almonds.

Broad Beans and Peas with Cream and Lettuce

Serves 4–6

1–2 shallots, peeled and finely
  chopped
1 oz / 30 g butter
1 Little Gem lettuce, shredded
8 oz / 230 g shelled peas
8 oz / 230 g shelled broad beans

3 fl oz / 85 ml single cream
finely chopped basil or summer savory
finely chopped parsley
salt
freshly ground black pepper

Cook the shallots in the butter in a saucepan without browning them. When they are soft and translucent, stir in the lettuce. Add the peas and beans and a splash of boiling water, no more than 2 tablespoons. Cook the vegetables for 2–3 minutes over a high heat, then add the cream, herbs and seasoning to taste. Stock can be used in place of cream, if preferred; in which case, do not add water but simply the boiling stock.

Broccoli with Tomato and Soy Butter

Serves 4

*This dish, with a slightly oriental touch both in its method of cooking
and in its flavours, is good enough to serve on its own as a starter.*

1 lb / 455 g broccoli
2 tsp sesame oil
1 tbsp salt
2½ fl oz / 70 ml water or vegetable
  stock

3 tbsp soy sauce
1 tbsp rice vinegar or sherry vinegar
3 oz / 85 g chopped tomato flesh
2 oz / 60 g chilled unsalted butter, diced
freshly ground white pepper

Separate the broccoli into florets and stalks. Peel the stalks and slice them on the diagonal to give a large cooking surface. Bring a saucepan of water to the boil with the sesame oil and salt. Drop in the broccoli, bring it back to the boil and boil for 30 seconds. Drain quickly and plunge the broccoli into chilled water, or at least rinse it well under running cold water to cool it quickly.

Heat the water or stock with the soy sauce and vinegar in a wok or large frying pan. Add the broccoli, cover, and steam until just tender. Remove the broccoli, and keep it warm over hot water, leaving the cooking juices in the wok or frying pan. Add the tomato and quickly reduce to 2–3 tablespoons. Off the heat, add the cubes of butter, one at a time, and whisk into the sauce until it emulsifies and thickens. Season with a little white pepper. (Extra salt should not be required because of the salt in the soy sauce.) Serve the sauce and broccoli separately or together, as you wish.

Braised Cabbage with Bacon, Cheese and Tomatoes

Serves 4–6

This dish goes very well with grilled polenta cakes and grilled sausages. For vegetarians, the bacon can be replaced with extra cheese and tomatoes.

1 Savoy or winter cabbage
4 tbsp olive oil
4 oz / 110 g smoked streaky bacon *or* a piece of ham or bacon, derinded and cut into small strips or chunks
1 small onion, peeled and finely chopped

4 dried tomato halves, soaked in hot water, drained and cut into strips, *or* 3 fresh tomatoes, peeled, deseeded and chopped
sprig of thyme, rosemary or marjoram
3 oz / 85 g Gruyère or Jarlsberg (or other cheese with similar melting qualities), diced

Remove any damaged leaves from the cabbage. Quarter it, cut out the thick stem, and slice into ½ in / 1 cm shreds. Rinse thoroughly and put in a saucepan with a tight-fitting lid. Cook the cabbage in just the water clinging to the leaves, which in effect steams it, for 2–3 minutes. Drain and put to one side. Heat half the olive oil in a large lidded frying pan. Add the bacon or ham and onion and fry for a few minutes. When the onion is soft, add the cabbage and the tomato. Add the rest of the olive oil and the herbs. Put the lid on, shake the pan, and then allow to cook for about 5 minutes, until the cabbage is just tender but not soggy. Stir the cheese into the cabbage until just beginning to melt into strings, then transfer to a warm serving dish. Serve very hot.

Sweet and Sour Cabbage

Serves 4

2 oz / 60 g butter
1 lb / 455 g white cabbage,
shredded

1 tbsp brown sugar
2 tbsp fruit vinegar or sherry vinegar

Heat the butter in a heavy frying pan or wok. Stir in the cabbage, and after a minute or so, add the brown sugar. Cook a little longer and then add the vinegar. Raise the heat, and stir vigorously for 20 seconds. Serve while the cabbage is still slightly crunchy and with the pan juices poured over it.

Variation ∾ Use red cabbage, and layer it with slices of onion and apple (use a sharp variety) in a baking dish, sprinkling each layer with the vinegar and sugar and a little red wine, freshly grated ginger, ground cinnamon and salt and pepper to taste. Dot the top with butter, and bake at 180°C / 350°F / Mark 4 for 1–1½ hours.

Lemon-Glazed Carrots

Serves 4

Marmalade makes an excellent glaze with plenty of flavour of its own to add a subtle bitter-sweet taste. Try lemon marmalade with carrots, orange marmalade with parsnips or beetroots and lime marmalade with turnips or swedes.

1 lb / 455 g carrots
1 oz / 30 g butter
1–2 tbsp lemon marmalade

salt
freshly ground white pepper
1 tbsp finely chopped chives or parsley

Peel or scrub the carrots, as appropriate. Slice them, cut them into batons or leave whole, depending on size. Put them in a saucepan with 1 in / 2.5 cm water and simmer gently until almost tender. Stir in the butter, marmalade and seasoning and raise the heat. Allow the cooking juices to amalgamate to a glaze, then transfer to a serving dish. Sprinkle with herbs before serving.

Celeriac with Lime

*This dish complements chicken very well. The preparation is a little
time-consuming, but the end result is worth it.*

1 lime with a good skin	salt
1 lb / 455 g celeriac	freshly ground white pepper
2–3 oz / 60–85 g unsalted butter	

Carefully pare the zest only from the lime, and slice this into fine shreds. Peel
the celeriac, cut it into thin strips, and slice each into fine shreds. Gently cook the
celeriac in the butter for 2–3 minutes, just to blanch it and heat it through. Season
it lightly, stir in the lime zest, and heat it through so that the essential oils are
released to flavour the celeriac.

Glazed Chestnuts

*Although chestnuts are not a vegetable, I have included a recipe for
them here as they are often served as such.*

1 lb / 455 g chestnuts, peeled	1–2 oz / 30–60 g butter
1 pt / 570 ml vegetable stock or fruity white wine	1 oz / 30 g light muscovado sugar

Cook the chestnuts in the stock or wine until tender. Drain them, reserving the
cooking liquid for soup or stock for another dish. Return the chestnuts to the pan
with the butter and sugar, cover and set over a low heat until the sugar has
dissolved. Shake to glaze the chestnuts.

Steamed Chinese Leaves and Mangetout

Serves 6

1 head of Chinese leaves
3 oz / 85 g mangetout
2 star anise

Dressing
2 tbsp toasted sesame oil
2 tbsp soy sauce
2 tbsp brown sugar
2 tbsp rice vinegar

Remove any damaged outer leaves from the Chinese leaves. Top and tail the mangetout. Shred the leaves across and mix them with the mangetout. Place them in a steamer basket with the star anise buried in the middle. Steam for 5 minutes. Meanwhile, mix together the ingredients for the dressing and pour it into a serving bowl. Drain the vegetables and toss in the dressing while still hot.

Stewed Cucumbers

Serves 6

2 onions
2 cucumbers
3 oz / 85 g unsalted butter,
    softened
2 tsp plain flour
6 tbsp fish, chicken or vegetable
    stock

2 tbsp white wine
1 blade of mace or pinch of
    ground mace
salt
freshly ground white pepper

Peel and thinly slice the onions. Cut the cucumbers in half lengthways, scoop out the seeds, and then slice the cucumber halves. Melt 2 oz / 60 g butter in a frying pan, and mix the rest with the flour to make *beurre manié*. Fry the onion in the melted butter for a few minutes until wilted, and then add the cucumber. Fry together for a few minutes more. Add the stock, wine and mace, then gradually stir in the *beurre manié* in small pieces. Shake the pan, then let all the ingredients stew together for a few minutes. Season and serve.

Fennel with Cheese Sauce

This is not based on any dish I have ever come across in Italy, but the inspiration certainly comes from the Italian way with vegetables, which is to treat them as an important part of any meal.

4 fennel bulbs, about 8 oz / 230 g each
1 oz / 30 g butter
2 shallots, peeled and finely chopped

¼ pt / 140 ml full-cream milk
4 oz / 110 g Gorgonzola or Dolcelatte cheese
4 oz / 110 g Fontina or Caciotta cheese
4 oz / 110 g ricotta cheese

Trim the feathery tops from the fennel bulbs, and if in good condition, reserve some for garnishing. Remove any bruised or broken leaves. Bring a large saucepan of lightly salted water to the boil. Cut the fennel bulbs in half down the middle, and put them in the boiling water. Bring back to the boil and simmer for 10–20 minutes until just tender. The length of cooking time will depend on how fresh and juicy the fennel was to begin with.

When the fennel is cooked, drain it. Remove the leaves in the centre of each piece, taking great care not to break them. Leave one complete layer of leaves so that a small bowl is formed, in which to pour melted cheese. The leaves you have removed will served as scoops to eat the cheese with. Some of the broader ones can be cut in half down the middle. Put the separated leaves in a colander, cover and set over hot water to keep them warm.

Melt the butter in a small saucepan and gently fry the shallots until soft. Pour on a little of the milk. Crumble in the blue cheese, cut the Fontina or Caciotta into small cubes, and put these in the pan together with the ricotta. Stir together, heating gently until melted, adding more milk, if required, to give the sauce a homogeneous, creamy consistency. Pour into the fennel 'bowls', and finish under a hot grill so that the cheese *just* begins to brown and bubble. Put on individual plates, garnish with sprigs of fennel tops and serve with the reserved fennel leaves.

Stir-fried Greens with Preserved Ginger and Sesame Seeds

Serves 6

1 lb / 455 g spring greens
½ head of Chinese leaves
1 lb / 455 g spinach
½ in / 1 cm fresh root ginger, peeled
2–3 garlic cloves, peeled
1 star anise
2–3 tbsp groundnut (peanut) oil
4 spring onions, trimmed and thinly sliced

1–2 tbsp soy sauce
1 tbsp rice wine
1 tbsp rice wine vinegar
2–3 pieces of preserved ginger, thinly sliced
2 tsp toasted sesame oil
1 tbsp toasted sesame seeds

Wash, trim and shred the vegetables, keeping them in separate piles. Fry the fresh ginger, garlic and star anise in the oil in a wok or large frying pan for 4–5 minutes. Discard the seasonings, and put the spring greens into the hot oil. Stir-fry for 2–3 minutes before adding the Chinese leaves. After stir-frying for 2–3 minutes, add the spinach and spring onions. When the spinach has collapsed, add the soy sauce, wine, vinegar and preserved ginger. Cover with a lid and steam for a few minutes more. Stir in the sesame oil, and then serve scattered with sesame seeds.

Deep-fried Leeks

1½ lb / 680 g leeks
groundnut (peanut) or sunflower oil for frying

Trim the leeks, and remove the coarse tops and outer skin. Cut into 3 in / 7.5 cm lengths, and slice in half lengthways. Shred the leeks into long, thin strips. Rinse and dry them thoroughly. Put oil in a wok or deep frying pan to a depth of about 3 in / 7.5 cm, and heat until a cube of bread sizzles as soon as it is dropped in. Fry the leeks in batches for about 20 seconds each, and drain them on kitchen paper before serving.

Braised Lettuce

4 Little Gem lettuces
4 oz / 110 g smoked streaky bacon
  rashers, derinded
1 onion or shallot, peeled and finely
  chopped

2½ fl oz / 70 ml water, white wine or
  stock
freshly ground black pepper
1 tbsp chopped chervil, parsley or
  summer savory

Quickly wash the whole lettuces, and remove any damaged outer leaves. With a sharp knife, cut a small conical plug from the base of each lettuce, excavating to a depth of about 1 in / 2.5 cm. Cut one of the bacon rashers into four. Roll up each piece tightly and stuff one into each of the cavities you have made in the lettuce hearts. Wrap the rest of the bacon around the lettuces, and secure with cocktail sticks or cotton. Heat a lidded frying pan and gently fry the onion for 5 minutes or so, then add the bundles. Moisten with the liquid and grind on a little black pepper. Cover and simmer for 10–15 minutes until the lettuces are wilted and tender. Remove the bundles from the pan with a slotted spoon, and place them in a heated serving dish. Remove the cocktail sticks or cotton. Boil down the cooking liquid and onion until reduced to 2–3 tablespoons. Pour it over the lettuce and sprinkle on some herbs before serving.

Marinated Mushrooms

It is a curious fact that mushrooms, which contain a lot of water,
actually give up some of their moisture when quickly boiled in water.
I suggest cooking them in a mixture of water and wine, which will
produce an excellent mushroom broth that can be used as a base for
mushroom soup (substitute for vegetable stock in recipe on page 8).

2 lb / 900 g fresh mushrooms
¾ pt / 430 ml good dry white wine
¾ pt / 430 ml water
4 tbsp white wine vinegar
2 bay leaves
1 tbsp peppercorns
1 small cinnamon stick

1 tsp sea salt
3 in / 7.5 cm strip of orange zest
¼ pt / 140 ml good olive oil
salt
freshly ground black pepper
chopped parsley, to garnish

Wipe the mushrooms carefully, and trim off the bases of the stems. Put the rest of the ingredients, except the olive oil, seasoning and 1 tablespoon wine vinegar, into a large saucepan. Bring to the boil, and simmer for 5 minutes. Put the mushrooms into the pan, bring back to the boil, and simmer for 6–7 minutes. Strain the liquid into a bowl and reserve for soup. Drain the mushrooms, then dry them by placing them on several layers of kitchen paper or an absorbent tea-towel. When dry, put them into a serving bowl with the olive oil and the remaining wine vinegar. Season to taste, and garnish with the chopped parsley.

Fried Puffballs

*This is one of my favourite wild mushroom recipes; quantities are not
given because who knows how many you will find?*

puffballs	flour	paprika
eggs	salt	butter
milk	freshly ground	olive oil
nutmeg	black pepper	finely chopped parsley

Peel and slice the puffballs about ¼ in/0.5 cm thick. Beat the eggs, milk and
nutmeg in a shallow dish, as if you were making French toast. Sift the flour, salt,
pepper and paprika on to a plate. Heat a mixture of butter and olive oil in a frying
pan. Dip the puffball slices into the egg mixture, then into the flour, and finally into
the egg mixture once more. Fry the slices in a single layer, turning them once.
Serve sprinkled with parsley.

Variation ∿ If you have only a small harvest of puffballs, say one or two, peel
and dice them, cook as described above, and use them in place of croûtons in a
bowl of salad greens, or mix them with other mushrooms into a bowl of freshly
made pasta.

Honey-Glazed Stilton Potatoes

Serves 4

4 large baking potatoes
2 oz / 60 g butter
freshly ground black pepper

4 oz / 110 g Blue Stilton, thinly sliced
1–2 tbsp honey

Scrub and dry the potatoes, and prick them all over. Bake towards the top of a preheated oven at 200°C / 400°F / Mark 6, until they feel soft when squeezed slightly. Cooking time will depend on the size and thickness of the potato but can be speeded up by inserting a small metal skewer into each potato at its thickest point so that heat is conducted to the centre more quickly. When cooked, remove the potatoes from the oven and cut a slice from the broadest surface of each one. Scoop the soft flesh out into a bowl, keeping the skins intact. Mix in the butter with a fork, and pepper to taste. Spoon back into the potato skins and smooth the surface, leaving enough room to lay thin slices of Stilton on top. Trickle honey over the cheese and put under a hot grill for 2–3 minutes for the honey and the cheese to melt and bubble. Serve immediately.

Roast New Potatoes and Garlic

Serves 4

4 heads of garlic
extra virgin olive oil

1 lb / 455 g new potatoes, scrubbed
  and pricked
coarse sea salt

Peel the outer skin from the garlic heads, but leave them whole. Slice a cap off the top, brush with olive oil and replace. Oil a roasting tin, and put in the garlic and new potatoes, sprinkling with a little salt. Roast in a preheated oven at 180°C / 350°F / Mark 4 until both are tender. To eat, break cloves off the garlic, and squeeze the soft flesh out of the skin to eat with the potatoes.

Variation ∾ Bake the scrubbed potatoes with peeled whole cloves of garlic and a little olive oil and seasoning in foil-wrapped parcels. This should take about 40 minutes at 180°C / 350°F / Mark 4. Put 4–5 potatoes and 2 large garlic cloves in each parcel.

Grilled Radicchio

*This is good served with a sprinkling of sea salt, a little more olive oil,
and a splash of lemon juice or balsamic vinegar.*

14–16 oz / 395–455 g radicchio, 2   salt
  firm round heads   freshly ground black pepper
4–6 tbsp good olive oil

Remove any bruised or wilted leaves and roots from the radicchio. Wash the heads and cut into quarters. Brush each piece with olive oil, season lightly and place under a moderate grill until cooked through, turning occasionally.

Variations ～ Grill lettuce in the same way. Use a firm, crisp lettuce, and, in addition to the olive oil and seasoning, sprinkle the cut surfaces with crushed garlic and grated cheese (Gruyère, Parmesan and Cheddar are good), before grilling.

Aubergines, courgettes, pepper and potatoes are all good grilled. Slice the aubergines and courgettes lengthways, brush each slice with olive oil, season, and grill on both sides. Quarter and deseed peppers, oil and season, and again grill on both sides, removing the skin as it peels off. Parboil, drain and dry potatoes before brushing with oil, seasoning and grilling on both sides. If the potatoes are large, slice them after parboiling.

Creamed Turnips

2 lb / 900 g turnips   salt
3 oz / 85 g unsalted butter   freshly ground white pepper
6 oz / 170 g crème fraîche or soured
  cream

Scrub the turnips and boil until tender. Peel, and put in a food processor with half the butter and cream. Process, and gradually add the rest of the butter and cream. Season to taste and reheat gently if necessary.

Variation ～ Use 1 lb / 455 g turnips and 1 lb / 455g potatoes.

MAIN COURSES

Artichoke and Potato Casserole

Serves 6

1 onion, peeled and thinly sliced
4 tbsp extra virgin olive oil
2½ lb / 1.10 kg new potatoes,
   scrubbed and dried
12 baby artichokes *or* 3 medium
   artichokes

12 garlic cloves, peeled
¼ pt / 140 ml dry white wine
sea salt
freshly ground black pepper
1–2 tbsp finely chopped parsley

Fry the onion gently in half the olive oil, using a flameproof casserole. Add the potatoes and fry all over, then turn down the heat, and continue to cook, partly covered, while you prepare the artichokes. Small ones just need trimming and rinsing before putting in the pan. Larger ones should be trimmed down by about a third, the outer leaves and stalk removed, and then quartered. The choke can then be pulled out. As you prepare each artichoke or piece, drop it into acidulated water to stop it discolouring. Drain the artichokes, and add to the casserole together with the garlic cloves and half the white wine. Season lightly, and simmer very gently until the vegetables are just tender, adding more wine and the remaining olive oil from time to time. Check the seasoning, scatter on the chopped parsley and serve direct from the pan.

Variation ∾ To make this into a more substantial dish, asparagus tips, freshly shelled peas and small pieces of ham can be added towards the end of the cooking time. A sprig of tarragon cooked with it gives a good flavour.

Aubergine, Okra and Tomato Stew

As well as being a hearty vegetarian main course when served with rice or another grain, this rich vegetable stew is an excellent accompaniment to grilled fish and meat dishes. It has even more flavour if made the day before required and eaten cold (but not chilled) with hot pitta bread. If you like such things chilli hot, then cook a small green or red chilli in the stew but carefully remove the seeds first.

1 medium onion, peeled and sliced
2½ fl oz / 70 ml extra virgin olive
   oil
1 lb / 455 g aubergines
6 garlic cloves, peeled
8 oz / 230 g okra

1 lb / 455 g peeled tomatoes, fresh or
   canned
2 sprigs thyme
salt
freshly ground black pepper
chopped flat-leaved parsley or coriander

Fry the onion gently in some of the olive oil in a flameproof casserole until it browns. Dice the aubergines into ½ in / 1 cm chunks, and add to the pan, together with the garlic. Add more olive oil, as the aubergine absorbs it like blotting paper. Trim the okra, carefully paring away the stalk end, and add it to the pan with the tomatoes, thyme and a little salt and pepper. Cover and cook over a low heat or in a low oven for 2–3 hours, until the vegetables are soft. Towards the end of the cooking time, stir in any remaining olive oil. Before serving, hot or cold, stir in the parsley or coriander.

Cabbage Stuffed with Wild Mushrooms

Serves 4

This is a rather grand recipe for cabbage. If you can get fresh wild mushrooms, so much the better. If not, the flavour of dried wild mushrooms is an important addition and worth the extra money. Dried wild mushrooms are really quite economical, go a long way and keep well. Just one small piece of dried porcini snipped into a soup or casserole immediately enhances the flavour.

½ oz / 15 g dried wild mushrooms
½ pt / 280 ml boiling vegetable or
   ham stock
8 large cabbage leaves
12 oz / 340 g fresh mushrooms
4 oz / 110 g ricotta
2 shallots

1 egg
salt
freshly ground black pepper
6 juniper berries
sprig of rosemary
2–3 tbsp extra virgin olive oil

Cut the dried mushrooms into small pieces, place them in a bowl, and pour on the boiling stock. Cut the hard central rib from each cabbage leaf, blanch the leaves thoroughly in boiling water, then drain. Wipe the fresh mushrooms, only peeling if absolutely necessary, and chop them very finely (I use a food processor at this point). Mix thoroughly with the ricotta. Peel and finely chop the shallots and add these to the mushroom and cheese mixture. Separate the egg. Beat the egg yolk lightly, and stir this into the mixture. Season to taste. Whisk the egg white, and fold this in. Strain the dried wild mushroom pieces, reserving the liquor, and stir them in gently.

Divide the stuffing between the eight cabbage leaves, and roll into neat parcels. Place in a lightly oiled baking dish. Scatter the juniper berries, and lay the sprig of rosemary on the cabbage parcels, and sprinkle with mushroom liquor and olive oil. Cover with foil, and bake in a preheated oven at 190°C / 375°F / Mark 5 for 25 minutes. Serve hot.

Celeriac, Pumpkin and Walnut Crumble

Serves 8

1 lb / 455 g celeriac
1 lb / 455 g pumpkin, peeled and
    deseeded
2 onions, peeled and finely chopped
2 tbsp olive oil
2 tbsp finely chopped parsley

8 oz / 230 g button mushrooms
5 oz / 140 g butter
2 oz / 60 g fresh breadcrumbs
3 tbsp finely chopped chives
3 oz / 85 g walnuts, finely chopped

Peel and slice the celeriac and blanch it immediately in lightly acidulated boiling water. Drain. Slice the pumpkin fairly thickly. Sweat the onions in the olive oil until soft, and then add the sliced vegetables. Cover with a lid, and let the vegetables 'steam' on top of the onions until tender. Transfer them to a buttered baking dish, sprinkling each layer with parsley.

Preheat the oven to 220°C / 425°F / Mark 7. Wipe and slice the mushrooms, and fry in half the butter until soft. This should be done over a high heat to evaporate the liquid. When cooked, finely chop the mushrooms. Mix them with the breadcrumbs, chives, walnuts and remaining butter, and spoon over the vegetables in the baking dish. Bake for 10–12 minutes in the top of the oven.

Variation ❧ Layer the cooked celeriac, pumpkin and onion in individual, ovenproof serving dishes, top with the mushroom, breadcrumb and walnut crumble mix, and finish off under a hot grill, rather than in the oven.

Wild Greens and Barley 'Risotto'

Serves 4–6

Many of the best edible green plants grow wild in relative profusion. Use a guide book to help you identify them, and only pick what you can be absolutely certain of identifying, thus avoiding the few plants that are poisonous. Pick well away from roadside verges and recently sprayed areas. Always wash well and dry all wild greens thoroughly (see method) before cooking. The strong flavour of wild greens goes well with pasta or a grain, such as rice or barley, as in this inexpensive and sustaining dish and the crumble recipe that follows.

2 lb / 900 g freshly picked wild greens, such as nettles, dock leaves, Jack-by-the-hedge, hogweed, fat hen, alexander stems, ground elder, chickweed, wood sorrel, orach and dandelion leaves
1 small onion *or* 2 shallots, peeled and chopped

2 oz / 60 g butter
2 tbsp extra virgin olive oil
12 oz / 340 g pearl barley
½ pt / 280 ml white wine
1½ pt / 850 ml hot vegetable stock
salt
freshly ground black pepper
freshly grated Parmesan cheese

First wash the wild greens thoroughly in several changes of warm water, and then dry them on kitchen paper or in a salad spinner. Toss them into boiling water to blanch them. Tender leaves, such as chickweed, fat hen, wood sorrel, orach and Jack-by-the-hedge, will need only the briefest blanching for about 1 minute. Tougher, stronger leaves, such as dock and nettles, should be blanched for 2–3 minutes. Drain, rinse, dry thoroughly and roughly chop. Leave on one side.

Gently fry the onion or shallots in half the butter and the olive oil in a large saucepan. Stir in the barley, add half the wine, and stir until it has been absorbed. Add the remaining wine, and cook gently until that too has been absorbed. Stir in the vegetable stock, a little at a time, allowing each batch to be absorbed before adding the next. After adding two or three batches of stock, stir in the prepared greens, and continue cooking until the barley is tender and all the stock is used up. Season to taste, and just before serving, stir in the remaining butter and the Parmesan cheese.

Wild Greens and Wild Rice Crumble

Serves 4–6

The wild greens in this recipe can be supplemented with bolted lettuce, spinach, watercress, Swiss chard or beet or turnip tops. For information on wild greens, see the recipe for Wild Greens and Barley 'Risotto' on page 154.

4 oz / 110 g wild rice
3 lb / 1.35 kg wild greens, such as chickweed, fat hen, wood sorrel, orach, Jack-by-the-hedge, nettles, dock leaves, hogweed, alexander stems, ground elder and dandelion leaves
2–3 shallots or small onions, peeled and chopped
2 tbsp extra virgin olive oil

1 tbsp finely chopped herbs, such as thyme, marjoram and rosemary
6 oz / 170 g hard cheese, grated
4 eggs
¼ pt / 140 ml buttermilk or single cream
salt
freshly ground black pepper
2 oz / 60 g fresh breadcrumbs
2 oz / 60 g nuts, finely chopped

Put the wild rice in a saucepan with about four times its volume of water, bring to the boil, and simmer until the rice is tender. Drain if necessary. Wash, blanch, drain and dry the leaves, as described in the recipe for Wild Greens and Barley 'Risotto' (see page 154). Place them in a large saucepan, cover and cook over a fairly high heat, stirring frequently, until the greens have collapsed. Drain them.

Sweat the shallots or onions in the oil in a large saucepan, and then mix in the cooked rice and greens, the herbs and most of the grated cheese. Beat the eggs with the buttermilk or cream, and mix this thoroughly with the vegetables. Season to taste, and spoon into an oiled ovenproof dish. Smooth the top, and sprinkle on the remaining cheese mixed with the breadcrumbs and chopped nuts. Dot with extra butter or oil, if you wish, and bake in a preheated oven at 180°C / 350°F / Mark 4 for about 45 minutes.

Mushroom and Potato Pie

Serves 4

You can make this with fresh mushrooms, but it has a richer flavour if made with a mixture of fresh and dried mushrooms. Use just one variety of dried mushroom or mix them, as you wish. They must be well soaked before cooking. I recommend pouring plenty of boiling water over them and leaving for an hour at least. Chinese flower mushrooms take longer, and I would poach them for an hour after an hour's soaking. Canned or bottled wild mushrooms can, of course, be used with no preparation.

1 lb / 455 g fresh and dried mushrooms, ready to use	salt
3–4 lb / 1.35–1.80 kg potatoes	freshly ground black pepper
6 oz / 170 g butter	½ pt / 280 ml stock, milk or single cream

Cut the mushrooms into small pieces. Peel the potatoes and slice as thinly as possible. Layer the potatoes and mushrooms in an ovenproof dish, dotting with butter and seasoning each layer of potatoes. Pour on the liquid, cover with foil, and bake in a preheated oven at 180°C / 350°F / Mark 4 for about 1 hour, less if the potatoes are wafer-thin; more if they are chunky.

Leek, Potato and Parmesan Strudel

Serves 6

3 oz / 85 g flaked almonds	2 cloves
2 oz / 60 g ground almonds	1½ lb / 680 g potatoes
6–8 oz / 170–230 g butter	salt
12 oz / 340 g leeks (white parts only)	freshly ground black pepper
½ pt / 280 ml milk	4 oz / 110 g Parmesan cheese, freshly grated
1 bay leaf	4 sheets filo or strudel pastry

Separately fry the flaked and ground almonds in a little of the butter, and put to one side to cool. The flakes should be crisp and golden, not brown. Peel, trim and thinly slice the leeks. Wash thoroughly to remove any grit, shake excess water from them, and put in a saucepan with the milk, bay leaf and cloves. Cook until the leeks are just tender, then drain and put to one side. Reserve the milk, and discard the bay leaf and cloves. Peel the potatoes and boil in lightly salted water. Drain, and mash them with a little of the milk in which the leeks were cooked and some more of the butter. Season lightly with salt and pepper, and stir in 1 oz / 30 g of the Parmesan and the cooked leeks. Melt the remaining butter.

To assemble the dish, liberally brush each sheet of pastry with melted butter. Lay the first sheet on top of the second, and then scatter the flaked almonds, ground almonds and 2 oz / 60 g Parmesan over the whole surface. Lay the remaining two buttered sheets on top. Spoon the mashed potato and leek mixture in an even line about 2 in / 5 cm from one long edge of the pastry. Roll up carefully, and transfer to a buttered and floured baking sheet, curving it slightly to fit if necessary. Brush the top with the remaining melted butter, sprinkle with Parmesan, and cook in the top half of a preheated oven at 190°C / 375°F / Mark 5 for about 40 minutes, until golden brown.

Winter Vegetable Gratin

Serves 6–8

1 lb / 455 g celeriac	2 cloves
1 lb / 455 g onions	1 blade of mace or piece of nutmeg
1 lb / 455 g potatoes	1 tsp cornflour
1 lb / 455 g leeks	1 tbsp water
8 oz / 230 g fennel	¾ pt / 430 ml thick Greek yoghurt
8 oz / 230 g jerusalem artichokes	4 oz / 110 g cheese, grated
1 pt / 570 ml vegetable stock	2 oz / 60 g ground hazelnuts
1 bay leaf	2 oz / 60 g chopped mixed nuts
	2 oz / 60 g fresh breadcrumbs

Peel and slice all the vegetables. Bring the stock, bay leaf, and spices to the boil, and cook the vegetables in it for 8–10 minutes, adding more boiling water, if necessary. Meanwhile, mix the cornflour and water and stir it into the yoghurt. Bring to the boil and simmer for 5–8 minutes, thus stabilizing the yoghurt. Remove from the heat. Transfer the vegetables to a lightly oiled or buttered baking dish. Boil the stock to reduce to about ¼ pt / 140 ml, removing the spices and bay leaf first. Stir in the yoghurt, and cook for 2–3 minutes before pouring it over the vegetables. Mix the cheese, nuts and breadcrumbs, and scatter over the top. Bake in a preheated oven at 180°C / 350°F / Mark 4 for 20 minutes or so.

Ratatouille

*Vegetables brought to a plump, sweet ripeness by the hot, late-summer
sun are some of the best partners for olive oil, and the Provençal dish
of* ratatouille *demonstrates this perfectly. Most cooks agree that a
ratatouille should include onions, garlic, aubergine and sweet peppers,
but here the certainty ends. Some leave out tomatoes; others leave out
courgettes. Paul Bocuse leaves out peppers, and inexplicably includes
carrots. I prefer to use all the Mediterranean vegetables.*

*As this is such a time-consuming dish to make, I have given
quantities for 10 servings. It is a good idea to make this amount, even
if you are serving fewer people. Any left over will keep well in the
refrigerator for several days, if covered. It could then be reheated and
served as a side dish with meat or fish, or used in the Vegetable
Crumble recipe on page 159).*

1½ lb / 680 g aubergines
1½ lb / 680 g onions, peeled and
　sliced
6 garlic cloves, peeled and crushed
½ pt / 280 ml olive oil
1 lb / 455 g green and red peppers,
　peeled
1½ lb / 680 g courgettes, sliced

2½ lb / 1.10 kg firm, ripe tomatoes,
　peeled, deseeded and chopped
1 bay leaf
sprig of thyme
3 parsley stalks
salt
freshly ground black pepper
3–4 tbsp extra virgin olive oil

Do not peel the aubergines, but slice them thinly and put them in a colander.
Sprinkle with salt, and let them drain for 30–40 minutes. Meanwhile, cook the
onions and garlic in 2–3 tablespoons oil in a frying pan until the onion is soft and
translucent. Transfer to a large flameproof casserole and set over the lowest
possible heat, using a heat diffusing mat if necessary. Halve the peppers, remove
the seeds, and cut the flesh into thin strips. Add a little more oil to the frying pan,
and gently cook the peppers, stirring from time to time, without letting them
brown, for about 20 minutes. Using a slotted spoon, transfer them to the casserole.
Rinse the aubergine slices, and dry them thoroughly by pressing them between
pieces of kitchen paper. Add rather more oil to the frying pan this time, and heat it
so that the aubergine slices sizzle and seal as soon as they are put in the pan. If the
oil is not hot enough, the aubergine will absorb it like blotting paper, but once the
slices are sealed you can turn down the heat and allow them to cook for 5–10
minutes. Again using a slotted spoon, transfer the aubergine to the casserole.

Cook the courgettes in more olive oil in the frying pan for 5–10 minutes, and transfer to the casserole. Add the tomatoes to the frying pan with the herbs, and cook for 15 minutes or so, until a good thick sauce is produced. Pour it over the vegetables in the casserole. The tomato sauce will seep down through all the layers of vegetables. Set the casserole over a slightly higher heat now, add a little more oil, if necessary, and cook, uncovered, for about 10 minutes. Add salt and pepper to taste, and stir in the extra virgin olive oil before serving. The *ratatouille* is delicious hot, warm or cold, as a starter, as a vegetable accompaniment to grilled fish or meat, or as a separate vegetable course.

Variation ~ A slightly quicker but less authentic method of preparing this dish, is to cook all the vegetables together, adding them one after the other to the same pan. Start by cooking the onions and garlic a little, then add the aubergine slices with a little more oil and cook for a few more minutes, then add the chopped tomatoes and strips of pepper, and finally add the courgettes, the whole cooking eventually to a meld of rich flavours with a soft consistency.

Ratatouille Crumble

Serves 4–6

5 oz / 140 g plain flour
1 heaped tbsp finely chopped
  parsley
1 oz / 30 g ground almonds or
  hazelnuts
2 oz / 60 g butter, diced

2 oz / 60 g Parmesan cheese, freshly
  grated
good pinch of nutmeg
1½ lb / 680 g *ratatouille* (see page 158)
3 oz / 85 g mozzarella cheese

Sift the flour, parsley and nuts together. Add the butter, and rub it in lightly and loosely until the mixture resembles irregular breadcrumbs. Stir in the Parmesan and nutmeg. Oil or grease a baking dish, and spoon in the *ratatouille*. Slice the mozzarella, and lay the pieces on top of the vegetables. Spoon the crumble topping evenly on the cheese, and bake in a preheated oven at 190°C / 375°F / Mark 5 for 20–25 minutes. Serve hot, while the mozzarella is still soft and melting; it becomes rubbery as it cools.

Vegetable Couscous

Serves 6–8

1 onion, peeled and chopped
3–4 garlic cloves, peeled and
    crushed
1 tbsp cumin seeds
½ tbsp ground coriander
1 tsp ground cardamom
1 tsp freshly ground black pepper
4 cloves
2 tbsp olive oil
1 medium aubergine, diced
2–3 courgettes, sliced

12 oz / 340 g ripe tomatoes, skinned and
    chopped
2 small turnips, peeled and diced
1 green or red pepper, deseeded and
    sliced
2 carrots, peeled and sliced
½ pt / 280 ml water or stock
8 oz / 230 g couscous
12 oz / 340 g cooked chick peas
2 tbsp chopped coriander
salt, to taste

Fry the onion, garlic and spices in the olive oil in a large saucepan for 2–3 minutes, and then add the remaining vegetables together with the water or stock. Bring to the boil, and simmer until the vegetables are tender but not mushy. Meanwhile, steam the couscous (see page 214).

Just before serving, stir the chick peas and coriander into the vegetable stew, bring back to the boil, and season to taste. Heap the steamed couscous on to a warmed serving platter, spoon the hot stew over it, and serve immediately with harissa or hot sauce handed separately for each person to take as they wish. If you cannot obtain harissa, you can make an equivalent hot sauce yourself.

Hot sauce
2 tbsp tomato or vegetable purée
1 tbsp olive oil
2 tbsp lemon juice

½ tsp ground coriander
¼ tsp cayenne pepper or chilli powder
2 garlic cloves, peeled and crushed

Mix all the ingredients together thoroughly, and let this stand for 20 minutes or so to let the flavours develop before using. A much more authentic and powerful hot sauce can be made by pounding fresh, hot red chillies to a paste, and mixing it with the other ingredients.

VEGETABLE TERRINES

Asparagus Terrine

This is good eaten hot or cold, but is best of all just warm. Serve it alone or with a homemade tomato or watercress sauce. A hollandaise sauce would be delicious, but very rich, as would a garlicky mayonnaise.

Pancakes
2 oz / 60 g plain flour
1 egg
¼ pt / 140 ml milk
oil for frying

Filling
12–18 stems of asparagus (depending on thickness), trimmed to fit the loaf tin lengthways

4 oz / 110 g tomatoes, peeled, deseeded and diced
2 eggs
¼ pt / 140 ml milk *or* 3 tbsp thick yoghurt and 2 tbsp water
1 tbsp finely chopped parsley
salt
freshly ground black pepper

Beat all the pancake ingredients, except the oil, together to make a smooth batter, and use it to make four large thin pancakes. Use three of them to line a well-oiled 1 lb / 455 g loaf tin, keeping one to cover the filling.

Wash the asparagus and boil rapidly in salted water for 3 minutes. Drain and refresh under cold running water. Scatter half the tomato dice over the bottom of the lined loaf tin and then put in the asparagus stems lengthways. Spread the rest of the tomato dice on top. Beat the eggs with the milk or the yoghurt and water, stir in the parsley, and season lightly. Pour this mixture over the vegetables.

Fold the overhanging pancakes over the filling, and cut the last pancake to fit neatly on top. Cover with oiled foil, and bake in a bain-marie in a preheated oven at 170°C / 325°F / Mark 3 for 50–60 minutes, testing with a knife point to see if it is cooked through. When it is done, the knife point will come out clean. Let the loaf cool slightly in the tin, then turn out, and leave to rest for an hour before slicing and serving.

Variation ❧ Replace the asparagus filling with a mushroom filling. Use wild mushrooms if available. Slice 1 lb / 455 g mushrooms, and fry with a little chopped onion or leek in olive oil until slightly softened. Use this mixture instead of the cooked asparagus stems when filling the terrine. This is very good with a fresh tomato sauce or a warm vinaigrette.

Aubergine and Red Pepper Terrine

Serves 6–8

A fresh tomato sauce or a spicy tomato and onion salad is very good with this, as is a bowl of warm couscous salad, flavoured with chopped fresh coriander and mint leaves, spring onions, tomatoes and olives (see page 214).

6 Swiss chard or large spinach
  leaves, stems removed
3–4 large aubergines, trimmed
juice of 1 lemon
salt

freshly ground black pepper
extra virgin olive oil
3–4 large red peppers
2 oz / 60 g parsley, finely chopped

Blanch the spinach or chard leaves in boiling salted water for 3–4 minutes. Drain, rinse in cold water, and pat the leaves dry. Slice the aubergines lengthways, about ¼ in / 0.5 cm thick. Brush each slice all over with lemon juice to prevent it discolouring, season lightly with salt and pepper, and brush all over with olive oil. Place the slices on an oiled baking sheet, and bake at the top of a preheated oven at 200°C / 400°F / Mark 6 for 15–20 minutes or until the aubergine is soft. Meanwhile, quarter the peppers, remove the stem, pith and seeds, and place, skin-side up, on an oiled baking sheet. Bake for 10–15 minutes in the top of the oven, moving the aubergines to a lower shelf. The skin on the peppers will blister and can easily be stripped off. To assemble the terrine, brush a 2 lb / 900 g loaf tin with olive oil, and place a long strip of foil down it lengthways to help turn out the terrine. Line the tin with the spinach or chard leaves, keeping one back to cover the terrine. Line the sides and bottom with slices of aubergine, and sprinkle on some parsley. Build up layers of red pepper and aubergine, scattering parsley between them and seasoning lightly, and finish with a layer of aubergine. Top with the remaining spinach or chard leaf, cover with foil or cling film, and weight it down with cans. Refrigerate overnight to let the flavours blend. Turn it out, slice, and bring back to room temperature before serving.

Black Mushroom Roulade

Caroline Yates, one of the senior staff at Leith's School of Food and Wine, produced this when I joined the principals and teachers there for lunch one day. She used very mature mushrooms, almost black, which resulted in a stunning combination of dark roulade filled with a white cream. It would make an excellent cold starter or main course, and can be prepared several hours in advance.

2 oz / 60 g unsalted butter	salt
1 oz / 30 g plain flour	freshly ground black pepper
2–3 shallots, peeled and finely chopped	4 eggs, separated
	3 oz / 85 g cream cheese
2 lb / 900 g mushrooms, roughly chopped or sliced	¼ pt / 140 ml double cream
	3 oz / 85 g pinenuts, toasted

Line a shallow rectangular Swiss roll tin with buttered baking parchment, and flour it lightly. Make a roux with half the butter and the flour, and put it to one side. In a very large frying pan, sweat the shallots in the remaining butter, and then add the mushrooms. Cook them thoroughly on a fairly high heat to extract as much of their moisture as possible. Cool slightly and put in a food processor with the roux, a little seasoning and the egg yolks. Process until smooth. Whisk the egg whites until stiff, and gently fold them into the mushroom mixture. Turn this into the prepared baking tin, smooth over, and bake in the top half of a preheated oven at 180°C / 350°F / Mark 4 for 12–15 minutes. When cooked, the sponge will feel springy to the touch and will shrink slightly from the sides of the tin. Lay a sheet of greaseproof paper on a worktop, and turn the sponge out on to it. Carefully peel off the baking parchment, and replace with a fresh sheet of greaseproof paper. Loosely roll the sponge between the two sheets of greaseproof paper while still warm. This will keep it pliable and will stop it sticking together.

Soften the cream cheese, and whip the double cream. Fold together, and at the same time fold in the toasted pinenuts. Unroll the sponge when cool, spread the cream on it, and reroll. Cover and refrigerate until required. Slice and serve.

Tomato Puddings

Serves 10

This is one of my favourite recipes for high summer, when tomatoes are most likely to be at their sweetest. I first read a description of it in Jennifer Paterson's food column in The Spectator. *It has evolved since then. Unlike summer pudding, the filling should not be cooked.*

3 lb / 1.35 kg ripe tomatoes
sea salt
freshly ground black pepper
extra virgin olive oil

sherry vinegar
12–15 slices firm white bread, crusts
   removed
herbs, to garnish

Peel the tomatoes, and cut them in half. Scoop out the seeds, juice and pulp and put in a food processor with the skins. Process the pulp and skin mixture, then rub it through a sieve to extract maximum juice and flavour. Pour half the resulting liquid on to the chopped tomato flesh. Taste the mixture, and then add just enough salt and pepper to season and a generous splash of olive oil. Mix the remaining tomato liquid with a little sherry vinegar. Add salt and pepper to taste. Cut the bread into wedges, dip it into the juice, and use it to line 10 small moulds as if making individual summer puddings. Spoon in the chopped tomato flesh, and cover with a round of bread. Cover the puddings, weight them down, and refrigerate for 6–8 hours or overnight. To serve, turn out each pudding on to a chilled plate, garnish with herbs, and serve with more juice. A large tomato pudding can be made in the same way.

THE TIMES COOK IN SRI LANKA

FOR TWO weeks, in 1991, I was invited by the British Council to take part in a British Food Festival at the Colombo Hilton in Sri Lanka. I can think of few better ways of building bridges between people than in the exchange which goes on in a busy kitchen. My introduction to Sri Lankan food started with a breakfast of string hoppers and white potato curry, washed down with fresh mango juice and tea from Nuwara Eliya.

Lunchtimes would find me in the pastry kitchen baking batches of scones for afternoon tea. Then it was time to go to the main kitchen to prepare Toad-in-the-Hole, Cottage Pie and Southend whitebait.

In enlightened self-interest, when asked to devise a cookery competition, I suggested 'a taste of Sri Lanka for a visiting English cook'. The six finalists proved a rich source of inspiration for my cooking. They explained and demonstrated the myriad uses of the coconut – the flesh, the milk and the sugar – in sweet and savoury cooking. Jaggery or palm sugar is a rich, soft dark brown sugar derived from the nectar of the coconut palm and the kitul palm. It has a wonderfully fruity, sappy caramel flavour, for which dark muscovado sugar, available here, is a substitute in terms of texture, but without the flavour. Jaggery is sometimes used in a thick liquid form, like treacle, and is served with curds or yoghurt, as one of Sri Lanka's favourite desserts.

I learned about the fragrant underlying flavour of many of the savoury dishes obtained from frying three leaves in oil – curry leaves, *rampe* (pandanus or screw-pine) and lemon grass. All three came back in my shopping bag, as did a roll of banana leaves for wrapping and steaming food, and some vacuum packs of Maldive fish. This is made from tuna fish, dried in the sun and pounded to a powder. It is the Sri Lankan version of anchovy paste and indispensable for adding a subtle, savoury and yet unfishy flavour. It is an important ingredient in the pickles, *mallungs* and *sambols*, the spicy relishes and accompaniments served with the traditional Sri Lankan meal of curry and rice. I have adapted the mint *sambol* to serve with roast lamb (see page 169). Once when I cooked a best end, I used some of the spices I had brought back from the markets in Kandy and Nuwara Eliya, and, like the tea, far fresher than we can ever buy here. Cooking lamb with cinnamon and cloves was a revelation. I can't recommend it highly enough: the sweet spices combine with the sweet, tender meat to perfection.

One of the biggest surprises for me were the vegetables. Expecting all manner of exotic pods, leaves and roots, of which there were indeed plenty, I also met more familiar leeks, broccoli, cabbage, carrots and beetroot. These are often 'tempered', not by the same method as used for Japanese tempura, but from the seventeenth-century, Portuguese kitchen when vegetables were *temporado*. I find myself cooking spicy vegetarian food often, using the techniques, spices, leaves and flavourings I brought back.

It is the sort of food that is as easy to cook for a crowd as for a couple. The ingredients are not expensive, especially if you have a prolific vegetable garden or allotment, or if you have access to a good street market. The food does not take very long to cook, and preparation is not complicated. Six or eight vegetable dishes, a platter of boiled or baked rice, some pickles and chutneys, a bowl of yoghurt, plus some good flat bread (nans, parathas and, at a pinch, pitta bread, and a stack of freshly made pappadoms), and you have an unusual meal that carnivores will enjoy as much as vegetarians.

While authenticity is an important factor, I was pleasantly surprised to see how much adapting of ingredients goes on in the Sri Lankan home. Recognizing that the coconut is a source of saturated fat, alternative oils are used. In the north, *gingelly* or sesame oil is common. This is not the toasted oil used in oriental cooking but a cold pressed and only lightly flavoured oil which is available in Britain. Other suitable cooking oils are sunflower oil, groundnut (peanut) oil, grapeseed oil and safflower oil. They are neutral in flavour and high in poly- or monounsaturates. Since they are not important for flavouring, use as little as possible for the cooking and lubricating process. Coconut milk adds a characteristic flavour to curries. Soya milk or vegetable stock will reduce the saturated fat but also the flavour.

Spices are best bought in small quantities and freshly ground for use in curries. I find a pestle and mortar invaluable. Look for green cardamoms, as these have more fragrance than the white or black pods. Turmeric can sometimes be bought fresh, like green ginger, and also as a dry root. I use it so little that I tend to use a small amount of curry powder for the yellow colouring.

Oriental and Asian shops are the places to look for lime leaves, lemon grass, pandanus leaf, curry leaves, galangal and chillies. Galangal, a rhizome resembling ginger, does not keep very long, but dried galangal has quite a pronounced flavour, unlike, for example, dried curry leaves. Lemon grass and pandanus freeze well.

Souring agents are important in curries. Tamarind pulp is available in Asian and oriental shops. A little of this is soaked in hot water, and the liquid used for cooking. Lemon or lime juice, and coconut vinegar are also used in curries. Sherry vinegar is a very useful substitute.

The recipes that follow are adaptable; more or less chilli can be used and different combinations of spices can be tried. I strongly recommend that you make more Tempered Beetroot (see page 167) than you need. While the leftovers are still warm, dress with olive or walnut oil and sherry vinegar. It makes a marvellous salad, which I have served with crisply cooked samphire on a bed of salad leaves. The brown and white curries, together with any leftover dhal and chick peas can be put in a blender with vegetable or chicken stock, then strained and chilled. Serve hot the next day as mulligatawny. But it is even better served chilled.

Tempered Beetroot

Serves 6–8

1 lb / 455 g raw beetroot
1 small onion, peeled and thinly
   sliced
2–3 fresh green chillies, deseeded
   and sliced
1 tbsp groundnut (peanut) or
   sunflower oil

sprig of curry leaves *or* 1 bay leaf,
   crumbled
1 tbsp ground coriander
1 tsp sugar
1 tbsp vinegar
½ pt / 280 ml coconut milk
   (see page 41)
salt

Peel and thinly slice the beetroot, cut it into thin strips or coarsely grate it in a food processor or with a grater. Fry the beetroot, onion and chilli in the oil until the liquid is absorbed and the beetroot glossy. Add the curry leaves or bay leaf, the coriander, the sugar and the vinegar, and cook for a further 5–10 minutes. Pour on the coconut milk, season with salt, and cook until the beetroot is tender.

White Potato Curry

Serves 6–8

2 tbsp groundnut (peanut) or
   sunflower oil
sprig of curry leaves *or* 2 bay leaves,
   crumbled
piece of lemon grass
1 in / 2.5 cm cinnamon stick
2 tsp ground coriander
¼ tsp ground turmeric
½–1 tsp chilli powder

2 fresh green chillies, deseeded and
   shredded
1 onion, peeled and thinly sliced
1 lb / 455 g potatoes, peeled and cut
   into 1 in / 2.5 cm chunks
½ pt / 280 ml coconut milk
   (see page 41)
salt

Heat the oil in a saucepan, add the curry leaves or bay leaves, the lemon grass and spices, and fry for a few minutes. Add the chillies and onion, and fry until the onion is wilted. Stir in the potatoes, and cook for a few minutes more. Add the coconut milk, and cook until the potato is tender. Add salt to taste and serve.

Dhal

Serves 4–6

1 onion, peeled and thinly sliced	2–3 cloves, ground
1 tbsp oil	8 oz / 230 g red lentils
2 tsp cumin seeds, ground	1 pt / 570 ml water
1 tsp coriander seeds, ground	salt

Fry the onion in the oil in a saucepan until wilted, and then add the spices, and fry for a few minutes. Stir in the lentils, and when they are coated with oil and spices, add most of the water. Bring to the boil, cover and simmer until the lentils are almost tender. Add salt at this stage and the rest of the water. If you prefer a soupy dhal, add a further ¼ pt / 140 ml water.

Aubergine and Okra Brown Curry

Serves 4–6

1 lb / 455 g aubergine, diced	2 tsp cumin seeds, ground
1 medium onion, peeled and thinly sliced	1 in / 2.5 cm cinnamon stick
1–2 tbsp oil	1 tsp anchovy paste or pounded dried fish (Maldive fish) (*optional*)
8 oz / 230 g okra	1 tbsp tamarind water or lime juice
1–2 fresh green chillies, deseeded and chopped	½ pt / 280 ml coconut milk (see page 41)
2 tsp brown mustard seeds	salt

Gently fry the aubergine and onion in the oil in a saucepan, and while these are cooking, trim the okra. Add the chillies, the rest of the spices and, if using it, the anchovy paste or dried fish to the pan, and cook for 5 minutes. Take care with the mustard seeds, as they pop and spit. Put in the okra and tamarind water or lime juice, mix well, and pour on half the coconut milk. Bring to the boil, and simmer until the vegetables are tender. Add more coconut milk as necessary, and season to taste.

Tempered Spinach and Chick Peas

Serves 4–6

2 lb / 900 g spinach, picked over
  and rinsed
2 tbsp oil
1 small onion, peeled and chopped
2–3 garlic cloves, peeled and
  crushed
1 chilli, deseeded and chopped

1 tsp grated fresh root ginger
1 tbsp lemon juice
1 tsp cumin seeds, ground
½ tsp coriander seeds, ground
3–4 tbsp coconut milk (see page 41)
1 lb / 455 g cooked chick peas

Squeeze the spinach dry between pieces of kitchen paper. Heat the oil in a large frying pan or wok, and fry the onion, garlic, chilli and ginger for a few minutes. Stir in the lemon juice and the spices, and fry for a further 5 minutes over a gentle heat, and then stir in the spinach. Stir-fry for 5 minutes or so until the spinach has collapsed, then add the coconut milk and the chick peas. Mix thoroughly, cover, and simmer together for a few minutes.

Variation ∾ You can replace the spinach with bolted garden greens.

Mint Sambol

Serves 4–6

1 oz / 30 g mint leaves
4 black peppercorns
½ tsp coarse sea salt
½ tsp sugar
1–2 fresh green chillies, deseeded
  and chopped

3–4 garlic cloves, peeled and chopped
2 tbsp toasted desiccated coconut
lime juice, to taste

Put the mint leaves, peppercorns, salt and sugar in a mortar, and pound to a paste. Add the chillies and garlic, and pound until well mixed. Scrape into a bowl, mix in the coconut and stir in lime juice to taste.

Variation ∾ Omit the peppercorns, replace the garlic with one finely chopped shallot, add a tablespoon of ground almonds, and instead of just the mint, use a mixture of chopped fresh leaves, chosen from chives, coriander leaves, parsley, mint, watercress and rocket.

Coconut Crisps

Makes 18–24

2 egg whites
3 oz / 85 g caster sugar
3 oz / 85 g desiccated coconut

1 oz / 30 g spray-dried coconut milk or
    skimmed cow's milk powder

Beat the egg whites until frothy but still loose, and then add the sugar and desiccated coconut. Sift in the powdered milk, and mix thoroughly. Drop spoonfuls on to a baking sheet lined with baking parchment, and flatten with a palette knife. Bake in the middle of a preheated oven at 180°C / 350°F / Mark 4 for 12–15 minutes, then turn off the heat and let the biscuits finish cooking in the bottom of the oven for a further 10–15 minutes. Remove and cool on a wire rack. The biscuits will become crisp as they cool.

Pasta and Noodles

Mixing flour with water or egg into a dough, and fashioning it into ribbon-like lengths, or one of a myriad other shapes, which are then either boiled in water while still fresh or allowed to dry for storage and later cooking, must be one of the oldest culinary techniques, and one which is, it is generally believed, common to many nations. There is every indication that Marco Polo was already familiar with various types of pasta when he went to China. How else would he have recognized the 'good lagana' (lasagne) he described eating there? The Etruscans, the ancient Greeks and the 3,000-year-old Shang Dynasty in China all left records, in one form or another, showing that pasta or noodles were a dietary staple for them. There also exists a long history of pasta-making in the Arab world and in Central Asia. Pasta is a simple recipe that cannot be improved upon, so it is hardly surprising that it is so ubiquitous.

Once upon a time, if you wanted to eat good, authentic Italian pasta, you had to fly off to Milan, Bologna or Palermo. Then gradually it became possible to find quality Italian dry goods such as rice and pasta, as well as the spectacular salamis, hams and cheeses, outside Italy, and so, armed with our oily, floury copies of Ada Boni and later Marcella Hazan, we taught ourselves to make creamy risotto and passably good pasta. Now there are fresh pasta shops churning it out by the metre in every shape and colour.

But it has been decided that this ancient recipe *can* be improved upon. It is mixed with spinach, with beetroot, with dried mushrooms, with herbs, with squid ink and even curry powder. Stuffed pastas have been known to come with such fillings as chicken tikka masala. All this is part of an effort to make us pay more for the 'added value'. Do not be taken in. None of this is better than the *pasta secca*, good, Italian, factory-made pasta made from hard or durum wheat. Do not assume that 'fresh' is best. Often fresh pasta is made from soft, low-protein flour, which when cooked can produce a gluey mass. On the whole, I think it is only worth making your own pasta if you have a special filling you want to try out. Homemade pasta is not at all difficult to make, but it is best undertaken in dry conditions, otherwise the pasta can be rather sticky to work with.

Sauces for pasta come in as great a range as pasta itself. Whilst there are no hard and fast rules about it, certain sauces are best suited to certain pasta shapes. If you were to serve a thick chunky pasta with a thin *pesto* or tomato sauce, the balance would be all wrong: too little sauce and too much pasta. Chunky meat or vegetable sauces are better with the thicker, larger pasta shapes, such as *penne* and *rigatoni*, or with those which nicely enfold a sauce such as the broad *pappardelle* or *festonati* with fluted edges.

In Italy, where wheat is the staple grain, it is natural that the pasta will be made with wheat flour (although much of the wheat now comes from Canada). In the Far East, noodles and sheets of pasta are made with whatever is the staple grain of the area. Thus one finds buckwheat noodles (*soba*) in Japan, as well as wheat flour noodles (*ramen* and *udon*). In China, one finds noodles made from wheat flour, rice flour, and bean starch.

Flour and water is not always made into various types of noodles or pasta. Sometimes it forms the basis for dumplings, such as the Italian *gnocchi* and German *knödeln*. In Alsace and southern Germany, *spaetzle*, a cross between a noodle and a dumpling, are made.

Whatever its name or shape, pasta is lovely, inexpensive, comforting, homely food.

PASTA DOUGHS

Homemade Lemon Pasta

Serves 4, as a main course

Pasta is not difficult to make by hand. This is a good all-purpose
recipe. The lemon oil or zest can be omitted.

10 oz / 280 g strong white flour   4 eggs
4 oz / 110 g fine semolina   2 tsp lemon oil *or* 1 tbsp finely grated
                                        lemon zest

Make the dough either by hand or in a food processor. For the first method,
heap up the dry ingredients on a work surface, and make a well in the centre. Slide
in the eggs and lemon oil or zest, and work in the flour gradually with your
fingertips until thoroughly mixed. Knead for about 10–15 minutes, working on a
floured board, to form a smooth, elastic dough. If using a food processor, simply
put all the ingredients in the bowl and process, in short bursts, for 30 seconds or
so. The texture will be crumbly but soft. Scoop it all together, and form it into a
ball. Cover the dough with cling film and let it rest in a cool place for 15 minutes.

Cut off a piece of dough about the size of an egg, and roll it out as thinly as
possible, about ⅛ in / 0.2 cm thick, on a lightly floured surface. Repeat this with
the rest of the dough. Let the rolled-out dough rest for 20 minutes before cutting
into the desired shape with a sharp knife. If using a pasta machine that rolls and
cuts, put the first rolled piece to one side while you roll out the rest of the pasta.
When you have finished rolling, the first piece of rolled pasta will be dry enough
for you to feed through the cutter. For *tagliatelle*, the rolled-out sheets of pasta
dough should be cut into ribbons about ¼ in / 0.5 cm wide. For *fettucine* or
tagliolini, they should be almost half that width, and for *pappardelle*, about ½ in /
1 cm wide. Hang up the strands of pasta as you make them, or loosely curl them
into nests. When ready, cook in plenty of boiling salted water for 3–5 minutes,
depending on thickness. When pasta is cooked, it should be *al dente*, that is tender
but still slightly firm to the bite. Serve with one of the simple sauces suggested on
pages 177 to 179.

For shaping pasta dough to make *ravioli* and *tortellini*, see the recipes on pages
175 and 198.

Pumpkin Ravioli

Serves 4 as a starter; 2 as a main course

Pasta
7 oz / 200 g strong plain white flour
2 eggs

You can make the dough very easily if you have a food processor. Put the flour into the bowl, add the eggs and process, in short bursts, for 30 seconds. The texture will be crumbly but soft. Scoop it all together, and form it into a ball. Let it rest, covered in cling film, in a cool place for 10–15 minutes. If you make the dough by hand, heap the flour on to a marble slab or your usual surface for making pastry. Make a well in the centre of the flour and slide in the eggs. Work into a dough with your fingertips, and form it into a ball. Let it rest, covered in cling film, in a cool place for 10–15 minutes.

Cut off a piece of dough the size of an egg, and roll it out as thinly as possible, ideally no thicker than ⅛ in / 0.2 cm. I find it easier to work with small pieces of dough, although accomplished pasta makers work with large quantities and still manage to roll it out thinly, using their hands to stretch the dough as they go. When you have a sheet of thin pasta, stamp out circles with a 2–4 in / 5–10 cm pastry cutter. The size is not particularly important; if you cut out large circles, you will probably only want two per serving, four or five if small. Repeat until you have used up all the pasta dough. Place the pasta rounds in a single layer, and not touching, on a board or tray covered with a clean tea-towel, and cover them with a barely damp tea-towel while you prepare the filling.

Filling

8 oz / 230 g cooked, drained pumpkin	1 tbsp *mostarda di frutta*, finely chopped (see note below)
2 oz / 60 g ricotta cheese, sieved	freshly ground black pepper
3 oz / 85 g ground almonds	freshly grated nutmeg

Blend all the ingredients together well.

Sauce
3–4 sage leaves
2 oz / 60 g unsalted butter, melted

Infuse the sage leaves in the butter over a low heat for 5–10 minutes, without burning the butter.

Ravioli

Place 1–2 teaspoons of the filling on to each pasta circle. Dampen the edges, fold over, and seal, to form half-moon shaped ravioli. Bring a large pan of water to the boil, salting it lightly or not, as you prefer. Add the ravioli and cook for 3–4 minutes until just tender. Drain, stir into the warm sauce, and serve with a grating of nutmeg and a sprinkling of Parmesan.

Note: Mostarda di frutta or *Mostarda di Cremona*, as it is sometimes called, is a unique condiment from northern Italy, made by preserving fruits in a mustard syrup. A little apricot jam mixed with mustard proves a useful substitute. Mostarda is available in most Italian food shops and good delicatessens, but it is expensive. Traditionally, it is served with the famous Italian dish of boiled meats, the *bollito misto*.

Variations ∽ Make the filling using 3 oz / 85 g crumbled or grated goat's cheese, 2 oz / 60 g ground hazelnuts, 2 peeled and crushed garlic cloves, a sprinkling of freshly ground black pepper and grated orange zest, and a tablespoon of finely chopped chives. Blend together well.

Instead of shaping the ravioli as above, leave the rolled out sheets of pasta dough whole, spoon out heaps of the filling at regular intervals on to half the sheets of dough. Place a second sheet on top. Press down around the edges and around the heaps of filling, and cut into filled squares or lozenges with a fluted pasta cutter.

SIMPLE PASTA SAUCES

THE SIMPLEST way to make a sauce for freshly cooked pasta is to stir in uncooked ingredients, such as extra virgin olive oil, crushed garlic, chopped olives, tomatoes and anchovies, crumbled or diced cheese and shredded fresh herbs. The heat of the pasta is sufficient to melt the cheese and heat through the other ingredients. Good combinations are extra virgin olive oil with crushed garlic, shredded basil leaves and chopped olives or tomatoes; olive oil, garlic, chopped anchovies and shredded chillies or sun-dried tomatoes; crumbled Gorgonzola and ricotta with diced mozzarella and grated Parmesan (a near classic *quattro formaggi*); shredded rocket leaves with olive oil, toasted pinenuts and shredded *prosciutto*; cream, *petit pois* and shredded *prosciutto* or smoked salmon; and, grandest of all, soured cream, vodka and caviar, with perhaps a little finely chopped tomato.

Broccoli and Anchovy Sauce

Stir-fry small florets of broccoli with finely chopped onion and garlic in extra virgin olive oil over a high heat for a few minutes, then stir in a couple of tablespoons of white wine, cover, and allow the broccoli to cook in the steam. When cooked, stir in chopped anchovies or anchovy paste, to taste, and fold this sauce into freshly cooked pasta. Serve with freshly grated Parmesan sprinkled over. Strips of sun-dried tomatoes that have been kept in oil can be added just before steaming the broccoli. This sauce is particularly good with thick chunky pastas, such as *penne* or *rigatoni*.

Celery and Sun-Dried Tomato Sauce

Gently fry a little finely chopped onion and garlic in extra virgin olive oil for a few minutes, until just beginning to turn golden brown, but without burning the garlic. Stir in a couple of handfuls of finely sliced celery and some strips of sun-dried tomato that have been soaked in hot water for 10–15 minutes. Pour on the soaking water, and simmer until all the liquid has been absorbed and the celery is cooked. Stir in some white wine and a little more olive oil, and cook for a few minutes more. *Fusilli* is a good pasta to serve with this sauce. Instead of Parmesan, crumble some goat's cheese on top.

Hazelnut Sauce

Put some shelled hazelnuts with a little hazelnut oil, some melted butter, a little crushed garlic and salt, freshly ground black pepper and freshly grated nutmeg, to taste, in a blender or food processor, and process until smooth. For a coarser texture, do not leave the motor on continuously, but switch it on in short bursts until the required texture is achieved. The more hazelnuts you add, the stiffer the sauce will be; the more butter and oil you add, the runnier the sauce will be. A similar sauce can be made with walnuts. Heat the sauce in a small saucepan before stirring it into freshly cooked pasta. Try it with *tagliatelle* or a short, chunky pasta, such as *penne* or *rigatoni*.

Herb Butter

Put equal quantities of chopped nuts and diced hard butter into a blender or food processor with a handful of chopped fresh herbs and a little salt and freshly ground pepper. Process until smooth and creamy. Blend this into freshly cooked pasta just before serving. It goes well with fine pastas, such as *linguine* and *tagliolini*, and will keep well in the refrigerator if covered. I think it is best not to use the more pungent, oily herbs, such as thyme, sage and rosemary, but you may feel otherwise. Fennel and almonds go well together, as do basil and pinenuts, coriander and walnuts, and chives and almonds. Experiment to suit your taste.

Herb and Gorgonzola Sauce

Tear up a handful of fresh herbs, and, using a pestle and mortar, pound them to a pale green paste with a couple of chopped spring onions and a little coarse sea salt. Stir this into freshly cooked fine pasta, such as *linguine* or *tagliolini*, and then stir in cubes of Gorgonzola cheese until the cheese melts. Serve immediately. Chervil, basil and lovage are good in this sauce, as are fennel, chives and marjoram.

Lemon Sauce

Infuse some pared lemon zest in butter over a low heat for 5–10 minutes, without the butter burning. Remove the zest, stir in some cream and grated lemon zest and cook gently until you have a well-flavoured cream. Stir in freshly ground white pepper and a little lemon juice to taste, and stir into freshly cooked pasta. Fresh pasta is best for this rich, creamy sauce. Try it with *tagliolini*.

Sausage Sauce

Use the best quality sausages you can find for this sauce. They should have a high meat content. Squeeze the sausage meat out of the sausages, and fry it over a gentle heat until the fat begins to run, then raise the heat, and allow the meat to brown. Remove the meat from the pan, leaving a little of the fat behind, and fry a little onion and garlic in it. Stir in a can of chopped tomatoes, cook until most of the liquid has evaporated, and then stir in the cooked sausage meat, a sprinkling of chopped oregano or marjoram and a glass of red wine. Simmer gently for 20–30 minutes. Season to taste, and stir into freshly cooked spaghetti. Serve with freshly grated Parmesan cheese sprinkled over.

Yellow Tomato Sauce

Sweat a little finely chopped onion, leek, carrot and celery in some extra virgin olive oil over a low heat, without browning, until soft. Add about a dozen roughly chopped yellow tomatoes, cover and cook until the tomatoes have collapsed. Add water from time to time if the mixture shows signs of sticking, but do not add too much or this will dilute the intense flavour. Rub through a sieve into a clean pan, reheat and season to taste. This is very good with freshly cooked *tagliatelle*.

PASTA AND NOODLE DISHES

Pasta with Ham and Asparagus 'Peas'

Serves 4, as a main course

1 lb / 455 g dried spaghetti or a
  short chunky pasta shape, such as
  fusilli, conchiglie or *penne*
4 oz / 110 g fresh asparagus tips
4 oz / 110 g Parma ham trimmings

3–4 oz / 85–110 g crème fraîche, soured
  cream or double cream
freshly grated nutmeg
freshly ground black pepper
salt
1 tbsp finely chopped parsley

Put a large saucepan of lightly salted water on to boil and cook the pasta
according to the directions on the packet. Meanwhile, slice the asparagus tips into
½ in / 1 cm pieces, and shred the ham. When the pasta needs only 3–4 minutes
more cooking time, drop in the asparagus 'peas', finish cooking, and drain. Put the
cream in the still hot pan, and return the pasta and asparagus to the pan. Turn
them thoroughly in the cream, stir in the ham, season to taste with nutmeg, pepper
and salt, and scatter over the parsley. Serve immediately in heated shallow soup
plates or from a large heated tureen or bowl.

Spaghetti Genoese Style

Serves 4, as a main course

1 lb / 455 g small new potatoes,
  scrubbed
1 lb / 455 g dried spaghetti
8 oz / 230 g slim green beans,
  topped and tailed

2 tbsp extra virgin olive oil
3–4 tbsp pesto
freshly grated Parmesan cheese

Bring a large saucepan of lightly salted water to the boil, put in the potatoes
and boil for 7 minutes. Add the spaghetti and boil for 8 minutes, then add the
beans, broken into pieces if you wish, and boil for 4–5 minutes. By this time, each
ingredient should be perfectly cooked. Drain and put in a heated serving bowl
containing the oil. Turn in the oil, and then add the pesto. Serve immediately, with
the Parmesan sprinkled over.

Pasta with Asparagus, Broccoli and Salmon Butter

Serves 4, as a main course

14 oz / 395 g packet dried
 spaghetti
3 oz / 85 g asparagus tips
2 oz / 60 g broccoli florets
1 tbsp olive oil or cream

Salmon butter
3 oz / 85 g cooked salmon

2 oz / 60 g butter
1 shallot, peeled and finely chopped
1 tbsp finely chopped parsley
freshly grated nutmeg
salt
freshly ground black pepper

First make the salmon butter. Put all the ingredients in a food processor and blend until smooth. Pack into a bowl, cover and refrigerate.

Bring a large saucepan of lightly salted water to the boil, and put in all the spaghetti. Bring back to the boil and boil for 2 minutes. Drop in the vegetables, boil for 30 seconds more, then remove from the heat, cover the pan with a tightly fitting lid, and allow to stand for 9 minutes. The spaghetti and vegetables will be perfectly cooked. Set a large sieve over the serving bowl and drain in some of the cooking water to heat it. Drain the spaghetti and vegetables, and return them to the saucepan. Stir in the salmon butter and the olive oil or cream. Empty the water out of the serving bowl, and pour in the spaghetti and vegetables. Serve immediately.

Pasta Val d'Arciere

Serves 4, as a main course

I learned this method of cooking dried pasta from Eva Agnesi, the president of one of Italy's largest pasta manufacturers. It works every time. If you use thick pasta like ziti *or* rigatoni, *it should be boiled for 3 minutes, not 2.*

1 lb / 455 g red-coloured dried
  pasta
1 red onion, peeled and chopped
4 tbsp extra virgin olive oil
2–3 cooked beetroot, peeled and
  diced
freshly ground black pepper
1 tsp finely chopped oregano or
  sage

3–4 tbsp red wine
2 tbsp balsamic vinegar
3–4 oz / 85–110 g Parma ham
  trimmings, (from the knuckle end),
  shredded or chopped
freshly grated Parmesan cheese
chives or flat-leaved parsley, to garnish
  (optional)

Bring a large saucepan of water to the boil, and put in the pasta. Bring it back to the boil and boil for 2 minutes. Remove from the heat, cover with a tight-fitting lid (place a folded tea-towel beneath the lid, if necessary, to ensure a tight fit), and let it cook for the full length of time given on the packet. While the water is first coming to the boil, prepare the sauce in a large pan by gently frying the onion in the olive oil until soft. Add the beetroot, pepper and herbs, and when they are well coated in the oil, add the red wine. Let the mixture cook until the wine has almost evaporated before adding the balsamic vinegar. Lower the heat as far as possible at this stage, and let it cook for the time the pasta cooks. Drain the pasta, and stir it into the sauce together with the Parma ham. Transfer to a large heated bowl or individual bowls. Sprinkle a little Parmesan cheese on top, and brighten it with chives or a leaf or two of parsley, if you wish.

Variations ∽ Instead of red pasta, red onion, beetroot, red wine and oregano or sage, use yellow pasta, white onion, charred and skinned yellow peppers, white wine and a few threads of saffron.

Or, use green pasta, with white onion, courgettes, white wine and watercress.

Fusilli Tricolore

Serves 4, as a main course

If you can't get fusilli, *use another short chunky pasta shape that will hold a sauce well.*

4 tbsp extra virgin olive oil
8 oz / 230 g fine green beans,
  shelled broad beans or shelled
  fresh peas
8 oz / 230 g white button
  mushrooms

8 firm, ripe tomatoes
4 garlic cloves, peeled and crushed
¼ pt / 140 ml vegetable or chicken stock
1 lb / 455 g mixed green, white and
  orange *fusilli*
chopped herbs

First make the vegetable sauce. Heat the olive oil in a heavy-based saucepan or frying pan. Top and tail the beans, and snap them in three or four places, depending on length. Wipe and quarter or slice the mushrooms. Peel and deseed the tomatoes and cut the flesh into strips about ¼ in / 0.5 cm wide. Stir the beans or peas into the hot oil, and cook for 3–4 minutes, add the mushrooms and tomatoes, and cook for 2 more minutes. Stir in the garlic and the stock. Allow to bubble quite fiercely so that the stock and oil emulsify and the sauce thickens. Meanwhile, cook the *fusilli* in plenty of lightly salted boiling water according to the directions on the packet, usually a minute or so for fresh pasta and 8–10 minutes for dried. Drain the *fusilli*, sprinkle on a few drops of oil and stir in the vegetables. Serve in heated shallow soup plates, sprinkled with fresh herbs.

Pappardelle with Hare Sauce

Serves 4, as a main course

Pappardelle *are broad, flat noodles which, when cooked, wind and fold themselves around a chunky meat sauce, as in this dish, based loosely on a traditional Tuscan one. If you cannot get or make* pappardelle, tagliatelle *or* fettucine *can be used instead. This is an ideal recipe for using up forequarters of hare if you have casseroled or roasted the saddle and legs. I have also eaten a similar dish up in the northern hills of Tuscany one wintry day, when wild boar was the meat cooked in this rich, dark sauce.*

2 hare forequarters
1 onion, peeled and chopped
1 celery stalk, trimmed and finely chopped
2–3 garlic cloves, peeled and finely chopped
1 tbsp extra virgin olive oil
¼ pt / 140 ml game, beef or chicken stock

1½ oz / 40 g bitter chocolate
1–2 sprigs marjoram *or* pinch of dried oregano
2 oz / 60 g seedless raisins
2 oz / 60 g pinenuts (optional)
1 tbsp balsamic vinegar
1 lb / 455 g fresh *pappardelle*

Strip the meat from the bones, and dice it. Fry the vegetables and garlic in the olive oil until wilted. Raise the heat, add the meat, and brown it briefly. Add the stock, the chocolate and the herbs. Simmer for about 40 minutes, uncovered, until the meat is tender and the sauce reduced. Stir in the raisins and pinenuts (if using), and cook for a few minutes to let the flavours mingle. Finally, add the balsamic vinegar. Stir the sauce into freshly cooked and drained pasta. It is the balsamic vinegar which leads me to describe the dish as being loosely based on the Tuscan classic. In Tuscany a red wine vinegar would be used; balsamic vinegar comes from over the Apennines in Emilia-Romagna. The deep, fruity complexity is a perfect counterpoint to the chocolate, however.

Spaghetti with Mussels and Watercress

Serves 4, as a main course

2 lb / 900 g fresh mussels
14 oz / 395 g dried spaghetti
2–3 oz/ 60–85 g trimmed, washed
  watercress

3–4 tbsp extra virgin olive oil
freshly ground black pepper

Scrub the mussels, knock off any barnacles, and tug off the 'beards'. Rinse the mussels thoroughly and discard any that fail to close when tapped. Put them in a saucepan, cover tightly and steam over a high heat for 2–3 minutes. Drain the mussels in a colander set over a bowl to collect the cooking juices. Discard any that fail to open. When cool enough to handle, shell the mussels and put them in a bowl of warm water to stop them drying out. Strain the cooking juices into a large saucepan, and add sufficient water to cook the spaghetti. Bring the water to the boil, and add the spaghetti. Bring back to the boil, and boil for 2 minutes. Stir, remove from the heat, and cover the pan with a tight-fitting lid. (See the method on p. 182.) Leave the spaghetti to continue cooking for the full time stated on the packet. Three minutes before the time is up, add the drained mussels and the watercress. Stir once more, replace the lid and leave for the allotted time. This is just sufficient to wilt the watercress to a soft, bright green and heat the mussels through. The pasta will be perfectly cooked. Drain it and transfer immediately to a heated serving dish. Stir in the olive oil, and grind on some black pepper. A little salt may be needed, but the mussels will probably be briny enough without it.

Variation ⮌ In July and August, when samphire is in season, I love to cook the small, cleaned sprigs with the spaghetti instead of watercress. The mussels can be replaced with clams.

Spaghetti alla Norcina

Serves 2, as a main course

*St Valentine was the martyred bishop of Terni. Terni is in Umbria,
not far from Norcia, which is famous for its black truffles. Here the
truffles are said to be at their best approaching carnival time, just
before Lent, which makes them a fitting dish to serve for St
Valentine's Day. I thought of this as I sat in a very ordinary restaurant
not too far from Terni, eating a plate of Spaghetti alla Norcina. It was
the only thing on the menu that tempted me, and such was the
restaurant that I had no great expectations of the dish. It looked like
spaghetti with a dark mushroom sauce, but when I ate a mouthful,
there, amongst the mushroom, was the unmistakable chippiness of
finely chopped truffle. Even a small amount of truffle will flavour and
perfume a staple such as pasta to make it all taste of truffle. In the
hope that someone might buy you a truffle for Valentine's Day, here is
what to do with it.*

2 oz / 60 g button mushrooms,
  wiped and finely chopped
1 shallot, peeled and finely chopped
3 tbsp extra virgin olive oil

1 truffle, scrubbed and chopped
8 oz / 230 g dried spaghetti
salt
freshly ground black pepper

Fry the mushrooms and shallot in half the olive oil until soft. Stir in the truffle,
and cook over a low heat for 8–10 minutes. Meanwhile, cook the spaghetti,
according to the directions on the packet or according to the method on p. 182,
drain it, and toss in the remaining olive oil. Stir the sauce and pasta together,
season lightly, and serve in heated bowls.

Tagliatelle alla Giuditta

Serves 4, as a main course

*This recipe was created by Giuditta Fini, and is served at the
restaurant Fini in Modena, which belongs to the family.*

1 small onion or shallot, peeled and
  finely chopped
1½ oz / 40 g butter
4 oz / 110 g piece of raw ham, such
  as Parma or San Daniele
6 ripe tomatoes, peeled, deseeded
  and finely chopped

freshly ground black pepper
14 oz / 395 g fresh *tagliatelle*
3 oz / 85 g Parmesan cheese, freshly
  grated

Gently fry the onion or shallot in the butter in a saucepan until soft. Cut the
ham into small dice, and cook it with the onion for a few minutes. Add the
tomatoes, and cook gently for about 30 minutes, seasoning to taste with pepper.
About 10 minutes before the end of the cooking time, cook the pasta according to
the directions on the packet or the method on p. 182, drain it, and stir it into the
sauce, adding the Parmesan. Serve immediately.

Vegetable Lasagne

The sauces can be made the day before required. If it is more convenient, the lasagne can be assembled 2–3 hours in advance and refrigerated until you are ready to bake it. It is worth making plenty of tomato sauce, as any surplus can be kept for another day.

Tomato Sauce
3–4 garlic cloves *(optional)*
1 onion
2 carrots
2 celery stalks
1 leek (white part only)
2 oz / 60 g fennel
2–3 tbsp olive oil

2 large (2 lb / 900 g) cans plum
    tomatoes
2 bay leaves
2–3 parsley stalks
sprig of thyme
sprig of sage or rosemary
salt
freshly ground black pepper

Peel and chop the vegetables, and sweat in the olive oil until the onion is just beginning to colour. Add the tomatoes and herbs, and cook, uncovered, for 2–3 hours on a very low heat. Allow to cool slightly before blending in a food processor or blender, or simply rubbing through a sieve. Season to taste.

Béchamel Sauce
2 oz / 60 g butter
2 oz / 60 g plain flour
1½ pt / 850 ml boiling milk

salt
freshly ground white pepper
pinch of freshly grated nutmeg

Put the butter in a heavy saucepan, and melt it over a low heat. Stir in the flour until you have a smooth paste. Do not allow the flour to colour. Pour on a little of the milk, and stir until smooth, then gradually add the rest, stirring continuously to avoid any lumps forming. When smooth, season to taste with salt, pepper and nutmeg, and cook gently for 8–10 minutes, stirring from time to time. Cool, cover and refrigerate until required.

Lasagne

1 lb / 455 g aubergine, trimmed

1½ lb / 680 g baby courgettes, trimmed

12 oz / 340 g baby leeks, trimmed

1 lb / 455 g lasagne

3 tbsp olive oil

8 oz / 230 g mozzarella cheese, diced

8 oz / 230 g ricotta, crumbled

4 oz / 110 g Parmesan or other hard cheese, freshly grated

Cut the aubergine into ¼ in / 0.5 cm slices. Bring a large saucepan of water to the boil, lightly salted or not, as you prefer, and put in the aubergine slices. After 2–3 minutes, put in the courgettes and leeks and boil for a further 2 minutes. Lift out the vegetables with a slotted spoon, put them in a colander, and refresh under cold running water to stop them cooking any further. Put to dry on layers of kitchen paper. Cook the lasagne sheets according to the directions on the packet, a few sheets at a time, if necessary, in the same saucepan of water in which you cooked the vegetables. If using freshly made lasagne that is still soft and supple, cook for 2 minutes only. Lay the cooked lasagne sheets on a clean tea-towel.

Liberally oil a square or rectangular ovenproof dish, and spread some béchamel sauce on the bottom. Cover with a layer of lasagne sheets, then a layer of vegetables, then some mozzarella and ricotta, and some tomato sauce. Spoon on another layer of béchamel, top with another of lasagne, and so on, finishing with sheets of lasagne topped with the remaining béchamel sauce. Sprinkle with the grated Parmesan, and bake in a preheated oven at 180°C / 350°F / Mark 4 for 50–60 minutes. Turn up the heat for the last 10 minutes, if necessary, to brown the top. Serve very hot.

Rich Vegetable and Pasta Pie

Serves 6–8

*In the past I have cooked this as the centrepiece for a vegetarian meal.
It is based on the rich pasta pies of Emilia-Romagna, which date back
to the Renaissance.*

Sweet Shortcrust Pastry	2 oz / 60 g caster sugar
8 oz / 230 g plain flour	4 oz / 110 g unsalted butter, cubed
pinch of salt	4 egg yolks

Mix the dry ingredients together, make a well in the centre and add the butter
and egg yolks. Gradually mix these in with your fingertips and gather the dough
together into a ball, trying not to handle it too much. Cover and chill for 1 hour.

Tomato Sauce	two 14 oz / 395 g cans tomatoes
1 tbsp olive oil	3–4 garlic cloves, peeled and chopped
1 medium onion, peeled and	¼ pt / 140 ml red wine
chopped	½ tsp dried thyme or oregano
1 celery stalk, trimmed and finely	salt
sliced	freshly ground black pepper

Heat the olive oil in a saucepan, and fry the onion and celery until translucent.
Add the tomatoes, with their juice, and garlic, the red wine and herbs. Cook on a
moderate heat until the vegetables are soft. Rub through a sieve and cook down
further if necessary until you have about 1 pt / 570 ml sauce. Season to taste, cool
and refrigerate until required.

Custard Sauce	1 tbsp caster sugar
¾ pt / 430 ml milk	3 egg yolks

Heat the milk and sugar together in a saucepan. Whisk the egg yolks in a bowl
and gradually stir in the hot milk. Strain the custard back into the saucepan, and
stir it continuously over a low heat with a wooden spoon until it thickens enough to
coat the back of the spoon, taking care not to curdle it by overheating. Pour it into
a bowl, and when cooled slightly, cover the surface with cling film to stop a skin
forming. Cool completely, then refrigerate until required.

Filling

1½ lb / 680 g dried pasta
olive oil
4 oz / 110 g mushrooms, sliced
4 oz / 110 g radicchio or chicory,
  shredded
4 oz / 110 g baby leeks, trimmed
  and cut into 1 in / 2.5 cm lengths
1 oz / 30 g butter

4 oz / 110 g blue cheese or goat's cheese
4 oz / 110 g mozzarella cheese
4 oz / 110 g Fontina, Edam, Gouda or
  Jarlsberg cheese
salt
freshly ground black pepper
2 tbsp finely chopped herbs
2 oz / 60 g Parmesan cheese, freshly
  grated

Cook the pasta in plenty of boiling water according to the direction on the packet. Drain it, and toss in a little olive oil to stop it sticking. Put to one side. Fry the vegetables in the butter for a few minutes until just wilted, and put them to one side. Cut the cheeses into small cubes. Use a large mixing bowl to assemble the filling. Put the cooked pasta in the bowl. If you have used long pasta, cut it into 2 in / 5 cm lengths. Stir in the vegetables, cheese and tomato sauce. Add the salt, pepper, herbs and Parmesan.

Pie

Roll out the pastry carefully, and line a deep, oiled cake tin with a removable base, leaving enough pastry to make a lid. Spoon in the filling, and heap it up to form a mound in the centre. Spread the custard sauce over it. Roll out the remaining pastry, and cover the pie, using the trimmings for decoration. Brush with an egg and milk glaze, and bake in the centre of a preheated oven at 190°C / 375°F / Mark 5 for 40 minutes. When cooked, carefully ease out of the tin, and transfer to a warm serving plate.

Hokkien Mee
(Fried Noodles Hokkien-Style)

Serves 4–6

This recipe is based on one given to me by Violet Oon, Singapore's first lady of food, who is not only a first-class Nonya cook, but the editor, publisher and main feature writer of The Food Paper, *a monthly tabloid of what's going on in Singapore's kitchens.*

1 lb / 455 g fresh or dried thin noodles

8 oz / 230 g medium-sized raw prawns, usually sold headless and frozen

5 tbsp groundnut (peanut) oil

8 oz / 230 g belly pork in a piece

1 medium onion

6 garlic cloves

8 oz / 230 g bean sprouts

2 oz / 60 g garlic chives

2 thin leeks

2 tsp salted soya beans, rinsed and drained, or Japanese miso paste

½ tsp salt

½ tsp sugar

2 tsp light soy sauce

2 tsp dark soy sauce

freshly ground black pepper

Cook the noodles according to the directions on the packet. Refresh under cold running water, and leave in a colander set in a bowl of cold water until ready to use. Wash the prawns, peel them (reserving the shells) and remove the intestinal veins. Dry the prawns and put to one side. Pound the prawn shells, and fry them in 2 tbsp oil in a large heated wok or deep frying pan until bright red. Pour on ½ pt / 280 ml water, bring to the boil, and strain for stock. Discard the shells. Put the piece of pork in the wok, cover with water, bring to the boil, and simmer for 30 minutes. Drain off the stock and reserve. When the pork is cool enough to handle, shred it finely, and put to one side. Peel, chop and pound the onion and garlic to a paste in a mortar. Blanch the bean sprouts in boiling water for 2–3 minutes, drain and put to one side. Wash the chives and leeks, and slice them thinly.

To assemble the dish, place the wok or frying pan over a high heat. Fry the onion and garlic paste in the remaining oil until fragrant and golden brown. Stir in the soya beans or miso paste, and fry until the oil separates out again. Add the pork, and stir-fry until browned. Add the prawns and stir-fry until they become pink and opaque. Add the leeks and garlic chives with the two stocks from the pork and the prawns. Bring to the boil, and simmer for 1–2 minutes. At this point, add the salt, sugar, soy sauces and a grinding or two of black pepper. Drain the noodles thoroughly, and add them and the bean sprouts to the pan. Stir-fry until bubbling nicely. Serve immediately.

Schinkernfleckerl
(Pasta with Ham)

*One of the most popular dishes served in the evenings in Viennese
restaurants is* schinkernfleckerl, *a soothing dish of pasta with chopped
ham. In Vienna, it is made with small squares of pasta, but you could
make it with macaroni. In fact, it bears a close resemblance to
macaroni cheese.*

1 oz / 30 g butter	4 oz / 110 g cooked ham
½ oz / 15 g plain flour	2 tbsp chopped tomatoes
½ pt / 280 ml warm milk	14 oz / 400 g dried macaroni
3 oz / 85 g grated cheese	

Melt the butter in a saucepan, sprinkle in the flour and cook gently for a few
minutes, stirring constantly. Gradually add the milk, stirring continuously until you
have a smooth white sauce. Cook for 10 minutes, then stir in the cheese, ham and
tomatoes until the cheese has melted. Meanwhile, cook the macaroni according to
the directions on the packet. Drain and mix with the sauce. Spoon into an ovenproof dish or individual dishes. Bake in the top of a preheated oven at 220°C / 425°F /
Mark 7, or put under the grill until the top is golden brown. Serve very hot.

GNOCCHI

Potato Gnocchi

Serves 4, as a main course

1 lb / 455 g cooked mashed potato
about 8 oz / 230 g plain flour

Put a large saucepan of salted water on to boil. Mix the potato and flour until you have a kneadable dough. More or less flour may be required, depending on the amount of moisture in the potatoes. Knead the dough lightly for a few minutes, and allow it to rest, covered, for 30 minutes. Divide the dough into four, and roll out each piece, using your hands. Cut into cherry-sized pieces. Roll the pieces down the back of the prongs of a fork, and make a small indentation in the centre of each with your thumb. Drop a few gnocchi at a time into the pan of simmering water, and remove with a slotted spoon as soon as they rise to the surface.

These gnocchi are good tossed in melted butter or a fresh tomato sauce. You will need about 3½ oz / 100 g melted butter or ¼ pt / 140 ml tomato sauce for the quantity of gnocchi in this recipe. Hand round freshly grated Parmesan to sprinkle over the gnocchi.

THE TIMES COOK IN ITALY

ALTHOUGH I have travelled widely in Italy and love Liguria, Rome and Sicily, Emilia Romagna, and particularly Modena, is my favourite.

Modena, a Renaissance city, is one of the gastronomic and culinary treasure houses of Italy. In a wonderful symbiosis, the lush plains feed the cattle which produce milk for Parmesan cheese (Parmigiano Reggiano, to give it its correct title). The whey left over from cheese-making is fed to the pigs, and they in turn provide the raw material for the excellent hams and sausages for which the region is renowned – cured ham from Parma, Colorno and Langhirano, and the famous *zampone*, a boned pig's trotter stuffed with a salami-like mixture, which is poached gently and served hot as part of the traditional *bollito misto*, a mixture of boiled (or rather poached) chicken, tongue, sausage, pork, ham and beef. *Bollito misto* is served in restaurants from special trolleys wheeled to your table – not a dish, alas, for the home cook.

Modena is famous for another speciality, balsamic vinegar. Made from the must of local grapes, it is cooked slowly and acetified before undergoing a lengthy ageing process, not unlike a sherry *solera*, in which vinegar is drawn from the oldest barrel for bottling and that barrel is topped up from the preceding year's barrel, and so on until six or seven barrels have been tapped and topped up. I have tasted vinegar perhaps 80 years old in the Casa del Balsamico owned by Giorgio Cattani, who also let me smell some vinegar made by his great-grandfather, which he estimated was 130 years old. One or two terracotta jars went back to the seventeenth century. Aged in fruit woods such as mulberry and cherry, and hard woods like ash and oak, the type of wood, the barrel size and the length of ageing all help to give a particular characteristic to this rich, fragrant, complex, sweet-sour brew.

When buying balsamic vinegar, beware of the difference in quality. *Aceto balsamico tradizionale di Modena* is expensive. *Aceto balsamico di Modena* is a different thing altogether. Commercially made, often coloured with caramel, without the same lengthy ageing and without the complexity and richness of the traditional product, it is, nevertheless, an interesting ingredient for salads, casseroles and fish dishes.

There are more gastronomic treasures to be found in Modena's restaurants. The famous *pasticcio di tortellini* is still served in Fini, the city's much respected restaurant. A sweet, shortcrust pastry is filled with meat *tortellini* in a cream sauce, a pastry lid is put on top, and the whole baked until golden brown. This is a rich dish of the kind that would have been served in the ducal households of bygone days. Cucino del Museo is a tiny restaurant tucked down by the side of the Palazzo da Musei. There, Paola Corradi cooks both a traditional menu and a 'creative' menu, salads of nasturtium flowers in the summer, pumpkin soup and pumpkin ravioli in the autumn. Just outside Modena, the Lancellotti family, who own a small hotel and restaurant, grow their own vegetables and herbs. Their food is simple, fresh and good.

We once went to visit our friends the Lancellottis as the weather turned cold, when the persimmons, pomegranates and quinces were ripening in their garden. The *zucca* were growing in such profusion that Angelo was giving them away, as well as making them into marvellous soup, filling for *tortellini* or ravioli and simply baking pieces of this rich golden squash in the oven to serve as a vegetable.

In the kitchen, Mama, her daughter-in-law Zdena and Angelo, her son, gave me cookery lessons. Zdena taught me how to make cakes, *tortas*, truffles and *amaretti*. Angelo taught me a marvellous recipe for stuffed liver, and how to make the filling for *tortellini in brodo* (see page 198). He emphasized that the meats should be lightly browned first and the fat drained off, which makes for a lighter filling and a more developed flavour. And, even more important, he said that the meat should be chopped by hand, rather than using a mincer or processor. The filling should have enough texture to be able to taste the three separate flavours. The importance of texture was highlighted again when Zdena prepared the almonds for the *amaretti*, again chopping by hand rather than using the grinder.

Mama Lancellotti showed me how to make pasta dough and then shape *tortellini* and make *maccheroni ai pettine*, squares of pasta shaped around a towel and rolled over a comb-like utensil. She used the flour of the region, not semolina, heaped it on to a board, and to *un etto* (about 3½ oz / 100 g) of flour, added one egg. She was not impressed when I said I made pasta dough in a food processor and rolled it out in a hand-cranked machine. In her kitchen it is mixed by hand on a large, smooth board, kneaded at length by hand and rolled out, all in one piece to a fine elastic sheet, about the thickness of a 20-pence piece. It takes time, but as I discovered when I did it in my own kitchen, it is relaxing and takes on its own rhythm.

Fillet of Beef in Balsamic Vinegar

Serves 6

six 5 oz / 140 g fillet steaks
4 tbsp balsamic vinegar
2 tbsp finely chopped herbs
freshly ground black pepper

2 tbsp olive oil
2 tbsp water
salt

Brush the steaks all over with a little of the balsamic vinegar. Sprinkle with herbs and a little black pepper and press well in. Heat the oil in a frying pan, and when it is hot, fry the steaks on both sides, until done to your liking. Remove the steaks, and keep warm while you finish the sauce. Put the rest of the balsamic vinegar and water in the frying pan, and bring to the boil, scraping up any caramelized residue stuck to the pan. Salt to taste, and serve spooned over the steaks.

Variations ➷ For extra interest, fry some very finely sliced onion or shallot in the pan before frying the steaks. More gravy can be made by adding stock or wine to the frying pan, and it can be turned into a thicker sauce by reducing it and then whisking in about 1 oz / 30 g butter, cut into cubes.

Radicchio and Parmesan salad

Serves 6

This will do duty as a starter, as a salad to follow a main course or as part of a cheese course; it also makes an excellent accompaniment to beef.

2–3 heads of radicchio, depending
  on size
4 oz / 110 g Parmesan cheese

3–4 tbsp extra virgin olive oil
sea salt
freshly ground black pepper

Remove any wilted or damaged leaves from the radicchio, and then take off all the leaves and wash and dry them, first in a salad spinner and then on kitchen paper. Arrange the leaves on plates. With a sharp knife or special cutter, shave the cheese into the finest slices possible, and lay them on top of the leaves. Trickle olive oil over the cheese, and then sprinkle with salt and pepper. Serve immediately.

Tortellini in Brodo

Filling (il ripieno)
4 oz / 110 g Parma ham, with about
    ¼ in / 0.5 cm fat around it
4 oz / 110 g pork
3½ oz / 100 g mortadella
1 tbsp grapeseed oil

1 egg
½ tsp salt
½ nutmeg, freshly grated
5 oz / 140 g Parmesan cheese, freshly
    grated
2 oz / 60 g fine fresh breadcrumbs

Cut the meat into 1 in / 2.5 cm dice, and brown lightly in the grapeseed oil, cooking it for 8–10 minutes. Drain the meat, and put it on a chopping board. Chop the meat finely, then mix in the egg, salt, nutmeg, Parmesan and finally the breadcrumbs. Mix by hand, and knead and work it for 5 minutes until the mixture is too soft.

Put the filling in a bowl, cover and keep until required. Use the same day.

Pasta
a generous 10 oz / 280 g plain flour
3 eggs

Pile the flour on to a work surface, make a well in the centre, and slide in the eggs. Working with your fingertips, gradually draw the flour from the edge to the centre, and blend with the egg by hand until a dough is formed. Sprinkle with more flour if the mixture is sticky, which it may well be if you are working in a humid atmosphere. Knead for 5–10 minutes until the dough is smooth and elastic. Cover and let it rest for 15 minutes at room temperature.

Roll out the pasta on a floured working surface to a thickness of approximately ⅛ in / 0.2 cm, stretching and rolling the dough over the rolling pin. (A long narrow pin, or *matarella*, is used in Italy.) It is easier to roll out smaller pieces of dough unless you are very practised at it. With a fluted cutting wheel, cut out squares of dough. Place a small, pea-sized ball of filling in the centre of each square of dough. Fold one corner over to the opposite and pinch the two edges of the triangle together very hard to seal them. Bend the central point of the triangle up and draw the other two points together around your finger. Pinch together to seal. Put the completed *tortellini* on a damp cloth until you have made them all.

Broth (il brodo)

This is a simple and excellent recipe for broth, which can also be used for other soup recipes. The chicken and beef can be used in a simple *bollito misto*.

1 chicken	chervil
2 lb / 900 g beef on the bone, such as a rib	2–3 in / 5–7.5 cm piece of celery
10 pt / 5.70 l water	1 small onion, peeled and halved
a little salt (unless you intend to use some of the broth for a reduced meat sauce)	1 garlic clove

Put all the ingredients in a large saucepan, bring just to the boil, skim off the foam, and simmer for 2–2½ hours, skimming fairly frequently. Remove the meat, and strain the broth into a clean saucepan. Bring to the boil, put in the freshly made *tortellini* and simmer for 2–3 minutes. Ladle the soup into a heated tureen. The pasta will continue cooking in the hot broth and will be just right by the time you serve it.

Torta di Riso
(Rice Cake)

1¾ pt / 990 ml milk
6 oz / 170 g arborio rice
pinch of salt
5 oz / 140 g sugar
2 oz / 60 g blanched almonds
3–4 bitter almonds *(optional)*
2 eggs, separated
grated zest of 1 lemon

2 oz / 60 g candied citron and orange
  peel, diced
1 oz / 30 g pinenuts
1 tsp vanilla essence
fine dry breadcrumbs
4 tbsp maraschino *(optional)*
icing sugar *(optional)*

Boil the milk in a heavy saucepan, add the rice, salt and half the sugar, and simmer gently for 20–30 minutes, stirring occasionally, until the rice is tender and the milk absorbed. Let it cool. Toast the almonds under the grill, and chop them finely. Beat together the egg yolks and the rest of the sugar, then add the rice, lemon zest, candied peel, pinenuts, almonds and vanilla essence. Beat the egg whites until stiff and fold in.

Butter a 10 in / 25.5 cm springform tin and coat the inside with breadcrumbs. Pour in the rice mixture and bake in a preheated oven at 170°C / 325°F / Mark 3 for about 1 hour, until brown on top. Let the cake cool, then prick it all over and pour on the maraschino, if using. Leave for 24 hours, then turn out, and, if you wish, dust all over with icing sugar before serving.

Grains and Pulses

When I started thinking about rice, grains and pulses, I checked my store-cupboard, which my husband, Tom, calls 'hoarder's corner', and was surprised at the range I found. Not counting the flours for baking, I found polenta and yellow cornmeal, the same thing but with different names in Italy and America; basmati rice, to serve plain with curries or as a scented, golden *pillau*; arborio rice for risottos; Calasparra rice from Valencia to make paellas; round grain rice for puddings; brown rice; wild rice; and even a bag of black glutinous rice, brought back from Singapore. There was also pot barley and the more refined pearl barley, which I use in casseroles and cook like rice in a version of risotto (see page 204). There was oatmeal for baking and for breakfast porridge, sharing shelf-space with grits, hulled and milled from corn; the grits, too, are for breakfast when I feel like making southern American food.

There was also a jar of couscous, made from semolina grains that have been dampened, rolled into small balls or 'grains', and coated with a finer wheat flour. It is, of course, properly speaking, a pasta, but as it is treated as a grain, I deal with it in this, rather than the previous chapter. Because it is processed, it simply needs moistening or steaming before serving. This makes the cereal swell and become tender. I serve it with meat and vegetable *tagines*, fragrant, spicy stews in the Moroccan style. Bulgar wheat, sometimes called *pourgouri*, cracked wheat or burghul, is also a partially processed grain that is further cooked by moistening with boiling water or steaming. It can be served in the same way as couscous, or as in Cypriot restaurants, with grilled lamb kebabs and salad. Both grains also make excellent salads. When they have swollen to their full size, I mix in olive oil, chopped mint and coriander or parsley, perhaps stoned, chopped black olives, diced, seeded tomato and spring onions or shallots. Add seasoning and a little lemon or lime juice (see page 214). Millet, too, and quinoa, can be prepared in this way, although they are equally good accompaniments for meat or fish dishes in place of rice or potatoes. Millet is much nicer than its bird seed connotations might lead you to believe. Quinoa is a similarly tiny, round grain, about the size of a sesame seed, and, like millet when cooked, yields about four times its original volume of a fluffy, delicately flavoured grain. The more unusual grains are to be found in healthfood shops.

Whole grains and seeds, too, such as raw buckwheat groats and wheat berries, can be cooked and eaten in place of other starches. Because, like brown rice, the hard outer coating has not been removed, they take longer to cook and have more nutritional value.

I have to record a notable lack of success with toasted buckwheat, however. It is an acquired taste, and I do not like it. Because it has already been partially processed, it cooks to a mush very readily, and has something of the thick, coating texture of refried beans, one of the few pulse dishes which I also do not like.

Any of these grains can be added to bread recipes for variety. Hard, unprocessed grains will need soaking or precooking before doing so, and I would not add more than a handful or so for each loaf. Grains and seeds can also be sprouted very easily, and these make an excellent and nutritious addition to winter salads and sandwiches.

The family of dried beans and peas, known as pulses, provides some of the most versatile ingredients to be found on the shelves of small specialist shops, healthfood stores and supermarkets. When cooked alone, they have an agreeable, but often rather bland, flavour, which makes them ideal companions to stronger flavours. The Mediterranean flavours of thyme, tomatoes and garlic combine with beans in Italian soups, French cassoulets and Spanish casseroles. Fiery chilli peppers liven up bean dishes in Mexico and Texas. Olive oil, lemon, sesame and coriander provide a subtle foil for chick peas and beans in Greek, Turkish and Middle Eastern dishes.

Once the mystique attached to bean cookery is dealt with, all these rich and flavoursome dishes can be brought into your repertoire. In fact, there is no mystique. In order for dried beans to become edible, their moisture content must be restored. This is done by allowing them to absorb as much water as possible. Cooking instructions and recipes in the past invariably called for overnight soaking. This was when beans were sold loose, and you did not know how long they had been stored. Nowadays, if you buy beans regularly from a stockist with a frequent turnover, you can be fairly certain of getting fresh (that is this year's) beans. Six hours soaking will usually be adequate, except for chick peas and soya beans which may need longer, and lentils which need little or no soaking. On the other hand, if it is more convenient to do so, overnight soaking will shorten the cooking time. Soaking in warm water is a quicker way of getting beans to the cooking stage. Another way is to pour plenty of boiling water over the beans and to soak for 2 hours, by which time the water will be cold. Even more effective is to bring them slowly to the boil, then allow to cool in the water. There are also those who advocate long, slow cooking of beans and those who favour the pressure cooker. There is no right or wrong way. It depends on the dish, the bean and your own preferred method. Some cooks recommend adding salt at the beginning; others say that doing this toughens the skins. I prefer to season towards the end of cooking so that the intrinsic flavours of the dish are allowed to develop first.

Beans and peas make excellent purées, soups and vegetable accompaniments, as well as colourful salads, for example by combining pale green flageolets, red kidney beans and cream cannellini beans.

RICE

Risotto

*This is one of my favourite rice dishes. Nutritious, economical,
versatile and easy to prepare, the soft, creamy texture of this northern
Italian classic makes it the perfect comfort food. Basically, it consists of
Italian short grain rice gently simmered and stirred until it absorbs its
flavoursome cooking liquid. Different meats, fish and vegetables can be
added to vary the dish as you wish.*

*To achieve the correct consistency, always use a good risotto rice,
such as arborio. You will need a large, heavy saucepan, preferably
with a rounded bottom to prevent the rice sticking at the corners, and
a wooden spoon for stirring. The heat should be kept constant and
moderate. If risotto cooks too quickly, the rice will be too soft and
'chalky', and if it cooks too slowly, it will have a sticky, glutinous
texture. Keep the stock simmering, so that it is always hot when you
add it, to avoid any temperature variations while cooking.*

Basic Method

Heat butter or olive oil in the pan, and coat the rice well in it before adding any
liquid. Then gradually add the simmering stock, about ¼ pt / 140 ml at a time,
always allowing one batch of stock to be absorbed before adding the next. Stir
constantly. Keep adding stock in this way until the rice is cooked. This should take
about 20–25 minutes. You may find that the risotto is cooked to your taste before
adding all the stock asked for in a recipe. The more liquid you add, the creamier
the risotto will be, but the rice should remain just firm to the bite or *al dente*. If
necessary, remove the pan from the heat, cover and allow to stand for a few
minutes to absorb any liquid remaining in the pan. Season to taste, and serve
immediately. Various flavourings, vegetables, meat and fish can be added during
the cooking process, as in the following recipes.

Broccoli, Broad Bean and Mint Risotto

Serves 4

1 medium onion, peeled and finely
   chopped
1 tbsp extra virgin olive oil
10 oz / 280 g arborio rice
4 oz / 110 g small broccoli florets
2½ pt / 1.45 l simmering vegetable
   stock
4 oz / 110 g shelled broad beans

1 tbsp finely chopped parsley
8 mint leaves, finely shredded
salt
freshly ground black pepper
1 oz / 30 g unsalted butter
2 oz / 60 g Parmesan cheese, freshly
   grated

Fry the onion in the olive oil in a large, heavy pan until soft and golden. Stir in
the rice and broccoli, until well coated in the oil, then gradually add the simmering
stock, as in the Basic Method on page 204. Continue until you have used up about
half the stock. Then, with the next batch of stock, add the broad beans and
parsley. Continue adding more stock and cooking it to absorption until the rice is
almost tender. Stir in the mint and seasoning, and cook in more stock until the rice
is cooked to your taste. Stir in the butter and Parmesan cheese, and serve
immediately.

Variations ∾ Leave out the broccoli, beans and mint, and instead use finely
diced courgettes and chervil, tarragon or chives. White wine can be added towards
the end instead of some of the stock.

Pumpkin Risotto

Serves 4–6

12 oz / 340 g piece of pumpkin,
  deseeded and skinned
2 tbsp extra virgin olive oil
1–2 shallots or 1 small onion, peeled
  and chopped
12 oz / 340 g arborio rice

2 pt / 1.15 l simmering vegetable or
  chicken stock
1 oz / 30 g unsalted butter
2 oz / 60 g Parmesan cheese, freshly
  grated

Coarsely grate the pumpkin. Heat the oil in a large, heavy pan, and cook the shallots or onion until translucent. Stir in the pumpkin and the rice. When the rice and pumpkin are well coated in oil, gradually add the simmering stock, as in the Basic Method on page 204 until the rice is done to your liking. I prefer a very creamy risotto and tend to add more liquid than some might like. Stir in the butter and Parmesan just before serving in heated soup plates.

Variation ∾ Instead of the pumpkin, use a mixture of grated carrot and very finely chopped celery. I once ate a risotto like this in Florence, and it was exquisite.

Mushroom and Red Wine Risotto

*This is such a robust, powerful and unusual dish that, on the whole, I
think it stands best on its own with perhaps a salad, cheese and fruit
to follow for a simple lunch or supper. As to the wine that you use, I
would suggest a cabernet sauvignon or a chianti, but I have the feeling
that it is a dish which would lend itself to experiment. For
mushrooms, use wild or cultivated, one single variety or a mixture.
Shiitake, oyster and cup mushrooms are a fine combination.*

3 oz / 85 g unsalted butter
1 onion or 3 shallots, peeled and
   thinly sliced
12 oz / 340 g mushrooms, cleaned
   and sliced
12 oz / 340 g arborio rice
½ pt / 280 ml red wine

2 pt / 1.15 l simmering vegetable or
   chicken stock
salt
freshly ground black pepper
2 oz / 60 g Parmesan cheese, freshly
   grated
parsley or chervil, to garnish *(optional)*

Melt half the butter in a large, heavy pan, and fry the onion or shallots until
translucent. Add the mushrooms, and make sure they are well coated with butter
before stirring in the rice. Bring the wine to the boil, and pour half of it over the
rice. Cook, stirring, until it has been absorbed, then add the rest. Once all the wine
has been absorbed, gradually add the simmering stock, as in the Basic Method on
page 204. You may not need to use all the stock. The rice may be cooked to your
taste after you have put in about 1¾ pt / 990 ml. Season and stir in the rest of the
butter and the Parmesan cheese, and serve immediately in heated soup plates.
Garnish with parsley or chervil if you wish.

Variation ∾ Omit the mushrooms, and stir in a bay leaf and a few sprigs of
rosemary with the rice. Use ¾ pt / 430 ml wine and only about 1¾ pt / 990 ml
stock. Sprinkle each serving with a little balsamic vinegar.

Treviso Risotto with Smoked Salmon, Grappa and White Truffle Oil

Serves 4

This is based on a dish served at the Atlanta Ritz-Carlton, one of Chef Gunther Seeger's creations.

6 oz / 170 g bacon, derinded and
    cut into matchsticks
1 heaped tbsp finely chopped
    shallots
1 head of radicchio, shredded
2 tbsp extra virgin olive oil

12 oz / 340 g arborio rice
2 pt / 1.15 l simmering chicken or
    vegetable stock
1–2 tbsp grappa
4 thin slices smoked salmon
dash of white truffle oil

Sweat the bacon, shallots and radicchio in the olive oil, using a large heavy pan, until the shallots are translucent and the radicchio wilted. Stir in the rice until well coated in oil, then gradually add the simmering stock, as in the Basic Method on page 204, until the rice is done to your taste. Stir in the grappa. Spoon the risotto into shallow heated soup plates, lay the smoked salmon on top and drizzle white truffle oil over the salmon. Serve immediately.

Smoked Oyster Risotto

Serves 4

1 medium onion, peeled and finely
    chopped
2 tbsp extra virgin olive oil
10 oz / 280 g arborio rice
good pinch of saffron threads,
    soaked in a little hot water
2 pt / 1.15 l simmering vegetable,
    fish or light chicken stock

3 oz / 85 g cooked peas *(optional)*
3 oz / 85 g peeled prawns *(optional)*
small can red pimentos, drained
1 can smoked oysters, drained
salt
freshly ground black pepper

In a large, heavy pan, cook the onion in the olive oil until soft. Stir in the rice, and when it is well coated with oil, add the saffron and soaking water and about ¼ pt / 140 ml simmering stock. Stir until the rice has absorbed the liquid, then continue adding the simmering stock, as in the Basic Method on page 204, until the rice is cooked to your liking. Stir in the peas and prawns, if using. Cut the pimentos into strips, and stir these in with the smoked oysters. Season to taste, and serve immediately.

Squid Risotto

Serves 4

With the ink sacs from 6–8 squid and their chopped tentacles and wings (see page 320 on how to prepare squid), you can make a marvellous black, Venetian-style risotto.

1 medium onion, peeled and finely chopped
1 tbsp extra virgin olive oil
tentacles and wings from 6 medium-sized squid, about 6 in / 15 cm long
10 oz / 280 g arborio rice
½ pt / 280 ml white wine
2 pt / 1.15 l simmering fish stock or water

ink sacs from 6 squid
salt
freshly ground black pepper
2 oz / 60 g unsalted butter
2 ripe tomatoes, peeled, deseeded and chopped
1 tbsp finely chopped parsley

Fry the onion in the olive oil in a large, heavy pan until translucent. Chop the squid tentacles and wings, and add these to the pan. They will turn opaque and begin to curl up. Pour in the rice, and stir it until well covered with oil. Bring the wine to the boil, and pour half on the rice. Allow to cook over a fairly high heat, stirring continuously, until the rice has absorbed the wine. Pour on the remaining wine, and cook until it, too, has been absorbed. Start gradually adding the simmering stock or water, as in the Basic Method on page 204. Once half the stock or water has been added, crush the ink sacs with 2–3 tablespoons of stock or water, and stir into the rice. In fact, it will colour the rice grey rather than black. Continue adding the stock or water as before, until the rice is done to your liking. Season to taste, stir in the butter, and serve in heated shallow soup plates, with a little chopped tomato and parsley on top.

Chicken and Asparagus Risotto

Serves 4–6

6 oz / 170 g skinless, boneless
chicken breast
3 oz / 85 g unsalted butter
1 medium onion, peeled and sliced
12 oz / 340 g arborio rice
2 pt / 1.15 l simmering chicken or
vegetable stock

8 oz / 230 g trimmed asparagus (tender
green parts only), cut into ½ in / 1 cm
lengths
3 tbsp dry white wine
2 oz / 60 g Parmesan cheese, freshly
grated

Dry the chicken on kitchen paper, and slice it into short, thin slivers. Melt half
the butter in a large, heavy pan, and fry the onion until translucent. Add the
chicken pieces, and fry these until coloured all over. Pour the rice into the pan, and
turn this in the melted butter until coated all over. Add ¼ pt / 140 ml simmering
stock, and stir continuously until the stock is absorbed. Add the asparagus, and
continue adding the simmering stock, as in the Basic Method on page 204, until the
rice is almost cooked and the risotto is beginning to be creamy. Add the wine, and
cook, stirring constantly, until the rice is cooked to your liking. Stir in the rest of
the butter and the Parmesan, and serve immediately.

Variation ∾ Omit the chicken, and use 1 lb / 455 g asparagus and vegetable
stock for a delicious vegetarian risotto.

Paella Valenciana

Here is an authentic recipe for paella valenciana, *as cooked for me by Tinuca Lasala at the Alambique cooking school in Madrid. Unlike the 'Spanish Flag' version of so many* paellas *seen outside Spain and in the Spanish coastal resorts, it is quite a plain-looking dish. There are no* strips of sweet pimento and olives (that is strictly for tourists), and there is no *mixing of meat and fish in the same dish. In this dish, Tinuca used chicken and rabbit, a very good combination. It should be cooked in a large, shallow pan, which has an absolutely flat base and is in even contact with the heat.*

¼ pt / 140 ml olive oil
salt
2 lb / 900 g chicken breasts and
  thighs, each cut into 2–3 chunks
1 lb / 455 g rabbit joints (hind legs
  or back), cut into neat serving
  pieces
8 oz / 230 g green beans, blanched
  and drained

4 oz / 110 g ripe tomatoes, peeled and
  chopped
2 garlic cloves, peeled and finely
  chopped
½ tsp mild paprika
2 pt / 1.15 l water
1 lb / 455 g cooked flageolet beans
good pinch of powdered saffron
1 lb / 455 g calasparra or arborio rice

Heat the oil in a large, flat-based, shallow pan. Put in a pinch of salt and the pieces of chicken and rabbit. Cook over a steady heat until the meat is a rich golden brown, then add the green beans, tomatoes and garlic. Cook for a few minutes more, then stir in the paprika, the water, the flageolet beans and saffron. Bring to the boil and allow to simmer for about 40 minutes, until the meat is almost tender. Add the rice in the traditional way, in the shape of a cross on the surface. Stir it in and cook over a high heat for 10 minutes, then over a low heat for a further 10–15 minutes, until the rice is tender. Remove from the heat, cover loosely and let it stand in a warm place for 10 minutes before serving.

Variations ❧ Rabbit alone can be used. Asparagus can be added, as can rinsed snails. I much prefer these to the shellfish and chicken paellas where the shellfish, particularly the squid, is invariably overcooked.

Kedgeree

Serves 6

*Originally a breakfast dish of rice and lentils from the days of the Raj,
this also makes an ideal lunch or supper dish. I particularly like to
serve it for a late leisurely breakfast.*

1 tbsp extra virgin olive oil or
  clarified butter
1 medium onion, peeled and thinly
  sliced
crushed seeds from 6 cardamom
  pods or ¼ tsp ground cardamom
3 cloves

12 oz / 340 g basmati rice
1½ pt / 850 ml water or fish stock
12 oz / 340 g cooked or raw fish
3–4 eggs
chives, curry powder, melted butter or
  cream, to finish

Heat the oil or butter in a heavy saucepan or flameproof casserole and fry the
onion until wilted and lightly browned. Add the cardamom, cloves and rice, and
stir until the rice is coated and shiny with oil. Add the water or stock, bring to the
boil, turn the heat right down, cover the rice with a very tightly fitting lid, or in its
absence, two thicknesses of foil, and let the rice cook for about 20 minutes by
which time it will have absorbed all the water. If using cooked fish, remove the
bones, and lay it on top of the rice, cover again and let it heat through in the steam.
If using raw fish, slice it very thinly, stir it into the rice and let it cook through for
about 5 minutes. Meanwhile, boil the eggs for 4½–5 minutes. Run cold water over
them until cool enough to handle, then shell and roughly chop them. Add them to
the rice and fish mixture. Add whatever garnish you prefer, and serve immediately.
If using curry powder, this should be stirred into the rice 5–10 minutes before the
end of the cooking time.

Basmati Rice
(cooked by the absorption method)

Serves 4

This is the best method for cooking rice to accompany curries.

1 small onion, peeled and finely chopped	2 tbsp ground cumin
2 tbsp ghee or clarified butter	4 cloves and the seeds of 3 cardamom pods
1 tsp salt	10 oz / 280 g basmati rice
	1 pt / 570 ml water

Fry the onion in the ghee or butter in a heavy saucepan, and when golden brown, add the salt and spices. Continue frying for a few minutes, without burning. Stir in the rice until well coated with the ghee or butter. Pour in the water, bring to the boil, cover with a tight-fitting lid, and cook over the lowest heat possible for 30 minutes, or in a preheated oven at 180°C / 350°F / Mark 4 for about 25 minutes.

OTHER GRAINS

Bulgar Wheat

Serves 4

Cracked wheat, burghul and pourgouri are other names for this very good cereal. It is often served as an accompaniment to grilled or casseroled lamb in Cypriot restaurants.

1 tbsp olive oil	6 fl oz / 170 ml water or stock
1 small onion, peeled and thinly sliced	pinch of salt
6 oz / 170 g bulgar wheat	herbs, such as flat-leaved parsley, coriander or mint

Heat the oil in a heavy saucepan, and gently fry the onion for about 10 minutes until it is soft and brown but not burnt. Stir in the bulgar wheat until it is well coated with oil. Pour on the water or stock, add the salt, bring to the boil, cover and turn the heat right down. Cook for about 20 minutes or until the wheat is tender and has absorbed all the liquid. Serve sprinkled with herbs.

Couscous

Most of the couscous on sale in our shops is precooked and does not require further cooking. To serve hot, say as an accompaniment to spicy fish, meat or vegetable stews, simply place in a colander or sieve over a pan of boiling water, and allow to heat up and moisten in the steam for 20–30 minutes. About 8 oz / 230 g couscous will be sufficient for four or six people. It also makes an excellent salad (see below).

Couscous Salad

Serves 4–6

8 oz / 230 g couscous
¼ pt / 140 ml water
6 spring onions, trimmed and finely
    sliced
3 firm, ripe tomatoes, peeled,
    deseeded and diced
12 black olives, pitted and halved
1 tbsp shredded mint leaves

1 tbsp finely chopped coriander or
    parsley
2–3 garlic cloves, peeled and crushed
3 tbsp extra virgin olive oil
2 tsp lemon or lime juice
salt
freshly ground black pepper

Put the couscous in a bowl, and sprinkle most of the water over it. As it begins to swell and dry, break up the lumps with your fingers. Add a little more water if necessary. Stir the spring onions, tomatoes, olives, herbs, garlic, olive oil and lemon or lime juice into the couscous. Season to taste and serve.

Variation ∾ A salad of bulgar wheat can be made in the same way.

Creamy Cep Polenta

*Bradley Ogden is one of the best chefs in the San Francisco area. I love
his food. This is based on one of his recipes.*

¾ pt / 430 ml water
¾ pt / 430 ml chicken or vegetable
   stock
sprig of rosemary
8 oz / 230 g yellow polenta flour
   (cornmeal)
4 oz / 110 g unsalted butter
8 oz / 230 g fresh ceps, cleaned,
   trimmed and cut into ¼ in / 0.5
   cm slices

2 garlic cloves, peeled and finely
   chopped
1 tbsp sea salt
1 tbsp freshly ground white pepper
3 tbsp finely chopped herbs, such as
   parsley, sage and marjoram
¼ pt / 140 ml soured cream

Preheat the oven to 180°C / 350°F / Mark 4. Bring the water and stock to a
rolling boil in a large flameproof casserole. Add the rosemary and polenta flour,
and cook for 5–10 minutes, stirring continuously with a wooden spoon to ensure
there are no lumps. Cover and cook in the oven for 45 minutes, stirring from time
to time. Remove from the oven, and add half the butter. Stand the casserole in a
roasting tin full of hot water to keep warm. Melt the remaining butter in a frying
pan, add the mushrooms, and fry them for 2 minutes. Add the garlic, and season
with the salt and pepper. Cook for another 2–3 minutes until the mushrooms are
soft. Add the mushrooms to the polenta with the herbs and the soured cream.
Serve immediately.

Variation ⁓ See also Grilled Polenta Slices with Mushrooms on page 66.

Tamales

This is a good dish to serve at a party. It was inspired by a visit I made to the Carullo supermarket headquarters in Bogota. After I had had a tasting of all manner of exotic fruits, I was taken round the staff canteen. The cooks were preparing tamales *for the evening shift, and I'd have loved to stay to eat with them. If possible, try to get one or two helpers. Ideally, the* tamales *should be wrapped in banana leaves or corn husks, but foil or greaseproof paper will do.*

1 lb / 455 g yellow polenta flour (cornmeal)
4 tbsp plain flour
1 tsp salt
2 tbsp olive oil
2 tbsp wine vinegar
½ tsp cumin seeds
chicken or beef stock, to mix
1 lb / 455 g raw boneless chicken
1 lb / 455 g pork spare-rib chops
1 lb / 455 g lean pork

8 oz / 230 g belly of pork, derinded
8 oz / 230 g chipolata sausages
1½ lb / 680 g onions, peeled and chopped
1 lb / 455 g tomatoes, peeled, deseeded and chopped
12 olives, pitted and chopped
2 oz / 60 g capers, drained
3 oz / 85 g seedless raisins
12 oz / 340 g cooked haricot, cannellini or other white beans

Sift the polenta, flour and salt together into a bowl. Mix in the olive oil, vinegar, cumin seeds and enough stock to make a smooth paste that is firm enough to handle. Dice the chicken and all the pork and sausages. Cook in a heavy saucepan with a little of the onion and tomato for about 30 minutes. In a separate pan, cook the remaining onion and tomato until soft, in a little oil if necessary.

Cut greaseproof paper into eight or ten 8 in / 20.5 cm squares. Spoon 3–4 tablespoons of the polenta paste into the centre of each, and flatten it to about ½ in / 1 cm thick. On top, pile a little meat, some of the tomato and onion mixture and some olives, capers, raisins and beans. Top with some more polenta paste, and smooth the top and bottom together to seal the filling inside. Carefully wrap the greaseproof paper around the tamale so that it is watertight. Wrap each parcel in the same way, tying if necessary. Steam for 2 hours.

The tamales can be served with a hot sauce, if you like, made by mixing finely chopped spring onion or leek, tomato, fresh chillies and fresh coriander leaves with lime juice or vinegar. Eat in the fingers when cooled a little, or with knife and fork.

Quinoa and Lentil Strudel

Serves 4–6

Quinoa is a tiny, round, lens-shaped seed, originally from the Andes, but now cultivated in the United States and China. Highly nutritious and with a delicious flavour, it is an excellent addition to the repertoire of grain cookery.

2 oz / 60 g fresh breadcrumbs
2 oz / 60 g almonds, finely chopped
2 oz / 60 g butter
4 tbsp extra virgin olive oil
2 leeks (white parts only), trimmed and sliced
2–3 garlic cloves, peeled and crushed
4 oz / 110 g shiitake mushrooms, sliced
3 ripe tomatoes, peeled, deseeded and chopped

12 ripe black olives, pitted and chopped
2 tsp green peppercorns
finely chopped parsley
finely chopped basil, chervil or coriander
6 large sheets filo pastry
6 oz / 170 g quinoa, cooked and cooled
6 oz / 170 g green or Puy lentils, cooked and cooled
1 mozzarella cheese, diced
3 oz / 85 g pinenuts, toasted

Fry the breadcrumbs and almonds in half the butter and a spoonful of olive oil. Put to one side. In half the remaining olive oil, sweat the leeks until soft, and stir in the garlic and mushrooms. When the mushrooms are almost cooked, stir in the tomatoes, olives, peppercorns and herbs. Melt the remaining butter, and mix with the remaining olive oil. Brush the sheets of filo pastry with it, and layer them on top of each other, scattering a little almond and breadcrumb mixture between each layer. Leaving a 1 in / 2.5 cm border, spread the quinoa over the pastry, then the vegetable mixture, the lentils and finally the diced mozzarella and toasted pinenuts. Roll up and carefully transfer to a baking sheet. Alternatively, spoon the filling into a rectangular heap in the middle of the pastry, and fold it like a parcel. Brush all over with melted butter, and bake in a preheated oven at 200°C / 400°F / Mark 6 for 10 minutes, then turn down the heat to 180°C / 350°F / Mark 4 for a further 10–15 minutes.

PULSES

Real Baked Beans

Serves 6–8

These are very good with baked potatoes.

1 lb / 455 g dried haricot or
  cannellini beans
8 oz / 230 g salt pork
1 large onion, peeled and sliced
2 bay leaves
2 oz / 60 g muscovado or molasses
  sugar

2 tsp mustard powder
½ tsp ground ginger
1 tsp freshly ground black pepper
1 pt / 570 ml hot water

Soak the beans in plenty of water in a large saucepan for 6–8 hours, or overnight if it's more convenient. Bring the beans and water to the boil, and boil rapidly for 10 minutes. Drain and rinse under cold running water. Cut the salt pork into 1 in / 2.5 cm chunks, and place half on the bottom of a deep, greased casserole. Lay half the onion slices on top, cover with the beans and put the rest of the pork on top. Bury the bay leaves in the middle of the beans. Stir the rest of the ingredients into the hot water, and pour the mixture over the beans. If necessary, add more hot water to reach the top of the beans. Cover and cook for 5–6 hours in a preheated oven at 150–170°C / 300–325°F / Mark 2–3. Once the beans are tender, add further salt if you think it necessary, bearing in mind that the pork was salted. Allow to cook into the mixture for 10 minutes. Serve from the casserole.

Linsenspeck
(Lentils with Bacon)

*This is often served as a quick one-dish lunch in Vienna, sometimes
with potato, sometimes with sliced fried dumplings.*

12 oz / 340 g green or brown lentils	8 oz / 230 g piece smoked streaky bacon
1 onion, peeled and thinly sliced	1½ pt / 850 ml bacon stock or water
1 tbsp oil	1 bay leaf

Rinse and pick over the lentils, pour boiling water over them to cover, and soak
for 30 minutes. Fry the onion in the oil in a large flameproof casserole until golden
brown. Put in the piece of bacon, and fry it all over until nicely browned. Add the
lentils, and any remaining soaking liquid. Cover with stock or water, add the bay
leaf, and bring to the boil. Lower the heat, and simmer gently until the lentils are
cooked.

Variation ❧ See also Bacon and Lentil Soup on page 32.

Cassoulet

Cassoulet's ingredients and its authenticity are debated in minute detail. Are partridge and mutton admissible in a cassoulet? Yes, for the Toulouse version, according to Ann Willan and, long before her, to Samuel Chamberlain, the loving chronicler of French regional cooking in his Bouquet de France, *a book based on a gastronomic tour of France, undertaken just after the war. Should goose or duck be used? Are tomatoes permitted? In truth, the cassoulet is properly a rustic dish of the Languedoc rather than the subject of academic discussion. When made in the hill villages of the Bas Languedoc, it will probably have lamb in it as an extra because sheep graze the hillsides; lowland villages will probably have pork in their cassoulets, both as sausages and as chunks of meat. Confit of duck or goose will add a touch of luxury. But none of these will be as important as the beans. As with most essentially peasant dishes, the meat is a seasoning for the staple. In times of plenty, the cassoulet would be full of meat; on lean days, it might not be much more than beans and a little sausage. Indeed, one of the names of the dish is* las moutsetos de coucanho, *the beans of Cocagne. A version of the dish which was common long before haricot beans were introduced from America, was goose and lentils, in which the small bluey-green* lentilles du Puy *were cooked in goose fat and stock with leeks, onion, carrot and garlic, before pieces of goose confit were added, which is why I have included the recipe here rather than in the meat or poultry chapters.*

2 lb / 900 g dried haricot beans or cannellini beans, soaked overnight and drained
3–4 pt / 1.70–2.30 l water
8 oz / 230 g pork rind, cut into squares
8 oz / 230 g knuckle of bacon or piece of streaky bacon
1 lb / 455 g breast of lamb, in a piece

1 onion
2 cloves
1 carrot
1 bouquet garni
6 joints of confit of duck or goose (see Note below)
3 lb / 1.35 kg lamb shoulder chops or pork spare-rib chops or a mixture of the two

1½–2 lb / 680–900 g Toulouse
   sausage or other meaty pork
   sausage
14 oz / 395 g can chopped plum
   tomatoes *(optional)*
garlic, peeled and crushed, to taste

½ bottle good dry white wine
3–4 oz / 85–110 g soft white
   breadcrumbs
salt
freshly ground black pepper

Put the beans in a large saucepan with the water, pork rind, bacon and breast of lamb. Peel and halve the onion, and push a clove into each half. Peel or scrub the carrot, and add the vegetables to the pan with the bouquet garni. Bring to the boil, skim any scum from the surface, cover and simmer gently for about 2 hours. Drain, reserving the cooking liquid.

Heat the confit gently in a frying pan to loosen it, and divide each joint in two. Pour the melted fat into a pot, and keep for another use. In the fat remaining in the pan, brown the meat and the sausage. Cut the sausage into 3 in / 7.5 cm pieces and the chops in half. The meat should still be in good-sized chunks.

For the next stage of cooking, discard the carrot, onion, pork rind, bacon and breast of lamb. Lightly grease a large earthenware dish with goose or duck fat. With a slotted spoon, transfer half the beans to the dish. Arrange the pieces of meat, poultry and sausage on top, add the tomatoes, if using, and the garlic, and cover with the remaining beans. Pour on the wine and enough of the liquid in which the beans cooked, almost to cover the beans. Sprinkle half the breadcrumbs on top, and bake in a preheated oven at 170°C / 325°F / Mark 3 for 1½–2 hours. Remove from the oven. Taste the liquid and season if necessary. Scatter on the remaining breadcrumbs, and bake for a further hour or so. Extra time will not harm it. The finished dish should be quite liquid with the meat very tender, and the beans remaining whole, with a crisp golden crust of breadcrumbs on top. The cassoulet is served from the dish in which it was cooked.

Note: If you do not have confit, I suggest partially roasting a duck, and using the drumstick and thigh quarters.

Dhal Tart with Cumin Pastry

Pastry
6 oz / 170 g plain flour
1 tsp ground cumin
pinch of salt
3 oz / 85 g butter, lard or vegetable
   shortening
1 egg yolk, lightly beaten
iced water

Filling
12 oz / 340 g thick, cooked spicy dhal
   (see page 168)
1–2 tbsp chopped coriander, basil or
   mint
3 eggs, lightly beaten

To make the pastry, sift the flour, cumin and salt together, and then rub in the fat lightly until the mixture resembles breadcrumbs. Stir in the egg yolk and enough iced water to bind to a dough. Cover and allow to rest in a cool place for 30 minutes or so before rolling out and using to line a 10 in / 25.5 cm flan ring set on a baking sheet. Prick the base of the tart, cover with foil or greaseproof paper, add a layer of dried beans, and bake blind in a preheated oven at 180°C / 350°F / Mark 4 for 15 minutes. Remove from the oven, take out the paper and beans, and leave to cool.

To make the filling, mix all the ingredients together, having first seasoned the dhal with salt, pepper and any other spices you think it needs. Spoon the filling into the pastry case, and bake in the oven at 180°C / 350°F / Mark 4 for about 20 minutes, until just set.

THE TIMES COOK IN NIGERIA

MY DIARY for one day in July 1966 describes the naming ceremony for baby Oluwoyo, the infant son of my neighbour Janet who taught with me in Ondo, Nigeria. Resonant Yoruba names, Bolanle Olubusola Abieke, were conferred upon the child, as he was presented with symbolic gifts of kola nuts, fish, salt, palm oil, meat and pepper. This was followed by a lunch of *akara*, *ebe*, egusi soup, *moyin-moyin*, Jolloff rice, goat, liver and chicken.

That, I'm afraid, is the sole mention of food in my diary for that year. It was certainly the gastronomic high point of my year in Nigeria. The rest of the time I lived on yam, beans, plantains and groundnuts, with the occasional pepper, chicken and rice when I was in funds. I was glad of the peppers, for it would have taken me a long time to adapt to eating cassava, yams, tannia, taro and all the other starchy roots that are not potatoes. Peppers are not native to West Africa, but were brought from South and Central America by European explorers and traders, particularly the Portuguese, who probably also introduced the cassava from Brazil. The Brazilian link still exists in Lagos, where one of the local dishes is *imoyo elaja*, fish marinated with lime juice, red peppers, garlic and onion, not unlike an *escabeche*. *Frejon* is another such dish, called *rejoada* in Yoruba, and consists of a stew of cowpeas (black-eyed beans), various meats and coconut milk, very like the present-day *feijoada* of Brazil and Portugal. Further to the west, in Benin, *cosido*, based on the Portuguese *cocido*, is considered a local dish now.

I was glad too, of the papaya tree which grew outside the kitchen door. Breakfast was half a papaya and fresh lime, and I used the leftover skins to tenderize beef. It needed it. The cattle used to walk most of the way from the northern provinces. Carcasses were hung in the market, and on the rare occasions that I could afford to eat meat, I quickly learned where to find the fillet, as all the beef was the same price, and the fillet was the portion least affected by the 1,000-mile walk.

Ondo market was noisy. Cattle bellowed in the pens, and high-life music was played at full volume. The market traders, all women, touted their wares in fine voice. I would usually part with a few *kobos* or copper pennies for a small, dusty heap of tomatoes or a larger pile of oranges. It was only years and years afterwards that I realized how lucky I was to live on green, untreated, unsprayed oranges for that year, instead of the uniformly orange oranges that we are used to.

As I write about the market, I can still smell the street food, my favourite of which was *akara*, small, savoury deep-fried cakes of bean paste in which there were buried mean shreds of chilli, very filling and very good. They make good 'small chop', snacks to serve with drinks. Some of the other recipes which follow will do very well on a buffet, particularly the peppery Groundnut Stew (see page 227) and the Jollof Rice with Chicken and Prawns (see page 228), which has long been a party dish in Nigeria. Egusi soup (see page 226) is also popular for entertaining. Hulled melon seeds, from *citrullus colocynthis* of the watermelon family, are an important ingredient. If you cannot get them, shelled unroasted pumpkin seeds are an appropriate substitute. Teabush and partminger are wild herbs with a pungent flavour much used in West African cooking; they are not unlike basil which I have suggested as a substitute.

The first two recipes are based on a paste made from ground, raw cowpeas or black-eyed beans. First the beans should be hulled or skinned. To do this, soak the pulses for 10 minutes in a bowl of cold water, and then rub handfuls of the beans between the palms of your hand several times to make sure that the coats are rubbed off all the beans. Fill the bowl with water again, and scoop out the skins, which will float to the surface. Repeat the draining, rubbing and floating process until all the skins have been removed.

The next process depends on whether the paste is to be deep-fried, as for *akara* (see page 225), or to be steamed, as for *moyin-moyin* (see page 226). For the first, the beans are drained and then ground with as little water as possible to make the paste. For steamed dishes the beans can be soaked for several hours, and then drained and ground. A food processor is invaluable for the grinding, which should result in as smooth a paste as possible. Use about an equal volume of water to beans to make the paste. After grinding, the paste should be whisked to lighten it to an airy texture. Other ingredients are lightly folded in at the last minute so that the paste will not 'fall'.

Palm oil is used extensively in Nigerian cooking. In its refined, concentrated version, it is a white, partially hydrogenated fat, with a texture somewhat like dripping. And, like dripping, it is high in saturated fat. For frying, I would use groundnut (peanut) oil instead, but for flavouring and enriching, for which palm oil is also used, as in *moyin-moyin*, I might use chicken fat, butter, dripping, olive oil or even one of the nut oils. Only palm oil, as you buy straight from the market, bright red, thick, almost solid, like shoe polish, with an agreeable nutty flavour, will impart absolute authenticity. *Moyin-moyin*, to which other flavourings can be added, is usually eaten with a grain dish, particularly bread or *eko*, which is made from cornstarch. A spoonful of pepper stew livens it up no end.

Akara
(Black Bean Fritters)

Makes 12–18

8 oz / 230 g black-eyed bean paste, made as described on page 224

1 egg, separated

1 heaped tbsp finely chopped onion or shallot

1 small red pepper, deseeded and finely chopped *or* ½ tsp dried chilli flakes

½ tsp salt

groundnut (peanut) oil for frying

Put the bean paste in a bowl, and whisk in the egg yolk. Continue whisking, adding warm water until a light, thick batter of dropping consistency is attained. Fold in the onion or shallot, red pepper or chilli flakes and salt. Whisk the egg white, and fold into the mixture.

Heat the oil to 180°C / 350°F, and drop in spoonfuls of the batter. When browned on the underside, turn the fritters over, and fry until uniformly golden brown. Remove from the oil, and drain on crumpled kitchen paper to absorb excess oil. Serve while still very hot.

Moyin-Moyin
(Steamed Bean Paste)

Serves 2–4

8 oz / 230 g black-eyed bean paste,
  made as described on page 224
2 tbsp warm fat or oil, such as
  chicken fat, butter, dripping or a
  nut oil
1 egg
1 small onion, peeled and finely
  chopped

1 scant tsp salt
dried chilli flakes or finely chopped
  fresh chilli, to taste
optional additions: cooked fish, prawns,
  chicken or ham (about 2–3 oz /
  60–85 g flaked, chopped or
  shredded); diced tomatoes; sliced,
  cooked okra; chopped spinach

Put the paste in a bowl, and beat in the fat or oil and the egg. Whisk in enough warm water to make a batter of custard consistency (that is thick enough to coat the back of a wooden spoon). Fold in the rest of the ingredients, and spoon into oiled ramekins. Cover each with foil. Place on a trivet in a saucepan with water not touching the dishes, put on the lid, and steam until just set and a knife point inserted into the middle will emerge clean. Serve in the ramekins or unmould. *Moyin-moyin* is traditionally steamed in leaves.

Egusi Soup

Serves 4–6

This is more of a stew than a soup.

2 lb / 900 g chicken portions
6 oz / 170 g dried hulled melon or
  pumpkin seeds
3 tbsp groundnut (peanut) oil
1 small onion, peeled and finely
  chopped

2 firm, ripe tomatoes, peeled, deseeded
  and chopped
2 red chillies deseeded and chopped
handful of basil, shredded
salt

Chop the chicken into small pieces, and put in a saucepan. Cover with water, bring to the boil, and skim any impurities from the surface. Lower the heat, and simmer, partially covered, for about 40 minutes until the chicken is tender. Remove any bones from which the meat has fallen, together with any skin, and remove the pan from the heat. Allow the fat to rise to the top, then skim off as much as possible. Put the soup on to simmer once more, uncovered to reduce the liquid. Grind the melon or pumpkin seeds. Heat the oil in a small frying pan, and fry the onion until wilted. Add the tomato and chillies, and stir in the ground seeds. Moisten with a little stock from the saucepan, and stir to a paste. Stir this into the soup, bring to the boil, and simmer for 10 minutes or so, until the soup thickens. Add the basil to the soup with salt to taste. Serve in heated shallow soup plates. Boiled yams, potatoes, bread or other starch is served with the soup.

Groundnut Stew

Serves 4

1 lb / 455 g blade steak	8 oz / 230 g skinned toasted or
1 onion, peeled and thinly sliced or	untoasted groundnuts (peanuts)
chopped	4 canned plum tomatoes, drained
4 small aubergines *or* 1 larger one,	2 tsp anchovy paste
about 12 oz / 340 g	1 tsp dried chilli flakes

Dice the beef, and put it in a saucepan with the onion. Just cover with water, bring to the boil, and skim the surface. Reduce the heat and simmer gently for 15–20 minutes. Halve small aubergines, or dice the larger one, and add to the pan. Grind the nuts, and work to a smooth paste with a little of the beef stock. Rub the tomatoes through a sieve, mix with the anchovy paste, nut paste and chilli flakes and stir the mixture into the beef. Continue cooking until the beef is tender and the sauce has thickened. Serve in heated shallow soup plates accompanied by steamed or boiled rice.

Jollof Rice with Chicken and Prawns

In Nigeria this dish is always served at celebrations. Originally it came from the Gambia.

1 lb / 455 g ripe tomatoes, peeled and chopped
1 onion, peeled and chopped
1–2 fresh red chillies deseeded and chopped
1 tsp freshly ground black pepper
freshly grated nutmeg

4 tbsp groundnut (peanut) oil
4 lb / 1.80 kg chicken, jointed into 8–10 pieces
14 oz / 395 g long grain rice
1¼ pt / 710 ml water or chicken stock
¼ pt / 140 ml peeled prawns

Fry the tomatoes, onion, chillies and spices in most of the groundnut oil in a saucepan for 5–10 minutes. Add the chicken pieces, raise the heat, and cook for about 10 minutes until they lose their rawness. Pour in the rice and the water or chicken stock. Bring to the boil, cover with a tightly fitting lid, and lower the heat as far as possible. Cook for 20–25 minutes, and then remove from the heat. Fork the rice to lighten it, and then cover once more, and let stand for the flavours to develop for up to 1 hour. Just before serving, dry the prawns, and fry them in the remaining oil for 2–3 minutes. Serve on top of the rice.

Eggs and Cheese

EGGS

EGGS ARE one of the cook's most valuable ingredients. Highly nutritious, yet relatively inexpensive, they are easy to cook and supremely versatile. The egg contains many valuable properties, and we use it in various cooking processes. We use it for aeration, thickening, emulsifying, stabilizing and coagulating. We could not make soufflés, custard, hollandaise sauce and pancakes without eggs.

On the whole, however, we also cook eggs because they taste so good. As with much fresh food, it is hard to improve on what nature has produced. A poached or boiled egg, served with buttered toast or wholemeal bread is a simple luxury.

Moreover, with just a few additions, eggs can be turned into elaborate dishes for special occasions, such as soufflés (see page 234) and trifle (see page 522), or into simple, rustic dishes such as a tortilla, a frittata (see page 240) or a Batter Pudding (see pages 52, 242 and 513).

Duck, goose, quail and even gull eggs are available, but I tend to use only hen eggs and to choose the medium to large sizes.

For many people, breakfast wouldn't be breakfast without eggs, so I have begun this chapter with some of my favourite egg dishes to start the day with. But, of course, they can be eaten at any time. I use free-range eggs in all my cooking.

BREAKFAST DISHES

Poached Eggs

Use very fresh eggs at room temperature and a wide shallow pan. A frying pan is quite deep enough; a sauté pan is perfect. Fill the pan three-quarters full with water and bring to a full rolling boil, then turn it down to a simmer. Break the eggs, one at a time, into a saucer, and slide them into the simmering water. With a large spoon, immediately draw the white back towards and over the yolk to envelope it. Add more eggs and treat in the same way. Simmer for 3 minutes and transfer to a bowl of warm water until needed. Remove with a slotted spoon, blot with kitchen paper, and trim off any ragged edges. Serve on hot buttered toast or use to make Eggs Benedict (see page 231).

Eggs Benedict

Split a lightly toasted plain muffin, butter it if you wish, lay on it a slice of ham, top with a poached egg, spoon on a thick coating of hollandaise sauce and flash it under a hot grill before serving.

Oeufs en Meurette

Serves 2

Cooking en meurette *is a speciality of Burgundy and the regions to the east, and food so cooked is served with a sauce made from the red wine in which it was first poached. Eels and river fish are cooked this way, as is chicken or veal, but one of the best-known dishes has eggs as the main ingredient. The most sumptuous version of* oeufs en meurette *that I have ever tasted is served at La Cote St Jacques in Joigny, where, as well as the usual accompaniments, Michel Lorain cooks small cubes of calves' liver, and, if my memory is correct, the mushrooms were wild mushrooms.*

3 oz / 85 g streaky bacon, derinded
  and cut into small pieces
8 small onions, peeled
1 oz / 30 g butter
10 button mushrooms, wiped and
  sliced or quartered

1 bottle good red wine
2 eggs
salt
freshly ground black pepper

Heat the bacon gently in a small frying pan, and when the fat runs, add the onions. Cook on a low heat until the onions are almost tender. Add the butter, raise the heat slightly, and fry the mushrooms. Remove from the heat while you poach the eggs. Pour the wine into a shallow pan (another frying pan or sauté pan is ideal) and bring to the boil. Crack the eggs, and slide them into the wine from opposite sides of the pan. Let them cook until the white has just set, completely enclosing the yolk. Carefully remove with a slotted spoon, and drain on kitchen paper. Boil the wine fiercely to reduce it by at least half, and pour it into the pan with the onions, bacon and mushrooms and season to taste. Cook for a few minutes more. Meanwhile, neaten up the eggs, trimming off any ragged portions of white. Place on pieces of toast or fried bread in heated soup plates and spoon the hot sauce over.

Poached Eggs in Field Mushrooms

Serves 4

4 large hollow field mushrooms
3 oz / 85 g butter, melted
4 eggs
2–3 tbsp grated cheese

salt
freshly ground black pepper
paprika

Brush or peel the mushrooms, as necessary. Remove the stalks, trim off the ends and chop finely. Brush the mushroom caps all over with melted butter. Place the chopped trimmings in the centre of the caps together with any remaining butter, and grill or bake the mushrooms until tender. Meanwhile, poach the eggs (see page 230), and drain them on kitchen paper. Place a poached egg on each cooked mushroom, sprinkle with grated cheese, salt, pepper and paprika to taste, and finish off under the grill until the cheese melts.

Variations ∾ Place a slice of ham in the mushrooms, before the egg, a spoonful of pesto, a smear of mustard, a splash of cream, or if you can get quail eggs, you can try miniature versions of this dish, using cap or button mushrooms.

Colazione alla Contadini
(Italian Country Breakfast)

Serves 1 (generously)

*This also makes a very good lunch or quick supper. Traditionally, it
would not be served as the first meal of the day, which would be
coffee and bread or a sweet bun, but at around 10 a.m., after working
for a couple of hours.*

2–3 rashers streaky bacon, derinded
1 shallot or small onion, peeled and
    thinly sliced, *or* 3–4 spring
    onions, trimmed and chopped

2 eggs
1 tbsp balsamic vinegar

Put the bacon and shallot or onion in a small frying pan, and cook first on a low heat, and then higher to cook the bacon, but without burning the onion. Crack the eggs, and slide them carefully into the pan without breaking the yolks. Cook the eggs until done to your liking, and add the balsamic vinegar before sliding the contents of the pan, now all held together by the egg white, on to a heated plate. Serve immediately.

Eggs Casho

Serves 6–8

1–2 tbsp sunflower or walnut oil
1 celery stalk, trimmed and thinly
   sliced
1 carrot, peeled and shredded
1 leek *or* 6 spring onions, trimmed
   and thinly sliced diagonally
4 oz / 110 g oyster, shiitake or
   button mushrooms, cleaned and
   sliced or quartered

4 oz / 110 g bean sprouts, blanched and
   drained
8–10 eggs
2–3 tbsp soy sauce

Heat the oil in a wok or large frying pan, and toss in the celery and carrots. Stir-fry for 2–3 minutes, then add the leek or onions and the mushrooms. Stir-fry for a further 2–3 minutes, then add the bean sprouts. Beat the eggs with the soy sauce, and pour over the vegetables. Turn with a spatula until just beginning to set. Serve immediately.

Variation ∽ Cold, this makes a delicious filling for slightly hollowed out wholemeal bread rolls.

Bacon, Egg and Sausage Pie

Serves 4–6

8 oz / 230 g sausages, cut into 1 in /
  2.5 cm pieces
8 oz / 230 g bacon, derinded
12 oz / 340 g shortcrust pastry

4–6 eggs
freshly ground black pepper
beaten egg or milk, to glaze

Fry the sausages gently in a non-stick frying pan until much of the fat has run out. Drain well. Grill or fry the bacon for 3 minutes, again until a good deal of the fat has been rendered. Allow the sausages and bacon to cool. Divide the pastry into two, roll out one piece and use to line a 10 in / 25.5 cm pie dish or plate. Arrange the bacon in the bottom of the pie and the pieces of sausage on top. Carefully break the eggs, one at a time, into a cup, and slide each one into the pie, distributing them as evenly as possible. Sprinkle with pepper. Roll out the second piece of pastry and use it to make a lid for the pie. Press the pastry edges together to seal, and trim off any over-hanging pastry. Make a small slit or two in the centre to allow steam to escape. Use the pastry trimmings to decorate the pie if you wish. Brush with egg or milk to glaze, and bake in a preheated oven at 190°C / 375°F / Mark 5 for about 30 minutes. If you are using a ceramic or pottery pie dish, the bottom of the pie will bake more thoroughly if you place it on a baking sheet in the oven.

SOUFFLÉS

WHENEVER I make a soufflé, I am always so pleased with the result that I promise myself to make them more often. But I never remember to do so. Yet we all, almost certainly, have all the ingredients necessary in our store-cupboards or refrigerators: eggs, milk, flour, butter and a little something to add in the way of texture and flavour are all it takes to create a fine impressive dish. A soufflé will fit into any part of a meal, as starter, main course, cheese course or pudding.

Soufflés are easy to make. Peter Kromberg, of the InterContinental Hotel in London, is the acknowledged expert, and a few years ago, I spent several weeks in his kitchen, where I picked up a number of tips on how to create the perfect soufflé:

- Use egg whites that are 4–5 days old for the best results, and always make sure the whisk you beat them with is scrupulously clean and grease-free.
- Fold the whisked egg whites into the basic mixture while it is still warm, as this helps the soufflé to rise.
- When filling the soufflé dish, do it carefully so that no drips hit the edge of the soufflé dish. This interferes with the rising action, 'anchoring' the soufflé to the dish.
- A soufflé dish can be prepared in different ways according to the type of soufflé. It should be well buttered, and then dusted with grated Parmesan, with breadcrumbs, pin-head oatmeal or sugar, depending on whether you are making a savoury soufflé, a seafood one, a fairly hearty one, or a sweet soufflé. This preparation also makes it easier to remove small soufflés from ramekins if you want to serve them sitting in a pool of sauce.
- The correct consistency of a soufflé should be soft enough in the centre so that each serving from a large soufflé will have some of the firmer outer portion, together with a little of the soft centre, which will be almost like a sauce.

Basic Savoury Soufflé

Serves 6–8

1 pt / 570 ml milk	2 oz / 60 g butter
salt	8 eggs, 6 of them separated
freshly ground black pepper	2½ oz / 70 g plain flour, sifted
freshly grated nutmeg	3 oz / 85 g cheese, grated

Butter a soufflé dish or dishes, and dust with a little grated Parmesan. Put three-quarters of the milk in a saucepan with the seasoning and butter. Bring to the boil. Beat the two whole eggs with the six egg yolks, the flour and the remaining milk, and stir slowly into the boiling milk over a low heat. Stir continuously until the mixture thickens but does not curdle. Remove from the heat. Whisk the egg whites until stiff. Stir the cheese into the sauce, and then fold in the egg white. Pour into the prepared dish or dishes, and bake in a preheated oven at 200°C / 400°F / Mark 6 for 12–22 minutes, depending on the size of the dish(es).

Savoury Soufflé Variations

One of the most famous soufflés must surely be the spinach soufflé with anchovy sauce served at Langan's Brasserie in London. It has been on the menu since Richard Shephard joined some six months after the restaurant opened in 1976. He thinks they must have cooked about 340 soufflés a week since then. Some of Peter Kromberg's specialities include an artichoke soufflé baked in its shell with a warm mustard vinaigrette; an aubergine soufflé with a red pepper and mint sauce; and a celery, pear and walnut soufflé with a port and Stilton sauce, which sounds a very agreeable combination. Strongly flavoured cheeses produce very good soufflés, I find. Michel Bourdin of the Connaught Hotel in London serves individual Stilton soufflés baked in pastry cases. Alice Waters at Chez Panisse in Berkeley, California, devised a recipe for a shallow soufflé with goat's cheese. This is a delightfully homely dish when baked in rustic earthenware. It cooks more quickly because the mixture is not as deep as the classic soufflé.

I feel much the same way about soufflés as I do about omelettes when it comes to deciding what to put in them. Rather than scraps of cooked meat, I much prefer to use fish, cheese or vegetables, alone or in combination. I would make an exception for juicy, cooked ham, and perhaps serve it with a leek sauce. Peter Kromberg does a 'family size' macaroni soufflé, in which he takes a half portion of basic savoury soufflé mix and folds into it, before adding the egg whites, strips of ham, cooked macaroni and extra grated cheese, with which he also tops the soufflé. This makes an excellent, inexpensive and impressive-looking main course, a grander version of macaroni cheese. Undyed smoked haddock is probably my favourite filling for a soufflé, but I like mussels, too, or prawns with a dill sauce poured in the middle. And, although it sounds unlikely, potatoes are just as good in a soufflé as they are in an omelette; diced, cooked firm waxy salad potatoes, and some well-flavoured fairly hard goat's cheese, such as Mendip, added to the basic savoury soufflé mix before folding in the egg whites. Serve the soufflé with a fresh tomato sauce.

Sauces with Soufflés

Opening the top of a soufflé at the table and pouring in a hot sauce has a spectacular effect, causing it to puff up in its dish, to *souffler* in fact. With a spoon in each hand, gently prize apart the top crust, and immediately pour in the sauce.

The same uncooked sauces that go well with pasta can also be used with savoury soufflés. Try fresh tomato and basil sauce, nothing but the shredded herb mixed with peeled, seeded and diced tomatoes and a little seasoning, with a cheese soufflé. Or pour pesto thinned down with a little olive oil or vegetable stock into a Parmesan soufflé. A simple mixture of melted butter, lemon juice and fresh mace is all that a good crab soufflé needs, or indeed a prawn, mussel or lobster soufflé.

Cheese Soufflés in Paper Cases

Makes 12

*These miniature soufflés can be served as a cheese course or as a
savoury with drinks before dinner.*

2 tbsp melted butter or sunflower oil	7 fl oz / 200 ml milk, boiled
1 oz / 30 g butter	3 oz / 85 g hard cheese, grated
1 oz / 30 g plain flour	1 egg yolk
	2 egg whites

Brush 12 fluted paper bun cases with the melted butter or oil, and place on a baking sheet. Make a thick, smooth white sauce with the butter, flour and milk, and cook for 5–10 minutes. Remove from the heat, add the cheese, and stir until melted. Beat in the egg yolk. Whisk the whites until firm, and fold into the egg and cheese mixture. Spoon into paper cases to within ½ in / 1 cm of the top, and run a knife tip or teaspoon around the top edge of the mixture to help it rise. Bake in a preheated oven at 180°C / 350°F / Mark 4 for 10–15 minutes.

OMELETTES

Crab and Courgette Omelette

Serves 1

This simple summery dish is good for lunch, supper or even
a late breakfast.

1 smallish courgette
1 tsp unsalted butter
2–3 eggs
salt
freshly ground black pepper

1 tbsp prepared crab meat
chopped chives
1 tomato, peeled, deseeded and
  chopped

Top and tail the courgette, and grate it into shreds. Heat the butter in a small frying pan or omelette pan and add the grated courgette. Cook over a gentle heat for about 5 minutes. Lightly beat the eggs. Raise the heat under the pan, and pour in the beaten egg. Draw the egg back to the centre from the edges as it sets to allow the uncooked egg to run to the edges and cook through. When still moist on top, season lightly and add the crab meat. Fold the omelette over and slide it on to a heated plate. Garnish with the chopped chives and tomato.

Variations ∾ For small vegetable-stuffed omelettes, I suggest making two or three vegetable purées, such as leek, asparagus and broad bean, and mixing each with a little crème fraîche or cream cheese and some chopped fresh herbs. Make single egg omelettes, and allow each one to cool slightly before rolling round a tablespoon of purée. These have been a summer favourite ever since I read Elizabeth David's *Summer Food*, which I remember buying on a June day in 1976 when the temperature was in the 90s. Served cold, the omelettes make a lovely hot weather dish; served freshly made and warm, they are most comforting.

Spanish Omelette

Serves 4

This does duty as a substantial starter, as a picnic dish or a main course. When cut into squares, it is most appetizing with a cool glass of fino *before lunch.*

2 tbsp olive oil
1 small onion, peeled and thinly
  sliced
4 oz / 110 g cooked spinach,
  squeezed dry and chopped

4 oz / 110 g cooked potatoes, diced
8 eggs
salt
freshly ground black pepper

Heat the olive oil in a deep heavy frying pan, about 8–9 in / 20.5–23 cm in diameter, and fry the onion until golden brown. Add the potatoes and spinach, and distribute the vegetables evenly over the base of the pan. Lightly beat the eggs. Raise the heat under the pan, pour the eggs over the vegetables, and season lightly with salt and pepper. Draw the egg back from the edges as it sets, to allow the uncooked egg to run to the edges and cook through.

When the omelette is almost set all the way through, invert a large plate over the frying pan. Tip the frying pan upside down and allow the omelette to fall on to the plate, cooked side uppermost. Place the pan back on the heat, adding a little more oil, if necessary, and when hot, slide the omelette back in to cook the second side. When fully cooked, turn out on to a plate and allow it to cool. To serve, cut into wedges.

Variations ⁓ Brown the diced potato with the onion, and instead of the spinach, use cooked asparagus, chopped into ½ in / 1 cm lengths.

Brown the diced potato with the onion, and while they are browning, sprinkle over a little turmeric, ground cumin, ground coriander and a few crushed cardamom pods. Substitute chopped watercress or rocket for the spinach. Season with a little cayenne pepper, as well as with salt and black pepper.

Pipérade

2 red peppers

1 green pepper

1 onion, peeled and finely chopped

2 tbsp olive oil *or* 1 oz / 30 g butter

8 oz / 230 g ripe tomatoes, peeled,
 deseeded and chopped

6 eggs

salt

freshly ground black pepper

cayenne pepper or chilli powder, to
 taste

Char and skin the peppers, then deseed and chop them. Cook with the onion in the olive oil or butter until soft. Add the tomatoes, and continue cooking until you have a thick purée. Lightly beat the eggs. Lower the heat under the pan, and once the mixture is no longer boiling, stir in the eggs. Season with salt and pepper, and cayenne or chilli powder, and continue stirring over a low heat until the eggs are cooked to a cream. They should not be lumpy but should have amalgamated with the purée and thickened it. Serve immediately with toast or fried bread.

Frittata of Wild Greens

8 oz / 230 g wild greens, washed,
 blanched, dried and chopped (see
 page 154)

2 tbsp olive oil

1 oz / 30 g butter

6 eggs

freshly ground black pepper

salt

Gently fry the greens for a few minutes in the oil and butter in an omelette pan. Lightly beat the eggs, with a little pepper and salt, and pour over the greens. When the underside is set, turn the frittata over and cook briefly on the other side before sliding it on to a warm serving plate.

Variations ✎ Cheese can also be added to the beaten egg – grated Parmesan, crumbled blue cheese or diced mozzarella.

Diced potatoes fried in the pan before the greens will turn this into a more substantial dish similar to a Spanish omelette.

FLANS AND BATTER PUDDINGS

Onion Flan

Serves 6–8

3 rashers smoked streaky bacon,
   derinded and cut into matchsticks
1 lb / 455 g onions, peeled and
   thinly sliced
1 oz / 30 g butter
1 tsp plain flour
¾ pt / 430 ml single cream or
   full-cream milk

salt
freshly ground black pepper
freshly grated nutmeg
3 eggs, lightly beaten
12 oz / 340 g shortcrust pastry

Fry the bacon gently in a heavy frying pan until all the fat runs out. Take the bacon from the pan, and drain it on kitchen paper. Gently fry the onions in the remaining fat, adding butter if necessary. Cook until the onions are soft, wilted, translucent and just beginning to brown. Remove from the heat, sprinkle on the flour and gradually stir in the cream or milk. Bring to the boil, stirring all the time, and cook for 5 minutes. Season with salt and pepper, and a little nutmeg. Stir in the beaten egg.

Roll out the pastry and use to line a 10 in / 25.5 cm greased quiche or flan tin. Put the bacon in the bottom of the flan and pour in the onion mixture. Place the tin on a baking sheet and bake in a preheated oven at 200°C / 400°F / Mark 6 for about 35 minutes, until the top is golden brown. The flan can be served at any temperature, but I prefer it warm.

Ham and Herb Custard Flan

Serves 4–6

8 oz / 230 g shortcrust pastry
5 oz / 140 g cooked ham, diced
  bacon or shredded Parma ham
3 egg yolks
¾ pt / 430 ml full-cream milk
4 spring onions, trimmed and finely
  chopped
3 tbsp chopped watercress

1 oz / 30 g cooked, drained spinach,
  finely chopped *(optional)*
2 tbsp finely chopped parsley
1 tsp chopped thyme or oregano
salt
freshly ground black pepper
pinch of freshly grated nutmeg

Roll out the pastry, and use it to line a 9 in / 23 cm flan tin. Scatter the ham over the base. Beat the egg yolks and milk together, and stir in the rest of the ingredients. Pour into the pastry shell. Place the flan tin on a baking sheet and bake in a preheated oven at 200°C / 400°F / Mark 6 for 10–15 minutes, and then at 180°C / 350°F / Mark 4 for 30–35 minutes or until a skewer inserted in the centre comes out clean. Remove from the oven, and cool on a wire rack before serving.

Gruyère and Courgette Batter Pudding

Serves 4–6

*Traditionally a sweet dish made with cherries, the recipe adapts well
to savoury ingredients.*

3 tbsp strong plain white flour
¾ pt / 430 ml full-cream milk
3 eggs
2 oz / 60 g butter
6 oz / 170 g Gruyère cheese, diced

4 oz / 110 g courgettes, trimmed and
  sliced
salt
freshly ground black pepper

Beat the flour, milk and eggs together to make a smooth batter, and let it stand for 30 minutes. Use half the butter to grease a flan dish. Scatter the diced Gruyère and the courgette slices over the base of the dish. Season the batter with salt and pepper, and pour it into the dish. Dot the rest of the butter on top. Bake in a preheated oven at 200°C / 400°F / Mark 6 for 30 minutes, and then at 180°C / 350°F / Mark 4 for another 20 minutes. Remove from the oven; the mixture will have risen and become puffy when first taken from the oven, but will then sink. Do not worry; it is meant to do this. Serve warm.

Variations ∾ Other vegetables and cheeses can be experimented with.

Courgettes and cheese are also good when baked in a custard rather than a batter mixture. Beat together 3 eggs and ½ pt / 280 ml milk, season, and pour this over the courgette slices and cheese in the flan dish. Bake for 30 minutes at 180°C / 350°F / Mark 4, and serve warm.

Rigodon

Serves 4–6

A speciality of the Beaujolais region, this is a perfect companion to the wine of the region.

7 oz / 200 g cooked meat, such as pork or ham
1 oz / 30 g butter
4 eggs
2 oz / 60 g plain flour
1 pt / 570 ml milk

salt
freshly ground black pepper
pinch of ground mace or nutmeg
1 sage leaf, finely chopped, *or* a pinch of dried sage

Cut the meat into small pieces. Use half the butter to grease a 2½–3 pt / 1.45–1.70 l baking dish, and lay the meat in the bottom. Beat the eggs and flour together to make a smooth, thick batter. Bring the milk just to the boil, and, whisking all the time, pour it slowly into the batter. Add the seasoning, mace or nutmeg and sage, and pour the mixture into the baking dish. Dot with the remaining butter and bake in a preheated oven at 180°C / 350°F / Mark 4 for 40–50 minutes, until well risen and dark golden brown. Serve warm, rather than hot or cold.

PANCAKES

PANCAKES are extremely versatile. They can be served with a huge variety of toppings and fillings, both sweet and savoury, as starter, a main course or a dessert. When we were children, my mother would make pancakes for my brother and me on Shrove Tuesday. We would smear them with butter, then sprinkle them with lemon juice and sugar, and roll up and eat them as fast as she could make them. Later, as a student in Southern Germany, I learned how to make the most economical use of the expensive fat, white stalks of asparagus by wrapping them first in a slice of ham, then in a pancake, which I would blanket with cheese sauce and bake under the grill.

Ham, cheese, chicken, sausage, artichoke hearts, asparagus, spinach, mushrooms, onions, tomatoes, smoked fish and shellfish, all make good fillings for savoury pancakes, either alone or combined. Jam, marmalade, maple syrup, honey, liqueurs, stewed and fresh fruit, yoghurt, cream and crème fraîche can be made into delicious toppings and fillings for sweet pancakes (see also the recipes for dessert pancakes on pages 556 and 557). Let your imagination flow freely. Louis le Roy, a Breton chef, prepares a remarkable filling for buckwheat galettes (see recipe on page 246). He spreads them with a creamy sorrel sauce on which poached monkfish cheeks are arranged. Another wonderful idea comes from a winner of the Lady Chef competition in Holland, Ida van den Hurk. She makes a pancake filling by mashing Stilton cheese with honey and cream; the pancakes can either be served cold or be warmed in the oven for 8–10 minutes before eating.

Whilst making pancake batter is relatively easy, achieving a thin pancake that doesn't stick first time is not. I usually plan for at least the first two to go into the waste bin. I find a well-seasoned, cast-iron crêpe pan is best for the job. I bought one in France which I only use for pancakes. I never wash it, only oil it.

Pancakes
(Basic Recipe)

Makes 6–8

4 oz / 110 g plain or self-raising
  flour
pinch of salt
1 large egg

½ pt / 280 ml milk
grapeseed or other neutral oil for
  cooking

Sift the flour and salt together into a bowl. Stir in the egg, and gradually add
the milk, beating until a smooth batter is formed, then whisk to lighten it. Cover
the batter and allow to stand for at least 1 hour before using.

Heat a crêpe pan or heavy, flat-bottomed frying pan and brush the inside
surface with a little grapeseed or other neutral oil. Pour on just enough batter to
coat the base of the pan thinly. Cook until the underside is lightly browned and the
top is bubbling. Flip the pancake over, and cook on the other side for 15–20
seconds only. Brush the pan lightly again with oil before cooking the next pancake.
As they come out of the pan, stack the pancakes on a plate over a pan of hot water
and cover with a clean, folded tea-towel until required. Spread with the filling of
your choice, roll or fold up, and serve.

Another way of serving pancakes is in the style of an old-fashioned quire, where
thin pancakes sandwiched with filling are piled one on top of the other, and then
cut into wedges like a cake.

Variation ⁓ For walnut pancakes, use an extra egg to make the basic batter,
and then stir in 2 teaspoons walnut oil and 3 oz / 85 g finely chopped walnuts.
Leave this batter to stand for at least 1 hour, then cook the pancakes as above.
These are good served with honey or maple syrup, or a syrup made by heating
together clear honey, walnut oil and orange juice with a little grated nutmeg.

Buckwheat Galettes

Makes 6–8

4 oz / 110 g buckwheat flour
pinch of salt
1 large egg

1 tbsp grapeseed oil
½ pt / 280 ml warm water

Put the flour in a bowl. Make a well in the centre, and put in the salt, egg and oil. Gradually stir in the warm water until you have a smooth paste. Beat vigorously for a few minutes, and then allow the batter to stand for 1 hour. This resting time, together with the beating and the temperature of the water, helps the flour to swell, which produces the correct texture for the batter.

Cook the pancakes as in the previous recipe, and serve with the filling of your choice. Buckwheat galettes are usually served with a savoury filling; smoked fish is particularly good. These are sturdy, substantial wodges, not lacy delicate crêpes.

CHEESE

BEING ABLE to watch food created from its raw materials and to attend every stage of the process can be a curiously moving experience. Early one autumn morning, I went to the Caseificio San Giovanni in the Modenese countryside to watch Parmesan cheese 'being born'. I now eat that cheese with a deep respect for the people who make it: those who rise before dawn to milk the cows and those who are at the dairy before 7 a.m. every day during the cheese-making season (15 April to 11 November) to receive the milk for their cheese and butter.

Silvano Bergianti has been making Parmesan cheese for just over 50 years, having taken over from his father. There is, however, no one to take over from him. His sons, whilst respecting their parents for their hard work, their seven-day week, do not want it for themselves. And in a curious way, I think their parents do not want it for them either, although they do not want the cheese-making to end. Parmesan cheese has been made in the region since the eleventh or twelfth century. The local version of its origins recounts that one of the Lucio Friars milked his goats and set the pail under a lemon tree, thus leaving nature to do the rest by introducing the coagulating acid of the windfall lemon into the waiting milk. Cheese-making throughout the world is surrounded by such myths. I remember hearing similar stories about the origins of Roquefort when I went to watch that cheese being made.

Whatever the type of cheese, they all have similar properties when cooked. One of the first things I cooked for friends after I was married and first had a kitchen of my own was *raclette* – grilled, melted cheese – which I planned to serve with new potatoes, boiled in their skins, and gherkins. A late supper was planned for after the theatre, and, being of a practical nature, I decided to prepare as much in advance as possible. This extended, I am ashamed to say, to melting the cheese in advance, to reheat later.

That evening taught me several valuable lessons about cooking cheese. As I began to reheat the melted cheese, it solidified into a block of rubbery protein, sitting in a pool of yellow oil. Fortunately, I was not put off cooking with cheese, and we went on to enjoy many a merry fondue evening and *raclette* supper, cooking and eating from the communal pot. This kind of cooking and entertaining is fun, and I'm never surprised by its popularity.

Cheese dishes are by their nature rich, and I think it is best, if serving one as a main course, to accompany it only with a salad of green leaves and herbs. It is said that anything cold that follows cheese will cause it to set into a solid indigestible mass. Perhaps a cup of herb tea would be just the thing as a *digestif*, followed by a long pause before bringing on the ices, sorbets and chilled fruit salads that one might well want to eat after such rich, filling food.

Cheese in Olive Oil

Take a piece of hard cheese, such as Emmental, Parmesan, Cantal or Cheddar, and remove enough thin slices for the number of servings you require. Lay the cheese in a shallow dish, and cover with extra virgin olive oil. Leave for several hours, and then serve the cheese from the dish, or arrange on plates with salad leaves.

Drained Cheese Flavoured with Herbs and Garlic

Makes 12 oz / 340 g

*This is a very simple method of producing a 'house-made' cheese that
is delicious to eat with salads or on crispbreads. You will need a
pierced mould which can be bought from a good kitchenware supplier.
You can also improvise with a scrupulously clean flower pot or by
piercing holes in the bottom of an empty fromage frais or yoghurt
container.*

1 lb / 455 g fromage frais or thick
   plain yoghurt
1–2 tbsp finely chopped herbs
1–2 garlic cloves, peeled and
   crushed

sea salt
freshly ground black pepper

Mix all the ingredients together. Line the mould with scalded muslin and pour
in the mixture. Balance the mould over a container to collect the whey which will
drain from the fromage frais or yoghurt. Let it stand for at least 8 hours to drain.
To serve, turn the cheese out on to a plate and remove the muslin. The whey can
be saved for making pancakes or scones, preferably savoury ones since it will have a
hint of garlic about it.

Variations ∾ If you make this without the herbs, garlic and seasoning, you can
serve it the way they do in Lyons, with sugar and cream, as a dessert.

Another Lyonnais version of the same idea is to serve the cheese undrained in a
bowl to be eaten with a spoon.

Cheese and Herb Creams

Serves 4–6, as a starter

If you have any of these left over, they can be shaped into a log, rolled
in cumin seeds or coarsely ground black pepper and served as a cheese
the next day.

1 oz / 30 g mixed 'soft' herbs, such
   as parsley, chervil, tarragon, dill
   and coriander
5 oz / 140 g plain cottage cheese
5 oz / 140 g plain yoghurt

5 oz / 140 g soft blue cheese
2 garlic cloves, peeled and crushed
fine sea salt
freshly ground white pepper
5 fl oz / 140 ml double cream

Put the herbs in a sieve, and pour boiling water over them to blanch them.
Rinse under cold running water, and then firmly pat dry between layers of kitchen
paper. Chop the herbs finely, and put to one side. Rub the cottage cheese through
a sieve, and mix with the yoghurt and blue cheese until smooth. Stir in the garlic
and herbs, and season lightly with salt and pepper. Whip the double cream, and
fold it into the cheese mixture. Spoon it into a sieve lined with scalded muslin, and
leave to drain for a few hours. Shape into *quenelles* (neat egg shapes) with two
tablespoons, and arrange one or two on individual plates with some salad leaves.

Traditional Baked Rarebit

Serves 4

1 oz / 30 g butter
8 oz / 230 g farmhouse Lancashire
  cheese, crumbled
2½ fl oz / 70 ml real ale

pinch of English mustard powder
dash of Worcestershire sauce
freshly ground white pepper
4 slices bread, toasted on one side

Melt the butter in a saucepan, and stir in the cheese, ale, mustard powder, Worcestershire sauce and pepper. Stir until the cheese has melted and the mixture is creamy. Put each slice of toast in a small heated ovenproof dish, toasted side down, and pour the mixture over the top. Put briefly in a hot oven, or under the grill, to brown lightly. Serve immediately.

Variations   Some variations include a slice of ham under the cheese; others add a poached egg on top of the browned cheese. I am not sure that either is an improvement. However, because tomato goes so well with cheese, I might serve a grilled half tomato or a spoonful of tomato chutney with the rarebit. Lancashire is not the only cheese for a rarebit, but I think it is the best; you may prefer Cheshire, Caerphilly or Wensleydale.

Grilled Goat's Cheese on Country Bread

Serves 8

8 slices rustic bread
1 large garlic clove, peeled
extra virgin olive oil

8 slices goat's cheese *or* 8 whole Crottin
  de Chavignol cheeses, or similar

Put the bread under the grill, and toast one side only. Rub the untoasted side quickly with garlic, brush with olive oil, and put a piece of cheese on each piece of bread. Put back under the grill and toast until the cheese is browned and bubbling. The heat will be sufficient to soften the cheese to a spreading consistency. Serve immediately.

Variations   After rubbing the untoasted side of the bread with garlic, place a few leaves of radicchio on each piece, sprinkle liberally with olive oil, season, and place under the grill until the radicchio has browned slightly. Lay the cheese on top of each slice, and return to the grill for a few minutes until the cheese is lightly browned and bubbling.

Cheese Fondue

Serves 4

*For fondues, there is no hard and fast rule about which cheese to use.
Many are suitable. Amongst the hard cheeses, Emmental and Gruyère
are the most commonly available. The semi-hard cheese Appenzell has
a rich, strong fruitiness which combines well with some of the milder
cheeses. Try Tilsit, the French Beaufort, the Norwegian Jarlsberg or
the Italian Fontina, either alone or in combination.*

1 garlic clove	1–1½ lb / 455–680 g hard or semi-hard
¾–1¼ pt / 430–710 ml very dry	cheese (see above), grated
white wine	freshly grated nutmeg
1 tbsp arrowroot or potato flour	1–2 crusty loaves of bread, cut into
4 tbsp kirsch	1 in / 2.5 cm cubes

Cut the garlic clove in two, and rub the inside of a heavy saucepan or fondue pot
with the cut surface. Pour in the wine, and place over a gentle heat. Blend the
arrowroot or potato flour with the kirsch, and put to one side. As soon as there is a
fine, bubbly foam on the surface of the wine, but it is not yet boiling, start to stir in the
cheese, a little at a time. Stir constantly and do not allow the mixture to boil. When all
the cheese has been added and has blended in, stir in the kirsch and arrowroot
mixture, and continue to cook, stirring, until the fondue begins to thicken. Stir in
nutmeg, to taste, then quickly transfer the bubbling fondue, in the cooking pot, to a
spirit lamp on the dining-table. Spear the cubes of bread on long forks, and dip into
the hot, bubbling fondue before eating.

Variations ∾ There are, of course, many variations on the above. The Genevois
fondue might contain finely chopped dried morels, and that of the eastern cantons of
Switzerland may be made with dry cider instead of wine. I have come across a recipe
for pink fondue in which a dry rosé is used instead of white wine. Black truffles,
cayenne pepper, mustard, tarragon, peeled and chopped tomatoes and even curry
powder and diced pineapple are other published variations, none of them an
improvement on the original. The *fondue de l'armailli* is rather nice; in it the cubes of
bread speared on forks and dipped into the fondue are replaced by potatoes boiled in
their skins. Kirsch is not the only *eau de vie* used in the fondue; one based on pears
and plums might be used. If I made the fondue with cider instead of wine, I would
use Calvados as the spirit.

Fonduta

Serves 4, as a starter

*This Italian recipe is lighter than fondue, and is good served on toast
or poured over grilled polenta slices (see page 66). You could also try
it with steamed new potatoes and a mixture of baby vegetables as a
starter.*

3 eggs
½ pt / 280 ml full-cream milk
2 oz / 60 g unsalted butter
5 oz / 140 g hard cheese (see
   suggestions for Cheese Fondue on
   page 251), grated

salt
freshly ground black pepper
freshly grated nutmeg

Beat the eggs with half of the milk and put in an enamel saucepan with the
butter, cheese and remaining milk. Set over a low heat and stir continuously until
the cheese has melted and a thick cream is produced. Season to taste with salt,
pepper and nutmeg.

Aligot
(Cheese and Potato Purée)

Serves 4–6

*Here is another favourite dish, from Central France, that will send
welcoming smells from the kitchen in the winter; I do not feel it is a
summer dish. The traditional recipe used butter and cream. However,
olive oil and thick Greek yoghurt make excellent substitutes.*

2 lb / 900 g potatoes, scrubbed
4 oz / 110 g butter *or* 4 fl oz / 115 ml
   extra virgin olive oil
4 tbsp cream or yoghurt

8 oz / 230 g Gruyère, Lancashire or,
   traditionally, Cantal cheese, grated
salt
freshly ground black pepper

Boil the potatoes until tender, then drain. When cool enough to handle, scoop
out the cooked potato into a saucepan and mash until smooth. With a wooden
spoon, beat in the butter or oil, keeping the pan over a low heat. Stir in the cream
or yoghurt, and then add the cheese, stirring until it has melted into the potatoes.
Season to taste and serve immediately.

Farmhouse Cheese Pie

Serves 6–8

*I developed this recipe as a means of tempering some Dutch farmhouse
cheese that was very mature and almost too powerful in flavour to eat.
It is a good way of using up odds and ends of cheeses. Alter the
balance of grated cheese and cottage cheese if your main cheese is
fairly mild.*

12 oz / 340 g puff pastry
1 celery stalk, trimmed and finely
  chopped
1 small onion, peeled and finely
  chopped
½ oz / 15 g butter

6 oz / 170 g plain cottage cheese
6 oz / 170 g hard cheese, grated
freshly ground black pepper
1–2 tbsp chopped herbs or watercress
beaten egg or milk, to seal and glaze

Divide the pastry in half, roll out each piece and cut it round a dinner plate (an
octagonal plate makes a well-shaped pie). Place one piece of pastry on a greased
and floured baking sheet. Gently cook the celery and onion in the butter for about
5 minutes, then mix with the cottage cheese and grated cheese. Add the pepper
and herbs, and pile on to the pastry on the baking sheet. Spread the mixture to
within ½ in / 1 cm of the edge of the pastry, and moisten the edge with beaten egg
or milk. Give the remaining piece of pastry another roll or two so that it will cover
the filling and meet the edges of the bottom piece of pastry. Press the edges
together, and trim them with a sharp knife, making clean cuts without dragging the
pastry. In this way you will get a well risen finish. Make several slits in the top to let
steam escape, and brush with beaten egg or milk. Bake in the top half of a
preheated oven at 190°C / 375°F / Mark 5 for 25–30 minutes, moving it to a lower
shelf if it shows signs of overbrowning. Serve the pie warm.

THE TIMES COOK IN THAILAND

AFTER ONE visit to Thailand, where I went as guest cook to the Dusit Thani Hotel in Bangkok, I came back with my usual bulging shopping bag. I had pale fawn, round cakes of palm sugar to use for sweetening coconut custards and crème brûlées, and a large roll of banana leaves, which I cut and shaped into small cups in which to steam fish 'custards' (these make an excellent starter). But by far the most space in my bag was taken up by herbs and spices, bundles of long, pale, fat stems of lemon grass, twigs of kaffir lime leaves and a hank of pandanus leaves.

I use these herbs and spices, not only to cook authentic Thai recipes, but also in my own dishes. Sometimes I want the taste of kaffir lime leaves, but not in a Thai green curry, though I find this dish quite marvellous, almost addictive in fact, and make sure I bring back the right ingredients to prepare it. Whenever possible I was in the Thai kitchen watching lunch and dinner being prepared. On my last day there, a large pot of green curry paste and one of red curry paste were being made, and the cooks vacuum-packed a sizeable portion of each for me. Sometimes I use the curry paste, sparingly, when I am frying a chicken or duck breast; I add just a little to a sauce made from the pan juices and some cream.

At other times, quite often in fact, I exhibit all the classic symptoms of the 'been to' syndrome and make a complete Thai meal as authentically as possible. Sudden urges to eat food flavoured with lemon grass and lime leaf come over me. I look for the smallest, meanest chillies I can find, and wish I was on my way to Chatuchak market, near the airport in Bangkok, rather than on my way to the local supermarket. Still, even there I can find small packets of Thai herbs and spices, such as red and green chillies, *krachai* (a type of ginger) or garlic chives, lemon grass and lime leaves. I also buy fresh basil, mint, coriander and ginger, and, from the salad bar, pick a shredded cabbage, carrot, cucumber, coriander, bean sprout and peanut salad, which makes a perfect filling for the many types of spring and rice rolls from Bangkok.

The Thais, I came to realize, love to wrap food, whether in banana leaves, delicate webs of omelette or rice flour pancakes and wrappers. Rice flour wrappers or papers store well, and can be found in oriental food shops. They can be wrapped around a filling to make spring rolls, which can then either be served fresh, just as they are, or deep-fried. The wrappers should be made pliable first by dipping them in water and laying them on a damp tea-towel. You can also use them instead of making the rice flour pancakes in the Rolled Pancakes and Dipping Sauces recipe (see page 256). This is a most sociable dish to prepare and eat. Follow it with a spicy red curry (see page 259).

I watched Khun Sununta, the chef in the Dusit Thani's Benjarong restaurant, prepare red curry for lunch one day, crosshatching the chicken breast so that it would absorb the spices and cook quickly and thoroughly. She used no oil for frying, since the coconut cream used in most Thai curries has plenty of oil in it. As any good cook does, she tested the meat by pushing it with her finger. I worked with some of her colleagues on the vegetable *mis-en-place*, learning how to tie a blanched yard-long bean into a tight double knot; the knot is made at one end, clipped off, and the remaining length of bean knotted in the same way. Blanched morning glory, mangetout, baby sweetcorn and pea-sized aubergines were also prepared for the curries and a chilli-based dip called *nam prig*.

Fresh mangoes, served with sweetened sticky rice, or caramelized or glazed bananas, served warm in coconut milk, are the perfect way to end a Thai meal. Or, you could try coconut custard (see page 260), grilled or steamed. Otherwise, choose a selection of cut tropical fruits, fashioned, if you feel inclined, into the traditional, exquisite flower and leaf shapes of Thai royal cuisine.

Rolled Pancakes and Dipping Sauces

Makes 8–10

Rice Flour Pancakes	pinch of salt
2 oz / 60 g fine rice flour	2 egg whites
1½ oz / 40 g self-raising flour	7 fl oz / 200 ml water

Sift the flours and salt together into a bowl. Beat in the egg whites, and gradually add the water until you have a smooth batter of pouring consistency. Cover and leave to stand for about 1 hour. Heat a well-seasoned pan, and wipe it with an oiled pad of kitchen paper. When hot, pour on a very thin layer of batter, swirling the pan around to get an even coating. Cook until the surface of the pancake looks dry, then turn it over with a spatula, and cook the other side. Stack up the pancakes as you cook them, separated by sheets of greaseproof paper, on a plate over a pan of hot water, and cover with a clean, folded tea-towel until required.

Pork and Prawn Filling	6 oz / 170 g peeled raw prawns
1 onion, peeled and finely chopped	2 tbsp groundnut (peanut) oil
1 carrot, peeled and finely chopped	1 tbsp soy sauce or fish sauce
1 celery stalk, trimmed and finely chopped	1–2 garlic cloves, crushed
6 canned water chestnuts, drained, *or* a Jerusalem artichoke, peeled and finely chopped	1 tsp grated fresh root ginger
	1 tsp grated fresh galangal
	1 tsp finely chopped lemon grass
6 oz / 170 g lean pork tenderloin, diced	

Put half the vegetables with the pork and prawns in a food processor. Process briefly until it has the texture of mince. Mix in the rest of the vegetables, and fry the mixture in the oil for 10–15 minutes. Season with the rest of the ingredients, and pile into a bowl.

Herbs and Vegetables	basil leaves
Prepare a selection of:	mint leaves
peeled cucumber, cut in half, deseeded, and cut into thin strips	finely sliced celery
shredded or sliced spring onions	blanched bean sprouts
coriander leaves	garlic chives

Chilli Sauce

4 tbsp rice vinegar or lime juice

2 tbsp water

1 tbsp sugar

3–4 chillies, finely sliced

Mix the vinegar or lime juice, water and sugar, and add the chillies.

If you would like a ginger or garlic sauce, as well or instead, prepare as above, but substitute 2 tbsp finely grated fresh root ginger or 2–3 peeled garlic cloves crushed with a little salt, for the chillies.

Coconut Sauce

1 small onion, peeled and thinly
    sliced

2–3 in / 5–7.5 cm thick end of
    lemon grass, thinly sliced

1 tsp crushed coriander seeds

1 tbsp groundnut (peanut) oil

3 oz / 85 g creamed coconut, broken off
    a block

about 3 tbsp stock.

Fry the onion, lemon grass and coriander in the oil until the mixture is fragrant. Stir in the creamed coconut, and when it has melted, add enough stock to give the sauce a good consistency for dipping.

If you would like a peanut dipping sauce, substitute peanut butter for the coconut cream.

To assemble the pancakes, which is very similar to the way one tackles Peking duck, spoon on some pork and prawn mixture, and then add some of the herbs and vegetables. Roll up the pancakes, turning in both ends to close them, and eat after dipping in one of the sauces. These rolls can also be deep fried.

Thien Duong Salad with Pork and Tiger Prawns
(Goi Buoi Tom Tit)

Serves 6–8

Although I learned this recipe in Bangkok, it is a Vietnamese dish.

slice of fresh root ginger
1 garlic clove, peeled
1 in / 2.5 cm piece lemon grass stalk
6–8 oz / 170–230 g piece pork
  tenderloin, thinly sliced

8 fresh tiger prawns
herbs, to garnish

Salad
lettuce or radicchio
1 cucumber
2 tsp salt
1 pomelo
1 carrot, peeled and cut into
  julienne strips
3 oz / 85 g bean sprouts, blanched
  and drained
1 small red onion *or* 2 shallots,
  peeled

1 tsp grated fresh root ginger
1 lemon grass stalk, thinly sliced
fresh lime juice, to taste
sugar, to taste
fish sauce, to taste
coriander leaves, shredded
mint leaves or basil leaves, shredded
1–2 red or green chillies, sliced
2 oz / 60 g dry roasted peanuts, crushed

Put the ginger, garlic and lemon grass in a saucepan with about ½ pt / 280 ml water. Bring to the boil, and simmer for a few minutes. Lower the heat, drop in the pork, and poach for 3–5 minutes. Remove with a slotted spoon, drain, and put to one side. Poach the prawns in the same stock until just firm, opaque and pink. Remove and drain them. When cool enough to handle, peel and de-vein the prawns, and chop into two or three pieces.

Line a platter or salad bowl with lettuce or radicchio leaves. The cucumber can be prepared either as long shreds taken off with a potato peeler, 2–3 in / 5–7.5 cm strips or by quartering lengthways. Place in a sieve, sprinkle with salt, and leave to drain for 20–30 minutes. Peel the thick skin from the pomelo, and then remove the tough thin skin from each segment. Break the segments up into small pieces, and put in a bowl with the carrot, bean sprouts, onion, ginger and lemon grass. Rinse and dry the cucumber, and add to the vegetables. Mix together the lime juice, sugar and fish sauce, and stir in the shredded herbs and chillies. Add water if necessary to thin down the mixture. Stir this into the salad, and add the pork and prawns. Let the mixture stand for a while so the flavours can develop, and then spoon into the salad bowl. Scatter the crushed peanuts on top, and garnish with more herbs before serving.

Simple Thai Red Curry with Chicken
(Pad Nang Gai)

Serves 4–6

Curry Paste
1 tsp coriander seeds
1 tsp cumin seeds
1 tsp white peppercorns
1 tsp coarse sea salt
3 garlic cloves, peeled and roughly chopped

1–2 lime leaves, finely shredded
1 lemon grass stalk, finely sliced
1 in / 2.5 cm piece of fresh galangal or fresh root ginger
4–6 fresh red chillies, deseeded and roughly chopped
1–2 tsp shrimp paste

3–4 chicken breasts
¼ pt / 140 ml coconut milk (see page 41)
2 lime leaves, finely shredded
2 tsp light muscovado or palm sugar

¼ pt / 140 ml chicken stock
2 tbsp fish sauce
1 tbsp dry roasted peanuts, crushed
basil leaves, shredded

First make the curry paste. In a mortar, grind the dry spices together, then add the salt, and grind in the garlic, lime leaves, lemon grass and galangal. The salt will help make grinding easier. Pound in the chillies and the shrimp paste.

Skin and bone the chicken breasts, and cross-hatch the smooth side several times with a sharp knife. Rub the curry paste into the chicken. In a well-seasoned frying pan or wok, fry the chicken on both sides for 2–3 minutes, which will bring out the spice aromas. Remove from the pan. Add the rest of the ingredients, except the peanuts and basil leaves, and half the stock, to the pan. Stir and bring to the boil, put the chicken pieces back, and simmer gently until the chicken is cooked through, adding the remaining stock if necessary. Serve sprinkled with the crushed peanuts and shredded basil leaves.

Grilled Coconut Custard

Serves 8

Whole eggs can be used in this dish, but egg whites alone keep the custard pale.

¾ pt / 430 ml coconut milk (see page 41)	5 egg whites
2 oz / 60 g caster sugar	4 oz / 110 g light muscovado or demerara sugar

Put the milk in a bowl and stir in the caster sugar. Beat in the egg whites, and strain into small lightly oiled ramekins. Place in a bain-marie and bake in the middle of a preheated oven at 180°C / 350°F / Mark 4 for about 20 minutes. Allow the custards to cool and set. Sprinkle with muscovado or demerara sugar, and grill until the sugar melts and caramelizes. Serve warm or chilled.

Variation ∾ Alternatively, the custards can be steamed for 10–15 minutes.

Fish and Shellfish

I wish we could all seek out and support a fishmonger. Fish is very good for us, highly nutritious, low in fat, and, best of all, it is absolutely delicious and quick and easy to cook.

Many people don't realize just how immensely varied fish is in its flavours and textures. Even within the large cod family, for example, there is a difference between cod and haddock. Whiting, of the same family, is delicate, and, although liable to break up easily, is invaluable as a basis for mousses and terrines. Monkfish is dense in texture with a sweet flavour. Mackerel, herring, tuna and other oily fish can take strongly flavoured accompaniments, such as the gooseberry sauce traditionally served with mackerel, the Mediterranean flavours of garlic and tomatoes, or the oriental tones of ginger, soy sauce and sesame oil. As well as all these familiar fish and the whole range of smoked fish, shellfish and freshwater fish, there are new fish coming into our shops all the time, such as the brightly coloured tropical fish from the Seychelles, the cod-like hoki from New Zealand and those from more northern waters, like the Arctic char and the zander or pike-perch with its sweet, firm, white flesh.

Fish is expensive when compared with meat, but in many ways you cannot compare the two sources of protein. The methods of getting them to our table are also very different. Do not be tempted to buy fish being offered for sale at far lower prices than you would expect. Be suspicious, for example, if you see halibut being offered for half its normal price; it might well have been around for some time. My advice is to get to know your fishmonger, and pay good prices for good fish.

I am lucky enough to have a very good fishmonger where I live. Each time I go into his shop, he points out not just the expensive fish, like the Dover sole, the turbot, the halibut and the sea bass, but also the mackerel and the herring, the squid and the lemon sole. He also sells a wide range of the more unusual fish, such as John Dory and red mullet, as well as swordfish steaks and well-trimmed fillet of tuna for his discerning Japanese customers. He sells shellfish and smoked fish in season when it is good, and he cooks his own crabs and lobsters to make sure they are absolutely fresh. I buy wild salmon, in season from spring until the end of August. It is also now possible to find salmon that is farmed on an extensive rather than intensive scale.

It is perhaps, then, hardly surprising that I cook fish two or three times a week. I have used most cooking methods from steaming and poaching to grilling, frying, baking and even serving raw. I love raw fish, and often serve it that way when I am confident that it is really fresh and sound. Do not serve fish raw unless you have this confidence. And, as with meat, when in doubt, don't. Sometimes I serve raw fish with just a little seasoning, so that the texture is little changed and it remains translucent. At other times, I prepare it with chillies and lime juice, as the Ceviche on page 302, in which the marinade ingredients almost 'cook' the fish.

Smoked fish is very popular in our house, and it is something I like to feature when I go abroad as a guest cook. First of all, it pleases expatriates to see kippers on the menu, but also people are surprised at the wide range of smoked fish available. When buying kippers and smoked haddock, I look for undyed fish. It makes no sense to me to colour a piece of smoked haddock with yellow dye derived either from the crocus (crocein) or from the seed of a South American tree (anatto). Kippers, salmon and haddock are all cold smoked while mackerel, trout, Arbroath smokies and others are hot smoked. In principle, hot smoked fish needs no further cooking, but occasionally I will put it in a pie or wrap it in pastry. Smoked salmon is not usually cooked further either, although kippers and smoked haddock are. On the other hand, I have come across a way of just flash grilling or frying thick vertical cuts of smoked salmon which makes it quite delicious. Smoked fish, too, can be turned into a very quick, easy starter by mixing the flesh, minus as many bones as possible, with butter, seasoning and perhaps some chopped onion and yoghurt. Such fish pâtés or pastes are particularly good with fresh wholemeal bread.

STEAMED AND POACHED FISH

Steamed Fish

Serves 6

*A small cod, hake, grilse (small salmon) or salmon trout in season, sea
bass, grey mullet, grouper or rainbow trout can be cooked in this way.
You can change the flavourings if you wish, adding coriander leaves,
star anise, or dried tangerine peel.*

2½–3 lb / 1.10–1.35 kg round fish, gutted but left whole with the head intact
1 bunch spring onions or baby leeks, trimmed
2 in / 5 cm piece fresh root ginger

2–3 garlic cloves, peeled and thinly sliced
3 tbsp soy sauce
2 tbsp good dry sherry or rice wine
1 tbsp toasted sesame oil

Rinse and dry the fish thoroughly. Split the spring onions or leeks lengthways, and lay half of them on an oval plate or dish large enough to take the fish and of a size to fit your steamer. Lay a few slices of ginger and garlic on top of the spring onions or leeks, and put a few slices in the fish. Put the fish in the dish, and sprinkle the remaining ginger and garlic on top. Cover with more spring onions or leeks. Pour over 1 tbsp of soy sauce, and place in a steamer. Steam for 8–12 minutes. Boil up the rest of the soy sauce with the sherry or wine. Remove the fish from the steamer, uncover it, and put the remaining onions or leeks around it. Pour the soy mixture over the fish and sprinkle on the sesame oil. Serve immediately.

Variations ∽ Instead of using ginger, garlic and soy sauce, season the fish with salt and pepper. Then steam it on a bed of washed and trimmed samphire, instead of leeks or spring onions, and serve it with a sauce prepared by heating a little garlic, olive oil, balsamic vinegar and fish stock or the cooking liquor together. Skate is good prepared this way. When cooked, remove the skin and then the long strand of flesh from the cartilage, and arrange these on top of the steamed samphire. Pour the hot sauce over, and serve with steamed new potatoes.

To steam monkfish fillet, season it with salt, pepper and lemon juice, and leave it to stand for 30 minutes before cooking. Cut horizontal slits in the top, and place strips of smoked salmon in these. Then steam on a bed of fresh dill, and serve with a sauce made by bringing lightly seasoned single cream to the boil and stirring in finely chopped dill.

Skate in Brown Butter
(Raie au Beurre Noisette)

Serves 4–6

2 lb / 900 g skate wings
4 oz / 110 g butter
3 tbsp finely chopped parsley

3–4 tbsp capers, thoroughly rinsed if in
  brine
3 tbsp wine vinegar

Cut the skate into four or six pieces, and poach gently in water or a wine and herb flavoured *court bouillon*. When cooked, transfer to a hot serving plate. Pour the water out of the pan, and brown the butter in the pan with the parsley. Pour the hot butter over the fish, and scatter on the capers. Bring the vinegar to the boil in the same pan, and pour it over the fish. Serve immediately. This is also extremely good done with olive oil, although it does not, of course, change colour.

Cold Poached Salmon, Glazed with Cucumber and Fresh Mint Jelly

Serves 6–8

4 lb / 1.80 kg salmon (or salmon
   trout), gutted
2 cucumbers
1 tbsp sea salt

large bunch of mint
4 leaves gelatine *or* 4 tsp powdered
   gelatine

Court Bouillon
1 onion, peeled and finely chopped
2 celery stalks, trimmed and finely
   chopped
1 leek, trimmed and finely chopped
1 carrot, peeled and finely chopped
2 bay leaves

handful of parsley stalks
2 sprigs thyme or tarragon
2 sprigs mint
1 bottle dry white wine
3 pt / 1.70 l water
1 tsp peppercorns
2 tsp sea salt

First make the court bouillon. Put all the ingredients in a saucepan, and simmer for 20 minutes. Strain into a jug, and allow to cool slightly.

Put the fish on the rack in a fish kettle, and pour the court bouillon over it, adding more water to cover if necessary. Bring gently to the point where the surface of the water bubbles just two or three times, then turn the heat down as low as possible. Cover and poach for 35 minutes. Lift the rack out of the kettle, and gently ease the fish on to a large board or platter for serving. Allow to cool before skinning.

While the fish is poaching, prepare the cucumbers by peeling them as thinly as possible with a vegetable peeler. Cut the cucumbers in half lengthways and scoop out the seeds. Slice as thinly as possible, put in a sieve over a bowl, and sprinkle with salt. Leave for 30 minutes, and then rinse and press dry between layers of kitchen paper.

While the fish is cooling, make the mint jelly. Put 1 pt / 570 ml of the fish cooking liquid in a saucepan, and bring to the boil. Put in about 1 oz / 30 g mint, stalks and leaves, keeping the best sprigs for garnish. Simmer for 1 minute, and then remove from the heat. Leave to infuse for 10 minutes, and then strain. Soften the gelatine in a little water or stock, and then stir it into the infused stock until dissolved. Pour into a jug set in a bowl of ice cubes to encourage it to cool as quickly as possible, but do not allow it to set completely. To glaze the salmon and the cucumber, it should be firm, yet still enough of a liquid consistency to be painted on with a pastry brush.

Skin the salmon and blot off any excess moisture. Brush on a layer of jelly, and when it is tacky, begin to arrange the cucumber over the fish to resemble scales. Dip each piece of cucumber into the jelly first. Brush a final layer of jelly over the cucumber scales, and allow to set. Pour the remaining jelly into a shallow dish, and when set, chop it finely. Garnish the platter with sprigs of mint and chopped jelly, together with other decorative edible flowers and herbs.

Variation ⁓ Serve the poached salmon hot with a sauce made by boiling about ¾ pt / 430 ml of the court bouillon until reduced by half, and then stirring in 4 tablespoons of capers and 3 tablespoons of balsamic vinegar; reduce a little more, then gradually stir in cubes of unsalted butter until a creamy sauce is formed.

Brill with Lentils in a Cider Sauce

Serves 4

4 oz / 110 g green lentils, preferably
   Puy lentils
½ pt / 280 ml fresh fish stock
½ pt / 280 ml water
1 oz / 30 g chopped onion
4 oz / 110 g unsalted butter

about 1¼ lb / 570 g fillets of brill or
   other flat white fish
7 fl oz / 200 ml dry cider
salt
freshly ground black pepper
lemon juice

Put the lentils in a saucepan, and add equal quantities of fish stock and water just to cover. Allow to simmer for about 20 minutes until the lentils are almost tender and all the liquid has been absorbed. Meanwhile, soften the onion, without colouring, in 2–3 oz / 60–85 g of the butter in a wide shallow pan. Add the fish fillets, and then pour in the remainder of the fish stock and half the cider. Add just enough water so that the fish is nearly covered with liquid. Bring to the boil, and simmer gently for about 4 minutes, until cooked. Remove the fish from the pan, and keep hot. Add the remaining cider to the liquid in the pan, and boil to reduce to 4 fl oz / 110 ml. Cut the remaining butter into small cubes, and whisk it into the liquid, a few cubes at a time, taking care not to boil. Season to taste with salt, pepper and a touch of lemon juice. Divide the lentils between four plates, and place the fish fillets on top. Coat the fish with the sauce and serve.

Lettuce-Wrapped Fish Fillets
Steamed with Mint

Serves 4

1½ lb / 680 g skinned fish fillets
salt
freshly ground black pepper
juice of ½ lemon
12 large lettuce leaves
handful of mint

Sauce
¼ pt / 140 ml fish stock
2 tbsp dry vermouth
1 oz / 30 g chilled butter, diced

Dry the fillets thoroughly and cut into four pieces. Season lightly on both sides with salt, pepper and lemon juice. Prepare the lettuce leaves by draping them over a large colander, and gently pouring boiling water over them to blanch them. Cool under cold running water, and dry carefully on kitchen paper. Cut out any central ribs that still remain firm and that would make it difficult to roll the leaves. Lay three leaves on the worktop, overlapping slightly. Put a mint leaf in the centre, a fish fillet on top and another mint leaf on top of the fish. Fold the lettuce leaves around the fish, enclosing it completely. Do the same with the remaining fish and lettuce leaves, and place the parcels in a steamer basket. Bring a saucepan or steamer of water to the boil, put in the rest of the mint sprigs, and place the steamer above the water level. Cover tightly and steam for 5–8 minutes, depending on the thickness of the fillets.

To make a sauce to serve with the fish, boil up the stock and vermouth until reduced to a few spoonfuls of shiny syrup. Whisk in the butter, one piece at a time, and pour a little sauce on to each heated dinner plate, alongside the fish parcel.

Variation ∞ Omit the mint, and sprinkle the pieces of fish fillet with a little diced tomato and finely chopped shallot before wrapping them in the lettuce leaves. For the sauce, omit the vermouth, and boil up the fish stock with a little of the juice from the diced tomato. Then stir in some saffron liquor, which is prepared by soaking a pinch of saffron threads in a little hot water or fish stock, and season to taste.

Poached Halibut with Prawns and Sandefjord Sauce

Serves 4

Sandefjord sauce is a classic Norwegian sauce made with cream and butter. I once came back from Norway with a bag of freshly cooked prawns, which I had bought straight from a boat moored in Trondheim harbour. Those and the Sandefjord sauce did wonders for a piece of halibut I cooked the next day.

1–1½ lb / 455–680 g halibut steak
½ lemon
salt
freshly ground black pepper
2–3 pt / 1.15–1.70 l fish stock

Sauce
2½ fl oz / 70 ml whipping cream
4 oz / 110 g unsalted butter, chilled and diced
2 tbsp chopped chives
3 oz / 85 g peeled cooked prawns

Rub the piece of halibut with the cut lemon and lightly season. Put in a deep frying pan or roasting tin, cover with the stock, bring gently to simmering point and hold there for 3 minutes. Turn off the heat, cover the pan, and put on one side while you make the sauce. Bring the cream to the boil, and beat in the diced butter, a little at a time. Whisk the sauce until light and smooth and do not allow it to boil. Just before serving, stir in the chives and prawns. Carefully remove the halibut from the pan, and divide it by removing the skin and the central bone. This gives four even pieces. Serve with the sauce poured over.

Variation ∾ Instead of the Sandefjord sauce, serve the fish with a mushroom and tarragon sauce. To make this, melt 1 oz / 30 g butter in a pan and fry 3 oz / 85 g sliced mushrooms in it. When the mushrooms are soft, stir in a few sprigs of finely chopped tarragon and ½ pt / 280 ml fish stock. Boil until reduced by half, and then add a little lemon juice and seasoning to taste.

GRILLED AND FRIED FISH

Charred Tuna Fish

Serves 6–8

Ideal for summer days when you decide to have a barbecue, tuna fish
is best when just seared on the outside and still raw inside.

1½–2 lb / 680–900 g tuna fish in a
   piece
2 tbsp sherry vinegar
6 tbsp extra virgin olive oil
salt
freshly ground black pepper

Orange Mayonnaise
1 tbsp orange juice
1–2 tsp grated orange zest
¼ pt / 140 ml mayonnaise

Tuna fish is sometimes sold in a thick fillet, and sometimes cut across the bone into a steak. If the latter, this divides neatly into four by removing the central bone and cutting each of the two fillets in half. Cut the fish into even-sized pieces as thick as possible. Six thick chunks cooks far more satisfactorily than twelve neat slices. Brush the fish with the sherry vinegar and olive oil. Season lightly and put to one side while the grill or barbecue heats up. The fish should be cooked at as high a temperature as possible, as quickly as possible, but, of course, cooked through as much or as little as you like. While the tuna is cooking, combine the mayonnaise ingredients. Serve the tuna hot with orange mayonnaise.

Grilled Salmon in Orange Butter Sauce

Serves 4

*Fillets of sea bass, sole or turbot prepared in this way are equally good.
It is important that the fillets are roughly the same shape, size and
thickness.*

2 oranges
1 small onion *or* 2 shallots
salt
freshly ground black pepper
4 salmon fillets, about 8 oz / 230 g
  each, with skin left on

1 oz / 30 g chilled butter, cut into cubes
herbs, watercress, capers or samphire,
  to garnish

Grate the zest from the oranges on to a plate, and squeeze on the orange juice. Peel and thinly slice the onion or shallots and place in a single layer on the plate. Season the salmon fillets very lightly and place, flesh-side down, in the orange and onion marinade. Leave to marinate for 30–40 minutes. Heat the grill. Remove the fillets from the marinade, and place on the grill rack, skin-side up. Grill for 5–8 minutes, depending on the thickness of the fillet and how well done you like fish.

Meanwhile, strain the marinade into a shallow pan and boil until reduced and syrupy. Beat in the cubes of chilled butter, one at a time, and heat through without boiling. Divide the sauce between four heated serving plates and lay a piece of fish alongside it. Garnish with whatever you have available.

Spiced Grilled Skewers of Fish

Serves 4, as a starter

Use monkfish, conger eel and trimmed scallops, if possible. For a main course, serve with brown rice and a salad.

1 lb / 455 g firm-fleshed fish, off the bone
2 tbsp orange or grapefruit juice
1 tbsp orange or grapefruit marmalade
2 tsp sesame oil
1 tsp soy sauce

freshly ground black pepper
¼ tsp ground allspice
¼ tsp ground cardamom
2 tbsp toasted sesame seeds
coriander or parsley, and orange or grapefruit slices or segments, to garnish

Cut the fish into 1 in / 2.5 cm cubes, or leave the scallops whole, if using them. Heat the juice and marmalade together in a saucepan, and then strain it into a bowl. Mix in the sesame oil, soy sauce, seasoning and spices, and stir in the fish until it is well coated. Leave to marinate for 30–40 minutes. Thread the fish on to skewers, and cook under a moderately hot grill for about 8 minutes, turning and basting with marinade from time to time. When done, arrange the skewers on individual plates, sprinkle with the toasted sesame seeds and garnish with herbs and fruit.

Sole à la Meunière

Le Repertoire de la Cuisine, *the indispensable manual for those working in a classical French kitchen, lists nearly 350 ways of preparing sole. Some sound less appealing than others. Sole Archiduc, for example, has the sole poached in Madeira, whisky, port and fish stock. The cooking liquor is reduced, and butter, cream and a* brunoise *of truffles and vegetables are added, and the fish is coated with this sauce. Not all dishes, however, are so rich and complicated. Sole Bordelaise has the sole poached in red wine with shallots, and then coated with the reduced cooking juices. I think, on balance, that sole is at its best cooked as simply as possible, and that* à la meunière *shows it off to perfection. Other flat fish, fish fillets and cutlets can be cooked in the same way.*

2½ fl oz / 70 ml milk
pinch of salt
2 whole sole, 10–12 oz / 280–340 g
    each, skinned, cleaned and
    trimmed

3 tbsp plain flour
freshly ground black pepper
3 oz / 85 g butter
1 tbsp finely chopped parsley or chervil
lemon wedges

Put the milk in a shallow dish with the salt, and dip the fish in it, then in the flour, coating them well. Season lightly with pepper. Heat the butter until hot, but not burning, in a frying pan, and fry the fish on both sides until done to your liking. Serve on heated plates with the butter poured over the fish, some chopped herbs and the lemon.

Pesce al Arancia
(Fish with Orange Sauce)

Serves 2

This is based on soglia al arancia, *which was on the* menu del giorno *one New Year's Day at Ristorante Fini in Modena. Red mullet is my favourite fish for it, although it can be adapted to most fish fillets. The oranges I like best to use are navel oranges or blood oranges. If you can get limes with good skin, try using them instead. In Southern Spain Seville oranges are used; try them in this recipe.*

2 red mullet fillets	salt
2–3 tbsp extra virgin olive oil	freshly ground black pepper
1 navel orange	¼ pt / 140 ml fish stock

Remove any scales left sticking to the fish skin, and larger bones that might come out easily. Brush the fillets on both sides with a little olive oil. Peel off two or three broad strips of zest from the orange, and grate the rest over the fish. Squeeze on some of the juice. Season lightly, and leave it while you cut the zest into long, thin curls. Simmer them in the stock until softened, then drain, reserving the stock. Heat a well-seasoned or non-stick frying pan over a moderate heat, and place the fish fillets, skin side down, in the pan. Cover with a lid, and sweat the fish for about 8 minutes, depending on the thickness. Transfer the fish to warm plates, and put the curls of orange zest on top. Pour the stock into the frying pan, add a little more orange juice, and boil until reduced to a few tablespoons. Whisk in the remaining olive oil, bring to the boil and serve the sauce with the fish.

Pan-fried Salmon Fillets with Basil and Mostarda Mayonnaise

Serves 4

4 pieces of salmon fillet, 5 oz /
   140 g each, skinned
salt

freshly ground black pepper
olive oil or butter

Mayonnaise
1 egg yolk, at room temperature
¼ pt / 140 ml preferred oil for
   mayonnaise
lemon juice or balsamic vinegar
1 tsp mostarda syrup (see p. 176)
½ tsp mustard

salt
freshly ground black pepper
1 piece of crystallized fruit in mostarda
   syrup
shredded basil leaves

First make a mayonnaise by gradually whisking the oil into the egg yoke until it thickens and emulsifies. Season with the lemon juice or vinegar, mostarda syrup, mustard, salt and pepper. Chop the crystallized fruit as finely as possible and stir into the mayonnaise together with the basil. Cover, and put in a cool place until ready to serve.

Season the fish, and cook gently in the oil or butter on both sides until done to your liking. The fish can be served hot, but it is, I think, better at room temperature, served on a plate with salad leaves. Serve the mayonnaise separately.

Variations ⁓ Serve with a tomato vinaigrette, instead of the mayonnaise. Prepare this by mixing 3 peeled, deseeded and finely chopped tomatoes with 2 tablespoons hot sherry vinegar and 4 tablespoons extra virgin olive oil. Bring the mixture to the boil, then remove from the heat, allow to cool sightly, and stir in a few shredded basil leaves before serving with the fish.

You could also prepare a cucumber vinaigrette as an alternative to the mayonnaise. Roughly chop a cucumber and put most of it in a pan with ¼ pt / 140 ml fish stock or white wine, a little salt and pepper and some finely chopped fresh tarragon. Simmer for 10 minutes, cool slightly, and blend with the uncooked cucumber and a little more chopped tarragon. Heat this cucumber liquid with 2 tablespoons sherry vinegar and 4 tablespoons extra virgin olive oil until boiling, and then allow to cool slightly, before adding a little more chopped tarragon and serving with the fish.

Salmon with Apples and Lime

Serves 6

6 escalopes of salmon, 7 oz /
  200 g each
3 crisp, firm dessert apples
6 oz / 170 g unsalted butter
2 oz / 60 g sugar

3 tbsp dry white wine
2–3 limes
salt
freshly ground black pepper
plain flour for dusting

Rinse and dry the salmon and put to one side. Peel, core and thinly slice the apples. Thickly butter an ovenproof dish or cast-iron frying pan, and put the apple slices in it, together with the sugar and white wine. Cook in a preheated oven at 180°C / 350°F / Mark 4 for 10 minutes, and then remove and keep the apples warm.

To make the sauce, decant the apple cooking juices into a saucepan. Peel the zest from the limes and reserve it. Squeeze the fruit, and add 2½ fl oz / 70 ml of the juice to the pan. Cook the liquid over a low heat to reduce slightly, then gradually add most of the remaining butter, a little at a time, whisking it to blend and emulsify the ingredients. Keep the butter sauce warm while you quickly cook the salmon. Lightly season the fillets, and dust with flour. Fry them in the remaining butter for about 5 minutes. Arrange the apple slices on plates with the salmon on top, and spoon over the sauce. Garnish with the reserved lime zest, shredded.

Charentais Salmon with Tarragon Sauce

Serves 4

*Fresh tagliatelle or boiled rice would go well with this recipe, acting as
a foil to the rich fish and unusual sauce.*

4 skinned salmon fillets, 5 oz / 140 g
  each
salt
freshly ground black pepper
1–2 tsp lemon juice

1½ oz / 40 g chilled unsalted butter, cut
  into cubes
2 tsp chopped tarragon leaves
4–5 tbsp Pineau des Charentes
4 sprigs tarragon, to garnish

Lightly season the salmon, and brush with lemon juice. Melt ½ oz / 15 g butter in a frying pan large enough to take the fillets in one layer. Keep the heat low. Put the fish in the pan, cover with a lid and allow the fish to sweat and cook in their own juices for 2–3 minutes. There is no need to turn the fish over. Add the chopped tarragon, re-cover and cook for 2–3 minutes before adding the wine and swirling it round the pan. Remove the fish and arrange on warm plates. Add the butter to the pan juices, a piece at a time, stirring well until it is all amalgamated.

Cod with Mussels and Herbs

Serves 6

3 lb / 1.35 kg mussels
¼ pt / 140 ml dry white wine
6–8 dill or coriander stalks
1 small onion, peeled and finely
   chopped
6 pieces of cod fillet or cod cutlets,
   6–8 oz / 170–230 g each

salt
freshly ground black pepper
12 oz / 340 g leeks
2 oz / 60 g unsalted butter
1 heaped tbsp finely chopped dill or
   coriander
4 tbsp cream *(optional)*

Scrub the mussels under cold running water, and knock off any barnacles with the back of a knife. Discard any mussels that do not close. Rinse the mussels and put them in a large saucepan with the wine, dill or coriander stalks and onion. Put the lid on, and put over a high heat for 2–3 minutes, just sufficient to steam open the mussels. Discard any which remain closed. Strain the cooking juices through a fine sieve and reserve it. When the mussels are cool enough to handle, remove them from their shells and place in a bowl covered with cling film to prevent them from drying out.

Skin the fish fillets or cutlets, and season lightly with salt and pepper. Put to one side while you prepare the leeks. Cut off the roots and the green tops as well as removing the coarse outer layers. Either slice the leeks into thin rings or cut into 3 in / 7.5 cm lengths, split and shred into fine strips. Wash thoroughly to get rid of any soil and then dry on kitchen paper. Melt the butter in a large, heavy frying pan, cover tightly and sweat the leeks until just tender. Push the leeks to one side of the pan, and add the pieces of cod in a single layer. Cover and cook the fish gently until done to your liking. With a fish slice, carefully lift out the pieces of fish, and keep them covered in a warm place. Add the mussel juices to the pan, and boil it up to reduce it somewhat. Stir in the chopped dill or coriander and cream, if using, and cook for 2–3 minutes more. Add the mussels, and let them just heat through before spooning the sauce, leeks and mussels over the cod. Serve immediately.

Variation ∾ Monkfish, haddock, plaice fillets and other white fish are all very good cooked in this way with mussels.

Cod with Parsley Sauce

Serves 4

The sauce in this recipe is enriched and finished with extra virgin olive oil instead of cream or butter. Mashed potatoes are a very good partner for this dish.

4 cod cutlets, 6–8 oz / 170–230 g
  each
salt
freshly ground black pepper
juice of ½ lemon or orange
1–2 tbsp extra virgin olive oil

Sauce
3 garlic cloves, peeled
1 oz / 30 g parsley, roughly chopped
2 tsp lemon or orange juice
1 tsp Dijon mustard
4 tbsp extra virgin olive oil
salt
freshly ground black pepper

Lightly season the fish, squeeze on some lemon or orange juice, and brush with olive oil. Allow it to stand for 10–15 minutes while you start making the sauce. Cut the garlic cloves into two or three pieces and put in a small saucepan with 2–3 tablespoons water. Simmer until the garlic is tender. Stir in the parsley, and let it cook for just 3–4 minutes, retaining its bright colour but becoming tender. Allow to cool slightly, and then blend until smooth. Sieve into a bowl set over a pan of hot water or into bain-marie. Stir in the fruit juice and mustard, and keep the sauce warm while you cook the fish. Using a heavy, lidded sauté or frying pan, cook the fish over a low heat for about 5 minutes, depending on thickness; a little longer may be required. The fish will be lubricated enough to cook in its own juices without burning. Strain fish juices into the parsley purée. Remove the fish from the heat, but keep it covered and in a warm place. Gradually whisk the olive oil into the purée, drop by drop, so that it will emulsify and thicken like a hollandaise sauce. Season lightly, and serve with the fish. If the sauce separates, don't worry; it still tastes very good, even though it might not look quite as it should.

Variations ∾ You can make a watercress or coriander sauce in the same way as the parsley sauce, or one from mixed herbs and spinach, for example.

For a complete change, serve the fish with a red wine sauce. Make this by adding a little finely chopped shallot and 2 glasses of good red wine to the juices left in the pan after removing the cooked fish. Boil fiercely, scraping up any bits stuck to the bottom of the pan, until the wine has reduced by a half. Then gradually stir in 1 oz / 30 g unsalted butter, cut into small pieces. Season, and serve over the fish.

Deep-Fried Mixed Fish and Vegetables

*No other method of cooking can reproduce the crisp, dry, flavoursome
sensation of deep-fried food. Yet the statistics are enough to put
anyone off deep-frying. A half-litre bottle of oil, whether one of the
'baddies' containing saturated fatty acids or one of the 'goodies' rich in
poly or monounsaturated fatty acids, represents 4,500 calories. The
secret, therefore, when deep-frying, is to make sure that most of the fat
stays on the outside and is not absorbed into the food. One of the
ways to do this is to make sure the food is cooked at the right
temperature, and for this a thermometer is useful. Maintain the oil
temperature by frying in small batches and by making sure the food is
completely dry, either by wiping it on kitchen paper or dipping it in
flour first. Flour also helps batter cling to the food, and I like food to
be battered before deep-frying, as this also prevents oil from being
absorbed. Groundnut (peanut) oil, soya oil, sunflower oil, olive oil
and grapeseed oil are all low in saturated fats and are particularly good
for deep-frying because they are stable at temperatures of around
200°C / 400°F.*

use some or all of the following,
 allowing 3–4 oz / 85–110 g
 prepared raw fish and 6 oz / 170 g
 prepared vegetables per person:
squid, cleaned and cut into rings
 (see page 320)
prawns, peeled and deveined
oysters, shucked
monkfish fillet, cut into 1 in /
 2.5 cm cubes
button or cup mushrooms, wiped
courgettes, sliced ¼ in / 0.5 cm
 thick

onion rings
baby leeks, cut into 2 or 3 pieces
broccoli florets
1–1½ pt / 570–850 ml oil for frying (see
 note above for type of oil)
flour for coating
lemon wedges, to serve

Light Batter
1½ oz / 40 g cornflour
1 egg
good pinch of salt
6 fl oz / 170 ml soda water

To make the batter, whisk all the ingredients together and use immediately.
Pour the oil into a wok or deep-frying pan, and heat it to 185°C / 365°F. While the
oil is heating, dip the prepared fish and vegetables first in the flour and then in the
batter. Shake off excess batter, and deep-fry in the hot oil in small batches for 2–3
minutes. Drain on kitchen paper, and serve immediately with lemon wedges.

Variation ∽ Instead of the lemon wedges, serve with a dipping sauce of
crushed garlic and ginger, soy sauce, sesame oil and rice vinegar.

Moroccan-Style Roast Salmon with Saffron–Onion Compote and Preserved Lemon

Serves 6

Rice, bulgar wheat and couscous are all excellent partners for this spicy fish dish. Whichever you choose would be best prepared before the dish and kept warm over steam. The flavour of fresh mint is right with the other flavours in this dish and sprigs of it could be used to garnish the plates.

1½–2 lb / 680–900 g salmon fillet
1 tsp cumin seeds
1 tsp coriander seeds
seeds of 6 cardamom pods
2 tsp coarse sea salt
½ tsp black peppercorns

4 tbsp extra virgin olive oil
2 large mild onions, peeled and thinly
   sliced
pinch of saffron threads, soaked in 2
   tbsp hot water
6 tbsp chopped preserved lemons

With a pair of tweezers, remove any fine bones from the salmon, and cut it into six even-sized pieces. In a small, heavy frying pan, lightly toast the spices, including the salt and pepper, for 2–3 minutes, and then grind in a mortar or clean coffee grinder. (This is a very nice spiced salt mixture to have on hand, and you may prefer to make it in larger quantities and store it.)

Brush the pieces of salmon all over with oil, and season them with the spice mixture. Put to one side while you prepare the onions. Heat the rest of the oil, and cook the onions until soft, wilted, much reduced and just beginning to caramelize. Add the saffron and soaking liquid, and cook just until the water has evaporated. Cover a baking sheet with foil, brush it lightly with oil, and lay the salmon on it; skin-side up. Preheat the oven to 200°C / 400°F / Mark 6, and roast the salmon in the *top* of the oven for about 8 minutes. Timing will, to a large extent, depend upon the thickness of the fish. The skin should be an attractive, golden brown and the flesh still slightly translucent. Transfer to heated serving plates, and serve with the saffron onion compote and the preserved lemon.

Baked Sea Bream

Serves 4

*This is a dish we like to prepare at my parents' house in Gozo, where
fennel grows wild in great abundance all over the island.*

2 bream, 1½ lb / 680 g each
extra virgin olive oil
sea salt
freshly ground black pepper

1 onion or 2 shallots, peeled and thinly
  sliced
fennel tops
2½ fl oz / 70 ml good dry white wine
splash of Pernod *(optional)*

Scale and clean the fish. Brush with olive oil, inside and out, and season lightly.
Put a few slices of onion or shallot in the bottom of an oiled ovenproof dish. Put
the fish on top with a few fennel sprigs tucked into the cavities and around the fish.
Cover with more onion rings, and splash on the wine and a little more olive oil.
Cover with foil and bake in a preheated oven at 180°C / 350°F / Mark 4 for about
30 minutes, depending on the thickness of the fish. As soon as the dish comes out
of the oven, remove the foil and sprinkle with Pernod, if using. The alcohol will
quickly evaporate, but the anise scent and flavour will remain.

Baked Mackerel with Fennel and Gooseberry Sauce

Serves 4

4 mackerel, cleaned and gutted,
  heads and backbones removed
extra virgin olive oil
salt
freshly ground black pepper

4 tbsp cider
8 oz / 230 g gooseberries
1 fennel bulb, trimmed and chopped
2 oz / 60 g butter, cut into small cubes

Brush the fish with olive oil, season it and sprinkle it with cider. Place in an
oiled ovenproof dish and bake in a preheated oven at 180°C / 350°F / Mark 4 for
about 20 minutes. Meanwhile, make the sauce by cooking the gooseberries and
fennel until soft in just enough water to stop them burning. When soft, sieve the
purée into a clean saucepan. Drain any cooking juices from the fish into the sauce,
and reheat. Beat in the butter until well mixed, and serve with the fish.

Sardines in Vine Leaves

Serves 4–6

12 sardines

24–36 vine leaves, depending on
  size

2–3 tbsp mustard

salt

freshly ground black pepper

6 tbsp olive oil

Make sure all the scales have been removed from the sardines. Blanch the vine leaves in boiling water for 2 minutes, refresh them under cold running water, drain and pat them dry. Spread a little mustard on each sardine and season lightly. Wrap each sardine in vine leaves, and arrange them in a single layer in a lightly oiled ovenproof dish. Sprinkle the rest of the olive oil over the parcels, and bake in a preheated oven at 190°C / 375°F / Mark 5 for about 25 minutes. Serve hot, cold or, perhaps best of all, just tepid with slices of sweet onion and tomato.

Cod Steaks with Bacon and Red Wine Sauce

Serves 4

8 very thin rashers of smoked or
  unsmoked streaky bacon,
  derinded

4 cod steaks, skinned

4 tbsp extra virgin olive oil

freshly ground black pepper

¼ pt / 140 ml red wine

Wrap the bacon rashers around the cod steaks and secure with cocktail sticks. Brush the fish all over with olive oil, and use the rest to oil an enamelled gratin dish. Lightly season the fish with pepper, and place in the dish. Pour on the red wine. Bake in a preheated oven at 190°C / 375°F / Mark 5 for 10–15 minutes, depending on the thickness of the steaks and how well done you like your fish. Remove from the oven, and transfer the fish to a warm serving dish. Cover and keep it warm while you boil up and reduce the cooking juices to make the sauce. Serve separately or poured around the fish, as you wish.

Baked Hake with Green Sauce

Serves 4

Once when I cooked this, I served it with steamed spinach and mashed potatoes. The dish has a slightly Basque feel to it and a fruity Jurançon Sec 1990 is the perfect accompaniment, as it is also to the creamy blue cheese from St Agur, which followed the dish.

4 hake cutlets, 6–7 oz / 170–200 g
   each
extra virgin olive oil
Sauce
3 spring onions, trimmed and sliced
8 mint leaves
small bunch of coriander (about
   1 oz / 30 g)
parsley sprigs
2–3 sprigs lemon thyme

1 lemon grass stalk, trimmed and thinly
   sliced
piece of green chilli *(optional)*
2–3 garlic cloves, peeled and chopped
½ tsp coarse sea salt
freshly ground black pepper
pinch of sugar
1 tbsp lemon juice
2 tbsp extra virgin olive oil
1–2 tbsp warm water

First make the sauce. Put the spring onions in a food processor or mortar, together with the mint leaves, coriander leaves stripped from the stems, parsley and lemon thyme. Add the lemon grass, chilli (if using), garlic, salt, pepper and sugar. Pound or process until you have a dark green mass. Blend in the lemon juice, oil and water to make a sauce-like paste.

Brush an ovenproof dish with olive oil, and spoon a little sauce over the base. Place the fish on top, brush with oil, and spread the rest of the sauce over the fish. Bake in a preheated oven at 180°C / 350°F / Mark 4 for about 12 minutes, depending on the thickness of the fish; small thick cutlets will take longer than thin broad cutlets.

Cod Fillet with Beetroot Sauce

Serves 2

2 thick pieces cod fillet, 6–7 oz /
  170–200 g each
2 tbsp olive oil
salt
freshly ground black pepper
2 garlic cloves
4 cardamom pods
fresh chervil, coriander or flat-
  leaved parsley, to garnish

Sauce
1 small onion, peeled and sliced
1 tbsp olive oil
½ stick celery stalk, trimmed and thinly
  sliced
2 oz / 60 g beetroot, peeled and diced
2 oz / 60 g ripe tomatoes, peeled,
  deseeded and roughly chopped
6 tbsp white wine
salt
freshly ground black pepper

First make the sauce. Gently fry the onion in the olive oil, then add the other
vegetables and pour on the wine. Simmer, uncovered, until the vegetables are
tender, then make a purée in a blender or food processor, and sieve into a clean
saucepan. Season to taste.

Skin the fish fillets and brush them all over with olive oil. Use the rest to lightly
oil an ovenproof dish, and lay the fillets flat in the dish. Crush the salt, pepper,
garlic and cardamom pods together, and sprinkle this mixture over the cod fillets.
Cover with foil or greaseproof paper and bake in a preheated oven at 180°C /
350°F / Mark 4 for 8–10 minutes.

Pour off any cooking juices from the fish into the sauce, and then gently heat it.
Spoon the hot sauce on to heated dinner plates, lay a fish fillet on top, and garnish
with the chervil, coriander or parsley.

Salmon Steaks with Fennel Stuffing and Saffron Sauce

Serves 4

1 fennel bulb, about 8 oz / 230 g, trimmed and sliced

3 shallots or 1 medium-sized onion, peeled and finely chopped

2 oz / 60 g unsalted butter

½ pt / 280 ml fish stock

pinch of saffron threads

¼ pt / 140 ml good dry white wine

4 salmon steaks, about 6 oz / 170 g each, 1½ in / 4 cm thick

3 tbsp double cream

Cook the fennel and shallots or onion in half the butter in a small saucepan until soft. Pour a tablespoon or so of fish stock into an egg cup, and soak the saffron in it. Boil the remaining fish stock and the wine together until reduced by two thirds. Butter an ovenproof dish, and lay the salmon steaks in it. Season them lightly and cover with buttered paper. Bake in a preheated oven at 180°C / 350°F / Mark 4 for 10–15 minutes. Remove from the oven and carefully take out the central bone from each salmon steak. Fill the cavities with the fennel mixture. Pour the cream and saffron liquid into the reduced wine and stock, and bubble until syrupy. Spoon this over the salmon steaks and then brown them quickly under a hot grill before serving.

Salmon or Sea Trout with Redcurrants

Serves 6

6 pieces of centre-cut fillet of sea
   trout or salmon, 5 oz / 140 g each
1 leek, trimmed and finely chopped
½ cucumber, finely chopped
1 oz / 30 g parsley, finely chopped
3 small carrots, peeled and
   shredded

salt
1–2 tbsp chopped mint
5 oz / 140 g redcurrants, stripped from
   their stalks
dry white wine
1 oz / 30 g unsalted butter
sprigs of mint, to garnish

Skin the fish, and remove any fine bones with a pair of tweezers. Mix together
the leek, cucumber, parsley and carrot. Place the vegetables in a baking dish, and
sprinkle with salt and chopped mint. Scatter over the redcurrants, and add enough
wine to cover about three-quarters of the vegetables. Place the fish on top, dot with
butter, cover with foil, and bake in a preheated oven at 200°C / 400°F / Mark 6 for
about 15 minutes. Serve garnished with mint sprigs.

Baked Salmon Trout with Orange Butter and Mint

Serves 6

*This is very good served with new potatoes, boiled or steamed in their
skins and dressed in a little walnut oil and orange juice.*

6 pieces of skinned salmon trout
   fillet, 6 oz / 170 g each
3 oz / 85 g unsalted butter
salt
freshly ground black pepper
12 sprigs mint

grated zest of 1 orange and 1 tbsp
   orange juice
1 tbsp finely chopped preserved
   kumquats or peel from coarse-cut
   marmalade

Trim the pieces of fillet to a neat shape, and remove any bones. Use a little of
the butter to grease an ovenproof dish. Lightly season the fish fillets, and place
them in a single layer in the dish with a mint leaf under each one. Reserve six leaves
or sprigs for decoration. Mix the rest of the butter with the orange zest, juice and

finely chopped preserved kumquats or orange peel. Spread the mixture over the fish, place another mint leaf on top of each fillet, and cover with foil or buttered paper. Bake in a preheated oven at 180°C / 350°F / Mark 4 for 10–15 minutes. Remove the foil or paper, and the wilted mint leaves, from the top of the fish. Spoon the cooking juices over the fish and garnish with mint before serving.

Mousseline of Fish with Fresh Tomato Sauce

Serves 1

Any white fish can be used, such as coley, cod or haddock. If you are feeling extravagant, use sole, turbot, hake or halibut. Parsley or watercress sauce can replace the tomato sauce if preferred.

½ oz / 15 g butter	salt
2 tsp plain flour	freshly ground black pepper
2 tbsp double cream	squeeze of lemon juice
2 tbsp fish stock	2 eggs, separated
3 oz / 85 g fish fillet, skinned	1 tbsp fresh tomato sauce

Melt the butter in a small, heavy saucepan, add the flour and stir until smooth. Pour on the cream and fish stock and cook until smooth and free from lumps, stirring continuously. When the mixture is thick and leaves the sides of the pan, remove it from the heat. Cut the fish fillet into pieces, and put it in a food processor with the seasoning, lemon juice, egg yolks and thick sauce. Process until smooth. Rub the mixture through a fairly fine wire sieve into a bowl. (This is a somewhat tedious process but necessary for a smooth, velvety texture to the mousseline.) Beat the egg whites until stiff, and fold into the fish mixture. Lightly butter a small soufflé dish, timbale or other ovenproof dish and half-fill with the mixture. Cover with a circle of greaseproof paper, and cook in a bain-marie in a preheated oven at 180°C / 350°F / Mark 4, or on the hob for 18–20 minutes, until risen and firm to the touch. Remove from the heat, lift the dish out of the water, and allow the mousseline to stand and settle for a minute or two. Turn it out on to a heated plate and pour the tomato sauce around it before serving.

Turbans of Sole with Dill Mousseline and Lime Sauce

Serves 4

4 fillets from a 1½ lb / 680 g Dover
  sole, skinned
2 oz / 60 g butter
1 plaice, or whiting fillet, about
  6 oz / 170 g, skinned
2 tbsp chopped dill
6 tbsp double cream or crème
  fraîche

½ pt / 280 ml well-flavoured fish stock
juice and finely shredded zest of 1 lime
salt
freshly ground black pepper
chopped chives *(optional)*

Trim the sole fillets to a neat shape. Thickly butter four small ramekins or ovenproof moulds, and line them with the sole fillets, pressing well to the side. Put any sole trimmings together with the plaice or whiting fillet, dill and 4 tablespoons of the cream into a food processor. Process until smooth, and rub through a sieve. Divide the mixture between the four ramekins and tap them sharply to settle the mixture. Cover with a sheet of foil or buttered paper and stand in ½ in / 1 cm hot water in a roasting tin. Cook in the top half of a preheated oven at 180°C / 350°F / Mark 4 for about 15 minutes, until just set to the touch. Remove the ramekins from the oven and keep them warm while you make the sauce. Carefully pour the cooking liquid from the ramekins into a shallow saucepan, and add the fish stock and the rest of the cream. Boil to reduce to a small amount of creamy concentrated sauce, then add some very finely shredded lime zest, lime juice and seasoning to taste. Add some chopped chives, if you wish.

Carefully turn the turbans of sole out on to heated dinner plates, pour on a little sauce, garnish with dill, lime and chives, and serve immediately.

Variations ﹋ I like to put a spoonful of fresh crab meat in the mousseline, and use the broken-up crab claw shells in the stockpot for an extra intense and rich version of this dish.

The turbans can also be made in individual ring moulds, and when turned out on to a plate, the centre filled with more prawns.

A large mould can also be used for 6–8 servings, in which case double the quantities which you use.

Fillets of Sole with Mushroom Stuffing

Serves 4, as a starter; 2 as a main course

4 fillets from a 1½ lb / 680 g Dover
  sole, skinned
salt
freshly ground black pepper
6 oz / 170 g button mushrooms
  wiped
2 shallots or 1 small onion, peeled
  and roughly chopped

1 garlic clove, peeled
1 tbsp finely chopped parsley
¼ pt / 140 ml fish stock or good white
  wine
a little freshly grated nutmeg

Season the fish lightly and set aside in a cool place. Put the mushrooms, shallots or onion and garlic into a food processor and chop very finely without making a purée of them. Cook the vegetables in a frying pan (preferably non-stick), moistening them with a little stock, if necessary, to stop them sticking. When cooked, allow to cool slightly, then stir in the parsley and season to taste. Lightly oil an ovenproof dish. Place one of the sole fillets, smooth-side up, on a work surface, and place a quarter of the mushroom mixture on one half of it. Fold over the other half and place it carefully in the oiled dish. Repeat with the other three fillets and the remaining mushroom mixture. Cover the dish with foil and bake in a preheated oven at 220°C / 425°F / Mark 7 for 8 minutes. Meanwhile, boil the stock or wine until syrupy and reduced to 3–4 tablespoons. Remove the fish from the oven, and carefully drain the cooking juices into the reduced sauce without letting the mushroom filling escape. Put the fish on individual plates. Season the sauce, strain it over each of the fish fillets, grate a little fresh nutmeg on top, and pop under a very hot grill for just long enough for the glaze to brown a little. Serve hot.

Variation ❧ Lemon sole or plaice can be used instead of Dover sole.

Baking en Papillote

Fish cooked *en papillote* or *al cartoccio* is found on fancy French and Italian menus, but, in fact, paper-bag cookery is not at all difficult. It requires the minimum of utensils and equipment – simply an oven, a flat baking sheet and greaseproof paper or baking parchment. Sometimes foil is used, but I do not like the sound of metal cutlery on foil, and would not recommend it. Because the food cooks in its own juices and vapours, this method of cooking is essentially another way of steaming, and is therefore a very healthy way of preparing food.

As with most simple cooking techniques, it works best with good quality, fresh ingredients that will taste of themselves. Rich, elaborate sauces have no place here. Anything sharp, pointed or awkward in shape will not do either. Choose fish fillets rather than whole fish. Remember, too, that this is not like a casserole. You cannot remove the lid and add a little more wine or seasoning. Everything must be wrapped up in the parcel at the beginning, so that the scent and flavour is only released as you open up the parcel just before eating its contents.

Fresh sardines that have been descaled, gutted, and stripped of their backbone; pieces of cod, haddock and salmon fillet; and skinned fillets of plaice, sole, brill and red mullet are excellent baked *en papillote*. Simply cut out greaseproof paper circles, about 12 in / 30.5 cm in diameter, and brush them with olive oil or melted butter. Place the fish on one half of each circle, and sprinkle it with lemon or lime juice, seasoning and a little more olive oil or melted butter. Fold the paper circles over to enclose the fish, folding and twisting the edges together to make a tight seal. Place the parcels on a baking sheet, and bake in a preheated oven at 180°C / 350°F / Mark 4 for 8–10 minutes. Serve immediately on heated dinner plates, allowing each person to open their parcel themselves.

Extra flavourings and vegetables can be added. Try adding a little white wine or fish stock or a few chopped spring onions or some herbs. Add these, together with matchstick strips of courgette and finely chopped, peeled and deseeded tomato, to a parcel of brill fillet, or add thin slices of parboiled potato and finely shredded cabbage to a parcel of red mullet smeared with basil butter. Thinly sliced or diced parboiled potato is also good with rainbow trout fillets; roll each fillet around a spoonful of a mixture of finely chopped Parma ham and sage leaves before placing in the parcel. Also try fillet of wild salmon with some finely shredded leek and thin slices of parboiled turnip mixed with crème fraîche and a little chopped dill.

FISH PIES AND STEWS

Fish and Potato Pie

Serves 4

2–2½ lb / 900 g–1.10 kg potatoes,
  peeled
6–8 garlic cloves, peeled
salt
freshly ground black pepper
3 tbsp olive oil
2 lb / 900 g mussels

12 oz / 340 g undyed smoked haddock
  fillet, thinly sliced
2 ripe tomatoes, sliced
¼ pt / 140 ml whipping cream or thick
  plain yoghurt
finely chopped parsley

Boil the potatoes and garlic together until soft. Drain and mash them with salt
and pepper to taste, and most of the olive oil. Use the rest of the olive oil to brush
a fairly shallow ovenproof dish. While the potatoes are cooking, scrub the mussels,
tug off their beards, and knock off any barnacles with the back of a knife. Discard
any mussels that remain open. Rinse the mussels thoroughly and put them in a
saucepan. Cover tightly and steam over a high heat for about 3 minutes, until the
mussels open. Discard any that remain closed. Drain the mussels and strain the
cooking liquor through a fine sieve. When the mussels are cool enough to handle,
remove them from their shells and put to one side. Spread half the mashed potato
over the bottom of the oiled dish, and arrange slices of smoked haddock down one
side and the mussels down the other. Top with the rest of the mashed potatoes,
and arrange the tomatoes slices on top. Whisk the cream or yoghurt with 3–4
tablespoons of the mussel liquor, and pour it over the pie. Bake in a preheated
oven at 180°C / 350°F / Mark 4 for 25–30 minutes. Scatter with chopped parsley
and serve.

Artichoke and Seafood Pie

Serves 4–6

1½ lb / 680 g Jerusalem artichokes
1 oz / 30 g plain flour
½ tsp salt
¼ tsp freshly ground black pepper
2 oz / 60 g butter
4 oz / 110 g mushrooms, wiped
8 oz / 230 g peeled prawns
6 scallops

1 lb / 455 g firm white fish, such as
    conger eel, monkfish or coley
1 tbsp finely chopped parsley
4 tbsp dry white wine
6 oz / 170 g shortcrust or puff pastry
milk, to glaze
4–5 tbsp cream (*optional*)

Scrub the artichokes and parboil them in their skins for 10 minutes. Meanwhile, season the flour with salt and pepper. Drain the artichokes, and when cool enough to handle, peel them, cut them in half or quarters, depending on size, and roll them in the seasoned flour. Use half the butter to grease a pie dish, and put the artichokes in the bottom. Lay the mushrooms and prawns on top of the artichokes. Rinse the scallops carefully, and remove the thin black intestine encircling them and the white muscle pad. Cut in half, if they are large. Put into the pie dish. Skin and bone the fish, dry it thoroughly, and cut it into 1 in / 2.5 cm cubes. Add it to the pie, sprinkle with parsley and white wine and dot with the remaining butter. Roll out the pastry and use to cover the pie, trimming and sealing the edges. Roll out the pastry trimmings and use to decorate the pie, if liked. Make a pencil-sized hole in the pastry, and keep it open by inserting a short roll of foil or greaseproof paper (or use a pastry funnel). Brush the pastry with milk, and bake the pie in a preheated oven at 200°C / 400°F / Mark 6 for 10 minutes, and then at 180°C / 350°F / Mark 4 for 15–20 minutes. Remove the pie from the oven, and take out the paper roll. If using cream, carefully pour it into the hole, and return the pie to the oven for a few minutes for the sauce to reheat. Serve hot.

Variation ⌁ Use potatoes instead of artichokes, and omit the scallops and mushrooms, but use an extra 8 oz / 230 g white fish. Sprinkle the cubes of white fish with a little orange juice, and then season with salt, pepper and paprika, before putting into the pie dish.

Salmon and Saffron Pie

Serves 4–6

1½ lb / 680 g wild salmon fillet
   from the thick end, skinned
1 tsp caster sugar
1 tsp ground cumin
1 tsp ground mixed spice
½ tsp ground cardamom
½ tsp freshly ground black pepper
½ tsp sea salt
½ tsp ground ginger
12 oz / 340 g shortcrust or rough
   puff pastry

2 tbsp couscous
1 large apple
juice of ½ lemon
3 oz / 85 g sultanas or seedless raisins
   (optional)
2 oz / 60 g butter
beaten egg yolk and milk, to glaze
good pinch of saffron threads
½ pt / 280 ml single cream
2 eggs

Remove as many bones as you can from the fish and cut it into 1½ in / 4 cm cubes. Mix together the sugar, spices and seasoning, and use to coat the salmon. Roll out the pastry, and use half of it to line a pie dish, about 9 in / 23 cm in diameter. Scatter the couscous over the base. Peel, core and slice the apple paper thin, dip it into lemon juice mixed with water to stop it browning, and then blot on kitchen paper. Use half the slices to line the base of the pie dish. Place the salmon pieces on top, and scatter the dried fruit in the spaces between, if using. Grate the lemon zest over the salmon, and top with the remaining apple slices. Dot with the butter. Roll out the remaining pastry and use to cover the pie making sure the edges are well sealed. Use any pastry trimmings to decorate the pie. Cut a small hole in the top, and keep it open with a roll of foil or greaseproof paper (or use a pastry funnel). Brush with beaten egg and milk, place the pie on a baking sheet, and bake in a preheated oven at 180°C / 350°F / Mark 4 for 20 minutes.

Meanwhile, infuse the saffron in a little boiling water, mix it with the cream, and beat in the eggs. Remove the pie from the oven, and turn the heat up to 200°C / 400°F / Mark 6. Remove the roll of foil or paper and carefully pour the saffron custard mixture into the pie, stopping when it shows signs of overflowing. Return the pie to the oven for 10–15 minutes to set the custard.

Variation ∽ If you do not like the combination of fruit with savoury food, use chopped and fried mushrooms instead of the raisins, and sorrel leaves in place of the apple.

Seafood Lasagne

The fish filling for this dish cooks rather more quickly than a meat filling would, so you need to precook the lasagne for slightly longer than you would normally. It is also a dish which can adapt itself to suit your pocket and your fishmonger. I have served it as the main course at a dinner party using scallops, mussels, prawns and monkfish. Cod or haddock would work well because they are firm-fleshed fish; whiting fillets would simply break up and go soft. Turbot or sole would be a treat, but I would hesitate to use such fine, delicately flavoured fish in this way. Oilier fishes, such as mackerel and herring, would not be as successful. Whatever I use, I always add some shellfish – prawns, mussels, scallops – for the extra flavour and slightly different texture.

2 oz / 60 g butter
1 tsp salt
1 tbsp oil
12 oz / 340 g lasagne sheets, dried, fresh or homemade

2–2½ lb / 900 g–1.10 kg prepared fish and shellfish (see above)
1½ pt / 850 ml thick béchamel sauce made with fish stock, cream or milk

Butter very liberally a rectangular ovenproof dish. (I use an old, rough, glazed, deep earthenware dish which does the job perfectly.) Bring a large saucepan of water to the boil, and add the salt and oil to stop the pasta sticking. Drop in the lasagne sheets, two or three at a time (not more, as they may stick together), and cook for 8 minutes if fresh, 6 minutes if freshly homemade, or according to the directions on the packet, plus 2 more minutes, if dried. Drain and set aside. Cut the fish into chunks of about 1 in / 2.5 cm. Dry very thoroughly, as most fish gives off quite a lot of liquid while it cooks.

Spread a few spoonfuls of béchamel sauce on the bottom of the prepared dish, and cover with a layer of lasagne. Put a layer of fish on the lasagne, and cover this with more sauce and another layer of lasagne. Continue until you have used up all the fish and all the lasagne. You may like to keep the different fish in separate layers or mix it all together. The top layer should be the last of the béchamel. Cook towards the top of a preheated oven at 200°C / 400°F / Mark 6 for 30–40 minutes, until brown and bubbling on top. Serve at once.

Fish Stew

Serves 6

Use a mixture of firm-fleshed fish, such as halibut, conger eel, or monkfish. Pieces of salmon can be added, as well as a mixture of shellfish, such as fresh mussels, scallops and prawns.

1 tbsp olive oil
3 leeks (white parts only), trimmed,
    sliced and cleaned
1 celery stalk, trimmed and sliced
6 garlic cloves, peeled and crushed
1 lb / 455 g ripe tomatoes, peeled,
    deseeded and roughly chopped
1 orange

1 tsp fennel seeds
1½ pt / 850 ml fish stock
3 lb / 1.35 kg prepared fish and shellfish
4 tbsp dry vermouth
salt
freshly ground black pepper
1–2 tbsp chopped parsley, chives,
    chervil or coriander

Heat the olive oil in a large heavy saucepan or flameproof casserole, and sweat the leeks, celery and garlic until soft but not brown. Add the tomatoes, and cook until most of their juice has evaporated. Carefully pare off two or three long curls of orange zest, then cut the orange in half, and squeeze out the juice. Put the juice and peel in the pan together with the fennel seeds and a little of the fish stock. Cover and cook gently for 15 minutes. Where necessary, cut the fish into 2 in / 5 cm chunks, and arrange all of it on top of the vegetables. Pour on the vermouth and remaining fish stock. Bring gently to the boil, then simmer for 2–3 minutes until the fish is just cooked. Season to taste, stir in the herbs, and serve immediately with plenty of crusty bread.

Spicy Fish Stew with Couscous

Serves 6

Do not let my mention of dried persimmons in the fish stew put you off trying this marvellous recipe. I used them because I had them. Rather than substitute dried apricots or peaches, which have a very pronounced flavour, I would use dried apples or pears, or simply a couple of handfuls of sultanas or seedless raisins. Almonds can be substituted for the pinenuts. If you cannot get grouper, use monkfish or the thick end of a cod fillet – something with plenty of depth, texture and density. For the spice mixture, I have not been too specific, since it is a matter of taste. I like to use plenty of cardamom and cumin, but you might prefer to use more cinnamon and cloves. You can make up the mixture from ground spices, or pound your own with a pestle and mortar. Chillies, too, are a matter of personal preference.

ground spice mixture, made up of 1 tbsp of some, or all, of the following, in proportions to suit your palate: cardamom, coriander, cumin, black cumin, cinnamon, cloves

2 tbsp olive oil

1 onion, peeled and thinly sliced

1–2 green or red chillies, deseeded and sliced

1 aubergine, trimmed and diced

1 celery stalk, trimmed and thinly sliced

8 oz / 230 g courgettes, trimmed and thickly sliced

4 oz / 110 g dried fruit, such as persimmons

1 tbsp chopped preserved lemon (*optional*)

1 pt / 570 ml fish stock

8 oz / 230 g couscous

a few mint leaves, shredded

a few coriander or basil leaves, shredded

1 tsp grated fresh root ginger

1–2 tsp sugar

8 oz / 230 g cooked, drained chick peas

3 oz / 85 g pinenuts or flaked almonds

1½–2 lb / 680–900 g firm fish fillets, cubed

mint, olives and toasted almonds, to garnish (*optional*)

Fry the spice mixture in the olive oil in a large sauté pan or wok for a few minutes, and then stir in the onion and chillies. Add the aubergine, celery and courgettes to the pan together with the dried fruit, lemon and half the stock. Cook for about 20 minutes. Put the couscous on to steam (see page 214), and add the shredded herbs, ginger, sugar, chick peas and nuts to the stew. Cook for a further

10–15 minutes, adding the remaining stock. Put the fish pieces on top, replace the lid, and let the fish just cook through, which will take 6–8 minutes, depending on the thickness.

Transfer the stew to a heated serving dish, garnish with mint, olives and toasted almonds, if you wish, and serve with the steamed couscous.

Variation ➤ Another way to present this dish is to spoon the cooked couscous into an oiled ring mould, press it down, then turn it out on to a heated platter, and spoon the fish stew into the centre.

SALTED AND SMOKED FISH

Salt Cod Cooked in Olive Oil and Sherry Vinegar

Serves 6

This was inspired by Pierre Roudgé at Vanel in Toulouse. Preparation should start at least the day before.

1½ lb / 680 g thick fillet of salt cod
1 lb / 455 g new potatoes
8 oz / 230 g ripe tomatoes
¼ pt / 140 ml extra virgin olive oil

2–3 tbsp sherry vinegar
flat-leaved parsley, chopped
freshly ground black pepper

Soak the salt cod for *at least 24 hours* and up to 48 hours in several changes of cold water. Drain, put it in a shallow saucepan and cover with fresh cold water. Over a low heat, bring the water just to the point where the surface breaks. Remove from the heat, and put to one side. The fish will continue to cook without toughening. Meanwhile, scrub and boil the potatoes until tender, then drain. Peel, deseed and chop the tomatoes. Drain the fish and flake it. Heat the olive oil in a frying pan over a moderate heat. Turn the fish in the olive oil until well coated, and add the sherry vinegar, potatoes, tomatoes and some of the parsley. Bring to the boil, season with pepper (the dish is unlikely to need further salting), and serve garnished with the rest of the parsley.

Petits Piments Farcis à la Morue de Chez Ithurria

(Red Pimentos Stuffed with Salt Cod)

Serves 4

I like to serve these with a few salad leaves and a simple warm vinaigrette made by heating some more extra virgin olive oil and whisking in some lemon juice or a balsamic or sherry vinegar.

12 oz / 340 g salt cod, soaked for 24–48 hours
4 garlic cloves, peeled and crushed
2–3 tbsp extra virgin olive oil
10 small red pimentos

2 oz / 60 g plain flour
¾ pt / 430 ml boiling milk
salt
freshly ground black pepper
freshly grated nutmeg

Poach the salt cod in water until tender. Drain, reserving the cooking liquid. Sweat the garlic in the olive oil, then add two of the pimentos, finely chopped. Stir in the flour, and make a roux. Gradually add the milk to make a thick binding sauce, using some of the cooking liquid if necessary. Pound the salt cod to a cream, and mix into the sauce. Season to taste with salt, pepper and nutmeg. Cut the tops off the remaining pimentos and scoop out the seeds and membranes. Stuff the pimentos with the salt cod mixture, cover and refrigerate overnight to let them set. When ready to cook, steam for 8–10 minutes and serve.

Smoked Mackerel Pâté

Makes 1 lb / 455 g

12 oz / 340 g undyed smoked mackerel
4 oz / 110 g softened unsalted butter or sunflower margarine
1 orange, lemon or lime

2 shallots or 2 spring onions, finely chopped
freshly grated nutmeg
freshly ground black pepper

Remove the skin and bones from the mackerel, and place it in a food processor or bowl and combine it with the softened butter or margarine. Grate some of the citrus zest into the mixture, then squeeze in about 2 tablespoons of citrus juice.

Add the shallots or spring onions and spices to the smoked mackerel mixture, and make sure it is thoroughly blended. Pack into small ramekins or jars and refrigerate until required, covered with an airtight lid, foil, cling film or a layer of melted butter to seal it.

Smoked Eel Terrine from Beddingtons

Serves 6

This is based on a version served at Beddingtons in Amsterdam. Jean Beddington serves it with a roasted red pepper salad, dressed in a little red wine vinegar and olive oil. As she says, this gives a nice complementary smoky sweetness with the eel.

9 oz / 255 g smoked eel fillets

Filling
12 oz / 340 g smoked eel fillets
9 fl oz / 260 ml fish stock

6 leaves gelatine *or* 6 tsp powdered
    gelatine
salt
freshly ground white pepper
lemon juice
6 fl oz / 170 ml double cream

Choose a small terrine, capacity 1½ pt / 850 ml, and line it with the fillets. If they are thick, place them between two sheets of cling film and flatten them carefully by beating with a mallet or rolling pin. Trim off the overhanging pieces and reserve.

To make the filling, purée the eel fillets and trimmings with half the fish stock in a blender. Dissolve the gelatine in the remaining stock, and add it to the purée. Push it through a fine sieve, and season with salt, pepper and a little lemon juice. Leave it to cool. Beat the cream until it makes soft peaks, and when the eel purée begins to set, fold in the cream. Pour into the eel-lined terrine and leave in the refrigerator until set. To turn out, dip in hot water until loose.

Smoked Haddock with Spinach

Serves 4–6

*This is a delicious combination, in pies, in roulades and in this dish
which has an airy soufflé topping. It can be baked in a large dish, or
the mixture divided between individual ovenproof dishes. I often use
frozen spinach for this. It is economical and tastes almost as good as
fresh. Buy finnan haddock or undyed smoked haddock for the best
flavour. Poach it in milk in a frying pan or roasting tin covered with
foil. Keep ½ pt / 280 ml cooking liquid for the soufflé mix.*

1 lb / 455 g cooked smoked
  haddock
½ oz / 15 g butter, softened
1 lb / 455 g cooked, well-drained
  spinach
4–6 eggs

Soufflé Topping
1 oz / 30 g butter
1 oz / 30 g plain flour
½ pt / 280 ml milk
3 eggs

Carefully remove any bones from the smoked haddock. Butter an ovenproof
dish or dishes and arrange the spinach on the bottom. Make four or six depressions
in the spinach and carefully slide an egg into each. Arrange the smoked haddock
on top. To make the topping, melt the butter in a saucepan, stir in the flour and
cook for 3–4 minutes. Gradually add the milk, stirring all the time to stop any
lumps forming. When all the milk has been added, let the sauce cook for another
few minutes. Separate the eggs. Beat the egg yolks into the sauce. Whisk the egg
whites until firm, and carefully fold into the sauce. Spread it over the smoked
haddock, making sure that it touches the edges of the dish. Bake in the top half of
a preheated oven at 190°C / 375°F / Mark 5 for 10–15 minutes, until the top is risen
and golden. The eggs inside should be just lightly set.

Warm Smoked Salmon with Cucumber

This recipe is based on one of the very best things we ate at Ballymaloe (the lovely country house hotel near Cork in Ireland), from one of the chef's special menus. Not a fan of many cooked smoked salmon dishes, I was quite won over by this treatment. Of course, the chef had the excellent local smoked salmon to work with, and it is really only possible to do it if you have a whole side of smoked salmon, since it is sliced straight down through the thickness of the fillet to the skin, in small, firm slices, not obliquely or horizontally as smoked salmon is usually sliced. Since the salmon really is just warmed through, and barely touches the pan, prepare the cucumber well in advance.

1 small or medium-sized cucumber	freshly ground white pepper
1–2 tsp salt	8 slices smoked salmon, 1–2 oz /
3 fl oz / 85 ml whipping cream	30–60 g each, cut as above
2 tsp finely chopped dill	extra dill, to garnish *(optional)*

Peel the cucumber, cut it in half lengthways, and scrape out the seeds. Finely dice and place in a sieve set over a bowl. Sprinkle with salt, and leave for up to 2 hours to disgorge its bitter juices. Rinse and dry thoroughly. Put the cream, dill and cucumber in a saucepan, and bring to the boil. Season to taste with white pepper, and keep the sauce warm while you prepare the salmon. Heat a non-stick or well-seasoned frying pan, large enough to hold all the salmon slices in a single layer, and put in the fish. Each side should come into contact with the pan only long enough to turn the surface opaque and no more – literally a few seconds on each side. Divide the sauce between four heated dinner plates and arrange the fish alongside it. Extra dill can be used to garnish, if liked.

MARINATED AND CURED FISH

Ceviche

(Marinated Fish with Onions, Tomatoes and Peppers)

Serves 4

Use plaice, lemon sole, cod, coley or haddock.

1 lb / 455 g white fish fillets,
  skinned
1 medium onion, peeled and very
  finely sliced
1 green pepper, deseeded and very
  finely sliced

1 small chilli, finely chopped
juice of 2 large limes
sea salt
freshly ground white pepper
a few coriander leaves
2 ripe tomatoes

Rinse and thoroughly dry the fish. Cut it into smallish cubes or strips, and put in a china or glass bowl. Put the onion with the fish and stir, then stir in the green pepper and chilli. Squeeze in the lime juice, and grind on a little salt and pepper. Tear most of the coriander leaves into shreds and add these. Mix together, cover and leave to stand in a cool place or refrigerator for 4–6 hours, stirring occasionally to make sure that all the fish comes into contact with the lime juice. When ready to serve, peel, deseed and chop the tomatoes. Serve the fish, together with its liquid, in bowls or on plates with a spoonful of diced tomato and the remaining coriander leaves for garnish.

Variation ∞ Sometimes this is served on a bed of lettuce with diced avocado, or in half an avocado. In Colombia, it is often served like this with a few prawns added. Perhaps this is where the ubiquitous avocado and prawns originated.

Mackerel Marinated in Lime and Coconut

Serves 4

*The texture and flavour of very fresh raw mackerel, just lightly
marinated, is quite exceptional.*

1 coconut	freshly ground black pepper
½ pt / 280 ml boiling water	2 limes
4 mackerel fillets	salad leaves
sea salt	

Puncture the coconut and pour the liquid into a jug. Crack the nut and, with a
sharp knife, zester or canelle knife, remove a few strips or curls of coconut flesh,
and put on one side for garnishing the dish. Grate the rest of the white coconut
flesh and put it in a bowl. Pour on the boiling water, and leave to stand for 30
minutes. Then sieve, pressing down vigorously to extract the maximum amount of
flavoured liquid or 'milk' from the grated coconut. Mix this liquid with the liquid
you have already extracted from the coconut, and allow it to cool completely. Cut
the mackerel fillets into very thin slices, as if you were slicing smoked salmon. (The
thin slices will marinate more quickly.) Arrange in a single layer in a flat dish,
sprinkle lightly with salt and pepper, and pour on the coconut milk, making sure
that all the fish is covered. Leave for 1 hour. Remove a few shreds of zest from one
of the limes and reserve for garnish. Cut both limes in half, and squeeze the juice
all over the fish. Using a wooden spoon so that the fish slices are not torn, stir
gently to spread the marinade all over the fish. Cover and refrigerate for a further
hour. Arrange on the salad leaves, garnish with the reserved strips of coconut and
lime zest and serve.

Variations ∾ Salmon, trout or fresh fillets of plaice can be prepared in the
same way.

Instead of the coconut and lime marinade, use one prepared by simmering
½ pt / 280 ml white wine vinegar with a little finely chopped carrot, onion and
garlic, a bay leaf, a few sprigs of parsley and thyme, a few cloves, peppercorns and
coriander seeds and a pinch of sea salt for 40 minutes. Pour this over the fish while
still hot, then leave to cool completely, chill and serve.

Marinated Smoked Haddock

Serves 10

1 fillet of undyed smoked haddock,
    about 1¾ lb / 795 g
4 fl oz / 115 ml hazelnut oil
sea salt

freshly ground black pepper
freshly squeezed lime juice
aged rum or malt whisky *(optional)*
salad leaves

Trim the fillet by removing the bones and then cutting away the thin (belly) side and the tail end so that you are left with a centre cut about 3 in / 7.5 cm wide and 10 in / 25.5 cm long. (The trimmings can be used for other things – smoked haddock tartare, omelette filling or kedgeree.) Cut the fish vertically into slices just under ¼ in / 0.5 cm thick. Lay on a platter. Brush with hazelnut oil, sprinkle with a little salt and pepper, and leave for 2–3 hours. About 30 minutes before serving, brush with lime juice and a little rum or whisky, if liked. To serve, arrange five or six pieces on a plate with a few small salad leaves. I often serve it with pickled samphire.

Jamaican Escoveitch Fish

Serves 8

This is traditionally served for breakfast on Sunday morning. Prepare the day before it is required.

8 sardines, small mackerel or
    herrings, cleaned and gutted
2 limes
salt
freshly ground black pepper
oil for deep-frying
2 chayotes or courgettes

2 onions
3 chillies
7 fl oz / 200 ml vinegar
3 tbsp sunflower, groundnut (peanut) or
    olive oil
12 allspice berries

Rub the fish with the juice of the two limes, salt and pepper. Fry in deep hot oil until brown, then drain on kitchen paper and arrange in a serving dish. Cut the chayotes or courgettes into 2 in / 5 cm batons. Peel and thinly slice the onions, and deseed and slice the chillies into rings. Put the vegetables in a saucepan with the vinegar, oil and allspice. Bring to the boil, and simmer very gently for 10 minutes. Pour the hot marinade over the fish, allow to cool, and then refrigerate overnight.

Variation ∿ For a similar dish, season the fish with cayenne pepper, ground coriander, ground cumin and ground cinnamon before frying. Make a marinade by mixing olive oil and lemon juice with finely chopped spring onion, tomato, garlic and chilli, and a little seasoning. Pour this over the fish, and then cover and refrigerate overnight.

Cured Salmon with Mustard Mayonnaise

Serves 6–8

2–2½ lb / 900 g–1.10 kg boned and
   scaled tail fillets of salmon
bunch of fresh dill *or* 3 tbsp dried
   dill seed or dill weed
2 tbsp coarse sea salt

1 tbsp granulated sugar
1 tbsp coarsely ground black or white
   pepper
1 tbsp cognac *(optional)*

Remove all the pin bones from the salmon. Spread a third of the dill in the bottom of a dish. Mix the salt, sugar and pepper, and sprinkle a third of it over the dill. Place one of the salmon fillets on top, skin-side down. Sprinkle half the remaining seasoning over the fillet, and lay half the remaining dill on top. Sprinkle on the cognac, if using it. Place the other fillet on top, sprinkle with the rest of the seasoning, and put the rest of the dill on top. Cover with foil, and weigh down. Refrigerate and keep for up to four or five days, though the salmon is good to eat after just 12 hours or so. To serve, wipe the dill and seasoning off the salmon, and cut into oblique or vertical slices. A sweet mustard mayonnaise is the traditional accompaniment (see below).

Variation ∿ Omit the dill, and add a few crushed cardamom pods, cumin seeds and coriander seeds to the mixture of salt, sugar and pepper.

Mustard Mayonnaise
2 hard-boiled egg yolks
1–2 tbsp mustard
1 tsp light muscovado sugar

8 tbsp olive or sunflower oil
2 tbsp wine vinegar
salt
freshly ground white pepper

Break down the egg yolks, and mash until smooth. Stir in the mustard and sugar until there are no lumps. Gradually add the oil, a drop at a time, until the mixture begins to thicken. The oil can then be added in larger quantities. Add the vinegar, a splash at a time, in between additions of oil. Finally, season to taste with salt and pepper. A little chopped dill can be stirred in if you wish.

Marinated Salmon and Scallops

Serves 6

This makes an excellent starter, served with wedges of lemon or lime and hot toast, warm bread or pumpernickel. It can be prepared 2–3 hours in advance.

1 lb / 455 g thinly sliced fresh salmon from the fillet

9 or 12 scallops (white parts only), sliced horizontally into 2 or 3 pieces

2–3 firm ripe tomatoes, peeled, deseeded and chopped

1 shallot, peeled and finely chopped

2–3 tsp grain mustard

5 tbsp hazelnut or extra virgin olive oil

¼ tsp salt

¼ tsp freshly ground black pepper

1 tsp lime or lemon juice

Arrange the salmon on individual serving plates, leaving a space in the middle. Arrange the scallop slices, in overlapping circles, in the middle of each plate. Mix the tomatoes and shallot, and spoon a small heap on to the centre of each plate. Mix together the rest of the ingredients, and brush liberally over the fish. Cover each plate with cling film and refrigerate until required.

Salmon Tartare with Cucumber Sauce

Serves 4, as a starter

12 oz / 340 g salmon, skinned
1 shallot, peeled and finely chopped
  (optional)
2 tbsp extra virgin olive oil
salt
freshly ground black pepper
1–2 ripe tomatoes
1 cucumber
1 tsp grated fresh horseradish
1 tbsp cream, thick yoghurt or
  buttermilk

Chop the salmon into very small pieces. If you prefer to use a food processor, process the salmon only very briefly, otherwise salmon paste will be the result. If using the shallot, mix it with the salmon and a spoonful of olive oil. Season lightly, cover and put to one side. Peel the tomatoes and cut in half. Scoop the seeds and pulp into a sieve and set over a bowl, and rub through the liquid. Cut the tomatoes into strips or dice, and reserve for garnish. Peel the cucumber and halve it lengthways. Remove the seeds, and chop or slice the cucumber. Fry the cucumber in the remaining oil for 5–6 minutes, and then put in a blender or food processor with the horseradish and cream, yoghurt or buttermilk. Blend until smooth.

Mix the salmon with enough of the tomato liquid to add a slight note of acidity, and spoon on to plates, or shape using ring moulds. Spoon the sauce around it, and add the tomato for garnish.

Variation ∾ Use fresh tuna fillet instead of the salmon. You can also make a good tuna fish tartare, by replacing the olive oil with toasted sesame oil and stirring in some finely chopped garlic and fresh coriander and a splash each of sherry and soy sauce. The cucumber sauce would not go down well with this version.

TWO SAUCES FOR FISH

Sun-Dried Tomato Hollandaise
(for grilled fish)

Serves 4

6–8 pieces sun-dried tomato,
  soaked until soft
freshly ground black pepper

1 tbsp sherry vinegar
3 egg yolks
4 oz / 110 g butter

Rub the tomato through a sieve, and discard the skin and seeds. Season with pepper, and mix in the sherry vinegar. Put the egg yolks in a blender with 1 tsp of the tomato mixture. Heat the butter in a saucepan until hot and foaming, but without letting it burn. Switch on the blender, and gradually add the hot butter. The mixture should thicken as the egg yolks and butter emulsify. Stir in the rest of the tomato mixture.

Parsley and Chive Sauce
(for grilled or poached fish)

Serves 4

1½ oz / 40 g parsley
½ pt / 280 ml single cream
2 shallots, peeled and finely
  chopped
1 oz / 30 g unsalted butter

2 fl oz / 60 ml dry white wine
12 chives
sea salt
freshly ground white pepper

Wash thoroughly and dry the parsley, either in a salad spinner or between layers of kitchen paper. Remove the stalks and put them in a small saucepan with the cream. Bring to the boil, remove from the heat, and leave to infuse for 15–20 minutes. Meanwhile, in another saucepan, sweat the shallots in the butter until they are soft and translucent. Add the wine to the shallots, and cook until reduced to 1 tablespoon. Chop the parsley leaves as finely as possible (a food processor is invaluable for this) and snip the chives very small. Strain the cream over the shallots and add the herbs. Cook for 5 minutes, then add salt and pepper to taste.

SHELLFISH

THROUGHOUT the autumn, winter and spring, shellfish is readily available. Indeed, with the increase in oyster farming, one no longer has to wait for an 'R' in the month to be able to enjoy them. If only farming them would bring the prices down! Mussels and clams are considerably cheaper and can be used in certain recipes instead of oysters. I had to do the opposite in Hong Kong. When I wanted to put my Celeriac and Mushroom Salad with Mussels (see page 111) on the buffet menu of the hotel where I was cooking, I was asked if I would mind using oysters instead, as the mussels, the large, green, lipped variety flown in from New Zealand, were far too expensive. Oysters *or* mussels make very good salads.

You might like to consider some of the unusual ways of using shellfish. Rather than serving them on their own as a starter, why not revive the old custom of serving a savoury at the end of a dinner party? Oysters or mussels wrapped in a small thin piece of streaky bacon and grilled is one of the classics. Shellfish combine with meat again in that Dickensian sounding Steak, Kidney and Oyster Pie (see page 388). This is a very good way of making a few small oysters go a long way. At a pinch, you could use canned or smoked oysters, and frozen oysters would not be a bad substitute. A close cousin is a wonderful Portuguese dish, Alentejo Pork with Clams (see page 326), liberally flavoured with fresh coriander, which is always our first choice at the bar in Gambrinus, our favourite restaurant in Lisbon. We wash it down with a bottle of Alvarinho de Monçao, Portugal's classiest vinho verde.

Mussel Tart

Serves 4–6

2 leeks, (white parts only), trimmed,
    sliced and washed
1 oz / 30 g butter
1 tbsp plain flour
¾ pt / 430 ml milk
12 oz / 340 g shortcrust pastry

4 egg yolks
salt
freshly ground black pepper
8 oz / 230 g freshly cooked shelled
    mussels

Sweat the leeks in the butter until soft. Stir in the flour and enough milk to make a thick sauce. Cook gently, adding the rest of the milk and stirring continuously to avoid lumps. Remove from the heat. Roll out the pastry, and use to line a 9 × 10 in / 23 × 25.5 cm flan ring or quiche dish. Beat the egg yolks into the sauce. Add salt and pepper, to taste, and the mussels. Pour this into the lined dish, and bake in a preheated oven at 190°C / 375°F / Mark 5 for 40–50 minutes, turning the heat down if the surface browns too much. It should be golden brown.

Cider-Steamed Mussels

Serves 4

The classic moules marinière *is made with dry white wine. Cider is a good alternative.*

4 lb / 1.80 kg mussels
2 shallots or 1 small onion, peeled
    and finely chopped
1 celery stalk, trimmed and finely
    sliced

¼ pt / 140 ml dry cider
2 tbsp fine, soft, white breadcrumbs
2 tbsp finely chopped parsley
freshly ground white pepper
1 oz / 30 g butter

Scrub the mussels under cold running water, discarding any that remain open. Tug off the 'beards' wedged in the straight sides of the shells, and knock off any barnacles with the back of a knife. (It is worth doing this, otherwise the barnacles may get dislodged during cooking and release sand into the pan.) Rinse the mussels again very thoroughly, drain them, and put into a large saucepan with the shallots or onion and celery. Pour on the cider, put the lid on, and put the pan on a high heat. Steam the mussels for 2–3 minutes, shaking the pan occasionally. Remove the lid, toss in the breadcrumbs and parsley, and replace the lid for 30 seconds, shaking vigorously. Transfer the mussels to a large tureen or individual bowls with all the cooking liquid, discarding any mussels that have not opened during cooking.

Stuffed Mussels

Serves 4

12 large mussels
4 oz / 110 g butter, softened
2 tbsp good dry white wine
1 shallot, peeled and finely chopped
1–2 garlic cloves, peeled and
   crushed

1 tbsp finely chopped parsley
salt
freshly ground black pepper
small pinch cayenne pepper

Scrub the mussels under cold running water, discarding any that remain open. With a strong, short-bladed knife, prize open the shells, cutting through the muscle. Take care not to spill any of the juice, but sieve it into a basin, and mix it with the rest of the ingredients to a smooth paste. Discard the top shells and divide the mixture between the 12 shells containing the mussels. Smooth the surface of each with the back of a knife. Arrange the stuffed shells on a baking sheet. (A layer of salt or sand spread on it will enable you to balance the shells perfectly, but is not essential.) Place towards the top of a preheated oven at 220°C / 425°F / Mark 7 and bake for 3–4 minutes, until the mixture is just bubbling. If you cook them for much longer, the mussels will become tough.

Variation ∾ Use oysters instead of mussels.

Cockle Pie

3 lb / 1.35 kg cockles in the shell *or*
  1 lb / 455 g cooked shelled
  cockles
¼ pt / 140 ml water
12 oz / 340 g shortcrust or flaky
  pastry

1 bunch spring onions *or* 6 baby leeks
8 oz / 230 g streaky bacon
freshly ground black pepper
¼ pt / 140 ml single cream
2 egg yolks

If using fresh cockles, rinse them thoroughly, and put in a saucepan with the water. Steam for 10 minutes or until the cockles are all open, discarding any that remain closed. Put a fine sieve over a bowl, and pour the cockles into it. Reserve the liquor. Remove and discard the shells when cool enough to handle. Rinse the shelled cockles to remove any grit.

Roll out the pastry, and use to line a 9–10 inch / 23–25.5 cm pie or quiche dish. (There will be pastry left over for the lattice top.) Wash and slice the spring onions or leeks. Remove and discard the bacon rind, and cut the bacon into matchsticks. Fry it gently for a few minutes, and then drain. Layer the cockles, spring onions and bacon in the pie dish. Grind on a little pepper. Beat the cream and eggs together with a little cooking liquor if you have cooked the shellfish from scratch, or 2–3 tablespoons water if not. Pour the custard over the filling. Roll out the remaining pastry, cut strips and use to make a lattice top. Bake in a preheated oven at 200°C / 400°F / Mark 6 for about 15 minutes then turn down the heat to 180°C / 350°F / Mark 4, and cook for a further 15–25 minutes.

Note ❧ Only use fresh or freshly boiled cockles for this; not cockles preserved in brine or vinegar.

Oysters in Champagne Jelly

Makes 12

1 cucumber	½ pt / 280 ml champagne
2 tsp salt	12 oysters
2½ leaves gelatine *or* 2½ tsp	freshly ground white pepper
powdered gelatine	chervil or dill, to garnish *(optional)*

Peel the cucumber and use a vegetable peeler to shave the flesh into long paper-thin strips, stopping when you get down to the seeds. Put the cucumber in a sieve over a bowl, sprinkle with salt and leave to drain for 2–3 hours. Rinse and dry thoroughly in a clean tea-towel. Meanwhile, soften the gelatine in half of the champagne, and then heat gently until it dissolves. Pour into a bowl. Prize open the oysters, and strain the juices into the bowl of champagne and gelatine. Stir in the remaining champagne and season lightly with pepper. Put in the coldest part of the refrigerator. Loosen the oysters from their shells, and put in a bowl. Scrub the oyster shells to use as containers. Arrange coarse sea salt on a platter, decorate with seaweed if you have been able to get some from your fishmonger, and arrange the oyster shells in it, as level as possible. Put a few shreds of cucumber in each shell, and place an oyster on top. By now the jelly should have begun to set. Spoon some on top of each oyster and garnish with some fresh herbs, if you wish, before serving.

If you need to refrigerate the oysters until required, try not to do so for longer than 30 minutes or so, as the briny flavour and scent is quite fleeting.

Variation ∞ You can just use water with a pinch of sea salt in it instead of the champagne, and call the dish Oysters in Seawater Jelly.

You could also allow the oysters to set in the jelly in small moulds or ramekins, with 2–3 oysters in each. Serve by turning out on to plates and spooning a little crème fraîche mixed with a few finely chopped shallots or chives on top.

Baked Potatoes with Oysters

Makes 12

12 potatoes, 2–2½ oz / 60–70 g
  each
2 oz / 60 g butter, melted
salt
freshly ground black pepper

12 oysters
chilled crème fraîche or whipped cream
  (optional)
dill or parsley, to garnish *(optional)*

Scrub rather than peel the potatoes which should, however, be as unblemished as possible. Cut a thin slice off the bottom so that they will stand firm on a baking sheet. Parboil the potatoes for 10–12 minutes, drain and, when cool enough to handle, cut a slice off the top of each one and use a pointed teaspoon or melon baller to scoop out a hollow large enough to hold an oyster. Brush the potato cases all over with melted butter and season. Place on a baking sheet in a preheated oven at 200°C / 400°F / Mark 6 for about 8 minutes until golden brown and sizzling. Prize open the oysters, and strain the juices into a bowl. Remove the oysters from their shells. At this point, there are two ways of proceeding. One is to pop a very cold oyster in a very hot potato and serve immediately with a little of the oyster juice sprinkled over it. Alternatively, if you prefer a cooked oyster, once they are in the potato cases, spoon a little crème fraîche or cream on top and put back in the oven for 3–4 minutes just to heat through. Serve garnished with dill or parsley if you like.

Variation ∾ Prawns, mussels or queen scallops can be used in this way in place of oysters. If using mussels, steam them open first and discard any which remain closed; if using queen scallops, steam or marinate them briefly before using.

Prawns in Orange Mayonnaise

Serves 4, as a starter

1¼ lb / 570 g whole cooked prawns
7 fl oz / 200 ml thick mayonnaise
1 orange with fine unblemished skin
2–3 garlic cloves, peeled and
  crushed

salt
freshly ground white pepper
1 shallot or spring onion, finely chopped
herbs, for garnish

Peel all but four of the prawns. Put the mayonnaise into a bowl, and grate the orange zest into it. Squeeze the orange, and stir in enough juice to give the mayonnaise the consistency of thick pouring cream. Stir in the rest of the ingredients and the peeled prawns. How you present the dish now is up to you. Perhaps place a lettuce leaf in four scallop shells, and spoon the mixture into them, garnishing with herbs and prawns; or arrange the mayonnaise on top of the salad leaves on a plate; or on shredded lettuce in a glass dish.

Variation ∞ Use cooked mussels or clams, or fresh cockles or oysters, or crab or lobster meat instead of the prawns.

Prawn and Coconut Curry

Serves 4

1 large onion, peeled and thinly sliced	½ tsp ground turmeric
2 tbsp ghee or groundnut (peanut) oil	½ tsp mustard seeds
	¼ pt / 140 ml water
4 oz / 110 g desiccated coconut *or*	2 tbsp plain yoghurt
2 oz / 60 g grated creamed	1 lb / 455 g peeled and deveined prawns
coconut (from a block)	juice of ½ lemon *or* 1 tbsp tamarind
4 garlic cloves, peeled and crushed	liquid

Fry the onion until golden in the ghee or groundnut (peanut) oil. Add the coconut, garlic and spices, and cook for a further 5 minutes. Stir in the water and yoghurt, and cook until the onion is soft. Add the prawns and lemon juice or tamarind liquid, and continue cooking for a further 5–8 minutes. Serve immediately on a bed of steamed or boiled rice.

Variations ∞ Instead of the spices used above, use a small stick of cinnamon, a few whole cloves, a few teaspoons of grated fresh root ginger and, if you have it, a few pieces of lemon grass stalk. Omit the yoghurt, and add 3 oz / 85 g each of mangetout, oyster mushrooms and bean sprouts with the water, and cook until the vegetables are just soft. Then, instead of lemon juice or tamarind liquid, stir in a teaspoon of soy sauce and a teaspoon of toasted sesame oil with the prawns. If you like spicy food, you can also add a little chopped chilli with the spices.

Use small queen scallops or chunks of monkfish instead of the prawns.

Prawn-Stuffed Mushrooms

Serves 4–6, as a starter

*I learned how to make this dish in Chan Fat Chee's kitchen at the
Fung Lum in Shatin in Hong Kong's New Territories, when he
invited me to learn about Cantonese food. Only raw prawns should be
used. These are usually sold frozen, but fresh ones can sometimes be
found.*

18 fresh shiitake mushrooms, about
  1½ in / 4 cm in diameter
2 tsp cornflour
1 lb / 455 g raw prawns, thawed if
  frozen, and peeled
1 egg white

large pinch of salt
small pinch of freshly ground black
  pepper
finely grated fresh root ginger and
  chopped chives or spring onion, to
  garnish

Remove the stalks from the mushrooms, and wipe the caps clean. Avoid
washing them if possible. Sprinkle cornflour lightly over the inside of each
mushroom cap. Put the prawns, most of the egg white, the remaining cornflour, the
salt and pepper in a food processor and process until you have a smooth paste.
Spoon the filling into each mushroom cap, and then smooth it over with a finger or
thumb dipped into the remaining egg white. Place in a steamer basket, and steam
for 8 minutes. Remove and garnish before serving.

Baked Scallops

Serves 4

12 scallops, shelled
4 oz / 110 g unsalted butter
4 oz / 110 g fresh white
  breadcrumbs

salt
freshly ground black pepper
sprigs of watercress
lemon wedges

Clean the scallops, remove the thick pad of muscle, and dice the white and
orange pieces. Thickly butter four ramekins or scallop shells, and line them with
some of the breadcrumbs. Divide the scallops between the four containers, and
cover with the remaining breadcrumbs and butter. Sprinkle with a little salt and
pepper. Bake at the top of a preheated oven at 220°C / 425°F / Mark 7 for 8
minutes. Serve very hot, garnished with the sprigs of watercress and lemon wedges.

Scallops with Julienne of Vegetables

Serves 2

This is another way of serving scallops, either as a starter or as a main course.

6–8 plump, shelled scallops
1 garlic clove, peeled and crushed
1 in / 2.5 cm piece of fresh root
   ginger, peeled and shredded
1 carrot, peeled and cut into very
   fine strips
1 leek, trimmed and cut into very
   fine strips

1 celery stalk, trimmed and cut into very
   fine strips
salt
freshly ground black pepper
½ lemon
2 tbsp fish stock
1 tbsp soy sauce

Clean the scallops by rinsing thoroughly under cold water to wash away any sand. Remove the intestine and the thick muscle. Pat dry on kitchen paper, and place in a shallow pie dish. Scatter the garlic and ginger over the scallops, then heap the carrot, leek and celery on top. Season lightly. Squeeze on just a few drops of lemon juice and moisten with the fish stock and soy sauce. Place the pie dish on an upturned saucer in a frying or sauté pan. Pour in 1 in / 2.5 cm or so of water, and cover with the lid or a sheet of foil. Bring to the boil, and steam for 5–7 minutes, depending on how plump the scallops are and how well done you like them. Remove the scallops and vegetables, and keep these warm on a serving plate. Boil the cooking juices until slightly reduced, and serve immediately.

Salmon and Scallop 'Chops'

Serves 6

*I learned to make this dish in the kitchens of the Hotel du Palais
in Biarritz, where Michel Gautier of Le Rouzic in Bordeaux was
teaching a* stage. *It is very good served on a nest of deep-fried leeks
(see page 145).*

1 long strip of salmon about 10 in /
   25.5 cm long, weighing about
   14 oz / 395 g and cut from the
   centre of the fillet
12 scallops, shelled and trimmed,
   with roe removed
salt
freshly ground white pepper
2 shallots, peeled and finely
   chopped

blade of mace
¼ pt / 140 ml dry white wine
1 tbsp white wine vinegar
2 egg yolks
4 oz / 110 g chilled butter, diced
3 ripe tomatoes, peeled, deseeded and
   chopped *or* sprigs of chervil, chives or
   dill

Skin the fish, and slice it into six long equal strips. Wrap each strip around two
scallops to form the letter 'B'. Secure with a wooden skewer pierced through the
centre. Lightly season, and put to one side while you make the sauce. Put the
shallots, mace, wine and vinegar in a saucepan, and boil to reduce by two-thirds.
Remove the mace and, off the heat, whisk in the egg yolks as for a sabayon sauce.
Whisk in the butter, a piece at a time, and, when well incorporated, season lightly
with a little white pepper. Heat a grill, griddle or heavy frying pan, and quickly
cook the fish on both sides. Serve on warm plates with some of the sauce and the
chopped tomatoes or herbs.

Variation ∾ For a much lighter sauce, reduce the wine and vinegar as
described above, and then whisk in fruity extra virgin olive oil instead of the egg
yolks and butter.

Grilled Scallops in a Light Mousseline Sauce

This dish can be partially prepared in advance. The scallops can be cleaned and put to marinate and the sauce base can be made a few hours in advance. The final preparation is then very quick.

16–24 medium-sized scallops, shelled
4 tbsp extra virgin olive oil
good pinch of freshly ground black pepper
4 ripe tomatoes, peeled, deseeded and chopped
½ oz / 15 g butter
2 tbsp white wine vinegar

2 tbsp fish stock
6 tbsp light soy sauce
¼ tsp Tabasco sauce
good pinch of fine sea salt
3 oz / 85 g chilled unsalted butter, cut into cubes
2 tbsp whipped cream
fine strips of courgette, to garnish

Make sure you have removed all the pads of muscle from the scallops and dry the scallops well. Marinate them in the olive oil and pepper. To make the sauce, cook the tomatoes in the butter for 2–3 minutes, add the vinegar, fish stock, soy sauce and Tabasco and boil for a further 2 minutes. Blend and sieve the mixture back into a pan. I find that a small frying pan is perfect for making this kind of sauce. Spread over a broader surface, the sauce reduces more quickly.

Salt the scallops, and grill them for 1 minute on each side, or less if they are fairly large and thin rather than small and chunky. Remove from the heat and keep them warm while you finish the sauce. Gently heat the sauce and gradually add the cubes of butter. Shake the pan with a swirling wrist motion to 'mount' the sauce, that is amalgamate the butter with the tomato base without it separating. At the last moment, fold in the whipped cream. Arrange the scallops and sauce on heated dinner plates, garnish with the fine strips of courgette, and serve with steamed or boiled rice.

Octopus and Squid

Octopus needs careful cooking and should be tenderized before cooking if it is not to be rubbery. Fishermen in the Mediterranean, when they have caught and killed the octopus, beat it against a rock to tenderize it. Thumping it with a rolling pin will do the same, or you can leave it to your fishmonger. In Galicia, I learned that you can also tenderize octopus by putting it in the freezer for 3 days and then simmering it for 28 minutes precisely.

Squid is rather easier to prepare and is a more tender fish anyway. It is well worth trying squid if you have never had it before. When cooked, the flesh is white and firm, yet tender, with a very sweet, pleasant flavour. And, of course, it has no bones. You can often buy it ready prepared, that is cut into rings which are excellent for paella or deep-frying. Alternatively, the uncut, cleaned out squid bodies are perfect for stuffing. If you clean them yourself, however, you can extract the ink sac, and use it to add to the sauce.

Describing how to prepare squid actually takes much longer than the preparation itself.

To Prepare Squid

Work at the sink with the squid in a colander. If you are right-handed, hold the body of the squid in your left hand, and pull off the head and tentacles with your right hand. Cut the ring of tentacles from the head, and put these to one side, discarding the rest of the head. Sometimes some of the entrails come away when you pull off the head. Before discarding these, look for the ink sac. It is a small, thin, elongated silvery sac which should be removed without breaking and placed in a separate bowl. Take the body of the squid, and squeeze out the remaining contents, as you would squeeze a tube of toothpaste. Check it for the ink sac if you have not already found it. Remove and discard the transparent 'quill' from the body cavity. Rinse the body thoroughly and peel off any skin. Remove the two triangular flaps or 'wings' and put these with the tentacles. Continue until you have cleaned all the squid.

The pile of tentacles and wings can be chopped up and used in risotto (see page 321), and the bodies can be stuffed with cooked rice, chopped tomatoes and mushrooms and baked; or sliced into rings, dipped in batter and deep-fried to serve with lemon; or sliced into rings and shallow-fried with olive oil, onions, tomato and garlic and served as a squid stew; or allowed to go cold and served as a salad (see page 109). You can keep the prepared raw squid until next day if you marinate it in white wine and olive oil and refrigerate it.

Fried Squid with Steamed Vegetable Risotto

Serves 4, as a main course, or 6–8, as part of a Chinese meal

*One of the things that I have learned from Chinese cooks is how to
cut squid so that it will curl most decoratively when cooked. But it is
not only for decoration. Cutting it in the way I describe below exposes
more surface area to the heat, so that it cooks more quickly and thus
stays tender.*

4 squid, about 6–8 in / 15–20.5 cm
  long
6 in / 15 cm piece of mooli (white
  radish)
2 long, straight carrots
1 parsnip
4 oz / 110 g celeriac
2 celery stalks
2 leeks
salt
freshly ground black pepper

2 tbsp soy sauce
1 tbsp sesame oil
2 tbsp rice wine or amontillado sherry
1 tbsp groundnut (peanut) oil
3 spring onions, trimmed and cut into
  1 in / 2.5 cm lengths, and then into
  shreds
1 in / 2.5 cm piece of fresh root ginger,
  peeled, sliced and shredded
1 tbsp concentrated fish stock or oyster
  sauce

Prepare the squid as described on page 320. Put the tentacles and wings on one
side. Cut open the bodies, and then cut in two down the middle. Lightly score the
flesh with a sharp knife in straight lines about ¼ in / 0.5 cm apart. Score across
these with the knife blade held at an oblique angle. Cut into triangular pieces, and
put with the tentacles.

Prepare the vegetables by washing, peeling and trimming them. Shave the root
vegetables into ¼ in / 0.5 cm ribbons. Slice the celery into long, thin shreds.
Quarter the leeks lengthways and separate into ribbons, cutting the wider ones in
half. Lightly season the vegetables, steam for 5 minutes, and then toss them in the
soy sauce, sesame oil and rice wine or sherry, which you first mix and heat in a
saucepan. Pile the vegetables in a dish and cover. Heat the groundnut (peanut) oil
in a wok or frying pan, and quickly stir-fry the squid for 2–3 minutes. Add the
spring onions and ginger and cook for another minute before adding the fish stock
or oyster sauce. Stir briskly, and serve poured over the vegetable ribbons.

THE TIMES COOK IN PORTUGAL

OF ALL THE kitchens in Europe, that of Portugal has been least influenced in recent times by France. *Cucina nuova* is to be found, to the regret of many, in restaurants all over northern Italy. *Neue Küche* flourishes in Bavaria. But I am glad to report that there are no signs of *novo cozinha* in Lisbon.

Every visit produces exactly the same dishes we have eaten there regularly over the past 20 years – the 'dry' soups, or *açorda*, thickened with bread; salt cod 365 ways (although my friend, Eduardo, maintains that there are only three ways to cook it – boiled, baked or spoiled); impossibly rich puddings made of little more than sugar and egg yolk; stuffed squid; *dobrada* or tripe stew; *cataplana*, cooked in the traditional hinged pan; *porco alentejana*, or Alentejo pork with clams, an unusual and very good combination (see page 326).

The food shops are also old-fashioned. Along Lisbon's rua do Arsenal, by the waterfront, are all the dry goods stores. They sell several varieties of beans, red, black and speckled. Dark, shiny, red paprika-flecked *chouriços* hang from the ceilings, as do natural casings for making sausages. Portuguese extra virgin olive oil, smoked sardines, almonds from the Algarve, plums from Elvas, arrowroot and *goiabada* or guava paste from Brazil and homemade quince paste or *marmelada* are all worth bringing back with you.

In the centre of each small, sawdust-floored shop is a heavy butcher's block, topped with marble, where the shopkeeper saws the plank-hard salt cod. Dried skate, squid, octopus, tuna and croaker add their pungent smells.

Food shopping in Lisbon reminds you of how it used to be. What is there is strictly seasonal, and to eyes that are used to seeing everything available, all the time, curiously restricted in choice. On an autumn visit, there would be chestnuts, quinces, plaits of garlic, necklaces of dried chillies, some bunches of coriander, persimmons, and several varieties of greens and potatoes. The potatoes come in waxy, lemon-fleshed varieties for steaming and boiling, and white floury varieties for use in *caldo verde*, the cabbage and potato soup.

Balmy weather brings out the barbecues. Whenever I smell charcoal, I am immediately transported to the old quarters of Lisbon above the River Tagus. With the spring, life begins to be lived outdoors again, and that includes cooking over small charcoal braziers. More often than not, fat silver sardines are being grilled (see page 323) as a prelude to dinner. They are the taste of Portugal, washed down with a glass of vinho verde. But salt cod, too, is the taste of Portugal (see page 323). Not that easy to find, it is easy to prepare, and although it takes time to soak, it makes for very good dishes. After a meal in Portugal we will sometimes choose a cake for dessert or one of the small egg sweets, but sliced oranges provide a refreshing note on which to end. If you want something more substantial, I suggest chilled rice pudding (see page 515).

Grilled Sardines

Serve 2 sardines per person

*I like to serve these with olives, rings of raw mild onion and lemon
wedges, or with a tomato salad. It is a good idea to serve plenty of
bread, too, to help down any tiny bones.*

fresh sardines	salt
extra virgin olive oil	freshly ground black pepper
1 lemon	bay leaves

Scale the fish, and gut them or not, as you wish. Brush with olive oil, squeeze
on a few drops of lemon juice, and season them lightly. Arrange them on a rack in
a grill pan, and tuck bay leaves between them. Preheat the grill until it is hot, and
grill the sardines on both sides, turning them carefully, for 10–15 minutes in all,
depending on the thickness.

Portuguese-Style Salt Cod

Serves 4

*This is very good indeed served with plain boiled or steamed new
potatoes. A jug of extra virgin olive oil and some halved lemons might
also accompany the fish.*

1–1½ lb / 455–680 g fresh cod fillet	3 tbsp extra virgin olive oil
4 oz / 110 g coarse sea salt	freshly ground black pepper
1 mild onion, peeled and thinly sliced	handful of olives
	chopped coriander

Take a shallow lidded box for the refrigerator. Cut the fillet into four pieces to
fit in the box in a single layer. Put half the salt in the bottom of the box, lay the fish
fillets on top, and spread the remaining salt over them. Cover and refrigerate for 2
days before use. Pour off the brine, and keep the fish in clean cold water for 8–15
hours, changing it from time to time. Skin the fish and dry thoroughly. In a large
frying pan, gently fry the onion in the olive oil until soft and golden. Add the fish,
and cook until it becomes just opaque. This takes only a few minutes. Season with
pepper, and add the olives and coriander. Cover with a lid, and shake the pan, the
steam causing the coriander to release its fragrant oils. Serve.

Variation ⁓ Garlic, peeled and thinly sliced, can be cooked with the onion.

Stuffed Squid

Serves 4–6

16–20 squid, about 4 in /10 cm long
3–4 tbsp extra virgin olive oil
1 onion, peeled and finely chopped
3 garlic cloves, peeled and crushed
2 ripe tomatoes, peeled, deseeded
  and chopped

salt
freshly ground black pepper
2 tbsp finely chopped coriander leaves
  or parsley
8 oz / 230 g cooked rice
3–4 tbsp dry white wine

Prepare the squid as described on page 320, chopping up the tentacles and wings and leaving the bodies whole, ready to be stuffed. Heat 1 tablespoon olive oil in a frying pan, and cook the onion in the oil for a few minutes, then add the chopped squid tentacles and wings and the garlic. Stir until the squid becomes opaque. At this point, add the chopped tomatoes, seasoning, some of the herbs and the cooked rice. Mix in and remove from the heat. Allow to cool. Spoon the rice mixture into the prepared squid bodies until loosely stuffed. Secure the ends closed with cocktail sticks or toothpicks.

Butter or oil a shallow ovenproof dish, and lay the stuffed squid in it in a single layer. Pour the wine over, and trickle the rest of the olive oil on top. Cover with foil or buttered paper, and bake in the middle of a preheated oven at 180°C / 350°F / Mark 4 for 20 minutes. Serve straight from the baking dish, sprinkled with the remaining herbs, and with a green salad to accompany it.

Sopa de Pedra
(Stone Soup)

Serves 6–8

One of my favourite legends is that about sopa de pedra, *a Portuguese speciality from the Alentejo. The story goes that a priest knocked on a door and asked the lady of the house for a pot of water to be put on to boil for him to make soup with. He took a handsome smooth stone out of his habit, and put it into the pot. Aghast, the lady asked if he would not also like a ham bone and some cabbage. Well, yes, she could put those in the pot if she wished, but they were not necessary. And what about some beans and sausages? Really, the stone was quite sufficient, but if she wanted to, and so on . . . The pot was filled up with more and more good things, each time the priest protesting that it was not necessary. After enjoying his rich, hearty soup, he carefully retrieved his stone, washed it, dried it, tucked it back into his pocket, and went on his way, knowing he would never have to go hungry.*

4 pt / 2.30 l water
1 ham bone or knuckle of bacon
marrow or beef bones
chicken carcass
1 celery stalk, trimmed and chopped into 3 pieces
1 carrot, peeled and chopped into 3 pieces
2 onions, peeled
3 cloves
8 oz / 230 g soaked white beans or chick peas
8 oz / 230 g shredded cabbage
8 oz / 230 g potatoes, peeled and sliced
4 oz / 110 g lean bacon or ham, diced
2–3 tbsp chopped coriander
8 oz / 230 g black pudding or spicy sausage
salt
freshly ground black pepper

Put the water, bones, celery and carrot in a large saucepan. Stud one of the onions with the cloves, add it to the pan and bring to the boil. Skim the surface of any impurities and simmer for 3–4 hours, partially covered, skimming from time to time. Carefully pour the stock through a fine sieve into a clean saucepan. Discard the vegetables. Put the beans or chick peas into the stock. Chop the remaining onion and add it to the pan with the remaining vegetables and the bacon or ham. Simmer for an hour or so until the beans are tender. Add the coriander and sausage, and cook for 20–30 minutes more, before seasoning to taste and serving. This is a thick soup, almost a meal in itself, to be served with thick crusty bread.

Porco Alentejana
(Alentejo Pork with Clams)

Serves 4

*If you cannot get the small Venus clams, use cockles, or small mussels,
not the large clams which have a tendency to toughness and, in any
case, are the wrong size for this dish.*

1 medium-sized onion, peeled and
  finely chopped
3 garlic cloves, peeled and finely
  chopped
12 oz / 340 g ripe tomatoes, peeled,
  deseeded and chopped
4 tbsp extra virgin olive oil
2 lb / 900 g Venus clams
2 lb / 900 g pork tenderloin
1 tsp ground coriander
1 tbsp roughly chopped coriander or
  parsley

Gently stew the onion, garlic and tomatoes in 3 tbsp of the olive oil for 20–30
minutes until the onions have more or less disintegrated. Meanwhile, scrub the
clams well under cold running water. Put them in a heavy saucepan with a lid,
4 oz / 110 g at a time, so that you do not risk overcooking them. With just a few in
the pan, they should all open at about the same time. Cover the pan with the lid,
and place over a high heat for 1–2 minutes, shaking the pan once or twice.
Carefully tip the clams into a colander over a bowl to collect the cooking liquor.
Open all the clams and leave in the colander, covered loosely, until ready to use.
Trim away any fat and gristle from the pork, and cut it into ½ in / 1 cm pieces.
Heat the rest of the olive oil in another frying pan and, when hot, add the cubes of
pork. Fry over a moderately high heat for 5 minutes or so, until nicely browned.
Sprinkle in the ground coriander and then add the onion, garlic and tomato
mixture. Cook together for another 5 minutes, then pour into a large heated
serving dish. Stir in the clams, and sprinkle with chopped coriander or parsley.

Poultry and Game

ecipes in this chapter vary from those for high days and holidays to those for simple weekday meals. A roast goose is dealt with in some detail, for a bird like this represents a considerable investment in money and time – a worthwhile investment too, and immensely satisfying when you consider all the other things that can be done with the various bits and by-products, such as rendered fat and giblets. I have learned from experience that, to be on the safe side, if you want a goose for Christmas, it is not too early to put your name down at birth as it were (that is at the goose's birth in the spring), though you might still get one if you ask nicely in September. Free-range and organic farm turkeys should be ordered well in advance of any festivities, too, to be sure of getting what you want. As with everything, it is worth paying more for a free-range, humanely reared, slow-growing bird, which has been fed on what birds normally eat.

For the purpose of these recipes, I am assuming that fresh poultry and game are being used, and I have not, therefore, given thawing times. I have also assumed that you will be using traditional, free-range birds which have plenty of muscle, and which, therefore, take longer to cook than intensively reared birds.

Although jointed poultry is readily available, and I use it occasionally, I find it is worth the extra time it takes to buy whole birds and joint them myself. That way, I have the carcass and trimmings to use for stock. I would certainly make an exception, though, for the Grilled Lemon-Marinated Chicken Wings on page 339.

Quail and guinea fowl are now being reared on a large scale, but it is still possible to buy free-range, organic guinea fowl. Ducks, too, come in a much wider variety than before. No longer do we have just the Lincolnshire breed, but also the very tasty Barbary duck and the cross-breed Gressingham duck. The duck recipes are interchangeable, as indeed are many of the recipes in this chapter. For example, I have often done a chicken version of the Boodles' Roast Stuffed Quail on page 359, which in fact started life as a recipe for partridge. Guinea fowl can be used for many chicken recipes and vice versa. Chicken cooked in cider is very good indeed, using the guinea fowl recipe on page 358.

CHICKEN

Poached Chicken

This is the best way to cook chicken to serve cold in a salad, although it also makes a very nice hot dish. The broth produced is excellent, and can be used either for soup, or as the basis for a sauce to serve with the chicken, or to make a clear jelly to garnish the cold fowl with.

4–5 lb / 1.80–2.30 kg chicken
1 carrot, peeled and chopped
1 celery stalk, trimmed and sliced
1 onion, peeled and chopped

1 leek, trimmed and sliced
parsley stalks
1 tsp peppercorns
a few sprigs of tarragon

Clean the chicken, and, instead of trussing it, insert four metal skewers into it, making sure they go through the thickest, densest parts of the chicken, particularly the thighs. The skewers will help conduct the heat right through the chicken. Place the bird in a large saucepan, and cover with water. Add the rest of the ingredients, and bring slowly to the boil. Lower the heat and, if you intend to serve the chicken hot, allow it to simmer very, very gently for 10 minutes per 1 lb / 455 g, and serve with boiled or steamed rice. If you intend to serve it cold, simmer it very, very gently for only 20 minutes, then remove the pan from the heat, and let the chicken go cold in the stock. The surface of the water should scarcely move, let alone bubble, while the chicken is cooking.

Variations ∽ Use different vegetables to vary the dish. Potatoes or barley and leeks, plus prunes and a few bay leaves, cooked with the chicken, will produce a version of cock-a-leekie. For more of an Italian flavour, you might cook courgettes, beans and a quartered cabbage with the chicken.

One of my favourite versions of this dish comes from Hainan, the large tropical island off the south China coast. The chicken is cooked simply in water, and allowed to cool. The broth is served piping hot with fried onion, slices of fresh ginger and spring onions floating in it, and a bowl of steaming rice accompanies the chicken, which has been chopped into small pieces of a size to be picked up with chopsticks. It is served with a remarkable condiment – fresh ginger, pounded with salt. You eat a mouthful of rice, then the cool, velvety, tender chicken, dipped in the ginger salt, followed by a spoonful of hot broth. It is a stunning combination of tastes, textures and temperatures.

Roast Chicken

*The simplest of all chicken recipes, this is one of the best. Basting with
butter produces a richly flavoured bird, with a burnished, appetizing
skin.*

3–4 lb / 1.35–1.80 kg chicken	twist of lemon zest
salt	handful of parsley stalks
freshly ground black pepper	1 oz / 30 g butter
bay leaf	4 tbsp good dry white wine *(optional)*

Remove excess fat from the body cavity of the chicken. Lightly season the bird
inside and out, and put the bay leaf, lemon zest and parsley stalks inside the cavity.
Carefully ease the skin away from the breast, and with your fingers spread the
butter over the flesh under the skin. Place the bird on a rack in a roasting tin, lying
it on one side of the breast, and pour over the wine, if using. Roast in a preheated
oven at 200°C / 400°F / Mark 6 for 20 minutes. Turn the bird over on to its other
breast, and return it to the oven for a further 20 minutes. Turn the bird breast-side
up, and continue roasting for another 20 minutes or so, until the juices run clear
when a skewer pierces the innermost part of the thigh. Strain the cooking juices
into a pan, bring to the boil, add further wine or water if necessary, and simmer
gently while you carve the chicken. Serve as a simple gravy with the chicken.

Variations ∾ For an oriental flavour, you can rub the chicken, before roasting,
with a mixture of crushed garlic, fresh ginger, soy sauce, toasted sesame oil and
five-spice powder.

A fragrant roast chicken is made by inserting fresh herbs under the skin instead
of the butter. Tarragon, chervil, coriander, thyme, savory and bay are particularly
successful. Allow the chicken to stand, covered and refrigerated, for 48 hours to
allow the scent of the herbs to permeate the flesh. Because of this waiting period,
you must use a very fresh chicken. Roast as above, smearing the butter on the
outside of the chicken before putting it in the oven.

Try the chicken with oyster stuffing to create a more festive dish. Remove the
crusts from six slices of bread, and then tear the bread into small pieces. Trim and
dice two celery stalks and peel and dice two shallots, and blanch them in boiling
water for 2 minutes. Chop up six shelled oysters and a little fresh dill, and mix
these together with the vegetables, bread and oyster juices. Mix in an egg yolk,
season, and spoon the mixture into the cavity of a seasoned chicken. Pack well in,
and close the end with cocktail sticks or thread. Roast as above, smearing the
chicken with melted butter and lemon juice before cooking.

Tarragon Jellied Chicken and Ham

*This is one of those useful 'cut and come again' dishes that keeps well
in the refrigerator, ready for use whenever an impromptu meal or
snack is called for. It is also useful for a large gathering or party.*

1 ham or bacon hock, about 2 lb /
   900 g
1½ lb / 680 g chicken portions, on
   the bone
1 pt / 570 ml dry white wine
1–2 bay leaves
a few parsley stalks

peppercorns
1 slice fresh root ginger *(optional)*
1 small celery stalk
6 leaves gelatine *or* 6 tsp powdered
   gelatine
1 tbsp finely chopped French tarragon
1 tbsp finely chopped parsley

Soak the ham or bacon overnight to get rid of any excess salt. Rinse and put in
a large saucepan. Remove any fat from the chicken joints and put them in the pan
with the ham. Pour on the wine and enough water to cover, about 2–3 pt / 1.15–
1.70 l. Add the herbs, spices, ginger and celery, bring to the boil, and simmer for
an hour or so, removing the chicken after 35–40 minutes, or when cooked. Take
the meat off the bone, in large pieces, and return the bones to the pan. When the
ham is cooked, remove from the pan, and when cool enough to handle, strip the
meat from the bones, discarding the skin. Strain the liquid through a sieve lined
with muslin or a jelly bag, and measure out 1½ pt / 850 ml. Soak the gelatine in
2–3 tablespoons water until soft, and then mix into the hot stock. Stir until
dissolved, reheating if necessary. Pack the meat into a wet 2 lb / 900 g loaf tin, and
scatter each layer with tarragon and parsley. Taste the stock and adjust the
seasoning, if necessary. Carefully pour into the tin, making sure all the air bubbles
are tapped out. Cover, cool quickly and refrigerate until set.

Variation ⁓ For an oriental-style variation, cook the meat in rice wine, water
and a little soy sauce, flavoured with ginger, lemon grass and star anise.

Pot-Roast Chicken with 40 Garlic Cloves

Serves 4

One of my favourite ways of cooking chicken is to pot-roast it with as much garlic as you can tuck into the pot with the bird. The end result is not at all as overpowering as the amount of garlic might suggest. And the carcass makes a wonderfully flavoured chicken and garlic broth for the next day. Of course, you do not have to use exactly 40 cloves of garlic, 20 or 30 will do – or 60!

4–5 heads garlic	1–2 sprigs French tarragon
3½–4 lb / 1.60–1.80 kg chicken	½ oz / 15 g butter
½ lemon	1 tbsp olive oil
salt	1 tbsp cognac
freshly ground black pepper	3–4 tbsp white wine

Separate and peel the garlic cloves, and put to one side. Remove any excess fat from the chicken cavity and neck. Rub the chicken all over with lemon juice, and put the half lemon inside the cavity. Lightly season the bird inside and out, and put the tarragon inside. Heat the butter and oil in a large flameproof casserole, and brown the chicken all over. Pour on the cognac and light it. When the flames have died down, tuck the garlic cloves around and under the chicken, and pour on the wine. Cover and cook in a preheated oven at 190°C / 375°F / Mark 5 for about 1¼ hours. The chicken can be served as it is with the clear juices and whole garlic cloves or a creamy sauce can be made by blending the two together.

Variations ∾ Use diced apple with only 10 cloves of garlic and calvados instead of the 40 cloves of garlic and the cognac.

Make a sweet and sour version by omitting the tarragon, using Muscat wine, and sprinkling with sorrel leaves.

Remove the chicken from the casserole after browning it, and line the casserole with vine leaves. Put in some pitted olives, a handful of herbs and about 20 garlic cloves before returning the chicken to the pot. Do not add any further garlic, but simply flame the chicken in cognac, pour on the wine, and continue as in the recipe above.

Fresh ripe tomatoes and new season's garlic cloves make a good bed on which to pot-roast a chicken. When cooked, the garlic and tomatoes can be rubbed through a sieve to make a sauce.

Chicken with Garlic Potatoes

Serves 8–10

1 tbsp dark muscovado sugar

1 tbsp tomato purée

2 tsp ground paprika

pinch of cayenne pepper or chilli
   powder

2 tsp ground cumin

½ tsp ground cardamom

2 tsp soy sauce

4 tbsp olive oil

2 tbsp wine vinegar or sherry
   vinegar

2 chickens, 3 lb / 1.35 kg each, jointed

juice of 1 lemon

salt

freshly ground black pepper

3 lb / 1.35 kg potatoes

1 head garlic

parsley, watercress or rocket

lemon wedges

Mix together the sugar, tomato purée, spices, soy sauce, half the olive oil and the vinegar to make a marinade. Rub the chicken pieces all over with lemon juice, and season them lightly. Turn the chicken pieces in the marinade until well coated. Cover and refrigerate for a couple of hours or overnight if more convenient.

Preheat the oven to 200°C / 400°F / Mark 6. Arrange the chicken pieces on a rack in a roasting tin, and place in the top half of the oven. Meanwhile, peel the potatoes and cut into 1 in / 2.5 cm chunks. Separate, peel and roughly chop the garlic cloves. Oil an earthenware or other ovenproof dish, put in the potatoes and garlic and add enough of the remaining oil to moisten them well. Put in the oven with the chicken. Turn the chicken pieces after 15–20 minutes, and drain away any fat. After another 15–20 minutes, turn the heat down to 180°C / 350°F / Mark 4, and continue cooking until the potatoes and chicken pieces are cooked. Stir the potatoes and garlic from time to time, and pour on some of the chicken juices to stop them drying out. Serve the chicken pieces on a large platter, surrounding the pile of garlic potatoes. Garnish with parsley, watercress or rocket and some lemon wedges.

If you wish, you can make a gravy by sprinkling a teaspoon or so of flour over the browned juice in the roasting tin and cooking for a minute or two, before adding boiling water with a little wine or some stock and stirring to scrape up the residues. Boil for 3–4 minutes, and then strain into a jug or gravy boat.

Variation ∽ Instead of marinating the chicken pieces, just season them, dip them in beaten egg and then coat in fine breadcrumbs before baking them. This is particularly good with baked sweet potatoes instead of the garlic potatoes.

Tandoori Chicken

Serves 4–6, as a starter

3 lb / 1.35 kg chicken, skinned and jointed	¼ pt / 140 ml plain yoghurt
2 tsp salt	½ tsp chilli powder
6 garlic cloves, peeled and crushed	2 tbsp tandoori spice mixture
	1 tbsp tomato purée

Make two or three small cuts in each piece of chicken, and rub half the salt and garlic into them. Mix the rest of the salt and garlic with the other ingredients in a bowl. Place the chicken pieces in the mixture, cover and leave to marinate for at least 6 hours. Remove the chicken pieces from the yoghurt mixture, letting the excess drip back into the bowl. Place the pieces in a single layer on an oiled baking sheet, and bake in a preheated oven at 180–190°C / 350–375°F / Mark 4–5 for 40–45 minutes. Pour off any excess juices which accumulate during cooking, as the chicken should be slightly dry on the outside and juicy (but cooked through, of course) on the inside. Serve with salad leaves, onion rings and lemon wedges.

Coq au Vin de Cahors

Serves 6–8

We were served a dish similar to this by my friend Michèle, who lives in a small hamlet in Languedoc, where her neighbours' chickens and cockerels run around her yard.

5–6 lb / 2.30–2.70 kg cockerel (or hen, which changes the dish to *Poule au Vin de Cahors*)	1 bay leaf
	sprig of thyme
	2–3 parsley stalks
6 oz / 170 g belly pork	3–4 garlic cloves, peeled
12 small onions *or* 1 large onion	2 tsp black peppercorns
2 leeks	2 cloves
2 carrots	piece of pork skin, cut into 2 in / 5 cm squares
small glass of cognac	
2 bottles Cahors red wine	salt

Joint the bird into eight pieces, and chop the remaining carcass into two or three. These pieces can be cooked with the casserole to add extra flavour. Remove the rind from the belly pork, and cut it into matchsticks. Fry gently in a large frying pan until the fat runs. Meanwhile, peel the onions, and if using a large one, slice it. Trim the leeks, and slice the white parts only, discarding the green tops. Peel and slice the carrots. Fry the vegetables with the pork, and when just beginning to brown, transfer to a large flameproof casserole. In the fat remaining in the pan, brown the chicken pieces on both sides, and transfer to the casserole. Pour on the cognac and light it. In another large saucepan, bring the wine to the boil, light it, and let it flame for a minute. Cover with a lid to extinguish the flames. Pour a little into the frying pan to deglaze it, scraping up all the cooking residues. Pour over the chicken, together with the rest of the wine. Tie the herbs, garlic and spices in a piece of muslin (or put them in a coffee filter paper, fold over and staple to keep it closed), and put this in the casserole, together with the squares of pork skin. Bring to the boil, cover, and cook in a preheated oven at 150°C / 300°F / Mark 2 for about 3 hours, or cook it on the hob on a heat diffusing mat, until tender.

When almost ready, strain the cooking juices into a frying pan, and reduce over a high heat until you have the consistency and flavour you like. Salt it only at this stage. (The sauce can also be thickened by stirring in a small amount of flour mixed with equal quantities of softened butter.) Arrange the pieces of meat in a serving dish, and pour the sauce over it. The coq au vin can be garnished with fresh or fried parsley and triangles of bread fried in duck or chicken fat or olive oil.

Variation ∽ Coq au Riesling is an Alsace dish, which is quite delicious and based on the above recipe without the belly pork, and with white wine replacing the dark red wine of Cahors. Serve it with sauerkraut and noodles.

Chicken in Salmorejo

Serves 4–6

3–4 lb / 1.35–1.80 kg chicken
2 lb / 900 g tomatoes
6 garlic cloves

¼ pt / 140 ml extra virgin olive oil
4 tbsp sherry vinegar
salt

Roast the chicken whole (see page 330), or if you have a char-grill or barbecue, joint it, and grill the pieces. Peel and deseed the tomatoes, and put them in a blender with the garlic, oil, vinegar and salt to taste. Blend until smooth. If you have roasted the whole chicken, joint it. Put the chicken portions in a deep casserole or earthenware dish, and pour the sauce over it. Cover and leave to stand for several hours in a cool place or, preferably, the refrigerator. Allow to come back to room temperature before serving.

Chicken Breasts with Fennel and Walnuts

Serves 4

*Make this dish in the autumn when the first of the walnuts
are available.*

4 skinless, boneless chicken breasts
2 tbsp walnut oil
juice and grated zest of 1 orange
1 small fennel bulb
2–3 garlic cloves
2–3 tbsp chicken stock or water

2 oz / 60 g fresh wet walnut halves
2 tbsp fromage frais
freshly ground white pepper
salt
finely chopped walnuts or mild paprika,
  to garnish *(optional)*

Brush the chicken breasts all over with walnut oil and pour half the orange
juice over them. Allow to marinate for at least 30 minutes while you prepare the
sauce. Trim any discoloured portions from the fennel. Remove and reserve any
nice, fresh-looking feathery tops for garnish, and slice and dice the bulb. Peel and
roughly chop the garlic. In a non-stick pan, sweat the vegetables over a very low
heat until soft. Moisten with the rest of the orange juice, and the chicken stock or
water and the orange zest. Remove as much skin as you can from the walnuts.
(Fresh wet walnuts are relatively easy to peel, and it does improve this delicate
sauce if you can remove the bitter skin.) Put the soft vegetables in the blender with
the cooking juices, the walnuts and the fromage frais. Blend until smooth and sieve
or not, as you prefer. Put the sauce in a double saucepan, or a heatproof bowl set
over a pan of hot water. Let the sauce heat up gently as you cook the chicken. This
is simply done by putting the breasts in a single layer in a non-stick frying pan,
covering with a lid or foil and letting them cook in their own juices for 12–15
minutes. ('Sweating' really is the best word to describe this method of cooking
done without fat.) When the chicken breasts are done, drain the cooking juices into
the, by now, hot sauce and season it to taste. Transfer the chicken breasts to a
heated serving dish or individual plates. Serve the sauce separately or poured over
the chicken, or indeed in a pool under the chicken. Garnish with the reserved
fennel leaves and some finely chopped walnuts if you like, or more simply with a
fine powdering of mild paprika.

Stir-Fried Chicken with Celeriac and Mushrooms

Serves 4–6

Whilst celeriac is a favourite addition to casseroles and makes a traditional slow-cooked braised vegetable to serve with game or roast beef, it also lends itself well to a simple stir-fry. The flavour given to the rest of the ingredients is that of celery, but the texture is quite different. It is important to slice it thinly for quick cooking.

3 skinless, boneless chicken breasts, 5 oz / 140 g each
amontillado sherry or rice wine
pinch of five-spice powder or ground fennel
12 oz / 340 g celeriac
1 carrot
4 oz / 110 g shiitake, oyster or cultivated mushrooms

3–4 spring onions or baby leeks
3 garlic cloves
1 tbsp sunflower oil
1–2 tbsp soy sauce
2 tsp toasted sesame oil
2 tsp toasted sesame seeds

Cut the chicken into oblique strips, no more than ½ in / 1 cm thick and about 1½ in / 4 cm long. Marinate them in the sherry or wine and spice while you prepare the vegetables. Peel and slice the celeriac, and then cut it into fine strips, or shave it into strips with a potato peeler. Deal with the carrot in the same way, or cut it into very thin oblique slices. Wipe the mushrooms and slice them. Trim and slice the onions or leeks, and peel and crush the garlic. With a slotted spoon, remove the chicken from its marinade, and let this drip back into the bowl for use later. Dry the chicken on kitchen paper. Heat the sunflower oil in a wok or frying pan, and when it is hot, stir in the chicken pieces and cook for 2–3 minutes. Add the celeriac and carrots, and stir-fry these for a few minutes more. Add the mushrooms, spring onions or leeks and garlic. Stir continuously for another couple of minutes or so, then put the lid on to let it all steam for another few minutes. Add 2 tbsp water, the soy sauce and sesame oil, stir to blend all the flavour, and then turn out into a serving dish. Scatter on the sesame seeds (which you can toast yourself by heating gently in a heavy frying pan). This is very good served with crisp green vegetables, such as broccoli, green beans or Chinese flowering cabbage (*choy sum*).

Mushroom-Stuffed Chicken Breasts

Serves 4

2 oz / 60 g dried ceps
4 dried Chinese mushrooms
¼ pt / 140 ml boiling water
4 skinless, boneless chicken breasts
4–5 tbsp Noilly Prat
pinch of freshly ground allspice
¼ tsp freshly ground black pepper
8 oz / 230 g fresh cup, button,
   oyster or brown mushrooms
2 oz / 60 g unsalted butter

1 tbsp olive oil
2–3 sprigs lemon thyme or basil leaves
2 garlic cloves, peeled and crushed
   (*optional*)
1 tbsp finely chopped flat-leaved parsley
salt
freshly ground black pepper
¼ pt / 140 ml chicken stock
butter, chilled and diced (*optional*)
finely chopped flat-leaved parsley, to
   garnish

Put the dried mushrooms in a bowl, and pour on the boiling water. Rub the chicken all over with half the Noilly Prat, and season lightly with the allspice and pepper. Wipe and slice the fresh mushrooms, and fry them in half the butter and oil. Add the lemon thyme or basil, and cook with the mushrooms for about 8 minutes. Strain the soaked dried mushrooms carefully to keep the juices, and then rinse if necessary to remove any grit. Slice, discarding any woody bits, and add to the mushrooms and herbs in the pan. Cook until all are tender and well amalgamated. Crushed garlic can be added, if liked. Remove from the heat, put to one side, and stir in the parsley. With a sharp knife, cut a long, deep pocket in each chicken breast. Season the mushroom mixture, and spoon it into the pocket in each breast, securing the openings with cocktail sticks. Heat the remaining butter and oil in a frying pan, and fry the chicken breasts on both sides until golden brown. Lower the heat, partially cover and cook for a further 15–20 minutes, until the juices show clear when the flesh is pierced with a knife. Transfer the meat to a warm plate, and cover with foil while you finish off the sauce. Deglaze the chicken frying pan with the rest of the Noilly Prat, and add the stock. Reduce by half, and pour on the soaking liquid from the dried mushrooms. Reduce by at least half again, and check the seasoning and consistency. Reduce further or add a splash of water, as necessary. The sauce can be 'buttered' at this stage; that is, 'mounted' with small pieces of chilled butter stirred in, or it can be left plain and clear. Spoon on to warm plates with the chicken breasts, and garnish with parsley.

Variations ∽ Chicken breasts can be prepared in this way with a variety of different stuffings. Here are some suggestions:

Simply stuff the breasts with a little crushed garlic, some chopped fresh tarragon and thin slices of mozzarella cheese. Season the breasts, and fry in butter on each side for about 8–10 minutes. Serve immediately with the pan juices poured over, or make a sauce as above using white wine or vermouth and water as the liquid.

Stuff the breasts with slices of ripe avocado and mozzarella cheese. Season lightly, and then instead of frying the breasts, bake them *en papillote* (see page 290) with a few sprigs of fresh thyme or marjoram and a splash of vermouth or white wine, for 15–20 minutes at 190°C / 375°F / Mark 5.

Stuff the breasts with fresh basil leaves, ricotta cheese and a little grilled, peeled and chopped red pepper. Season, and this time steam for about 20 minutes either on a shallow dish in a steamer or on a steamer rack in a saucepan, with a few pieces of softened liquorice root in the steaming water. To make a sauce, simmer some chicken stock with another piece of softened liquorice root for about 15 minutes. Remove the liquorice root, strain in the cooking liquid from the chicken, and reduce to about half. Enrich with cream or butter if you wish, and serve poured over the chicken. If you don't like liquorice, try using herbs, ginger or citrus zest instead.

Grilled Lemon-Marinated Chicken Wings

Serves 6–8

24 chicken wings	2 tbsp clear honey
2 tbsp soy sauce	pinch of five-spice powder
2 tbsp lemon juice	2 star anise
grated zest of 1 lemon	3–4 garlic cloves, peeled and crushed
1–2 tbsp lemon grass stalks, trimmed and thinly sliced	½ tsp Szechuan peppercorns or freshly ground black pepper
2 tbsp dry sherry or rice wine	1 tbsp toasted sesame oil

Put the chicken wings in a large bowl. Mix the rest of the ingredients together, and pour over the chicken, turning to coat thoroughly. Cover, refrigerate and leave overnight. When ready to grill the meat, drain the pieces, letting the marinade drip back. Grill the chicken wings, brushing with the marinade from time to time. Remove and pile on a platter. Boil the marinade for 3–4 minutes, and serve with the chicken.

Spring Vegetable and Chicken Casserole

Serves 8–10

2 chickens, 3 lb / 1.35 kg each,
  jointed
2 tbsp olive oil
1 large onion, peeled and chopped
1½ lb / 680 g new potatoes,
  scrubbed
6 oz / 170 g carrots, peeled and
  thickly sliced
1 head garlic, peeled and chopped
  (optional)
1 pt / 570 ml dry white wine

2–3 sprigs tarragon
8 oz / 230 g green beans, topped and
  tailed
1 lb / 455 g small courgettes, thickly
  sliced
6 oz / 170 g baby sweetcorn
4 oz / 110 g mangetout or sugar snap
  peas
sea salt
freshly ground black pepper
chopped chervil, parsley or tarragon

Trim excess fat from the chicken pieces, and fry them in the olive oil in a frying pan until just browning all over. Transfer the pieces to a large flameproof casserole. Fry the onion until golden brown, and put with the chicken. Put about ¼ in / 0.5 cm cold water in the frying pan, bring to the boil and scrape up all the caramelized bits stuck to the bottom of the pan. Pour over the chicken. Add more water to come halfway up the chicken, cover and simmer gently for 15–20 minutes. Add the potatoes, carrots, garlic, if using, wine and tarragon, and cook for a further 10 minutes before adding the rest of the vegetables. Continue cooking until the vegetables are just done. Season to taste, and scatter on the herbs before serving.

TURKEY

Braised Turkey, Stuffed with Herbs, Garlic and Truffle

Serves 8

6 garlic cloves, peeled
1 truffle, scrubbed *or* 1 oz / 30 g
   dried porcini, soaked for 30
   minutes and drained
6 lb / 2.70 kg fresh turkey
herbs, such as chervil, tarragon,
   coriander or parsley, or a mixture
   of these
2½ fl oz / 70 ml white port or fino
   sherry

4 tbsp extra virgin olive oil or melted
   butter
salt
freshly ground black pepper
8 oz / 230 g belly pork
1 onion, peeled and sliced
1 carrot, peeled and chopped
1 celery stalk, trimmed and sliced
1 leek, trimmed and sliced
½ pt / 280 ml turkey stock

Cut the garlic in thin slivers, and thinly slice the truffle or cut the porcini into thin slivers. Ease the skin away from the flesh of the turkey, over breast, thighs and drumsticks. Arrange the garlic, truffle or mushroom pieces and the herbs over the flesh. Draw the skin back into place and secure with a cocktail stick.

Mix the port or sherry and olive oil or butter, and brush it over the bird. Lightly season the surface and inside the cavity. Remove the rind from the belly pork, cut it into small strips, and fry in a flameproof casserole large enough to hold the turkey and vegetables. Lightly brown the belly pork, and add the vegetables, letting them fry until the onion just begins to change colour. Place the turkey on top of the vegetables. Pour on the stock and any remaining port and olive oil, bring to the boil, cover with a tight-fitting lid and transfer to a preheated oven at 170°C / 325°F / Mark 3 for about 3 hours. Test for thorough cooking by piercing the inner thigh. The juices should run clear. If using a meat thermometer, it should read 71–77°C / 160–170°F. The lid can be removed for the last 20 minutes or so to brown the breast. Transfer the turkey to a carving board, making sure to drain all the juices out of the cavity into the casserole as you lift it. Cover with foil, and keep it in a warm place while you make the gravy. Strain the cooking juices into a shallow pan, and reduce the liquid until it has the flavour and consistency you desire. Pour into a heated jug.

Pork and Chestnut Forcemeat Balls

Serves 6–8

*You can roast a turkey in much the same way as you would a chicken
(see page 330), but it is probably better to cover the bird with a
buttered cloth (cheesecloth or muslin that has been dipped in melted
butter) rather than to spread butter under the skin. At 180°C /
350°F / Mark 4, allow 3–3½ hours for a 6–8 lb / 2.70–3.60 kg bird,
and 3¾–4½ hours for a 10–14 lb / 4.50–6.30 kg bird. Stuffing the
body cavity is not recommended; serve with these forcemeat balls
instead.*

1 lb / 455 g chestnuts	finely grated zest of 1 lemon
milk	¼ tsp ground allspice
6 oz / 170 g belly pork	salt
1 turkey liver	freshly ground black pepper
2 tbsp soft breadcrumbs	1 egg yolk
1 tbsp finely chopped parsley	1 tbsp brandy

To peel the chestnuts, make a slit at the tip of each nut, and put them under a
hot grill or in a heavy frying pan to roast them until the shell becomes brittle
enough to remove. Peel off the bitter brown skin underneath, and cook the
chestnuts in milk until they are tender. Remove the skin from the belly pork and
cut the pork into chunks. Remove any sinews and discoloured parts from the liver
and mince or process it with the pork. Drain the chestnuts and, depending on
whether you like a smooth or more textured forcemeat, sieve or process the
chestnuts or break them up with a fork. Mix with the meats and the rest of the
ingredients. Form into balls with wet hands, and bake alongside the turkey for the
last 30–40 minutes.

Bread Sauce

Makes 1 pt / 570 ml

This is also traditionally served with roast turkey.

1 small onion, peeled
6 cloves
1 pt / 570 ml full-cream milk
1 bay leaf
4 oz / 110 g fresh white
  breadcrumbs

1 oz / 30 g butter
salt
freshly ground white pepper
freshly grated nutmeg

Stud the onion with the cloves, and put it in a saucepan with the milk. Add the bay leaf, bring to the boil, then remove from the heat, cover and leave to infuse for 20–30 minutes. Stir in the breadcrumbs and butter, and cook gently for 15 minutes. Remove the onion, cloves and bay leaf and season to taste with the salt, pepper and nutmeg.

Variation ∾ Replace the 1 oz / 30 g of breadcrumbs with 1 oz / 30 g of ground almonds.

Turkey and Olive Casserole

Serves 6

Marinade
1 pt / 570 ml good dry white wine
1 carrot, peeled and thinly sliced
1 onion, peeled and thinly sliced
1 leek, trimmed and thinly sliced
1 celery stalk, trimmed and thinly
  sliced
2 tbsp extra virgin olive oil
4 garlic cloves, peeled and crushed

2 lb / 900 g uncooked turkey meat, off
  the bone
1 bay leaf
6 firm ripe tomatoes, peeled, deseeded
  and cut into strips
4 oz / 110 g green or black olives

First, make the marinade. Bring the wine to the boil with the carrot, onion, leek, celery and most of the olive oil. Allow to cool and then stir in the garlic.

Cut the meat into 1 in / 2.5 cm pieces, and pour the marinade over the meat, add the bay leaf, tomatoes and olives. Allow to bubble once or twice, then turn the heat down very low. Cook for 45 minutes or until the meat is tender.

Turkey Bstila

*This crisp, golden, flaky, filo pie has long been a favourite of mine,
and makes a lovely lunch or buffet dish. It is based on a Moroccan
sweet and savoury pie. The amount of sugar and spices and fruit it
contains might surprise you, but I urge you not to stint on these.
Leftover turkey meat becomes a real treat prepared this way.*

5 eggs
½ pt / 280 ml strong turkey stock
4 oz / 110 g butter, melted
18 sheets filo pastry
3 tbsp sugar
4 oz / 110 g flaked almonds, cooked
  in butter
1 tsp ground cinnamon
1½ lb / 680 g cooked turkey meat,
  off the bone

4 oz / 110 g chopped dried fruits, e.g.
  apricots, etc.
2 oz / 60 g pickled lemons, chopped
  (optional)
1 tsp cardamom seeds
1 tsp cumin seeds
1 tsp ground cumin
2 tsp coriander seeds
1 tsp ground coriander
almonds, olives and mint, to garnish

Beat the eggs with the stock, and cook gently in a non-stick frying pan, almost
as if you were making scrambled eggs, stirring continuously. When lightly set,
remove the pan from the heat and allow to cool.

Brush a shallow 10 × 8 in / 25.5 × 20.5 cm dish with melted butter. Brush two
sheets of filo pastry with melted butter and fit into the dish with edges overlapping.
Fit in four further sheets of pastry, cut to the size of the dish, and individually
brushed with melted butter. Sprinkle on half the sugar, almonds and cinnamon.
Pour the egg mixture over this, reserving 3 tablespoons. Lay six more sheets of
pastry on top, trimmed to fit the dish and each one brushed with melted butter.

Cut the turkey into ½ in / 1 cm chunks. Mix it with the dried fruit, pickled
lemons, if using, cardamom, cumin, coriander seeds and the rest of the sugar,
almonds and cinnamon. Lay on top of the pastry. Spoon the remaining egg mixture
over the top, and smooth over. Cut four more sheets of pastry to fit the dish, brush
with melted butter, and lay over the filling. Fold over the overlapping pastry as
neatly as possible, and fit the remaining two trimmed and buttered sheets on top.
Bake in preheated oven at 180°C / 350°F / Mark 4 for 40 minutes. Increase the
temperature to 200°C / 400°F / Mark 6 for 10 minutes to cook to golden brown.

To serve, turn the bstila on to a serving platter, and garnish with almonds,
olives and mint leaves. Serve hot or cold.

DUCK

Grilled Duck Breasts

Serves 4

4 duck breasts
1 carrot, peeled and chopped
1 onion, peeled and chopped
1 celery stalk, trimmed and sliced
2–3 garlic cloves, peeled and
   crushed

sprig of fresh thyme
½ pt / 280 ml dry white wine
¼ pt / 140 ml unsalted duck stock
finely chopped parsley or chervil
salt
freshly ground black pepper

Trim any fat and membranes from the duck breasts. Leave on or remove the skin, as you prefer. Put the meat in a dish in a single layer and spread the vegetables, garlic and thyme over it. Pour on the wine, cover and leave to marinate overnight in the refrigerator.

When ready to cook, bring the meat back to room temperature. Heat the grill very hot and lightly oil the rack. Remove the meat from the marinade and wipe it dry. Grill on both sides, browning the meat well, and then turn down the heat to continue cooking until done how you like it. Transfer the meat from the grill to a plate, loosely cover it, and keep it in a warm place while you finish the sauce. Drain any cooking juices into a small frying pan, strain in the marinade, and boil it until it has reduced by half and the alcohol has evaporated. Add the stock, and boil until the sauce is of the right consistency. Stir in the chopped herbs and season to taste. To serve, either slice the meat or leave the breasts whole. I like to serve a little gooseberry or redcurrant jelly with it and some steamed vegetables. Courgettes, kohlrabi, broccoli and beans would all go well.

Roast Duck with Glutinous Rice Stuffing

Serves 4

You should start preparation the day before.

6 lb / 2.70 kg Lincolnshire or
   Barbary duck

Marinade
¼ pt / 140 ml wine or dry sherry
3 tbsp soy sauce
2 tbsp clear honey
1 tbsp rice vinegar or sherry vinegar
1 celery stalk, trimmed and sliced
1 garlic clove, peeled and chopped
1 shallot, peeled and chopped
½ oz / 15 g fresh root ginger, peeled
   and chopped

Stuffing
3 oz / 85 g belly pork
3 oz / 85 g short grain rice
duck heart, gizzard and liver, chopped
¼ tsp five-spice powder or ground
   aniseed
2 cloves
2 in / 5 cm piece of tangerine peel,
   finely chopped
6 fl oz / 170 ml stock or water
freshly ground black pepper
salt

Remove any loose fat from the duck cavity. (If you like this kind of thing, and I do, duck fat is excellent for cooking. Prepare it by melting it very gently in a frying pan and pour it into a container which you can refrigerate once the fat has cooled.) Prick the duck all over with a larding needle or sharp pointed knife. Put all the marinade ingredients in a saucepan and simmer gently for 10 minutes. Allow to cool, and strain it, reserving the vegetables. Put the duck in a shallow dish, breast-side down, and pour on the marinade. Turn once or twice, cover loosely, and leave in the refrigerator for at least 12 hours and preferably 24 hours.

Next day, prepare the stuffing. Cut the belly pork into small ¼ in / 0.5 cm cubes, leaving the skin on as this gives the right sort of stickiness to the stuffing. Fry it gently until the fat runs, and then raise the heat to brown the meat a little. Stir in the rice, the duck heart, gizzard and liver, spices, tangerine peel and vegetables from the marinade, and cook for 2–3 minutes. Pour on half the stock or water, season and bring to the boil. Cover and simmer gently until the rice is almost cooked. (You may need to add more stock.) Allow the stuffing to cool slightly before spooning it into the duck. Place the duck on a rack in a roasting tin, having dried it thoroughly, and roast it in a preheated oven at 190°C / 375°F / Mark 5 for 1½ hours, turning up the heat to 200°C / 400°F / Mark 6 for the last 10 minutes or so. Allow the duck to rest for 10–15 minutes before carving.

A bowl of steamed or stir-fried mixed vegetables goes very well with the duck. I like to do a mixture of green beans, broccoli, mangetout, baby sweetcorn, carrot strips, celery and perhaps some bean sprouts.

Variations ∽ You may insert slivers of garlic into the skin of the bird, and vary the stuffing by omitting the belly pork, browning the chopped heart, gizzard and liver in a little butter, and replacing the five-spice or aniseed and tangerine peel with a little grated apple, some sultanas, a handful of pinenuts or chopped almonds and a little chopped thyme or oregano.

Stuffed Orange-Glazed Duck Breasts

Serves 4

4 duck breasts
juice and grated zest of 1 orange

1 tbsp orange marmalade
2 tbsp Southern Comfort or whisky

Stuffing
5 oz / 140 g cooked rice *or* 3 oz / 85 g soft breadcrumbs
1 small onion, peeled and finely chopped
1 celery stalk, trimmed and finely chopped

4 dried apricots, soaked, drained and chopped
1 tbsp pinenuts or chopped walnuts
1 tbsp finely chopped parsley
salt
freshly ground black pepper

Remove the fillets from the duck breasts, and use in another recipe. With a sharp knife, make a deep pocket in each duck breast to hold the stuffing, taking care not to pierce the flesh around the edges. Score the duck skin quite deeply, diagonally and across. This will help the fat to drain away as the meat cooks. Mix the grated orange zest with half of the orange juice, the marmalade and liqueur. Brush the duck breasts with this mixture. Mix the stuffing ingredients with the rest of the orange juice and spoon into the pockets in the duck breasts. Brush the meat with more of the basting liquid, and arrange the duck breasts on a wire rack in a roasting tin. Roast towards the top of a preheated oven at 220°C / 425°F / Mark 7 for 12–15 minutes, depending on the thickness of the meat and how well done you like it. Brush the meat twice during cooking with the orange mixture. Remove from the oven, and allow the meat to rest in a warm place for 5–10 minutes. Serve with a watercress salad and plain boiled or steamed potatoes in their jackets.

Duck Breasts with Pumpkin Seed Sauce

Serves 4

*I was once taken to Rosa Mexicana, said by many to be the best
Mexican restaurant in Manhattan, and was served an exquisitely
subtle dish of duck in pumpkin seed sauce or* pipian. *The elusive
sharpness came from the green tomato or tomatillo, with its papery
husk. This is not easy to find here. You could use physalis or Cape
gooseberry which is a close relation, but it will change the colour of
the sauce. I have retained the rich green colour of the sauce and
slightly altered the flavour by using a firm under-ripe kiwi fruit, or
alternatively, you could use a squeeze of lime juice. This recipe works
well with chicken, with duck and with wild duck. Wild rice makes a
very good accompaniment.*

4 duck breasts, off the bone
salt
freshly ground black pepper
3 oz / 85 g toasted pumpkin seeds
1 medium onion, peeled and
 chopped
1–2 green chillies (or more to taste),
 seeded and chopped

3 garlic cloves, peeled and crushed
1 tbsp sunflower oil
1 oz / 30 g coriander, chopped
1 oz / 30 g watercress leaves, chopped
2½ fl oz / 70 ml duck stock or water
1 firm, under-ripe kiwi fruit

Remove the skin from the duck breasts, season lightly, and poach in stock or
water for 5–8 minutes. Remove and put to one side. To make the sauce, gently fry
the seeds, and then the onion, chillies and garlic in the oil, until the onions are soft
and wilted. Stir in half the coriander and watercress and the stock or water and
simmer for a few minutes. Peel the kiwi fruit, roughly chop, and put in a blender or
food processor with the sauce and the rest of the coriander and watercress. Blend
until smooth, then return the sauce to the pan set over a gentle heat. Put the duck
breasts in the sauce, and cook the two together for 4–5 minutes before serving.

Duck Breasts with Redcurrant Sauce

Serves 4

4 duck breasts
1–2 shallots, peeled and finely
  chopped
4 oz / 110 g oyster mushrooms
4 oz / 110 g redcurrants, removed
  from stalks and washed
4 tbsp dry white wine

4 tbsp chicken, duck, veal or vegetable
  stock
salt
freshly ground black pepper
2 oz / 60 g chilled butter, diced
  (*optional*)

Place the duck breasts in a saucepan, skin-side down, and cook over a gentle heat until the fat runs. Add the shallots and mushrooms, then put them to one side. Drain off most of the duck fat from the pan and add most of the redcurrants, reserving a few berries to add to the sauce just before serving. Raise the heat, and cook just long enough to crisp the skin of the duck, and then turn the meat over and fry for a few minutes on the underside. Cooking will depend on the thickness of the meat and how well done you like it. Remove the duck breasts, and keep them warm while you finish the sauce. Deglaze the pan with the wine and stock, crushing the juice out of the redcurrants. Sieve the sauce into a small, clean saucepan and bring to the boil. Season to taste, and add the shallots, mushrooms and reserved redcurrants. Place the duck breasts on heated plates, and spoon on the sauce. If you want to enrich the sauce, do this by adding the chilled butter to the sauce, a piece at a time, before putting in the mushrooms. Make sure each piece of butter is absorbed into the sauce before adding the next piece. Stir the sauce, and swirl it, off the heat, to emulsify the mixture.

Variations Use elderberries in place of redcurrants for a rich dark sauce. Blackberries, blueberries or cranberries can also be used.

To Salt and Poach Duck Breasts

Serves 4

This is a Welsh recipe that comes from The First Principles of Good
Cookery *by Lady Llanover, first published in 1867. It is a curious
book, written in the person of a hermit passing on the principles of
good cookery to the traveller, and covering such diverse matters as the
management of hedgerows, the rearing of goats and beekeeping, as
well as the art or science of making soup and how to 'potch a dish of
eggs for a weak stomach'.*

4 duck breasts
2–3 oz / 60–85 g coarse sea salt

Rub the duck breasts all over with the salt, and put them in a shallow dish.
Cover and refrigerate for 3 days. At least once a day, rub the salt in again. On the
third day, rinse all the salt off, and put the meat in an ovenproof dish in a roasting
tin. Pour on enough water just to cover the duck breasts, and then pour 1–2 in /
2.5–5 cm water into the roasting tin. Bring the water in the roasting tin to the boil,
then turn the heat down as low as possible, or transfer to a preheated oven at 150°C
/ 300°F / Mark 2. Poach, uncovered, for about 1½ hours. The duck will be tender
and cooked through rather than pink. Serve hot with an onion sauce, or allow to
cool, slice and serve with salad.

Duckling Casserole

Serves 6

2 ducklings, 5 lb / 2.30 kg each
piece of celery
slice of fresh root ginger
2 bay leaves
2 onions, peeled and sliced
4 cloves

1 sprig of thyme
½ pt / 280 ml dry white wine
1 lb / 455 g mixed root vegetables, such
    as parsnips, carrots, turnips, potatoes
    and celeriac, scrubbed or peeled and
    cut into chunks

Remove the wish bone from each duckling, then with a sharp knife, remove
each breast. Refrigerate these, and use for another meal (see pages 347–350). Cut
off the wings and the legs. Divide the leg joints into thighs and drumsticks, and cut
the wings into three joints. Remove as much of the skin and fat as possible from the

duckling legs and carcasses, and put it in a casserole or ovenproof dish, setting aside a little of the fat for the casserole ingredients. Chop up the carcasses and put in a large saucepan with the smallest wing joints, the piece of celery stalk, slice of fresh root ginger and a bay leaf. Cover with water and boil to make stock. (If you have giblets with the ducklings, add the necks to the stock ingredients.)

Fry the onions in the reserved duck fat in a flameproof casserole, and then brown the meat. If you have giblets, add the heart, gizzard and liver. Add the cloves, remaining bay leaf and thyme, and the white wine. Bring to simmering point, add the vegetables, cover and cook in the middle of a preheated oven at 150–180°C / 300–350°F / Mark 2–4 until the meat is tender. About 45 minutes at the higher temperature you will find should be sufficient, and about 1½ hours at the lower temperature.

While the casserole is cooking, put the dish containing the fat and skin in the bottom of the oven to melt the fat. This will take at least as long as the casserole takes to cook. When all the fat has been rendered, strain into a container, and refrigerate when cool. This fat is excellent in pastry- and scone-making and for frying potatoes. I fry potatoes perhaps once or twice a year, and when I do, I like something tasty to fry them in. The remaining bits of skin and meat in the dish can be chopped, transferred to a frying pan and crisped up to serve as lardons with a frisée salad. Thus, nothing is wasted.

Strain the stock into a jug, cool, cover and refrigerate it, so that it is ready for using in another recipe.

Braised Duckling with Turnips

Serves 4

4–5 lb / 1.80–2.30 kg duckling, jointed

1 medium onion, peeled and thinly sliced

1 lb / 455 g small fresh turnips (the purple or white and pale green variety), peeled and thinly sliced

3 in / 7.5 cm piece of orange zest

¾ pt / 430 ml stock, water or good wine

2½ fl oz / 70 ml port or vermouth

1 tsp arrowroot

salt

freshly ground black pepper

chopped parsley, to garnish

In a deep heavy, frying pan or *sauteuse*, lay the pieces of duckling, skin-side down, and cook for 10–15 minutes, until the fat runs free. Remove the pieces and put to one side. Drain off most of the fat (which can be kept for other cooking purposes). Fry the onion in the fat remaining in the pan until browned lightly, then add the turnips and cook for a few minutes. Lay the pieces of duckling on top, skin-side up, add the orange zest and pour on the stock, water or wine. Bring to the boil, remove any scum which forms on the surface of the liquid, cover and simmer very gently for 45–50 minutes, until the meat is tender. Mix the port or vermouth with the arrowroot, and stir this into the liquid. Bring back to the boil, season to taste and serve in a heated serving dish sprinkled with parsley. New potatoes or rice would go very well with this.

GOOSE

SOME YEARS AGO, I was to cook a goose for Christmas dinner at my parents' home in Derbyshire, and asked them to order a goose from their butcher. I marinated it, stuffed it and roasted it carefully to a burnished golden brown. Marvellous trimmings were prepared, and it made its crisp, golden appearance on the table. My father took up the knives and his carving position, while the rest of us looked on with expectation. But the bird was so tough that it was impossible even to pierce its skin. It turned out to have been an old farmyard goose, probably someone's 'guard dog', for they are an excellent deterrent to intruders. If you intend to cook goose, therefore, always look for one born within the year.

In spite of that experience, I can certainly recommend goose, both at Christmas and at Michaelmas (29 September), when serving it is an old English tradition that is said to bring prosperity for the coming year. By then, goslings born in the spring will have had five or six months to fatten up and will be just ready for the table.

A gosling, or a 'green goose', weighing around 7–10 lb / 3.20–4.50 kg, is eaten at about six months old, and an adult bird, weighing up to 18 lb / 8.15 kg, is sold for the table up to about 18 months old. Goose is still very much seasonal and has largely been spared intensive rearing, hence its relatively high cost. Pound for pound, it also has less meat on it than a chicken or turkey, and can at first seem an extravagance. A 12 lb / 5.45 kg goose will only feed four, or six at a pinch, but you should also have about 1½ lb / 680 g meat pickings from the carcass, which can be potted (see page 355) or used to make Parmentier of Goose (see page 356), and about 1 lb / 455 g clean white fat from the cavity, which makes a fine shortening for pastry, and another large pot of fat drained from the roasting, which you can use for roasting potatoes or for frying. The carcass makes a good soup and the giblets a rich sauce (see page 356). You can even bone and stuff the neck to make a sausage if you have the patience.

To Roast a Goose

This is how I cook a 12 lb / 5.45 kg (table weight) goose to serve four people. Remove any giblets and the clean white fat from the cavity, and keep these for later use. Fill the cavity with a bunch of mixed herbs. Line a large roasting tin with a piece of foil, large enough to come up the sides of the goose, and cut an extra piece to lay lightly on top of the bird to stop the breast from browning too much. Swaddle the drumsticks with pieces of foil, since they do not have a thick skin and layer of fat and are liable to dry out. Prick the bird all over, particularly at the sides, at the neck and at the vent end, where most of the fat is concentrated.

Preheat the oven to 180–200°C / 350–400°F / Mark 4–6. I prefer to use the lower temperature, but some experts say you should use the higher one. Put the goose on its back in the roasting tin, and put the tin on a rack just below the centre of the oven. After an hour, turn the goose breast-side down, and roast it for another 2–2½ hours, then finally on its back for 30 minutes to brown it. Keeping it breast-side down for most of the cooking time will keep it juicy. The fat should be drained off periodically during cooking, and stored in a bowl. If you want a shiny bird, baste it with a mixture of honey and sherry vinegar. Once the bird is cooked, let it rest, covered, in a warm place for 15–20 minutes. This will make carving much easier.

Carving a goose can be quite a shock for someone whose only experience of carving is the Christmas turkey. The breast bone is reached much more quickly. Long slices should be taken from the whole length of the breast.

Apple and Pistachio Stuffing

Serves 4

*Moving away from traditional English accompaniments, I often serve
goose with green lentils, polenta, red cabbage or even spiced fruit. I
also make this stuffing. If you cannot get pistachios, use extra
almonds.*

8 slices wholemeal bread, crusts
  removed, 8–10 oz / 230–280 g in
  all
1 large apple, peeled, cored and
  grated
3 tbsp calvados
1 medium onion, peeled and finely
  chopped

1 tbsp roughly chopped almonds
1 tbsp pistachios
1 tbsp chopped sage
1 tsp chopped lemon thyme
1 egg yolk, lightly beaten
2 tbsp goose stock or white wine
salt
freshly ground black pepper

Let the bread dry out for a day, and then tear it into small pieces. Soak the
apple in the calvados for 15 minutes, and then mix with the rest of the ingredients.
Grease a soufflé dish or other ovenproof dish with a little goose fat, and spoon in
the stuffing. Bake it in the oven with the goose for 45 minutes–1 hour.

Potted Goose

Makes 1½ lb / 680 g

14 oz / 395 g cooked goose meat
3 sage leaves or a sprig of rosemary
  or thyme, finely chopped
12 oz / 340 g goose fat, melted

salt
freshly ground black pepper
freshly grated nutmeg

Shred the meat, or put it in a food processor and process on 'pulse' until the
meat is just chopped to an even size but not mushy. Stir the herbs into the meat
together with the goose fat. Season to taste with salt, pepper and nutmeg, and pack
into individual ramekins or other suitable containers. To keep it longer, a layer of
melted fat can be poured over the top which will be sealed when the fat sets. Keep
in the refrigerator.

Giblet Sauce

Serves 2, as a main course; 4 as a starter

*Giblets are giblets, and there is no elegant term in English for a giblet
salad or stew. I make mine into a sauce to serve with pasta.*

1 onion, peeled and chopped	¼ pt / 140 ml goose stock or red wine
1 celery stalk, trimmed and sliced	1 bay leaf
1 tbsp goose fat	1 tbsp chopped parsley
1 goose heart, gizzard and liver	salt
1 tsp tomato or vegetable purée	freshly ground black pepper

Fry onion and celery in the goose fat. Remove any skin, piping, membrane and
discoloured parts from the giblets. Slice and dice, and first add the gizzard to the
frying pan. Cook it with the onions and celery, raising the heat to brown the meat
all over and then lowering it. After 10 minutes, add the heart and liver pieces, and
brown these before stirring in the purée and the stock or wine. Bring to the boil,
add the bay leaf, cover and simmer very gently for 30–40 minutes. Stir in the
chopped parsley and season to taste. This is even better if cooked the day before
required, in which case only add the parsley just before serving the sauce stirred
into a bowl of freshly cooked and drained pasta.

Parmentier of Goose

Serves 4–6

Inspiration for this comes from Bruno Loubet, whose very good book *Cuisine
Courante* has a recipe for confit of duck baked in a mashed potato crust. Leftover
meat stripped from the carcass of goose can be cooked in a similar fashion,
provided you add some of the goose fat and gravy. First boil 2–3 lb / 900 g–1.35 kg
potatoes. Mash with salt, pepper and enough rendered goose fat to make it
appetizing. Spoon half of it into a greased pie dish. Lay pieces of cooked goose in
it, dotted with goose fat, and moistened with plenty of gravy, and spread the rest of
the mashed potato over the top before baking in a preheated oven at 220°C / 425°F /
Mark 7 for 20–30 minutes, until cooked through and the top is nicely browned.

GUINEA FOWL AND QUAIL

Herb-Stuffed Pot-Roast Guinea Fowl with Garlic and Onion Sauce

Serves 4

3 lb / 1.35 kg guinea fowl
fresh herbs, such as tarragon,
    chervil, basil, parsley and thyme
½ lemon
salt
freshly ground black pepper

1–2 heads of garlic
2 oz / 60 g butter
1 onion, peeled and thinly sliced
measure of cognac
3 tbsp dry white wine
cream *(optional)*

Gently ease the skin away from the breasts and thighs of the guinea fowl, inserting your finger between skin and flesh at the neck end of the bird. Push the herbs under the skin. Peel off thin strips of lemon zest, and put this inside the cavity, together with any extra herbs. Squeeze the lemon and rub the juice over the bird, then season it lightly inside and out. Separate and peel all the garlic cloves, and fry them in the butter in a deep flameproof casserole with the onion slices for a few minutes without letting them brown. Turn the guinea fowl in the hot butter, pour on the cognac, and flame it. Add the white wine, cover with a lid, and cook in a preheated oven at 170°C / 325°F / Mark 3 for about 1½ hours. Transfer the bird to a heated serving dish, whole or jointed, as you prefer. Skim the fat from the cooking juices. Rub the garlic, onion and cooking juices through a sieve, and bring to the boil. Add more seasoning, if necessary, cream if you like, or boil to reduce if you prefer a thicker sauce. Serve with the bird.

Guinea Fowl in Cider with Quinces

Serves 4

3 lb / 1.35 kg guinea fowl
3 garlic cloves (*optional*)
½ lemon
salt

freshly ground black pepper
paprika
½ pt / 280 ml strong dry cider
2 small quinces, halved

Trim the guinea fowl of excess fat. Cut off the tips of the wing pinions, and loose skin and do whatever else needs to be done to make your guinea fowl presentable for the table. Peel and slice the garlic, if using, and cut each slice into thin slivers. Insert them at intervals under the skin of the guinea fowl. Rub the half lemon all over the guinea fowl, squeezing the juice on to it. Sprinkle with salt sparingly, more liberally with pepper and paprika. Put the cider in a small saucepan and reduce by half, getting rid of the alcohol and concentrating the flavour. Heat a non-stick frying pan, add the bird and fry until browned all over. Put the halved fruit inside the guinea fowl, and then put the guinea fowl in a lidded casserole. Pour the cider over it, cover and cook in a preheated oven at 200°C / 400°F / Mark 6 for about 1 hour. When cooked, remove the guinea fowl from the casserole, and keep it warm on a carving plate. Reduce the cooking juices until syrupy, and serve these separately in a heated sauce boat.

Variation ∾ If you like, you could cook some carrot sticks together with the guinea fowl for the last 30 minutes of cooking, and serve them as one of the accompanying vegetables.

Boodles' Roast Stuffed Quail

Serves 4

If you decide to serve 2 quails per serving, increase the stuffing ingredients.

2 oz / 60 g butter
4 oven-ready quails
½ tsp salt
1 tsp freshly ground black pepper
2 ripe bananas, peeled
2 thick slices wholemeal bread or
  cornbread

2 tsp finely chopped tarragon
1 tbsp finely chopped onion, shallot or
  spring onion
2½ fl oz / 70 ml dry white wine

Rub the butter over the quails and put some inside. Lightly salt the quails inside and out. Mix the pepper into the bananas, mashing them until fairly smooth. Cut the crusts from the bread, and crumble it into the bananas. Mix in the tarragon and onion. Spoon the mixture into the quails. Put them on a rack in a roasting tin, and roast in a preheated oven at 190°C / 375°F / Mark 5 for 45 minutes. Remove from the oven and keep the quails warm while you make a little gravy. Skim the fat from the roasting tin, and pour in the white wine. Set it on the heat, and bring to the boil, scraping up any bits of dripping stuck to the tin. Add 2–3 tablespoons water, and cook for 5 minutes, until reduced to about half. Serve with the quails.

Spatchcocked Quails

Serves 6

If you decide to serve 2 quails per serving, increase the marinade ingredients.

6 oven-ready quails
1 tbsp marmalade
1 tbsp sherry vinegar
2 tbsp extra virgin olive oil

pinch of chilli powder
¼ tsp freshly ground black pepper
1 tsp soy sauce

With a pair of poultry scissors, cut the quails open down the backbone. Turn over and press down on the breast bone to flatten the birds. Wipe them all over. Mix the remaining ingredients and brush all over the quails. Cover and marinate for an hour or so, and then, having drained them, put on a hot grill. Turn the birds during cooking, and brush on the marinade from time to time, or if there is little left, brush with olive oil. If cooking on a barbecue, these quails are particularly good served with whole bananas baked in the embers, or slices of grilled plantain, and roast corn on the cob.

GAME

KNOWING THAT I often cook game and write about it, someone asked me if I thought game was elitist food. I said no and was then asked why, in that case, did not more people eat it. Availability is one reason, but even that can be overcome by ordering what you want from your local butcher. The supermarkets, too, are stocking an ever-increasing range of both feathered and furred game.

It is not expensive when you compare it with other meat and poultry. A whole hare weighing 5–6 lb / 2.30–2.70 kg should cost no more than a similar-sized chicken, and often much less. It has tender meat on the saddle for roasting, the hindquarters for jugged hare, plenty of carcass to make good rich soup, and meat on the forequarters to combine with belly pork, liver and spices for a well-flavoured terrine or coarse pâté.

One of the reasons I enjoy cooking and eating game is that it is so versatile in the dishes that you can create around it, hot or cold, elegant or rustic, light or substantial. It is no more difficult to prepare than any other meat or poultry, and a bonus is that it is usually very lean meat, and therefore lower in saturated fat and cholesterol.

Butchers and game dealers will prepare the meat on request, skinning or plucking as necessary, and also making sure that it is hung. Supermarkets sell their game ready-prepared in neat packages, as they do chickens and turkeys, and there is scarcely any need to get your hands 'dirty', which was why, I think, many people avoided cooking game.

One of the disadvantages of buying game oven-ready off the shelf, however, is that you cannot apply to it any of the tests that help distinguish a younger bird from a wily old bird that has escaped the guns for a season or two. When in doubt, my advice is to cook it slowly in a sealed pot so that, with luck, it will stay moist and juicy. An alternative method, with a dryish bird like pheasant, is to cook the breasts only (so you will need two birds to feed four people) by frying them on a high heat perhaps having marinated them first. They should be well cooked on the outside but just cooked inside.

Vegetables that go well with game are either the sharp, powerful flavours of spiced red cabbage or sauerkraut, or the mellow, earthy flavours of braised vegetables such as celery, celeriac, fennel and parsnips. Instead of potatoes, I like to serve polenta made from yellow cornmeal, either straight from the pan in a soft heap, or I let it go cold in a loaf tin, and then slice and grill or fry it (see page 66). It's marvellous for soaking up a good gravy. Other foods that go well with game are apples, pears and chestnuts. Fresh walnuts add an unusual texture to game casseroles and terrines.

Steamed Stuffed Pheasant Breasts

4 pheasant breasts
16 large lettuce leaves
¼ pt / 140 ml cider
apple peelings
1 bay leaf
sprig of sage

Stuffing
4 tbsp cooked brown, white or wild
  rice

2 tbsp chopped, peeled, deseeded
  tomatoes
2 tbsp grated apple
salt
3 oz / 85 g ricotta or sieved cottage
  cheese
freshly ground black pepper
1 tbsp finely chopped parsley
2 tbsp cider

First make the stuffing. Mix all the ingredients together and put on one side.

Skin the pheasant breasts, and slit each one almost in half horizontally. Open out, butterfly fashion, and press flat. Using a non-stick frying pan, cook the meat over a high heat for 30 seconds on each side until lightly browned. Blanch the lettuce leaves by draping them over a colander and pouring boiling water over them. Pat dry on kitchen paper. Spoon the stuffing on to the pheasant breasts, and fold the meat back over to enclose it, securing the breasts closed with half cocktail sticks. Wrap each one in lettuce leaves, and place the parcels in a single layer in a steamer basket. Steam over the cider, apple peelings and herbs for roughly about 15 minutes.

Pheasant Breasts with Berry Fruit Sauce

Serves 4

4 pheasant breasts, marinated
    overnight in wine and olive oil, if
    you like
2 shallots, peeled and finely
    chopped

2 tbsp fruit jelly, such as redcurrant,
    cranberry, blackberry or gooseberry
½ pt / 280 ml unseasoned pheasant
    stock
2 oz / 60 g chilled unsalted butter,
    cubed

Dry the pheasant breasts thoroughly. Heat a non-stick pan and fry the meat on both sides, then cook gently for 15–20 minutes or until the meat is tender. Remove the meat, and keep it warm while you finish the sauce. Add the shallots, jelly and stock to the frying pan. Boil quite fiercely, scraping up any cooking residue from the bottom of the pan, and reduce to 4–5 tablespoons. Add the butter, a cube at a time, swirling the pan after each addition to amalgamate the butter and cooking juices. Slice the pheasant breasts, or not, as you wish, and serve with the sauce.

Pheasant and Rabbit Casserole

Serves 4–6

4 pheasant legs
1 lb / 455 g boneless rabbit *or*
    1½–2 lb / 680–900 g rabbit
    portions
1 tbsp olive oil
16 pickling onions, peeled
8 oz / 230 g mushrooms, wiped
¼ pt / 140 ml dry red or white wine

¼ pt / 140 ml pheasant stock
1 bay leaf
1 sprig of thyme
8 peppercorns
salt
chopped parsley and triangles of fried
    bread, to garnish

Remove the meat from the bones and cut into even-sized pieces (or as near even as possible, given the particular shape of muscle involved), and remove the sinews. (Bones and sinews should go into the stockpot.) Heat the olive oil in a frying pan, and fry the meat all over, a batch at a time, to the point where it just loses its raw colour. Transfer to a flameproof casserole. Fry the onions until just browning a little, which will give the casserole a good colour. Add to the casserole.

Fry the mushrooms, and then put them with the meat and onions. Deglaze the pan with wine, scraping up any residues stuck to the pan. Add the stock, bring to the boil, and pour over the meat. Add the herbs and peppercorns, cover and cook over a low heat or in a preheated oven at 170°C / 325°F / Mark 3 until the meat is tender. Season with salt to taste and garnish with parsley and triangles of fried bread. If you want a slightly thicker and richer sauce, pour most of it off into a shallow saucepan, and boil up to reduce it before pouring it back into the casserole. This should be done *before* adding any salt.

Pigeon Breasts with Sweet and Sour Vegetables

Serves 4

4 plump, tender pigeons	freshly ground black pepper
3 celery hearts or 6 celery stalks	juniper berries, crushed
8 oz / 230 g white cabbage	1 tbsp soy sauce
2 carrots	2 tbsp unrefined brown sugar
2 leeks	1 tsp lemon juice or wine vinegar
6 oz / 170 g mushrooms	

Carefully remove the breasts from the pigeons. Peel and finely slice or shred the vegetables, reserving the trimmings. Brown the rest of the pigeon carcasses in a heavy saucepan, and add 3 pt / 1.70 l water and the trimmings from the vegetables. Simmer gently until you have a rich tasty stock to be used as the base for a game soup or mushroom risotto. Season the breasts with pepper and crushed juniper berries. Place the vegetables in a steamer basket with the mushrooms on top, and steam until tender but not soggy.

Meanwhile, cook the pigeon breasts, either in a non-stick frying pan, a well-seasoned cast-iron pan or under a hot grill, for 3–4 minutes on each side. Allow to rest on a plate in a warm place. When the vegetables are cooked, tip them into a bowl. Mix the soy sauce, sugar and vinegar, and stir this into the vegetables until they are well coated and the sugar has melted. Divide between four heated dinner plates. Slice each breast in two, and arrange four slices on each plate, pouring over any cooking juices collected on the plate. I like to serve them with steamed brown rice or potatoes.

Pot-Roast Partridge

This recipe can simply be multiplied by the number you wish to serve.
One partridge serves one person.

1 oz / 30 g butter, softened
½ tbsp finely chopped herbs
salt
freshly ground black pepper
1 partridge

1 tsp brandy
1 tbsp port, vermouth or good red wine
1 tsp fruit jelly
slice of toast, cut to a round, to serve

Mix the butter, herbs and seasoning. Smear some over the partridge breast, and put the rest inside the cavity. Heat a little more butter in an ovenproof saucepan or flameproof casserole, and fry the bird all over until nicely browned. Pour on the brandy and set alight. Add the port, vermouth or wine. Cover with a lid or foil, and cook in a preheated oven at 190°C / 375°F / Mark 5 for 35 minutes or so. Drain off the cooking juices into a small saucepan, add the fruit jelly, cook and reduce until syrupy. Serve the partridge on a small round of toast with a spoonful or two of sauce.

Variations ∾ Blend a little lemon zest and chopped garlic with the butter and herbs, and brown a thinly sliced shallot with the bird. Omit the brandy, and use Muscat wine instead of port, pouring it over the bird with a tablespoon of chicken or game stock. Peel a handful of large Muscat grapes, cut them in half, remove the pips, and add these to the casserole for the last 10 minutes of cooking. Omit the fruit jelly, and simply reduce the cooking juices to make a sauce.

Do not use herb butter, but simply season the bird and brown it with a little chopped onion. Cut a trimmed celery heart in half, and place the two halves under the bird in the casserole. Scatter a few juniper berries on top, and flame with gin rather than brandy. Add a bay leaf and water instead of the port or wine, and cook as above. To make a sauce, simply reduce the cooking juices.

Pheasant, guinea fowl, and of course, chicken can be cooked in the same way.

Beef and Pigeon Crumble

*A favourite variation on the pie theme is the crumble.
Here the meat, which is better cooked the day before required, is
topped with a savoury crumble that takes minutes to make and is
then baked in the oven.*

1–1½ lb / 455–680 g shin of beef
8 pigeon breasts
1 oz / 30 g seasoned flour
1–2 tbsp olive oil
1 large onion, peeled and thinly
   sliced
½ pt / 280 ml dry red wine or
   Guinness
½ pt / 280 ml pigeon or beef stock
1 head of celery, trimmed and sliced
2 bay leaves

6 allspice berries
3 cloves
salt
freshly ground black pepper

Crumble topping
6 oz / 170 g plain flour
2 oz / 60 g butter
1 tbsp chopped herbs
1 oz / 30 g hard cheese, freshly grated

Remove the tough outer skin from the beef, and cube both meats. Toss the meat in the seasoned flour. Brown the meat all over in the oil in a frying pan or flameproof casserole, remove from the pan and put to one side while you lightly brown the onion in the same pan. Pour on the wine or Guinness, and boil it, scraping up any cooking residues stuck to the pan. Add the stock and celery, and bring to the boil. Put the meat in a lidded casserole with the bay leaves and spices, and pour over the stock and celery. Cook in a preheated oven at 150–170°C / 300–325°F / Mark 2–3 for 2–3 hours or until the meat is tender. Season, allow to cool, and refrigerate until required.

To make the crumble, rub the flour and butter together, and stir in the herbs and cheese. Put the meat into an ovenproof dish, spoon the topping evenly over it, and bake in a preheated oven at 180°C / 350°F / Mark 4 for 20–25 minutes.

Variation ❧ Instead of the crumble topping, use a scone topping to make a beef and pigeon cobbler. For this, sift together 8 oz / 230 g plain flour, 4 teaspoons baking powder and a pinch of salt. Rub in 2 oz / 60 g butter, and then blend with plain yoghurt to form a soft dough. Knead lightly, and roll out to about ¾ in / 2 cm thick on a floured surface. Cut out 2 in / 5 cm rounds with a pastry cutter. When you are ready to make the cobbler, heat up the beef and pigeon stew in the casserole. Arrange the uncooked scone rounds on top, overlapping slightly, and bake in a preheated oven at 200°C / 400°F / Mark 6 for 10–15 minutes.

Sussex Woodman's Pie

Serves 4–6

One year, there was correspondence on The Times' *letters' page about that great rural nuisance, the grey squirrel. 'A rat with good public relations' was one memorable description. And from another reader came a suggestion that they be made into Brunswick stew (see page 560). I had already given a recipe for Brunswick stew the previous winter after a visit to friends in Birmingham (USA), who served us the Alabama version on our first night with them. A favourite one-pot meal throughout the southern states, it is traditionally made with squirrel, as well as corn, beans and other vegetables. Faintheartedly, I suggested various substitutes for squirrel and I was taken to task by a reader who, living in West Sussex, is plagued with squirrels. She has an arrangement with a friend, a warden for the National Trust, that she will take as many of the 'little beasts' that he can shoot; the front halves he keeps for his ferrets and the hindquarters he gives to her. The squirrels are only good for eating in the autumn, she tells me, 'when they have been stuffing themselves on a strictly vegetarian diet, but squirrel back legs stack up very neatly in the freezer and keep extremely well'. My correspondent then kindly gave me her recipe for a pie which I give below.*

3 squirrel hindquarters	1½ oz / 40 g butter
8 pigeon breasts	1½ tbsp plain flour
1 large bottle (about a litre) strong dry cider	14 oz / 395 g can chopped tomatoes
	8 oz / 230 g button mushrooms
1–2 bay leaves	salt
1 tsp black peppercorns	freshly ground black pepper
2 medium onions, peeled and sliced	8 oz / 230 g puff pastry

Marinate the meat in the cider with the bay and peppercorns for 24 hours. Cook in the marinade in a low oven, about 150°C / 300°F / Mark 2, until the meat is tender and comes away from the bone. Allow to go cold in its cooking juices. Strip the meat from the squirrel joints (taking care to remove the tiny bones and any shot), and pull the pigeon breasts into pieces. Strain and keep the liquor. Gently fry the onions in the butter until soft, sprinkle on the flour, and make into a sauce with the strained cooking juices. Add the tomatoes and mushrooms, and bring to simmering point. Season to taste after 10 minutes, stir in the meat, and transfer the mixture to a pie dish or other suitable receptacle. Cover with a puff pastry lid, making a hole in the centre to let the steam escape. Glaze and decorate it if you wish and bake in a preheated oven at 190°C / 375°F / Mark 5 for 20–25 minutes until the pastry is crisp and golden brown.

Variation ➣ If you cannot get hold of squirrel, use rabbit, preferably wild rabbit.

Roast Saddle of Hare with Apple and Chestnut Sauce

Serves 2–4

You can occasionally find frozen saddles of hare, but it is far better to buy the whole hare and have your butcher joint it, leaving the whole saddle. With the rest, forelegs, hindlegs, and giblets, you will have plenty of ingredients for game soup, pâté or a sauce for pasta.

1 saddle of hare
½ pt / 280 ml apple juice
1 onion, peeled and sliced
1 tbsp juniper berries
chives or other herbs

Sauce
1 onion, peeled and sliced
a little olive oil
1 dessert apple, peeled, cored and sliced
liver from the hare, chopped
2 oz / 60 g unsweetened chestnut purée
salt
freshly ground black pepper

Marinate the saddle overnight in the apple juice together with the onion, juniper berries and herbs. Next day, remove the hare from the marinade. Strain the marinade and set aside for the sauce. The final cooking takes very little time so you should have ready everything else that you will be serving with the hare. Preheat the oven to 230°C / 450°F / Mark 8. With a sharp knife, ease the two fillets away from either side of the backbone, without removing them. This makes carving easier. Put the hare in a roasting tin and roast in the oven for 15 minutes. Meanwhile, make the sauce. Fry the onion in the olive oil until lightly browned. Add the apple slices, liver and chestnut purée. Cook together to make a rich stew, adding the reserved marinade and letting it reduce considerably. Season to taste.

Rich Hare Casserole

Serves 6–8

1 large, plump hare
1 onion, peeled and sliced
1 tbsp olive oil
2 tbsp plain flour
1 tsp salt
1 tsp freshly ground black pepper
½ tsp paprika
¼ pt / 140 ml full-bodied red wine

½ pt / 280 ml game or beef stock
1 oz / 30 g plain chocolate (the least
   sweet possible)
2 oz / 60 g seedless raisins or sultanas,
   soaked in brandy
1 bay leaf
sprig of thyme

Joint the hare, and divide the saddle into four pieces. Fry the onion in the olive oil until golden brown, using a large *sauteuse* or flameproof casserole. Mix the flour, salt, pepper and paprika, and coat the pieces of hare in it before adding them to the pan and browning them all over. Pour on the wine, and scrape up any cooking residues. Add the rest of the ingredients. Bring to the boil, and skim the surface. Cover and simmer over the lowest possible heat, or cook in a preheated oven at 130°C / 275 °F / Mark 1 for 2½–3 hours, in both cases, until the meat is tender.

Roast Saddle of Rabbit, Boned and Stuffed with Herbs and Ricotta

Serves 4

1 large rabbit, about 3 lb / 1.35 kg
   when skinned
salt
freshly ground black pepper
2 oz / 60 g bunch watercress
4 oz / 110 g ricotta or sieved cottage
   cheese

1 tbsp chopped herbs, such as chervil,
   basil or tarragon
1 tsp Dijon or other good strong
   mustard
1 garlic clove, peeled and crushed

Ask the butcher to joint the rabbit, leaving the saddle whole. Use the legs for pâté or in a casserole. Bone the saddle by cutting with a sharp knife on each side of the backbone and scraping along and down over the ribs, easing the flesh off the bones. When you have finished, you should have two long fillets of lean meat, each with a thin flap. Season the meat lightly, and lay one piece next to the other, flaps overlapping. Remove any damaged or yellowing leaves and the coarsest stalks from the watercress. Wash, dry and finely chop it and mix it with the ricotta or cottage cheese, the herbs and mustard. Add the garlic. Spoon the mixture on to the overlapping flaps of rabbit meat and spread evenly. Slip four or five lengths of string under the meat, bring the two edges together, and tie together as a roll, making sure that the filling is not oozing out of the ends. Slip the meat inside a roasting bag, slit the bag in one or two places, secure it tightly closed, and place on a baking sheet. Roast in the centre of a preheated oven at 180°C / 350°F / Mark 4 for 30–35 minutes. Remove from the oven and allow to rest in a warm place for 15 minutes before slicing the rabbit into neat rounds and serving with any cooking juices and some vegetables.

Saupiquet de lapin

I learned to make a very good sauce for rabbit in Anne Majourel's kitchen at Le Ranquet in Tornac in that empty quarter of France just where the olive groves cease and the chestnut forests begin. Anne is a Languedocienne, taught to cook by her grandmother, and feels it is important to maintain cooking traditions, while recognizing how they can be adapted to modern needs with no sacrifice of integrity. What we made in her kitchen was *saupiquet de lapin*, a rich sauce thickened with the rabbit liver and redolent of garlic and the *garrigue* outside, acres of wild thyme. We ate it with roast rabbit and steamed potatoes. One rabbit liver will make enough sauce for two to three people. Anne fried the liver in grapeseed oil, not olive oil, which was a surprise until I remembered that her father is a wine-maker in Corbières, and he makes his own oil after the wine making is over. A handful of fresh thyme and a bay leaf also went into the frying pan, and the liver was cooked until just pink inside. A couple of heads of garlic were peeled, two thirds of them simmered until soft in a little stock and vinegar, the remaining garlic crushed raw. The raw garlic, the cooked liver and its cooking juices without the herbs, were put in a food processor and blended until fairly smooth, and then the cooked garlic and stock was added and processed until a smooth sauce was obtained. Anne's *grandmère*, she told me, would then enrich the sauce further, beating in egg yolk and oil as for a mayonnaise. When she reheated it, Anne simply stirred in a little aïoli before serving and pronounced it *unctus*, a most descriptive word in the *langue d'oc*.

Rabbit with Lavender

Serves 4

saddle from a 3½ lb / 1.60 kg rabbit
4 oz / 110 g ricotta
3 oz / 85 g cucumber, peeled and
  diced

2 tbsp finely chopped parsley
salt
freshly ground black pepper
30 sprigs lavender

Carefully remove the two fillets and flaps from each side of the backbone, scraping down from the backbone and over the ribs with a sharp knife. Trim the two pieces to regular shapes. Place the fillets side by side, flaps overlapping, leaving a 'channel' for the stuffing. Mix the ricotta, cucumber, parsley and seasoning, and lay it between the two fillets. Slide seven or eight pieces of string underneath, form the meat into a roll, and tie it together at regular intervals, pushing back any stuffing that escapes.

Pour 1 pt / 570 ml water in a saucepan, and bring to the boil. Drop in most of the lavender, keeping a little back for garnishing. Turn the heat off and allow the lavender to infuse for 15 minutes. Place the rabbit in a steamer basket over the lavender infusion. Slowly bring the water back to the boil, and allow the rabbit to steam gently for 30 minutes.

Slice the rabbit, placing two or three rounds on each of four serving plates, and serve with wild rice (or brown rice if you can't get wild) and some lightly steamed green beans. Garnish with the reserved lavender.

Rabbit Pie

Serves 4

2 lb / 900 g rabbit portions
1 medium onion, peeled and sliced
3 tbsp sunflower or extra virgin
  olive oil
8 oz / 230 g fennel
¾ pt / 430 ml stock, water or white
  wine
salt

freshly ground black pepper
12 oz / 340 g field mushrooms, wiped
  and sliced or quartered
sprig of tarragon
grated zest of ½ lemon
6 oz / 170 g soaked prunes *(optional)*
6 oz / 170 g shortcrust pastry
milk or cream, to glaze *(optional)*

Fry the rabbit and onion in 2 teaspoons oil in a flameproof casserole until golden brown. Trim the fennel, and slice into ¼ in / 0.5 cm pieces. Put it with the rabbit and onion. Cover with stock, water or wine, and bring to the boil. Season very lightly, and turn the heat down to the merest simmer. Cover and cook gently for about 45 minutes. The dish can be prepared to this point the day before, in which case strain and reduce the cooking juices to about ¼ pt / 140 ml, and then cool as quickly as possible before refrigerating until required, keeping the rabbit and vegetables separate from the stock. Remove the rabbit from the bone, if preferred. Fry the mushrooms briskly in the rest of the oil until they give off most of their moisture. Lightly oil or butter a pie dish, and lay the pieces of rabbit in the bottom, then a layer of mushrooms, a layer of fennel and onion and finally the remaining mushrooms. Tuck a few tarragon leaves into the filling, and sprinkle lemon zest on top. Add the prunes, if using. Spoon the, by now, jellied stock over the filling. Roll out the pastry and use to cover the dish, pressing well down to seal it. Make a hole in the top for steam to escape, and decorate with pastry leaves or other trimmings. Brush with milk or cream, to glaze, if you wish, and bake in a preheated oven at 190°C / 375°F / Mark 5 for 35 minutes. Serve hot or warm with green vegetables or a crisp salad.

Variations ∾ For a more substantial dish, put a layer of sliced parboiled potatoes in the bottom.

An even more substantial dish, which is particularly good cold and, therefore, excellent for a brave spring picnic expedition, can be made by lining the pie dish with pastry.

Rabbit and Saffron Rice

Serves 4

Like me, you have probably got a cupboard or a drawer full of dried herbs, spices, nuts and fruit. Use them in this very fragrant dish. It is marvellous for putting in a slow oven and forgetting about while you go to the cinema. The oven does not need to be preheated so you can even do this on an automatic timer. For preference, cook in a very well soaked clay pot, a chicken brick or a Römertopf.

pinch of saffron threads *or* ¼ tsp
  powdered saffron
1 large mild onion
1 large rabbit, jointed (use the
  hindlegs, shoulders and saddle,
  cut into 3 or 4 pieces)
2 tbsp sultanas or chopped dried
  apricots

2 tbsp blanched almonds or pinenuts
8 oz / 230 g patna or basmati rice
2 in / 5 cm cinnamon stick
2 bay leaves
1 pt / 570 ml chicken, rabbit, veal or
  vegetable stock

Soak the saffron threads, if using, in a small amount of boiling water. Peel and slice the onion, and place in the bottom of the clay pot. Put the rabbit pieces on top with the sultanas and nuts. Pour the rice in, shaking it down into the spaces, and add the powdered saffron or saffron threads and soaking liquid. Tuck the cinnamon stick and bay leaves well down into the casserole, and pour on the stock. Cover and cook slowly in the bottom half of the oven at 150°C / 300°F / Mark 2 for 2–2½ hours.

Medallions of Venison with Raspberries

Serves 6

In Norway I came across many uses of wild berries with game: black grouse with blueberries, ptarmigan with redcurrants, reindeer with raspberries. It is a combination that works well, and I particularly like the flavour of raspberries with the darker game meat, such as grouse, hare and wild duck. I have also tried it with venison.

6 venison medallions, 4 oz / 110 g each	6 peppercorns
4 oz / 110 g raspberries	2 tbsp walnut oil
2 tbsp raspberry vinegar, sherry vinegar or balsamic vinegar	1 oz / 30 g butter
	1 tsp sunflower oil
2–3 cloves	4 tbsp game stock
2–3 juniper berries	salt
	freshly ground black pepper

Put the medallions in a dish in a single layer. Set aside a few raspberries for garnish, if you wish, and crush the remainder with the vinegar and 2–3 tablespoons water. Crush the spices, and mix with the walnut oil into the raspberry marinade. Pour this over the meat, cover and refrigerate for several hours, turning it once. When ready to cook, bring the meat to room temperature, scrape off the crushed raspberries and spices, but reserve the marinade. Dry the meat well, and heat a frying pan with half the butter and all the oil (or use a non-stick frying pan). When hot, sear the meat on both sides, lower the heat, and cook until done to your liking. Remove the meat from the pan, and keep it in a warm place, loosely covered, on a plate. Sieve the marinade into the frying pan, and raise the heat. Allow to reduce slightly, then stir in the stock, and once that is bubbling, quickly add the remaining butter, and season to taste. Pour in any cooking juices that have drained out of the meat. Serve the sauce with the meat, some herbs and raspberries for garnish. Mashed potatoes and glazed kohlrabi slices make very good accompaniments.

Variation ∾ Instead of marinating the meat, simply fry it to your liking, and serve with a sauce made by cooking the raspberries with a little chopped onion in olive oil and butter until soft, adding ¼ pt / 140 ml each of red wine and water, cooking for 3 more minutes, and then passing through a sieve and reheating to serve. Use blackberries, blueberries or elderberries to replace the raspberries.

Venison and Stout Pudding

Serves 4–6

Suet Pastry
4 oz / 110 g self-raising flour
4 oz / 110 g fresh white, brown or
  wholemeal breadcrumbs
pinch of salt
4 oz / 110 g shredded fresh suet
¼ pt / 140 ml water

Filling
1 tbsp good olive oil
12 small onions or shallots, peeled

8 oz / 230 g celery hearts, trimmed and
  sliced
1¼ lb / 570 g lean stewing venison, cut
  into 1 in / 2.5 cm cubes
sprig of marjoram
1 bay leaf
2 tsp chestnut flour (arrowroot, potato
  flour or cornflour can be substituted)
¼ pt / 140 ml game stock
¼ pt / 140 ml stout
salt
freshly ground black pepper

To make the pastry, sift the flour into a bowl, and add the breadcrumbs and salt. Stir the dry ingredients together with a knife. Add the suet and sufficient water to make a firm but springy dough. Turn out on to a floured board, knead lightly, and form into a ball. Cover and stand it in a cool place while you prepare the filling.

Heat the olive oil in a heavy pan, add the onions and celery, and fry until just beginning to colour lightly. Add the venison and herbs. Sear the meat all over. Moisten the flour with a little of the stock, and stir it into the rest of the stock and the stout. Add this all to the pan, and bring to simmering point. Season to taste, and remove from the heat. Leave the meat to cool.

Grease a 2 pt / 1.15 l pudding basin. Roll out three-quarters of the pastry, and use this to line the pudding basin. Spoon in the cooled meat mixture. Roll out the remaining quarter of the pastry, and place this on top of the basin. Seal the edges. Cover the basin with a sheet of greaseproof paper, pleated in the middle to allow the pastry to rise slightly. Tie the paper securely round the top of the basin. Cover the pudding with a clean tea-towel, and tie it round the rim of the basin. Bring the ends up over the pudding, and tie into a knot. Put the basin in a large saucepan, pour in boiling water until it reaches halfway up the basin. Cover the saucepan with a lid, and simmer for 2 hours, replenishing the water in the pan with more boiling water, where necessary.

Pot-Roast Haunch of Venison

*Two of the finest roasts I have ever eaten have been venison. One was
a saddle of venison which was larded, marinated in port, olive oil,
wine, herbs and spices, and then roasted in a hot oven for about 15
minutes per 1 lb / 455 g, basting frequently. The other was this dish,
cooked for me by a Scottish doctor for a Sunday lunch.*

1 pt / 570 ml olive oil
¼ pt / 140 ml lemon juice
1 onion, peeled and sliced
8 juniper berries, crushed

7 lb / 3.20 kg haunch of venison
6 tbsp medium sherry
2 tbsp grated horseradish

Mix the olive oil, lemon juice, onion and juniper berries together to make a
marinade, and pour it over the venison. Leave for 24 hours, basting occasionally.
Remove the meat from the marinade, dry it, and sear it all over in a frying pan. Put
it in a large casserole. Boil the marinade to reduce it a little, then pour it over the
meat. Cook in a preheated oven at 150°C / 300°F / Mark 2 for 3–3½ hours.

Remove the venison from the casserole, and put it on a carving dish, covered,
in a warm place, while you finish off the sauce. Add the sherry to the juices in the
casserole, and boil to reduce and thicken. Stir in the horseradish just before serving
with the carved meat. Rowanberry or crabapple jelly are also ideal companions to
serve with venison.

Venison Chilli

Serves 8

1 lb / 455 g dried kidney or borlotti
   beans, washed, soaked overnight
   and drained
2 lb / 900 g lean stewing venison
2 tbsp olive oil or groundnut
   (peanut) oil
1 medium onion, peeled and sliced
3–4 garlic cloves, peeled and sliced
1–3 tsp cayenne pepper (according
   to taste)

1 tbsp paprika
1 tbsp cumin seeds
1 tbsp chopped fresh marjoram or
   oregano *or* ½ tsp dried
2 bay leaves
14 oz / 395 g can tomatoes, drained
salt
freshly ground black pepper

Put the beans in a saucepan with plenty of water. Bring slowly to the boil, and boil briskly for 15 minutes. Drain and rinse, put back in the pan, and cover with water. Bring to the boil and simmer for 1 hour. Meanwhile, trim the meat and cut it into very small cubes. In a non-stick frying pan, fry the meat until well browned. Remove from the pan and put into a flameproof casserole.

Heat the oil and fry the onion until golden brown. Add the garlic, spices and herbs, and fry for 5 minutes, scraping up any bits stuck to the bottom of the frying pan. Pour the contents into the casserole, together with the tomatoes and the beans and their cooking liquor. Bring to the boil, and simmer, uncovered, for 1 hour until the meat and beans are tender. Taste and add salt and pepper as necessary. You can use fresh chilli in place of the cayenne pepper, with caution.

THE TIMES COOK IN FRANCE

THE FIRST meal I ever ate in France is still vivid in my memory. It was a warm day in the year of *'les événements de mai'*, and I had arrived in Albi on the overnight train from Paris to begin a year at the École Normale as *assistante*. After meeting the formidable *directrice*, I was taken into the dining room for a solitary lunch.

It was late enough in the year not to bother with shutters, and the tall, generously proportioned windows let in the afternoon sun. About twenty round tables with bent-wood chairs were arranged around the cool tiled floor. At one end of the room was a long, wooden dresser on which woven red and green napkins and tablecloths were piled next to water jugs, bread baskets and litre bottles of red wine. The *table des prof* was laid for one. I was given a crisp, new napkin, and a bread basket lined with a red, linen cloth containing a newly baked *baguette* chopped into pieces by the guillotine at the end of the sideboard. I poured a glass of the rough red wine from Labastide de Levis and ate the plate of *blanquette de veau* put in front of me. It was followed by a perfectly ripe Passecrassane pear and a slice of Cantal. All this was a hint of what was to come in this tranquil establishment where the chef was paid more than the principal. This young man, not long out of his apprenticeship, was already well known in the region for the banquets he would prepare when off duty for christenings and first communions. He was not generous with his recipes and tuition, but would allow me into his kitchen to watch what he was cooking.

The experience of that year was very important to me, and I could not help being influenced by it. I learned about food that was new to me: mussels, oysters, sweetbreads, brains, skate and *choucroute*, not to mention the Languedoc specialities of *confit*, *cassoulet* and *brandade de morue*. It was a small school, not many more than 100 students and staff, and we ate wonderful food. Especially on Sundays, when most of the boarders had gone home, Chef would give us local asparagus with *sauce mousseline*, a whole poached salmon garnished with cucumber slices and lightly jellied stock, followed by homemade strawberry ice cream. We would still drink the same coarse wine, though. Only on birthdays would we club together to buy a bottle of champagne and *gâteaux sec* for an afternoon *vin d'honneur*. 'We', I should add, were the *assistante*, the three *surveillantes* and the assistant housekeeper.

Sometimes I would go off with my friend, Michèle, to her family in the country, where I learned about wild mushrooms, which we would gather in the fields nearby, toss in butter and serve for supper with an *omelette aux fines herbes*. *Memère* would serve us *reines claudes à l'eau de vie* at the end of these long rustic meals, and tell me about the small still where they were allowed to make three litres of *eau de vie* a year for private use.

That year taught me a great deal about food, about taste, about seasonality, about the importance of choosing the very best ingredients that one can afford. When we visited Michèle in 1991, for the first time since 1968, she cooked *coq au vin* for us, and it was clear that she, too, still put into practice all that she had learned at Albi. A version of her recipe can be found on page 334.

Twenty-five years of visiting France several times a year has meant that I have come to know well many parts of the country: Alsace, the Touraine, the Basque country, Burgundy and the châteaux country of Bordeaux.

In 1991, I was lucky enough to be able to spend some time visiting the kitchens and talking to the cooks who produce the lunches and dinners served to guests of several châteaux in Bordeaux. It was a delight to sample the food. Without exception, it was based on local and seasonal ingredients, unpretentious food (as far removed from *nouvelle cuisine* as it is possible to be), and cooked with skill and imagination.

At Château Mouton Rothschild, asparagus, a berry fruit salad and crisply roasted duck were served at a late spring luncheon. And for the first course, one of those dishes that are so simple you can't imagine why you didn't think of it too. I have given on page 445 the warm brioche filled with scrambled eggs and smoked cod's roe, more subtle and unusual than smoked salmon, and highly recommended.

The kitchen at Château Chasse-Spleen, like so many in the Médoc, has a deep open fireplace. It is a working fireplace, too. Vine cuttings are burnt to glowing embers, and meat is then grilled over them. When we lunched there one cold November, ten of us sat down to steak grilled in this way, chips, a classic *tarte aux pommes* and a fish terrine to begin with.

Josette Riondato has two kitchens at Château Loudenne, one in the main house with a large fireplace where the evening meals are cooked and often char-grilled, like the *magret de canard* we had one evening. The other is the 'vintage kitchen' where the vineyard workers eat lunch, together with those who might be attending a course at the École du Vin. This is a homely and practical kitchen with brass ceiling lamps, wall tiles, large chopping boards, a cool tiled floor in the *girondin* style and massive low stone sinks with capacity to hold the giant-size pots and pans Josette uses for large-scale entertaining. She is a calm, speedy cook, judging with her eye, tasting little, neat and economical in all she does. She described to me how she started to collect recipes and cook when she was about 12 years old. If she didn't know what the ingredient was, such as *chapelure*, she would leave it out. At 17, she went to work for a *pharmacienne* from whom she learned *la cuisine bourgeoise*, then went as cook to Château Castéra, and 25 years before had began cooking at Château Loudenne. All her food is local – rabbits for lunch were delivered as we talked. The ceps she had bought from the laundry mistress's husband, a great forager. She used to buy her milk from the farmer, then from the dairy, from the village shop, but now it comes in cartons from the supermarket, progress which she regrets.

Between Dax and Pau in *le grand sud-ouest* of France is the rich fertile area known as *les Landes* and within that area is Chalosse, a district famous for its poultry, whether ducks and geese for *confits* and *foie gras* or chickens reared in the open air and apparently at considerable liberty. In early June, the maize which fills every cultivated field is no more than two or three feet tall. Each farm has its rack of dried maize cobs from last year's harvest, and it is not difficult to understand why chickens from this part of France will more often than not be corn-fed birds. There are not many better ways of cooking such large, full-flavoured, well-fed, well-exercised chickens than the very simple Poule au Pot, given on page 381. Henri, Prince of Navarre, son of Jeanne d'Albert, grandson of King Henry of Navarre, and later King Henri IV of France is credited with this dish. Born in the Château of Pau, it was his wish that every French citizen would be wealthy enough to afford to eat chicken every Sunday. His entry to the world was marked in true Béarnais fashion with a drop of Jurançon wine and a clove of garlic rubbed on his lips. A Jurançon sec from Cauhapé would be the perfect companion to this satisfying dish which is indeed excellent for Sunday lunch.

The other recipes that follow are also not fashionable, but just very, very good, full of flavour and texture.

Légumes à la Grecque

Artichoke bottoms and baby artichokes, courgettes, green beans, celery, mushrooms, wild mushrooms and small onions are some of the vegetables that can be prepared in this way. Trim the vegetables as appropriate, cutting celery and courgettes into rounds or batons. Cooking time will vary: mushrooms and courgettes will need only a few minutes; onions and artichokes much longer.

Court bouillon
7 fl oz / 200 ml water or vegetable stock
3½ fl oz / 100 ml extra virgin olive oil
juice of 2 lemons *or* 3½ fl oz / 100 ml dry white wine

1 tbsp coriander seeds
1 tsp coarse sea salt
½ tsp white peppercorns
piece of fennel
celery top
sprig of thyme
bay leaf

Put the water or stock, oil, and lemon juice or wine in a large saucepan with the coriander, salt and peppercorns. Tie the fennel, celery top and herbs together in a bouquet garni and add it to the pan. Bring to the boil and simmer for 5 minutes, then add the vegetables and cook them for as long as necessary. Strain them, and leave both vegetables and cooking liquor to cool. Mix together again when cold.

Note ∾ This is an extremely good *court bouillon* for poaching fish, such as mackerel or salmon fillets, and for chicken.

Poule au Pot

Serves 4–6

1 large chicken, about 4¼ lb /
  1.90 kg
1 veal bone or pig's trotter
large sprig of lemon thyme or
  thyme
1 celery stalk
1 onion, peeled and studded with 4
  cloves
salt
freshly ground black pepper
bay leaf
parsley stalks
12 young carrots, peeled or
  scrubbed
12 small turnips, peeled
12 pickling onions or shallots,
  peeled
1 small cabbage, cut into wedges

Stuffing (optional)
6 oz / 170 g belly pork, derinded
  and minced
2–3 garlic cloves, peeled and
  crushed
1 onion or shallot, peeled and finely
  chopped
1 oz / 30 g parsley, finely chopped
6 oz / 170 g breadcrumbs
2 egg yolks
freshly grated nutmeg

First make the stuffing, if using. Mix all the ingredients together with the finely chopped heart, liver and gizzard from the chicken. If the chicken is trussed, remove the string and spoon the stuffing into the cavity, having first removed any excess fat. Either sew up the vent or secure it closed with cocktail sticks or skewers.

Put the chicken (stuffed or not), veal bone or pig's trotter, thyme, celery stalk and onion in a large stockpot or saucepan and cover with water. Add a little seasoning, the bay leaf, parsley stalks and the neck and wing tips and other trimmings from the chicken. Bring the water just to the boil, skim any foam from the surface, lower the heat and poach the chicken gently for 1 hour. The water should not boil. Then remove the herbs, celery and onion, and add the prepared vegetables. Bring back to the boil, lower the heat, and poach until the vegetables are just cooked. Skim the surface occasionally to remove any impurities.

Transfer the chicken to a carving board, and the vegetables to a serving platter. Cut up the chicken, and arrange on the platter with the vegetables, moistening with a little of the broth. Serve the broth first with a slice of stuffing, if using, in each bowl, and then the meat and vegetables together with either rice, homemade noodles, dumplings or new potatoes.

Variation ∾ The veal or pig's trotter will provide enough gelatine in the broth for you to serve a cold *poule au pot*, if you wish. Make this by arranging the vegetables, chicken and stuffing in a deep platter, and pour over it the strained, reduced stock. Cool, then chill until just set. Or layer in a loaf tin, adding blanched green beans, pour on the strained, reduced stock, cool, then refrigerate until set.

Oeufs à la Neige

Serves 4–6

3 eggs, separated	1 vanilla pod
3½ oz / 100 g vanilla sugar	toasted flaked almonds and caramel
1 pt / 570 ml full-cream milk	threads, to decorate *(optional)*

Whisk the egg whites with the sugar until it forms firm peaks. In a shallow pan, such as a deep frying pan or sauté pan, bring the milk to the boil with the vanilla pod. Make 'egg' shapes of meringue with two tablespoons, and place them in the simmering milk. Poach for 2 minutes, and then gently turn the meringues over with two forks. When they are firm to the touch, remove them with a slotted spoon, and drain them on a clean tea-towel. Strain the milk and use to make a custard of pouring consistency with the egg yolks and a little more sugar. Pour it into a glass bowl. Float the meringues on top and serve chilled. You can decorate the meringues with toasted flaked almonds, if you wish, and threads of caramel.

Meat and Offal

In another book, *The Real Meat Cookbook*, I have covered the subject of meat and poultry very thoroughly. Today's cook is concerned not only with the buying, preparing and cooking of meat but also with how it is produced and the animals reared. Free-range and organic meat is more expensive than intensively reared, or why not call it 'factory farmed', meat. I continue to argue that if we ate much less meat than we do now, then we could afford to pay for meat which had come from humanely reared animals, and this includes free-range veal. A diet which included meat every day would be a very dull one. You only have to look at earlier chapters in this book to see what you would be missing.

The recipes here range from simple dishes that can be cooked with the minimum of effort when you get home from work, such as Grilled Spiced Pork Chops (see page 414) and Grilled Marinated Lamb Cutlets (see page 403), to good-tempered casseroles, which can be left to cook for several hours (see pages 428–431).

On the whole, I have used the less expensive cuts of meat. There is only one recipe for fillet of beef (see page 385), but it is worth including, for you can use it as the basis of an elegant meal that takes relatively little time to cook, and makes a good standby for impromptu entertaining.

As always, I have paid attention to leftovers, particularly important if you are cooking a large joint. Thus I have included my recipes for potted beef (see page 385), for vegetables stuffed with lamb (see page 405) and for a homely shepherd's pie or cottage pie (see page 404). And I have included some of my favourite recipes for meat stews, such as *bigos*, the Polish hunter's stew (see page 421), Boston baked beans (see page 420) and *feijoada* (see page 419), all of which are excellent for adapting to large-scale entertaining.

BEEF

Roast Fillet of Beef

Serves 4 with plenty of leftovers for sandwiches

2¼ lb / 1 kg fillet of beef
4 tsp olive oil
2 tsp wine vinegar
1 tbsp clear honey

1 tsp Angostura bitters
1 tsp soy sauce
1 tsp Worcestershire sauce
4 tbsp crushed peppercorns

Trim any fat from the beef. Mix all the liquid ingredients, and brush this all over the meat. The meat can be marinated overnight or cooked after it has stood, covered, for 1 hour to absorb some of the flavours. Wipe off any excess liquid, and fry the meat until browned all over in a well-seasoned or non-stick frying pan. Roll the meat in the crushed peppercorns, pressing them well into the surface. Place the meat on a rack in a roasting tin, and roast in a preheated oven at 220°C / 425°F / Mark 7 for 20–30 minutes, depending on how well done you like your meat. Allow it to rest in a warm place for 10–15 minutes before carving.

Potted Beef

Makes about 1½ lb / 680 g

The quantities given here can be multiplied or divided according to how much beef you have. A food processor is very useful, particularly for large quantities.

1 lb / 455 g cooked beef
4 oz / 110 g unsalted butter
1 tsp ground mace
good pinch of freshly grated
  nutmeg

good pinch of freshly ground black
  pepper
1–2 tbsp port or Madeira
salt
1–2 tbsp clarified butter

Cut the beef into small cubes, first removing the fat or gristle. Place it in a food processor with the butter, spices and port or Madeira. Process until smooth. Season to taste, and pack into a jar. Pour clarified butter over the top to seal. Cool, cover and refrigerate.

Boeuf à la Ficelle
(Boiled Beef on a String)

Serves 6

*This is an old-fashioned French dish, but has much to recommend it
today, requiring the best-quality produce to be cooked as simply and in
as healthy a fashion as possible. Of course, what you serve with it
might change all that. I have a jar of 'hot horseradish mustard', which
I like to mix with unsalted butter or cream to serve with the beef, and
Fay Maschler, in her excellent book,* Eating In, *recommends
horseradish ice cream, made by whipping double cream with grated
horseradish and a squeeze of lemon juice and freezing it. Properly
cooked, the beef should be underdone. Choose a tender piece of beef
of roasting or grilling quality.*

2 lb / 900 g piece of rump or sirloin	1 bay leaf
4 cloves	
1 onion, peeled and quartered	*To serve*
1–2 carrots, peeled and cut into	watercress
batons	mustard
2 celery stalks, trimmed and sliced	horseradish sauce
1 turnip, peeled and sliced	gherkins
2 tsp salt	coarse sea salt
12 black peppercorns	

For this, you need a large saucepan or stockpot. Trim any fat from the meat
and tie the meat parcel-fashion into a neat shape with sufficient string to suspend
the meat either from the pan handles or from a wooden spoon laid across the top
of the pan. The meat should not touch the bottom of the pan. Test this before you
start to cook. Push a clove into each quarter of onion, and put in the pan with all
the other vegetables, the seasonings and bay leaf, and enough water to cover the
meat. Bring to a full rolling boil, and put in the meat. The water will immediately
go off the boil, but bring it back to boiling before turning the heat down to the
gentlest simmer to allow the meat to poach for about 30 minutes (15 minutes per
1 lb / 455 g). Have a hot serving dish ready and all the accompaniments. Transfer
the meat to the dish, slice and serve.

About half-way through the cooking time, boil separately a selection of baby
vegetables to serve with the meat if you wish. The vegetables cooked with the meat
will probably be too soft.

Spiced Topside Braised in Cider

Serves 8–10

This is a dish for a large gathering, unless you want a lot of leftovers. These are, though, delicious in sandwiches, salads or as potted beef (see page 385). It is also a good-tempered dish and can be left for several hours to cook in a slow oven. Start the preparation at least the day before and marinate the beef overnight. It can marinate for up to 72 hours. This is not unlike the traditional German sauerbraten.

4 lb / 1.80 kg boned and rolled topside or silverside
2 tsp salt
2 tsp ground cardamom
3 tsp ground ginger
¼ pt / 140 ml cider vinegar
¾ pt / 430 ml dry cider
1 medium-sized onion, peeled and sliced
1 medium-sized carrot, peeled and sliced

1 leek, trimmed, sliced and washed
1 celery stalk, trimmed and sliced
2 bay leaves
1 cinnamon stick
6 cloves
1 tbsp allspice berries
1 tbsp black peppercorns
1 tsp ground mace
2 tbsp olive oil
1 tsp plain flour
½ oz / 15 g butter, softened

Trim and wipe the beef. Rub it all over with the salt, cardamom and 2 teaspoons of the ginger, and place it in a large bowl. Place the vinegar, cider, vegetables, bay leaves, cinnamon, cloves, allspice, peppercorns and mace in a saucepan, bring to the boil and pour over the meat. Cool quickly, then cover and refrigerate for up to 72 hours, turning the meat occasionally.

When ready to cook the meat, choose a casserole only slightly larger than the joint. Remove the meat from the marinade and dry it all over. Heat the oil in a frying pan or in the casserole if it is flameproof. When the oil is hot, sear the meat all over until browned. Put it into the casserole, and add about half the marinade and vegetables. Cover and cook in a preheated oven at 170–180°C / 325–350°F / Mark 3–4 for 3½ hours. Check the liquid level after a couple of hours, and add more of the marinade and vegetables if you wish.

When the meat is cooked transfer it to a carving dish and keep it warm. Pour the pan juices and any remaining marinade and vegetables into a saucepan and bring to the boil. Simmer for a few minutes while you prepare a ginger *beurre manié* by mixing together the flour, softened butter and the remaining teaspoon of ginger. Drop the *beurre manié*, bit by bit, into the saucepan, stir and cook for a further 10 minutes. Slice the meat and strain the sauce over it or into a sauceboat.

Steak, Kidney and Oyster Pie

Serves 4

Start preparation the day before required.

1½ lb / 680 g rump steak	1 bay leaf
½ pt / 280 ml bitter ale or stout	½ pt / 280 ml beef stock
8 oz / 230 g veal or lamb kidney	salt
12 pickling onions *or* 1 large onion	freshly ground black pepper
1 tbsp olive oil	12 oysters (or more)
1 oz / 30 g seasoned flour	8 oz / 230 g puff, rough puff or flaky
1 sprig parsley	pastry
1 sprig thyme	beaten egg and milk, to glaze

Trim the fat and gristle off the meat, and cut it into 1 in / 2.5 cm cubes. Put the meat in a bowl and marinate it in the bitter or stout for about 1 hour. Remove any fat from the kidney and the fine membrane. Snip out the central core, and cut the kidney into small chunks. Cover and refrigerate until required. Peel the onions, slice the large one, if using, and, in a flameproof casserole, fry in the olive oil until golden brown. Drain the marinade from the meat, and put to one side. Dry the beef thoroughly, and toss it in the seasoned flour, shaking off and reserving the excess. Fry until browned all over. Tie the herbs together in a bouquet garni and put them together in the casserole with the beef and onion. Strain the marinade over the meat, and add half the stock. Bring to the boil, skim any foam from the surface, lower the heat, cover and simmer gently for about 1 hour or until the beef is tender. About 30 minutes after starting to cook the beef, toss the kidneys in the remaining seasoned flour, fry them briefly and add to the casserole. Season to taste, but remember that the oysters, which you add later, will be a little salty. Remove from the heat, cool as quickly as possible and chill overnight.

The next day, spoon the meat and onions into a suitable pie dish and the jelly-like gravy into a small saucepan. Add the remaining ¼ pt / 140 ml stock to the saucepan, bring to the boil and reduce until you have about 7 fl oz / 200 ml liquid, enough to make the pie filling nice and juicy. Allow to cool. Meanwhile, carefully open the oysters, and arrange these on top of the meat, distributing them in such a way that each portion of pie will contain some oysters when you cut it. Strain the oyster liquid over the filling, and pour the cooled reduced meat juices over it. Roll out the pastry (not too thin), and use to cover the pie, pinching it round the rim of the pie dish to seal it. Cut off any overhanging pastry, and from it, stamp out some form of decoration, to stick on top of the pie crust, if you wish. Brush the pastry with the glaze, and bake in a preheated oven at 200°C / 400°F / Mark 6 for 15 minutes. Turn the oven down to 180°C / 350°F / Mark 4 and bake for a further 15 minutes, moving the pie to a lower oven shelf if necessary.

Fajitas

Serves 6–8

2 tbsp soy sauce
juice of 1–2 limes
1 tsp Angostura bitters
3 tbsp tequila
3 tbsp extra virgin olive oil
2–3 garlic cloves, peeled and crushed
1–2 ripe tomatoes, peeled, deseeded and chopped

½ tsp freshly ground black pepper
½ tsp sea salt
pinch of chilli powder or dried pepper flakes
2 lb / 900 g piece of flank steak
4 green or red chillies
coriander leaves, to garnish

Mix together all the ingredients except the steak and chillies to make a marinade. Slash the meat two or three times on each side, and put it in a shallow bowl with the marinade. Leave for 2–4 hours. Heat the grill. Remove the steak from the marinade, reserve the marinade and grill for 5–6 minutes on each side, if you like it rare, 8 minutes for medium and 10–12 minutes for well done. At the same time, grill the chillies until charred. When cool enough to handle, skin them, cut them in half, remove the seeds and shred finely. Slice the steak thinly across the grain. Mix the steak and chillies with a little of the reserved marinade, and pile on a serving platter. Garnish with coriander and serve with warm tortillas or pitta bread. Refried beans would also be a traditional accompaniment which are quickly made by draining, rinsing and mashing a can of red kidney beans and frying them in a little olive oil or in a non-stick frying pan until just beginning to brown.

Marinated Grilled Skirt Steak with Mango Salsa and Chilli Salsa

Skirt steak is one of the tastiest pieces of beef imaginable, and very lean. It is at its best when quickly grilled or fried, and served rare. Longer cooking tends to toughen it a little. The Mango Salsa needs to be made at least a day in advance.

2 lb / 900 g piece of skirt steak
2–3 red or green chillies, deseeded
  and chopped
coriander sprigs, to garnish

Mango Salsa
1 large mango
3 oz / 85 g sultanas or chopped
  dried apricots
1 green pepper, grilled, skinned,
  deseeded and chopped
4 spring onions, trimmed and finely
  sliced
6 tbsp granulated or muscovado
  sugar
2½ fl oz / 70 ml white wine vinegar,
  rice vinegar or coconut vinegar
2 garlic cloves, peeled and crushed

1 tsp fresh root ginger
salt
freshly ground black pepper

Marinade
2 ripe tomatoes, peeled, deseeded and
  chopped
2 garlic cloves, peeled and crushed
4 tbsp rum or tequila
4 tbsp pineapple juice
4 tbsp olive oil

1 tbsp lemon or lime juice
2 tsp Worcestershire sauce
1 tsp Angostura bitters
½ tsp Tabasco sauce
½ tsp sea salt
½ tsp freshly ground black pepper

To make the Mango Salsa, peel the mango and slice the flesh away from the stone. Chop it and mix it with the rest of the ingredients. Put in a bowl, cover with cling film and refrigerate overnight, or preferably for 2–3 days.

To make the marinade, mix all the ingredients together. Slash the meat in two or three places on each side, place in a shallow bowl, and pour the marinade on top. Leave for several hours. When ready to cook, heat the grill, remove the meat from the marinade, reserve it, and make sure that the meat is not only back at room temperature but also reasonably dry. Grill for 5–8 minutes on each side for rare, 8 minutes for medium and 10–12 minutes for well done. Remove the steak from the grill, and allow to rest for 5–10 minutes before slicing it across the grain. Mix the meat with a little of the marinade. Strain the rest into a bowl, and stir in the chillies. Hand this and the Mango salsa separately, and decorate the meat with sprigs of coriander. Serve with flour tortillas or pitta bread.

Variation ❧ Use papaya or pineapple, instead of mango, in the salsa.

You could also cut the meat into small strips and stir-fry it. Serve this with steamed rice, rather than tortillas or pitta bread.

Rosy Jellied Beef

Serves 8

1 bottle good Provençal dry rosé
  wine
2 carrots, peeled and thinly sliced
1 celery stalk, trimmed and thinly
  sliced
1 onion, peeled, quartered and
  thinly sliced
4 garlic cloves, peeled and thinly
  sliced
3 fl oz / 85 ml ruby port or red
  vermouth

1 bay leaf
1 sprig lemon thyme
1–2 sprigs parsley
½ tsp crushed black peppercorns
2 lb / 900 g piece of skirt steak
2 tbsp extra virgin olive oil
4 leaves gelatine *or* 4 tsp powdered
  gelatine

Mix together all the ingredients, except the steak, the olive oil and the gelatine to make a marinade. Trim the beef of fat and sinews, place it in a bowl, and pour on the marinade. Cover and marinate overnight. Next morning, remove the meat from the marinade, dry it, and fry it in the olive oil in a flameproof casserole to brown it lightly. Pour on the marinade ingredients, and simmer on the lowest possible heat until done to your liking. I find that skirt is best served either rather rare, in which case 15 minutes will probably be sufficient, or well cooked very slowly. In this case you can cook it for 1½–2 hours, but it must be long, slow cooking or otherwise, the meat will be dry, grey and tough. Remove the meat from the pan, and let it rest for 15–20 minutes before slicing it. Juices will run out, and these should be added to the pan juices. Lay the meat, in overlapping slices, in a serving dish. Scoop some of the carrots and celery out of the pan, and arrange these with the meat. Soak the gelatine in a little cold water until soft. Strain the cooking juices through a very fine sieve or muslin to obtain as clear a juice as possible, and mix in the gelatine until dissolved. Pour over the beef. Cool and then chill, and serve when just lightly jellied.

Corned Beef Hash

Serves 6–8

1½ lb / 680 g old potatoes
1 medium-sized onion, peeled and
   thinly sliced
2 tbsp extra virgin olive oil or
   clarified butter
1 lb / 455 g corned beef

1 scant tablespoon Dijon mustard
1 tsp soy sauce
2 tbsp stock or red wine
salt
freshly ground black pepper

Peel the potatoes and cut into chunks. Boil until almost tender, then drain, dice small and place in a bowl. Fry the onion in the olive oil or butter in a heavy frying pan until soft and lightly browned. With a fork, mix the corned beef, onions and potatoes together, and add the mustard, soy sauce, stock or wine and seasoning. Stir well until thoroughly mixed. Heat the frying pan, and spoon in all the hash, pressing it well down. When cooked brown and crisp on the bottom, invert a plate over the frying pan, and flick the pan over so that the hash cake is on the plate, cooked side up. If necessary, add a little more oil or butter to the pan, and slide in the hash to cook the other side. When cooked, cut into wedges and serve. Some people like eggs with this, poached, fried or soft-boiled.

LAMB

Rack of Lamb with Mustard and Herbs

Serves 4

2 best ends of lamb, chined
4 garlic cloves, peeled and crushed
1 tbsp Dijon or mild made-up
 mustard
2 tbsp fresh brown breadcrumbs
1 tbsp lemon juice

1 tbsp olive oil
1 tbsp finely chopped parsley
pinch of chopped thyme, marjoram or
 rosemary
salt
freshly ground black pepper

Remove the skin and most of the fat from the joint. Mix together the rest of the ingredients and spread the mixture thinly over the outside of the joints. Place on a rack in a roasting tin and roast in a preheated oven at 220°C / 425°F / Mark 7 for 20–25 minutes. Cook for longer if you like your lamb well done. Remove from the oven, and leave to rest in a warm place for 15 minutes before carving.

Butterflied Leg of Lamb

Serves 6

5–6 lb / 2.30–2.70 kg leg of lamb,
 boned
¼ tsp coarse sea salt
small sprig rosemary
1 small can flat anchovy fillets,
 rinsed and chopped

2–3 garlic cloves, peeled and crushed
12 black or green olives, pitted and
 finely chopped
2 tbsp Dijon mustard
3 tbsp extra virgin olive oil

Use two or three skewers to skewer the meat flat, like an open book. Pull off any excess fat and membranes. In a mortar, grind the salt and rosemary, and mix with all the remaining ingredients. Spread this paste over the meat. Cover and marinate overnight or for several hours, if possible. Cook on a hot grill, turning carefully to ensure even cooking. If you have a meat thermometer, 60°C / 140°F indicates medium cooked, 54°C / 130°F is pinkly rare. Roast or barbecued lamb is marvellous with thick slices of grilled aubergine and roasted peppers.

Roast Lamb with Sweet Spices

Serves 6

3 best ends of lamb, chined
1 lemon
1 tsp crushed black peppercorns
1 tsp ground coriander
½ tsp ground cumin

½ tsp fine sea salt
½ tsp crushed brown mustard seeds or
   yellow mustard flour
1–2 cinnamon sticks
12 cloves

Trim most of the fat off the lamb joints. Cut the lemon in half, and squeeze the juice over the meat, rubbing it well into the fat. Mix the crushed and ground spices, and sprinkle over the lamb. Split the cinnamon sticks into slivers ½–1 in / 1–2.5 cm long, and insert into the fat and between the flesh and rib bones of the lamb. Stud the cloves diagonally across the back fat of each joint. Place on a rack in a roasting tin, and roast in a preheated oven at 200°C / 400°F / Mark 6 for 20 minutes. Remove from the oven, cover with foil, and keep the meat warm for 15 minutes to rest it – to allow the juices to fall back into the meat for a uniform pinkness when carved.

Variation ᴖ Use a 3–4 lb / 1.35–1.80 kg leg or loin of lamb, and roast it for about 1¼ hours.

Instead of spicing the lamb, simply season it lightly and rub with olive oil before roasting. Serve with mint sauce, made by pounding 2 or 3 sprigs of fresh mint, a little black pepper, a few celery seeds and fennel seeds and a pinch of dried oregano together in a mortar, putting this in a pan with 3 tablespoons each of good red wine and cider vinegar, a tablespoon of plum jam and a tablespoon of olive oil, and bringing to the boil. Simmer gently for 20 minutes, strain and serve.

Poached Leg of Lamb

4 lb / 1.80 kg leg of lamb
2 bay leaves
1 onion, peeled and studded with 6
    cloves
parsley stalks
1 carrot, peeled and sliced

1 small turnip, peeled and sliced
1 leek, trimmed, sliced and washed
1 celery stalk
salt
freshly ground black pepper

Trim any fat from the leg of lamb and tie it with string to hold it in shape. Fill a large saucepan with water, and add the rest of the ingredients. Bring to the boil, and put in the leg of lamb. When the water comes back to the boil, turn the heat down to the lowest possible simmer, and poach for 1 hour (15 minutes per 1 lb / 455 g). Remove the lamb from the pan, and put it to rest in a warm place for 10–15 minutes before carving.

There are any number of ways of embellishing this simple dish with sauces and garnishes. One I like very much is caper sauce, which can be made as an old-fashioned roux of flour and butter moistened with the lamb juices and a little thin cream into which you stir 2–3 tablespoons capers.

Laver sauce is a traditional accompaniment to lamb in Wales, its rich iodine flavour and dark silky texture making a wonderful contrast with the meat. Laver (an edible seaweed) is usually sold ready-cooked. To make a simple sauce, heat about 8 oz / 230 g laver with a knob or two of butter and 1 pt / 570 ml lamb stock and season to taste.

Onion sauce also goes well with lamb, whether roasted or poached. To make it, sweat a large chopped onion in butter until translucent, and then stir in a few cloves and allspice berries. Sprinkle on a tablespoon of flour and gradually stir in ½ pt / 280 ml milk until you have a smooth sauce. Cook until the onions are soft, and sieve or blend into a purée, depending on whether you like a smooth or chunky sauce. Season to taste.

Fillet of Lamb with Ginger and Coriander

Serves 6

1¼ lb / 570 g lamb fillet
4 tbsp dry sherry or rice wine
1 tbsp sherry vinegar or rice vinegar
2 tsp sesame oil
1 tsp soy sauce
1 tsp crushed coriander seeds
1 in / 2.5 cm piece of fresh root
  ginger, peeled and shredded

2 garlic cloves, peeled and crushed
3 spring onions, trimmed and thinly
  sliced
1 tbsp sunflower oil
salt
freshly ground black pepper

Trim the lamb and cut into diagonal slices, ¼ in / 0.5 cm thick. Mix the sherry or wine, vinegar, sesame oil, soy sauce and coriander seeds, stir in the ginger, garlic and spring onions, and pour over the lamb. Marinate for at least 8 hours.

Drain the meat, reserving the marinade, and dry the meat on kitchen paper. Heat the sunflower oil in a large frying pan or wok, and put in the lamb. Stir-fry for 2–3 minutes, until browned and cooked. Remove the lamb with a slotted spoon, and transfer to a dish or platter. Strain the marinade into the frying pan or wok, bring to the boil, and reduce a little. Season to taste, and pour over the meat. Serve with stir-fried vegetables, such as bean sprouts, shredded Chinese leaves, mangetout, spinach and sliced celery, carrots and mushrooms.

Spring Lamb and Vegetables with Herb Cobbler

Serves 10

4 lb / 1.80 kg trimmed weight leg, shoulder or neck fillet of lamb, off the bone
1 onion, peeled and studded with 6 cloves
1 large carrot, peeled
1 celery stalk, trimmed and cut into chunks
2 bay leaves
large sprig of thyme
parsley stalks
small sprig of rosemary
1 bottle Sauvignon Blanc
1 pt / 570 ml lamb stock

Vegetables
20 pickling onions, peeled
20 baby carrots, scrubbed
20 asparagus tips
8 oz / 230 g shelled broad beans

Cobbler Topping
1½ lb / 680 g self-raising flour
1 tsp salt
7 oz / 200 g butter
2 oz / 60 g chervil, parsley, tarragon and chives, finely chopped
buttermilk or plain yoghurt thinned with water

Brown the meat, and place it in a large flameproof casserole. Add the onion, carrot and celery. Tie the herbs together, and place in the casserole with the meat and vegetables. Pour over the wine and stock, bring to the boil, lower the heat and simmer gently for 1 hour.

Add the pickling onions and baby carrots to the meat and vegetables in the casserole, and cook for a further 15 minutes. Add the asparagus and beans, and cook for 10–15 minutes more until all the vegetables are cooked.

To make the cobbler topping, sift the dry ingredients together. Rub in the butter. Stir in the herbs, and when ready to bake, mix in enough liquid to give the consistency of scone dough. Quickly roll out to about ¾ in / 2 cm thick. Cut into rounds with a fluted scone cutter. Arrange close together on a baking sheet, and bake in a preheated oven at 200°C / 400°F / Mark 6 for 10–12 minutes. Serve one piece with each serving of meat and vegetables.

Variation ∞ Instead of serving the lamb on individual plates, serve it from the casserole in which it was cooked, having arranged the cobbler topping around the top and baked it as described.

Al's Café Lamb and Prune Tagine

Serves 4–6

Yuba City, the prune capital of the world, is where I ate and enjoyed this dish.

1½ lb / 680 g boneless lamb shoulder or neck fillet	¼ tsp ground cinnamon
1 tbsp extra virgin olive oil	¼ tsp freshly ground black pepper
1 large onion, peeled and chopped	½ pt / 280 ml water or lamb stock
2 garlic cloves, peeled and chopped	pinch of salt
½ tsp ground turmeric	6 oz / 170 g pitted prunes
	2 tsp lemon juice

Trim the meat, and cut into 1 in / 2.5 cm chunks. In a heavy pan, brown the lamb in the olive oil. Add the onions, garlic and spices and continue to fry until the onions are transparent. Add the water and salt, and bring slowly to the boil. Reduce the heat immediately, cover and simmer gently for 1 hour. Add the prunes and lemon juice, cover once more, and simmer for a further 45 minutes or so. Serve with couscous, bulgar wheat or basmati rice.

Lamb Paprika

Serves 4

If using lamb on the bone, ask your butcher to chop it for casseroling.

3½ lb / 1.60 kg lamb on the bone *or* 1½ lb / 680 g boned and cubed lamb, best end or middle neck	1 onion, peeled and sliced
1 oz / 30 g seasoned flour	2 celery stalks, trimmed and sliced
1 tbsp olive or sunflower oil	1 tbsp paprika
	1 tsp ground cumin
	½ pt / 280 ml stock or water

Trim any excess fat and gristle from the lamb. Put the seasoned flour in a strong paper bag, and shake the pieces of lamb in it, a few at a time. Remove the pieces from the bag, shake off any surplus flour, and put the meat to one side.

Repeat until all the meat has been coated. Heat the oil in a heavy flameproof casserole and, when hot, sear the meat, a few pieces at a time, until nicely browned all over. Remove the meat and put to one side. Fry the vegetables until golden brown, and put with the meat. Sprinkle the paprika and cumin into the pan, and cook for 1–2 minutes, stirring and scraping up the bits stuck to the bottom. Moisten with a little of the liquid and stir until smooth. Gradually add the rest of the liquid, then bring to the boil. Put the meat and vegetables back in the pan, cover, lower the heat and simmer very gently for 1–1½ hours, until the meat is tender. Alternatively, cook the casserole towards the bottom of a preheated oven at 200°C / 400°F / Mark 6 for about 1 hour.

Lamb and Kidney Hotpot

Serves 6

6 best end or loin lamb chops
3–6 lamb kidneys (according to taste)
1 onion, peeled and sliced
1 lb / 455 g potatoes, peeled and sliced
2–3 carrots, peeled and sliced
2–3 small turnips, peeled and sliced (optional)
2 celery stalks, trimmed and sliced
2 leeks, trimmed, sliced and washed
salt
freshly ground black pepper
4 cloves
1 bay leaf
½ pt / 280 ml dry cider, ale, white wine or stock
1 tbsp olive oil

Trim excess fat from the chops. Remove the fat and membrane from the kidneys, slice them in two horizontally and snip out the cores. Use some of the kidney fat to fry the chops and kidneys all over to brown them, or use a non-stick frying pan. Put the meat to one side. Arrange a layer of onion and potato slices on the bottom of a lightly greased casserole, put the chops on top, then add a layer of vegetables, the kidneys, and finish with a layer of potatoes. Lightly season each layer. Tuck in the cloves and bay leaf, pour on the liquid, and brush the top layer with olive oil. Cover and cook in the middle or bottom half of a preheated oven at 180°C / 350°F / Mark 4 for 2 hours. Remove the lid, raise the heat, and finish off nearer the top of the oven for another 20 minutes or so to brown the potatoes.

China Chilo

Serves 4–6

Looking for dishes to include in my occasional series on Great British Classics, I was much taken with a recipe I came across several times. Dorothy Hartley's Food in England *describes China Chilo as a clear white and green dish, 'much fancied by the ladies'. Eliza Acton gives a recipe for it in* Modern Cookery (1845), *and something rather similar features in Hannah Glasse's* The Art of Cookery Made Plain and Simple *of a century earlier. It is still a good dish today, perfectly suited to summer dining. I have based my recipe on Eliza Acton's. Originally mutton was used. If you can get it, use it.*

1 lb / 455 g lean boneless lamb
2 oz / 60 g butter
¼ pt / 140 ml white wine, lamb
  stock or water
1 cucumber
3 Little Gem lettuces, cut in half
  and washed

1¼ lb / 570 g shelled peas
8 spring onions, trimmed and sliced
4 oz / 110 g button mushrooms, wiped
  and halved or quartered, if you wish
salt
freshly ground black pepper
chervil or parsley, to garnish

Mince the lamb or dice it very small. Cook it in the butter until it loses its raw look. Pour on half the liquid, cover and simmer for 50–60 minutes. (Mutton will take longer.) Meanwhile, peel the cucumber, cut it in half lengthways, scrape out and discard the seeds, and dice the flesh. Slice the lettuces. Add the vegetables and remaining liquid to the lamb after it has cooked for 50–60 minutes, and cook for a further 20–30 minutes. Season to taste and serve in a ring of boiled or steamed rice, garnished with herbs.

Variation ∞ Sprinkle a little curry powder on the meat as it cooks in the butter at the beginning of the recipe.

Lamb and Artichoke Stew

Serves 6–8

3½–4 lb / 1.60–1.80 kg lamb
    shoulder chops
2 tbsp plain wholemeal flour
1 tsp paprika
½ tsp salt
½ tsp freshly ground black pepper
1 tsp ground cumin
1 tsp ground coriander
1 onion, peeled and sliced
2 tbsp sunflower oil

seeds of 6–8 cardamom pods
1 pt / 570 ml lamb stock
8 dried apricots
1 lb / 455 g Jerusalem artichokes, peeled
    and halved or quartered
1 bay leaf
salt
freshly ground black pepper
parsley or coriander, finely chopped

Trim any excess fat and membrane from the chops. Sift the flour and spices together, and use to dust the meat. Fry the onion in the oil until transparent. Remove and put to one side. Fry the cardamom seeds until they begin to release their fragrance, and then begin frying the meat, a few pieces at a time if necessary. When browned, add ¼ pt / 140 ml stock, and bring to the boil, scraping up any residues stuck to the bottom of the pan. Cut the apricots in half, and add them to the casserole with the artichokes. Pour on the rest of the stock, add the bay leaf, bring to the boil, and skim the surface. Lower the heat, cover, and simmer until the lamb is tender. If you want a more concentrated sauce, strain the cooking juices into a saucepan and reduce as appropriate. Mix it back in with the meat, and season to taste. Sprinkle with parsley or coriander and serve.

Irish Stew

Serves 6

*The classic proportions for this traditional dish are half as much onion
as meat, and twice as much potato.*

2 lb / 900 g middle or best end of
   neck chops *or* 1½ lb / 680 g
   boneless stewing lamb
3 lb / 1.35 kg potatoes, peeled and
   sliced
12 oz / 340 g onions, peeled and
   thinly sliced

salt
freshly ground black pepper
1 bay leaf
1 sprig of thyme
finely chopped parsley

Remove as much fat as possible from the meat. In an earthenware or similar
ovenproof casserole, build up layers of potato, meat and onion, seasoning lightly
and finishing with a layer of potatoes. Tuck in the bay leaf and thyme, and pour in
¼–½ pt / 140–280 ml water, enough to stop the contents burning in the initial
stages. Cover and cook in a preheated oven at 170°C / 325°F / Mark 3 for 2½–3
hours. Sprinkle with parsley, and serve.

Homemade Lamb Sausages

Serves 4–6

*These sausages are best made an hour or so before required, to allow
the flavours to develop.*

1 lb / 455 g lean, boneless lamb
12 oz / 340 g breast of lamb, off the
   bone
3 tbsp fresh breadcrumbs
1 egg yolk

1 tbsp finely chopped parsley
1 tsp finely chopped rosemary or thyme
salt
freshly ground black pepper

Mince or process the two meats as coarsely or as finely as required. Put in a
large bowl, and mix in the crumbs and egg yolk, and then the herbs and seasoning.
Make sure all is thoroughly mixed, and then fry a teaspoonful of it to check the

seasoning. With wetted hands, shape the mixture into round cakes or sausage shapes, or pack into sausage shapes around skewers. Cover and refrigerate until required. Cook under a hot grill or on a barbecue, to your liking.

Variations ～ Mix other seasonings, such as ground cumin or coriander, crushed garlic or chopped chilli, into the meat.

Grilled Marinated Lamb Cutlets

Serves 8

*Cutlets cut from the thoroughly trimmed and chined best end of lamb
are best for this recipe. They are more expensive but will save time,
for most of the fat will have been removed.*

1 tbsp mustard
4 garlic cloves, peeled and crushed
4 tsp olive oil
1 tbsp fortified wine such as port or
  sherry
1 tbsp soy sauce

1 tsp tomato purée or ketchup
2 tsp soft brown sugar or honey
freshly ground black pepper
16–24 best end lamb cutlets
several sprigs rosemary or thyme

Blend all the ingredients, except the meat and herbs, together until smooth. Brush over the cutlets, and lay them in a dish with the herb sprigs. Cover and refrigerate overnight. When ready to cook the cutlets, bring them back to room temperature, heat the grill and shake any surplus marinade from them. Grill for 2–4 minutes on each side, depending on thickness and how well done you like your lamb. Serve hot, warm or cold. The end of the rib bones can be bonneted with paper cutlet frills.

Shepherd's Pie

*This is an excellent dish for using up the leftover remains of a large
joint, although it can be made from scratch using raw minced meat.*

1 medium onion, peeled and finely
  chopped
1 tbsp olive oil
1½ lb / 680 g minced lamb, cooked
¼ pt / 140 ml meat stock or gravy
1–2 tbsp port or red vermouth
1 tsp soy sauce or Worcestershire
  sauce
pinch of ground mace or freshly
  grated nutmeg

pinch of ground allspice *(optional)*
pinch of chopped rosemary or thyme
1 tbsp finely chopped parsley or chives
salt
freshly ground black pepper
1½ lb / 680 g mashed potato (mashed
  with a little olive oil while still hot)

Fry the onion in the olive oil until lightly brown. Mix with the meat, stock or
gravy, port or vermouth, sauce, spices, herbs and seasoning, and spoon the mixture
into an ovenproof dish. Spread the mashed potato over the top, and score the
surface in lines with a fork. Bake in the top half of a preheated oven at 180°C /
350°F / Mark 4 for 40–45 minutes.

Variations ∾ Make a Cottage Pie by using beef instead of lamb.

Grated cheese, egg yolk, herbs, cream and spring onion are some of the things
that can be added to the mashed potato topping for variety.

Minced Lamb Kebabs

1 onion, peeled and finely chopped
3 garlic cloves, peeled and finely
  chopped
1½ lb / 680 g lean minced lamb
1 tbsp ground cumin

½ tbsp ground coriander
1 tbsp ground cardamom
1 tbsp freshly ground black pepper
2 tbsp finely chopped parsley or
  coriander

Mix the onion and garlic with the minced lamb. Mix in the rest of the ingredients, and fry a tiny piece to check whether the seasoning is to your liking. Add more spices if it needs it. Wet your hands and form the mixture into balls or sausage shapes around skewers or satay sticks. Heat the grill, and when hot, grill the kebabs until done to your liking. The length of time required will also depend on how thickly the meat is packed around the skewers.

Baked Stuffed Vegetables

*Stuffed vegetables are a tasty way of using up good-quality leftovers,
and provide an alternative to moussaka or shepherd's pie (see page
404).*

8 oz / 230 g cooked lamb, minced
  or diced
12 oz / 340 g cooked bulgar wheat
  (see page 213)
2 oz / 60 g finely chopped onion
2 oz / 60 g lightly toasted pinenuts
  or flaked almonds

2 oz / 60 g raisins or chopped apricots
  (optional)
finely chopped mint
good pinch of ground coriander
salt
freshly ground black pepper
1–2 tbsp extra virgin olive oil

Mix the ingredients together, and spoon into your chosen hollowed vegetable. Place in an oiled roasting tin or ovenproof dish, cover with foil and cook in the top half of a preheated oven at 180°C / 350°F / Mark 4 until the vegetables are tender.

Variations ∞ Spinach, cabbage and vine leaves can also be wrapped around the same mixture and baked.

Devilled Lamb's Kidneys

Serves 2, as a main course; 4 as a snack

*This has a fine Edwardian ring to it, the kind of food you might find
in a silver chafing-dish on the sideboard when you come downstairs to
a country house breakfast. It is also an inexpensive dish and quick to
cook, making it a useful addition to the lunch or dinner table.
Serve it on toast for a snack or with plain boiled rice for a more
substantial dish.*

Sauce
1 small onion or 2 shallots, peeled
  and finely chopped
½ oz / 15 g butter
1 tsp good curry powder
1 tsp plain flour
2½ fl oz / 70 ml stock, milk, water
  or beer
1 tsp mustard
1 tbsp mango chutney

6 lamb's kidneys
½ oz / 15 g butter *or* 1 tbsp olive oil
1 tbsp plain flour
1 tsp good curry powder
finely chopped parsley, to garnish

First make the sauce. Fry the onion or shallots gently in the butter until golden brown. Stir in the curry powder, and cook for 1–2 minutes, then stir in the flour. Gradually add the liquid, and stir continuously until you have a smooth sauce. Cook on a low heat for 10 minutes, then add the mustard and chutney.

While the sauce is cooking, remove the fat and outer skin from the kidneys. Split each kidney horizontally in two, and snip out the cores. Put the flour and curry powder in a paper bag, and shake the kidneys in it to coat them with seasoned flour. Heat the butter or oil in a frying pan and fry the kidneys gently until cooked to the degree you prefer. I cook them for about 5 minutes or less, as I like them pink. Serve them on toast or a bed of rice with some of the sauce and parsley for garnish.

Iscas
(Liver)

This is my version of Iscas, *the favourite way of preparing liver in Lisbon. Rather than calves' liver, which does not lend itself well to a marinade, use best-quality lamb's liver. The secret is to cook it very quickly so that it does not toughen.*

1½ lb / 680 g lamb's liver	1 mild onion, peeled and thinly sliced
3 tbsp good white wine	salt
3 tbsp olive oil	freshly ground black pepper

Remove any piping from the liver and cut first into slices and then into strips about the length and thickness of your little finger. Place in a bowl. Mix the wine with the olive oil, and pour this over the liver. Add the onion, and leave to marinate overnight.

Heat a flameproof casserole with a lid, and preferably with handles, on the hob. Drain the liver, reserving the marinade. Put the liver in the hot casserole, perhaps doing it in two or three batches to avoid crowding the pan, which would lower the temperature and the meat would steam instead of searing. Put the lid on, and shake the casserole vigorously. Return it to the heat to cook for not more than 3–4 minutes. Remove the liver and keep it warm. Proceed until you have cooked all the liver. When you have removed the last of the liver from the casserole, pour in the reserved marinade, boil until reduced by half, then season it and pour it over the liver. Serve immediately.

Braised Stuffed Lambs' Hearts

Serves 4

This is an inexpensive and delicious recipe which requires little advance preparation. Once in the casserole, the hearts can be left to cook on a very low heat for up to 2½ hours. A slightly higher temperature will cook them in 1½ hours, but they should be cooked gently to keep them tender. Calves' hearts can also be used.

4 lamb's hearts	½ tsp ground cumin
1 tbsp olive oil	¼ tsp ground cardamom
1 small onion, peeled and chopped	3 cloves
4 tbsp soft breadcrumbs or cooked rice	½ tbsp chopped coriander, basil or parsley
½ tbsp pinenuts or other chopped nuts	¼ pt / 140 ml stock, wine or water
½ tbsp raisins	salt
	freshly ground black pepper

With kitchen scissors, carefully cut out the centre 'core' of each heart, leaving an empty 'pocket' to take the stuffing. Finely dice the cores. Heat the olive oil in a flameproof casserole, and fry the diced heart and onion until just browned. Transfer to a bowl and mix with the breadcrumbs or rice, nuts, raisins, spices and herbs and spoon this mixture into the hearts. Close the tops with cocktail sticks. Fry the hearts all over in the oil that is remaining in the casserole. Pour on the liquid, bring to the boil, and then turn the heat right down. Cover and cook gently until the meat is tender. Drain the cooking liquid into a saucepan, boil until reduced by at least half, season to taste and serve with the stuffed hearts. This is very good served with spiced rice, couscous, polenta or bulgar wheat rather than potatoes. You could braise a dish of celery hearts in the oven at the same time.

GOAT AND KID

IT SEEMS to me a pity that when we have a good source of alternative meat, which is within the bounds of the culturally acceptable, we shy away from it and do not eat goat meat more often.

Most of the kid and goat available comes from young billy goats culled from milking herds. It is a pale, delicate, slightly gelatinous meat that might even be called bland without the addition of plenty of onions, herbs and spices. The meat from a fully mature animal is another matter altogether, tender and full of flavour. Although I have cooked and enjoyed dishes using young kid goat, I have only in recent years had the opportunity to cook the mature meat. My first experience with it brought home the importance of hanging meat properly. The joint I had came from an 18-month-old animal that had been slaughtered 9 days previously. I kept it in the refrigerator, loosely but carefully wrapped, for another 5 days. Twice I wiped it over with a cloth dipped in sherry vinegar. There was probably no need to do this, but some folk memory made it feel right to freshen and sweeten the meat in this way. By the time I cooked the meat, it was perfectly hung.

Rather than disguise the meat with spices and plenty of herbs, I decided to cook it in a simple fashion so that the flavour and texture could be savoured. Not having a baker's oven, which is marvellous for slow cooking, I cooked it, still *boulangère*-style, with potatoes and onions, in a chicken brick. The meat was lean, tender and juicy, fine-grained and full of flavour. Perhaps the best indication of the quality of the meat is that we served it with a bottle of 1981 Château Mouton Baron Philippe.

Leg of Goat Baked in the Oven

Serves 4

3 lb / 1.35 kg leg of goat
4 tbsp olive oil
2–3 carrots, peeled and cut into
  chunky batons
1 large head garlic, cloves separated
  and peeled
3–4 large potatoes, peeled and
  thickly sliced

2 large onions, peeled and thinly sliced
sprig of thyme or rosemary
a few parsley sprigs
salt
freshly ground black pepper
7 fl oz / 200 ml dry white or red wine

Brown the joint all over in 1–2 tablespoons of the olive oil. Arrange the carrots, garlic, potatoes and half the onion in the bottom of a well-soaked *Römertopf* or chicken brick. Lay the meat on top, and cover with the rest of the onions. Add the herbs, season lightly, and pour on the wine and the rest of the olive oil. Put on the lid, and cook in a preheated oven at 180°C / 350°F / Mark 4 for 2–2½ hours.

PORK

Roast Stuffed Loin of Pork

Serves 4–6

*This is a good-tempered roast, like most pork dishes, and can be left
well alone in the oven. Long, slow cooking is needed so an extra 15
minutes or so won't hurt. It is delicious hot or cold, but if you are
serving it cold, do not serve it straight from the refrigerator. Chilled
slices of meat are most unappetizing.*

3 oz / 85 g dried prunes
3½ lb / 1.60 kg loin of pork
1 onion, peeled and finely chopped
4 oz / 110 g soft breadcrumbs
2 oz / 60 g shelled and chopped
  walnuts

finely chopped herbs
salt
freshly ground black pepper
stock, to moisten

Put the prunes to soak in hot water. Remove the skin from the pork and bone
the joint. You can make stock with the bones. Remove a few of the loose pieces of
meat, and finely chop or mince them. Mix the onion with the chopped meat,
breadcrumbs and walnuts. Add the herbs and seasoning, and spread the stuffing
over the meat. Drain the prunes and remove the stones. Lay the prunes down the
middle of the joint, on top of the stuffing. Shape the joint into a roll, and tie it at
intervals with string to keep it together. Heat a non-stick frying pan and fry the
joint all over to seal it. Transfer to a casserole, moisten with stock and cook in a
preheated oven at 180°C / 350°F / Mark 4 for 1½ hours. Remove from the oven
and, if serving hot, allow to rest in a warm place for 10 minutes before carving. If
serving cold, it is delicious with a fruity chutney.

Pot-Roast Pork

Serves 4–6

*Ask your butcher to remove all the skin and some of the fat before
rolling the meat.*

2½ lb / 1.10 kg rolled, boned loin or
  half leg of pork
1 onion, peeled and sliced
6 cloves
6 garlic cloves

small sprig of rosemary *or* a handful
  of fennel
sea salt
freshly ground black pepper
1 pt / 570 ml full-cream milk

Heat a non-stick frying pan, and brown the meat all over. Remove and set
aside. Lightly fry the onion until just beginning to turn colour, and then lay it in the
bottom of a casserole just a little larger than the joint of pork. Push the cloves into
the pork fat at intervals. Peel the garlic and cut into slivers. Insert these into
horizontal incisions in the pork fat. Place the joint on top of the onions, tuck the
herbs around it and season lightly with salt and pepper. Bring the milk to the boil,
and pour it over the meat. Cover and cook in a preheated oven at 170°C / 325°F /
Mark 3 for about 2 hours. Remove from the oven and, if serving hot, allow to rest
for 10–15 minutes before carving. Serve with mashed potato or potato gnocchi (see
page 194). This is also delicious served cold with a potato and mushroom salad (see
page 100).

Pork Chop and Potato Casserole

Serves 4

4 lean chump, loin or spare-rib
  chops, about 6–8 oz / 170–230g
  each
2 lb / 900 g waxy potatoes, peeled
  and thinly sliced
2 onions, peeled and thinly sliced

salt
freshly ground black pepper
1 pt / 570 ml white wine
1 cinnamon stick, about 2 in / 5 cm
sprig of sage

Trim most of the fat from the pork, and use a piece of it to grease an ovenproof
dish or casserole large enough to hold the chops in a single layer. Arrange a layer of
half the vegetables in the dish, put the pork chops on top, and cover with the rest

of the potatoes and onions layered on top. Lightly season, pour on the wine and tuck the cinnamon and sage into the dish. Cover with foil or a close-fitting lid, and bake in a preheated oven at 180°C / 350°F / Mark 4 for 1–1½ hours, until the meat is tender and the potatoes are well cooked. You can remove the cover and brown the top for the last 20 minutes or so if you wish.

Pork Chops with Caper, Lemon and Parsley Sauce

Serves 4

4 pork chops or cutlets
1 tbsp olive, sunflower or
   groundnut (peanut) oil (or use a
   non-stick frying pan)
zest of ½ lemon, cut into narrow
   strips
2 tbsp capers, drained

2 tbsp finely chopped parsley
¼ pt / 140 ml dry white wine or water
2 tsp cream or crème fraîche *(optional)*
salt
freshly ground black pepper
freshly grated nutmeg

Fry the pork chops or cutlets in the oil until golden brown all over. Turn down the heat, and add the lemon zest, capers and half the parsley. Moisten with 3–4 tablespoons wine or water. Half cover the frying pan, and let the meat cook very gently for 15–20 minutes, until tender. Cooking time will depend on how thick the meat is, and which cut you have selected. Remove the meat from the pan, and keep it covered in a warm place while you make the sauce. Add the rest of the wine or water to the pan, and bring it to the boil, scraping up any caramelized residues, and reduce it until you have about 4 tablespoons. Stir in the cream, if using, and bring back to the boil. Season the sauce with salt, pepper and a little nutmeg, and stir in the rest of the parsley.

Serve the pork chops on heated dinner plates, with a spoonful of sauce. A purée of potatoes and garlic accompanies the meat very well, as do lentils.

Grilled Spiced Pork Chops

Serves 4

*This is a very quick and easy recipe to prepare. You can vary the
marinade and spices to suit your own taste and store-cupboard. I like
to serve the chops with boiled rice and a vegetable cooked in plenty of
juices, such as a* ratatouille *type of dish. Unlikely though it may
sound, cod cutlets are delicious marinated, cooked and served in the
same way, although they cook far more quickly.*

4 pork chops or cutlets
2 tbsp fruit chutney or apricot jam
½ tsp chilli sauce *or* ¼ tsp chilli
   powder
2 garlic cloves, peeled and crushed
1 tbsp good sherry

½ tbsp soy sauce
1 tsp Worcestershire sauce
1 tsp Angostura bitters
1 tsp ground cumin
1 tsp ground coriander

Trim excess fat from the chops or cutlets. Mix the rest of the ingredients
together and brush over the chops. Let them stand for at least 30 minutes to
absorb some of the flavours. (You can even prepare the meat in the morning, cover
it and refrigerate until required.) Heat the grill and cook the chops under the grill
until cooked through, turning once. Cooking time will depend on the thickness of
the meat, not its overall weight.

Braised Spare-Rib Chops

Serves 2–3

*If for any reason you are out of such essentials for Oriental cooking as
ginger, garlic and spring onion, and yet would still like to cook
something Chinese in taste, try this dish. Although so easy to prepare,
the end result is nonetheless pleasing, not least because of the subtle
vinegary touch in the sauce.*

1¼ lb / 570 g spare-rib chops, cut
   into large pieces
½ tsp salt
2 tbsp sugar
1 tbsp light soy sauce

1 tbsp dark soy sauce
1 tbsp rice vinegar *or* 2¼ tsp white wine
   vinegar
½ tbsp Shaoxing wine or amontillado
   sherry
½ pt / 280 ml water

Put the chops in a heavy pan or flameproof casserole. Season with the salt,
sugar, soy sauces, vinegar and wine or sherry, then add the water and bring to the
boil. Reduce the heat, cover and continue to simmer gently for 1½–1¾ hour,
turning the pieces over two or three times so that both sides absorb the seasonings.
If the liquid is evaporating too quickly, add a little more water. Test if the pork is
tender enough. Simmer for another 20 minutes, or longer, if necessary. Remove the
meat to a serving dish. If there is too much liquid left in the pan, reduce it over a
high heat, then pour the sauce over the pork. Serve hot.

This dish can be made a day in advance and kept in the refrigerator. Its taste
actually improves overnight.

Cucumber and Spare Ribs

Serves 4

*Here is another oriental recipe using spare-rib chops.
It is inexpensive and full of flavour. Use hairy cucumbers if
you can get them from Oriental supermarkets.*

8 dried Chinese mushrooms *or*
   12 fresh shiitake mushrooms
2 large cucumbers
1¼ lb / 570 g spare-rib chops

1 tbsp groundnut (peanut) oil
sea salt
freshly ground black pepper

Soak the dried mushrooms, if using, in ¼ pt / 140 ml water for 30 minutes. If
using fresh mushrooms, poach them for 5 minutes in the same quantity of water.
Drain and reserve the liquid. Slice the mushrooms. Peel the cucumbers and cut
into wedges (hairy cucumbers need scraping, not peeling). Dice the pork. Heat the
oil in a wok or large frying pan, and fry the pork until browned all over. Add the
vegetables and cook for a couple of minutes, then add half the mushroom liquid.
Cook for a further minute or two, season with salt and pepper and serve
immediately.

Variation ∿ You can use six medium-sized courgettes instead of the
cucumbers.

Pork Chops with Onion and Sauerkraut

Serves 6

1½ lb / 680 g onions, peeled and
   thinly sliced
2 oz / 60 g butter *or* 4 tbsp
   groundnut (peanut) oil or olive oil
6 pork loin chops

1 lb / 455 g sauerkraut
3 tbsp wine vinegar or cider vinegar
3 tbsp dry white wine or cider
pinch of thyme

In a large frying pan, gently fry the onions in half the butter or oil until lightly
caramelized. Remove with a slotted spoon, and put to one side. Add the rest of the
butter or oil, and fry the chops on both sides to brown. Reduce the heat, and cook
for 20–25 minutes or until done. Meanwhile, gently heat the sauerkraut. When

cooked through, drain it, and pile it on a serving plate. Arrange the pork chops and onions on top. Cover and keep warm while you finish the sauce. Deglaze the pan with the vinegar and wine or cider, scraping up the browned cooking residues. Add the thyme, bring to the boil, and pour over the pork. This is very good served with creamy mashed potatoes.

Spare-Rib Chops in Cider with Chestnuts and Potatoes

Serves 6

3 lb / 1.35 kg spare-rib chops
2 oz / 60 g plain flour
½ tsp salt
½ tsp freshly ground black pepper
¼ tsp ground cinnamon
¼ tsp ground mace
1–2 tbsp olive oil
20 small onions, peeled
1½ lb / 680 g small potatoes, scrubbed or peeled

1 lb / 455 g chestnuts, boiled and peeled
1 bay leaf
1 sprig sage
1 sprig parsley
1 sprig thyme
2 pt / 900 ml dry cider
2 apples
1 tbsp melted butter
2 tbsp finely chopped parsley

Trim any excess fat from the chops. Put the flour, seasoning and spices in a large paper bag, and shake the chops in the seasoned flour until lightly dusted. Fry the chops in the oil, a few at a time, until browned all over, and put them to one side. Brown the onions. Put half the onions, potatoes and chestnuts in the bottom of a casserole and arrange the pork chops on top. Cover with the rest of the onions, potatoes and chestnuts. (If you cannot get small potatoes, cut larger ones into pieces.) Tie the herbs together, and tuck down in the dish. Pour on enough cider to come almost to the top of the vegetables. Bring to the boil, cover and simmer very gently, or cook in a preheated oven at 170°C / 325°F / Mark 3 for about 1½ hours, until the meat is done. Peel and core the apples and slice into rings. Blanch them until tender, and arrange on top of the casserole. Brush with melted butter, and finish off under the grill just to caramelize the apples. Sprinkle with parsley and serve. If you prefer to have a thicker sauce, strain off the liquid before you add the apple. Boil until reduced to the thickness you require, pour back over the meat and proceed with the apples.

Pork and Rabbit Casserole

Serves 6

1½ lb / 680 g belly pork, in a piece
1 pig's trotter, if available
2 lb / 900 g rabbit, saddle and
   hindquarters only
1 onion, peeled and chopped
2 carrots, peeled and cut into sticks

¾ pt / 430 ml dry white wine
3–4 sprigs of French tarragon
2–3 parsley stalks
salt
freshly ground black pepper

Remove the rind from the belly pork, and cut the meat into 1 in / 2.5 cm cubes. Chop the trotter into two or three pieces so that it will fit in the casserole (or you could ask your butcher to do this). Chop the rabbit into pieces if it is not already portioned. Fry a handful of the belly pork until the fat runs, and in this fry the onion until golden brown. Add the rest of the pork and the rabbit, a few pieces at a time, and brown them all over. Transfer the onion, the meat, the pork rind and the pig's trotter to a lidded casserole. Add the carrots. Pour half the white wine into the frying pan in which you browned the meat, and deglaze the pan by bringing the wine to the boil and scraping up any residues stuck to the pan. Pour it over the meat, and add the rest of the wine. Keep back some of the tarragon and parsley for garnish, and put the rest in with the meat. Bring to the boil, cover and cook on a very low heat or in a preheated oven at 170°C / 325°F / Mark 3 for about 2 hours, until the meat is tender. Remove the pork rind and wilted herbs from the casserole, chop the rest of the tarragon and parsley, and stir it in, together with salt and pepper to taste. This is marvellous served with a bowl of lentils.

Feijoada

(*Brazilian Pork and Bean Stew*)

Serves 8–10

1½ lb / 680 g dried black beans
2–3 lb / 900 g–1.35 kg piece of
  gammon or knuckle of bacon
2–3 pig's trotters, chopped in half
2 lb / 900 g spare-rib chops
1 bay leaf
1 celery stalk
4 cloves

1 small onion, peeled and quartered
1 lb / 455 g cooked garlic sausage or
  chorizo
1 large onion, peeled and chopped
1 tbsp groundnut (peanut) or sunflower
  oil
6 garlic cloves, peeled and crushed
freshly ground black pepper

In separate pots, soak the beans and the gammon or bacon overnight, or for at least several hours. Drain the beans, and in a pan of fresh water, boil them for 10–15 minutes. Drain them once more, and put in a large flameproof casserole together with the gammon or bacon, the pig's trotters and the spare-rib chops. Add the bay leaf and the celery. Push a clove into each onion quarter and add to the pan. Cover with water, bring to the boil, skim any scum from the surface, and simmer, partially covered, for 2 hours, or until the meat and beans are tender. Remove the bay leaf, the celery and, if you can find them, the cloves and onion quarters. At this stage, the meat will have fallen away from the bones so remove as many bones as you can, together with the skin from the bacon knuckle, if you used one. Add the diced garlic sausage. Brown the chopped onion in the oil, but do not let it burn. Stir in the garlic and a couple of ladlefuls of cooked drained beans. Fry, and then mash with the back of a spoon. Stir this paste back into the stew to thicken it. Bring back to the boil, and season with pepper. Greens, boiled rice and a peppery sauce are traditional accompaniments.

Boston Baked Beans

This is excellent if cooked the day before required, and then carefully reheated.

1 lb / 455 g dried Boston, navy or
   haricot beans, soaked overnight
   and drained
8 oz / 230 g belly pork or salt pork
2 pt / 1.15 l boiling water
1 large mild onion, peeled and
   thinly sliced
2–3 garlic cloves, peeled and
   crushed

2 tbsp molasses
2 tbsp Dijon mustard
2 sprigs of thyme or a good pinch of
   dried thyme
2 bay leaves
2 tsp grated fresh root ginger
½ tsp freshly ground black pepper
salt

Boil the beans in plenty of water for 10 minutes. Drain and rinse them. Cut the belly pork, keeping the skin on, into 1 in / 2.5 cm pieces. Put all the ingredients, except the salt, in a large flameproof casserole, cover and bring to the boil. Lower the heat, simmer for 10 minutes, then transfer to a preheated oven at 130°C / 275 °F / Mark 1 and cook for about 12 hours. Add more water if the beans begin to show signs of drying out before they are cooked. Season with salt about 1 hour before the end of the cooking time.

Bigos

(Polish Hunter's Stew)

1 lb / 455 g spare-rib chops or
    boneless shoulder of pork

1 lb / 455 g *kielbasa* or other spicy,
    meaty cooking sausage

8 oz / 230 g onions, peeled and
    sliced

1 tbsp oil

½ oz / 15 g dried ceps, soaked for
    30 minutes and drained

2 lb / 900 g sauerkraut

6 cloves

2 in / 5 cm cinnamon stick

1 bay leaf

½ tsp dill seeds

8 oz / 230 g soaked prunes, pitted

4 canned tomatoes

water or stock

freshly ground black pepper

2–3 tbsp soured cream *(optional)*

fresh dill or parsley *(optional)*

Cut the meat and sausage into 2 in / 5 cm chunks. (You can toss in flour if you want to thicken the stew.) Fry the onions in the oil until nicely browned, and brown the meat in the same pan. A large, heavy, lidded flameproof casserole is best. Cut up the ceps and add them to the pan with their soaking liquid, the sauerkraut, spices, bay leaf, dill seeds and prunes. Rub the tomatoes through a sieve, and stir into the mixture. Add enough water or stock to cover all the ingredients, bring to the boil and simmer very gently for about 1½ hours. Alternatively, cook in a preheated oven at 150°C / 300°F / Mark 2. Uncover for the last 20 minutes to let the liquid evaporate as the stew should be fairly thick. Season with pepper, stir in the soured cream, if using, and serve the stew from the pot, brightened up with the dill or parsley, if liked. Baked potatoes go very well with this, as does rye bread. Beer or ice-cold vodka are the perfect accompaniments.

Meatloaf

1 onion, peeled and finely chopped
1 tbsp olive oil
12 oz / 340 g minced lean pork
12 oz / 340 g minced lean veal
12 oz / 340 g minced lean beef
3 oz / 85 g soft breadcrumbs
1 tsp fennel seeds
1 tsp crushed juniper or allspice
  berries

2–3 garlic cloves, peeled and crushed
1 tbsp finely chopped chives
1 tbsp finely chopped parsley
1 tsp chopped thyme or oregano
3 tbsp port, red wine or vermouth
3 tbsp rich meat stock
½ tsp freshly ground black pepper
¼ tsp salt

Fry the onion in the olive oil until soft, and mix with the rest of the ingredients. Pack the mixture into a 2 lb / 900 g loaf tin. Press well down to get rid of any pockets of air which would give the meatloaf a crumbly texture. Place the loaf tin in a roasting tin and pour about 1 in / 2.5 cm water into the roasting tin. Bake in a preheated oven at 180°C / 350°F / Mark 4 for 1–1½ hours, until a skewer inserted into the centre releases clear running juices.

Variations ∾ You can make meatballs using the same mixture. Simply wet your hands, take a walnut-sized piece of the mixture, and roll it into a ball. Continue until you have used up all the mixture, place the balls in a lightly greased roasting tin, and bake at 180°C / 350°F / Mark 4 for 30 minutes. Serve hot as hors d'oeuvre or in a fresh tomato sauce with spaghetti.

Use the mixture for stuffing cabbage leaves. Blanch the leaves first, and cut out the central stem to make them more pliable. Put a spoonful of the mixture on each leaf, and fold up to form a neat parcel. Place the parcels in a greased baking dish with some cider and chopped tomatoes, cover, and bake for 2–3 hours in a very low oven.

Sausage and Potato Pie

Serves 6–8

2 lb / 900 g potatoes, peeled and
    thinly sliced
½ pt / 280 ml milk
4 cloves
1 onion, peeled and thinly sliced
3 leeks, trimmed and sliced
1 bay leaf

12 oz / 340 g coarse pork sausages
12 oz / 340 g white pudding (*boudin
    blanc*)
12 oz / 340 g black pudding
freshly ground black pepper
sage leaves
8 oz / 230 g puff pastry

Parboil the potatoes for 5 minutes. Put the milk in a saucepan with the cloves,
onion, leeks and bay leaf, bring to the boil and simmer for 5 minutes. Prick the
sausages, white pudding and black pudding all over to stop them splitting and, one
batch at a time, immerse them in a pan of boiling water for a minute and then
plunge them into a bowl of ice cold water. This treatment firms them up for slicing.
Skin the black pudding if necessary. Slice the sausages, white pudding and black
pudding into ½ in / 1 cm pieces and sprinkle with black pepper.

Lightly grease an ovenproof dish large enough and deep enough to hold the
ingredients. Build up layers of potato and layers of sausage, white pudding and
black pudding, distributing some of the softened onion and leeks amongst them,
and, if you wish, burying the bay leaf and cloves in the pie. Finish with a layer of
potato and pour over a few tablespoons of the warm milk. Crumble or chop the
sage leaves and scatter on top. Roll out the puff pastry and use to cover the pie,
carefully sealing the edges. Make decorations from the trimmings, and stick on the
top with a little of the leftover milk. Make a slash or two in the pastry to allow
steam to escape. Brush with more of the milk, and bake in a preheated oven at
180°C / 350°F / Mark 4 for 40–45 minutes.

Pork Pie

Serves 10

*A traditional hot-water crust pork pie is not food for the faint-hearted,
containing, as it does, a couple of pounds of pork, some bacon, and
half a pound of lard. It is not food for everyday, but, once in a while,
it should do no harm. Although it does require some time spent in
preparation, it is a most satisfying thing to produce. When it is finally
turned out of its tin and sliced, it will be the subject of much
admiration with its dark golden, meltingly crisp, short pastry (which is
best achieved with lard), soft creamy white inner layer, and nuggets of
pink pork close-packed in a clear, firm jelly.*

Stock
1 pig's trotter, split in two
2 lb / 900 g pork bones
4 pt / 2.30 l water
1 carrot
1 celery stalk
12 peppercorns

Filling
1 lb / 455 g belly pork
4 oz / 110 g streaky bacon

1 lb / 455 g lean pork
1 tsp freshly ground black pepper
¼ tsp freshly grated nutmeg
1 tbsp finely chopped parsley
½ tbsp finely chopped sage or thyme

Hot-Water Pastry
1½ lb / 680 g plain flour
1 tbsp salt
9 oz / 255 g lard
7 fl oz / 200 ml water
milk or egg to glaze

First make the stock/jelly. Simmer all the ingredients together in a large
saucepan for 2–3 hours, then strain and reduce to 1 pt / 570 ml. Set aside to cool.

While the stock is simmering, remove the rind from the belly pork and bacon
(this can be added to the stockpot) and mince the meats together. Fry quickly, in
batches if necessary, just to remove the raw look. Dice the lean pork and fry in the
same way, draining off any liquid into the stock. Mix the meats together, and add
the spices and herbs. Cover and put in a cool place while you make the pastry.

Set aside about 5 tbsp flour and sift the remainder together with the salt. Put
the lard and water in a saucepan, and bring to the boil, stirring continuously and
slowly adding the flour to it. When dry and liquid ingredients are thoroughly
blended together in a hot, smooth rather than sticky mass, turn it out on to a
worktop, and knead, adding the reserved flour as necessary to form a smooth,
workable pastry. Cut off a quarter of the pastry to use as a lid, and press or roll out
the rest. With it line a 2 lb / 900 g loaf tin leaving about ½ in / 1 cm pastry hanging

over the rim of the tin. Fill with the pork mixture, slightly mounding it in the centre. Roll out the remaining pastry and use to cover the pie. Press the edges together, roll them over once inside the rim of the loaf tin (to make it easy to slide a palette knife all the way round the cold pie to ease it out of the tin) and make a fluted edge by pinching together at intervals. Roll out the pastry trimmings to make stick-on decorations if you wish. Make a pencil diameter hole in the top of the pastry, and keep it open with a small roll of greaseproof paper. Brush the pie with milk or egg to glaze it, and lay two or three layers of greaseproof paper or foil on top so that the crust does not bake too brown. Bake in the centre of a preheated oven at 170°C / 325°F / Mark 3 for 1¼ hours. Remove the paper or foil for the last 15 minutes. Let the pie cool for 2–3 hours, and then slowly pour in, through the hole in the pastry, as much of the rich stock as you can. Allow to cool completely, then wrap in foil or greaseproof paper to store. Do not keep it for more than 2–3 days in the refrigerator. Turn out of the tin, and cut into slices to serve.

Variations ➣ Instead of the pound of lean pork, use 8 oz / 230 g lean pork and 8 oz / 230 g rabbit meat.

Once, when I had neither pig's trotter nor pork bones, I made the stock with a chicken carcass, and then used gelatine to obtain a set. It worked very well and is, of course, quicker since the chicken carcass only needs an hour or so to simmer. For an even finer tasting jelly, you can replace some of the water used to make the stock with dry white wine.

VEAL

Roast Breast of Veal Stuffed with Sweetbreads and Herbs

Serves 6

Here is a very good recipe for roast veal. It requires time spent on it in preparation, but once it is in the oven, it needs little attention. Breast of lamb can be substituted for the veal, but it is fattier and needs more trimming. If you cannot get sweetbreads, use veal or lamb's kidney, neither of which needs blanching, but the fatty core should be removed.

12 oz / 340 g calves' sweetbreads
2½ lb / 1.10 kg breast of veal,
  boned
salt
freshly ground black pepper
1 lemon
4 oz / 110 g fresh spinach leaves
2 oz / 60 g parsley
handful of fresh sorrel *or* 4 lettuce
  leaves

2 garlic cloves, peeled and crushed
1 oz / 30 g softened butter
1 tbsp chopped fresh tarragon leaves
veal bones
1 carrot, scrubbed
1 onion, cut into quarters
1 celery stalk, trimmed
½ pt / 280 ml white wine

Soak the sweetbreads in cold water for 1–2 hours. Open out the boned breast of veal, and trim off any excess fat and gristle. Season lightly with the salt and pepper and finely grate lemon zest over the meat. Cover loosely and put to one side in a cool place while you prepare the stuffing.

Strip the spinach, parsley and sorrel or lettuce leaves from their stems, and place in a large colander. Pour enough boiling water over the leaves to blanch them, then drain them and put them in a bowl of ice-cold water for 30 seconds. Drain again and dry the leaves thoroughly by rolling them in a clean tea-towel. Chop them roughly and mix with the garlic, butter, and tarragon and a tablespoon of lemon juice. Spread this over the breast of veal, cover loosely, and put to one side while you prepare the sweetbreads.

Drain the sweetbreads and trim to remove any gristle and the membrane. Put in a saucepan, cover with cold water, add ¼ teaspoon salt and bring slowly to the boil. Hold at simmering point for 3 minutes, then drain and rinse the sweetbreads under plenty of cold running water. When cool enough to handle, lay them down the centre of the veal breast, roll up the meat and tie it with string at 1 in / 2.5 cm intervals. Put the veal bones in a roasting tin together with the vegetables and place the veal roll on top. Moisten with 4–5 tbsp of white wine. Roast in a preheated oven at 150–170°C / 300–325°F / Mark 2–3 for 3–3½ hours, moistening it from time to time with a little more white wine or water. Remove the meat from the oven, and let it rest in a warm place for 10–15 minutes before carving it. Pour off the cooking juices to make a gravy.

Veal 'Birds'

Serves 4

This is an economical, easy-to-cook meat dish similar to those found in many European and Eastern European kitchens. Beef, lamb or pork could replace the veal.

4 slices of veal from the leg, 4 oz / 110 g each
4 oz / 110 g minced veal
1 heaped tbsp fresh breadcrumbs
1 egg, lightly beaten
1 tbsp finely chopped parsley
½ tbsp finely grated onion
½ tbsp finely chopped almonds
1 tsp finely grated lemon zest

¼ tsp sea salt
¼ tsp freshly ground black pepper
¼ tsp ground cloves
¼ tsp freshly grated nutmeg
1 oz / 30 g unsalted butter
1 tbsp good dry white wine or vermouth
1 tbsp water
3–4 parsley stalks

Roll the slices of veal between pieces of cling film to flatten them, or pound them if you have a very blunt, soft instrument. Mix all the other ingredients, except the butter, liquid and parsley stalks, together. Spread the mixture on the four veal slices, and roll up and tie with string. Heat the butter in a flameproof casserole or frying pan, and fry the rolls on all sides until just golden brown. Add the liquid and parsley stalks, cover with a tight-fitting lid, and cook on the gentlest heat for 45 minutes, or cook in the bottom half of a preheated oven at 180–190°C / 350–375°F / Mark 4–5. These are also very tasty cold.

Calves' Liver with Sage and Balsamic Vinegar

Serves 2

1 tbsp plain flour
1 tsp fine sea salt
1 tsp freshly ground black pepper
pinch of ground ginger
pinch of ground allspice

8–12 oz / 230–340 g calves' liver
1 oz / 30 g unsalted butter
sprig of sage
2 tbsp balsamic vinegar
sage leaves, to garnish

Shake the flour, salt, pepper and spices together in a paper bag to make seasoned flour. Cut the liver into two or four pieces, and shake each one in the bag of seasoned flour. Melt half the butter in a heavy frying pan and, when hot, add the pieces of liver. Fry quickly on both sides until golden: 2–3 minutes should cook it to pink, but give it longer if you prefer it well done. Remove the liver and keep it warm. Add the rest of the butter, the sage and the balsamic vinegar. Heat together, stirring, to make a light sauce. Serve the liver with a little of the sauce and a sage leaf or two on heated dinner plates.

Variations ∾ Use raspberry, rice or sherry vinegar to replace the balsamic vinegar. This recipe method can also be used for cooking calves' or lamb's kidneys, which should be trimmed of all fat, membrane and core, and then sliced.

FAVOURITE CASSEROLES

I DECIDED to end this chapter with some of my favourite meat recipes. All are for casseroles that use some of the least expensive but tastiest cuts of meat. These are not large, dense pieces of meat, nor are they very fatty. Plenty of bone, gristle and sinew yields juices of an incomparably rich flavour and texture, when cooked slowly. For that is the secret. These cuts of meat will not make a big hole in your budget, but they will take time to cook, several hours in some cases. On the other hand, they are not dishes that will be spoilt by an extra half hour or so in the oven, and thus you can leave them cooking in a slow oven while you do something else. They can also be cooked the day before and reheated. Getting them into the pot will not take too long either, simply the time it takes to chop up a few vegetables.

Braised Knuckle of Veal

Serves 4

A large knuckle of veal makes a very good and inexpensive dish. The very end of the shank, which I chop off, yields a tasty stock after slow simmering. I scoop out the marrow and stir into the white risotto that I serve with this dish.

2 tbsp extra virgin olive oil
1 large onion, peeled and thinly
   sliced
1–2 carrots, peeled and thinly sliced
2 celery stalks, trimmed and sliced
3–3½ lb / 1.35–1.60 kg knuckle of
   veal in a piece
4 garlic cloves, peeled and crushed

2 tomatoes, deseeded and chopped
1 bay leaf
3 in / 7.5 cm twist of orange zest
small sprig of thyme or rosemary
½ bottle of good dry red wine
salt
freshly ground black pepper

Heat the olive oil in a flameproof casserole or heavy saucepan, and add the onion, carrots and celery. Fry them gently until soft and beginning to colour and be full of aroma. This is an important stage which adds extra depth of flavour.

Push the vegetables to one side, and lightly brown the piece of veal all over. Arrange it on top of the vegetables. Add the rest of the ingredients, except the seasoning, bring slowly to the boil, reduce the heat to the merest simmer, cover the casserole with a tightly fitting lid or foil, and cook very gently for 2½–3 hours, or until the meat is tender and falling away from the bone. Season after about 2 hours. Alternatively, you can cook this dish in the bottom half of a preheated oven at 170°C / 325°F / Mark 3.

When the meat is cooked, remove it to a warm serving dish. Reduce the cooking liquid to the consistency you prefer, and pour it over the meat. Finely chopped parsley mixed with finely chopped garlic and grated lemon zest – the Italian *gremolata* – makes a nice addition, not only as a garnish but as a spark of very fresh flavours. A white risotto made with arborio rice, veal stock and the stirred-in bone marrow is the perfect accompaniment. The stock can cook at the same time as the meat is braising, either in the oven or on the hob.

Variation ⁓ For a dish with oriental flavours, marinate overnight a pork knuckle in soy sauce, five spice powder, peppercorns, grated ginger, rice vinegar and demerara sugar. Braise on a bed or pre-soaked, par-boiled black beans, and serve garnished with fresh coriander.

Lamb Shanks with Leeks and Barley

Serves 4

1 large onion, peeled and sliced or
  chopped
1 tbsp olive or sunflower oil
2–3 garlic cloves, peeled and
  crushed (*optional*)
4 lamb shanks
½ pt / 280 ml red or white wine,
  lamb stock or water

1 tsp black peppercorns
2 bay leaves
1–2 sprigs thyme
6 oz / 170 g pearl barley
1 lb / 455 g leeks, trimmed and sliced
salt

In a flameproof casserole, fry the onion in the oil until golden brown, adding the garlic, if using. Add the lamb shanks and brown all over, then add the wine, stock or water, the peppercorns, bay leaves, thyme and barley. Bring to the boil, cover, and simmer for 1 hour. Add the leeks, and salt to taste, stir to cover them with juice, and continue cooking until the lamb, barley and leeks are tender. The casserole can also be cooked in a preheated oven at 180°C / 350°F / Mark 4 for about 2 hours, or for longer at a lower temperature if more convenient.

Oxtail Stew

Serves 4

3 lb / 1.35 kg oxtail in pieces
1 medium onion, peeled and sliced
7 oz / 200 g can of tomatoes
1 pt / 570 ml water, stock, beer or
  good red wine

sprig of thyme *or* ½ tsp dried thyme, or
  any other herb if you like
salt
freshly ground black pepper
herbs or watercress, to garnish

Remove as much fat as possible from the oxtail, and fry it in a heavy well-seasoned or non-stick pan until browned all over. Add the onion and fry until light brown. Rub the tomatoes through a sieve on to the meat and onion, and add the liquid and herbs. Bring to the boil, cover, turn the heat right down, and let it barely simmer for about 2 hours or until the meat is tender. Remove from the heat, allow to cool in the pan and refrigerate until next day.

About 30 minutes before you want to serve the stew, remove it from the refrigerator. The fat will have solidified on top and every scrap can be removed.

Gently reheat the stew, and simmer it for 15 minutes or so. Season to taste and garnish with some greenery. This is good served with braised or steamed celery hearts and mashed potatoes, or with broccoli and broad egg noodles. We also like it with flageolet, haricot or cannellini beans, presoaked and cooked as described in the next recipe. For a more refined version, you can, when the meat is reheated the second day, remove it from the bone.

Pork and Beans

Serves 6

It's a good idea to make plenty of this casserole. It tastes even better the next day, and leftovers make a delicious soup with the addition of stock. You do not have to use the cuts of meat I have suggested. A joint of boned spare rib alone can be used, or hand of pork or belly pork.

1 small piece of pork fat, about 1 oz / 30 g, removed from whatever meat you are cooking
2 onions, peeled and sliced
1½ lb / 680 g boned rolled joint of spare rib
1 lb / 455 g piece of pig's head
2 pig's trotters, split in two
1 lb / 455 g haricot beans, soaked overnight and parboiled for 20 minutes

1 lb / 455 g peeled tomatoes (fresh or canned)
4 garlic cloves, peeled and crushed
1 bottle dry white wine
pinch of salt
pinch of freshly ground black pepper
herbs for flavouring and garnish

Melt the pork fat in a large flameproof casserole, add the onions and fry until golden brown. Add the pieces of meat and fry until lightly browned all over. Add the rest of the ingredients and bring slowly to the boil. Cover and cook at the bottom of a preheated oven at 170°C / 325°F / Mark 3 for 2½–3 hours, until the beans and meat are tender. If, when cooked, the casserole is too liquid for your taste, pour off most of the liquid into a saucepan. Boil and reduce by half, then stir back into the casserole. Taste and add more seasoning if necessary. Serve garnished with fresh herbs of whatever variety you used to flavour the casserole.

THE TIMES COOK IN THE PHILIPPINES

I WAS invited as guest cook to the Manila Peninsula in June 1989. Outside, temperature and humidity levels hovered around the low 90s; although it was much the same in the kitchen, I kept getting requests for steak and kidney pudding, and one guest even asked if I was going to do steamed sponge pudding and custard. But, as someone else remarked, if you wait for cooler weather in the Philippines, you would never eat those dishes. I'm not sure I would want to, but there were clearly a lot of homesick expatriates in Manila, and I compromised by cooking bangers and mash and cottage pie.

In the kitchens of the Manila Peninsula Hotel, the chef and sous chefs were Swiss and German. Asking the Swiss butcher to make English sausages was one of the first hurdles. But he, too, compromised, and we made an excellent sausage, with plenty of ground pork and lightly flavoured with sage and black pepper.

Side by side with these traditional English dishes, I cooked my own dishes adapted for local ingredients. Pears were unavailable, so I adapted my Pear and Chocolate Tart (see page 554) to use green mangos. A dark-fleshed, mackerel-type fish, the *tanguingue*, was smoked and marinated in olive oil and *calamansi* juice, which has the taste of a fragrant, piercingly sour lime. At home, I often serve cod with a passion fruit butter sauce. In Manila, I cooked *lapu-lapu*, a very fine, firm white-fleshed grouper, in the same way. I also served it English-style with parsley sauce, and, on my last day, we served *lapu-lapu* with chips, sprinkled with palm vinegar and wrapped in copies of the *Manila Bulletin*.

When I was not cooking, I was watching the local cooks preparing Filipino dishes. Some of them are recognizably of Spanish origin, like the *adobong*, *calderetang*, *rellenong* and *almondigas*, stews, stuffed vegetables and meatballs. The desserts and pastries, too, could come straight from Spain – the *leche* flan, *yema*, *polvorón* and *pastillas de leche*, as well as the *ensaymada* and the *churros*, which you might well be served at a *merienda cena* or high tea.

But although *adobong* – pork, chicken or quail cooked with vinegar, soy sauce, garlic and spices – is often said to be the national dish of the Philippines, perhaps the most characteristically Filipino are the *sinigang* dishes, which are lightly boiled or poached and lightly soured. They can be made with a variety of ingredients, according to availability, pocket and taste. I used to enjoy the *sinigang na sugpo*, giant prawns cooked in rice water with fish sauce, swamp cabbage or *callaloo*, pieces of pineapple and slices of tamarind. It is the souring which is so particular to Filipino food, and it is extremely refreshing, especially when eaten with *milagrosa* rice as a foil, perhaps perfumed with pandanus leaf.

It is said that if you rely on vinegar or *calamansi* juice to sour your food, you are very lacking in imagination as a cook. And yet there is a wonderful range of vinegars to choose from in the Philippines, including the delicate coconut vinegar, and the *cala-mansi* has plenty of juice. But pineapple, green mangos, papayas, guavas, tomatoes, tamarind and a variety of leaves and flowers all add a note of refreshing acidity.

We refreshed ourselves in other ways, too, for example with *halo-halo*, a lurid confection of cooked fruit pieces and sweetened beans, corn and chick peas, mixed with milk and sugar and heaped over crushed ice, or with iced melon juice with coconut, jelly chunks, sago and coconut.

If sourness is the characteristic Filipino flavouring, purple is the favourite food colour. It comes from the *ube* or purple yam, the purée of which is used in ice creams, cakes, drinks and even in a purple vichyssoise.

But for more straightforward food, the Beef Steak Tagalog (see page 434) and Garlic Rice (below) couldn't be simpler, and they make an extremely tasty combination. This was my favourite lunch in the chef's dining room at the hotel. Other dishes show Chinese influences, such as the Pancit Molo (see page 434), which is best made for a large number. For dessert, I suggest a lime sorbet (use lime instead of orange juice in the recipe on page 540) or a mango jelly or fool. To make the jelly, use a juicer to extract the juice from ripe mangos, and mix it with apple juice and then gelatine. For the fool, purée the ripe mango flesh and mix it with whipped cream.

Garlic Rice

Serves 4

If this becomes a favourite dish, it is worth preparing a larger quantity of garlic and oil and keeping it in a cool, dark place. Serve with Beef Steak Tagalog (see page 434), or with fried chicken.

3 tbsp groundnut (peanut) or sunflower oil
4 garlic cloves, peeled and finely chopped
1 lb / 455 g steamed or boiled rice

Heat the oil in a frying pan very gently, and add the garlic. This must not brown too much or it will take on a bitter taste and spoil the rice. The secret is to keep the heat low and be prepared to spend time letting the garlic just turn gold. Stir in the rice, and when it is well coated with oil, allow it to heat through thoroughly before spooning it into teacups, pressing it down and turning it out on to plates.

Beef Steak Tagalog

Serves 4

4 slices rump steak, 4–6 oz / 110–
  170 g each and about ½ in / 1 cm
  thick
2 onions, peeled and thinly sliced
3 tbsp soy sauce

3 tbsp lime juice
freshly ground black pepper
1–2 tbsp corn oil or groundnut
  (peanut) oil

Trim any fat and gristle from the steak, and place it on top of a few pieces of onion in a shallow dish. Mix the soy sauce and lime juice with a good pinch of black pepper, and pour over the steak. Scatter a few more pieces of onion on the top and leave to marinate for an hour or so, turning once or twice.

Heat the oil in a frying pan, and remove the steak from the marinade, letting the juices drip back into the dish. Fry the steak with the remaining onion until done to your liking. Remove the steak and onions from the pan, and keep them warm. Pour the marinade and marinated onions into the frying pan, and stir up any caramelized residue on the bottom of the pan. Add 2–3 tablespoons water, and bring to the boil. Sieve and serve the sauce poured over the steak and onions. Garlic Rice (see page 433) makes the ideal accompaniment.

Pancit Molo
(Dumpling Soup)

Serves 6–8

1 onion
1 carrot
1 celery stalk
6 water chestnuts *(optional)*
4 oz / 110 g lean boneless chicken
4 oz / 110 g lean boneless pork

4 oz / 110 g cured lean ham or bacon
4 oz / 110 g peeled prawns
2 tbsp soy sauce
1 tbsp sesame oil
24 wonton wrappers
3 pt / 1.70 l chicken stock

Peel, trim and chop the vegetables, and put in a food processor with three quarters of the meat and prawns. Dice the rest and reserve. Process the meat, prawns and vegetables with the soy sauce and sesame oil until you have a smooth paste. Spoon a little into each wonton wrapper, wet the edges, and draw together to make a bundle. Pinch together to seal it. Bring the stock to the boil, and drop in the dumplings and the reserved meat and prawns. Simmer for 10 minutes and serve.

Baking

The first part of this chapter is not intended for those who already have a well-established routine for making their own bread. It is for those who would like to do so but who are put off by the mystique attached to it, by arcane terms, such as 'knock back', and what 'hollow' sounds like when you tap a baked loaf, and how exactly do you knead, and why?

In the rest of the chapter I have included my favourite 'bakes', including some very traditional yeast cakes and tea breads. This might give the impression that I bake a great deal. I do not, but I think it would be very sad if we forgot how to make the spiced loaves and tea cakes that our mothers and grandmothers knew how to bake. The one thing I do bake regularly, however, is bread. I love doing it, and will make time to do it, although in fact it takes much less time than you might imagine, and is easy once you get the hang of it.

Specialist breads can be expensive. A 3¼ lb / 1.50 kg bag of strong flour costs about a third of the price of a loaf of bread, and will make three loaves. I am not suggesting that the bread that you or I will make is as good as that made by bakers who have spent years learning and perfecting their craft, any more than I would claim that you or I could turn out 3-star Michelin dinners. But you will be able to produce good bread that will get better and better with practice. Mine is much, much better now than it used to be 10 years ago. And you will learn how to adapt recipes. By changing proportions and ingredients, you will be able to produce a variety of breads, carrying on a tradition of cheap and nutritious food, which is therapeutic to make.

BASIC BREADS

Basic Ingredients

Yeast Bread-making is not a mechanical, unchanging process. Yeast is a living organism, and does indeed have a life of its own. All we can hope to do in making bread is to use its properties and get it to work for us. It grows and expands when conditions, such as temperature, moisture and food supply, are right. And the carbon dioxide gas caused in the expansion is what 'raises' the loaf to give it its characteristically spongy, airy, crumb texture. Fresh yeast can sometimes be bought from bakers where bread is made on the premises. Health and wholefood shops are another source of fresh yeast. Fast-action dried yeast, available from supermarkets, is simply mixed with the dry ingredients, and the dough is only required to rise once. It gives good results. I use fresh yeast if I can get it, or active dried yeast, also available from supermarkets. It comes in granule form, is mixed with water, and then added to the dough, which is given two risings. Some recipes specify active dried yeast. If a recipe calls for fresh yeast, you can replace it with about two-thirds the quantity of dried yeast. Approximately ½ oz fresh yeast or 2 teaspoons of active dried yeast are needed per pound of flour or 20 g active dried yeast are needed per kilo. A 7 g sachet of fast action yeast will raise 750 g / 1 lb 10 oz strong flour.

Flour Gluten, produced from the protein in flour, is what gives bread the characteristic chewy texture. Strong wheat flour has the highest gluten content; rye flour also has gluten, but less. Other cereals, although containing protein, do not form gluten. Hard and rubbery, when flour and water is first mixed, the gluten becomes soft and elastic with kneading.

Other cereals can be used in bread-making, such as oatmeal and cornmeal, but not alone; they need to be mixed with a high proportion of wheat flour.

Strong flour, bread flour, unbleached strong flour, organic bread flour are some of the names under which you will find flour suitable for bread-making. It is useful also to look at the nutritional table on the packet. Strong flour will have a protein content of 11 to 13 per cent; plain flour, suitable for cake-making, will have around 9 per cent protein.

Salt Salt is used in bread-making to 'slow down', and thus control the action of yeast. It should be added at the rate of approximately 1½ teaspoons per pound of flour or 15 g per kilo.

Water The only other essential ingredient in bread-making is water, although liquid can be added in the form of milk, eggs, even cider, usually replacing a proportion of water. It is useful, when developing your own recipes, to remember, as a rule of thumb, that flour needs more than half its volume of water, that wholemeal flour absorbs even more water, and that on a humid day, you might need less water than on a dry day.

Terms and Techniques

Kneading Turning the heavy flour and water paste to a smooth, pliable, elastic, dough requires hard work, which is, nevertheless, quite manageable in small quantities. Domestic food processors can only mix, and do not perform the pummelling, stretching, tearing and gathering action, which is kneading although some electric mixers have dough hooks which perform something like a kneading action. It is a pleasure to feel the dough form under your hands, and unstick itself from your fingers as it becomes smooth and springy. On a floured worktop, hold the dough with one hand, and with the heel of your other hand, push the rest of the dough away from you. Give the dough a quarter or half turn, and repeat the process. Do this for 15 minutes, by which time all the dough will have had a thorough kneading.

Knocking back When the dough has had its first rising, all the air or gas is knocked out of it by turning it out on the table and thumping it around for a few minutes. It can also be given a further kneading, which will improve the quality of the baked product even further.

Proving This is the final rising of the dough once it has been shaped into loaves and put into prepared tins, moulds or on to trays. Proving should be done at the same temperature as the mixing and kneading, and the dough not allowed to form a hard skin. Covering with a damp muslin cloth is better than a tea-towel, which might hold down the loaf. Proving takes about 30 minutes in a warm room. Use this time to heat the oven so that the bread will go into a steady high heat at 240°C / 475°F / Mark 9. The tins are prepared by greasing and flouring.

Testing for 'doneness', the 'hollow' sound An undercooked loaf is still moist and heavy inside, without enough air trapped in it. When tapped on the bottom, it sounds soft and dull. When fully baked, light and airy inside, it will sound, when tapped, 'hollow'. A full tea caddy, when tapped, sounds different to the hollow ring of an empty tea caddy.

Optional additives Fat in the form of lard or butter, in the proportion of 1 oz / 30 g to 1 lb / 455 g of flour, will give a slightly softer crumb. A proportion of water can be replaced by milk (whole, skimmed or semi-skimmed), which will also produce a softer, lighter crumb. Honey, malt, syrup or treacle in the proportion of ½ oz / 15 g to 1 lb / 455 g will sweeten the bread and provide extra nourishment for the yeast.

Flavours

This is where you can let your creative instincts take over. Remember only that substantial liquid additions should be calculated as part of the overall water content, and dry absorbent additions as part of the dry ingredients. Thus, if you use eggs or olive oil, you will need slightly less water; if you use a handful or two of oatmeal or cornmeal, use less flour. Some additions, such as powdered saffron or chopped, fresh herbs, for example, will not affect the proportions one way or another.

Cheese bread Add finely grated, hard cheese, about 3 oz / 85 g to 1 lb / 455 g flour.

Tomato bread Add softened, chopped dried tomatoes or tomato purée to the dough.

Onion bread Add finely chopped onion, fried to a golden brown; mix some into the dough, and scatter the rest on top before baking after glazing the bread with egg yolk beaten with milk.

Seed and herb bread When added to wholemeal or mixed meal dough, seeds give a chewy, flavoursome bread. The seeds can be toasted, or not, as you prefer. I like to use sesame, pumpkin and sunflower seeds. In late summer when your herbs go to seed, these too can be added to bread. Basil, fennel, dill, coriander, and parsley are all worth trying, as, of course, are the finely chopped leaves of the plants.

Olive bread Mix chopped, pitted green or black olives into the dough. Traditional olive breads tend to keep the olives whole and unpitted, but this can be dangerous if you bite into an olive hidden in a thick slice of bread. Chopped rosemary is a perfect partner to the olives.

Golden bread This is another idea to save for the summer when you can shred nasturtium flowers and leaves and chop the seeds to mix into the dough. This bread makes lovely cream cheese sandwiches, as does bread into which you have stirred marigold petals.

Orange bread Stir into an enriched dough (see Variations on page 441) 2–3 tablespoons of dried-up, last year's marmalade. This makes an excellent tea or breakfast bread.

Fruit and nut bread Into an enriched dough (see Variations on page 441), stir in chopped, dried fruit and nuts, for example dates and walnuts, stoned prunes and flaked almonds or apricots and hazelnuts.

Saffron bread Pounded or soaked saffron threads, added to an enriched white dough (see Variations on page 441), can be made into buns or a loaf.

Basic White Bread

Makes 1 large loaf

1 lb / 455 g strong white flour, at
   warm room temperature
1½ tsp salt

½ pt / 280 ml warm water
2 tsp active dried yeast

Sift the flour and salt together into a large warm bowl. Pour half the water into a small bowl, and sprinkle the yeast on top. After a few minutes, it will begin to become active and bubble on the surface. Make a well in the flour and pour in the yeasty liquid, and then the remaining warm water. With your hands, or a wooden spoon, mix the flour and liquid together until it forms a sticky mass. Turn it out on to a floured worktop, and knead for 15 minutes. Put the dough into a large, warm oiled bowl, and cover the top of the bowl, not touching the dough, with a clean, damp piece of muslin or a light tea-towel. Leave in warm, draught-free place for about 40 minutes, after which time the dough will have more than doubled in volume. Knock it back, knead a little more, if you wish, and return it to the bowl to rest for 20 minutes. Turn it out on to a floured worktop, and quickly shape it to fit your tin or tray. You can be fairly heavy-handed at this stage, too, since no air should get rolled or folded into the dough. Cover again with a light, damp cloth, and leave to prove for 30 minutes. Bake in the centre of a preheated oven at 240°C / 475°F / Mark 9 for 15 minutes, then turn the oven down to 200°C / 400°F / Mark 6 for a further 15–20 minutes. Remove from the oven and turn out on to a wire rack to cool, but do not slice until cold.

Variations ∾ For enriched white bread, use 7 fl oz / 200 ml warm milk instead of the warm water. Sprinkle the yeast into half of it, and beat an egg and 2 oz / 60 g butter, melted, into the remainder before mixing it in.

For a sweet white loaf, mix in 2 tablespoons of honey.

To make flat olive oil bread, follow the recipe above until the dough has had its first rising, then knock it back, and put it on an oiled bake stone, set on a baking tray. (I have used a cast-iron griddle with satisfactory results.) Leave the dough, lightly covered with a damp cloth to rise for 20 minutes, then stretch it to fit the griddle or bake stone, and let it prove for 20–30 minutes more, covered. With your fingers, make hollows in the surface of the dough at regular intervals. Mix a little olive oil and warm water, brush it over the dough, sprinkle on coarse salt, and bake for 20 minutes or so in a preheated oven at 200°C / 400°F / Mark 6. Cool on a wire rack in the usual way.

Mixed Grain and Seed Bread

Makes 1 large loaf

8 oz / 230 g strong white flour	12 fl oz / 340 ml warm water
4 oz / 110 g wholemeal flour	2 tsp active dried yeast
1½ tsp salt	2 tbsp sunflower seeds
4 oz / 110 g medium oatmeal	2 tbsp pumpkin seeds

Sift the two flours and salt together. Mix the oatmeal with ¼ pt / 140 ml water, and let it stand. Sprinkle the yeast on to the remaining water, and let it stand for a few minutes. Make a well in the dry flours, and pour in the yeast mixture. Stir together, then add the wet oatmeal mixture and the seeds. Knead, and proceed as in the Basic White Bread recipe.

Grant Loaf

Makes 1 large loaf

*For those who prefer the denser chewiness and the added nutritional
value of bread made with wholemeal flour, there are many good
recipes available. I like a loaf made with half or two-thirds white flour
to appropriate proportions of wholemeal flour. But for a pure
wholemeal loaf, probably one of the easiest and most reliable recipes is
that for the Grant Loaf, developed by Doris Grant for her book* Our
Daily Bread. *It produces a soft, wet dough that you have to spoon into
the loaf tin. It is not kneaded, nor does it have a second rising, and it
is difficult to imagine that it will ever rise. It does a little. The secret is
to warm all the ingredients and the loaf tin. Once used to the recipe
and convinced that it will work, you can double the quantity. A food
processor is ideal for this mixture.*

a good 14 oz / 400 g wholemeal
   flour
1 heaped tsp salt

1 tsp sugar
1 tsp active dried yeast
12–13 fl oz / 340–370 ml hand-hot water

Mix the dry ingredients (except the yeast) using just half the sugar, and put
them to warm. Mix the remaining sugar with the yeast, sprinkle it into ¼ pt / 140
ml of the hand-hot water, and let it work for 10–15 minutes. Meanwhile, grease a 2
lb / 900 g loaf tin, and put it to warm. Warm the food processor by filling the bowl
with hot water or immersing it in a washing-up bowl of clean hot water. Once the
yeast has frothed up, re-assemble the food processor, and put in the warm dry
ingredients, the yeasty liquid and the remaining hot water. Process until you have a
smooth but wet dough. Spoon it into the prepared loaf tin, and put the whole thing
inside a large polythene bag. Leave to rise in a warm place for 25–30 minutes, by
which time the dough should have risen to the top of the loaf tin. Bake in the
middle of a preheated oven at 190°C / 375°F / Mark 5 for about 1 hour. Remove
the bread from the oven, and turn it out on to a wire rack to cool.

Variation ⁓ You can replace the sugar with honey or black treacle for an even
more distinctive loaf.

Cider Bread

Makes 3 large loaves

*This is the method for making bread by hand using fresh yeast. Use
farm or unpasteurised cider if you can, which still has plenty of yeast
activity in it. Otherwise, choose a dry commercial cider.*

3¼ b / 1.50 kg strong white flour
1 tbsp salt
1 oz / 30 g fresh yeast

1 tsp caster sugar or honey
1½ pt / 850 ml farm cider

Sift the flour and salt together into a large bowl, and make a well in the centre.
Cream the yeast and sugar or honey together, and stir in a third of the cider. Pour
into the well. Gather in enough of the flour to make a thin batter without breaking
the flour 'wall'. Sprinkle some of the flour over the top, and let the yeast work for
about 20 minutes until the batter breaks through the surface. Stir the yeast mixture
into the flour, adding the rest of the cider until you have a workable mass of dough.
Turn out on to a floured worktop and knead for 20–30 minutes. Put the bread into
an oiled bowl, cover with a clean, damp cloth, oiled foil or oiled cling film, and
leave to rise for a couple of hours in a warm place. (Alternatively, let it rise slowly
in the refrigerator for up to 24 hours.)

Turn the dough out on to a floured worktop again, and give it a second
kneading, but only for about 5 minutes this time. Shape into loaves, and put in
oiled tins or on oiled baking sheets, cover once more, and let it rise for about 45
minutes. (With this dough, I like to use some for loaves, some for bread rolls and
some for pizza bases which can be frozen at this stage.)

Bake the loaves in a preheated oven at 200°C / 400°F / Mark 6 for about 40
minutes. Turn out and cool on a wire rack before slicing.

Oatmeal Soda Bread

Makes 1 loaf

These two quickly made breads do not contain any yeast. The raising agents are cream of tartar, bicarbonate of soda, and baking powder.

12 oz / 340 g strong white flour
2 oz / 60 g wholemeal flour
2 oz / 60 g medium oatflakes
2 tsp bicarbonate of soda
2 tsp cream of tartar

1 tsp salt
1 oz / 30 g lard or butter
½ pt / 280 ml buttermilk (or milk soured with 1 tbsp lemon juice)

Sift the dry ingredients together into a bowl. Cut up the lard or butter, and lightly rub it into the flour with your fingertips until the mixture resembles fine breadcrumbs. Make a well in the centre, pour in the buttermilk, and mix until you have a soft, pliable, but not sticky, dough. Add more liquid or flour as necessary. On a floured worktop, knead the dough lightly, and flatten it slightly into a circle, about 7–8 in / 18–20.5 cm across. Place it on a floured baking sheet, mark a deep cross in the centre, and bake for about 30 minutes in a preheated oven at 200°C / 400°F / Mark 6. Allow to cool slightly on a wire rack, but serve while still fresh and warm.

Cornbread

Makes 1 loaf or 6 muffins

4 oz / 110 g plain flour
4 oz / 110 g cornmeal or polenta
1 tsp salt
4 tsp baking powder

8 fl oz / 230 ml buttermilk
1 egg
2 tbsp groundnut (peanut) oil or melted butter

Sift the dry ingredients together into a bowl. In a separate bowl, thoroughly mix the buttermilk, egg and oil or butter. When you are ready to bake the cornbread, mix the wet and dry ingredients. Spoon the mixture into hot greased muffin tins or a shallow cake tin, and bake in the top half of a preheated oven at 230°C / 450°F / Mark 8 for 15 minutes if muffins, 20–25 minutes if in a cake tin. Remove from the oven, allow to cool slightly in the tin, then turn out on to a wire rack to cool slightly. Eat while still warm.

Quick Saffron Bread

Makes 1 large loaf or 8–10 rolls

few saffron threads
¼ pt / 140 ml boiling water
1½ lb / 680 g strong white flour
2 tsp salt

1 sachet (7 g) fast-action dried yeast
4 tbsp extra virgin olive oil
½ pt / 280 ml cold water

Put the saffron in a bowl, and pour on a little boiling water. In a bowl or food processor, mix the dry ingredients, and add all the liquids, including the oil and the saffron liquor. When it is thoroughly mixed, knead it for 10 minutes on a floured surface until smooth and elastic. Quickly shape it to fit your oiled loaf tin or baking sheet, or divide into 8–10 small pieces, shape these into rounds and place on an oiled baking sheet. Cover with a damp tea-towel, and leave to rise until doubled in volume. Bake in a preheated oven at 230°C / 450°F / Mark 8 for 35–40 minutes if a large loaf, or 15–20 minutes for rolls. Cool on a wire rack before using.

Individual Brioches

Makes 8–10

8 oz / 230 g strong white flour
½ tsp fast-action dried yeast
½ tsp salt

2 eggs, lightly beaten
2–3 oz / 60–85 g butter, melted
beaten egg and water, to glaze

Sift the dry ingredients together into a bowl, and then mix in the eggs and melted butter. On a floured surface, knead for about 5 minutes until the dough is smooth and elastic. Brush 8–10 brioche tins with melted butter, and in each one place a ball of dough, with a smaller ball pushed into the top. Brush with egg wash and cover with a damp cloth, or place the tins on a tray in a large polythene bag. Leave them to rise in a moderately warm place for about 40 minutes. Glaze again, and then bake in a preheated oven at 230°C / 450°F / Mark 8 for about 15 minutes. Serve warm, cut open and lightly buttered. Or scramble some eggs and stir in a little shredded smoked salmon, smoked trout or smoked cod's roe; spoon this mixture into a warmed, partly hollowed-out brioche, and serve immediately. Another good filling is fresh fruit, such as slices of banana, apple or peach, or stoned cherries, or summer berries. Pour over a little hot syrup, made by boiling clear honey with a little butter and grill lightly before serving with cool yoghurt or crème fraîche.

Boxty
(Potato Bread)

Here baking powder is the raising agent, though, in fact, this bread hardly rises at all, and is more like a potato cake.

8 oz / 230 g potatoes, peeled
2½ fl oz / 70 ml water
8 oz / 230 g mashed cooked
   potatoes
8 oz / 230 g plain flour

1 tbsp baking powder
3 oz / 85 g butter, melted
salt
freshly ground black pepper

Grate the peeled potatoes into a bowl containing the water. Stir with a fork, and then pour through a fine sieve into another bowl, pressing down well on the potatoes. Dry the grated potatoes on a clean tea-towel, and mix with the mashed potato. Let the potato starch in the water settle, and carefully pour off the water. Mix the starch with the potatoes and the rest of the ingredients. Shape the mixture into a ball and roll or pat it into a round, flat cake. Make a cross on top, dividing the loaf into four. Bake on a greased and floured baking sheet in a preheated oven at 180°C / 350°F / Mark 4 for 40–45 minutes. Serve hot, pulled into four pieces, split and spread with butter.

SAVOURY YEAST BAKING

Tomato Tart

Serves 6–8

A bread-making session led to this recipe. I had dough left over, and used it to make a tart case. I also had sweet, ripe tomatoes, some new season's garlic and extra virgin olive oil. Together they made an exquisite dish.

6 oz / 170 g white bread dough
  (see page 440)
2–3 tbsp extra virgin olive oil
12 oz / 340 g firm, ripe tomatoes,
  sliced
2–3 garlic cloves, peeled and thinly
  sliced

½ tsp sea salt
freshly ground black pepper
shredded basil or finely chopped
  parsley, to garnish

Lightly grease and flour a large baking sheet. Roll out the bread dough to form as wide a circle as you can without tearing it, and, of course, not bigger than the baking sheet. Carefully transfer the dough base to the baking sheet. Pinch up the edges all round to hold the filling in. Liberally brush olive oil over the base and sides. Arrange the tomato slices, slightly overlapping and interspersed with slices of garlic, on the base. Sprinkle with salt and pepper, and bake the tart in the top half of a preheated oven at 180°C / 350°F / Mark 4 for 20–25 minutes. Serve hot or warm, with basil or parsley sprinkled over.

Variations ∽ Instead of tomatoes, you could use aubergines, red peppers or courgettes. You should blanch the aubergines and courgettes after slicing them, and, if you can bear it, peel the peppers. For a really spectacular dish, you could make a single tart using all four vegetables.

A tomato tart can also be made using shortcrust pastry instead of bread dough. Use the pastry to line a 10 in / 25.5 cm flan ring or quiche dish, and bake blind for 5–10 minutes before brushing with olive oil and filling with garlic and tomatoes. Bake for 15–20 minutes only.

Tomato and Sausage Loaf

Serves 6–8

1 lb / 455 g strong white flour
2 tsp fast-action dried yeast
1 tsp salt
½ pt / 280 ml tepid water
4 tbsp olive oil
2 tsp tomato purée
3–4 pieces dried tomato, cut into
　small pieces *(optional)*
2 tbsp Dijon mustard
beaten egg and milk, to glaze
　(optional)

Sausage Filling
1½ lb / 680 g coarsely ground lean
　sausage meat
2 shallots *or* 1 small onion, peeled and
　finely chopped
2–3 garlic cloves, peeled and crushed
sprig of sage or rosemary
sprig of thyme
sprig of lovage or celery top
3 tbsp soft breadcrumbs
2 tbsp egg yolk
1 tbsp sunflower oil

Sift the dry ingredients together into a bowl, and make a well in the centre. Pour in the water, oil, tomato purée and pieces of tomato, if using, and mix until you have a fairly slack dough. Using extra flour on the worktop, knead until the dough is smooth, satiny and elastic. Place in a greased bowl, cover with a clean, damp tea-towel, and leave to rise until at least doubled in volume. This can be done overnight in the refrigerator or in a couple of hours at normal room temperature. If the weather is hot and dry, you may need to remoisten the tea-towel to prevent a hard crust forming on the dough. While the dough is rising, prepare the filling.

Mix all the filling ingredients together, except for the sunflower oil, stripping the herbs from their stems and chopping as necessary. Roll into a slightly flattened sausage shape of a size that will fit your frying pan. Fry the meat all over in the sunflower oil to brown it, remove from the pan, and put aside to cool.

Turn the dough on to a floured worktop, knock it back and knead it smooth again. Roll it out to a square large enough to enclose the sausage. Wet the edges. Spread the dough with Dijon mustard, place the sausage in the centre, and draw the two edges over, pinching together to seal. Close the two ends as well, and turn the sausage loaf on to a greased baking sheet, with the seam underneath. Slash lightly in two or three places, and brush if you like with a milk and egg yolk glaze.

Bake in a preheated oven at 200°C / 400°F / Mark 6 for 15 minutes, and then turn down to 170°C / 325°F / Mark 3 for a further 15 minutes. Cool on a wire rack, before slicing and serving. It can be served warm or cold, and makes a very good picnic or buffet dish.

Sausage Calzone

Serves 2 as a starter

6 oz / 170 g white bread dough (see page 440)

2 meaty pork sausages

1 small onion or shallot, peeled and finely chopped

2–3 tbsp tomato purée

2 oz / 60 g mozzarella cheese slices

a few anchovy fillets, capers and pitted black olives *(optional)*

thyme, basil, sage or other herbs, finely chopped

freshly ground black pepper

Roll out the dough to a circle, about ¼ in / 0.5 cm thick, and arrange it half on and half off a floured baking sheet (the over-lapping half will be folded over the filling). Squeeze the meat from the sausages, and fry with the onion or shallot for 5 minutes. Spread tomato purée on the half of the dough on the baking sheet, leaving a ½ in / 1 cm border, and then put the sausage meat on top, then the slices of cheese and the anchovies, capers and olives, if you are using them, and finally the herbs and a few grindings of pepper. Moisten the border of dough with water, fold over the other half, pinch the edges together to seal, cover with a damp cloth, and leave to prove for 30 minutes. Bake in a preheated oven at 180°C / 350°F / Mark 4. Serve while hot.

Glamorous Pizzas

Makes 2

*These are best made when you are making bread. The bases can be
frozen until required.*

6–8 oz / 170–230 g white bread
   dough (see page 440)
2 tbsp extra virgin olive oil
coarse sea salt
freshly ground black pepper

3–4 oz / 85–110 g cream cheese
4 oz / 110 g smoked salmon, thinly
   sliced
lemon or lime wedges, to serve

Cut the dough in half and roll out two circles. Place them on an oiled baking
sheet, brush them with olive oil, and sprinkle with salt and pepper. Allow to rise
for 20–30 minutes, and bake in the top half of a preheated oven at 200°C / 400°F /
Mark 6 for about 10 minutes, until crisp and puffy. Remove from the oven, and
allow to cool slightly before spreading with cheese and laying the slices of smoked
salmon on top. Serve with wedges of lemon or lime.

Variations ⇒ There are a number of variations on this theme of a warm base
and uncooked topping. A few suggestions are goat's cheese spread on the pizza
base, topped with peeled, deseeded and chopped tomatoes, chopped black olives
and torn up basil leaves; soured cream or cream cheese mixed with a little mustard
spread on the base, and topped with thin slices of prosciutto, salami or coppa; and
a sweet mustard mayonnaise topped with paper thin slices of raw tuna fish, raw
salmon or raw fillet of beef, with suitable garnishes on top.

The size given is suitable for a snack or a light main course. Smaller versions
can be made as canapés.

YEAST CAKES, SWEET BREADS AND SCONES

Scotch Pancakes

8 oz / 230 g plain flour
1 tbsp baking powder
2 tbsp caster sugar
pinch of salt

8 fl oz / 230 ml soured milk or
　buttermilk
1 egg
2 tbsp melted butter

Sift the dry ingredients together into a bowl, and stir in the liquids. Beat until you have a thick batter of a dropping consistency. Heat the griddle or frying pan and grease it. Spoon the mixture on to the surface, a tablespoon or a soupspoon at a time, cooking three or four pancakes at once. When the underside is smoothly brown, and the top surface dry and bubbled, turn and cook on the other side. Remove and cool on a wire rack, or keep wrapped in a tea-towel, and serve warm.

Sally Lunn Buns

1 lb / 455 g plain flour
1½ tsp salt
1 tsp fast-action dried yeast
2 oz / 60 g butter, lard or vegetable
　shortening

¼ pt / 140 ml warm milk
2 egg yolks, lightly beaten
beaten egg, to glaze
granulated sugar, to finish

Sift the flour, salt and yeast together into a bowl. Rub in the fat, and mix in the milk and egg yolks. Knead until you have a smooth, soft dough, working in extra flour as necessary to absorb any excess moisture. The longer you knead, the better texture you will have. Shape the dough to fit greased baking rings about 6 in / 15 cm in diameter, or use greased sandwich cake tins for larger buns. Cover and leave to rise until doubled in volume. Bake in a preheated oven at 220°C / 425°F / Mark 7 for 15–20 minutes. Halfway through baking, brush with beaten egg. At the end of baking, remove from the oven and sprinkle granulated sugar on top.

They are traditionally served hot, split and filled with whipped cream. I like smaller versions of dough flattened into balls about 3 in / 7.5 cm in diameter.

Edith Bissell's Nut Roll

Makes 1 large or 2 small rolls

In my mother-in-law's household in western Pennsylvania, festival food preparation always begins with the baking of the 'nut roll', a sweet, yeasty dough rolled around a filling of crushed walnuts and sugar, shaped into a crescent, egg-washed and baked to a shiny gold. She learned this recipe from her mother whose baking was renowned and done on a grand scale to feed a large family.

1½ lb / 680 g strong white flour
1 sachet (7 g) fast-action dried yeast
1 tsp salt
2 oz / 60 g caster sugar
4 oz / 110 g butter
½ pt / 280 ml scalded milk
1 egg, lightly beaten

beaten egg and milk, to glaze
melted butter, to finish

Filling
8 oz / 230 g walnuts, freshly ground
2–4 oz / 60–110 g sugar, to taste
a little warm milk, to mix

Sift the dry ingredients into a bowl, including the yeast. Melt the butter in the milk and stir this into the flour together with the egg. The dough can be mixed by hand or in a food processor. Turn on to a floured worktop and knead for 5–10 minutes, adding more flour if necessary, to obtain a firm but elastic dough. Put it into a large oiled bowl or in a large polythene bag, cover and leave to rise until doubled in volume.

Meanwhile, to make the filling, mix the ground walnuts with the sugar and enough warm milk to make a spreadable paste.

Roll the dough out very thinly, dividing it into two if you want two smaller rolls. It should be ¼ in / 0.5 cm thick when rolled out. Spread the filling over the surface, and roll it loosely, bending it gently into a crescent shape. Place on a baking sheet, glaze the top with milk and egg, and bake in a preheated oven at 190°C / 375°F / Mark 5 for 20–30 minutes, until well risen, golden and hollow-sounding when you tap the base. Remove from the oven, brush a little melted butter over the top, and then cover with a clean tea-towel for 5 minutes. Remove the cloth, and allow to cool completely before cutting.

Variations ∾ Try the roll with a poppy-seed filling. Instead of the walnuts, use 6 oz / 170 g ground poppy seeds and 3 oz / 85 g raisins. Cook these with the sugar in about ¼ pt / 140 ml warm milk for a minute or two until thickened. Cool the mixture, and beat in 1 oz / 30 g softened butter and a little ground cinnamon. Add a teaspoon of rum to this filling if you wish.

Crumpets

Crumpets, like blini (see page 57), are made from a thick batter that is raised with yeast. The batter is poured into special crumpet rings that are placed on a hot greased griddle, and not allowed to spread out.

¾ pt / 430 ml water
1 tsp active dried yeast
pinch of sugar

10 oz / 280 g plain flour
scant tsp salt

Warm ½ pt / 280 ml water, sprinkle the yeast on to it, and add the sugar. Set aside until the yeast is bubbling, then stir in the flour and salt, and mix until you have a smooth, soft dough or firm batter. Cover with a damp cloth, and leave to rise in a warm, draught-free place for an hour or so. Warm the rest of the water, and stir it into the mixture until you have a looser batter. Cover and let it prove for 10–15 minutes more. Heat the griddle, grease it and place the crumpet rings on it. Pour in the batter to half-fill the rings. Cook until holes appear on the top, the surface is dry and the underside nicely browned. Remove and keep them warm in a cloth-lined basket until you have cooked the rest of the crumpets. These are best served hot and freshly made, although they can be toasted the next day.

Date and Cornmeal Muffins

Makes 24

*Unlike English Muffins, which use a yeast-risen dough, these
American-style muffins are sponge-like and rise because of the raising
agents in baking powder. I like the texture obtained from strong bread
flour, but you can also use self-raising flour and omit the baking
powder. These are good for teatime as well as breakfast, and can be
varied at will.*

12 oz / 340 g self-raising flour
4 oz / 110 g cornmeal or polenta
2 tsp baking powder
2 tbsp caster sugar *(optional)*
pinch of salt

3 oz / 85 g butter, melted
2 eggs, lightly beaten
milk or buttermilk
4 oz / 110 g chopped pitted dates

Sift the dry ingredients together into a bowl. Stir in the butter and eggs, and
enough liquid to form a batter of dropping consistency. Stir in the dates, and spoon
the mixture into greased bun tins or paper cases set on a baking sheet, filling them
about two-thirds to three-quarters full. Bake in a preheated oven at 190°C / 375°F /
Mark 5 for 15 minutes. Serve warm and freshly baked.

Dried Fruit Muffins

Makes 18

9 oz / 255 g strong white flour
4 tsp baking powder
6 tbsp Greek yoghurt
6 tbsp sunflower or groundnut
   (peanut) oil

3 eggs
8 tbsp light muscovado sugar
4 tbsp mincemeat *or* 9 tbsp seedless
   raisins, dried cranberries or dried
   cherries

Sift the flour and baking powder together into a bowl. Beat the yoghurt and oil
together, and then beat in the eggs and sugar until the mixture is smooth. Stir in
the mincemeat or dried fruit, and then combine wet and dry ingredients until well
blended. Arrange 18 paper cases in a deep muffin tin, and spoon in the mixture.
Bake in a preheated oven at 200°C / 400°F / Mark 6 for 20 minutes. Serve warm.

Variations ～ Wholemeal flour can be substituted for part of the white flour, as can fine yellow cornmeal or blue cornmeal. Nuts and/or spices can be added, different dried fruits can be substituted, or use freshly grated apple. Replacing the dried fruit with chopped walnuts, and about 1½ oz / 40 g of the flour with an equal amount of sifted cocoa powder, would make very good teatime buns.

Yorkshire Fat Rascals

Makes 12–15

1 lb / 455 g self-raising flour
½ tsp salt
8 oz / 230 g butter, lard or
vegetable shortening
2–3 oz / 60–85 g caster sugar

3 oz / 85 g seedless raisins, sultanas or
mincemeat
1 heaped tbsp yoghurt
1 egg
¼ pt / 140 ml milk

Sift the flour and salt together into a bowl, and then rub in the fat. Stir in the sugar and dried fruit or mincemeat. Beat together the yoghurt, egg and milk, and stir into the flour and fruit mixture until just bound together into a soft dough. Quickly roll out the dough on a lightly floured worktop to about ½ in / 1 cm thick. Cut into rounds with a scone cutter, place on a greased baking sheet, and bake in a preheated oven at 220°C / 425°F / Mark 7 for 10 minutes.

Potato Scones

Makes 12

1 lb / 455 g potatoes, peeled
pinch of salt

½ tsp baking powder
sifted flour, to mix

Boil the potatoes and when cooked, drain and mash them. Put on a floured worktop, and sprinkle on the salt and baking powder. Work in as much flour as needed to make into a fairly stiff dough. Roll out and cut into triangles or rounds, about ½ in / 1 cm thick. Lightly grease a heated griddle or flat, cast-iron frying pan, and cook the scones, turning them once. They should be quite doughy in the middle. Serve hot or warm, with butter, cream cheese or soured cream. They are very good with smoked salmon.

Variation ⁓ If you use a large proportion of potato to flour, you can shape the dough into cakes, and shallow fry these in a mixture of butter and oil. These potato cakes are then very good served with freshly cooked asparagus and poached egg.

Rich Apricot and Cardamom Scones

Makes 12

12 oz / 340 g plain flour
4 tsp baking powder
1½ oz / 40 g caster sugar
½ tsp ground cardamom
pinch of salt
4 oz / 110 g butter

3 oz / 85 g dried apricots, finely
   chopped
1 egg
4–5 fl oz / 115–140 ml milk
beaten egg and milk, to glaze

Sift the dry ingredients together into a bowl. Rub in the butter quickly and lightly with your fingertips. Stir in the apricots. Beat the egg and half the milk together, and mix into the dry ingredients, adding more milk as necessary until you have a soft dough. On a lightly floured worktop, quickly knead the dough until smooth, roll out to about ¾ in / 2 cm thick and cut in 2–2½ in / 5–6.5 cm rounds. Place the scones on a lightly greased and floured baking sheet, just touching each other. Brush with egg and milk glaze, and bake in a preheated oven at 220°C / 425°F / Mark 7 for 10 minutes or until well risen and golden brown.

Strawberry and Almond Split

Serves 4–6

1 lb / 455 g firm ripe strawberries
1 tbsp orange liqueur
2 tbsp icing sugar
8 oz / 230 g plain flour
4 tsp baking powder
½ tsp salt
3 oz / 85 g unsalted butter

¼ pt / 140 ml soured milk
milk for brushing
1 oz / 30 g flaked almonds
¼ pt / 140 ml double cream
¼ pt / 140 ml whipping cream
icing sugar for dusting

Hull the strawberries and slice into a dish. Sprinkle on the orange liqueur, and sift up to a tablespoon of icing sugar on to them, less if they are very sweet and ripe. Mix the dry ingredients in a bowl or food processor, including the rest of the icing sugar. Rub the butter into the flour and stir in enough milk to form a firm dough. Knead lightly and roll out into a circle about ¾ in / 2 cm thick and 6–7 in / 15–18 cm in diameter. Place it on a buttered and floured baking sheet, brush the top with milk, and scatter on the flaked almonds, pressing them down lightly. Bake in a preheated oven at 200°C / 400°F / Mark 6 for 12–15 minutes, covering it loosely with buttered paper after 5 minutes to stop the nuts burning. Cool the scone on a wire rack, and then split it horizontally in two.

Drain the strawberry juices into a bowl, add the double and whipping cream, and whisk until firm peaks are formed. Spread half the cream on one half of the scone, arrange the sliced strawberries on top, and spread the rest of the cream over them. Place the other half of the scone on top, dust with a little icing sugar, and then serve.

CAKES

Lemon Grass and Coconut Cake

Makes one 9 in / 23 cm cake

*I rarely think of using herbs when making puddings and cakes, but a
jar of dried lemon grass was next to the small bottle of sweet lemon
oil when I went to get out my baking things one day. I had planned to
make a moist, lemon-flavoured coconut cake. A pinch of lemon grass
made it even more fragrant.*

6 oz / 170 g unsalted butter,
   softened
6 oz / 170 g light muscovado sugar
3 eggs, separated
3 oz / 85 g self-raising flour
pinch of salt

1 tsp baking powder
4 oz / 110 g desiccated coconut
1 tsp ground or rubbed dried lemon
   grass
½ tsp lemon oil

Grease a 9 in / 23 cm square cake tin, and line the base with greaseproof paper.
Cream the butter and sugar together, and beat until pale and fluffy. Beat in the egg
yolks, one at a time, and then fold in the dry ingredients. Whisk the egg whites
until stiff, and then fold into the cake mixture with a large metal spoon together
with the lemon grass and lemon oil. Pour into the prepared tin and bake in a
preheated oven at 170°C / 325°F / Mark 3 for 40–50 minutes, or until a fine skewer
inserted into the middle of the cake comes out clean. Allow the cake to cool slightly
in the tin before turning it out on to a wire rack to cool completely.

Variations ∞ Dried lemon balm and grated lemon zest would give much the
same effect as the lemon grass and lemon oil.

Ice the cake with a lemon water icing, made by blending together icing sugar,
lemon juice and water.

Make a lemon syrup from lemon juice, granulated sugar and water, and pour it
over the cake while it is still warm. Cut into wedges, and serve as a pudding with
chilled thick yoghurt or cream.

Cinnamon-Strewn Hazelnut Cake

Makes one 9 in / 23 cm round or 7½ in / 19 cm square cake

This is a very quick, easy cake to make, especially with a food processor. Served warm with a bowl of chilled yoghurt or buttermilk, it makes an excellent pudding, but is just as good with mid-morning coffee or a cup of tea in the afternoon. You need not use hazelnuts – almonds, walnuts or pistachios can be used for the topping and ground almonds in the cake.

2 oz / 60 g ground hazelnuts
4 oz / 110 g self-raising wholemeal
 flour
2 oz / 60 g cornflour
1 tsp baking powder
½ tsp salt
2½ oz / 70 g demerara sugar,
 ground in a coffee grinder
4 oz / 110 g polyunsaturated
 margarine or unsoftened butter

6 tbsp buttermilk *or* 3 tbsp plain
 yoghurt and 3 tbsp water
1 egg, lightly beaten

Topping
1½ oz / 40 g plain flour
1 tbsp ground cinnamon
2 oz / 60 g demerara sugar
1 tbsp roughly chopped hazelnuts
1½ oz / 40 g polyunsaturated margarine
 or butter

Make the topping first by mixing together the dry ingredients, including the hazelnuts, and then rubbing in the margarine or butter until the mixture resembles breadcrumbs. To make the cake batter, sift all the dry ingredients together into a bowl, and then blend in the margarine or butter, the liquid and the egg. Beat well; the mixture will be quite soft. Spoon it into a greased and floured cake tin, either a 9 in / 23 cm diameter round tin, or a 7½ in / 19 cm square tin. Strew the topping on the surface, and bake in a preheated oven at 180°C / 350°F / Mark 4 for 35–40 minutes or until a skewer inserted in the middle of the cake comes out clean.

Beetroot and Almond Cake

Makes one 8 in / 20.5 cm cake

*Knowing that carrots make a deliciously moist and rich cake that does
not taste at all carroty, I finally got around to making a cake I had
either dreamed about or imagined – a beetroot cake – a really rich red
cake that I thought would be splendid for all kinds of festive
occasions. One could even make a red heart-shaped cake for St
Valentine's Day. It took me a long time to find uncooked beetroots, as
most greengrocers boil them before selling them. I now know why.
Raw beetroot takes a very long time to cook, much longer than cake
batter takes to bake. However, finely grated, parboiled beetroot did
give the effect I was looking for. As I stirred it into the cake mixture,
the juices dyed the batter a deep crimson, and it contained even deeper
flecks of crimson root. In the same way that some of the crimson
disappears if you cook beetroot in* bortsch *for a long time, so it did in
the cake, and it was really only the grated root which gave the colour.
The outer part of the cake browned, of course, as it baked. However,
it was worth making, had a very good flavour and texture, to which
the ground and flaked almonds certainly contributed, and it looked
very unusual when cut.*

8 oz / 230 g butter, softened
8 oz / 230 g caster sugar
4 eggs, separated
6 oz / 170 g self-raising flour
2 tbsp crème de cassis, crème de
  mûre or blackcurrant juice drink
1 tsp baking powder
4 oz / 110 g ground almonds
2 oz / 60 g flaked almonds

10 oz / 280 g beetroot, parboiled,
  peeled and grated

Topping and Filling
8 oz / 230 g cream cheese
1 tbsp clear honey, warmed
1 tbsp crème de cassis
1 oz / 30 g flaked almonds, toasted

Lightly butter two 8 in / 20.5 cm sandwich cake tins, and line the bases with
greaseproof paper. Cream the butter and sugar together until pale and light in
texture. Beat in the egg yolks, one at a time, adding a little flour each time to help
prevent the mixture curdling. Stir in the crème de cassis. Sift in the rest of the flour
and the baking powder, and mix thoroughly. Fold in the ground and flaked
almonds, and the beetroot. Whisk the egg whites to peaks, and gently fold into the
cake mixture with a large metal spoon. Spoon into the prepared tins, and level the
tops. Bake in a preheated oven at 180°C / 350°F / Mark 4 for about 40 minutes or

until a skewer inserted into the middle of the cake emerges clean. Remove from the tins, and cool on wire racks. Beat the cream cheese, honey and crème de cassis until light and fluffy, and use half of it to sandwich the cakes together. Spread the rest on top, and scatter on the toasted flaked almonds.

Variation ∾ For a more finished effect, brush the side of the cake with honey and roll in extra toasted almonds.

An alternative, simpler way of finishing the cake is to sandwich it with raspberry jam or blackcurrant jelly, and sift icing sugar over the top.

Chocolate Jonathan

Serves 6–8

3 eggs
2 oz / 60 g light muscovado or demerara sugar, ground fine in a coffee grinder
1 oz / 30 g cocoa powder
2½ oz / 70 g self-raising flour
1 tbsp strong coffee, rum or Tia Maria

Chocolate Mousse Filling
10 oz / 280 g good-quality dark chocolate
1 tbsp strong coffee, rum or Tia Maria
2 oz / 60 g unsalted butter, softened
3 egg whites
pinch of salt

Preheat the oven to 190°C / 375°F / Mark 5. Line a 10 × 14 in / 25.5 × 35.5 cm Swiss roll tin with buttered greaseproof paper. Put the eggs and sugar into a pudding basin set over a saucepan of barely simmering water. Whisk together until pale, foamy and much increased in volume. Sift the cocoa powder and flour together and fold gently into the egg and sugar mixture. Stir in the coffee or liqueur. Pour into the Swiss roll tin, level it off and bake in the top half of the oven for about 10 minutes. Remove and turn out on to a wire rack. Peel off the paper and leave to cool. To prepare the mousse melt the chocolate in a clean pudding basin over hot water, and beat in the coffee or liqueur until thoroughly mixed. Remove from the heat, cool slightly, and mix in the softened butter. Whisk the egg whites with a pinch of salt until stiff and fold into the chocolate.

Cut the sponge into pieces and use to line a 1 lb / 455 g loaf tin, leaving a slice to fit over the top. Line the tin with the shiny surface of the cake towards the centre. Pour the filling in and cover with the final slice of sponge. Cover with cling film or foil and refrigerate for several hours until set. Turn out on to a board, slice and serve on individual plates with a spoonful of crème fraîche and a dusting of icing sugar.

White Chocolate Mousse and Orange Flower Roulade

Serves 6–8

4 oz / 110 g caster sugar
4 eggs, separated
1 tbsp orange flower water
grated zest of 1 orange
4 oz / 110 g self-raising flour, sifted

Filling
3½ oz / 100 g white chocolate
1 tsp orange flower water

¼ pt / 140 ml double cream
1 egg white

To decorate
icing sugar
fresh edible flowers or crystallized
  flowers

Preheat the oven to 180°C / 350°F / Mark 4. Grease a Swiss roll tin and line with greaseproof paper. Put half the sugar in a pudding basin set over a saucepan of hot water. Add the egg yolks, and whisk until thick and pale. This will take about 5 minutes, during which time you should also whisk in the orange flower water. Whisk the egg whites, together with half the remaining sugar until peaks form. Fold in the rest of the sugar, and whisk until firm and glossy. Fold the orange zest and sifted flour into the egg yolk mixture, then fold in the egg white mixture. Spoon into the Swiss roll tin, shaking to fill it evenly. Bake for 10–12 minutes, until just firm to the touch. Turn out on to a clean tea-towel. Peel off the paper, and trim off the firm edges. Roll up loosely, from one of the short ends, wrapping the tea-towel with it. Leave to cool while you prepare the filling.

Break the chocolate into small pieces, and put in a heatproof bowl. Bring the orange flower water and half the cream to the boil, and pour over the chocolate. Stir until the chocolate has melted, and allow to cool. Whip the remaining cream, and separately whisk the egg white. Fold the two together, and fold into the white chocolate mixture. Unroll the sponge, spread the filling over and reroll it. Place on a long platter, and sift icing sugar over the top. Decorate with fresh (if possible), or crystallized flowers.

Orange and Almond Cake

Makes one 8 inch / 20.5 cm cake

*Cakes made with olive oil can sometimes be heavy, which is why this
one contains a little extra baking powder to help lift it. Folding in the
whisked egg whites at the end also helps it rise.*

1 oz / 30 g flaked almonds	2 oranges
7 oz / 200 g self-raising flour	7 tbsp light olive oil
1½ tsp baking powder	2 tbsp milk
9 oz / 255 g caster sugar	4 tbsp almond liqueur, such as
2 oz / 60 g ground almonds	Amaretto
3 eggs, separated	

Grease an 8 in / 20.5 cm diameter deep cake tin with a loose bottom, and line
the base with a circle of buttered greaseproof paper, buttered-side up. Scatter the
flaked almonds over the base. Sift the flour, baking powder, two-thirds of the sugar
and the ground almonds together into a bowl. Mix the egg yolks with the juice and
grated zest of one orange, the olive oil and milk, and stir the liquid ingredients
except the liqueur into the dry ones until you have a smooth batter. Whisk the egg
whites to firm peaks, and fold into the cake batter. Spoon the mixture into the
prepared cake tin, smooth the surface, and make a slight depression in the centre.
Bake in the middle of a preheated oven at 180°C / 350°F / Mark 4 for 50–55
minutes, until the cake is firm to the touch and well risen.

While the cake is baking, make the syrup by melting the remaining sugar in the
juice of the second orange, and grating in a little orange zest as well, if you like.
Boil for a few minutes until it begins to thicken, then remove from the heat, allow
to cool, and stir in the liqueur. Remove the cake from the oven and pour the syrup
over it. Allow the cake to cool in the tin, then transfer it to a plate, turning it
upside-down in the process, so that the underside of the cake now becomes the
top, with a coating of golden brown flaked almonds. You may need to level the top
of the cake slightly before turning it, to allow it to sit flat on the plate.

Sharon's Caramel Walnut Cake

Makes one 8 inch / 20.5 cm cake

6 oz / 170 g unsalted butter,
  softened
4 oz / 110 g light muscovado sugar
3 eggs, separated
8 oz / 230 g self-raising flour
2 tbsp golden syrup
6 tbsp full-cream milk
pinch of salt

For the Caramel Filling and
  Topping
12 oz / 340 g light muscovado sugar
2 tbsp single cream
2 oz / 60 g unsalted butter
4 oz / 110 g chopped walnuts
walnut halves, to decorate

Butter two 8 in / 20.5 cm sandwich cake tins, and line the bases with greaseproof paper. Cream the butter and sugar together until pale and fluffy. Beat in the egg yolks, one at a time, sprinkling on some of the measured quantity of flour and mixing thoroughly after the addition of each egg yolk to prevent curdling. Mix in the syrup and milk, and then fold in the remaining flour and the salt. Whisk the egg whites to peaks, and then gently fold into the cake batter with a large metal spoon. Divide the mixture between the cake tins and level the surface with the back of a spoon. Bake in a preheated oven at 180°C / 350°F / Mark 4 for 30–35 minutes, until a warmed skewer inserted in the centre of each cake emerges clean. Remove from the oven, turn out and cool on wire racks. The cakes, when cold, can be stored in an airtight container and assembled the next day.

To make the caramel, put the sugar, cream and butter in a saucepan, and heat gently until the sugar has melted. Bring to the boil, stirring continuously, and boil for 7 minutes. Away from the heat, beat the caramel to thicken it. Sandwich the two cakes with some of the caramel and the chopped walnuts. Pour the rest of the caramel over the top of the cake, and decorate with walnut halves.

Toffee Cake

Makes one 8 inch / 20.5 cm cake

Shortbread Base
4 oz / 110 g butter, softened
2 oz / 60 g caster sugar
6 oz / 170 g plain flour

Topping
2 tbsp golden syrup
14 oz / 395 g unsweetened condensed
  milk
5 oz / 140 g good-quality chocolate

Cream the butter and sugar together. Mix in the flour, and form into a ball. Press into an 8 in / 20.5 cm round cake tin, 1½ in / 4 cm deep, or a tin of roughly the same size. Cook in a preheated oven at 190–200°C / 375–400°F / Mark 5–6 for 12–15 minutes. Remove the tin from the oven, and leave the shortbread in it.

To make the toffee, put the golden syrup and condensed milk into a saucepan, bring to the boil, and boil for precisely 7 minutes, stirring all the time. Spread the mixture over the shortbread, and allow it to cool. Melt the chocolate, and spread it over the cooled toffee, marking into small triangles, squares or fingers, as appropriate, before the chocolate has set. Cut when cold.

Teisen Lap

Makes one 9 inch / 23 cm cake

The name of this recipe means 'moist cake' in Welsh. It is a simple, everyday cake recipe and a good standby. Currants were traditionally used, but raisins are now far more readily available. It can be made in the food processor.

1 lb / 455 g plain flour
1 scant tbsp baking powder
4 oz / 110 g butter, diced
4 oz / 110 g lard
6 oz / 170 g light muscovado sugar

freshly grated nutmeg, to taste
4 eggs
¼ pt / 140 ml milk, yoghurt or
  buttermilk
8 oz / 230 g seedless raisins

Sift the flour and baking powder together into a bowl. Rub in the fat, then add the sugar, nutmeg, eggs and enough liquid to give a soft consistency. Stir in the raisins, spoon into a greased 9 in / 23 cm cake tin, and bake in a preheated oven at 180°C / 350°F / Mark 4 for about 1 hour.

Madeira Cake

Makes one 8 inch / 20.5 cm cake

8 oz / 230 g unsalted butter
6 oz / 170 g caster sugar
3 eggs

10 oz / 280 g self-raising flour
scant ¼ pt / 140 ml milk
candied lemon peel

Beat the butter to a cream. Add the sugar, and cream together thoroughly with the butter. Add the eggs, one at a time, alternating with a tablespoon of the flour. Beat each addition into the mixture very thoroughly before adding the next. Add the milk and the remaining flour and incorporate this well into the mixture. Line a 8 in / 20.5 cm cake tin with two or three layers of greaseproof paper, pour in the cake mixture, and bake in a preheated oven at 180°C / 350°F / Mark 4 for about 1 hour. Halfway through cooking, lay strips of lemon peel on top of the cake, return it to the oven, and continue cooking for another 30 minutes or until the cake is firm and golden brown.

Spiced Ginger Loaf

Makes a 2 lb / 900 g loaf

6 oz / 170 g plain unbleached flour
6 oz / 170 g wholemeal flour
4 oz / 110 g rolled oats, or fine to
  medium oatmeal
1 tsp bicarbonate of soda
½ tsp ground mace
½ tsp ground allspice or mixed
  spice
freshly grated nutmeg
1 tsp ground ginger

6 oz / 170 g light muscovado or
  demerara sugar
8 oz / 230 g treacle or golden syrup
4 oz / 110 g butter, lard or vegetable
  shortening
1 tbsp chopped preserved ginger or
  crystallized ginger
1 egg, lightly beaten
6 tbsp milk or soya milk

Stir together the dry ingredients in a bowl. Warm the treacle or syrup and fat together until just melted, and stir into the dry ingredients. Add the chopped ginger, egg and milk. Spoon into a 2 lb / 900 g loaf tin, and smooth the surface. Bake in a preheated oven at 180°C / 350°F / Mark 4 for 30 minutes, then turn the oven down to 150°C / 300°F / Mark 2 for about 30 minutes. Remove from the oven, and cool in the tin before turning out.

Banana and Carrot Loaf

Makes a 1½ lb / 680 g loaf

6 oz / 170 g sunflower margarine or
    unsalted butter, softened
6 oz / 170 g light muscovado sugar
4 eggs, separated
2 tbsp yoghurt
8 oz / 230 g self-raising wholemeal
    flour

1 tsp baking powder
1 tsp ground allspice
½ tsp ground cinnamon
¼ tsp freshly grated nutmeg
3 oz / 85 g pinenuts or flaked almonds
6 oz / 170 g carrots, peeled and grated
2 ripe bananas, peeled and mashed

Grease a 2 lb / 900 g loaf tin and line with greaseproof paper. Cream the fat
and sugar together in a bowl or food processor until pale and light, then beat in the
egg yolks and yoghurt. Sift the flour, baking powder and spices together, and stir
into the cake batter. Add the nuts, carrots and bananas, mixing thoroughly. Whisk
the egg whites until stiff, and fold into the cake mixture. Pour into the loaf tin,
making a slight depression down the centre of the mixture to prevent it rising too
much in the middle and cracking. Bake in the centre of a preheated oven at 180°C /
350°F / Mark 4 for about 1½ hours. Lay buttered paper or foil over the top if the
cake looks as if it is browning too much. Leave to cool in the tin for 10 minutes or
so after removing it from the oven. Turn on to a wire rack, and remove the paper.
Slice when cold.

Variation ∽ The cake can also be baked in a round cake tin, cut in half and
spread with a cream cheese filling which can also be used to frost the top. Flavour
it with honey, cinnamon, orange zest, brown sugar or fruit syrup, according to your
own taste.

Plum and Apple Cake

Makes one 8–9 inch / 20.5–23 cm cake

2 eggs, separated
5 oz / 140 g light muscovado sugar
5 oz / 140 g plain yoghurt
3 tbsp sunflower oil
6 plums, stoned and thinly sliced

2 dessert apples, peeled, cored and
    thinly sliced
5 oz / 140 g self-raising wholemeal flour
1 scant tsp baking powder
pinch of salt

Beat the egg yolks and sugar together until pale and foamy. Whisk the egg whites to firm peaks. Mix the yoghurt and oil into the egg and sugar, and then add the fruit. Sift the dry ingredients together, and stir into the mixture, finally folding in the egg whites. Pour into a greased 8 or 9 in / 20.5 or 23 cm cake tin, and bake in a preheated oven at 200°C / 400°F / Mark 6 for about 30 minutes. Serve warm as a pudding, with poached plums, apple purée or yoghurt, or serve cold as a cake.

Variations ∽ Variations on this theme can be played with different combinations of fruit. It is very good with pears, and chopped walnuts.

Twelfth Night Cake

Serves 6

5 oz / 140 g ground almonds
3 oz / 85 g unsalted butter,
    softened
3 oz / 85 g caster sugar

2 tsp orange flower water
10 oz / 280 g puff pastry
1 china bean or dried haricot bean
beaten egg and milk, to glaze

Mix the almonds, butter, sugar and orange flower water together. Roll out the pastry to two circles about 8–9 in / 20.5–23 cm in diameter. Place one circle on a baking sheet lined with greaseproof paper, and spread the almond mixture over it, leaving a ¾ in / 2 cm border. Push the bean into the almond mixture and smooth over it. Brush around the border with a little of the egg and milk glaze, and lay the second circle of pastry on top. Press down lightly with the prongs of a fork to seal. Prick the top in one or two places, and decorate with pastry trimmings, or by marking it decoratively with a sharp knife. Brush with the glaze. Bake in a preheated oven at 200°C / 400°F / Mark 6 for 15–20 minutes until well risen and golden brown. The finder of the bean becomes king or queen of the Twelfth Night festivities.

Light Simnel Cake

The simnel cake, a dense, rich confection of dried fruit and spices, was traditionally served on Mothering Sunday, and now more often at Easter time.

4 oz / 110 g unsalted butter, softened

2½ oz / 70 g demerara sugar

3 eggs

6 oz / 170 g fine wholemeal flour

pinch of salt

1 tsp ground mixed spice

½ tsp baking powder

4 oz / 110 g dried apricots, pears or peaches, or a mixture chopped

4 oz / 110 g sultanas

2 tsp lemon juice

grated zest of ½ lemon

Almond Paste

7 oz / 200 g ground almonds

4 oz / 110 g unrefined caster sugar

grated zest of ½ lemon

1 tsp lemon juice

1 oz / 30 g unsalted butter, melted

1 egg, lightly beaten

First make the almond paste. Mix all the ingredients together thoroughly, using only as much egg as is needed to bind the mixture. Knead lightly and put to one side, loosely covered.

Grease and line a 8 in / 20.5 cm cake tin and preheat the oven to 170°C / 325°F / Mark 3. Cream the butter and sugar together, and beat in the eggs, one at a time. Sift the dry ingredients together and fold into the mixture. Stir in the dried fruit, lemon juice and zest, and mix thoroughly but gently. Pour half the mixture into the prepared cake tin. Roll out slightly less than half the almond paste, and cut out a circle 6½ in / 16.5 cm diameter and about ¼ in / 0.5 cm thick. Place in the cake tin, pressing down lightly. Spoon on the rest of the cake mixture, smooth the top of the cake and make a slight depression in the centre so that the cake will bake flat. Bake in the centre of the oven for 1–1¼ hours, or until a skewer inserted into the middle comes out clean. Allow the cake to cool in the tin before removing it to decorate it. Roll out the rest of the almond paste and cover the surface of the cake with it so that it overlaps by about ½ in / 1 cm. With the trimmings, make suitable decorations – eleven small balls to represent the eleven faithful apostles, eggs, nests, chickens, whatever you think suitable. Brush the top of the cake with the remaining beaten egg and put under a hot grill for 8–10 minutes to glaze, taking care not to let the surface burn.

Almond Cake for Mothering Sunday

Makes one 8 inch / 20.5 cm cake

*As an alternative to simnel cake on Mothering Sunday, I suggest this
almond cake which has a lovely flavour and texture. Serve it after
lunch with coffee or as a teatime cake. It would also make a very
good present.*

8 oz / 230 g unsalted butter,
  softened
8 oz / 230 g caster sugar
5 eggs, separated
6 oz / 170 g plain flour, sifted

4 oz / 110 g ground almonds
1 tbsp Amaretto *or* 1 tsp almond essence
  (optional)
1 oz / 30 g flaked or halved blanched
  almonds

Grease and line an 8 in / 20.5 cm cake tin, and preheat the oven to 180°C /
350°F / Mark 4. Cream the butter and sugar together until pale and fluffy. Beat the
egg yolks in a heatproof bowl set over a saucepan of hot water until light and
foamy. Whisk the egg whites. Mix the egg yolks into the creamed mixture, and
then fold in the flour, ground almonds and Amaretto or almond essence, if using.
Lastly, fold the egg whites very gently into the mixture, which should now have a
dropping consistency. Spoon it into the prepared cake tin and level the top, making
a slight depression in the centre. Arrange the almond halves on top, or simply
scatter the flakes at random. Bake for about 1¼ hours or until a warmed skewer
inserted deep into the middle of the cake comes out clean.

Gâteau de St Honoré

Makes one 10 inch / 25.5 cm cake

Choux Pastry
¼ pt / 140 ml water
2 oz / 60 g butter
pinch of salt
2½ oz / 70 g plain flour
2 eggs, lightly beaten

5 oz / 140 g sweet shortcrust pastry
4 oz / 110 g granulated sugar
¼ pt / 140 ml water

To finish
sweetened whipped cream
toasted almonds
chopped angelica

First make the choux pastry. Put the water, butter and salt in a saucepan and bring to the boil. When it does so, tip in all the flour at once, stirring vigorously with a wooden spoon. As you stir, the mixture will dry and become smooth to the point where it leaves the sides of the pan. Remove from the heat, and beat in the eggs, a little at a time, making sure each addition is thoroughly incorporated. Keep stirring until you have a smooth paste. Cover the surface with damp greaseproof paper to stop a crust forming.

Roll out the shortcrust pastry to make a circle about 10 in / 25.5 cm across, and place it on a buttered and floured baking sheet. Prick the pastry all over with a fork. Using three-quarters of the choux pastry, spoon or pipe it on to the pastry base, forming a ring about 2 in / 5 cm inside the edge of the pastry circle. On a separate lightly buttered baking sheet, use the rest of the choux pastry to make 6–8 small balls. Bake the cake base in a preheated oven at 220°C / 425°F / Mark 7 for about 25 minutes, and then the choux buns at the same temperature for 15 minutes or so. (You cannot bake them at the same time since the buns take less time than the base, and the secret to the successful baking of choux pastry is to cook it at an even temperature without opening the oven door.) While the pastry is baking, make a light toffee by melting the sugar in the water and boiling it to the 'crack' stage (140°C / 280°F or when a drop of syrup forms brittle threads in cold water). When the base and the buns are cooked, place them to cool on a wire rack. Dip the buns in the toffee, and stick them to the choux pastry surround, arranging them at intervals. Brush the tops with the rest of the toffee, and allow the cake to cool. Fill the centre with the sweetened whipped cream, and decorate with the toasted almonds and chopped angelica.

Bûche de Noel

Serves 6–8

*As an alternative to Christmas pud, I might look back to my time
spent in France, and make a* bûche de Noel *or Christmas log. It is so
easy to make that one year I did a Christmas branch, making six
sponges, filling and rolling them, and shaping them as a knotted
branch. It was a very effective finale to Christmas lunch.*

3 eggs
3 oz / 85 g caster sugar
2 oz / 60 g plain flour
1 oz / 30 g cocoa powder

Cream Filling and Covering
3½–4 oz / 100–110 g best-quality
    plain chocolate

½ pt / 280 ml double or whipping
    cream
2 tbsp dark rum, orange-flavoured
    liqueur or any other liqueur or spirit
    that you like to use

Whisk the eggs and sugar together for about 8 minutes in a bowl over a
saucepan of hot water until pale and much increased in volume. Sift the flour and
cocoa powder together and gently fold into the egg mixture. Pour into a 10 × 14 in /
25.5 × 35.5 cm Swiss roll tin which you have previously lined with buttered and
floured greaseproof paper. Bake in a preheated oven at 190°C / 375°F / Mark 5 for
10–12 minutes. Remove the cake from the oven, and turn out on to a clean tea-
towel. Carefully peel off the paper and remove the edges of the cake with a sharp
knife (this part of the cake is much firmer than the rest, and if you do not remove
it, the cake will be more inclined to crack when you roll it up). Loosely roll the
sponge in the tea-towel and put to one side. Meanwhile, make the cream filling and
covering. Melt the chocolate in a bowl over hot water. Remove from the heat and
whisk the chocolate to lighten it (by beating air into it). Leave to cool. Whip the
cream, flavour it with the liqueur, and fold it into the cooled chocolate. Unroll the
sponge and spread over it between a third and a half of the mixture. Roll up the
sponge and place it on a serving dish. Spread the rest of the chocolate cream over
the cake. Lightly run a fork over it to give the effect of tree bark. Decorate as you
wish in a seasonal fashion.

FRUIT CAKES

Eight Treasures Fruit Cake

Makes a deep 10 inch / 25.5 cm round cake or a 9 inch / 23 cm square cake

*Eight is an auspicious number in China, and I have devised
this celebration cake with an oriental flavour using eight dried
fruits and nuts.*

12 oz / 340 g unsalted butter,
   softened
12 oz / 340 g light or dark
   muscovado sugar
14 oz / 395 g plain flour
4 eggs
juice and grated zest of ½ lemon
1 tsp lemon oil *(optional)*
1 tsp ground cinnamon
1 tsp ground mixed spice
¼ tsp Chinese five-spice powder
¼ tsp ground cardamom

¼ tsp freshly grated nutmeg
3 lb / 1.35 kg dried fruit and nuts, using
   8 from the following list: sultanas,
   seedless raisins, pitted prunes,
   apricots, cherries, cranberries,
   crystallized ginger, pecans, walnuts,
   almonds, papaya, mango, citron peel,
   sweet preserved kumquats, limes or
   mandarins, bananas
3 tbsp amontillado sherry or Shaoxing
   wine

Cream together the butter and sugar, and when soft and light, beat in the flour
and eggs alternately. Stir in the rest of the ingredients. Spoon into a 10 in / 25.5 cm
round or 9 in / 23 cm square cake tin lined with buttered greaseproof paper. Bake
in a preheated oven at 180°C / 350°F / Mark 4 for 3½–4 hours, and cover the
surface of the cake with brown paper or foil to prevent the top from burning too
much. Alternatively, two smaller cakes can be made, which will take about 2 hours
to bake.

Rich Dark Christmas Cake

Makes a deep 9 inch / 23 cm round cake or 8 inch / 20.5 cm square cake

13 oz / 370 g currants
6 oz / 170 g lexia raisins
6 oz / 170 g sultanas
6 oz / 170 g pitted prunes, chopped
3 oz / 85 g chopped dates
4 oz / 110 g flaked almonds
2 tsp grated lemon zest
1 tsp ground allspice
1 tsp ground mace or nutmeg

½ tsp ground cinnamon
2 tbsp orange juice
2½ fl oz / 70 ml brandy, whisky or
   orange liqueur
8 oz / 230 g unsalted butter, softened
8 oz / 230 g dark muscovado sugar
4 eggs, lightly beaten
12 oz / 340 g plain flour

Line a 9 in / 23 cm round or 8 in / 20.5 cm square cake tin with a double thickness of greased greaseproof paper with a 2 in / 5 cm collar. Tie a double thickness of brown paper round the outside, and put the tin on a baking sheet.

Pick over the fruit, and mix it with the almonds, lemon zest and spices. Stir in the orange juice and spirit, making sure the fruit is well moistened all over, and leave to stand. Cream the butter and sugar together until pale and soft. Beat in the eggs, a little at a time, adding a little flour after each addition to stop the mixture curdling. When you have finished mixing in all the flour and eggs, stir in the prepared fruit. (This is the time for everyone to give the cake a stir and make a wish.) Spoon the cake batter into the prepared cake tin, smooth over the surface with the back of a spoon, and make a slight hollow in the centre of the cake so that it will bake level. Bake on the lowest shelf of a preheated oven at 150°C / 300°F / Mark 2 for 3–3½ hours. Lay a circle of foil or greaseproof paper lightly over the cake if it shows signs of browning too much, and turn the oven down slightly. Test for complete cooking by inserting a warmed skewer into the centre of the cake; it should emerge clean.

Remove the cake from the oven, and let it cool completely in the tin. When cold, spoon a little brandy over it (or whatever spirit you have used in the cake), and wrap it carefully in greaseproof paper, then in foil. Store it in a cool, dry place, 'feeding' it every couple of weeks with a couple of spoons of spirit, if you wish, but make sure that the cake is rewrapped very carefully. When required decorate as you wish.

Variation ∾ For a paler, less rich cake, I would use 13 oz / 370 g sultanas, 3 oz / 85 g chopped dried pears and 6 oz / 170 g each of muscatel raisins, currants and chopped dried apricots for the fruit, and use light, rather than dark, muscovado sugar.

Rich Black Bun

Makes one 10–12 inch / 25.5–30.5 cm cake

*A dark fruit cake enclosed in dough, this is traditionally eaten in
Scotland at Hogmanay.*

Dough
3 tsp dried yeast
¾ pt / 430 ml warm skimmed milk
2 lb / 900 g strong plain flour
½ tsp salt
12 oz / 340 g unsalted butter

Filling
1 lb / 455 g currants
1 lb / 455 g seedless raisins
8 oz / 230 g stoned prunes,
   chopped

8 oz / 230 g chopped figs or dates
6 tbsp coarse marmalade
4 oz / 110 g flaked almonds
2 tsp ground cinnamon
2 tsp ground cloves
2 tsp ground ginger
1 tsp ground cardamom
4 tbsp whisky

Glaze
1 egg yolk
1 tbsp skimmed milk

First make the dough. Sprinkle the yeast on the milk, and let it work for 10–15
minutes. Sift the flour and salt together into a bowl, and then rub in the butter
until the mixture resembles fine breadcrumbs. Mix in the yeasty liquid and knead it
until smooth on a floured worktop. Place the dough in an oiled bowl, cover with a
clean tea-towel wrung out in hot water, and put it to rise in a warm, draught-free
place until doubled in size. However, if it suits your timetable better, let it rise in a
cold place over a longer period. Mix together all the ingredients for the filling, and
leave to stand while the dough is rising.

Divide the dough into two pieces, one half the size of the other. Flatten the
larger piece on a floured worktop, and lay the filling on it. Knead the filling and
dough together until thoroughly incorporated, and shape into a large bun. Roll out
the other piece of dough to a circle, large enough to enclose the bun. Place the bun
in the centre of the dough and wrap the edges towards the centre. Pinch to seal.
Line a 10–12 in / 25.5–30.5 cm cake tin with greaseproof paper, and put the bun in
it, smooth-side up. Cover with a damp tea-towel, and let the dough prove for a
further 30–40 minutes. Prick all over with a larding needle or skewer, right through
the cake. Beat the egg yolk and skimmed milk together. Brush over the surface, and
bake in a preheated oven at 180°C / 350°F / Mark 4 for about 2 hours.

BISCUITS AND COOKIES

Olive Oil Shortbread

Makes 8 pieces

*I occasionally experiment by using olive oil instead of butter in my
baking. Try the following recipe. It is delicious. Use a mild olive oil,
perhaps a pure olive oil rather than extra virgin.*

5 oz / 140 g plain flour   pinch of salt
1 oz / 30 g fine semolina or ground   2 oz / 60 g sugar
   rice   4 fl oz / 110 ml olive oil

Mix the dry ingredients together with a fork. Gradually pour in the olive oil
and stir to bind the mixture together. Press it into the bottom of an 8 in / 20.5 cm
cake tin and smooth the surface. Cut through to the bottom of the tin into eight
wedges, and prick all over with a fork. Chill the mixture for about 30 minutes, and
then bake in the bottom half of a preheated oven at 150°C / 300°F / Mark 2 for
about 1 hour, until golden brown. Serve cold.

Variation ∾ Extra flavour can be added by stirring in a couple of teaspoons of
fennel seeds or ground cardamom. I have tasted similar biscuity things in Seville
and Liguria, both made with olive oil.

Lavender Biscuits

Makes 12–15

1 tbsp lavender flowers   2 oz / 60 g ground almonds
4 oz / 110 g caster sugar   1 tbsp rice flour, potato flour or
1 egg white   cornflour

Put the lavender and sugar in a clean coffee grinder, and grind to a powder.
Whisk the egg white lightly, and fold in the dry ingredients. Line baking sheets
with non-stick baking paper, and put spoonfuls of the mixture on to them, well
spaced out. Flatten them slightly and bake in a preheated oven at 180°C / 350°F /

Mark 4 for about 15 minutes, until just golden brown. Remove from the oven, and leave the biscuits to cool on the baking sheets for 10 minutes before transferring them to a wire rack and leaving them to cool completely. Store in an airtight container until required. These biscuits will keep well for up to two weeks.

Wholemeal Fruit and Nut Biscuits, American Style

Makes 18–24

These 'biscuits' are, essentially, what the British would call scones.

2 tsp active dried yeast
2 tbsp warm water
1¼ lb / 570 g self-raising wholemeal flour
1 oz / 30 g light muscovado sugar
½ tsp baking powder

4 oz / 110 g sunflower margarine or other shortening, plus extra for brushing
8 fl oz / 230 ml buttermilk
4 oz / 110 g chopped nuts
4 oz / 110 g dried fruit, chopped

Grease a roasting tin or baking sheet, and preheat the oven to 200°C / 400°F / Mark 6. Dissolve the yeast in the warm water. Mix the flour, sugar and baking powder together, and rub in the fat until the mixture forms lumps the size of hazelnuts. Mix the buttermilk and yeast mixture together, and add it to the dry mixture together with the nuts and fruit. Stir together with a fork until the dough just binds. Roll out to ½ in / 1 cm thick on a floured worktop. Cut out with a 2 in / 5 cm pastry cutter, and place close together in the roasting tin or on the baking sheet. Cover with a clean, damp cloth, and leave to prove for 1 hour. (The dough will rise but not double in volume.) Bake for 15–20 minutes, until golden brown. Brush the tops with melted margarine or butter, and serve hot or warm.

Hazelnut Macaroons

Makes 15–20

*Macaroons are the answer if you are sick of looking at a depleted bowl
of nuts or bored with cracking them and getting pieces of shell all over
the carpet. Crack them all and grind them in the food processor. You
can mix the nuts, but I think a single flavour is to be preferred.
Hazelnuts make a welcome change from the more usual almonds.*

4 oz / 110 g ground hazelnuts
4 oz / 110 g caster sugar
1 egg white

Mix the ground nuts and sugar together, and then stir in the egg white to form
a stiff paste. Line a baking sheet with rice paper. Take a piece of paste the size of a
marble, roll it into a ball, and place it on the rice paper. Continue with all the paste
in this way, leaving plenty of space around each ball, as they are to be flattened.
You can do this simply with oiled fingers or use a decorative stamp, covered loosely
in oiled clingfilm, to make a design on top of the macaroons. The final size should
be about 1½ in / 4 cm in diameter and ¼ in / 0.5 cm thick. Bake towards the top of
a preheated oven at 180°C / 350°F / Mark 4 for 15 minutes, until just lightly golden.
Switch off the oven, leave the door ajar, and place the macaroons on the bottom to
allow them to dry out for 15–20 minutes. Remove and allow to cool on the baking
sheet. They will harden, and you can remove them with the rice paper.

Amaretti

Makes 4 dozen

*Apricot kernels are used in the authentic version of these biscuits. It is
possible to buy these in oriental food shops.*

12 oz / 340 g blanched almonds
2 egg whites
8 oz / 230 g caster sugar

Line baking sheets with non-stick baking parchment or rice paper. If you have
blanched the almonds yourself, dry them out in a low oven. Chop the almonds very
fine, but do not use a grinder or food processor as the almonds must not become

oily, and there should be some variety in the texture – coarse, fine and medium. Whisk the egg whites to firm peaks, then fold in the sugar and the almonds. Put teaspoonfuls of the mixture on the baking sheets at 2 in / 5 cm intervals. Bake in the top half of a preheated oven at 180°C / 350°F / Mark 4 for 10–15 minutes until faintly coloured all over, no more than a pinkish-gold blush. You could try baking these at a lower heat over a longer period, if preferred.

Biscotti di Vino
(Crisp Wine Biscuits)

Makes 10–12

A food processor makes short work of this recipe; first mix the dry ingredients and then add the liquid. It makes a rather soft, pasty dough. And if you use red wine, the dough turns an alarming and unappetizing blue-grey. This changes on baking to a nice warm brown.

1 lb / 455 g plain flour
5 oz / 140 g caster sugar
1 tsp salt
1 tbsp baking powder
6 tbsp olive oil

6 tbsp muscat wine, port, sherry or
  full-bodied dry red table wine
3–4 oz / 85–110 g plain flour for
  kneading and rolling out

Sift the dry ingredients together into a bowl. Make a hollow in the centre, and pour in the oil and wine. Mix thoroughly and knead lightly on a floured worktop until smooth. Break off a walnut-sized piece of dough, and roll it into a rope about 4 in /10 cm long. Pinch the ends together to form a ring, and place on a greased and floured baking sheet. Continue with the rest of the dough. Bake in the top half of a preheated oven at 180°C / 350°F / Mark 4 for 20 minutes, and then for a further 15–20 minutes towards the bottom of the oven at 150°C / 300°F / Mark 2. Remove the biscuits and allow to cool on a wire rack. When completely cold, store in an airtight container.

Variations ～ A variation on this recipe is to replace the wine with a water and Pernod or Pastis mixture, brushing the biscuits with a sugar and water glaze after the first baking and sprinkling on fennel or anise seeds.

If you prefer not to bake with olive oil, you can use melted butter.

Cantuccini
(Almond Dipping Biscuits)

Makes about 48

When cooled completely, these hard biscuits, full of almonds,
keep very well in an airtight tin, so it is worth making them
in large quantities.

1 lb / 455 g whole unblanched
  almonds
10 oz / 280 g golden granulated
  (unrefined) sugar
8 oz / 230 g plain flour
1 tsp ground cinnamon *(optional)*

2 tsp baking powder
3 tbsp melted butter
2 eggs, lightly beaten
1 egg yolk and 4 tbsp milk, beaten
  together, to glaze

Place the almonds in a shallow roasting tin and toast them in the oven. Grind a quarter of the almonds with a quarter of the sugar, and put into a large bowl. Stir in the flour, all the remaining sugar, the cinnamon, if using and baking powder, and mix well. Coarsely chop half the remaining almonds and stir into the mixture with the remaining whole almonds. Add the melted butter and beaten eggs, and knead lightly until the dough is thoroughly combined. Divide the dough into four pieces and, with your hands, roll out each piece into a log. Flatten to about ¾ in / 2 cm thickness, then carefully transfer to a buttered and floured baking sheet. Brush with the glaze and bake in the top of a preheated oven at 190°C / 375°F / Mark 5 for 20–25 minutes until golden brown and a skewer inserted in the middle comes out clean. Cut into diagonal slices about ¾ in / 2 cm wide. Switch off the oven, and let the biscuits stand in the bottom of the oven for 15 minutes. Transfer the slices to a rack to cool even more. Allow them to get completely cold, and then store in an airtight container.

Straccia Denti
(Very Hard Almond Biscuits)

Makes 4 dozen

1 lb / 455 g almonds
14 oz / 395 g honey
10 oz / 280 g plain flour

3 egg whites
a little butter

Blanch the almonds, remove the skins, and slice the nuts lengthways, or split them. Mix with the honey and flour, keeping back a tablespoon of the flour. Whisk the egg whites to stiff peaks, and fold into the almond mixture. Butter and flour baking sheets, and put spoonfuls of the mixture on to them, leaving space for it to spread. Bake in a preheated oven at 170°C / 325°F / Mark 3 until the biscuits are a pale gold. Let them cool on the baking sheets and then remove, and when completely cold, store in an airtight tin.

Lemon Clove Cookies

Makes 4 dozen

The original recipe for these came from Chez Panisse.

8 oz / 230 g unsalted butter,
   softened
6 oz / 170 g caster sugar
1 tsp pure vanilla essence
1 egg

1 tbsp finely grated lemon zest
18 oz / 500 g plain flour
pinch of salt
¼ tsp ground cloves, or to taste

Cream the butter and sugar together until pale and fluffy. Beat in the vanilla, egg and lemon zest, then gradually work in the flour, adding the salt and cloves, until you have a soft dough. Divide in two, and roll each into a cylinder 2 in / 5 cm in diameter. Wrap in cling film, then with foil, and chill for at least 2 hours, or overnight if more convenient. Preheat the oven to 180°C / 350°F / Mark 4. Unwrap the dough, and slice it about ¼ in / 0.5 cm thick. Place the cookies on baking sheets with ½ in / 1 cm between each, and bake for 8–10 minutes, until pale golden brown on top and a slightly darker colour underneath. Cool on a wire rack.

Variations ∞ The cloves can be replaced with crushed cardamom seeds, and the lemon zest with orange zest.

Rose and Coconut Macaroons

Makes 12

1 teacupful clean, dry, scented rose
    petals
3 oz / 85 g sugar
4 oz / 110 g shredded or desiccated
    coconut

1 tbsp double cream
1 egg white
few drops rosewater *(optional)*

Put the petals and sugar in a food processor and work until smooth. Tip into a
bowl and stir in the coconut, cream and egg white. Add the rosewater if you think
the flavour needs a little boost. Lightly butter 12 small madeleine moulds (or bun
tins) and spoon in the mixture, smoothing the top into a gentle curve. Bake in the
centre of a preheated oven at 170°C / 325°F / Mark 3 for about 20 minutes, until
set and just tinged golden brown on the top. Alternatively, you can pile the mixture
into small pyramids on a baking sheet lined with rice paper.

Chocolate Meringues

Makes 6–8

2 oz / 60 g icing sugar
1 tbsp cocoa powder
2 egg whites
2 oz / 60 g caster sugar

Mousse
4 oz / 110 g high quality plain chocolate
2 oz / 60 g unsalted butter, at room
    temperature
2 egg yolks
2 egg whites

Sift the icing sugar and cocoa together into a bowl. Whisk the egg whites to
firm peaks, adding a tablespoon of caster sugar after a minute or two. When the
whites are firm, gently whisk in the remaining sugar, and then carefully fold in the
cocoa mixture. Butter two baking sheets and dust with flour. Spoon on the
meringue mixture in neat ovals, using two tablespoons to shape it. Bake in a
preheated oven at 150°C / 300°F / Mark 2 for about 1 hour. Take care that the
meringues do not become brown. Turn the baking sheets to ensure regular baking.
When the meringues are cooked, remove them from the oven, and allow them to
cool and dry out.

Meanwhile, melt the chocolate in a bowl set over a saucepan of hot water. Remove from the heat, and beat in the butter until smoothly incorporated. Thoroughly mix in the egg yolks, and when the mixture is cool, whisk the egg whites, and gently fold in the chocolate mixture. Use this mousse to sandwich the meringues together in pairs.

Pumpkin Seed Cookies

Makes about 24

American cookbooks are a good source of sweet pumpkin recipes – pies, puddings, meringues, soufflés and ice-creams, not to mention cookies. This one is based on a recipe from a book called The Joy of Cooking. *I have gradually changed almost every ingredient in it but still followed the same basic method.*

12 oz / 340 g golden syrup
4 oz / 110 g unsalted butter
generous 4½ oz / 125 g plain flour,
   sifted

½ tsp salt
3–4oz / 85–110 g toasted pumpkin seeds

In a small, heavy saucepan, boil the syrup and butter together for 30 seconds or so, and remove from the heat. Tip in half the flour and the salt, and beat vigorously until there are no lumps. Add the remaining flour, and beat the mixture until it is smooth and leaves the side of the pan. Stir in the pumpkin seeds. Drop heaped teaspoonfuls of the mixture on to two well-greased baking sheets. Bake in a pre-heated oven at 180°C / 350°F / Mark 4 for 12–15 minutes. The cookies will be soft when you transfer them to a rack but will firm up as they cool.

Variations ⌘ Golden syrup can be replaced with molasses, maple syrup or thick syrup made of muscovado sugar.

Replace the pumpkin seeds, a couple of tablespoons of flour and a little of the butter with peanut butter, smooth or crunchy, and peanut butter addicts will be your friends for life.

Use hazelnut or walnut oil in place of some of the butter, and some chopped hazelnuts or walnuts for very elegant biscuits.

Crisp Violet Biscuits

Makes about 18

4 oz / 110 g chopped almonds
1 oz / 30 g crystallized violets, plus
    18 for decoration
2 oz / 60 g icing sugar

1 tbsp plain flour, sifted
pinch of salt
2 egg whites

Lightly process the almonds and 1 oz / 30 g crystallized violets in a blender or pound in a mortar. Mix in the sugar, flour and salt. Whisk the egg whites, and fold into the dry ingredients. Line baking sheets with rice paper, and drop teaspoons of the mixture on to it. Flatten slightly with a wet teaspoon or palette knife, and place a crystallized violet in the centre of each. Bake on the middle shelf of a preheated oven at 150°C / 300°F / Mark 2 for about 30 minutes. The biscuits should not brown, as you want the violet colour to show through. If you take the biscuits out of the oven at this stage and allow them to cool on wire racks, they will still be slightly chewy inside when cold. To dry them completely, turn off the oven, place the baking sheets of biscuits on the floor of the oven and leave them for another 30 minutes or so with the door slightly ajar. Remove and cool on wire racks.

Jam and Almond Tarts

Makes 12

3 oz / 85 g plain flour
5 oz / 140 g unsalted butter
4 oz / 110 g ground almonds

3 oz / 85 g caster sugar
iced water
homemade jam

Sift the flour into a bowl and rub in 3 oz / 85 g of the butter, until it resembles breadcrumbs. Mix in half the ground almonds, half the sugar and enough iced water to make a firm dough. Cover and refrigerate for 30 minutes. Handling it as little as possible, roll out the pastry, and use to line 12 greased and floured tart tins. Prick the base of each with a fork. Mix the rest of the almonds, sugar and butter together to form a paste. Divide amongst the tarts, and press into the base. Place a teaspoon of jam in each tart, place the tart tin on a baking sheet, and bake in the top of a preheated oven at 190°C / 375°F / Mark 5 for 15–20 minutes. Remove and allow to cool on a wire rack.

THE TIMES COOK IN MALTA AND GOZO

LOOK THROUGH most books on Mediterranean cooking, and you will be unlikely to come across recipes from Malta. This is a pity, for the traditional dishes of Malta and Gozo have great appeal. Some, such as the *ravjul, mqarrun,* and *rikotta,* remind one of the islands' proximity to Sicily and Italy. The many dishes using *ful* or broad beans, fresh and dried, so like Egyptian dishes, hint at ancient links with the Islamic world, as do the almonds and semolina much used in pastries, and the spices and fresh mint used in fish dishes.

My parents live on Gozo, the smaller of the two main islands, and we go there several times a year, at all seasons. I like the late spring best, when the wild flowers are in full bloom, the new season's vegetables are just ready, and there are plenty of lemons, so that my mother can spare me some to bring home to make lemon curd (see my recipe on page 566) and a piercingly lemon marmalade (see page 566).

In one sense, Gozo is no different from all other places we travel to. The market is one of the main focal points of our day. The markets in Malta and Gozo do not display the rich opulence of French or Italian markets. Fruit and vegetables are small, having had to fight for survival in a hot, dry climate, but are nevertheless full of flavour.

We get to the market early, by 7 a.m. in summer, to wait for the fishermen to set up their stalls with the night's catch. There are usually no lobsters, as these go to the restaurants and hotels, but there will be a few prawns, small striped pilot fish, colourful bream and, if you are lucky, magnificent, large, red scorpion fish (the *chapon* of expensive restaurants in Nice), which we take home and bake with bundles of wild fennel, fresh, green garlic and the local white wine. In mid-August, the *lampuki* season opens, and for the next few days there is always a scramble at the market to get the first of these delicate and beautiful fish, whose flesh is not unlike that of a fine herring. We grill *lampuki* for breakfast and eat the rest cold for lunch with sweet, freshly picked tomatoes, still warm from the sun. One letter from my parents describes how they had picked well over 150 lb / 68 kg of tomatoes from their small garden in just a few weeks. 'Tomato Bob', as my father is called by the neighbours, is an object of wonder and of not a little amusement among the local farmers, for his strange English ways, such as watering his tomato plants at dawn and dusk each day.

Vegetable dishes are very much a feature of traditional Maltese cooking – curly endive fried with garlic, gourd fritters, broad bean casserole, sweet and sour aubergines and a marvellous potato and artichoke casserole. Despite the lack of rain, vegetables are plentiful if not varied. There are tiny, round courgettes, lettuces, cucumbers and beans. Nothing is graded, however, or washed. It comes straight from the fields, piled into boxes. That is why you have to get to the market early, so that you have the pick of the best produce, the soundest figs, the biggest plums, the juiciest lemons.

On our way home, we will stop at the baker's for the best bread in the world. Fresh, crusty and hot, it comes straight from the brick oven. The bread, especially that of Gozo, for which it is justly famous, is perhaps the most characteristic of all the food on the island. Nowhere else produces such good bread. Made with leavening, left to rise slowly, and baked on the floor of a wood-fired, brick oven, it emerges hard, golden and crusty on the outside and moist, full of flavour and chewy on the inside.

The bakery is the other focal point of village life in Gozo, especially on a Sunday. After the baker has taken out the morning's bread, into the oven go trays and tins of small pies or *pastizzi*, made with a variety of fillings, such as quail, pigeon, cheese, vegetables or ricotta. There will be *timpana*, the national dish, a baked pasta in meat sauce (see page 488), and rabbits to be roasted, which is the favourite Sunday lunch. The women from the village carry their trays of prepared food covered with white cloths up to the bakery, for few of them will have ovens, and even if they do, they recognize that cooking their food in a wood-fired oven will give it an incomparable flavour. It is also a place to stop and chat with the baker and your neighbours, in the warm, dry, dark bake shop, with wonderful smells emerging from the oven.

We take our bread back for lunch, and eat it with small, fresh local sheep's cheese, *gbejniet*, and some tomatoes. Bread and fresh tomatoes make one of the most delicious of all Mediterranean dishes. In fact, it is so simple that it hardly needs a recipe. What you need is good, fresh crusty bread, extra virgin olive oil, garlic, salt and pepper in whatever quantities and proportions you think fitting. Slice the bread quite thick, and pour on plenty of olive oil. Roughly chop the tomatoes, and spread them on top of the bread. Crush the garlic with a little salt, and distribute this amongst the tomato pulp. Grind on some pepper. If you let this sit for 15 minutes, the bread will be well soaked with fruity, fragrant, oily juices. It is only a little less delicious when eaten immediately. *Pan catalan* and *pan bagnat* are its Spanish and French names. In Gozo it is called *hobz bis-zeit*, and the bread there makes it the best version. *Ftira* on page 487 is similar.

Ftira
(Flat Bread Sandwich)

Serves 4–6

14 oz / 400 g strong plain flour
1 tsp salt
1 tsp fast-action dried yeast
2 tbsp olive oil
7 fl oz / 200 ml hand-hot water

Filling
3–4 tbsp extra virgin olive oil, plus any
   or all of the following: ripe, firm,
   sweet tomatoes, sliced; shredded
   lettuce; sliced cucumber; peeled and
   thinly sliced mild onions; peeled and
   thinly sliced garlic; coarse sea salt

Sift the dry ingredients together into a bowl and stir in the olive oil and water. Mix until the dough binds together. Turn on to a floured worktop and knead for 10 minutes until the dough is smooth and elastic, adding more flour if necessary. Oil a sandwich cake tin, about 9 in / 23 cm in diameter, and roll out the dough to fit it. Mark two or three deep parallel slits in the top of the dough, cover with a clean, damp tea-towel, and leave to rise in a warm place until it doubles in volume. Bake in a preheated oven at 190–200°C / 375–400°F / Mark 5–6 for 25–30 minutes. Remove from the tin, and allow to cool on a rack. Slice in half, and scoop out some of the crumbs to provide a slight hollow for plenty of filling.

Trickle olive oil over the inner surfaces of the bread, and lay the filling in it, piling it quite high. Season to taste, and then replace the top half of the bread. Cover it with cling film, and weight it down for an hour or so to get the bread well soaked with the juices. Serve cut into wedges.

Timpana

Serves 6–8

2 onions, peeled and finely chopped
2 tbsp olive oil
2–3 garlic cloves, peeled and
  crushed
8 oz / 230 g lean pork, minced or
  finely chopped
8 oz / 230 g lean beef, minced or
  finely chopped
½ pt / 280 ml meat stock or red
  wine

12 oz / 340 g canned plum tomatoes
8 oz / 230 g chicken livers
1 lb / 455 g macaroni or bucatini
salt
1 lb / 455 g flaky or puff pastry
freshly ground black pepper
3 eggs, lightly beaten
2 oz / 60 g Parmesan cheese, freshly
  grated

Fry the onions in the olive oil until soft and golden. Add the garlic, pork and
beef to the onions, and fry until browned all over. Add the stock or wine, and cook
on a fairly high heat until most of the liquid has evaporated. Add the tomatoes.
Bring to the boil, and simmer gently for 1–1½ hours. (You can prepare the sauce to
this point the day before required.) Trim the chicken livers, separate the lobes and
cut each in half. Quickly fry the chicken livers in a non-stick frying pan until just
sealed all over and firm. Remove and put to one side. Boil the pasta in lightly salted
water until barely tender. (It should be 'fearlessly undercooked' for the finished
timpana to cut correctly.) Drain the pasta and refresh it under cold running water.
Roll out 12 oz / 340 g pastry to line an 8 in / 20.5 cm diameter cake tin or
ovenproof dish, about 2½ in / 6.5 cm deep. Mix the pasta with the meat sauce,
season it, and stir in the eggs and grated cheese. Put half the mixture in the lined
tin, and arrange the chicken livers on top. The rest of the pasta and sauce should
be poured on top. Roll out the remaining pastry to make a lid. Cover the pie, seal
the edges, and make one or two slits in the top to allow steam to escape. Put the
dish or tin on a baking sheet, and bake in a preheated oven at 180°C / 350°F /
Mark 4 for 1–1½ hours. Allow the timpana to stand for 30 minutes after removing
it from the oven, and then carefully turn it out on to a plate before slicing it.

Gaghaq Tal-Ghasel
(Semolina and Treacle Rings)

Makes 18–24

Filling
1 lb / 455 g black treacle
16 fl oz / 455 ml water
3 oz / 85 g light muscovado sugar
1 tbsp chopped candied peel
1 tbsp marmalade
1 tbsp orange flower water
grated zest of 1 lemon
grated zest of 1 orange
½ tsp ground cloves

½ tsp ground allspice
7 oz / 200 g semolina

Pastry
14 oz / 400 g plain flour
4 oz / 110 g butter or sunflower
  margarine
1 egg yolk
chilled water, to bind

Put all the filling ingredients, except the semolina, into a saucepan, and bring gently to the boil. Stir in the semolina to thicken the mixture; about half should be sufficient. Cook the mixture for a few minutes. Let it cool, and then put to one side until required. If it is made the night before, covered and refrigerated, it is very easy to handle when cold.

Make the pastry by sifting the flour into a bowl and rubbing in the butter. Stir in the egg yolk and enough water to bind it. Divide the pastry into two or three pieces for ease of handling. Roll it out, and cut into rectangles 7 × 4 in / 18 × 10 cm.

Take a tablespoon of the filling, and roll it into a thumb-thick sausage shape, 7 in / 18 cm long. Use some of the remaining semolina to prevent sticking, if necessary. Place in the middle of one of the pastry rectangles and fold the pastry over to seal in the filling. Bring the two ends together to form a ring. Make the rest of the rings in the same way. As each one is made, place it on a baking sheet which you have first greased and scattered with some of the remaining semolina. With a sharp knife, make half a dozen slashes in the pastry on the top surface of each ring. Bake in the centre of a preheated oven at 180°C / 350°F / Mark 4 for 20 minutes. If your oven tends towards hot, use a lower setting, for the pastry should not brown. As it bakes, the filling expands and spills through the slashes, providing a striking black and white contrast.

Almond Jelly

Almond trees grow all over the islands, but only some of them produce sweet almonds. The rest are inedibly bitter which is a pity, for almond pastries and cakes feature largely in the local repertoire. I have to make do with bought almonds if I want to make this delicate almond jelly. Although you can, at a pinch, use ready-ground almonds, you will be able to extract most flavour from those you blanch and grind yourself. Serve the jelly with a few sliced strawberries or perhaps a purée of greengages or apricots. You should start preparation the day before required.

8 oz / 230 g shelled but unblanched almonds
1 pt / 280 ml boiling water

2–3 oz / 60–85 g sugar
4 leaves gelatine *or* 5 tsp powdered gelatine

Blanch the almonds in boiling water to remove their skins. Pound them finely in a pestle and mortar or food processor. (It is *not* a good idea to use a coffee grinder, as it gets clogged up.) Put the ground almonds in a bowl, pour ¾ pt / 430 ml of the boiling water over them, and allow to infuse overnight. Melt the sugar in 2–3 tablespoons of the remaining water and put to one side. Soften the gelatine in the rest of the water, and then dissolve it over a gentle heat. Strain the almond 'milk' into a bowl, pressing as much liquid out as possible. Stir the gelatine and the syrup into the almond milk, and pour into a wetted mould. Refrigerate until set. Turn out, slice and serve with fruit.

Puddings and Pies

ere I have included many traditional recipes, from steamed puddings and
rice puddings to trifles, fools and syllabubs. For special occasions, and at the
right time of year, they will meet with great approval from your family and
friends. There are also plenty of fruity desserts, fruit salads and baked fruit dishes
which are inexpensive and easy to make. Ices, sorbets and granitas take up a good deal
of space in this chapter too. For these, I use whatever fruits are in season – that is, when
I do not choose a plain, pure, vanilla ice cream, which is probably my favourite.
Amongst the recipes for pies, you will find some using filo pastry, others using
variations on shortcrust and some using chocolate pastry, which is very good indeed.

Soufflés are much easier to make than you are sometimes led to believe, and I have
included several recipes for the hot variety. They make a spectacular ending to a rather
simple meal, and are in keeping with a more elaborate one. They are also immensely
versatile, and from the suggestions I have given, you will be able to make up your own
sweet soufflés very easily.

My travels are well reflected in this chapter. I have included Papos d'Anjo (see
page 533) from Portugal, Tiramisu (see page 520) and Ida Marverti's Lemon Pie (see
page 550) from Italy, Ile Flottante Josette (see page 521) and Cassolette de Cerises
Tièdes (see page 544) from France, numerous American-inspired pie recipes and some
recipes inspired by my travels in the Far East, such as Chilled Vanilla Tapioca Pudding
with Summer Fruits (see page 517) and the jasmine tea syrup for poaching fruit (see
page 498).

Note that some of the recipes, for custards, mousses and ice creams, use raw eggs.

FRUIT DESSERTS

Baked Bananas

For each person, take a large ripe banana, make a small lengthways slit down the top, enough to let the steam escape, and bake in a preheated oven at 180°C / 350°F / Mark 4 until tender. To eat, simply strip back a piece of the skin, and scoop out the soft flesh with a spoon. Serve with a pot of chilled yoghurt or cream, some brown sugar or honey and some cinnamon or nutmeg. Alternatively, you can peel the bananas and wrap them in foil or greaseproof parcels for baking, but moisten them first with a little orange or lemon juice, a splash of rum, some sugar and butter, all of which will cook together to make the sauce.

Baked Apricots with Vanilla

Serves 4

3 oz / 85 g unsalted butter
12 dried apricots, soaked for 2–3
  hours

1 vanilla pod
1 orange

Cut out four large greaseproof paper hearts, and butter them lightly. Place three apricots on one half of each paper heart. Cut the vanilla pod in four, and tuck each piece amongst the apricots. Grate the orange zest on top, and then squeeze the juice over. Dot with the remaining butter, fold over the paper hearts, and seal the edges to make parcels. Place the parcels on a baking sheet and bake in a preheated oven at 180°C / 350°F / Mark 4 for 15 minutes.

Variation ∾ Prunes and other dried fruit can also be baked in this way.

Baked Stuffed Apples

Serves 6

Baked apples are a really delicious autumn pudding, but only worth doing if you already have the oven on for other things. I like to use large, crisp, firm apples. They do not have to be cookers, although Howgate Wonder or Lord Derby would be perfect if you can find them. There is no hard and fast rule about what to stuff them with. A simple mixture of brown sugar, raisins and butter is good. A more elaborate version might include some almond paste or ground almonds and calvados. A spoonful of mincemeat mixed with rum is a speedily prepared stuffing to which you can add some crumbled almond macaroons. Here is another version, flavoured with rosewater.

6 medium to large, crisp, firm apples
3 oz / 85 g ground almonds
2 oz / 60 g butter, softened
2 tbsp light or dark muscovado sugar
good pinch of ground cinnamon
good pinch of ground cardamom (optional)
1 tbsp rosewater

Wash the apples thoroughly, and core them. Mix all the remaining ingredients, and divide the mixture into six, spooning it into each apple cavity. Place the stuffed apples in a lightly oiled or buttered roasting tin, and bake in a preheated oven at 180°C / 350°F / Mark 4 for 1 hour or until the apples are tender.

Variations ∾ Ricotta cheese mixed with sultanas, ground almonds and a little clear honey would also make a good stuffing. Also trickle some honey and lemon juice over the apples before you bake them.

Pears can also be stuffed and baked in the same way. Peel them first, and then core them by working from the base, first cutting out a small plug which can be replaced, and then enlarging the cavity. Spoon the stuffing in, and then replace the plug. The same stuffings suggested for apples are also good with pears, but I think a mixture of a blue cheese, such as blue Stilton, Roquefort or Gorgonzola, butter and a sprinkling of nutmeg is particularly good. The pears will only need to bake for about 30–40 minutes. Cover them with buttered paper while they cook.

Instead of stuffing apples and pears for baking, you can spike them with shreds of cinnamon sticks or, as the Parisian chef, Alain Passard, with split vanilla pods. Do not peel or core the fruit, simply wash it, then spike with the vanilla or cinnamon, smear with butter, sprinkle light muscovado sugar over, and cover the fruit in spirals of orange and lemon zest before baking.

Baked Sticky Prunes

Serves 6

18 large prunes
1 pot of hot, fragrant tea, such as
    Earl Grey or jasmine
3 oz / 85 g ground almonds

2 oz / 60 g icing sugar, sifted
2 oz / 60 g butter, melted
1 tbsp lemon juice
9 walnut halves *or* 18 blanched almonds

Steep the prunes overnight in the tea. Remove and dry the prunes, and take out the stones. Make an almond paste by mixing together the almonds, sugar, most of the butter and the lemon juice. Add a little hot water to bind it if necessary. If using walnuts, cut each one in half. Break the almond paste into 18 pieces, and mould each one around a piece of walnut or an almond. Stuff each prune with an almond-wrapped nut. Use the rest of the butter to grease an ovenproof dish or baking tray. Put the prunes in the dish or on the tray, and cover with buttered paper. Bake in a preheated oven at 200°C / 400°F / Mark 6 for 10 minutes. Serve hot with chilled yoghurt or cream.

Variation   You can sprinkle the prunes with port or syrup before baking.

Gratin of Berries

Serves 4

When you want something a little more elaborate than a bowl of berries, this simple gratin fits the bill perfectly.

1 lb / 455 g prepared berries, such
    as raspberries, strawberries
    (halved or quartered, if large),
    redcurrants and wild strawberries

1–2 tbsp kirsch or framboise
3 eggs
3 tbsp caster sugar

Divide the berries (which you can heat through if you wish, but do not cook them) between four shallow heatproof dishes. Sprinkle them with the kirsch or framboise. Whisk the eggs and sugar in a bowl set over a saucepan of hot water until thick, pale and foamy. Spoon the mixture over the berries, and place under a preheated grill long enough to brown the surface lightly. Serve immediately.

Apple and Elderflower Fritters

Serves 4

7 oz / 200 g plain flour
pinch of salt
2 tsp fast-action dried yeast
1 egg
¼ pt / 140 ml warm milk
1 apple, peeled, cored and finely
  diced

grated zest of 1 lemon
1–2 tsp lemon juice
2–3 oz / 60–85 g elderflowers, stripped
  from their stalks
oil for frying
icing sugar for serving

Mix the flour, salt and yeast, and then beat in the egg and milk until you have a smooth, thick batter. Stir in the apple, lemon zest and juice, and finally fold in the elderflowers. Heat the oil to 180°C / 350°F, and fry the mixture, scooping it up a dessertspoonful at a time, until golden brown. Drain on kitchen paper, and serve hot, dusted with icing sugar.

Variations ∾ Try fritters using plum and apricot halves or slices of apple. The batter can be flavoured with vanilla if you wish.

Apricots in Peppered Wine

Serves 6

1½ lb / 680 g apricots
½ vanilla pod
8 small bay leaves (fresh if possible)
1 tbsp peppercorns

2 tsp allspice berries
¾ pt / 430 ml good full-bodied white or
  rosé wine
sugar or honey, to taste

Peel the apricots by plunging them briefly into a pan of boiling water to loosen the skins. Put the vanilla pod, bay leaves and spices in a saucepan with the apricots and wine. Simmer gently until the apricots are tender but not woolly. This may take anything from 10–30 minutes, depending on the ripeness of the fruit. Remove the apricots with a slotted spoon, and transfer to a serving bowl. Boil the liquid to thicken it slightly, and sweeten with sugar or honey to taste. Scrape the seeds from the vanilla pod into the syrup, and pour through a strainer over the apricots. When cool, chill until ready to serve. The bay leaves can be used to decorate some of the apricots.

Variation ∾ Cloves and cinnamon can be used in place of the vanilla, pepper and allspice mixture.

Peaches with Wine Custard

Serves 4

4 firm peaches
½ pt / 280 ml sweet wine

2 egg yolks
1–2 tbsp double cream

Wash and dry the peaches and place them in a saucepan. Pour on the wine, cover and bring to the boil. Simmer gently for 10 minutes, then remove from the heat and allow the peaches to cool in the wine. Remove the peaches, peel them and slice or cut in half, removing the stones. Bring the wine back to the boil, and reduce it by half. Place the egg yolks in a bowl, beat in the cream and pour the boiling syrup slowly into the cream, whisking continuously. Strain the mixture back into the saucepan. Cook over a very low heat, stirring all the time with a wooden spoon, until just thick enough to coat the back of the spoon. Strain the custard over the peaches, chill and serve.

Variation ∾ Sugar and a little nutmeg can be added as you cook the custard, if you wish.

Pears in Red Wine

Serves 6

This recipe comes from Josette Riondato at Château Loudenne in Bordeaux.

5 oz / 140 g sugar
¼ pt / 140 ml dry red wine
6 firm pears

2 navel oranges
1 small lemon
butter

Make a syrup of the sugar and wine. Peel, halve and core the pears. Scrub the oranges and lemon and slice them. Put the fruit in the syrup, and simmer until the pears are tender. Transfer the fruit to a serving dish, and reduce the syrup slightly, stirring in a nut of butter to give the sauce a nice gloss. Pour it over the fruit and serve warm. Vanilla ice cream, crème fraîche or a warm sabayon are good accompaniments, but the fruit is also very good on its own. You will notice how good the oranges are cooked this way. I have sometimes just cooked oranges in the red wine syrup.

Variation ∾ Josette sometimes cooks prunes and dates with the fruit and garnishes the serving dish with grapes and toasted almonds.

Honey and Sage Poached Pears

Serves 4

*We always think of sage as a flavouring for savoury dishes, but
its warm, spicy fragrance can also enhance sweet dishes,
particularly fruits.*

4 even-sized pears
2 tbsp honey
2 tbsp water

1–2 small sprigs of sage
fresh sage leaves, to decorate

Peel the pears, and cut a thin slice from the base of each so that they will stand
upright in a heavy saucepan. Trickle the honey over the pears, and add the water
and the sage sprigs. Bring to the boil, cover and simmer gently for 15 minutes.
Remove the pears, and place them in individual bowls. Reduce the liquid until
syrupy, and pour a little over each pear. Decorate with fresh sage leaves. Chill and
serve.

Variations ∾ Use sprigs of rosemary instead of sage.

Use 3 tablespoons of honey and only 1 tablespoon of water, and omit the sage.
After removing the fruit, boil the syrup until it caramelizes, and then stir in ¼ pt /
140 ml double cream and cook for another few minutes. Pour this over the pears,
and serve.

Melon and Peaches in Jasmine Tea Syrup

Serves 6

3 oz / 85 g sugar
7 fl oz / 200 ml water
2 tsp jasmine tea leaves

6 firm, ripe peaches
1 ripe melon
lemon juice, to taste

Boil the sugar and water together to make a syrup, and pour it over the jasmine
tea leaves. Peel the peaches with a very sharp knife, and slice them into a glass
bowl. Cut the melon in half, remove the seeds and scoop the flesh out in small balls
or chunks, ensuring that the juice is not lost but caught in the glass bowl. When the
tea syrup is cool and well infused, strain it over the fruit, add lemon juice to taste,
and chill until required.

Variations ∾ Melon is also very good with slices of apple in a ginger and
honey syrup. To make the syrup, use 3 tablespoons of clear honey instead of the

sugar, and then stir in tiny strips of fresh root ginger. Simmer this for a few minutes, and allow to stand overnight before pouring over the prepared fruit.

You could also try melon on its own in mint syrup. For this you infuse a handful of fresh mint leaves in the sugar syrup, instead of the jasmine tea leaves. Prunes are also good in mint syrup. Put them directly into the hot syrup, allow to cool, and then leave refrigerated for at least 24 hours. Remove the now discoloured mint leaves before serving.

Experiment with different types of fruit in any of the syrups suggested. Try strawberries, for example, in the jasmine tea syrup. You can also experiment with the flavouring of the syrup. Strawberries are good in a red wine syrup, heightened with cinnamon, and sliced nectarines in a lime and honey syrup are also very good. Use lime zest and juice to flavour the honey syrup.

Cinnamon Plums

Serves 4

1 lb / 455 g firm, ripe plums
1–2 oz / 30–60 g unrefined sugar
¼ pt / 140 ml water

1 cinnamon stick *or* ½ tsp ground
  cinnamon
1 tbsp fresh orange juice

Remove any stalks from the plums, and rinse them. With a sharp knife, cut round the long circumference of each plum, right down to the stone, and twist the two halves in opposite directions to separate them. Ease out the stones and put to one side. Put the rest of the ingredients in a saucepan, and heat gently until the sugar has melted. Crack the plum stones to extract the kernels and add these to the syrup with the plums. Cook gently for 10–15 minutes, or a little longer if the plums were very firm. Remove from the heat, cool and then chill until required. Serve with cream, yoghurt or ice cream. The plum kernels add a delicate hint of almond to the dish. Whenever I make plum jam, I always add a few for each jar, just before the jam is about to reach setting point.

Dried Figs Poached in Jasmine Tea with Two Sauces

Serves 4

12–16 dried figs
1½ pt / 850 ml jasmine tea
2 bay leaves

honey or sugar *(optional)*
3½fl oz / 100 ml double cream

Put the figs in a sieve, and pour boiling water over them to remove any oil or preserving spray. Poach them gently until tender in the jasmine tea together with the bay leaves. Remove them from the syrup with a slotted spoon, and put them to one side. Discard the bay leaves. Reduce the liquid to about 7 fl oz / 200 ml, sweeten if you think it needs it, and reboil until syrupy. Pour off half into a jug, and with the remaining syrup boiling vigorously, stir in the double cream, and cook it until slightly thickened. Serve the figs, still warm, on individual serving plates with the clear syrup to one side and the cream sauce to the other.

Fruit and Nut Casserole

Serves 6–8

1½ lb / 680 g dried fruit, such as
   apricots, prunes, figs, peaches,
   pears and apples
4 pt / 2.30 l hot Earl Grey or
   jasmine tea
piece of lemon grass
2 bay leaves

12 allspice berries
2 oz / 60 g pinenuts
2 oz / 60 g hazelnuts
2 oz / 60 g flaked almonds
2 oz / 60 g walnut pieces
3 tbsp sweet muscat wine *(optional)*

Put the dried fruit in a lidded flameproof casserole, and pour on the hot tea. Add the lemon grass, bay leaves and allspice. Bring to the boil, cover and cook in a preheated oven at 170°C / 325°F / Mark 3 for 1½–2 hours. Remove from the oven, and allow to cool. Toast the pinenuts, hazelnuts, almonds and walnuts in a heavy frying pan until just crisp and gold. When the fruit is just warm, stir in the nuts, and the wine if using. This is very good served with chilled thick Greek yoghurt.

Kissel

Serves 4–6

I learned how to make kissel *from a landlady whose family had lived in Russia.*

1 lb / 455 g stoned cherries
2 pt / 1.15 l water

5 oz / 140 g sugar
2 oz / 60 g potato flour

Simmer the cherries in the water for 10 minutes. Crush in the pan, with a large wooden spoon, electric hand blender or potato masher, and cook for a further 2 minutes. Strain into a clean saucepan, add the sugar, and heat. Mix the flour with 2 tablespoons cold water, and stir into the juice as soon as it comes to the boil. Stirring all the time, let the mixture boil for 1 minute. Remove from the heat, and then pour into a bowl. The mixture will set to a soft, smooth, jelly-like texture as it cools. The mixture should not be allowed to boil for more than 1–2 minutes for its final cooking or the starches will break down and the mixture will remain liquid.

Variation ❧ Replace the cherries with redcurrants and other soft fruit. In winter, you could try using cranberries.

Golden Fruit Salad

Use some or all of the following in appropriate quantities: mango, papaya, kumquats, kaki or sharon fruit, mandarin oranges and other easy-peelers, golden russet apples, ripe star fruit, pineapple, golden muscat grapes, passion fruit, physallis, fresh dates, ripe Galia or charentais melon, soaked dried apricots
sweet wine, such as Muscat de Rivesaltes or Moscatel de Valencia
2–3 sheets 24-carat gold leaf *(optional)*

Prepare the fruit as appropriate, but keep it in distinctive shapes rather than dice it all – slices of star-fruit, long curving slivers of mango, orange segments, melon balls. Leave smaller fruit whole, and be prepared to put up with kumquat pips and grape seeds. Peel any fruit that needs it over a bowl to catch any juice. Mix this with the sweet wine, and crumble in the gold leaf, if using. Put the fruit into a large (glass) bowl, and pour over the gold flecked wine. Serve chilled.

Occitan Fruit Salad and Frosted Grapes

This is a dish to try when fresh purple figs are available. The other fruits used are ripe but firm pears, white muscat grapes and the sweetest black or red grapes you can find. Peel, core and slice the pears lengthways, and arrange in a shallow bowl. Cut the figs into quarters or eighths, peeling only if necessary, and place in the bowl, together with the grapes. The fruit can be arranged in an elaborate design or simply heaped up. Sprinkle the fruit with a little sugar and Armagnac, and pour over it the contents of a bottle of Blanquette de Limoux for absolute authenticity or other dry sparkling wine, as available. Leave to chill.

The large pale yellow muscats are the ones to use for the frosted grapes. Divide the bunch into sprigs of four or five grapes. Whisk one or two egg whites, and dip the grapes in to cover them completely. Remove them and dust with icing sugar or caster sugar. Place on a baking sheet lined with greaseproof paper, and let them dry in a low oven for 20 minutes. Remove, allow to cool, and then chill before serving on top of the chilled fruit salad. Fruit salads of this kind look particularly good served in china or glass pedestal bowls.

Variation ⌒ At Christmas put segments or slices of tangerines, clementines, pink grapefruit, blood oranges and whole kumquats in a syrup with mint leaves, and add a glass or two of sparkling dry wine just before serving.

Watermelon Pond

Take the biggest watermelon that you can fit in your refrigerator and find a container for it. Slice off the top quarter or fifth as a lid, scoop most of the flesh out of it and remove the seeds. Put the flesh in a blender. Put the 'lid' in a polythene bag, and chill it until required. With a melon baller, scoop the flesh out of the rest of the melon, finally scraping out the layer that is too thin to scoop into balls. Add these scrappy pieces of melon to the blender. Take a punnet each of strawberries, raspberries and blueberries (or of just one fruit), and hull and rinse, if necessary. Put the melon balls back into the melon shell, nicely mixed with the berry fruit. Put some icing sugar or sugar syrup in the blender with the melon pieces, and add the juice of an orange and a generous measure of an appropriate liqueur or *eau de vie*, and blend until smooth. Pour over the fruit in the melon shell. Cover and chill for 2–3 hours. Serve, with the lid on, or decorated with raspberry and strawberry leaves, or other attractive greenery. The sugar and *eau de vie* can be replaced with apple juice, pear juice or extra raspberries.

PUDDINGS

'BLESSED BE he that invented pudding, for it is a manna that hits the palates of all sorts of people,' wrote a French visitor to Britain, François Misson, in the late seventeenth century. The variety and content of our puddings intrigued him. Baked in the oven, boiled with meat, 'they make them fifty several ways', he declared, stating that flour, milk, eggs, butter, sugar, suet, marrow and raisins were 'the most common ingredients of a pudding'. I wonder which particular puddings M. Misson had eaten to draw forth such rapturous praises, for he goes on, 'Ah, what an excellent thing is an English pudding . . . give an English man a pudding and he shall think it a noble treat in any part of the world.' And it is a rare treat now. Looking at that list of rib-sticking, artery-clogging, tooth-decaying ingredients, it is not surprising that puddings are no longer a regular feature in our cookery repertoire. But it would be sad to let them disappear from our tables altogether, for they are, indeed, quite unique, and as M. Misson described, immensely varied.

Kirsch and Almond Pudding

Serves 4–6

3 oz / 85 g unsalted butter, softened
3 oz / 85 g sugar
3 eggs
2 oz / 60 g self-raising flour

3 oz / 85 g ground almonds
2 tbsp kirsch
1–2 tbsp milk
3 oz / 85 g bottled or frozen cherries, chopped

Cream the butter and sugar together until pale and fluffy. Beat in the eggs, a little at a time, alternating with flour and ground almonds, making sure that each egg is thoroughly incorporated before adding the next. Mix in the kirsch and enough milk to give a soft dropping consistency. Stir in the cherries, and spoon the mixture into a greased 2 pt / 1.15 l soufflé or other suitable baking dish. Bake in a preheated oven at 180°C / 350°F / Mark 4 for 40–45 minutes. Remove from the oven, and allow to cool slightly before slicing and serving. This is a substantial pudding with a cake-like consistency kept moist by the fruit and almonds. It can be dusted with icing sugar before serving. For a richer pudding, serve it with kirsch-flavoured whipped cream and a thin purée of cherries.

Variation ∾ To make an apple and fig pudding, omit the kirsch and almonds, use 5 oz / 140 g flour and stir in 2 oz / 60 g grated apple and 2 oz / 60 g chopped, dried figs instead of the cherries.

Lemon Sponge Pudding

Serves 4–6

2 large juicy lemons
4 oz / 110 g unsalted butter,
  softened
4 oz / 110 g light muscovado sugar,
  plus extra for sprinkling in the
  baking dish

4 oz / 110 g self-raising flour
2 eggs, lightly beaten

Thinly slice one lemon, and blanch the slices in boiling water for about 30 seconds. Dry, and put to one side. Grate the zest of the other lemon, and squeeze out the juice. Put both on one side. Grease a 2 pt / 1.15 l soufflé dish or other suitable baking dish, and sprinkle with sugar. Arrange the blanched lemon slices over the base. Cream the butter and sugar together until pale and fluffy, and add, alternately, the flour, lemon juice, lemon zest and eggs. Spoon the mixture into the prepared baking dish, smooth the top, and bake in a preheated oven at 180°C / 350°F / Mark 4 for 30 minutes until well risen and a knife point inserted in the centre will come out clean. This is very good served with lemon curd or warmed golden syrup blended with a little extra lemon juice.

Variation ∞ For a rich cranberry, pear and walnut pudding, instead of the lemon slices, place a handful of fresh cranberries, slices of pear and walnut halves in the base of the baking dish. Then make the sponge mixture without the lemon juice and zest, using self-raising wholemeal flour and an extra egg. Spoon this into the baking dish, smooth the top, and bake as above for 45 minutes.

Raisin, Rum and Pineapple
Upside-Down Pudding

Serves 6

Topping
1 small to medium pineapple
2 tbsp pineapple juice
1 oz / 30 g unsalted butter
1 oz / 30 g light muscovado sugar
2 tbsp rum
1 oz / 30 g seedless raisins

Pudding
4 oz / 110 g unsalted butter, softened
3 oz / 85 g light muscovado sugar
2 eggs
6 oz / 170 g self-raising wholemeal flour
1 tsp baking powder
2 oz / 60 g seedless raisins
2 tbsp milk
2 tbsp rum

For the topping, peel and slice the pineapple, remove the hard central core. Heat together the juice, butter and sugar until the sugar has dissolved. Remove from the heat, and stir in the rum. Pour into a buttered 8 in / 20.5 cm cake tin, and arrange the pineapple slices in the bottom, overlapping if necessary. Fill the gaps with raisins. Mix the pudding ingredients thoroughly, beating for 2–3 minutes. Spoon the mixture over the pineapple, and level the top. Bake in a preheated oven at 180°C / 350°F / Mark 4 for 45 minutes, until firm to the touch. Cool in the tin for 5 minutes and then turn out on to a serving dish, if you are serving the pudding hot or warm, or cool it on a wire rack if serving it cold.

Variation ∾ For a similar caramel, apple and pear pudding, first smear the inside of the cake tin liberally with about 1 oz / 30 g butter, and then sprinkle on a tablespoon of sugar. Place the tin over a low heat until the butter and sugar have melted. Arrange slices of apple and pear in the bottom of the tin, and spoon in the pudding mixture, made with raisins and rum but with an extra egg. Bake as above.

Apricot, Almond and Honey Pudding

Serves 6–8

4 oz / 110 g light muscovado sugar
4 oz / 110 g unsalted butter,
   softened
2 eggs, separated
3 oz / 85 g plain flour
1 oz / 30 g ground almonds
2 tsp baking powder

pinch of ground cinnamon or
   cardamom
6 oz / 170 g dried apricots, soaked,
   drained and chopped
3 oz / 85 g honey
2 tbsp Amaretto liqueur *(optional)*

Cream the sugar and butter together until pale and fluffy. Lightly beat the egg yolks and gradually beat them into the creamed mixture. Sift the flour, almonds, baking powder and spice together and fold into the mixture. Mix the apricots, honey and liqueur, if using. Spoon a quarter of the apricots into the bottom of a greased 2½ pt / 1.45 l pudding basin with all of the honey and liqueur mixture. Stir the rest of the apricots into the creamed pudding mixture. Whisk the egg whites to peaks and fold into the pudding mixture. Spoon over the apricots in the pudding basin, cover with a piece of greaseproof paper, and pleat the paper in the middle before tying it down securely. Cover with foil, and cook the pudding in a steamer or in a pan of simmering water that comes halfway up the sides of the pudding basin for 1½–2 hours, adding more boiling water to the pan as necessary. Leave the pudding in the basin for 5 minutes before turning out, and serving with clotted cream, thick yoghurt or crème fraîche.

Variations ∾ To make a persimmon pudding, omit the apricots, almonds, honey and liqueur, use 6 oz / 170 g flour and a pinch of ground allspice instead of the cinnamon or cardamom, and stir in 8 oz / 230 g ripe persimmon pulp, 2 oz / 60 g grated carrot, a little milk and, if liked, a few drops of vanilla essence.

For a delicious pear and chocolate pudding, make a creamy pudding mixture as above, omitting the almonds and spice, using 4 oz / 110 g flour and adding 1 oz / 30 g cocoa powder and 4 oz / 110 g chocolate, broken into small pieces. Lay thin slices of pear in the bottom of the pudding basin. Heat 1 oz / 30 g sugar and 1 oz / 30 g butter together until the sugar has dissolved, and pour this over the pear. Spoon the pudding mixture into the basin, and cover and steam as above. Serve with a sauce made by melting white chocolate with some cream or crème fraîche in a saucepan.

Very Superior Cabinet Pudding

This is based on one of Eliza Acton's recipes.

1 oz / 30 g unsalted butter
3 oz / 85 g good-quality glacé or
   crystallized cherries
12–16 oz / 340–455 g sponge cake
3 oz / 85 g amaretti, ratafias or
   other almond macaroons, roughly
   crumbled

3 eggs
1 oz / 30 g caster sugar
1 pt / 570 ml single cream
1 measure kirsch or Amaretto

Generously butter a 2 pt / 1.15 l pudding basin. Cut the cherries in half, and arrange them around the basin, pressing them into the butter. Slice the sponge cake, and line the bottom and sides of the pudding basin with it. Dice the rest of the cake, mix it with the amaretti and any remaining cherries, and put into the lined basin. Beat the eggs with the sugar, and stir in the cream and finally the liqueur. Strain this custard into the sponge-lined and filled basin, and let it stand for 20 minutes. Cover with greased foil, and tie this on firmly with string around the rim of the basin. Cook in a steamer or in a pan of simmering water that comes halfway up the sides of the basin for 1 hour, adding more boiling water to the pan as necessary. Remove the basin from the steamer, and let it stand for 5–10 minutes before removing the cover and turning out the pudding. Cream, custard or a thin fruit sauce can be served with it.

Classic Christmas Pudding

Serves 12

It is difficult to imagine that our present-day Christmas pudding has its origins in a medieval porridge, or pottage, as it was once called! It was the Victorians who introduced the dried vine fruits and candied peel that are used today. I think prunes are marvellous in Christmas puddings, and this recipe includes pitted prunes and prune flakes. The latter is a useful baking ingredient as it provides fibre and a rich dark colour. Concentrated apple juice is used as a sweetener, together with the honey and marmalade and can be bought from healthfood shops, as can the nut oils, which I use in place of suet.

8 oz / 230 g pitted prunes
8 oz / 230 g seedless raisins
8 oz / 230 g sultanas
8 oz / 230 g dried apricots
4 oz / 110 g prune flakes
4 oz / 110 g fresh wholemeal
  breadcrumbs
2 oz / 60 g chopped almonds
2 oz / 60 g flaked almonds
2 oz / 60 g ground almonds
1 apple, peeled, cored and grated
1 tbsp grated orange zest *or* 2 tsp
  sweet orange oil

½ tsp ground cinnamon
½ tsp grated nutmeg
½ tsp ground mace
½ tsp ground cloves
½ tsp ground allspice
¼ tsp ground cardamom
2 tbsp orange marmalade
3 tbsp walnut oil
4 tbsp concentrated apple juice
2 tbsp clear honey
4 eggs
2½ fl oz / 70 ml brandy
¼ pt / 140 ml oloroso sherry

Prepare and chop the dried fruit. Put all the dry ingredients and the apple and orange zest or orange oil in a large bowl, and mix thoroughly, either with a large wooden spoon or your hands. Put the marmalade, walnut oil, juice, honey, eggs, brandy and sherry in another bowl or in a blender or food processor, and beat until well blended and frothy. Pour the liquid over the dry ingredients. Mix again until the mixture is moist. Cover and let it stand for a couple of hours, at least, and, if possible, overnight to let the spice flavours develop. Oil or butter a 3 pt / 1.70 l pudding basin, and spoon in the mixture. As the pudding contains no raw flour, it is not going to expand very much during cooking, and you can fill the mixture to within ½ in / 1 cm of the rim. Take a large, square piece of greaseproof paper, oil or butter it, pleat it, and tie it over the top of the pudding basin with string.

Place the basin in a saucepan, standing it on a long triple strip of foil to help you lift the hot basin out of the saucepan once cooked. Pour in boiling water to reach halfway up the pudding basin, cover the saucepan, and bring it back to the boil. Lower the heat to keep the water at a steady simmer, and steam the pudding for 5–6 hours. Make sure the water is kept topped up and boiling. When the pudding is cooked, allow it to go completely cold before removing it from the basin and wrapping it in fresh greaseproof paper and foil. It will not keep longer than 2–3 months as there is so little added sugar.

When you want to serve it, steam for a further 2 hours.

Pear and Caramel Pudding

Serves 6–8

2 oz / 60 g unsalted butter	8 oz / 230 g plain flour
12 oz / 340 g pears, peeled, cored and sliced	2 tsp baking powder
	pinch of ground allspice
6 oz / 170 g caster sugar	4 oz / 110 g shredded suet
¼ pt / 140 ml whipping cream	7 fl oz / 200 ml milk

Gently melt the butter in a heavy saucepan or frying pan, and cook the pears in it for 2–3 minutes. Sprinkle with half the sugar and continue to cook gently, stirring from time to time, until the sugar has dissolved. Raise the heat, and boil until the sugar just begins to caramelize. Pour in the cream immediately, and stir to blend to a pale caramel sauce. Spoon some of the pears and most of the liquid into the bottom of a greased 2½ pt / 1.45 l pudding basin. Sift the dry ingredients together, stirring in the remaining sugar, then the suet and enough milk to give a soft dropping consistency. Layer this dough and the remaining fruit and caramel syrup in the basin, finishing with a layer of dough. Cover with a piece of pleated greaseproof paper, tie down and cook in a steamer or in a pan of simmering water that comes halfway up the sides of the pudding basin for 2½–3 hours, adding more boiling water to the pan as necessary. Leave it for 3–4 minutes before turning out and serving.

Raspberry Bread and Butter Puddings

Serves 6

When I suggested including an apricot bread and butter pudding in my cookery course at Ballymaloe in Ireland, I was asked, most tactfully, if that was not rather a heavy pudding for summer. I can be stubborn sometimes, and did indeed cook bread and butter pudding, of which everyone asked for seconds. Apricots not being available, however, I used fresh raspberries instead, which, when sprinkled with sugar and layered between the bread, cooked down to an exquisite, freshly flavoured jamminess. The puddings are best of all served warm.

½ pt / 280 ml milk
½ pt / 280 ml single or whipping cream
½ vanilla pod
2 eggs, lightly beaten

2 oz / 60 g unsalted butter
18 buttered slices of white bread, crusts removed
8 oz / 230 g raspberries
3 oz / 85 g sugar

Put the milk, cream and vanilla pod in a saucepan and scald. Remove from the heat, and let the vanilla pod infuse for 20 minutes. Remove and split the pod, scrape out the vanilla seeds, and return them to the milk. Beat in the eggs. Butter six individual ovenproof ramekins, and put a layer of bread, butter side up, in each, using the ramekin base or a pastry cutter to cut rounds of bread. Scatter on a few raspberries and a little sugar. Top with another round of bread. Pour on the custard mixture, a little at a time, letting each batch be absorbed before adding more. When all has been poured on, top with another round of bread, and let the puddings stand for 20–30 minutes before putting them on a baking sheet, and baking them in the top half of a preheated oven at 180°C / 350°F / Mark 4 for 15–20 minutes or until golden brown. Allow to cool slightly before turning the puddings out on to plates. They can be served with crème anglaise, whipped cream or raspberry sauce.

Variations ∽ Chopped apple, pear, plum, apricot, peach or stoned cherries can replace the raspberries.

At holiday times, when I buy the Italian yeast cake *panettone*, I use leftovers of that instead of the bread.

A simple variation on bread and butter pudding is to place small cubes of buttered toast in individual ramekins and pour a rich custard, sweetened with honey, over them. Leave to stand for 10 minutes, and then bake at 180°C / 350°F / Mark 4 until set and nicely browned.

Winter Pudding

12 oz / 340 g mixed dried fruit
1 cinnamon stick
3 cloves
6 grinds fresh nutmeg
3 in / 7.5 cm strip of lemon peel
2 pt / 1.15 l Earl Grey or other
    fragrant tea

6–8 slices of wholemeal bread, crusts
    removed
thick Greek yoghurt or double cream
toasted hazelnuts or almonds

Cut the fruit into smaller pieces and remove any stones. Gently poach the fruit, spices and peel in the tea until the fruit is plumped up and tender. (If it is more convenient, soak the fruit in the tea overnight to cut down on cooking time.) Strain the fruit, discard the spices and peel, and reserve the cooking liquid.

Cut each slice of bread into two wedge-shaped pieces, dip them in the cooking juices, and use about two-thirds of the bread to line a pudding basin. Spoon the fruit into the lined basin, place the remaining bread on top to fit as a cover, and pour on more cooking juices to moisten the bread thoroughly. Cover with foil and weight down with a heavy object. Cool, then refrigerate overnight until required. When ready to serve, turn the pudding out on to a shallow dish. Pour on more juice if there are any dry patches, and then spread the pudding with yoghurt or pour cream over it before sprinkling toasted nuts over the surface.

Variation ∿ For an early summer pudding, use white bread, and instead of the dried fruit mixture, fill the pudding with a delicious gooseberry and elderflower compote. Make this by cooking 2 lb / 900 g topped and tailed gooseberries with 1–2 heads of washed elderflowers in ½ pt / 280 ml water until the fruit is soft. Sweeten to taste, then sieve, letting the syrup trickle into a bowl. Use this to moisten the bread, and fill the pudding with the gooseberries and elderflower pulp.

Chocolate and Chestnut Pudding

Serves 10–12

This is extremely rich. You can use sweeteened chestnut purée,
but leave out the sugar.

1 lb / 455 g unsweetened chestnut purée	8 oz / 230 g best-quality plain chocolate
4 oz / 110 g icing sugar, sifted (or more to taste)	4 oz / 110 g unsalted butter, softened

Mix the chestnut purée and icing sugar until smooth. Melt the chocolate in a bowl set over a saucepan of hot water, and incorporate this into the chestnut mixture with the butter. The final blend should be a soft, dark, rich paste. Line an oiled 2 lb / 900 g loaf tin with a strip of foil or cling film to help you unmould the pudding. Spoon in the mixture, and tap the tin hard to settle it. Refrigerate overnight.

The next day, turn the pudding out on to a board or plate, and cut into slices with a sharp knife dipped in hot water. Dust it and the plate with a little icing sugar for extra effect, or serve it with a sauce.

A very quick sauce can be made by gently melting white chocolate, blending in some single cream or full-cream milk, a little at a time, until it is smooth pouring consistency. The sauce can be warm or cool. Certain types of fruit sauce would also go with the chocolate and chestnut pudding; soaked dried apricots can be made into a purée, as can bottled cherries or frozen raspberries, or try heating some marmalade with a tablespoon of rum and sieving it to make a clean, bitter-sweet rummy syrup.

Variation ∿ Add pure vanilla essence, brandy or rum to the pudding mixture.

Clafoutis

*Traditionally a harvest dish of central France, from the Limousin and
the Auvergne, I think it is a pity to wait until late summer to cook
clafoutis, since cherries are at their best earlier in the summer.*

1–2 oz / 30–60 g unsalted butter	½ pt / 280 ml milk
2 eggs	1 tbsp kirsch *(optional)*
2 egg yolks	2 oz / 60 g sugar
2 oz / 60 g plain flour	12 oz / 340 g stoned cherries

Generously butter a 9–10 in / 23–25.5 cm pie or quiche dish, place on a baking
sheet, and put in the oven. Heat the oven to 180°C / 350°F / Mark 4.

Meanwhile, mix all the ingredients, except the cherries, to make a smooth
batter. Remove the hot pie dish from the oven, pour in half the batter, and then
add the cherries and remaining batter. Return the dish on the baking sheet to the
oven as quickly as possible. Lower the heat to 170°C / 325°F / Mark 3, and bake
for 45–60 minutes. Serve warm with yoghurt, fromage blanc, crème fraîche or
cream.

Variations ∞ Other fruit can be used in clafoutis instead of the traditional
cherries. Sliced apples or pears, halved and stoned plums and apricots and stoned
greengages all work very well, particularly if a little *eau de vie* or liqueur is added to
the batter. Watery acidic fruits, such as rhubarb and gooseberries do not work
well, and I would not use soft fruit, except for blueberries and bilberries.

Pear and Blackberry Crumble

Serves 4–6

Crumbles are very easy, homely puddings to make, and they are very popular indeed. The same dish is called a crisp, not a crumble, in America. They are best served warm with chilled cream, crème fraîche or thick yoghurt.

4 oz / 110 g unsalted butter
1 lb / 455 g pears
juice of 1 lemon

3 tbsp unrefined sugar
6 oz / 170 g plain flour
4 oz / 110 g blackberries

Use a quarter of the butter to butter a pie dish. Peel, core and slice the pears. Toss them in lemon juice to prevent them browning, and sprinkle with half the sugar so that a good syrup is produced, and then put them in the pie dish. Dot with another 1 oz / 30 g of the butter. Rub the remaining butter into the flour until it resembles fine breadcrumbs. Stir in the remaining sugar. Mix the blackberries in with the pears, and spoon the crumble mixture on top, pressing it down a little. Bake in a preheated oven at 180°C / 350°F / Mark 4 for 30 minutes or so, until the crumble topping is golden.

Variations ∾ These are almost limitless, but some of my favourite substitutes for the pears and blackberries include gooseberries, plums and chopped hazelnuts, cherries with chopped almonds and kirsch, pears and chopped crystallized ginger, rhubarb and flaked almonds, blackcurrants and chopped mint leaves, and the very unusual combination of bananas and mangos, flavoured with rum, with coconut added to the crumble topping. Spices and chopped or ground nuts can be added to the topping mixture of any crumble if you wish.

MILK PUDDINGS, CUSTARDS, FOOLS AND CREAMS

Vanilla Rice Pudding

Serves 4–6

½ oz / 15 g unsalted butter
2½ oz / 70 g round grain or
  pudding rice
1½ pt / 850 ml full-cream milk
2 tbsp sugar

3 in / 7.5 cm strip of lemon zest
3 in / 7.5 cm cinnamon stick
½ vanilla pod
¼ pt / 140 ml single cream

Thickly butter a pie dish, and put in all the ingredients except the cream. Stir, and bake in a preheated oven at 150°C / 300°F / Mark 2 for 2–3 hours. Two or three times during cooking, stir in the skin which forms on the surface. After about 1½ hours, remove the cinnamon stick and vanilla pod. The lemon zest will almost have disintegrated and can be stirred in. Split the vanilla pod open, and scrape out the sticky seeds. Stir these into the pudding with the cream, and allow it to bake undisturbed for the rest of the cooking time. It is the slow cooking that gives the pudding its creamy texture.

Caramelized Milk Pudding

Serves 4–6

2 oz / 60 g sago, tapioca or pudding
  rice
1 vanilla pod
1 pt / 570 ml full-cream milk

demerara sugar, to taste
½ pt / 280 ml double or whipping
  cream

Cook the cereal and vanilla pod in the milk until the grains are tender. Remove the vanilla pod, split it, and scrape the seeds into the pudding. Stir in the sugar while the mixture is still hot, and allow it to cool. Whip the cream, fold it in, and spoon the mixture into ramekins. Sprinkle on a layer of sugar to cover the surface, and put under a hot grill until it melts and caramelizes. Remove from the heat and refrigerate. You can achieve a similar effect by cooking the sugar until it just caramelizes, and then pouring it over the chilled pudding. It should set to a nice glossy brittle surface.

Semolina Pudding with Redcurrant Sauce

Serves 4

The first time I was served semolina pudding in a grand restaurant I thought the chef was having a joke at my expense. Although it was called flameri de sémoule, *semolina pud is what it was. Since then I have come across it several times, and I must confess, I have enjoyed it. Each time it has been served chilled in a small glass dish or ramekin with a tiny amount of delicious sauce poured over and around it. How different from the bowls of wallpaper paste one used to be served at school. Hot or cold, this is an excellent pudding. I use redcurrants to serve with my version.*

½ pt / 280 ml milk
1 oz / 30 g semolina
caster sugar
3 tbsp single cream

4 oz / 110 g redcurrants, removed from
  stalks and washed
2–3 tbsp water
4 sprigs of redcurrants, to decorate

Mix a couple of spoonfuls of milk with the semolina to make a paste. Bring the rest of the milk to the boil, and stir in the semolina paste. Lower the heat, and cook very gently for about 10 minutes. Remove from the heat, and sweeten with caster sugar to taste. Stir in the cream until thoroughly mixed, and pour into glasses or small bowls. Cover, cool and then chill until ready to serve. Put the redcurrants in a saucepan with the water. Cook until just soft, and then stir in 2–3 oz / 60–85 g caster sugar until dissolved. Sieve and allow to cool. Run a thin layer of the sauce over the semolina, and chill until ready to serve. Decorate with fresh berries.

Variations ⁀ Raspberries, strawberries and other berry fruits can be used instead of the redcurrants.

Chilled Vanilla Tapioca Pudding with Summer Fruit

Serves 6

1 oz / 30 g tapioca
1¼ pt / 710 ml full-cream milk
1 vanilla pod

sugar, to taste
½ pt / 280 ml single cream
1 lb / 455 g prepared summer fruit

Put the tapioca, milk and vanilla pod in a heavy saucepan. Bring slowly to the boil, and simmer gently for 15–20 minutes, until the tapioca is cooked. Remove from the heat, and take out the vanilla pod. Split it, scrape out the sticky black seeds, and stir them back into the tapioca with a little sugar and the cream. Stir in the fruit and chill until required. The consistency, when chilled, should be quite loose and soupy, and thus you may need to add a little more cream or milk. Serve in glasses or glass bowls over crushed ice if you wish.

Sabayon of Single Malt

Serves 4–6

This very superior custard is a wonderful accompaniment to apple pie.

2 tbsp caster sugar
3–4 tbsp single malt whisky
4 egg yolks

Put the sugar and whisky in a heatproof bowl and set over a saucepan of simmering water without letting the bowl touch the water. Stir in the egg yolks, and then whisk until the mixture becomes pale, foamy and thick. The sabayon is ready when a ribbon of it, trailed from the whisk over the rest of the mixture, holds its shape for 5 seconds. Serve immediately. A less rich sauce is made by using two whole eggs instead of four egg yolks.

Lemon Custards with Raspberry Sauce

Serves 6

1 large lemon with thin,
  unblemished skin
6 oz / 170 g caster sugar
2 eggs

3 egg yolks
1 pt / 570 ml full-cream milk
1 lb / 455 g raspberries, rinsed and
  hulled

Finely grate the zest from the lemon into a bowl. Squeeze a drop of lemon juice over it, and mix in half the sugar. Let it steep for 20–30 minutes, then beat in the eggs and egg yolks. Bring the milk to scalding point, and pour it over the eggs, stirring continuously. Strain the custard through a not-too-fine sieve (you want the lemon zest to come through but not the white threads from the eggs) into wetted ramekins or dariole moulds. Place in a roasting tin filled with water to about halfway up the ramekins or moulds. Lay a piece of foil on top to cover, and bake in a preheated oven at 180°C / 350°F / Mark 4 for 30 minutes or until the custards are set.

Test for setting by inserting a skewer into the centre. When the custard has set, the skewer will emerge clean. Remove from the oven, allow to cool, and then chill until required. To make the sauce, heat the raspberries gently with the remaining sugar, and when it has dissolved, rub through a sieve. Spoon on to plates, turn the custards out, and place on top of the sauce.

Variation ∞ Make orange custards in the same way, and serve them warm with chilled strawberries, sliced or left whole.

Simple Rhubarb Fool

Serves 4–6

1 lb / 455 g rhubarb (trimmed
   weight)
½ tsp ground cinnamon or
   cardamom

honey or sugar, to taste
½ pt / 280 ml double or whipping
   cream *or* 8 oz / 230 g thick plain
   yoghurt

Cut the rhubarb into 1 in / 2.5 cm lengths, rinse underneath cold running
water, and put in a saucepan. Cover and simmer gently with the spice until the fruit
is soft. Stir in sugar or honey to taste, remembering that the rhubarb will be further
diluted by the cream or yoghurt. Cook a little longer until the sugar has dissolved.
Allow the fruit to cool completely. Whip the cream, and gently fold it into the fruit
pulp, or fold the fruit pulp into the yoghurt, if using it (fold the lighter texture into
the heavier). Spoon into bowls or glasses and chill until required.

Strawberry and Raspberry Fool

Serves 4–6

*Some of the very best puddings using soft summer fruits are simple
variations on the strawberries and cream theme. One of the richest is
Eton Mess – strawberries crushed with sugar and stirred into whipped
cream. An even nicer version is this uncooked fool recipe.*

8 oz / 230 g strawberries
8 oz / 230 g raspberries
3 oz / 85 g caster or icing sugar

1 pt / 570 ml whipping or double cream
1 tbsp rosewater

Put the fruit in a bowl, sprinkle on the sugar, and crush with the back of a fork.
Whip the cream, and stir the rosewater into the fruit. Stir fruit and cream together,
and pile into glasses or bowls to serve.

Caramel Cream

Serves 4–6

1 pt / 570 ml single cream	4 oz / 110 g sugar
1 vanilla pod	2 tbsp water
3 egg yolks	

Bring the cream slowly to the boil with the vanilla pod. Meanwhile, beat the egg yolks in a bowl with ½ oz / 15 g sugar. Pour on the hot cream, whisking all the time. Remove the vanilla pod, and wash and dry it for future use. In a small, heavy saucepan, melt the rest of the sugar in the water. When melted, raise the heat and allow to caramelize and go light brown. Pour the caramel quickly into four individual ramekins or a soufflé dish, swirling it around to cover the base and the sides of the ramekins. Strain the egg and cream mixture into the ramekins. Stand the dishes in a roasting tin containing a little water, and bake in a preheated oven at 180°C / 350°F / Mark 4 for 25–30 minutes. You will know when it is ready by sticking a knife point into the centre of the cream. It will come out clean when the creams are cooked. Allow to go completely cold, then refrigerate. To serve, turn out on to plates.

Tiramisu

Serves 6–8

8 oz / 230 g sponge fingers	4 oz / 110 g ricotta
¼ pt / 140 ml strong black coffee or espresso	3–4 oz / 85–110 g icing sugar
	1 tsp pure vanilla essence
3 tbsp cognac	2–3 egg whites
8 oz / 230 g Mascarpone or cream cheese	1 tbsp grated plain chocolate
	1 tsp finely ground coffee
4 tbsp thick yoghurt	

Dip half the sponge fingers in the mixed coffee and cognac, and place in the bottom of a glass serving bowl. Blend the Mascarpone, yoghurt, ricotta, sugar and vanilla essence until smooth. Whisk the egg whites until stiff, and fold into the creamy mixture. Spoon half of it into the glass bowl. Cover with the remaining sponge fingers dipped in the coffee and cognac mixture, and then spoon on the rest of the cream, smoothing the surface. Sprinkle the surface with chocolate and coffee, and then cover and refrigerate for several hours before serving.

Ile Flottante Josette

I watched Josette Riondato, the cook at Château Loudenne in
Bordeaux, at work in her kitchen one day, and was much taken with
her version of a French classic.

Meringue	Custard
5 oz / 140 g granulated sugar	just under 2 pt / 1 l full-cream milk
2½ fl oz / 70 ml water	½ vanilla pod, split in two
6 egg whites	6 egg yolks
2 oz / 60 g caster sugar	3½ oz / 100 g caster sugar
	1 scant tsp potato flour, arrowroot or cornflour

Boil the sugar and water together until caramelized, without letting it brown
too much. In the early stages of cooking the sugar, when you can safely leave it for
a minute or two, whisk the egg whites to firm peaks with the caster sugar. Slowly
pour the hot caramel on to the meringue, and continue beating, either with a fork
or in the bowl of an electric mixer. When thoroughly folded in, pour the meringue
into a buttered charlotte mould, and refrigerate until required.

To make the custard, scald the milk with the vanilla pod. Beat the egg yolks
and sugar, and thoroughly mix in the starch. Pour the hot milk over the eggs,
stirring continuously. Strain the custard back into the saucepan, and cook over a
gentle heat, stirring, just until the surface breaks once. Remove immediately from
the heat, and pour into a bowl. Cool and refrigerate until required. To serve, turn
the meringue into a shallow bowl, and pour the custard around it.

Eighteenth-Century English Trifle

Serves 10

Sponge
4 eggs, separated
generous 4 oz / 120 g icing sugar
generous 4 oz / 120 g self-raising
  flour, sifted

Custard
¾ pt / 430 ml milk
4 oz / 110 g caster sugar
1 vanilla pod
6 egg yolks

Trifle
apricot glaze *or* redcurrant jelly
12 amaretti
¼ pt / 140 ml cream sherry
1 pt / 570 ml whipping cream
toasted flaked almonds

Line a 10 × 14 in / 25.5 × 35.5 cm Swiss roll tin, with buttered greaseproof paper. To make the sponge, whisk the egg yolks over hot water with half the sugar until pale and thick enough to leave a ribbon. Whisk the egg whites, adding the remaining sugar. Fold the flour into the egg yolk mixture, and then fold the two mixtures carefully together. Spread in the prepared Swiss roll tin and bake in a preheated oven at 180°C / 350°F / Mark 4 for 10–12 minutes. Turn out flat on to a clean tea-towel, peel off the greaseproof paper, trim off the crisp edges, and roll up loosely. Put on one side.

To make the custard, put the milk and sugar in a saucepan with the vanilla pod, and bring to the boil. Pour it over the egg yolks, whisking continuously. Strain the mixture back into a clean saucepan. Retrieve and rinse the vanilla pod for further use, or split it and scrape some of the seeds into the custard. Gently cook the custard until it thickens, but without letting it curdle. Cover and put aside to cool.

Unroll the sponge and spread it with the glaze or jelly, then roll it up again and slice it. Line the bottom of a glass bowl with the sponge slices. Place the amaretti on top, and moisten with the sherry. Spoon on the custard, and chill to set slightly. Whip the cream, and spread on top. Arrange the flaked almonds around the edge and in a daisy pattern on top.

Quick Whipped Cream Desserts

These take but minutes to make and are a very sumptuous way to finish a meal, particularly if the preceding dishes have been somewhat frugal. Use double or whipping cream, and do not try to fold in anything too stiff. Thick honey, for example, should be softened first. Fresh strawberries can be sliced or chopped. Summer fruit from the freezer can be blended with a little sugar to a purée. Here are some possible combinations: honey, whisky and toasted oatflakes; chocolate flakes, rum and toasted flaked hazelnuts; toasted flaked almonds, crushed amaretti and Amaretto liqueur; sliced strawberries and kirsch; raspberry purée and kirsch; sweetened chestnut purée, which looks good when just lightly folded in for a marbled effect.

Ricotta with Apricot Sauce

Serves 4

6 oz / 170 g untreated dried apricots
12 oz / 340 g ricotta
1 oz / 30 g unsalted pistachios (optional)

Put the apricots in a small saucepan and cover with boiling water. Leave them to stand for 20-30 minutes, then bring back to the boil, cover and simmer gently until tender and plump. This can take from 5 to 30 minutes, depending on how dehydrated the apricots were to begin with. Make sure that they are kept covered with water. This will form part of the sauce. Cool the apricots with their cooking liquid, and then rub them through a sieve. Chill until required. Slice the ricotta into four neat shapes and place on dessert plates. Blanch and peel the pistachios, if using them, and roughly crush them with a rolling pin. Pour some of the sauce on to the ricotta, without completely covering it, and scatter the pistachios on the sauce. The contrast between the sharp, fruity sauce and the bland, smooth cheese is pleasing and delicious. Moreover, pistachios definitely go with apricots, which makes it worthwhile hunting out a source of unsalted ones. You will probably find them in a wholefood shop which is also a good place to buy the apricots, as you are more likely to find untreated ones there.

Variation ➣ Prunes can replace the apricots if you wish.

Lemon Syllabub

Serves 4

1 small lemon	freshly grated nutmeg
1 tsp clear honey	¼ pt / 140 ml chilled double cream
2 tbsp cognac	½ pt / 280 ml chilled whipping cream
3–4 tbsp rich oloroso sherry	

Grate the lemon zest into a small bowl and squeeze in 1 tablespoon lemon juice. Add the honey, cognac, sherry and a little nutmeg. Cover and refrigerate overnight. Next day, stir in the creams and whisk until foamy. Spoon into wine glasses and chill until required. Serve with sponge fingers, brandy snaps, almond biscuits or crisp cigarette-shaped wafers. If you leave the syllabub for several hours, it will separate into a thick cream on top and a clear liquorous whey at the bottom. It is very good like this but equally very good freshly whipped.

Variations ∽ Mix 3 tablespoons of fine-cut orange marmalade with 4 oz / 110 g sugar, 8 tablespoons of malt whisky and the juice of 2 lemons or 2 Seville oranges together. Leave to stand for several hours, and then stir in the creams and whisk as above.

Melt 6 tablespoons of honey, stir in 6 tablespoons of malt whisky, add the creams, and whisk as above. For a pink version, use cherry brandy.

Chilled Persimmon Creams

Serves 4

4 ripe persimmons with sound, unblemished skins	2 tbsp icing sugar
juice and grated zest of 1 small lemon	½ pt / 280 ml double cream

Cut a thin slice off the top of each persimmon to make a 'lid'. With a pointed spoon, carefully scoop out the pulp on to a plate. Make a purée of half of it in a blender together with the lemon juice and zest, and the icing sugar. Whisk the cream until firm, and blend in the persimmon purée. Roughly chop the rest of the fruit, and stir this into the cream. Divide the mixture among the fruit skins, replace the lids, and chill until required. The creams can, of course, also be served in wine glasses if the persimmon skins are not good enough to bring to the table.

Rose, Yoghurt and Cheese Hearts with Rhubarb Sauce

Serves 4

You can buy individual heart-shaped pierced moulds imported from France in good kitchenware shops. Like much kitchenware, they are worth looking out for when you are in France, as they tend to be cheaper. Line the moulds with damp muslin or cheesecloth to stop the mixture drying out too much. If you cannot obtain moulds, pierced yoghurt or cottage cheese cartons are a good substitute, but you will, of course, lose the heart shape. I use the pink, tender, forced rhubarb in this recipe.

Rhubarb Sauce
12 oz / 340 g rhubarb
caster sugar, to taste
freshly grated nutmeg

Rose Hearts
5 oz / 140 g thick, plain Greek-style
  yoghurt
4 oz / 110 g curd cheese or sieved
  cottage cheese
4 tsp rosewater
clear honey or caster sugar, to taste
2 egg whites

Chop the rhubarb into 1 in / 2.5 cm chunks, but do not peel it. Rinse it, and place in a saucepan with the sugar. Cook gently, partially covered, until the sugar has dissolved, and the fruit is tender. Rub through a sieve, sprinkle with nutmeg, and chill until required.

Blend the yoghurt and curd or cottage cheese, mix in the rosewater until smooth, and sweeten to taste. Whisk the egg whites to form peaks, and fold into the cheese. Spoon the mixture into lined moulds, place on a plate, and refrigerate for about 12 hours to drain and firm up. When ready to serve, turn out on to plates, and carefully peel the muslin from the moulded cheese mixture. Serve with the rhubarb sauce poured over.

Variations ⇛ In summer, use soft fruits instead of rhubarb to make the sauce.

Instead of rosewater, use orange flower water in the cheese mixture, or stir in freshly chopped mint. Mint hearts go well with a blackcurrant or raspberry sauce.

JELLIES, BLANCMANGES, MOUSSES AND COLD SOUFFLÉS

Pear Jelly

Serves 4

1 pt / 570 ml pear juice
4 leaves gelatine *or* 4 tsp powdered
   gelatine

1 large, firm, ripe, sweet pear, peeled,
   cored and sliced
juice of ½ lemon

Put 3 tablespoons of pear juice into a saucepan, add the gelatine and leave to soften. When soft, put it over a low heat, and stir until the gelatine has completely dissolved. Brush the pear slices with lemon juice to prevent them from discolouring. Mix the rest of the pear juice with the gelatine liquid. Dip the pear slices into this, and line individual moulds or one large mould with the slices. Refrigerate until set. Carefully pour in the rest of the liquid, and refrigerate until set. The pears may float away from the sides, but the jelly will still look good with the fruit suspended in it.

Variations ❧ Use red wine instead of pear juice and 6 oz / 170 g stoned sweet cherries instead of the pear. Omit the lemon juice, put the fruit directly into the mould or moulds, pour the jelly liquid over, and refrigerate until set.

For a clear port and rosemary jelly, omit the fruit and use a mixture of port and water to replace the pear juice. Put all this port and water mixture in a pan with a stick of cinnamon, several sprigs of rosemary, a splash of orange juice, the gelatine and sugar to taste. When the gelatine has softened, heat and stir until the gelatine and sugar has dissolved. Do not let it boil. Remove the cinnamon stick. Leave to stand for 30 minutes before pouring into the mould or moulds and allowing to set.

To make a lemon buttermilk jelly, soften then dissolve the gelatine in 3 table-spoons of water. Then heat ¼ pt / 140 ml fresh lemon juice with 6 oz / 170 g sugar until the sugar dissolves. Stir in the dissolved gelatine and ½ pt / 280 ml buttermilk, and pour into the mould or moulds and allow to set.

Fromage Blancmange with Peaches or Nectarines

Serves 6-8

You should make the blancmange at least 4 hours in advance.

5 leaves gelatine *or* 5 tsp powdered
  gelatine
10 oz / 280 g fromage blanc
¼ pt / 140 ml milk
5 oz / 140 g caster sugar
½ pt / 280 ml whipping cream
6 peaches or nectarines

7 fl oz / 200 ml white dessert wine, red
  wine or apple juice
2–3 oz / 60–85 g sugar
juice and grated zest of 2 oranges
2–3 cloves
small stick of cinnamon
1 oz / 30 g toasted flaked almonds

Put the gelatine in a bowl with a little water and leave to soften. Put the fromage blanc in a bowl, and beat until smooth. Put the milk and sugar in a saucepan, bring to the boil, and simmer until the sugar has dissolved. Stir in the softened gelatine until it, too, has dissolved, and remove from the heat. Pour this mixture into the fromage blanc, and stir until thoroughly blended. Allow to cool completely. Whip the cream, and fold into the fromage blanc. Pour the mixture into a wet charlotte or jelly mould. Smooth the surface, and refrigerate for about 4 hours until set. An hour before serving, peel, stone and slice the peaches or nectarines. Put in a bowl. Put the wine, sugar, orange zest and juice and spices in a saucepan. Heat until the sugar has dissolved, and then boil until the mixture just begins to thicken. Remove from the heat, cool, and pour over the fruit. Let this macerate for 30 minutes or so. Turn out the blancmange, spoon the fruit around it, and decorate with toasted almonds.

Ginger Mousse with
Lime and Honey Sauce

Serves 4

2½ oz / 70 g caster sugar
3 egg yolks
pinch salt
½ oz / 15 g fresh root ginger,
    peeled and grated
6 fl oz / 170 ml double or
    whipping cream
2 limes

3½ fl oz / 100 ml clear honey
3½ fl oz / 100 ml water
¼ tsp cornflour

To decorate (optional)
2 fl oz / 60 ml double or
    whipping cream
4 slices candied ginger

Whisk the sugar, egg yolks, salt and ginger until thick and foamy. Whip the cream until firm, and fold into the mousse. Spoon into serving glasses and chill until required.

To make the sauce, squeeze the lime juice into a saucepan, add the honey and most of the water and bring to the boil. Blend the cornflour with the rest of the water, and then add it to the lime syrup. Stir and cook for a minute or two more. Chill and serve with the mousse which can first be decorated with cream and candied ginger.

Vanilla Mousse with Strawberries and Vanilla Sauce

Serves 8

You can decide how plain or rich you want this mousse to be by making it with cream cheese and double cream for extra richness, with sieved and blended cottage cheese and fromage frais for a low-fat version, with curd cheese and thick yoghurt for a medium-fat version or any combination of your choice. The consistency, however arrived at, should be that of thick cream or yoghurt, that is a coating consistency. You need pierced moulds to hold the mixture.

1 pt / 570 ml single cream	1 lb / 455 g soft cheese (see above)
1 vanilla pod	2 egg whites
2–3 tbsp caster sugar	¼ pt / 140 ml fruity red wine
2 leaves gelatine *or* 2 tsp powdered gelatine	1 cinnamon stick
	freshly ground black pepper
2 tbsp water	2 lb / 900 g strawberries

Put the cream in a saucepan with the vanilla pod and 1 tablespoon sugar. Bring to the boil and remove from the heat. Scoop out the vanilla pod, split it open, scrape the seeds into the cream and allow to cool. Meanwhile, let the gelatine soften in the water in a small bowl. When it is soft, drain out half the water and place the bowl in a saucepan of water. Heat until the gelatine has dissolved. Blend the gelatine and a quarter of the vanilla cream with the soft cheese. Put the remaining vanilla cream on one side to serve as a sauce. Whisk the egg whites and fold carefully into the mixture. Line eight small pierced moulds with damp muslin, place them on a tray and spoon in the cheese mixture. Allow to drain and set in the refrigerator for at least 8 hours. Cover to stop the muslin drying out.

Make a syrup by heating the red wine with the rest of the sugar, the cinnamon and black pepper until the sugar has dissolved. Boil for a few minutes, then allow to cool. Sort the strawberries into three batches, discarding any rotten ones. The softest but still sound ones should be hulled and made into a purée. The larger firm ones should be hulled, sliced and marinated in the red wine syrup, and the small firm ones should be reserved with as much of their stem as possible to serve whole.

To assemble the dish, turn out the mousses on to dessert plates. Pour a little vanilla cream sauce over one side of the plate, and some strawberry coulis on the other. Decorate with fresh strawberries.

White Chocolate and Cheese Mousse with Blackberry Sauce

Serves 6

6 oz / 170 g white chocolate
2 oz / 60 g cream cheese
8 oz / 230 g fromage frais
3½ fl oz / 100 ml whipping or
    double cream

2 egg whites
12 oz / 340 g blackberries
icing sugar or syrup, to taste
cocoa powder and icing sugar, to
    decorate (*optional*)

Break the chocolate into a heatproof bowl, and melt over a saucepan of hot water. Allow to cool. Mix the chocolate with the soft cheeses. Whip the cream, and fold this in. Finally, whisk the egg whites to firm peaks and fold in. Line pierced moulds with damp muslin, and spoon in the mixture. Place the moulds on a plate, cover and refrigerate for several hours or overnight. When ready to serve, clean and pick over the blackberries, place them in a blender and purée them. Sieve, then sweeten to taste. To serve, turn out the mousses on to individual plates, and spoon some of the blackberry purée around them. The mousses can be sprinkled with cocoa powder and the dark sauce with icing sugar for extra contrast.

Variations ∾ The mousse can also be made with crème fraîche, drained and sieved cottage cheese, low-fat fromage blanc or Greek yoghurt in place of the fromage frais. It all depends on what is available and how rich you want the mousse to be.

The mousse can also be spooned into small ramekins. It will set but only lightly and should be eaten with a spoon. A layer of blackberry purée can be spooned over the top.

Chilled Pumpkin Soufflé

Serves 6–8

3 leaves gelatine *or* 3 tsp powdered
   gelatine
4 tbsp white rum or kirsch
½ pt / 280 ml milk
1 cinnamon stick
4 cloves
4 oz / 110 g caster sugar
4 eggs, lightly beaten
8 oz / 230 g cooked, mashed
   pumpkin

½ tsp ground cinnamon
½ tsp ground ginger
¼ tsp ground mace or grated nutmeg
¼ tsp ground cloves
½ pt / 280 ml double cream
toasted chopped nuts *or* crystallized
   fruit, to decorate (*optional*)

Put the gelatine and liqueur in a small bowl set over a pan of hot water, and leave to soften. Make a custard by scalding the milk with the cinnamon stick and whole cloves, then stirring in the sugar, and pouring it over the eggs, stirring continuously. Strain the custard into a clean saucepan, and cook it very gently, without letting it boil, until it thickens enough to coat the back of a wooden spoon. Put it to one side to cool.

Mix the pumpkin with the ground spices, then stir in the gelatine which should be completely dissolved (apply more heat, if necessary). Whip the cream. Fold the cooled custard into the pumpkin mixture, and then fold in the whipped cream. Oil a 6 in / 15 cm wide greaseproof paper strip, and tie it round a 2 pt / 1.15 l soufflé dish. Spoon in the mixture, and refrigerate until set. Carefully remove the paper collar. Decorate the soufflé, if you wish, with toasted chopped nuts or crystallized fruit.

Variation ∾ For an even lighter mixture, keep back 2 egg whites from the custard, whisk them, and fold in after the cream.

HOT SOUFFLÉS

Basic Sweet Soufflé

Serves 6–8

Fresh fruit purées are amongst the best to serve with sweet soufflés. Lemon or lime marmalade, heated with or without rum or whisky, makes a good sauce for a citrus fruit soufflé. Melted chocolate, dark or white, is excellent with a plain sweet vanilla soufflé. I am less keen on the sabayons, which are light custard sauces flavoured with wine or spirits. These rather over-egg, in my view, this rich dish.

1 pt / 570 ml milk
1 oz / 30 g butter
6 eggs, separated, plus 2 extra egg
  yolks

5 oz / 140 g caster sugar plain
3 oz / 85 g plain flour, sifted

Generously butter a 2 pt / 1.15 l soufflé dish or individual soufflé dishes, dust the inside with sugar and refrigerate until needed. Put three-quarters of the milk and the butter in a saucepan, and bring to the boil. Whisk the egg yolks and sugar together for a minute or two. Mix the flour and remaining milk to a paste, and whisk it into the egg yolks until well mixed. Stir this mixture into the boiling milk and butter, over a low heat, whisking all the time until the mixture thickens but does not curdle. Remove from the heat, fold in the egg whites, whisked to stiff peaks, and spoon into the prepared soufflé dish or dishes. Place in a roasting tin containing enough water to come about a third of the way up the sides of the dish or dishes, and bake in a preheated oven at 190°C / 375° F / Mark 5 for 30 minutes.

Variations ∾ To make a lemon soufflé, which is probably my favourite, grate the zest of two lemons, and squeeze the juice of one lemon into the mixture just before adding the beaten egg whites, and reduce the quantity of milk by the same volume as the lemon juice.

For a chocolate soufflé, coarsely grated or chopped chocolate can be added just before folding in the beaten egg whites.

Grated apple with Calvados, thinly sliced pears with *eau de vie de poire*, and dried or bottled cherries with kirsch can all be added, again just before the beaten egg whites, to make delicious fruit-flavoured soufflés. Again adjust the quantity of milk used to allow for any extra liquid added.

Try stirring in crushed amaretti or ratafia biscuits, moistened with the almond liqueur, Amaretto di Saronno, just before the egg whites.

Banana and White Chocolate Soufflé

Serves 4–6

2 oz / 60 g unsalted butter
2 oz / 60 g plain flour
½ pt / 280 ml full-cream milk
1–2 ripe bananas
2 tbsp caster sugar

2 egg yolks
4 egg whites
3–4 oz / 85–110 g white chocolate,
   broken into pieces

Butter a 1½ pt / 850 ml soufflé dish, and dust the inside with sugar. Make a thick white sauce with the butter, flour and milk. While it is cooking, peel the bananas and blend or mash thoroughly with the sugar. Stir into the cooked white sauce. Let the mixture cool slightly before beating in the egg yolks. Whisk the egg whites until stiff, and carefully fold into the banana base. Spoon half the mixture into the prepared soufflé dish, and lay the pieces of chocolate on the top. Spoon on the rest of the mixture, and put the soufflé dish in a roasting tin containing enough water to come about a third of the way up the side of the dish. Bake in a preheated oven at 180° C / 350° F / Mark 4 for about 30 minutes.

Papos d'Anjo (Angel Throats)

Makes 20-24

*This is a typical Portuguese dish, much easier to make than it might
seem, rich and eggy, and first cooked for me by my friend Teresa Grilo.*

8 oz / 230 g caster sugar
¼ pt / 140 ml water
½ vanilla pod

4 egg yolks
1 egg white

Butter and flour two bun tins. Dissolve the sugar in the water and cook it over a low heat with the vanilla pod. Meanwhile, beat the egg yolks until they are foamy and pale. Whisk the egg white until firm, and fold carefully into the egg yolks. Spoon the mixture into the bun tins – a scant tablespoon of the mixture in each should fill all 24 holes. Cook in the top of a preheated oven at 220° C / 425° F / Mark 7 for about 5 minutes or until just set. Remove the little soufflés from the tins, and allow to cool slightly on wire racks. Dip them, with two forks, into the hot syrup, and arrange them in a shallow glass or china dish. Pour the rest of the syrup over them, discarding the vanilla, cool and chill until required.

Pineapple and Rum Soufflés

Serves 4–6

8 oz / 230 g peeled fresh pineapple
2 tbsp water
1 oz / 30 g butter
1 oz / 30 g plain flour
¼ pt / 140 ml skimmed milk
1 tbsp caster sugar
3 eggs, separated
icing sugar for dusting

Sauce
3 tbsp orange juice
1 tbsp caster sugar
1 tsp cornflour
1–2 tbsp water
3 tbsp rum

Generously butter individual soufflé dishes and dust the insides with sugar. Refrigerate until needed. Dice a third of the pineapple, and put to one side. Chop the rest, and put in a blender with the water. Blend for a few seconds, and then pour through a sieve over a bowl. Press out as much juice as possible, and then put the pulp from the sieve with the diced pineapple. Melt the butter in a saucepan, and stir in the flour. Cook the roux for a few minutes, then blend in equal parts of pineapple juice (using no more than half) and skimmed milk until you have a smooth sauce. Cook for a few minutes until it thickens. Remove from the heat, and stir in the sugar, the diced and pulped pineapple and the egg yolks. Mix thoroughly. Whisk the egg whites to firm peaks, and fold in carefully. Spoon the mixture into the prepared soufflé dishes, and place them in a roasting tin containing enough water to come a third of the way up the sides of the dishes. Bake in a preheated oven at 200° C / 400° F / Mark 6 for 12–15 minutes. Meanwhile, make the sauce. Put the orange juice and sugar in a saucepan. Blend the cornflour with the water and add to the saucepan with the remaining pineapple juice. Bring to the boil, and cook for a few minutes until thickened slightly. Stir in the rum just before serving the soufflés. Dust the soufflés with icing sugar, and, as you serve each one, break open the top with a spoon and pour in a little sauce which will cause the soufflé to rise in its dish.

ICES

To Make an Ice Bowl

The ice bowl is a most effective way of keeping ice cream in good condition while serving it, and looks stunning on a bed of flowers or leaves. I have come across the idea before, but suspect that Myrtle Allen of Ballymaloe in Ireland originated it. Here is her method of making it, as described in *The Ballymaloe Cookbook*. She points out that for domestic purposes, it can be used two or three times if carefully wiped out with a damp cloth each time and then refrozen.

Take two bowls, one about double the capacity of the other. Do not use aluminium. Half-fill the big bowl with cold water. Float the second bowl inside the first. Weight it down with water or ice cubes until the rims are level. Adjust so that the smaller bowl stays in a central position by sticking pieces of flour and water paste on to its rim to widen it enough to hold it in place. The water should come within ½ in / 1 cm of the top.

An alternative method is to float the smaller bowl so that its rim is ½ in / 1 cm above the rim of the big bowl. Place a square of fabric over the top and tie it on with string under the rim of the lower bowl, as one would tie on a jam pot cover. Adjust the small bowl to a central position. The cloth holds it in place.

Put the bowls in the freezer, if necessary adjusting the position of the small bowl as you put them in. Leave for 24 hours.

To turn out the ice bowl, remove the cloth or wedges. Twist and shake the ice bowl free, and turn it out carefully. If disaster looms and the ice bowl splits, press it together firmly, and put it back in the big bowl to refreeze for about 15 minutes.

The ice melts at the base where it touches the serving dish so that a thick bottomed bowl is best. Serve, with the ice cream in it, on a folded serviette, to absorb moisture.

Vanilla Ice Cream

Serves 8

1 pt / 570 ml full-cream milk
1 vanilla pod, split
4 tbsp caster sugar

4 egg yolks
½ pt / 280 ml double cream

Put the milk and vanilla pod in a saucepan, and bring to the boil. Remove from the heat. Beat the sugar and egg yolks together, and pour on the scalded milk, stirring continuously. Strain the mixture into a clean saucepan, scrape in the vanilla seeds from the pod, and stir over a low heat until the custard thickens enough to coat the back of a wooden spoon. Remove from the heat, and allow to cool. Whip the cream, and fold into the cold custard. Pour into an ice-cream maker, and freeze according to the manufacturer's instructions. Or pour into a container, and freeze in a freezer or the freezing compartment of a refrigerator, in which case you will need to remove it after about an hour and beat it or blend it in a food processor until smooth and light, and then return it to the freezer for its final freezing.

Variations ∾ For a delicious cardamom and rosewater ice cream, replace the vanilla pod with the seeds from 8 cardamom pods, and after scalding these with the milk, leave to stand for 45 minutes. Use only two egg yolks, and stir 2–3 tablespoons of rosewater into the cooled custard just before folding in the whipped cream.

For lavender ice cream, first grind the sugar in a coffee grinder or with a pestle and mortar with ½ oz / 15 g fresh lavender buds, and scald this mixture in the milk. Beat the egg yolks on their own, and pour on the scalded lavender-flavoured milk, stirring continuously. Then continue as above.

The rich, dark, syrupy Pedro Ximenez wine, or PX as it is commonly known, is often used to sweeten the naturally dry amontillados and oloroso sherries for the northern European market. It is also a marvellous ingredient for the cook, and I use it to make a wonderful ice cream, which knocks rum and raisin ice cream into a cocked hat. Soak about 4 oz / 110 g raisins in about ¼ pt / 140 ml Pedro Ximenez wine for several hours, then stir this into the vanilla ice cream mixture, and freeze in the usual way.

Quick Banana and Cardamom Ice Cream

Serves 8

6 ripe bananas
juice of 1 lemon
¼ pt / 140 ml sugar syrup *or* 5 oz /
   140 g icing sugar, sifted

seeds of 10 cardamom pods
½ pt / 280 ml double cream
¼ pt / 140 ml single cream

Peel the bananas, and put in a blender with the rest of the ingredients. Blend until smooth, pour into an ice-cream maker, and freeze according to the manufacturer's instructions. Or pour into a container, and freeze in a freezer or the freezing compartment of a refrigerator, in which case you will need to remove it after about an hour, and beat it or blend it in a food processor until smooth and light, and then return it to the freezer for its final freezing.

Variations ❧ For a quickly made peach ice cream, use 1 lb / 455 g peaches, peeled and sliced, instead of the banana, and orange or apple juice instead of the lemon juice, and omit the cardamom.

Replace the banana with 1 lb / 455 g cooked blackberries or blueberries or other available berries, and omit the lemon juice and cardamom.

For a quick marmalade ice cream, gently heat about 1 lb / 455 g marmalade until runny, strain it into a bowl, stir in the creams until well blended, and then freeze as above.

You can make quick ice creams using scented flower petals and buds. Scented petals from carnations or clove pinks, that have not been sprayed, petals from old-fashioned roses, and lavender buds can all be used. Make a syrup using water and sugar, stir in the petals or buds, bring back to the boil, and leave to steep overnight. The next day, strain the syrup, add lemon juice, blend with double cream, and freeze as above.

Banana and Rum Tofu Ice Cream

Serves 4–6

If you like to eat puddings every day, it makes sense to look for low-fat and low-calorie alternatives to butter, cream and sugar. On balance, I prefer to eat puddings just occasionally and use the traditional ingredients rather than the 'ersatz'. Silken tofu is one of those derivatives of the useful soya bean. It is a pale, creamy substance with little flavour of its own and a texture like that of cream, but with only 2.6 per cent fat as against the 48 per cent of double cream.

4 ripe bananas
2 tbsp rum
2 tbsp honey (or more to taste)
juice of ½ lemon or 1 orange

1 packet silken tofu
pinch of ground cinnamon or grated
 nutmeg

Peel the bananas and put them in a blender with the rest of the ingredients. Blend until smooth, and then pour into an ice-cream maker, and freeze according to the manufacturer's instructions. Or pour into a container and freeze in a freezer or the freezing compartment of a refrigerator, in which case you will need to remove it after about an hour and beat it or blend it in a food processor until smooth and light, and then return it to the freezer for its final freezing.

Iced Terrine of Summer Fruits and Cheese

Serves 6–8

8 oz / 230 g cottage cheese
8 oz / 230 g ricotta
8 oz / 230 g fromage frais
icing sugar, to taste
few drops of pure vanilla essence

4 oz / 110 g raspberries
8 oz / 230 g strawberries
4 oz / 110 g blueberries (*optional*)
frosted mint leaves and redcurrants, to
 decorate

Put the cheeses in a blender, and blend until smooth. Sweeten to taste, and blend in the vanilla essence. Transfer to a bowl. Hull and pick over the fruit. Fold it into the cheese mixture, and pack it into a loaf tin lined with cling film. Cover and freeze until firm. Turn out and slice. Frosted mint leaves and redcurrants decorate this nicely, and a raspberry sauce made by blending and sieving raspberries, and sweetening, if necessary, makes a pleasant accompaniment.

Apple Sorbets

Tropical fruit sorbets are fashionable, but one can tire of their insistent flavours and vivid colours. For the very best sorbets, apples are hard to beat. In their infinite variety they provide a whole palette of colours, textures and aromas, as well as sorbets for every season. Even if you cannot find the apples to serve a Cornish Aromatic sorbet, a D'Arcy Spice sorbet, a Melcombe Russet or a Green Balsam, consider the perfumed sweetness of a Worceser Pearmain sorbet, or the dry nuttiness of an Egremont Russet. A Granny Smith makes a marvellously tart, mouth-tingling sorbet, and a really ripe flushed Golden Delicious, a mouthful of sweetness.

To prepare apples for a sorbet, quarter and core them, and then roughly chop, and put in a food processor or blender with a couple of tablespoons of water and a teaspoon or two of lemon juice to stop discolouring. I like to keep a little of the peel on for the flecked effect it gives. Blend to a purée, and then mix with the syrup as described below. I find it worthwhile keeping a bottle of syrup on hand for making sorbets.

To make the syrup, stir 2 ½ lb / 1.10 kg sugar in 1 pt / 570 ml water over a low heat, bring to the boil, and boil for 1 minute. Cool, bottle, and refrigerate.

To make sorbet, mix some syrup with an equal quantity of water, and add fruit pulp in equal volume to the liquid used. Stir in the juice of half a lemon. Blend thoroughly, pour into an ice-cream maker or sorbetière, and freeze according to the manufacturer's instructions. The mixture can also be frozen in a container in the freezer or ice-making compartment of a refrigerator. As the mixture freezes and crystals form, it will need to be stirred from time to time. To ensure a smooth sorbet, it is quite a good plan to give it its final stir in a food processor before putting it back in the freezer. Sorbets are best eaten within a few hours of being made.

I prefer to use raw apples, but interesting variations can be created with different apples cooked to a purée and then flavoured with cinnamon, cloves or cardamom. For another version, simply freeze cider into a sorbet.

If you have picked lots of apples or pears, it is worth freezing them for making instant sorbets. Peel, core and quarter the fruit, brush with lemon juice to stop it discolouring, and open-freeze it on a tray before putting into labelled bags. To make an instant sorbet, put the fruit pieces in a food processor with a little cold water (about 4 tablespoons per 1 lb / 455 g of fruit) and the sugar syrup to taste. Switch on and process until smooth. Pile into glasses and serve immediately.

Orange Sorbet

Serves 6

juice of ½ lemon

1 pt / 570 ml freshly squeezed
orange juice

icing sugar, to taste (see note below)

Campari (*optional*)

Mix all the ingredients together, stirring until the icing sugar has dissolved. Freeze in a sorbetière or ice-cream maker, according to the manufacturer's instructions. The mixture can also be frozen in a container in a freezer or the ice-making compartment of a refrigerator, in which case you will need to remove the mixture and beat it from time to time to ensure a smooth sorbet. It is preferable to give the final stirring in a food processor or blender, before returning to the freezer. Add a little Campari to this sorbet if you wish (see note on alcohol below). *Note:* Too much sugar will prevent the sorbet from freezing well, and too little will give it a grainy texture, like that of a granita. A proportion of one part sugar to two parts other ingredients is about right. However, different fruits and fruit juices contain different amounts of sugar. For example, just over 10 per cent of freshly squeezed orange juice is sugar. The mathematicians amongst you will be able to work out proportions for your own specific recipes.

Alcohol can be excellent in some sorbets but too much can also inhibit freezing, so be careful.

Variations ∾ For a lemon sorbet, replace the orange juice with about one-third lemon juice to two-thirds spring water. You can also add the flavour of lemon thyme to this. In that case, first pound a teaspoon of fresh lemon thyme leaves in a mortar with a little of the sugar, then stir in the freshly squeezed lemon juice before mixing with the water and the rest of the sugar and freezing. A grapefruit and mint sorbet can be made in a similar fashion, using fresh mint leaves instead of the lemon thyme, and grapefruit instead of the lemon juice. A little vodka or gin is very good in a lemon or grapefruit sorbet (see note on alcohol above).

For mango sorbet, blend the flesh of 3 ripe mangos with enough apple juice to make up to 1 pt / 570 ml, then stir in the icing sugar until dissolved, and freeze as above.

For banana sorbet, first prepare 1 pt / 570 ml sugar syrup, then blend in 3 chopped, ripe bananas, a little lime juice and, if you like, a little rum (see note on alcohol above).

To make a berry sorbet, for example with strawberries, raspberries, red or blackcurrants or cranberries, cover about 1 lb / 455 g picked-over fruit with water, simmer until soft, sweeten to taste, purée, sieve and cool. Stir in a little lemon juice, adjust the sweetness, if necessary, and freeze as above.

The fruit for a pineapple sorbet also needs to be cooked first. Roughly chop the flesh of a large pineapple, purée it in a blender or food processor with a little water, strain to collect as much juice as possible, and cook the pulp with about ½ pt / 280 ml water and 8 oz / 230 g sugar for about 5 minutes. Sieve to extract more juice, and discard the pulp. Mix together all the juice you have collected, make up to 1 pt / 570 ml with water if necessary, add a little lemon or lime juice, a splash of rum if desired (see note on alcohol above), and freeze as above.

Apricot and rhubarb sorbets use cooked fruit and a little gelatine. Cook 1 lb / 455 g halved, stoned apricots or chunks of rhubarb in 1 pt / 570 ml water or apple juice until soft. Soften 2 leaves gelatine or 2 teaspoons powdered gelatine in a little more water or apple juice, and stir this together with sugar to taste into the cooked fruit. Blend or process to a purée, and then freeze as above.

For a delicious fromage blanc sorbet, stir fromage blanc into a sugar syrup, add a little lemon juice and freeze as above.

Surprise Caprice

I found this recipe for deep-fried ice cream, faded and handwritten on a piece of paper that fluttered out of L'Art Culinaire Français, *when a friend gave it to me as a present. We could not trace the recipe to the Caprice restaurant in London but research by Robin Weir and Caroline Liddell for their book,* Ices, *traces deep-fried ice cream to the World's Fair in Chicago in 1893.*

2 egg yolks
2 oz / 60 g caster sugar
4 tbsp Marsala or other sweet wine
1 lb / 455 g block vanilla dairy ice cream
3 oz / 85 g cake crumbs
3 oz / 85 g ground almonds
icing sugar for dusting

Batter
4 oz / 110 g plain flour
pinch of salt
1 tbsp caster sugar
1 tbsp groundnut (peanut) or almond oil
¼ pt / 140 ml water
1 egg white
groundnut (peanut) oil for deep-frying

Beat together the egg yolks, sugar and wine. Slice the ice cream, and dip the slices into the egg mixture before coating them in a mixture of the cake crumbs and ground almonds. Freeze the slices very hard.

To make the batter, sift the dry ingredients into a bowl, and stir in the oil and water, beating until the batter is smooth. Allow it to stand for 1 hour. Whisk the egg white to firm peaks, and carefully fold into the batter.

Heat the oil to 190° C / 375° F. Dip the ice cream slices into the batter, allowing any excess to drip back. Deep-fry for approximately 30 seconds. Drain and serve immediately, dusted with icing sugar.

Mandarins with Pomegranate Granita

Serves 4–6

A granita has a coarser texture than a sorbet. The mixture should not be allowed to freeze too hard; it should have a soft, grainy texture when served. Granitas can be made by simply pouring fruit or vegetable juice into a shallow container, and freezing it, stirring from time to time so that the mixture freezes evenly. Vegetable granitas make unusual starters, garnished with a few fresh herbs. This pomegranate granita is a perfect match for the chocolate-coated mandarins.

2–3 pomegranates
¼ pt / 140 ml sugar syrup (see page 539)

8 mandarins
2 oz / 60 g good-quality plain chocolate

Halve the pomegranates, and extract the juice on a lemon squeezer. Mix this with the syrup, and freeze to a granita texture in an ice-cream maker or sorbetière, following the manufacturer's instructions, or pour into a container and freeze in a freezer or the ice-making compartment of a refrigerator, stirring the sides of the granita into the middle from time to time to ensure even freezing.

Squeeze two of the mandarins, and put the juice to one side. Peel the remaining fruit, break up into segments, and remove all the pith. Put half the segments in a bowl with the juice, and put the rest on one side. Melt the chocolate in a bowl over a pan of hot water, remove from the heat, and with the help of a couple of small forks or skewers, dip the segments of mandarin not in juice, one by one, into the chocolate, and put on one side on wax paper to harden.

To assemble the dessert, spoon the mandarin juice into shallow serving bowls, and arrange the segments of fruit in them in a petal fashion, alternating chocolate and non-chocolate segments. Pile some granita in the middle, and serve.

Variation ∽ Replace the pomegranate granita with a rosé champagne granita. Make this by stirring 3 tablespoons of sifted icing sugar into ¾ pt / 430 ml rosé champagne, and freezing the mixture as above.

Cassolette de Cerises Tièdes, Glace Amande

*This recipe is a complicated one to assemble. The cherries are stoned
and in place of the stalk is a small 'cigarette' roll of crisp biscuit. It is a
very good pudding but have someone give you a hand at the end,
sticking the rolls in the cherries. Alternatively, leave the biscuits
unrolled and serve them on a plate to accompany the cherries and ice
cream. It is based on a dish served at the Hôtel du Palais in Biarritz in
the early summer.*

Almond Ice Cream
½ pt / 280 ml milk
½ pt / 280 ml single cream
4 oz / 110 g almond paste, softened
8 egg yolks
3 oz / 85 g caster sugar
½ oz / 15 g glucose (*optional*)

Biscuits
generous 4 oz / 125 g unsalted
   butter, softened

6½ oz / 185 g icing sugar
generous 4 oz / 125 g plain flour, sifted
5–6 egg whites
pure vanilla essence

Cherries
7 fl oz / 200 ml water
7 oz / 200 g sugar
7 oz / 200 g unsalted butter
2 lb / 900 g stoned cherries
1–2 tbsp kirsch

Heat the milk, cream and almond paste in a saucepan. In a bowl, beat together
the egg yolks, sugar and glucose, if using. When warm, add a quarter of the cream
mixture to the egg mixture, and thoroughly incorporate. When the cream mixture
boils, pour it over the egg mixture, beating continuously.

Sieve the mixture into a clean saucepan, and cook gently until it will coat the
back of a wooden spoon. Cool, then freeze in an ice-cream maker or in a box in the
freezer. An ice-cream maker will turn the mixture and make it smooth. You will
need to stir the mixture by hand or in a food processor during the freezing process
for a really smooth ice cream, if you freeze the mixture in a container.

To make the biscuits, lightly cream together the butter and sugar, and then add
the rest of the ingredients, mixing to a paste. Rest the mixture in the refrigerator
for 15–20 minutes. Spread the mixture as thin as possible in 1½ in / 4 cm circles on
a buttered baking sheet. Bake in a preheated oven at 180° C / 350 ° F / Mark 4 for
8–10 minutes. As soon as you remove the sheet from the oven, roll up each small
biscuit while still warm.

For the cherries, put the water, sugar and butter in a clean, non-stick frying pan. Heat gently until the sugar has dissolved, and then cook the mixture until syrupy. Add the cherries and poach for 5 minutes, stirring in the kirsch right at the end. Pour the cherry syrup into shallow soup plates or dishes together with a portion of cherries. Place a biscuit 'cigarette' or roll in each cherry cavity, and serve with a scoop of almond ice cream on top.

Baked Ice Cream Cake with Blazing Fruit

Serves 6

1 lb / 455 g vanilla ice cream (see
   page 536)

Cake
2 heaped tbsp caster sugar
2 egg yolks
2 egg whites
2 heaped tbsp self-raising flour,
   sifted

Fruit
12 oz / 340 g stoned cherries or
   blueberries
1 oz / 30 g caster sugar, or to taste
4 tbsp kirsch or white rum

Meringue
3 egg whites
3 tbsp caster sugar

Scoop the ice cream into balls or quenelles, place on a tray and open-freeze very hard. To make the cake, beat the sugar and egg yolks together until pale and foamy. Whisk the egg whites to firm peaks. Stir the sifted flour into the egg and sugar mixture, and then fold in the egg whites. Spoon the batter into a greased and floured shallow 8 inch sponge tin, and bake in a preheated oven at 180° C / 350° F / Mark 4 for 12 minutes. Allow to cool slightly in the tin before turning out on to a wire rack to cool.

Heat the fruit and sugar with a little water until tender. Stir in 2 tablespoons of spirit, and put to one side. For the meringue, whisk the egg whites until firm but not granular. Stir in the sugar, and whisk until you have firm, glossy peaks.

Place a small ramekin in the centre of the cake on an ovenproof serving platter. Arrange the frozen balls of ice cream around it, and spread the meringue all over, sealing in the ice cream. Bake in the top half of a preheated oven at 200° C / 400° F / Mark 6 for 3–4 minutes, until the meringue is just golden. Remove from the oven. Spoon some of the warm fruit into the ramekin and, just before you are about to serve them, pour on the remaining kirsch or rum and light it. Hand the rest of the fruit around separately.

PIES, TARTS AND PANCAKES

Basic Sweet Pastry

Lines a 9 in / 23 cm tart tin or makes 24 2½ in / 6.5 cm diameter tartlets

3½ oz / 100 g butter, softened	7 oz / 200 g plain flour, sifted
2 oz / 60 g caster sugar	pinch of salt
1 egg	

Cream the butter and sugar together until light. Slowly add the egg and then the flour and salt. Lightly work the mixture together until it binds to a dough. Cover and refrigerate for at least 1 hour before use.

To make a tart to serve six, roll out the pastry to about ⅛ in / 0.2 cm thick, and use it to line a greased 9 in / 23 cm tart tin (or to make individual tartlets, line twenty-four 2½ in / 6.5 cm tartlet tins). Prick the pastry all over. Cover with greaseproof paper, and weight it down with a handful of dried or baking beans. Bake in a preheated oven at 200°C / 400° F / Mark 6 for 8–10 minutes. This is called 'baking blind'. Remove the greaseproof paper and the beans. The pastry case is now ready for you to add one of the fillings given below (or one of your own). When you have filled the tart case, bake in a preheated oven at 180° C / 350° F / Mark 4 for about 30 minutes (15–20 minutes for individual tartlets) until the filling has set and the top is lightly browned.

Lemon Tart

Peel 3 large, thin-skinned lemons, removing as much pith as possible. Slice them thinly, and remove the pips. Cover with 6 oz / 170 g sugar, and leave overnight. When ready to make the tart, drain the lemony syrup into a bowl, and beat in 4 eggs. Arrange the lemon slices in the prepared pastry case, pour on the egg mixture, and bake as above.

Coconut Tart

Beat 4 eggs with 1 oz / 30 g cornflour and 5 oz / 140 g caster sugar, and then stir in ¼ pt / 140 ml single cream and 5 oz / 140 g desiccated coconut. Mix well, pour into the prepared pastry case, and bake as above.

Banana Tart

Peel and slice 6 bananas, and soak them in a little lemon juice and 3 tablespoons of rum for 1 hour. Mix 4 eggs with 7 oz / 200 g sifted icing sugar, and stir in 7 oz / 200 g ground almonds. Arrange the drained banana slices in the prepared pastry case, mix any remaining rum and lemon juice mixture with the egg mixture, and pour this over the bananas. Scatter flaked almonds over, and bake as above.

Date Tart

Beat 4 eggs with 4 oz / 110 g light muscovado sugar and ¼ pt / 140 ml single cream, and then stir in 3 oz / 85 g ground almonds. Stone and halve 8 oz / 230 g dates, and arrange in the prepared pastry case. Pour the egg mixture over, and bake as above.

Apple or Greengage and Almond Tart

Mix 3 oz / 85 g ground almonds with 2 oz / 60 g caster sugar, and spread this mixture over the bottom of the prepared pastry case. Peel and thinly slice 1 lb / 455 g apples or halve and stone 1 lb / 455 g greengages, and arrange on top of the almond mixture. Beat 2 eggs with ½ pt / 280 ml full-cream milk and a little sugar to taste, and pour over the fruit. Bake as above.

Nut Tart

Beat 3 eggs with 2 oz / 60 g light muscovado sugar, 4 oz / 110 g melted butter and 4 tablespoons of golden syrup. When thoroughly mixed, beat in the juice and grated zest of 1 lemon. Arrange shelled nuts in the prepared pastry case, and pour over the egg mixture. Bake as above, but about 10 minutes before the tart is ready, remove from the oven, and quickly place a few more shelled nuts on top of the tart, and then continue baking.

Cheese and Fruit Tart

Mix 8 oz / 230 g grated apple with 2 oz / 60 g butter, melted, 1 oz / 30 g sugar and a little ground cinnamon. Smear a little mincemeat over the base of the prepared pastry case, spread about 4 oz / 110 g cream cheese on top, and finally spoon in the apple mixture. Dot with butter, and bake as above.

Brie and Saffron Tart

Soak a few saffron threads for 20 minutes in a little hot water. Mix 4 oz / 110 g curd cheese with 4 oz / 110 g brie with the rind removed. Melt 3 tablespoons of honey in the same amount of hot water. Mix this honey liquid with the cheese, then stir in the saffron liquid, and beat in 2 eggs. Pour the mixture into the prepared pastry case, and bake as above.

Apricot Bread and Butter Tarts

Makes 12

12 slices of bread
3 oz / 85 g butter, softened
2 tbsp light muscovado sugar

4 oz / 110 g thick Greek yoghurt or
    double cream
12 apricots, poached, cut in half and
    stoned

With a pastry cutter, cut out rounds of bread to fit individual tart tins. Grease the tins with half the softened butter, and spread the rest of the butter on the bread, one side only. Roll the edges of the bread in the sugar and fit them gently into the tart tins, butter side up, taking care that they don't break. Place a small piece of greaseproof paper in the base of each tart and a few dried beans on top. Bake the bread and butter tarts in the centre of a preheated oven at 200° C / 400° F / Mark 6 for 10 minutes, until crisp and golden brown. When cooked, remove from the oven and remove the paper and beans. Spoon yoghurt or double cream into each tart and lay the apricot halves on top. Serve hot or warm.

Green Tomato and Apple Pie

Serves 6

*This recipe is a good one for using up the end-of-season tomatoes that
never ripen.*

12 oz / 340 g shortcrust or flaky
  pastry
2 oz / 60 g unsalted butter,
  softened
2 oz / 60 g light muscovado sugar
pinch each of ground cinnamon,
  cloves, mace and allspice

½ grated zest of lemon
1 lb / 455 g green tomatoes, thinly sliced
1 lb / 455 g windfall or cooking apples,
  peeled, cored and sliced
milk and sugar, to glaze
2 tbsp Calvados or Cognac

Line a 9 in / 23 cm pie plate with half the pastry. Mix the butter, sugar, spices
and lemon zest together. Layer the tomatoes and apples in the pie dish, dotting
each layer with some of the creamed butter and sugar. Roll out the remaining
pastry, and cover the pie, sealing the edges well, and leaving a small hole in the pie
crust. Brush with milk, and sprinkle with sugar. Bake in a preheated oven at
220° C / 450° F / Mark 7 for 10 minutes. Remove the pie from the oven, and pour
in the spirit through the small hole left in the crust. Return the pie to the oven, and
continue baking for 30–35 minutes with the heat turned down to 180° C / 350° F /
Mark 4.

Variation ⤳ A rosehip and raspberry filling is also delicious. To make this, slit
8 oz / 230 g rosehips, and remove the seeds. Rinse, drain and simmer the rosehips
in a little water until tender. Drain and allow to cool, and then mix with 8 oz /
230 g fresh raspberries and 2–3 oz / 60–85 g sugar, according to taste. Stir in a
little lemon juice, a tablespoon of cornflour and a few gratings of nutmeg. When
the pie is removed from the oven, after the first 10 minutes of baking, pour ¼ pt /
140ml cream beaten with 3 egg yolks into the small hole left in the pie crust.

Ida Marverti's Lemon Pie

Serves 6

Pastry
6 oz / 170 g plain flour
pinch of baking powder
3 oz / 85 g unsalted butter,
    softened and cut up
1 oz / 30 g vanilla sugar
1½ oz / 40 g caster sugar
2 egg yolks

Lemon Cream
2 egg yolks
2 tbsp caster sugar
2 tbsp plain flour, sifted
7 fl oz / 200 ml full-cream milk
grated zest of 2 lemons

Heap the flour and baking powder on a worktop, and make a well in the middle. Put the pieces of butter in the well with the sugars and egg yolks. Draw in the flour with your fingertips, and work the ingredients together quickly to form a dough. Add more flour only if necessary. Cover the pastry, and let it stand while you make the filling. Cream the egg yolks and sugar together until pale and foamy. Thoroughly mix in the flour, and blend in the milk. Add the lemon zest.

Roll out two-thirds of the pastry and use to line an 8 in / 20.5 cm flan ring, leaving enough around the edges to overlap the lid. Pour in the lemon cream. Roll out a lid, and cover the pie, overlapping a neat edging of pastry. Seal on the lid with water. Prick the top to let the steam escape, and bake in the middle of a preheated oven at 180° C / 350° F / Mark 4, moving to a lower shelf after 20 minutes or so if the pie shows signs of browning too much.

Variation ∾ To make a lemon meringue pie, make the lemon filling with water rather than milk, stir in a little lemon juice as well as the zest and a little melted butter. Beat together thoroughly, and stir over a low heat until the mixture thickens. Remove, and allow to cool before pouring into the pastry case. Beat 3 egg whites until they begin to firm up, then fold in 2 tablespoons of caster sugar. Continue whisking until firm again, and then fold in another tablespoon of sugar. Whisk until this meringue is stiff and glossy, then spoon it over the lemon filling, heaping it up in the centre. Bake for 20–30 minutes until the meringue is golden brown. Serve warm.

Filo Pastry Apple Tarts

Serves 4

4 dessert apples, peeled, cored and
 diced
½ tsp ground cinnamon
4 cloves
seeds from 4 cardamom pods
brown sugar, to taste

3 oz / 85 g unsalted butter
3 oz / 85 g raisins, currants or sultanas
3 sheets filo pastry
2 tbsp apricot jam
1 tbsp water
1 oz / 30 g flaked almonds

Cook the apples gently for 5–8 minutes with the spices, a little sugar, half the butter and the dried fruit. Cut the sheets of pastry into four quarters, and trim each to a square. Laying the squares, one on top of the other, and brushing each with melted butter before you use it, line each of four small buttered ramekins with three sheets of filo pastry, each one placed on top of the other at a slight angle so that the twelve points show separately. Spoon the fruit into the pastry-lined ramekins, stand them on a baking sheet, and bake in the centre of a preheated oven at 180° C / 350° F / Mark 4 for 10–12 minutes. When just cool enough to handle, ease the pastries out of the ramekins, and transfer to small serving plates. Heat the apricot jam and water together, and spoon this glaze over the apple. Scatter hot toasted almonds on top, and serve immediately, with or without cream.

Tarte aux Poires

Serves 4–6

Pastry
4 oz / 110 g unsalted butter
6–7 oz / 170–200 g plain flour,
   sifted
pinch of salt
1 oz / 30 g caster sugar
1 egg yolk mixed with 3 tbsp cold
   water
1 egg white, lightly beaten

Filling
1 pt / 570 ml sweet white wine, such as
   Montbazillac or St Croix du Mont
half the juice and the finely grated zest
   of 1 lemon
blade of mace
1 bay leaf
6 firm ripe pears
3–4 tbsp apple or redcurrant jelly, or
   strained apricot jam

To make the pastry, rub the butter into the flour, salt and sugar until it resembles fine breadcrumbs, using your hands or a food processor. Make a well in the centre, pour in the egg yolk and water, and mix together with a knife until you have a ball of pastry. Wrap the pastry in greaseproof paper, and refrigerate for 20–30 minutes to firm it up.

When ready to bake, roll out the pastry and use to line a 10 in / 25.5 cm flan ring. Brush the base with lightly beaten egg white. Prick the base with a fork, and firm up again in the refrigerator. Preheat the oven to 190° C / 375° F / Mark 5, and bake for 18–20 minutes, until the pastry is cooked to a pale golden colour and just shrinking away from the flan ring. Turn the pastry case out of the flan ring, and leave to cool on a wire rack. While the pastry is cooking, and then cooling, prepare the filling.

Put the wine in a saucepan with the lemon zest, lemon juice, mace and bay leaf. Bring to the boil, and simmer for 5 minutes. Peel, halve and core the pears, and poach in the wine until just tender. Remove the pears, drain, and put to one side. Boil down the liquid until it has the consistency of a syrupy glaze. Allow to cool. Brush the inside of the pastry case with the jelly or strained jam. Slice the pears, and arrange in the flan. Brush over with the glaze.

Muscat Grape Tart with Melted Butter Pastry

Serves 4

This is a very simple recipe which breaks all the rules about having a chilled work surface and cool hands to make pastry, and was given to me by Sheila Clark, a gifted, inventive cook who lives in Kent. If you choose large, ripe grapes, then it is not too much of a chore to peel and deseed them.

3 oz / 85 g butter	7 oz / 200 g thick Greek yoghurt *or*
2 oz / 60 g sugar	6 tbsp whipped cream
grated zest of ½ lemon	1 lb / 455 g peeled, deseeded muscat
6 oz / 170 g plain flour	grapes

Melt the butter gently in a saucepan. Add the sugar and let it melt and amalgamate but not cook. Remove from the heat, and stir in the lemon zest, then begin to work in the flour. The mixture will eventually become a stiff dough. Press it with your fingers or the back of a wooden spoon into a buttered baking dish, flan tin or 9 inch / 23 cm flan ring on a baking sheet. Prick all over, and bake in a preheated oven at 200° C / 400° F / Mark 6 for 12–15 minutes, moving it to a lower shelf in your oven if it shows signs of burning.

When the base is cool and you are almost ready to serve the tart, spread the yoghurt or cream on the pastry and cover with the grapes. This is delicious served with a glass of chilled sweet muscat wine.

Tarte au Chocolat Barbara

Pastry
6 oz / 170 g plain flour
1½ oz / 40 g cocoa powder
4 oz / 110 g unsalted butter
2 oz / 60 g caster sugar
1 egg yolk, lightly beaten
iced water, to mix

Filling
2 tbsp kirsch, Amaretto, Mandarine or
  other *eau de vie* or liqueur
1 tsp cornflour
4 oz / 110 g dark, bitter chocolate,
  broken into pieces
2 egg yolks
3 egg whites

The pastry can be made by hand or in the food processor. Sift the flour and cocoa together and rub in the butter. Stir in the caster sugar, the egg yolk and enough water to combine the mixture into a smooth pliable dough. Chill for 15 minutes or so. Prepare a 10 in / 20.5 cm flan ring set on a baking sheet, or a deep cake tin of similar diameter with a loose bottom. Grease the baking equipment. Roll out the pastry as thinly as possible into a rough circle. Carefully transfer it to the flan ring or cake tin, and fit it round the base and up the sides. If using a deep cake tin, let the pastry sides come up about 1½–2 in / 4–5 cm, no more. Line the bottom with greaseproof paper, put a layer of dried beans on top, and bake blind in a preheated oven at 180° C / 350° F / Mark 4 for 15 minutes. Remove from the oven, discard the paper and beans, and allow to cool in the tin.

To make the filling, mix the liqueur and cornflour, and put with the chocolate in a bowl set over hot water. Let the chocolate melt. Remove from the heat, allow to cool, and beat in the egg yolks. Whisk the egg whites until firm, and carefully fold the two mixtures lightly together. Spoon into the pastry case and smooth out. Bake in the centre of a preheated oven at 200° C / 400° F / Mark 6 for about 15 minutes. Remove from the oven, and allow to cool in the tin for 10–15 minutes before sliding it out on to a plate. Before serving, dust with icing sugar. This is best freshly baked and still just warm.

Variations ∽ Bake the pastry case blind for 25 minutes instead of 15 minutes, and to replace the filling used above, bring ½ pt / 280 ml double cream to the boil with a vanilla pod. Remove the vanilla pod, and away from the heat, tip about 14 oz / 395 g high-quality plain chocolate, broken into small pieces, into the cream. Mix in thoroughly, and as the mixture cools, beat it vigorously to lighten it. Leave this mixture on one side, while you poach four pears, that have been peeled, halved and cored, until tender in a sugar syrup with a little lemon juice. Remove the fruit from the syrup, allow to cool and slice. Spoon the chocolate cream into the pastry case, arrange the pear slices on top, pour over some reduced syrup, and serve. Instead of the pears, you can use stoned prunes that have been cooked in a wine or sugar syrup, or slices of banana. If using banana, leave raw, but prepare a separate sugar syrup, and pour this over to glaze.

Rhubarb, Ginger and White Chocolate Tart with Cream

Serves 8–10

Pastry
2 oz / 60 g icing sugar
8 oz / 230 g plain flour
pinch of salt
2 tsp ground ginger
3 oz / 85 g firm cream cheese
2 oz / 60 g unsalted butter
iced water, to mix

Filling
2 lb / 900 g rhubarb, trimmed and
  peeled, if necessary
2–3 oz / 60–85 g light muscovado sugar
2 tbsp water
4 oz / 110 g white chocolate
½ pt / 280 ml thick Greek yoghurt or
  whipped cream
1 tbsp finely chopped preserved ginger
3–4 tbsp syrup from preserved ginger

To make the pastry, sift the icing sugar, flour, salt and ginger into a bowl, and rub in the cream cheese and butter until it resembles fine breadcrumbs. Stir in enough water to form a firm dough. Knead lightly, cover and put to cool for 30 minutes. Roll out and use to line a 12 in / 30 cm loose-bottom tart tin. Prick it all over, and line it with foil or butter wrappers, and weight it down with dried beans. Bake 'blind' in a preheated oven at 180° C / 350° F / Mark 4 for 30 minutes, until crisp. Remove and discard the foil or butter wrappers and the beans, turn out and leave to cool on a wire rack.

Cut the rhubarb into 6 in / 15 cm lengths, halving or quartering lengthways if the rhubarb is very thick. Put in a saucepan with the sugar and water, and cook gently until the rhubarb is just tender but not too soft. Drain, cool and reserve the cooking liquid. Melt the white chocolate, and brush this over the inside of the pastry case. Chill briefly to set. Mix the yoghurt with as much of the cooking juices from the rhubarb as it will hold and still remain fairly firm. Fold in the ginger and syrup. Spread the cream over the tart and arrange the rhubarb on top.

Apple and Blackberry Pancakes

Serves 4

4 oz / 110 g plain flour
2 eggs
1 oz / 30 g caster sugar
½ pt / 280 ml skimmed milk
2 tbsp beer, soda water or sparkling
   mineral water

melted butter for frying the pancakes
6 oz / 170 g blackberries
sugar or honey, to taste
2 large apples, peeled, cored and sliced
1 oz / 30 g butter

Mix the first four ingredients into a smooth batter, and allow to stand for at least 1 hour. Just before cooking the pancakes, stir in the beer, soda water or mineral water to give the batter an extra lightness. Use this batter to make eight large pancakes, following the method described on page 245, oiling the pan with the melted butter. Stack them up, and leave the stack, covered, over a pan of hot water until required. Pick over the blackberries, and cook them until soft in a little water. Rub through a sieve into a saucepan, and sweeten the sauce to taste. When ready to serve, fry the apple slices in the butter until golden. Put a generous spoonful of apple on each pancake, and roll up loosely. Quickly warm the blackberry sauce, and serve the pancakes on heated plates, with the sauce poured over.

Variation ∾ Instead of serving the pancakes with apples and blackberries, peel and chop up a small, sweet pineapple, reserving any juice, and mix with a crumbled 7 oz / 200 g block of creamed coconut. Heat gently, with any juice and perhaps a little water, until the creamed coconut melts. Use this as the filling for the pancakes.

Quire of Orange Pancakes with Marmalade Sauce

Serves 6

8 oz / 230 g plain flour
¼ tsp salt
¼ tsp ground mace
3 eggs
12 fl oz / 340 ml milk

4 tbsp orange liqueur
1 tbsp orange flower water
4–6 oz / 110–170 g marmalade
whipped cream, thick yoghurt or
    crème fraîche

Sift together the flour, salt and mace, and make a well in the middle. Gradually beat in the eggs and milk, first to a smooth paste and then until you have a smooth batter. Stir in the liqueur and orange flower water. Let the batter stand for an hour before using. Use a non-stick or well-seasoned frying pan or a lightly oiled crêpe pan, and use the batter to prepare a stack of very thin pancakes, using the method given on page 245. If the pancakes are too thick, the finished dish will be stodgy. If you cover the stack with foil and leave it over a pan of hot water, you can prepare to this point before dinner or lunch, and leave the pancakes while you get on with the rest of the meal.

To serve, spread the top pancake of the stack with the marmalade, and transfer to a serving plate. Spread the next pancake with marmalade and place on top of the first. Continue until you have a new pile of pancakes layered with marmalade, cut it into wedges like a cake and hand the cream or yoghurt separately.

Variations ∾ The orange and marmalade is but one version of this rather nice pudding. Jam, cream and icing sugar and honey, lemon juice and yoghurt are also good combinations.

The orange flavouring in the batter can be replaced with sherry, for example amontillado or oloroso, and the pile of pancakes served with cream whipped with sweet sherry.

You can also use the apples with blackberry sauce, and creamed coconut and pineapple mixture, described on page 556, with a quire of pancakes.

THE TIMES COOK IN THE USA

FOR MORE than 20 years now, I have been visiting the United States once or twice a year, to visit my mother-in-law, Edith, in Pittsburgh, or friends on both the east and west coasts and in between. It is always a culinary adventure, whether I'm with one of San Francisco's well-known women chefs or in a small café 'down east' in Maine, famous for its blueberry pie. And whilst I love dining in the latest fashionable places, trying imaginative and exquisite dishes, I also love shopping and cooking American-style.

During one visit, we spent a very agreeable domestic interlude with friends in Alabama. We had breakfast in the local coffee 'shoppe', ordering eggs and grits and waffles with whipped butter and maple syrup and 'all the coffee you can drink'. We visited the supermarket, a very good one too, with a fine array of imported olive oils and balsamic vinegars. Of much more interest to me, though, were all the different types of cornmeal and grits, including blue cornmeal, blue corn tortillas, and blue cornflakes. On the vegetable racks, the bitter greens and the varieties of sweet potatoes caught my eye. Our friend, Carolyn, and I shared the cooking. I used the lava stone grill to cook marinated mahi-mahi, although I was very tempted by the catfish, and I cooked black-eyed beans into what turned out to be a very passable version of Texas caviar (see page 559). Best of all, though, Carolyn taught me how to make cornbread (see page 444) and Brunswick stew (see page 560), not to mention Key Lime Pie (see page 561).

More often than not, cornbread is made in a skillet or frying pan made of cast-iron. The pan is greased and heated in the oven before the batter is in, rather in the same way that Yorkshire puddings are made. Although the dry ingredients and the wet ingredients can be mixed separately in advance, it is most important not to combine the two until you are ready to bake it, as the raising agent is produced by the action of the sour buttermilk on the baking powder. It is important to use cornmeal not cornflour, and this is available from healthfood shops and some delicatessens. You can use polenta which is also ground corn (or maize).

Another American classic is Brunswick stew which is somewhat like hotpot or Irish stew in that there are a number of variants. It clearly started life as a rustic one-pot meal, in which you put whatever you had in the way of meat and vegetables. It is said to have originated in the rural southern Appalachians, but is now cooked for smart dinners all over the south. Georgia claims to have the best version, but that is disputed by Virginia, and I thought our Alabama version very good indeed. Squirrel is what was used originally and is called for in some of my older cookery books. I have used chicken and beef. You could use pork, rabbit, lamb, and, of course, vary the vegetables. Corn and beans should be included if possible.

We cannot get the large juicy, almost sweet, Key limes in Britain, but the pie does not suffer too much from being made with ordinary limes.

I have also included the traditional Pumpkin Pie recipe (see page 561), which I learned from my mother-in-law, and the extraordinary Shaker Lemon Pie (see page 562). This is an acquired taste. Not everybody likes it. My husband, Tom, didn't when I was testing the recipe.

Traditional American desserts have become fashionable. Plates of chewy, home-made cookies will appear in the most elegant restaurants, along with peach pies, fruit cobblers and apple crisps (a more buttery version of our crumble), served with vanilla or cinnamon ice cream. They are easy to make (see page 562), and I often find them more popular when I serve them than a plate of elegant sorbets.

Texas Caviar

Serves 6–8

1 lb / 455 g dried black-eyed beans
bunch of spring onions
3–4 firm ripe tomatoes
2–3 garlic cloves
several fresh coriander stems

extra virgin olive oil
sherry vinegar or wine vinegar
coarse sea salt
freshly ground black pepper

Boil the beans for 10 minutes, drain, cover with boiling water, and leave for 2–3 hours. Final cooking should then take no more than 45–60 minutes, although if the beans are very old and hard, they may need longer. While the beans are cooking, prepare the rest of the ingredients. Trim, wash and slice the spring onions. Peel, deseed and dice the tomatoes, and peel and crush the garlic. Strip the coriander leaves from the stems and chop them; add the stems to the cooking beans, if you wish. When the beans are cooked, drain them and mix in oil, vinegar and seasoning to your taste. Stir in the rest of the ingredients and check the seasoning once more. Remember to discard the coriander stems before serving.

Brunswick Stew

1 onion, peeled and sliced
1 lb / 455 g shin of beef or flank
 steak
4 pt / 2.30 l water
3 lb / 1.35 kg chicken
14 oz / 395 g can of peeled plum
 tomatoes
1 bay leaf
sprig of thyme

2 cloves
2 lb / 900 g small potatoes, scrubbed
8 oz / 230 g okra, trimmed (*optional*)
3 corn cobs
6 oz / 170 g shelled broad beans
 (*optional*)
salt
freshly ground black pepper

Put the onion in a large stockpot or saucepan with the beef. Cover with the
water and simmer for 1 hour. Put in the chicken, having first removed any excess
fat from the cavity, the tomatoes and the herbs, and cloves. Simmer for another
hour. Remove the chicken and beef from the pot, add the potatoes and okra, if
using, and continue to simmer. Remove the meat from the bones, discarding these
and any skin and gristle. Chop each corn cob into three or four pieces, put it into
the pot with the broad beans, if using, and put back the meat. Bring back to the
boil, and simmer until the vegetables are tender. Season to taste. Serve in shallow
soup plates. You can, if you wish to have a thicker liquid, drain it off into another
saucepan, and boil it fast to reduce it to the desired consistency. It should,
nevertheless, be quite a wet stew, the juices to be mopped up with cornbread (see
page 444).

Variation ⮑ Some of the meat can be replaced with squirrel (see pages 366
and 558) for a truly authentic Brunswick Stew.

Key Lime Pie

Serves 6

3 eggs, separated
finely grated zest of 1–2 limes
4 fl oz / 115 ml fresh lime juice and
    pulp
8 fl oz / 230 ml can of sweetened
    evaporated milk

9 in / 23 cm baked blind Basic Sweet
    Pastry case (see page 546)
3 oz / 85 g caster sugar

Whisk the egg yolks until pale and fluffy. Beat the lime zest, juice and pulp with
the evaporated milk until thick and smooth. Combine with the beaten egg yolks.
Spoon the filling into the prepared pastry case. Whisk the egg whites until soft
peaks form. Sprinkle in half the sugar and whisk again until peaks form. Continue
adding the sugar and whisking until firm, glossy peaks form. Spoon the meringue
over the filling, covering right to the pastry edge. Fork up the surface into peaks or
a swirl. Bake in a preheated oven at 180° C / 350° F / Mark 4 for 15–18 minutes,
until just golden brown. Allow to cool for about 3 hours before serving.

Pumpkin Pie

Serves 6

8 oz / 230 g shortcrust pastry
10 oz / 280 g pumpkin, cooked and
    mashed
4 oz / 110 g golden syrup
2 oz / 60 g light muscovado sugar
¼ tsp freshly ground black pepper
½ tsp ground ginger

1 tsp ground cinnamon
1 tsp ground mixed spice
2 eggs, lightly beaten
½ pt / 280 ml full-cream milk or half-
    and-half mixture of milk and single
    cream

Roll out the pastry and use to line a 9–10 in / 23–25.5 cm pie dish. Mix the
pumpkin, syrup and sugar until thoroughly blended. Stir in the spices, and beat in
the eggs. Pour in the milk, and blend thoroughly before pouring into the pastry
case. Bake in a preheated oven at 220° C / 425° F / Mark 7 for 15 minutes, and
then turn down to 180° C / 350° F / Mark 4 for a further 35 minutes, or until set
and a skewer inserted in the centre comes out clean.

Shaker Lemon Pie

Serves 6

3–4 thin-skinned lemons
7 oz / 200 g sugar
3 eggs

12 oz / 340 g shortcrust pastry
beaten egg and milk, to glaze

Slice the lemons very thinly into a bowl, removing the pips. Sprinkle on the sugar, and leave overnight. When ready to bake the pie, beat the eggs, and stir them into the lemon and sugar mixture (by now the sugar will have dissolved). Divide the pastry in two, roll out one piece, and use it to line a 10 in / 25.5 cm pie or quiche dish. Pour in the lemon mixture. Roll out the remaining pastry, and use it to cover the pie, pressing the edges well down with the tines of a fork to seal. Cut a small cross in the centre of the pastry lid, and fold back the four corners. Brush with the egg and milk glaze, and bake in a preheated oven at 180° C / 350° F / Mark 4 for 15 minutes, then turn down the oven to 150° C / 300° F /Mark 2, and bake for a further 30 minutes.

Prune and Pumpkin Cookies

Makes 12

1½ oz / 40 g unsalted butter,
    softened
1 oz / 30 g light muscovado sugar
1 egg
½ tsp pure vanilla essence
4 oz / 110 g pumpkin purée

8 oz / 230 g plain flour
1½ tsp baking powder
1 tsp ground cinnamon
½ tsp freshly grated nutmeg
pinch of salt
5 oz / 140 g pitted prunes, chopped

Cream the butter and sugar together until light and fluffy, beat in the egg and vanilla essence and then the pumpkin. Sift the dry ingredients together and mix thoroughly with the pumpkin mixture. Stir in the prunes. Take heaped tablespoons of the mixture, and drop on to a greased baking sheet, spacing well apart (use two trays, if necessary). Bake in a preheated oven at 180° C / 350° F / Mark 4 for 20–25 minutes, until the cookies are springy to the touch and the bottoms lightly browned. Transfer to a wire rack to cool.

Preserves,
Sweets and Drinks

I am something of a hoarder. My husband, Tom, would hoot at the understatement. 'You were a squirrel in another life,' he tells me, for I have a larder whose shelves amaze me, they are so full of jars. This hardly fits with the image of a cook who so strongly advocates the use of fresh food, seasonal produce and frequent shopping. There are jars of sun-dried tomatoes, pickled samphire, preserved lemons, marmalade, damson jelly, plum jam and much, much more. I put it down to some atavistic urge, some trait inherited through the female line, to pot and preserve and build up stores against times of shortage. For that is why we preserve. It is a relic of the times when food was truly seasonal, when preserving was a means of dealing with nature's gluts, when we potted, pickled, jellied and preserved.

If you want to enjoy raspberries these days, you don't have to make do with raspberry jam or wait for the raspberry season. You can go to the supermarket and buy Chilean raspberries in February. But I still go on making raspberry jam in the summer and marmalade in the winter. That is when it begins for me, in late December, when the first of the citrus fruits come to us from southern Europe, the lemons and blood oranges from Sicily and Cyprus, then the big juicy navels from Valencia and the bitter oranges from Seville. The fragrant oils and sharp bite are a welcome antidote to the warm, comforting food of winter. Then there is rhubarb, and, much later, gooseberries and elderflowers.

It has always seemed to me that midsummer marks the final fling of activity before the lazy, dog days of July and August. In the countryside, hay-making goes on, and in the mountainous areas the sheep are taken up from lowland to mountain pastures until the end of the summer. In the kitchen, it is the peak time for pickling and preserving, as gardens and allotments move into full production. I have a faded piece of paper found in an old cookery book, which reads, 'Order extra salt for beans. Shallots – use earthenware 7 lbs jars. Put lavender to dry. Refill bags. Linen room, bathroom cupboards, shelves.' I have rarely read anything quite so evocative of another age, when there were fewer demands on us, and thus more time to devote to peaceful, domestic tasks.

Even though I have no garden full of beans and shallots waiting to be bottled, and I shall have to beg lavender from friends with gardens, I still like to capture some of the flavour of an English summer. My fishmonger sells samphire, which I preserve using a fairly sweet pickle mix (see page 577). Fresh, it makes a wonderful first course on its own, quite as good as asparagus and best cooked in the same way, steamed and served with melted butter. I like to mix tender samphire shoots with freshly cooked pasta, garlic, lemon juice and olive oil. And it is, of course, a superb accompaniment to fish and shellfish dishes. As a pickle, I serve it with smoked fish, fresh fish and fish salads.

Then comes the autumn with its glut of plums and damsons, and bilberries, blueberries, and wild hedgerow fruit, which I make into jellies (see page 571) to be given as presents or to serve with autumn and winter game dishes.

PRESERVES

Marmalades

The first time I wrote about marmalades in *The Times* was just as the Seville oranges were coming into the shops. I was taken aback by the passion which my comments and recipes provoked. Food-writer colleagues tell me that marmalade generates more letters than any other topic. We have come to the conclusion that it is the one thing in the culinary world about which the British feel really passionate. Everyone clearly feels he or she has the secret of the best marmalade. It's all in the soaking, the grating, the shredding, the skinning, the boiling or whatever.

Thus, in alternate years I have written a 'this is not about marmalade' column, describing the other uses for Seville oranges, giving recipes for using them with fish, with poultry, and in marinades and puddings. But I have finally succumbed. I am hooked on marmalade-making. Early spring visits to Jerez see me coming back with a bulging bag of bitter oranges, picked for free, just as we used to scrump apples when we were children. I also use lemons from my mother's tree in Gozo. It only produces small fruit, but it is immensely fragrant and makes exquisite marmalade. Whatever fruit I use, I now always follow the same method, the one that works best for me, and which I discovered by trial and error.

First I cook the whole fruit. By accident, the first time I made it this way, I forgot I had left the fruit on, and it cooked for nearly 8 hours on the lowest possible heat. By then I did not feel like dealing with it, so I left it overnight. Next day, the fruit was cold, and therefore easy to handle. When I quartered it, it was an easy matter to squeeze out the pips. The fruit had become jelly-like, having released all its pectin and the surplus I used to make a separate mango and tangerine marmalade. I cut tangerine peel into thin strips and cooked it until soft in the liquid before adding the tangerine pulp, chopped mango pulp and sugar. This pectin-rich liquid can also be used for making jams with low-pectin fruit, like strawberries.

To test for setting point, with all preserves, such as jams, jellies and marmalades, let a small amount drop on to a cold plate. When setting point is reached, the liquid will 'jel' on the plate, no longer runny. It can take anything from a few minutes to an hour for setting point to be reached.

Slow-Cooked Marmalade

Makes 5–6 lb / 2.30–2.70 kg

3–4 lb / 1.35–1.80 kg citrus fruits,   3–4 lb / 1.35–1.80 kg granulated sugar
  including at least a couple of
  Seville oranges and 1–2 lemons

Put the whole fruit in a large, heavy pan, cover with water, bring to simmering point, cover and cook on the lowest possible heat for 6–8 hours. Remove from the heat, keep covered, and leave overnight. Next day, measure out 1½ pt / 850 ml cooking liquid into a preserving pan. Reserve the rest of the pectin-rich liquid for use in making other jams and preserves (see earlier suggestion on p. 565). Quarter the fruit, remove the pips, and thinly slice it. It will be very soft, but should not be too soft to handle. If it is, just chop it. You can also chop it in the food processor if you are not particular about having shredded peel. Transfer the fruit to the preserving pan. Heat gently, and when warm, stir in the sugar. Keep on a low heat until the sugar has dissolved, and then bring to the boil. Boil until setting point is reached. Pour into clean, hot jam jars, cover with waxed paper discs and then cellophane, and label the jars.

Seville Orange Curd

Makes 2 lb / 900 g

6 Seville oranges with good skins   8 oz / 230 g unsalted butter, cut into
4 eggs, plus 2 extra yolks   small cubes
                                            12 oz / 340 g sugar

Grate the zest and squeeze the juice from the oranges into a bowl. Lightly beat in the eggs, and add the butter and sugar. Set the bowl over a saucepan of hot water (or cook in a double saucepan), and keep the water hot but not boiling. Stir from time to time until the butter has melted and the sugar has dissolved. Heat gently, stirring continuously, for 15–20 minutes, until the mixture thickens. Remove from the heat. Allow to cool slightly, and pour into clean, dry jars. Cover immediately, label, and when cool, refrigerate. It should be used within 3–4 weeks. *Variations* ∾ This recipe works equally well with lemons, limes or grapefruit, although the latter will not have quite the same intensity of flavour.

Strawberry Jam

Makes about 3½ lb / 1.60 kg

Homemade jams and jellies always taste nicer than commercial ones, even if they are made in exactly the same way. Like fruit vinegars (see page 580), they make lovely presents, too. My favourite strawberry jam recipe is based on one from Nell Heaton's A Calender of Country Recipes, *in which gooseberry juice is used as the setting agent.*

2 lb / 900 g strawberries
2 lb / 900 g sugar

¼ pt / 140 ml gooseberry juice (made from cooking 4 oz / 110 g gooseberries in ¼ pt / 140 ml water, then straining)

Layer the strawberries and sugar alternately in a large, heavy saucepan, cover and leave for 24 hours. Next day, heat through gently, and then add the gooseberry juice. Boil fast until setting point is reached. Cool, stir and pot in clean, hot jars, covering with waxed paper discs and sealing with cellophane covers. Label the jars.

Plum and Passion Fruit Jam

Makes about 3½ lb / 1.60 kg

2 lb / 900 g firm plums
7 fl oz / 200 ml water
4 passion fruit

juice of 1 lemon
2 lb / 900 g sugar

Wash the plums, halve them, and remove the stones. Cut each half into two or three pieces, and place in a wide, shallow pan with the water. Simmer gently until the fruit is soft. Rub the passion fruit pulp through a sieve on to the plums. Add the lemon juice, and stir in the sugar until it has dissolved. Bring the mixture to the boil, and boil rapidly until setting point is reached. Pot in clean, hot jars, cover with waxed paper discs, seal with cellophane covers, and label.

Passion Fruit Curd

Makes 2 lb / 900 g

4–5 large passion fruit
6 egg yolks

8 oz / 230 g unsalted butter, cut into
    small cubes
7 oz / 200 g caster sugar

Cut a slice off the top of each fruit, and carefully scoop all the pulp and seeds into a small saucepan. Add a tablespoon of water and heat gently. This will loosen the pulp. Place a fine sieve over a bowl, and rub the pulp and juice through it. Discard the seeds. Lightly beat the eggs into the juice, and set the bowl over a pan of hot water, keeping it hot but not boiling. Add a little of the butter and the sugar, stirring from time to time until the sugar has dissolved. Gradually stir in the rest of the butter. Raise the heat slightly, and cook the curd gently, stirring it until it thickens. Pour into clean, dry jars and cover immediately. Label and refrigerate. Eat within 3–4 weeks.

Cherry Jam

Makes about 3½ lb / 1.60 kg

¾ pt / 430 ml gooseberry or red-
    currant juice (made by cooking
    ¾ lb / 340 g fruit in ¾ pt /
    430 ml water, then straining)

1½–2 lb / 680–900 g granulated sugar
    (depending on the sweetness of the
    fruit)
2 lb / 900 g stoned cherries

Put ¼ pt / 140 ml juice and the sugar in a saucepan, and heat gently until the sugar has dissolved. Add the rest of the juice and the cherries, bring to the boil, and boil rapidly until setting point is reached. Spoon into clean, hot jars, cover with waxed paper discs, seal with cellophane covers, and label the jars.

Pear Cheese

Makes 3 lb / 1.35 kg

Although the mixture takes a while to cook, fruit cheese is easy to make, and worth doing because it keeps very well. The cheese, a firm paste which slices when cold, can be potted in small, straight-sided jars and sealed and labelled as you would jam. I like to make at least one batch in a loaf tin, which I turn out and keep in a rectangular dish in the refrigerator for slicing and serving as a sweetmeat after dinner or as an accompaniment to cheese. Pear cheese is particularly good with Lancashire cheese.

3–4 lb / 1.35–1.80 kg pears
¼ pt / 140 ml water
granulated sugar

Remove any stalks from the pears and wash the fruit. Quarter it, and simmer in the water until very soft. Remove from the heat, and rub the soft fruit through a sieve into a clean saucepan. Simmer it until reduced by about a third. Remove from the heat and weigh the pulp. Return it to the saucepan and stir in sugar to the same weight as you noted for the pulp. Stir until the sugar has dissolved, and then return the mixture to the heat, boiling it until it becomes glossy and firm enough to hold the trail of the spoon when drawn through it. Remove from the heat, and pot as described above.

Redcurrant Jelly

Makes about 4 lb / 1.80 kg

4 lb / 1.80 kg redcurrants
water
granulated sugar

Wash the redcurrants, and discard any rotten ones. Put them in a saucepan, and cover with water. Simmer for 45–60 minutes, then crush the fruit with a potato masher. (With one batch that I made, I also added some apple cores and peel, since I was preparing apples for a pie. This debris provides even more pectin.) Suspend a scalded jelly bag over a large bowl, and spoon in the crushed fruit and juice. Allow to drip for several hours. Do not squeeze the bag to encourage more juice to flow, as the pulp will make the jelly cloudy. Measure the liquid into a large pan, and for each pint of juice, stir in 1¼ lb / 570 g sugar. Dissolve the sugar over gentle heat, and then boil hard for 10 minutes or until setting point is reached. Remove from the heat. Scoop any foam from the surface, and pour the jelly into clean, hot jars. Cover with wax discs and then cellophane and label.

Quince Jelly

Makes about 4 lb / 1.80 kg

2 lb / 900 g quinces
3 pt / 1.70 l water
granulated sugar

Roughly chop the quinces, and put them – peel, stalks, core and all – into a preserving pan. Pour in the water, and simmer gently until the fruit is completely soft. This can take up to 2 hours. Ladle the mixture when soft into a scalded jelly bag suspended over a large bowl. I find a jelly bag hooked over the legs of a small, up-turned, four-legged stool works best. Let the liquid drop through of its own accord and preferably overnight. If you hurry it by squeezing and prodding, the resulting jelly will be cloudy. Measure the juice into a clean preserving pan, and for each 1 pt / 570 ml, stir in 1 lb / 455 g sugar. Heat very gently until the sugar has dissolved. You can warm the sugar before you add it, and it will dissolve more quickly. Once there are no sugar crystals to be seen, bring the mixture to the boil, and boil rapidly until setting point is reached. Remove from the heat, and put at once into clean, hot jars. Cover with wax discs and cellophane. Label the jars.

Hedgerow Jelly

Use whatever edible wild berries, fruit, hips and haws you can find, and if possible, use those of the same colour together to give red or purple jellies. On the other hand, real foragers will not be too bothered about this nicety, and will use a handful of this and a portion of that. Most wild fruits are sour and indeed quite inedible unless cooked with sugar, and most have enough pectin to give them a set. Elderberries, however, need added pectin, which is best obtained from windfall apples, cookers or crab apples. Hips, haws and rowanberries are not very juicy and again, it is a good plan to cook them with apples to give extra juice.

The ingredients could not be simpler: you need the fruit, a little water and, at the next stage, sugar. Cook the fruit until soft. The juiciest fruit needs only about 1 in / 2.5 cm water in the pan, drier fruit should have about half its volume of water, and the hardest fruit should be almost covered with water. When the fruit is soft, mash it to extract all the pulp and essences. Suspend a jelly bag over a bowl, and let the pulp drip through it overnight. Measure out the juice you collect, and for each 1 pt / 570 ml, weigh out a generous 1 lb / 455 g sugar. Put both in a saucepan, and heat gently until the sugar has dissolved. Then boil fast until setting point is reached. Pot in clean, hot jars, then seal and label.

If you have only a small amount of fruit and want to make spiced jelly to serve with game, cook the fruit not with water but with cider vinegar and a stick of cinnamon, a couple of cloves and a few cardamoms. This is an excellent way of using windfall apples.

Do not imagine, however, that you need to be in the heart of the country to hunt for wild food. In Jane Grigson's memorable description, you can find rowanberries 'in tamed crimplene comfort along suburban avenues', as well as in other less accessible haunts. My own London street boasts several rowan trees and an elderbush, and there is a blackberry patch not far away. Be careful not to pick from bushes that have been blasted with exhaust fumes, and wash everything very well in warm water.

Garlic Jelly

Makes about 3 lb / 1.35 kg

4 heads garlic cloves, separated and
  peeled
3 lb / 1.35 kg cooking apples

3½ pt / 2 l water
granulated or preserving sugar
juice of 1 large lemon

Crush the garlic with the blade of a knife. Chop the apples, and simmer both ingredients in the water until soft. Strain through a jelly bag suspended over a large bowl. Measure the juice collected, and pour it into a large saucepan. For every 3 pt / 1.70 l juice, stir in 2 lb / 900 g sugar. Heat gently until the sugar has dissolved, and then boil hard until setting point is reached. While the mixture is boiling and before it reaches setting point, add the strained lemon juice. Pot the jelly in small, clean, hot jars. Cover with wax discs and seal with cellophane covers. Label the jars.

Dried Apricot Jam

Makes 3–4 lb / 1.35–1.80 kg

1 lb / 455 g dried apricots
6 bitter almonds
12 sweet almonds

3 pt / 1.70 l water
3 lb / 1.35 kg granulated sugar,
  warmed

Soak the apricots overnight before using them. Drain and chop them. Crush the almonds, and tie in a piece of muslin. Put the fruit, almonds and 3 pt / 1.70 l water in a preserving pan, and cook until the fruit is soft. Remove from the heat, and stir in the sugar until it dissolves. Put the pan back on high heat, bring the mixture to the boil, and boil rapidly until setting point is reached. Remove the bag of almonds, and skim off any scum. Pot in clean, hot jars. Cover with waxed paper discs, and seal with cellophane covers. Label the jars.

Mincemeat

Makes about 2 lb / 900 g

*Some years I make my own mincemeat for Christmas, if I leave myself
enough time. This one is best left for a month or so to let the spirit
and spices mature the fruit. You can use the traditional beef suet or, of
course, a vegetarian suet. A healthy alternative to the suet is a few
tablespoons of olive oil which works very well.*

4 oz / 110 g dried apricots, soaked
  overnight

4 oz / 110 g sultanas

4 oz / 110 g lexia or muscatel raisins

4 oz / 110 g currants

4 oz / 110 g peeled, cored and
  grated russet apples

4 oz / 110 g finely chopped mixed
  peel or marmalade

4 oz / 110 g light or dark muscovado
  sugar

4 oz / 110 g grated suet

juice and grated zest of 2 lemons or 2
  oranges

5 tbsp rum or calvados

5 tbsp cognac

Chop, mince or lightly process the dried fruit, but take care not to turn it into a
paste. Mix with the rest of the ingredients in a bowl. Cover and allow the flavours
to develop for 2–3 days. Pack into clean jars, fill to the top, and place waxed paper
discs on top. Seal the pots with dampened cellophane covers, secured with rubber
bands. Or pot in Kilner jars. Store in a cool, dry, dark place.

PICKLES, CHUTNEYS AND KETCHUPS

ACCORDING TO Henry Sarson, whose book *Home Pickling* is one of my favourites, 'only a pickled peach can beat a good pickled walnut, and not always then'. The book was written in 1940 for all those who had forgotten or 'never knew how to make pickles like mother used to make', for the enthusiastic allotment diggers whose surpluses rotted in the tool shed, and for greenhouse owners whose last tomatoes failed to ripen in 'the fickle English sun'. Lord Woolton, then Minister of Food, welcomed the book, seeing it as an encouragement to the population to improve the restricted war-time diet by eating vegetables, to avoid waste and to reduce reliance on food imports. None of these reasons pertains to pickling now, but it is still worth doing to add different flavours and textures to our food.

The pickling process involves immersion first in salt or brine to draw out as much water as possible from the fruit or vegetable, which would otherwise dilute the vinegar, and then immersion in the vinegar. This can be ready-flavoured, or you can make your own pickling vinegar. To safeguard against spoilage, you need to use a strong vinegar for this. Malt vinegars and distilled or spirit vinegar can be used, and sherry vinegar is of the right strength but is more expensive, as is old wine vinegar. Non-brewed condiment is not a vinegar and has no place in a kitchen.

Standard Brine

Makes 1 pt / 570 ml

5 oz / 140 g salt
1 pt / 570 ml water

Dissolve the salt in the water, and use 1 pt / 570 ml for each 1 lb / 455 g vegetables. Small, 'drier' vegetables such as capers, nasturtium seeds and samphire can be given a dry salt treatment.

Sweet Pickling Vinegar

Makes 1 pt / 570 ml

*Pickling vinegars can be made in advance and kept until required.
Because the fumes of hot vinegar are so pervasive, it is a good idea to
make them on a day when you can have all the doors and windows
open. Like deep-frying, the aromas and essential oils linger in hair and
clothes for days. This sweet pickling vinegar is the one I like to use for
small cucumbers, onions and mixed vegetables. For samphire, which
has such an elusive flavour, I leave out the ginger, dill and coriander,
but keep the 'sweet spices'.*

1 pt / 570 ml vinegar
6 oz / 170 g light muscovado sugar
1 in / 2.5 cm piece of fresh root
  ginger, peeled
6 cloves

piece of cinnamon
6 cardamom pods
12 allspice berries
½ tsp coriander seeds
½ tsp dill seeds

Put ¼ pt / 140 ml vinegar, the sugar and spices in a stainless steel saucepan,
bring to the boil, and simmer for 30 minutes. Remove from the heat, and stir in the
rest of the vinegar. Cool, strain and bottle until required.

Variations ∽ For an aromatic pickling vinegar, omit the sugar, and flavour the
vinegar with 24 allspice berries, 1 teaspoon each of coriander seeds, cumin seeds,
mustard seeds and black peppercorns, 6 cloves, 6 bay leaves and 6 crushed juniper
berries. This is very good with walnuts, capers and nasturtium seeds. But as with so
many things, this is all a matter of taste.

With both vinegars, spices can be added or left out, as you prefer. Hotter
pickles can be made by increasing the amount of pepper, ginger, or mustard seed,
and with the addition of dried chillies.

Pickled Walnuts

Makes 2 lb / 900 g

*Here is a simple recipe for pickling walnuts. Leaving them in the sun
is what gives them the characteristic blackness. Green walnuts are
picked in late June or early July, before the shell begins to harden.*

2 lb / 900 g green walnuts
2 pt / 1.15 l Standard Brine (see
  page 574)

2 pt / 1.15 l unstrained Pickling Vinegar
  (see page 575)

Soak the walnuts in the brine for 4–5 days, drain them, and put them in the sun
for 2–3 days to dry and blacken. Pack them into jars. Pour boiling pickling vinegar
over the walnuts, and distribute the spices, evenly if possible, between the jars.
Cover and seal whilst still hot. The pickles should be kept for a month before using
in order to be fully mature; they will keep unopened for much longer, about 1–2
years.

Lemons Pickled in Oil

*I learned this simple method from Claudia Roden.
You can also use limes or Seville oranges.*

Scrub the fruit well, and slice or cut into wedges. Arrange on a tray, and freeze
overnight in a freezer or in the ice-making compartment of a refrigerator. Put the
frozen fruit in a colander set over a bowl. Salt generously and leave to drain for 1–2
hours. As the fruit thaws out, it will become soft and limp, and the pith will no
longer be bitter. Layer the slices or wedges in a glass jar, sprinkling with a little
paprika between each layer. Cover with a good-quality olive, nut or grapeseed oil,
and close the lid. The pickle will be ready in 2–3 days.

Summer Pickle

This colourful, piquant, sweet and sour pickle can be served with drinks, just as you would olives. Note that the olives and cherries are not stoned.

12 small onions, peeled	1 tbsp sugar
12 black olives	½ tsp ground cumin
12 green olives	½ tsp ground coriander
12 button mushrooms, wiped	cayenne, to taste (*optional*)
12 small radishes, topped and tailed	2 cloves
12 cherries	1 small piece of cinnamon
12 cherry tomatoes	¼ pt / 140 ml olive oil
2 heads garlic, cloves separated and peeled	2½ fl oz / 70 ml sherry vinegar or wine vinegar
1 tsp sea salt	1 tbsp kirsch (*optional*)

Blanch the onions in boiling water for 2–3 minutes, and then drain and put in a large glass jar or bowl with the rest of the vegetables and fruit. Put the salt, sugar, spices and liquids in a small saucepan, and bring to the boil. Pour over the vegetables and fruit, mix well and seal for 3–4 days before serving. (This need not be made in a preserving jar; a large glass bowl covered with cling film will do just as well, I have found.)

Pickled Samphire

2 lb / 900 g samphire	2 pt / 1.15 l Sweet Pickling Vinegar (see page 575)
6 oz / 170 g coarse salt	

Pick over the samphire, discarding any soggy pieces and roots. Rinse free of sand and mud, and gently towel dry. Put the samphire in a dish, and sprinkle with the salt. Leave overnight. Next day, pack into jars and pour the vinegar over. Cover and seal. This is actually ready to use within a few days, but it will also keep for several months.

Gooseberry Chutney

Makes about 6 lb / 2.70 kg

1 lb / 455 g onions, peeled and
    chopped
1 oz / 30 g mustard seed
6 lb / 2.70 kg gooseberries, topped
    and tailed

2 oz / 60 g salt
1 lb / 455 g brown sugar
1 lb / 455 g seedless raisins
1 oz / 30 g ground mixed spice
1 pt / 570 ml vinegar

Cook the onions in a very little water until soft. Crush the mustard seed, chop
the gooseberries, and put all the ingredients in the saucepan with onion. Cook until
thick and glossy. Pour into jars while still warm, and seal.

Cranberry, Kumquat and Juniper Chutney

Makes about 2 lb / 900 g

1 lb / 455 g onions, peeled and
    chopped
1 tbsp groundnut (peanut) oil
1 oz / 30 g butter
8 oz / 230 g kumquats
8 oz / 230 g cranberries

1 tsp juniper berries, lightly crushed
2 cloves
1 bay leaf
6 oz / 170 g light muscovado sugar
2–3 tbsp sherry vinegar

Cook the onion very gently in the oil and butter until soft and beginning to
caramelize slightly. Allow 30–40 minutes for this, and stir from time to time to
prevent the onions from burning. Meanwhile, halve the kumquats, discard the
seeds, and roughly chop the fruit. Simmer in 2–3 tablespoons water until tender.
When the onion is soft, stir in the kumquats and their cooking liquid, the
cranberries and juniper berries. Thread the cloves into the bay leaf and add to the
pan. Cover with a lid, and cook over a gentle heat until the cranberries have
popped. Remove the lid, raise the heat, and let the cooking liquid evaporate. Stir in
the sugar, and add the vinegar. Cook until thick and glossy, remove the bay leaf
and cloves, cool, pot and refrigerate.

Quince Purée

Makes about 2 lb / 900 g

4 lb / about 2 kg quinces
3 pt / 1.70 l water
1½ lb / 680 g sugar

3 in / 7.5 cm cinnamon stick
4 oz / 110 g butter
3 tbsp cider vinegar

Wipe, peel, quarter and core the quinces. (Use the peel, and core if you like, to make about ½ pt / 280 ml pectin-rich extraction, which can be used to make jam or jelly with rhubarb.) Put the quinces in a saucepan with the water, sugar, cinnamon and half the butter. Bring to the boil, and simmer for 15–20 minutes. Drain, reserving the syrup for another use, such as sorbets. Return the fruit to the pan, and continue cooking, with the vinegar added, until tender. Sieve the fruit, and stir in the remaining butter. Cool, pot, and store in the refrigerator until the purée is needed.

Cranberry Ketchup

Makes about 1½ lb / 680 g

1 lb / 455 g cranberries
1 onion, peeled and chopped
4 garlic cloves, peeled and chopped
¼ pt / 140 ml water
6 oz / 170 g sugar

¼ pt / 140 ml vinegar
¼ tsp sea salt
freshly ground black pepper
ground mace, paprika, allspice and
   cloves

Cook the cranberries, onion and garlic in the water until the cranberries pop. Make a purée in a blender or food processor, and sieve into a clean saucepan. Stir in the sugar, vinegar, salt, pepper and ground spices until the sugar has dissolved. Cook gently until the mixture thickens. Pour the ketchup into hot sterilized jars, seal and label.

VINEGARS

Fruit Vinegar

When there is a glut of fruit in the late summer and early autumn, make fruit vinegars to liven up winter salads. Put your chosen fruit in a bowl, crush it with a fork or potato masher, and pour on 1 pt / 570 ml wine vinegar for each 1 lb / 455 g fruit. Macerate the fruit and vinegar for a day or so, and then strain into clear bottles, and store for later use. Raspberry vinegar is one of my favourites, but I also think blackcurrant vinegar is very good.

Lavender Vinegar

Of all the herb vinegars, lavender is the one I like best. Before the blossoms are fully opened, take a faggot of lavender and put it in a bottle of white wine vinegar. Re-cork and leave, ideally on a sunny windowsill, for 2–3 weeks. The lavender can be removed or left in, as you wish. Other herb vinegars are made in exactly the same way, but the lavender is particularly good when used to dress delicate salads of herbs, such as chervil and purslane and other small leaves. And do not forget how good a sprig or two of lavender is with roast lamb in place of rosemary.

Garlic Vinegar

Use a large head of garlic to every 2 pt / 1.15 l wine vinegar. Peel, separate and bruise the garlic cloves and place them in a suitable bottle that has a well-fitting stopper. Pour on the vinegar, seal, and leave to infuse for at least 3 weeks before using. The garlic cloves can be left in the vinegar, or it can be strained into a clean container. Modern as this sounds, this is an Eliza Acton recipe, and she describes how shallots, green mint and horseradish can also be used in a similar way to flavour vinegar.

BUTTERS

Flower butter

With nasturtiums or marigolds, where it is mainly the colour I want, I put the flower petals in a food processor with butter, blend until thoroughly mixed, and then refrigerate until needed. To make a rose or lavender butter, which makes an unusual addition to the tea table with warm scones, wrap a block of unsalted butter in muslin and bury it in a bowl of fresh flower petals. Clove pinks with their strong scent can also be used in the same way.

Samphire Butter

Take two parts samphire to one or two parts softened butter. Rinse the samphire thoroughly and only use the tender shoots, not the woody stems. Drop it into a pan of boiling water to blanch for 30 seconds, and then drain and immediately plunge it into cold water to stop it cooking. Drain and dry thoroughly. Put it in the food processor with the butter, and process until thoroughly blended. Pack into ramekins, and cover with foil until ready to use. Serve with steamed, poached or grilled fish, rather than fried fish which is already rich in oils.

Brandy Butter

Makes about 8 oz / 230 g

6 oz / 170 g unsalted butter, softened
3 oz / 85 g icing sugar
4 tbsp cognac

Beat the butter until it is pale and creamy, and then, still beating, add the sugar and finally the cognac. Pack into decorative pots or ramekins. Cover with a waxed paper disc and cling film until required.

Variation ➴ Replace the cognac with 2–3 tablespoons *eau de vie de coing* and 2 tablespoons quince jelly for a fragrant quince butter.

DRINKS AND FRUITS IN ALCOHOL

Elderflower Cordial

Makes 3 pt / 1.7 l

If I had a large country kitchen, I would experiment with dandelion wine, and with elderflower wine which sparkles like champagne. Instead, I content myself with trying a little elderflower milk punch and using the dandelion flowers in fritters and small omelettes. I also make several bottles of very concentrated elderflower syrup or cordial, of which I never seem to make enough. It makes the most exquisite sorbets and refreshing summer drinks, flavours fruit salads, creams and custards, and adds a magical touch to salad dressings.

2 lemons
2 limes
2 oz / 60 g tartaric acid
12 elderflower heads, well washed
   and drained

3 lb / 1.35 kg granulated sugar
3 pt / 1.70 l water

Quarter the lemons and limes, squeeze the juice into a large bowl, and add the skins, together with the tartaric acid and the elderflower heads. Add the sugar and water, stir well, cover loosely, and let it stand for 24–36 hours, stirring from time to time. Remove the lemon and lime pieces. Pour the flowers and liquid into a large saucepan, and bring to the boil; hold there for 2–3 minutes. Remove from the heat, and allow to cool. Strain into bottles, and seal.

Variation ∾ Almond-scented hawthorn flowers can be used in the same way to make a cordial.

Elderflower Cooler

Makes 1.5 l

1 75 cl bottle dry white wine, chilled
4 tbsp elderflower cordial or more to taste (see page above)
1 75 cl bottle sparkling water, chilled

Mix the wine and cordial in a large glass jug, and pour in the sparkling water just before serving.

Sangria du Ranquet

Makes 75 cl

1–2 pink grapefruit
1 75 cl bottle sweet muscat wine, such as Muscat de Lunel or
Muscat de Rivesaltes

Cut the grapefruit into eight segments each, and then slice each segment. Put in a large bowl or jug, and pour on the wine. Chill and leave to macerate for several hours. Serve neat or with a splash of sparkling water for a more refreshing drink. This unusual combination comes from Le Ranquet in the Gard region of France.

Raspberry Cocktail

Serves 1

2–3 ripe raspberries
1 tsp icing sugar or sugar syrup

½ measure of *eau de vie de framboise*
tonic water, chilled

Put the raspberries in the bottom of a wine glass or cocktail glass. Sprinkle with icing sugar, and add the *eau de vie*. Top up with ice cold tonic water.
Variations ∾ A stronger version replaces the tonic water with sparkling wine, and the luxury version uses champagne.

Christmas Morning Cocktail

Serves 8–10

1 tbsp clear honey
1 miniature Orange Curaçao or
   Cointreau

12 blood oranges
1 bottle non-vintage Champagne,
   chilled

In a large glass jug, mix the honey and liqueur. Squeeze the oranges, and carefully pour the juice into the honey mixture, avoiding splashing the sides of the jug as much as possible. Pour in the champagne, mix and serve.

Herb Garden Punch

Makes about 1½ pt / 850 ml

2 sprigs each of mint, French
  tarragon and basil
1 pt / 570 ml water
10 oz / 280 g sugar
2 measures white rum

1 measure orange liqueur
juice of 1 lemon
juice of 1 lime
chilled sparkling mineral water

Put the herbs and water in a saucepan, bring to the boil, and simmer for 3 minutes. Strain the liquid into a large jug, and stir in the sugar. Cool and chill. Into a large glass jug, pour the rum, liqueur and fruit juices. Stir in the herb syrup, and then add the mineral water to taste.

Lemon Barley Water

Makes 2 pt / 1.15 l

2 unsprayed lemons
3 oz / 85 g pearl barley

2 pt / 1.15 l water
sugar or sugar syrup, to taste

With a potato peeler, thinly pare the zest from the lemons and put it in a saucepan with the pearl barley and half the water. Squeeze the lemons and reserve the juice. Pull out the pulp from the lemon halves and add to the pan. Bring to the boil, and simmer for 30–40 minutes. Remove from the heat, mash the pulp, and let it stand for an hour or so. Scoop out a tablespoon or so of barley, and put it in a large jug. Sieve the cooked pulp into it, add the squeezed juice and the rest of the water, and sweeten to taste. Cover and refrigerate. This is even better on the second day.

Iced Ginger Tea

Makes 2 pt / 1.15 l to be diluted

2 in / 5 cm piece of fresh root
   ginger, peeled and sliced
1 tbsp Ceylon or Darjeeling tea
2 pt / 1.15 l water, boiling

1 lb / 455 g granulated sugar
still or sparkling mineral water
fresh orange slices or wedges and mint
   leaves, to decorate

Put the ginger in a jug. Put the tea in another jug or teapot, and pour boiling water in each. Leave each to steep for 5 minutes, and then strain both into one large glass jug. Stir in sugar or syrup. Allow to cool, and then refrigerate. Dilute with water, decorate with orange and mint and serve.

Triple Orange

Makes 2 pt / 1.15 l

1 small can frozen condensed
   orange juice
1 tbsp orange marmalade
2–3 tbsp orange-flavoured liqueur

1 tsp Angostura Bitters
1¾ pt / 1 l bottle sparkling spring or
   mineral water
frosted mint leaves, to decorate
   (*optional*)

Put the first four ingredients in a blender and blend until smooth. Pour into a large chilled jug and top up with sparkling water. Frosted fresh mint leaves are suitable for decoration, if liked.

Variation ∽ An alternative version of this drink, for which you will have to think of another name, can be made from concentrated grapefruit juice, lime or lemon marmalade and a couple of measures of gin or vodka.

Hot Spiced Buttered Rum

Serves 1

1 tsp demerara or light muscovado
  sugar
¼ tsp finely grated lemon or orange
  zest

¼ tsp ground allspice
measure of rum
½ oz / 15 g unsalted butter

Warm a mug or Russian tea glass by pouring in boiling water. Empty it, and put in the sugar, zest, spice and rum. Fill with boiling water, and float the butter on top. Make sure the mug is not too large, or you will need to increase the other ingredients if they are not to be too diluted.

To Start a Rumpot

Summer is the time to start a rumpot or tutti frutti, if you are planning to serve it at Christmas. Good, sound unwashed fruit, starting with strawberries, sugar in equal proportions and rum to cover it all is what you need, as well as a deep earthenware jar with a lid. If you do not have one, a tall glass 'sweet jar' will do, as long as you have a dark place to store it.

2 lb / 900 g strawberries
1 lb / 455 g sugar
1¾ pt / 990 ml high proof rum

Make sure the strawberries are clean and unblemished and unsprayed if possible. If you have to wash the strawberries, they should be thoroughly dry before you put them in a bowl and sprinkle the sugar all over them. Leave overnight, and then put the strawberries and accumulated juice into the pot. Pour on the rum. The fruit should be weighed down to keep it below the level of the liquid. Keep it covered and in a dark place. Go on adding fruit and sugar throughout the summer and into the autumn, making sure that the last layer of fruit is always covered by 1 in / 2.5 cm rum. All the soft fruits, apricots, peaches, nectarines and greengages can go in, as well as melon pieces, plums and grapes. Avoid citrus fruit and only use one or two apples and pears. When the last fruit has been added, ideally about a month before Christmas, top up with more rum and keep covered.

Nocino
(Walnut Liqueur)

Makes 1¾ pt / 1 l

*San Giovanni, the Feast of St John and also Midsummer's Day, is
when walnuts are picked to make this traditional liqueur of the
Modena region in Northern Italy. Suave, dark and mellow with a
powerful undertow, my friend Angelo's homemade version has
legendary powers. He tells the story of a visiting businessman who
took a bottle back to England. On a return visit, when the* digestivos
and amari *were being offered, his face lit up 'Ah, nocino!' And could
he have another bottle? He was pleased with the last one, he said. His
bossy wife finished most of it after dinner one evening, and had slept
for three days.
The bottling alcohol used is the kind you buy in French grocers as
eau de vie de fruits. You could use vodka or brandy, but the end
result will not be quite the same. Green walnuts are those picked
before the shell has hardened.*

25 whole green walnuts	4 cloves
1¾ pt / 1 l bottle of alcohol	1 walnut leaf
3 in / 7.5 cm cinnamon stick	1⅓ lb / 600 g sugar

Cut each walnut lengthways into six wedges, and put them in a large glass
preserving jar with the alcohol (use two or more smaller containers if necessary),
the spices and the walnut leaf. Seal the jar, and leave it in a warm, sunny place for 2
months, shaking it from time to time. At the end of this period, strain the liquid
through muslin or a fine sieve. Make a syrup with half the sugar and 2 tablespoons
of water and, in another saucepan, caramelize the remaining sugar. When just
brown, but not burnt, remove from the heat and carefully pour in the boiling
syrup, stirring all the time. The mixture must not caramelize further. Allow it to
cool, and mix the caramel syrup with the filtered walnut extract. Seal it back in the
jar, and leave for 30–40 days more, shaking it occasionally, and then filter once
more before bottling. Traditionally, this liqueur is aged for a year, preferably two,
before drinking.

Apricots in Muscat

Makes about 2 lb / 900 g

2 lb / 900 g dried apricots
1 bottle good muscat wine

Pack the fruit into a preserving jar. Pour on enough wine to cover the fruit completely and close the lid. Top up with more wine as required.

One of the best wines to use for preserving apricots is the José Sala vin de liqueur from the south-west of France. It is inexpensive yet very good quality, and it has a lovely grapiness backed by a richer hint of orange marmalade which suits the apricots perfectly.

Queimada de la Casa
(Flaming Coffee)

Serves 8

2–3 tbsp sugar
7 fl oz / 200 ml *aguardiente*, brandy or rum
1 pot freshly made coffee for 8

Put the sugar in a warmed flameproof bowl or pan that is large enough to hold all the ingredients. Set it on a mat on the table, pour on the spirit, carefully light it and let it burn. Stir it from time to time with a long-handled spoon. It will burn for a good 5 minutes, melting the sugar and evaporating the alcohol. As the flames die down, pour on the coffee. Stir thoroughly and ladle into small coffee cups. Serve this drink immediately.

CHOCOLATES

THE QUALITY of chocolate used in cookery should, like wine, be at least of the quality you would eat or drink. The key to quality lies in the figure given on the packaging for the percentage of cocoa mass or solids. Briefly, the higher the percentage the better. The more cocoa mass, the less fat, sugar and other ingredients. If a chocolate bar contains 35 per cent cocoa solids, one might ask what makes up the other 65 per cent. The very best chocolate I have ever tasted contains 80 per cent cocoa solids, leaving a lower percentage to be made up with other ingredients. If you have never tasted a *grand cru* chocolate, be prepared for a revelation comparable to that of tasting a *grand cru* wine against a lesser wine. It is made with the same care, blending the *criollo* bean from South America and Indonesia, with its fine, fruity perfumed characteristic, and the robust *forastero* bean from Africa, which adds weight and strength. Good chocolate breaks with a crisp, dry snap. It melts in the mouth with a fine, smooth texture, soft and light without being fatty and cloying. Like good wine, it has a long finish, its fine subtle flavours lingering. It contains small amounts of caffeine, and theobromine which induce a feeling of well-being, comforting at the same time as being stimulating.

Chocolate and Hazelnut Truffles

Makes 24–36

14 oz / 400 g hazelnuts
14 oz / 400 g good-quality plain
  chocolate

2 tbsp pure olive oil
2–3 oz / 60–85 g cocoa powder

Lightly toast the hazelnuts, which can be blanched or not, but rub off any loose skin, and crush them. Melt the chocolate in a bowl set over hot water, and stir in the hazelnuts. Thoroughly mix in the olive oil, and put the mixture in the refrigerator to firm up. Take a dessertspoon or teaspoon, depending on what size truffles you want, and shape the mixture into balls. Roll them in cocoa, and place in paper cases. Keep in an airtight tin, and the truffles will last for up to a week.

Chocolate Rum Truffles

Makes 24–36

1 lb / 455 g good-quality chocolate
6 fl oz / 170 ml double cream
2–3 tbsp rum

1 oz / 30 g cocoa powder *or* 1 oz / 30 g
  sifted icing sugar *or* 6 oz / 170 g plain
  chocolate, melted

Grate or chop the chocolate into a bowl. Put the cream in a saucepan, and bring it just to the boil. Pour it on the chocolate and beat until incorporated. Stir in the rum and chill for 2–3 hours until firm. Scoop small pieces of mixture off with a teaspoon, and roll quickly and lightly into a ball, preferably on a marble slab. Roll in cocoa powder or icing sugar, or dip in the melted chocolate, letting any excess chocolate fall back. Continue with the rest of the chocolate mixture. Place the truffles in individual paper cases, and carefully store until required, separating each layer with foil or film. They will keep for 7–10 days in the refrigerator.
Variations ∾ Instead of coating the truffles in cocoa powder, icing sugar or chocolate, for a more spectacular effect, simply wrap each one in a sheet of gold leaf before placing it in a paper sweet case.
  Before you refrigerate the mixture, mix in finely chopped (*not* ground) almonds, and then chill and continue as above.
  You can omit the alcohol if you wish, or use another type of liqueur.

White Chocolate Truffles

Makes 24

*This is a rich, sweet treat for those who love chocolate. One at the end
of a delicious meal is hardly going to do much harm, however.*

12 oz / 340 g white chocolate
4 oz / 110 g unsalted butter

6 tbsp double cream
1 oz / 30g icing sugar, sifted

In a small, non-stick saucepan gently melt and stir together the first three ingredients. Allow to cool, and then put in the refrigerator or on ice cubes to make quite firm. Working quickly, scoop off small pieces with a teaspoon, and roll into small balls. Roll in the icing sugar, and place in individual paper sweet cases. Store in the refrigerator, and eat within 3–4 days.

Whisky and Walnut Toffee

Makes about 2 lb / 900 g

*Making toffee was always a favourite pastime for my brother and me
as children on the afternoon of Bonfire Night. Here is a grown-up
version, good to serve after dinner with coffee.*

6 oz / 170 g walnut halves
1 lb / 455 g demerara sugar
¼ pt / 140 ml water

4 oz / 110 g unsalted butter
2 tbsp whisky

Place the walnuts in a buttered or oiled cake tin or Swiss roll tin. Place the
sugar and water in a heavy saucepan. Melt the sugar over low heat, then bring to
the boil, and boil for 20 minutes. Add the butter and whisky and continue boiling
until a piece becomes brittle when dropped into cold water. Pour immediately over
the walnuts. When the toffee is almost set, mark into squares so that it can be
broken up more easily when cold.

THE TIMES COOK IN COLOMBIA

I WAS LUCKY enough to be invited to Colombia to take part in a British food festival, in Bogotá, during which my husband and I had ample time to explore the gastronomy of the country.

We sampled the richly flavoured and varied *costeño* cooking of Cartagena on the Caribbean coast, with its spicy fish stews and tropical fruit, and everywhere the sweet smell of fried coconut, which is so much a feature of Cartagena's kitchens. We ate grilled sweet lobster, were tempted by the Chinese *loncheriàs*, and bought fruit on the beach from the *palanqueràs*, vividly dressed women selling pineapples, mangos, bananas, medlars, limes, watermelons and papaya. Roadside stalls sold corn cakes, fried chicken and tropical fruit juice.

Life was much more sedate in the *sabañera*, the foothills of the Andes where Bogotá is situated, and the food less exuberant. Nevertheless, we liked it very much, particularly the national dish, *ajiáco*, a warming chicken stew or thick soup cooked with three kinds of potatoes together with a local herb or weed called *guascas*. Watercress makes a reasonable substitute.

One of the local food writers, Ettica Rosenbaum, took me under her wing, and arranged for me to visit markets and supermarkets. We learned about all the different varieties of potatoes and roots when we visited the huge wholesale market covering several acres to the south-east of Bogotá. We also saw plantains and tubers, such as yucca and yams, as well as the unusual *chuguas*, which resembled miniature pink beetroot, and *cubios*, which were like purple spinning tops. The fruit section was a revelation, with rich scents and vivid colours of fruits I had never even heard of, let alone seen before, together with many varieties of guavas, passion fruits, custard apples and tree tomatoes. Many of the fruits are sharp in flavour and are used for refreshing drinks, at breakfast or with traditional dishes.

With your *ajiáco* in Colombia, you are likely to be served a fruity milk drink, such as *sorbete de curuba*, made from a variety of passion fruit, or *sorbeta de guanabana*, made from soursop. If you make the guava paste in the way I describe on page 594, you will also be able to make *sorbete de guava* (see page 594). Guava paste is a very popular dessert in Colombia, but as fresh guavas are not easy to find outside the tropics and are expensive, I have made my paste with canned guavas. The result is quite acceptable. Guavas are one of the few fruits that retain their scent and some of their texture when processed.

However, Colombians like to eat hefty meat dishes, and after one of these, a platter of tropical fruits is refreshing, colourful, and easy on the digestion.

When it is cool, grey and misty high in the Andes, sophisticated Bogotános like to stop for a break in the afternoon. This *merienda* is taken with as much ceremony and enjoyment as, in more leisurely times, we might have taken tea. It is a small, relaxed meal, and I was introduced to it by Ettica Rosenbaum, when she took me to La Cofredia, a small restaurant in one of the smart areas of this vibrant city. Hot drinking chocolate was whisked and thickened with a wooden *molinillo*, or beater, and served in large cups. With this we ate small *tamales*, ground corn and a little meat steamed in a corn husk, and other little *colaciones* or baked goods, including *almojabana*, *calados*, and *pan de yuca*, a soft bread made from cassava flour. The most traditional accompaniment, which I liked very much, was soft, fresh cheese, not unlike a firm ricotta, pieces of which are dipped into chocolate and eaten in the fingers just as the cheese begins to melt. *Papayuela*, a small papaya-like fruit stewed in syrup, was one of the sweet accompaniments; *casquitas di limón*, lemon skins soaked to rid them of their bitterness and then cooked in sugar, the other.

Some of the 'short eats' in Chapter 2 would be eminently suitable for a *merienda*, the Mince Meat Pastries (see page 50), for example, or the Cheese and Asparagus Pastries (see page 52), the Llapingachos (see page 63) and small versions of the Tamales (see page 216). Here I include a recipe for rich drinking chocolate (see page 595), as well as a recipe for *churros* (see page 596), which are marvellous dipped into the chocolate.

Dulce de Guayaba
(Guava Paste)

Serves 4–6

1 lb / 455 g can guavas
about 7 oz / 200 g sugar
juice of 1 lemon

Drain and reserve the syrup from the can of guavas. With a teaspoon, remove the seeds from the centre of the guava halves. Put these in a bowl and reserve. They can be used with the syrup in the next recipe. Chop the guavas small or make a purée of them if you want a smooth paste. Put in a heavy saucepan with an equal quantity of sugar and the lemon juice. Heat through very gently until the sugar has dissolved and then bring to the boil. Cook until a line remains through the mixture when you draw the edge of the wooden spoon across the base of the pan. Pour the mixture into a shallow, greased dish and leave until set. Turn out, divide into pieces, and serve each one on a small plate with a slice of ricotta cheese.
Variation ∾ When set, cut into squares or sticks, roll in caster sugar, wrap individually in cellophane or greaseproof paper, and store in an airtight container.

Sorbete de Guayaba
(Guava Sherbet)

Serves 2–3

This is not a sorbet as we know it, but more of a thick drink. You could freeze it if you wish. It uses up the syrup and pulp from the previous recipe.

guava syrup (see previous recipe)   ½ pt / 280 ml milk or water
guava seeds and pulp (see previous   2 tbsp yoghurt
   recipe)

Put the syrup in a blender together with the seeds which will still have a good deal of pulp around them. Switch the motor on in short bursts to loosen the seeds from the pulp. Rub the mixture through a sieve and return it to the rinsed-out blender. Add the liquid and yoghurt. Blend, chill and sieve.

Canelazo
(Hot Cinnamon Punch)

Serves 4–6

¾ pt / 430 ml water
2 cinnamon sticks, 3 in / 7.5 cm
   each

¼ pt / 140 ml *aguardiente*
juice of ½ lemon
sugar for frosting

Put the water and cinnamon sticks in a saucepan, and bring to the boil. Turn down the heat and barely simmer for 8–10 minutes. Add the *aguardiente* and the lemon juice and remove from the heat after another 1–2 minutes. Moisten the rims of small wine glasses, dip them into the sugar to frost the edges and strain in the hot punch.

Chocolate Eugénie

Serves 10–12

This is named after Empress Eugénie, the Spanish wife of Napoleon III, who made chocolate a popular drink in France. It is still prepared and served this way at the Hotel du Palais in Biarritz for the merienda. After the Spanish had introduced chocolate from the New World, they could not keep it a secret very long, and it soon found its way over the Pyrenees to Bayonne and Biarritz, where still today you will find some of the world's best chocolatiers.

2 pt / 1.15 l full-cream milk
7 fl oz / 200 ml whipping or single
   cream
1 vanilla pod *or* 3 in / 7.5 cm stick
   of cinnamon *or* 2 blades of mace

pinch of salt
pinch of freshly ground black pepper
12 oz / 340 g good-quality plain
   chocolate

Put the milk and cream with the spice, salt and pepper in a saucepan, and bring to the boil. Break up the chocolate, put it in a bowl, and pour the milk over it. Stir until the chocolate has melted, and let it stand in a heated jug for a few minutes to infuse. Strain it into a heated jug, whisk to a froth, if you like, and serve. This is a very rich drink, to be served in small cups.

Churros

Serves 6–8

1 pt / 570 ml water
12 oz / 340 g flour, sifted
2 eggs, lightly beaten
½ tsp salt

sunflower or groundnut (peanut) oil for
    frying
icing sugar for dusting

Bring the water to the boil, and remove from the heat. Tip in the flour, and stir vigorously. Put back over the heat, and mix until smooth. Remove from the heat, and beat in the salt and the eggs, little by little, until the mixture becomes smooth and glossy. Spoon it into a large piping bag with a broad, fluted nozzle. Bring a large pan of oil to a temperature of 180°C / 350°F, and pipe in lengths of paste about 4–5 in / 10–12 cm long. Do not crowd the pan or the temperature will drop and the paste absorb oil. When done, the *churros* will be crisp and pale gold, taking no more than a few minutes to achieve this. Drain on kitchen paper, and serve very hot, dusted with icing sugar.

Entertaining

PLANNING FOR AN IMPORTANT MEAL

I HAVE never thought it very helpful to give a countdown to Christmas dinner or to any other grand occasion, such as a wedding or a Christening party, since everyone has a plan which works best for their own particular needs, whether a large or small gathering, a formal or informal one, or one with or without children. Rather than approach such events in the manner of a military-style campaign (you know the sort of thing – 06.00 light oven, 06.30 juggle 20-pound turkey into undersized oven, 06.35 retrieve turkey from kitchen floor, etc.), I thought I would offer a few suggestions that might save last-minute panics when the foil runs out or you can't find the cinnamon sticks for mulled wine. I have included some short-cuts and time-savers that no one will notice, but they will allow for a much more relaxing time for the cook who is not backed up by a *brigade de cuisine*.

Space

Put away, in the garage, under the bed, in the spare room, all the equipment that you know you will not use – the wok, the fish kettle, the pasta-maker and the other things that take up too much room. On the other hand, remember where you put them; otherwise, chaos will ensue if someone decides they want stir-fried brussels with the turkey or poached rather than baked salmon. Clear space in the refrigerator and freezer. Pot whatever can be potted, such as the odd piece of ham, cold roast beef or game. Deal similarly with heel ends of cheese that are not fit for another appearance on the cheese board but that can be grated on pasta or soups or, if quite soft, can be potted with butter, port and ground mace. While you are making those things, make up a batch of anchovy butter, too, for hot toast fingers to serve with aperitifs. Make sure you have room for extra ice, which you can either make or have delivered in time for the event. Make plenty of room for the bird, fish or joint so that it can be well covered and remain out of contact with everything else in the refrigerator. Clear out the salad drawers and start again.

Checklist for kitchen shopping

Buy more than you think you can possibly use of the following: foil (is it wide enough?), lace paper doilies, bin liners, plastic bags, cling film, kitchen paper (as well as mopping up spills, use it to blot up excess grease on the surface of stocks and sauces) and J cloths. A scalded J cloth will do just as well as muslin for straining stocks, sauces and jellies; also use squares of J cloth to tie up bundles of herbs or spices, such as when preparing a *bouquet garni* or a bundle of cinnamon, cloves, allspice berries, mace and orange zest for mulled wine.

Planning the meal

It is not a good idea to have all hot courses, unless you have plenty of kitchen help to share the tasks. A cold first course, followed by a hot main course, vegetables or salad, then cheese and finally one cold and one hot dessert, is a workable format for the single-handed cook.

Avoid having to plate every course, especially hot ones. This is fine if there are two or three helpers, but can be a disaster otherwise. It is, however, useful to choose cold first courses and desserts that can be prepared a few hours in advance, plated, covered in cling film and refrigerated until required.

Advanced preparation

Salad greens, such as lettuce, radicchio, endive, fennel and celery, can be trimmed and well washed, but leave the roots on and put everything, roots down, in a large bowl of water, to which you add some ice cubes from time to time. Keep this in a cool place, and they will stay fresh for a day or two, although they will lose some vitamins, of course.

If you peel, halve, deseed and thinly slice cucumber, then salt and drain it for several hours, and finally rinse and squeeze dry in kitchen paper, it will keep, covered, in the refrigerator, for 2–3 days.

Most vegetables can be washed, trimmed or peeled, sliced and blanched, and put in airtight containers in the refrigerator several hours before required. After blanching, put them in a bowl of ice-cold water, and then drain them. Again, loss of vitamins is the price to pay for convenience.

Most kinds of soups, hot or cold, can be made the day before, and the garnishes, such as cream, sherry, croûtons or snipped herbs, can be added at the last moment.

A tub of double cream or thick yoghurt mixed with half the quantity of good jam, jelly or marmalade can be frozen for a very acceptable ice cream. Above all, remember to leave enough time for ice cream to 'ripen off', that is thaw a little, before serving. Good vanilla ice cream can be used as a base for toppings of honey, chestnut purée, crumbled cake, rum-soaked raisins or chopped crystallized fruit.

If possible, prepare cold first courses a few hours in advance, then plate, cover with cling film, and refrigerate. You should also plate cold puddings of the fruit or chocolate terrine variety.

Checklist for the freezer

All of the following are worth having to make extra pies, savoury pastries or sandwiches: puff pastry, filo pastry, pitta bread and Indian flat breads.

Table decoration

Why not combine this with the sweet course. Decorate pine branches or a silver painted branch with decorative edibles. Crisp wine biscuits, wrapped chocolate truffles, small squares of cake wrapped in cellophane, kumquats, physallis, cherries and medjoul dates are just a few of the things which you can use, depending on the season, of course.

COOKING AN IMPORTANT MEAL

There are more similarities between cooking for six and sixty than might be, at first, apparent, and indeed if you plan large-scale entertaining in the same way as you plan a small dinner party, you can't go far wrong. Note that I say 'plan'. The execution of it is a different matter altogether. Although you do not need ten times as much assistance, cooking for sixty is not something to be undertaken single-handedly if it can be avoided. I speak from the experience I had when I cooked a Club dinner at Ninety Park Lane in London.

In the planning of the dinner I was careful to avoid too many hot dishes that would need last-minute attention, as this puts the kitchen under a strain. I wanted the food to reflect my style of cooking, with an emphasis on seasonal, local ingredients, and have some good, sharp flavours at the beginning to waken the appetite. For the same reason, I chose to put the sorbet as a pre-dessert, refreshing the palate after meat, cheese and red wine, before going on to the high point of the meal, the trifle with 1985 champagne La Grande Dame.

The first three courses were kept small, just four or five slivers of fish, a tomato pudding made in an espresso cup, and a small piece of skate. At the test meal (which, incidentally, is a good idea before a large-scale occasion), by the time we reached the skate salad, we realized that something crunchy was needed, and having tasted them before at the restaurant, I suggested beetroot crisps to be served as a garnish to the salad, actually more of an integral part of the dish, as I tend not to garnish my food very much.

Having prepared the tomato puddings the night before, on the evening of the dinner itself, I realized I had made a major mistake in the planning of the meal by suggesting broad beans as part of the spring vegetables with the lamb cobbler. Not only do broad beans have to be podded, but they also have to be slipped out of their skins. It took three of us an hour to prepare enough for sixty people. The planning of the cold dishes first was a good idea, and ensured that the meal got off to a smooth start. In fact, it ran smoothly throughout.

By the time the main course was served, there was time for a breather, and then it was all hands on deck to get out the rarebit, one person slicing cheese, another baking it, someone else cutting the toasted cheese, another person arranging it on each plate and then passing it to me to garnish with lamb's lettuce, and finally someone giving it a final inspection before handing it to the waiter to serve.

As well as having the Veuve Clicquot La Grande Dame, there was 1983 Veuve Clicquot to start, the 1983 rosé with the tomato pudding and a delicious 1983 Château Clerc Milon with the lamb.

This is the meal we cooked:

Marinated smoked haddock
with pickled samphire (see pages 304 and 577)

Tomato pudding (see page 164) with baby leeks

Skate salad with mint, honey
and cider vinaigrette (see variation page 108)

Spring lamb and vegetables with herb cobbler (see page 397)

Lancashire cheese rarebit (see page 250)
on saffron bread with lamb's lettuce salad

Rhubarb sorbet (see page 541)

Eighteenth-century English trifle (see page 522)

On the following pages are more menus for different occasions in different seasons, food that I like to put together, which may suggest other combinations to you.

SPRING MENUS
St Valentine's Day Dinner

Little Oyster Pies (see page 49)
or *Oysters in Champagne Jelly (see page 313)*

Spaghetti alla Norcina (see page 185)

Fennel and Pomegranate Salad (see page 96)

Rosé Champagne Granita (see page 543)
or *Rose, Yoghurt and Cheese Hearts*
with Rhubarb Sauce (see page 525)

Amaretti (see page 478)

Easter Lunch

Fresh Scallop and Jerusalem Artichoke Soup
(see page 21)

Roast Chicken with Oyster Stuffing
(see page 330)

Roast New Potatoes and Garlic (see page 148)
Steamed Chinese Leaves and Mangetout (see page 142)

Rhubarb, Ginger and White Chocolate Tart (see page 555)
or Simple Rhubarb Fool (see page 519)

Casual Supper

Hummus (see page 74)
Radishes with Three Butters (see page 74),
Cucumber and Mint Salad (see page 98)

Al's Café Lamb and Prune Tagine (see page 398)

Couscous (see page 214)

Orange, Onion and Olive salad (see page 97)
Chick Pea and Vegetable Salad (see page 106)

Pears in Red Wine (see page 497)

Sunday Lunch

Brandade of Smoked Trout (see page 75)

Roast Stuffed Loin of Pork (see page 411)

Leek, Potato and Parmesan Strudel (see page 156)
or Broccoli with Tomato and Soy Butter (see page 138)
Roast or Jacket Potatoes

Golden Fruit Salad (see page 501)

SUMMER MENUS

Picnic

Spanish Omelette (see page 239)

Tarragon Jellied Chicken and Ham (see page 331)

Rillettes de Porc (see page 80)

Quick Saffron Bread (see page 445)

Flask of Summer Vichyssoise (see page 38)

Banana and Carrot Loaf (see page 467)

Toffee Cake (see page 465)

A basket of fresh berry fruits

Barbecue

*Grilled Aubergine, Onion and Pepper Salad
with Warm Garlic and Pinenut Cream (see page 114)*

Charred Tuna Fish (see page 270)

or *Grilled Sardines (see page 323)*

Spatchcocked Quails (see page 359)
or *Grilled Lemon-Marinated Chicken Wings (see page 339)*
or *Butterflied Leg of Lamb (see page 393)*

*Grilled Goat's Cheese on Country Bread
(see page 250)*

Grilled Fruit Brioche (see page 445)

Elderflower Cooler (see page 582)

Sangria du Ranquet (see page 583)

Barbecue Marinades

The following marinade recipes are sufficient to marinate and baste a single set of ingredients for six people, that is, half a dozen fish steaks, quails or pork chops. The oriental marinade is particularly suitable for chicken, salmon, tuna fish, and sausages, kebabs and pork chops, the herb and lemon marinade for lamb and vegetables and the tandoori marinade for chicken, kebabs and lamb chops. But this does not mean that you cannot use the oriental marinade for vegetables or the hot and sweet marinade for quails.

Oriental marinade
4 tbsp sherry or rice wine
2 tbsp sherry vinegar or rice vinegar
1–2 tbsp soy sauce
1 tbsp sesame oil
1 tsp grated fresh root ginger
2–3 garlic cloves, peeled and crushed
1 piece of lemon grass stalk, crushed (*optional*)
1–2 chillies, deseeded and thinly sliced (*optional*)
½ tsp freshly ground black pepper

Herb and lemon marinade
6 tbsp extra virgin olive oil
2–3 tbsp lemon juice
3 tbsp finely chopped parsley and other herbs
salt
freshly ground black pepper

Hot and sweet marinade
3 tbsp tomato ketchup
3 tbsp cider vinegar
2 tbsp honey or light muscovado (soft brown unrefined sugar)
2 tbsp groundnut (peanut) oil
1 tbsp Worcestershire sauce
1–2 tbsp tabasco sauce
1 tsp ground cumin
½ tsp freshly ground black pepper
¼ tsp salt

Tandoori marinade
5 oz / 140 g plain yoghurt
4 spring onions, trimmed and finely chopped
2 garlic cloves, peeled and crushed
2 tbsp paprika
2 tsp ground chilli pepper (or more to taste)

Garden Party
(A Cold Buffet)

Salade Niçoise (see page 102)

Salade Huguette (see page 104)

Pear and Herb Salad with Raspberry Dressing
(see page 99)

Cold Poached Salmon Glazed with
Cucumber and Fresh Mint Jelly (see page 266)

Chicken in Salmorejo (see page 335)

Rosy Jellied Beef (see page 391)

Tomato Pudding (see page 164)

Gâteau de St Honoré (see page 471)

Watermelon Pond (see page 502)

Rose and Coconut Macaroons (see page 482)

Easy Summer Entertaining

Carrot and Peach Soup (see page 37)

Salmon Tartare with Cucumber Sauce (see page 307)
or Marinated Salmon and Scallops (see page 306)
or Smoked Salmon and Lentil Salad (see page 109)

Fajitas (see page 389)
or Mushroom-Stuffed Chicken Breasts (see page 338)

Broad Beans and Peas with Cream and Lettuce (see page 138)

Strawberry and Raspberry Fool (see page 519)

Olive Oil Shortbread (see page 476)
or Lavender Biscuits (see page 477)

AUTUMN MENUS

Game Dinner

Mushroom and Red Wine Risotto (see page 207)
or *Mushroom Terrine (see page 161)*

Pigeon Breasts with Sweet and Sour Vegetables (see page 3643
or *Pot-Roast Partridge (see page 364)*
or *Rich Hare Casserole (see page 368)*

Grilled Radicchio (see page 149)
or *Spiced Red Cabbage (see Variation page 140)*
Mashed potatoes

Cinnamon Plums (see page 499)
or *Apple Sorbet (see page 539)*

Feast for Free

Nettle and Barley Soup (see page 9)
or *Wild Greens and Barley Risotto (see page 154)*
or *Frittata of Wild Greens (see page 240)*

Cockle Pie (see page 312)
or *Sussex Woodman's Pie (see page 366)*

*White Chocolate and Cheese Mousse with
Blackberry Sauce (see page 530)*

Vegetarian Feast

Aubergine, Corn and Tomato Soup (see page 5) with
Savoury Batter Pudding (see page 52)
or *Vegetable Gumbo (see page 18) with*
Spanakopitta (see page 55)

Tomato Tart (see page 447)
or *Vegetable and Tofu Creams with*
Tomato and Basil Vinaigrette (see page 133)

Black Mushroom Roulade (see page 163)
or *Celeriac, Pumpkin and Walnut Crumble (see page 153)*

Quinoa and Lentil Strudel (see page 217)
or *Creamy Cep Polenta (see page 215)*

Ginger Mousse with Lime and Honey Sauce (see page 528)
or *Quick Banana and Cardamom Ice Cream (see page 537)*
or *Muscat Grape Tart with Melted Butter Pastry (see page 553)*

Coming In From The Cold
(A supper for Hallowe'en, Bonfire Night or after a long country walk)

Spicy Sausage Roll (see page 51)
or *Tomato and Sausage Loaf (see page 448)*

Boston Baked Beans (see page 420)
or *Venison Chilli (see page 376)*

Honey-Glazed Stilton Potatoes (see page 148)

Pear and Caramel Pudding (see page 509) with
Sabayon of Single Malt (see page 517)
or *Chilled Pumpkin Soufflé (see page 531)*
or *Baked Stuffed Apples (see page 494)*

WINTER MENUS
Leisurely Brunch

Grilled Scallop and Bacon Skewers (see page 70)

Bacon, Egg and Sausage Pie (see page 234)

Eggs Casho (see page 233)

Kedgeree (see page 212)

Poached Eggs in Field Mushrooms (see page 232)

Pancakes (see page 245) and Syrup

Oatmeal Soda Bread (see page 444)

Cornbread (see page 444)

Dried Fruit Muffins (see page 454)

Fruit and Nut Casserole (see page 500)

Supper Party for Vegetarians

Spiced Carrot and Parsnip Soup (see page 7) with
Stir-Fried Vegetables and Toasted Sesame Tartlets (see page 61)
or Raisin Tapenade Cigarillos (see page 59)

Llapingachos (see page 63)
or Aubergine and Red Pepper Terrine (see page 162)

Pumpkin Ravioli (see page 175)
or Vegetable Lasagne (see page 188)

Green Salad

Pineapple and Rum Soufflés (see page 534)
or Quire of Orange Pancakes with Marmalade Sauce
(see page 557)

30-Minute Dinner

Warm Mackerel and Cucumber Salad (see page 115)

Pasta with Celery and Sun-Dried Tomato Sauce (see page 177)

Calves Liver with Sage and Balsamic Vinegar (see page 428)
or Grilled Duck Breasts (see page 345)

Traditional Baked Rarebit (page 250)

Ricotta with Apricot Sauce (see page 523)

White and Gold Party

Snail Puffs (see page 48)
Mussels in Overcoats (see page 54)
Wontons (see page 53)

Smoked Haddock and Potato Soup (see page 28)
or Fish Soup (see page 22)

Homemade Lemon Pasta (see page 174)
with Lemon Sauce (see page 179)
or Pumpkin Risotto (see page 206)

Moroccan-Style Roast Salmon with
Saffron-Onion Compote (see page 280)
or Pot-Roast Chicken with
40 Garlic Cloves (see page 332)
or Rabbit and Saffron Rice (see page 372)

Carrot and Peach Salad (see page 95)
White Root Salad (see page 106)
Roasted Pepper Salad (see page 100)

Ile Flottante Josette (see page 521)
Caramelized Milk Pudding (see page 515)
Golden Fruit Salad (see page 501)
White Chocolate Mousse and Orange Flower Roulade
(see page 462)

CHRISTMAS MENUS

Traditional Christmas Dinner

With the aperitifs:
Little Oyster Pies (see page 49)
Roquefort Profiteroles (see page 56)
Minced Meat Pastries (see page 50)

Oysters on the half shell
or *Prawns in Orange Mayonnaise (see page 314)*

Braised Turkey (see page 341)
or *Roast Goose (see page 354) with*
all the trimmings (see pages 342, 343 and 355)

Glazed Chestnuts (see page 141)
Winter Vegetable Gratin (see page 157)

Classic Christmas Pudding (see page 508)
or *Bûche de Noel (see page 472)*

Vegetarian Christmas Dinner

With the aperitifs:
Gougère (see page 56)

Pumpkin and Almond Soup (see page 12)

Rich Vegetable and Pasta Pie (see page 190)

Fennel and Pomegranate Salad (see page 96)

Chilled Persimmon Creams (see page 524)

Cantuccini (see page 480),
Biscotti di Vino (see page 479) and
Straccia Denti (see page 481) with
a rich sweet dessert wine

Light Christmas Dinner

With the aperitifs:
Deep-Fried Oyster and Potato Bundles (see page 69)
or *Baked Potatoes with Oysters (see page 314)*

Salmon and Scallop 'Chops' (see page 318)

Roast Duck with Glutinous Rice Stuffing (see page 346)

Deep-Fried Leeks (see page 145)
Steamed Chinese Leaves and Mangetout (see page 142)

Hazelnut Macaroons (see page 478) with
Mandarins with Pomegranate Granita (see page 543)

CHRISTMAS FOOD PRESENTS

Food for Christmas presents is a favourite choice, and one in which every taste and price-range is amply met, from a single jar of preserved ginger to a luxury hamper. This might be a selection of foodstuffs packed into an attractive box or basket, designed to appeal to a particular culinary or gastronomic passion or it might be mustards and pickles, English cheese or a selection of extra virgin olive oils. But one of the nicest presents you can give is something you have made yourself, such as unusual jams and jellies, potted meats and fish, pâtés, biscuits and chocolates.

Here are some ideas for food presents. You will find the recipes throughout the book on the pages indicated. Remember to label such things clearly, and include storage instructions and an 'eat by' date (in *italics*), mentioning whether the product should be refrigerated, Ⓡ.

- Potted Crab *2–3 days* Ⓡ (see page 78)
- Chicken Liver Mousse *1 week* Ⓡ (see page 77)
- Redcurrant *or* Quince Jelly *indefinitely* (see page 570)
- Pear Cheese *indefinitely* (see page 569)
- Seville Orange *or* Lemon Curd *3–4 weeks* Ⓡ (see page 566)
- Passion Fruit Curd *3–4 weeks* Ⓡ (see page 568)
- Dried Apricot Jam *indefinitely* (see page 572)
- Mincemeat *12 months* (see page 573)
- Gooseberry Chutney *indefinitely* (see page 578)
- Cranberry Ketchup *indefinitely* (see page 579)
- Lemons Pickled in Oil *indefinitely* (see page 576)
- Quince Butter *3–4 weeks* Ⓡ (see page 581)
- Brandy Butter *3–4 weeks* Ⓡ (see page 581)
- Apricots in Muscat *1–2 years* (see page 588)
- Chocolate Rum Truffles *5–7 days* Ⓡ (see page 590)
- Whisky and Walnut Toffee *2 weeks* (see page 591)
- Pork Pie *5 days* Ⓡ (see page 424)
- Olive Bread *1–2 days* (see page 439)
- Quick Saffron Bread *1–2 days* (see page 445)
- Edith Bissell's Nut Roll *5–7 days* (see page 452)
- Toffee Cake *1 week* (see page 465)
- Madeira Cake *1 week* (see page 466)
- Spiced Ginger Loaf *2 weeks* (see page 466)
- Eight Treasures Fruit Cake *6–8 weeks* (see page 473)
- Cookies *2–3 days* (see pages 481, 483 and 562)
- Cantuccini *2 weeks* (see page 480)

LUCKY FOOD FOR THE NEW YEAR

Pork, herrings, greens, long noodles, beans, lentils and honey; in different cultures, all these foods, and many others, are symbolically associated with money, and thus encourage the acquisition of good fortune for the New Year.

Fish, because it swims forward, will help us make our way through the year. It is also a symbol of fertility and plenty, both in Chinese and Jewish cultures; herring, because of the way it swims in shoals is said to bring abundance, and is an important part of northern European celebrations at New Year. Lentils signify coins, and honey, sweetness and purity; both are consumed in Italy to ensure plentiful supplies of each. In Scotland, a rich dark fruit cake is traditionally served on New Year's Eve.

When I first went to America, I was introduced to the idea of eating pork for New Year's Eve. Unlike the chicken, which is another candidate for the holiday table, the pig does not scratch around for its living, and, with luck, neither will we. There is also an Afro-American attachment to greens as a symbol of money.

Here is my suggestion for a lucky menu for the New Year:

Brill with Lentils in a Cider Sauce (see page 267)

Pork Chops with Onion and Sauerkraut (see page 416)
or *Pot-Roast Pork (see page 412)*

Stir-Fried Greens with Preserved Ginger and
Sesame Seeds (see page 144)

Apricot, Almond and Honey Pudding (see page 506)

Rich Black Bun (see page 475)

MATCHING FOOD AND WINE

I shall never forget the time my father gave a treasured half bottle of fine claret from the legendary 1961 vintage to a business colleague whose wife then used it to make the gravy for the Sunday roast. I don't think my parents have ever forgotten it, either, for although it is true that in cooking with wine, you should at least use a wine that you would drink, the finest wines are for drinking with the meal, not for cooking.

Planning a meal around a special bottle can be quite a challenge, but one to be enjoyed rather than feared. Being married to someone who is passionate about wine, and who has built up a cellar over the years, has meant that I am faced with this agreeable challenge quite often. I have learned one or two rules, one of which is that there are always exceptions to the rules. If a dish is to be cooked in wine, the rule book has it that it should be the same wine as is served with it. I would modify that a little. A coq au vin might be served with a Charmes Chambertin, but I would cook with a bourgogne rouge. On the other hand, at the Hôtel de la Poste in Beaune, I have eaten M. Chevillard's wonderful sole cooked in red burgundy, while with it we drank a white burgundy.

Lamb may be the traditional partner for a fine claret, but I have also served salmon with claret. In the past, too, I have cooked salmon as the supporting act to a Grand Cru Chablis and to German Spätlesen of the fabled 1971 and 1976 vintages.

It is important to consider the guests, too. These are usually chosen with great care if a fine bottle is to be the centrepiece of the evening. And if it's only one fine bottle, then no more than six will sit down at table. But if your guests are traditional in their tastes, it is better to serve the lamb rather than the salmon with the claret. Farmhouse Cheddar was the only thing we dared served with a 1959 Giscours to one of our more conservative wine-loving friends.

Whether you are serving a fish dish with a great white wine or a meat dish with a good red wine, I have found that there are flavours and ingredients best avoided. Asparagus and leeks give wine a metallic taste, and globe artichokes make it taste sweet. Fennel and aniseed can overpower wine, and unless used with a very light hand, the more subtle but similar flavour of chervil and tarragon does the same, particularly when the herbs have matured in the sun and their essential oils have intensified in flavour. Some foods, such as ceps and other wild mushrooms, and also cultivated mushrooms, are particularly good with wine. The more delicate oriental flavours, such as ginger, garlic and lemon grass, used with a light hand, are a delight with the best white Rhônes, the Château Grillet and Condrieu.

Food from the same region as the wine will usually partner it best of all, as this is a combination which may have evolved over a very long time. If your chosen bottle is one of the super Tuscans, try milk-roast pork or a flavoursome *stracotta*. An old Dão or Reguengos from Portugal might be matched with a *chanfana*, a half leg of lamb braised in red wine. Roast lamb or noisettes of lamb would be my choice for claret, the roast if I planned to serve the meal family-style, noisettes if I wanted it to look more elaborate and if we were only four at table and not six. By the time you have arranged the sixth pretty plate, the rest are cold.

A chicken dish is one of the best partners for a really fine wine, not chicken as 'blotting paper', but chicken as a foil for a whole range of wines. Chicken will also cook nicely in red or white wine, whole, in casseroles or in elegant dishes based on supremes, with a range of herbs and spices, or as plainly as possible.

IMPROMPTU ENTERTAINING

It is often the small, impromptu meals that are the most enjoyable way of entertaining. Elevenses, afternoon tea or a leisurely, late breakfast are civilized and civilizing punctuation marks in the day, which have all but disappeared from our busy lives, with little time to pause and reflect with friends and family over a glass of crisp fino or warming oloroso sherry or a mug of turkey soup and a mince pie. Nor do we take an hour off from other pursuits to enjoy a traditional afternoon tea, with scones and clotted cream, thin finger sandwiches and a piece of fruit cake.

Apart from the leisurely and often impromptu nature of such meals, they do fit in extremely well with the sort of entertaining many of us do over holiday periods. A late breakfast is the perfect thing to serve if you are also planning a late dinner party the same day, and consider serving elevenses if, for instance, a big celebratory meal such as Christmas dinner is planned for the early evening.

The midnight Christmas dinner or New Year's Eve dinner that is so popular in France, and which I sometimes serve on Christmas Eve, can be awaited with pleasurable excitement rather than hunger pangs, if you prepare afternoon tea. This need not be elaborate, and is an excellent opportunity for impromptu entertaining. I also love to have a winter picnic, perhaps to take to a Boxing Day race meeting, with plenty of cold cuts and leftovers for sandwiches, flasks of hot soup and slab of Christmas cake.

A good way to overcome the feeling of anti-climax after the holidays is to have a party on the spur of the moment. An impromptu affair is not expected to have four or five elaborate courses, and could quite easily be arranged as a buffet. To lift it out of the ordinary, why not consider a Russian buffet and serve *zakouski*? These appetizing little dishes would normally be served as a prelude to a Russian dinner, but also make marvellous food for a buffet. I first came across them at a favourite restaurant in Paris, Dominique, in Montparnasse. Not being able to afford caviar, we ordered a stack of warm blini, the yeast batter pancakes which come with melted butter, sour cream, chopped onion, and *zakouski*. These came in six or eight small dishes on a silver platter. That, together with a small carafe of ice-cold vodka embedded in crushed ice, made a delightful supper.

It is a supper you can reproduce at home with just a little careful shopping and a minimal amount of cooking. Blini are essential to such a meal. However, if you do not want to make these yeast pancakes (see page 57), an ordinary pancake batter will do (see page 245). The sharp-eyed reader of recipes will notice the blini mixture is not very different from that of pikelets. If you can buy or make good pikelets, you can use those instead. To go with the blini, you do not have to serve caviar. Cured herrings and smoked fish are preferable to dyed lumpfish roe. Salmon and trout roes are more expensive but very good indeed.

A selection of *zakouski* can be made up by visiting your local delicatessen and also sorting through your store-cupboard. Serve them in small bowls, and let people help themselves to a spoonful of this and a morsel of that. As well as the blini, have some pumpernickel or other rye bread on hand. Here are some ideas to get you started:

- anchovy and potato salad, using perhaps the pink fir apple or other firm waxy potato
- shredded or sliced cucumber with dill and soured cream
- coleslaw
- sauerkraut salad, which is drained sauerkraut mixed with a little sugar, olive oil, grated apple and chopped celery, garnished with cranberries
- cold meat salad mixed with onion, chopped dill pickle, shredded carrot and mayonnaise
- herrings prepared in various ways, pickled, soused, marinated or chopped
- sardines mashed with butter, lemon juice, mustard, parsley and pepper
- stuffed hard-boiled eggs
- taramasalata

Index

Recipes suitable for vegetarians are marked with the symbol ⓥ in the index.

Note on vegetarian recipes: some of these indicated specify particular cheeses, which many vegetarians do not eat. Suitable cheese made from vegetable 'rennet' can be substituted.

Many of the recipes suggest vegetable or meat stock. These too I have indicated as suitable for vegetarians, as I also have in the case of a few recipes which include anchovies, for example. Vegetarians can omit the ingredient and substitute a small amount of soy sauce or yeast extract.